Elizabethan Espionage

Elizabethan Espionage

*Plotters and Spies in the
Struggle Between Catholicism
and the Crown*

Patrick H. Martin

McFarland & Company, Inc., Publishers
Jefferson, North Carolina

LIBRARY OF CONGRESS CATALOGUING-IN-PUBLICATION DATA

Names: Martin, Patrick H., author.
Title: Elizabethan espionage : plotters and spies in the struggle between Catholicism and the crown / Patrick H. Martin.
Description: Jefferson, North Carolina : McFarland & Company, Inc., Publishers, 2016. | Includes bibliographical references and index.
Identifiers: LCCN 2016012585 | ISBN 9781476662558 (softcover : acid free paper) ∞
Subjects: LCSH: Great Britain—History—Elizabeth, 1558–1603. | Espionage, British—History—16th century. | Spies—Great Britain—History—16th century. | Great Britain—Foreign relations—1558–1603. | Great Britain—Politics and government—1558–1603.
Classification: LCC DA356 .M28 2016 | DDC 327.1242009/031—dc23
LC record available at http://lccn.loc.gov/2016012585

BRITISH LIBRARY CATALOGUING DATA ARE AVAILABLE

ISBN (print) 978-1-4766-6255-8
ISBN (ebook) 978-1-4766-2359-7

© 2016 Patrick H. Martin. All rights reserved

No part of this book may be reproduced or transmitted in any form or by any means, electronic or mechanical, including photocopying or recording, or by any information storage and retrieval system, without permission in writing from the publisher.

Front cover image: George Cruikshank's 1754 engraving of Guy Fawkes lighting a fuse under the Houses of Parliament © 2016 golibo/iStock

Printed in the United States of America

*McFarland & Company, Inc., Publishers
Box 611, Jefferson, North Carolina 28640
www.mcfarlandpub.com*

To John M. Finnis

Acknowledgments

Professor John Finnis was my companion on the jouney of writing this book as well as my co-author of articles cited in the Bibliography. My wife, Ann Hingle Martin, has been highly supportive and encouraging through the many years of research and writing. She has read and commented helpfully on many drafts and has shared the frustrations of bringing the book into print. All responsibility for errors in fact and judgment rests on me alone. John Klause has read critically and sympathetically drafts of the manuscript and provided helpful insights. Fr. Thomas McCoog, S.J., was exceptionally helpful in providing access to materials in Archives of the Society of Jesus, London, during a period of research there and in supplying materials subsequent to the visit. Two researchers in foreign archives were invaluable. R. W. O'Hara collected documents in the National Archives at Kew. Ruth Jaeneke-Elyas collected copies of letters of and to William Sterrell housed at the Vienna Archives. Anthony Smith, president of Magdalen College, assisted on several trips to the College in search of Sterrell, and the Magdalen College Archivist Robin Darwall-Smith provided access to unique materials of the College as well as promptly responding to all inquiries. Paul Hammer gave useful guidance in response to reading a draft of an early article on William Sterrell. The research spanned some twenty years, portions of which were assisted by sabbaticals and research grants from the Louisiana State University Law Center.

Table of Contents

Acknowledgments	vii
Preface	1
1. The Persons-Campion Jesuit Mission of 1580–1581	5
2. Tainted in Blood	16
3. A Wolf by the Ears	21
4. The MP from Morpeth: Gentleman Pensioner and Assassin	29
5. Persecution of Catholic Gentry	38
6. Aboard the Ambassador's Boat	45
7. Mary Stewart and the Theatre of the World	50
8. The Spanish Armada and English Catholics	67
9. The Essex, Phelippes and Bacon Intelligence Initiative	79
10. In Spanish Lands: The Bisley-Moody Plot	95
11. The Parliament of 1593: Sterrell and Marlowe	107
12. Who Can Protect the Queen? A Rivalry over Assassins	120
13. The General Factor and Arbella Stewart	129
14. Co-opting the Privy Council	140
15. Trustworthy Men at the Fountainhead in the Council	147
16. The Network at Work: Tricks of Strong Imagination	161
17. Charles Paget, Meet Monsieur Boulant	167
18. Treaty Negotiations and Burgundian Jewels	175
19. Essex's Dismal Tumult	186
20. The War between the Priests	193
21. Scenes of a Dying Queen	208
22. Transitions and Treasons, 1603	218
23. From Intelligence to Entertainment	238
24. Measure for Measure: A Sermon to a King	249

25. Cecil's Interrogations: Phelippes's Lies and Sterrell's Equivocations	263
26. A Stir in Wales—The Whitsun Commotion, 1605	271
27. The Gunpowder Treason	275
28. Conclusion: The State of the English Counter-Reformation after Gunpowder	288
Chapter Notes	291
Bibliography	344
Index	353

Preface

Since September 11, 2001, it has become almost common to identify aspects of the English Counter-Reformation as terrorism. For example, Derek Wilson's *Sir Francis Walsingham: A Courtier in an Age of Terror* (Carroll & Graf, 2007), equates Counter-Reformation Catholics to modern terrorists: the Pope was a "religious leader in Rome urging state-sponsored terrorism and dispatching his mullahs into England to deflect Elizabeth's subjects from their loyalty." What is terrorism? A precise definition is elusive, but paragraph 3 of Resolution 1566, unanimously approved by the United Nations Security Council in October 2004, describes terrorism as "including [acts] against civilians, committed with the intent to cause death or serious bodily injury, or taking of hostages, with the purpose to provoke a state of terror in the general public or in a group of persons or particular persons, intimidate a population...." Terrorism then refers to violent acts against civilians that are intended to create fear and are perpetrated for a religious, political, or ideological goal. Who might be called a terrorist?

While the government-sponsored massacre of Huguenots (French protestants) in Paris in 1572 may have given rise to fear of something similar happening in England, terror was never a component of a plan or strategy advocated by any English Catholics. The closest political plan for mass violence was the Gunpowder Plot to blow up Parliament as it met in November 1605. The purpose was to overthrow the existing government rather than to create mass fear in the population as the Jacobins in the French Revolution, the Irish Republican Brotherhood, or Islamist jihadists.

State-sponsored terrorism has often been practiced throughout history. Agents of the English government engaged in mass murder from time to time during the Sixteenth Century. The burnings of English protestants by Mary Tudor's government was terrorist—public spectacles designed to strike fear into her non-Catholic subjects. The placing of the severed heads and limbs of English Catholic priests atop spikes on the city's walls by Elizabeth's government were acts of terrorism over a quarter century to cow into submission her Catholic subjects. In fact, the English Privy Council's policy of torturing and executing priests was explicitly adopted as their "punishment, to the terror of others." The only terrorism to be found in England during the reign of Queen Elizabeth was the barbaric torture and savage executions practiced by the government in its persecution of its Catholic subjects.

In lucid moments in *King Lear* Act V, the mad Lear reconciles with his faithful Cordelia as his kingdom has fallen into ruin. In expectation that they will be imprisoned together, he says they will sing like birds in a cage. "As if we were God's spies," they will take upon themselves the "mystery of things." God's spies are observers who stand apart from and outlast the "packs and sects of great ones that ebb and flow by the moon." Earlier Lear's steadfast lieutenant Kent had commented on another sort of spies. Rulers, he said, have in their midst "spies and speculations" (watchful agents, spies) in the guise of servants who provide intelligence on "our state."

Shakespeare's words were written in the immediate aftermath of the Gunpowder Plot. The aborted attempt to blow up Parliament and the royal family was as devastating to English Catholicism as the ruination of Cordelia by the actions of her sisters and father. *Lear* could well have been reflecting on the twenty-five years of religious strife that had preceded the performance of the play on December 26, 1606, before King James.

Intelligence and espionage, "spies and speculations," were important factors in the struggle over England's religious identity in the age of Elizabeth and Shakespeare. Two Elizabethan courtiers who served as secret agents are central to this book on Elizabethan spies and their activities. Both have escaped the scrutiny of history, in part because their high-ranking sponsors jealously guarded their secret services to preserve their own reputations. Though their loyalties were on opposite religious sides, both were unusually intrepid and resourceful. In other respects, too, they were similar. Both were from England's landed gentry. Both had lost a father at an early age. Both spent some years in close presence to Queen Elizabeth. Both were fond of Latin epigrams. If they were not well-acquainted, their paths surely crossed.

Their names were George Gifford and William Sterrell. Their spying was intimately connected with the Catholic seminaries established on the Continent to train young Englishmen. Gifford's brother and several cousins were educated and ordained overseas, and these relatives facilitated his anti–Jesuit efforts. Sterrell was instrumental in transporting students to the seminaries, and such activities contributed to his long-time association with the English Jesuits.

Elizabeth's principal strategy to end Roman Catholicism in England was to isolate the remaining Catholics. They were forbidden to exercise their religion, and the government sought to prevent them from having any communication with their co-religionists abroad. No new priests were to be trained or allowed into England. But exiles set up seminaries in Europe to educate young Englishmen and to ordain them so they could return to England to keep the church alive. William Allen and Robert Persons were the two most important men for this. Many of the men who worked with them were Oxford scholars like themselves. Allen founded the English College at Douay (relocated to Rheims 1578–1593) and an English College at Rome. Persons established seminaries in Spain. Catholic families sent their sons abroad, and other young men drawn to Catholicism were encouraged to cross the seas, for seminary. *Seminary* is rich in meaning: "n. 1. A piece of ground in which plants are sown (or raised from cuttings) to be afterwards transplanted; a seed-plot" (*Oxford English Dictionary*). Hundreds of the young English cuttings, now Catholic priests, returned to England from Flanders, France, Spain and Rome, transplanted back to their native soil. The government's response to their success was a campaign to extirpate them and to intimidate any who assisted them through fear of death, imprisonment, and ruinous fines.

Primarily through one official, Sir Francis Walsingham, the English government established an extensive intelligence apparatus to counter the missionary efforts arising from the seminaries. He placed spies (moles) into the seminaries and employed *agent provocateurs* to disrupt their work or to entrap the Catholics in crimes against the state. One agent was

George Gifford. Historians have treated Gifford as a man of status in the queen's household who was caught betraying his government but whose crimes were overlooked to avoid scandal. He was, instead, a very effective provocateur sent by Walsingham to the Duke of Guise in France to encourage an assassination plot. The successes of Walsingham caused the Catholics to seek their own sources to counter the spies set against them. They found such a man in William Sterrell.

At the end of January 1605, Robert Cecil, Secretary of State, Principal Minister to King James, interrogated Sterrell. This former Oxford University philosophy lecturer confessed to corresponding with England's enemies. Sterrell was, in fact, the key figure in a Jesuit-linked counter-espionage network connecting English Catholics with exiles in Europe. William Sterrell had been spying for persons overseas for two decades. Highly intelligent and useful, he was unusually well-connected. The king and Court would have been scandalized if the spying role were revealed to the public. Sterrell was allowed to return to his current employment, administering Court entertainments and diplomatic functions within the royal household for a great nobleman who was a favorite hunting companion and councilor to the King. Had Secretary Cecil known of Sterrell's aliases and activities over the years, he probably would not have gone free. Indeed, he later returned to his career in foreign intelligence. Now, for the first time, Sterrell's story can be told and placed in the context of the times in which he operated. His aliases have been penetrated and his activities laid out to examine.

In the pages that follow, we will meet a number of the agents who plied their trade in the last twenty-five years of the reign of Queen Elizabeth. For many, we will have only fleeting glances, and we can never be sure when they may have been playing tricks on us, deliberately leaving misimpressions.

This book explores the Elizabethan suppression of the Catholic religion followed by a substantial portion of England's own people. It traces the establishment of an intelligence network by resourceful English Catholics (within the country and abroad) to counter the government's activities, often violent and devious, to extinguish their religion. Despite some successes, the accession of James I and the failure of the Gunpowder Plot marked the end of this counter-espionage effort. The endnotes reflect the fact that this work is derived from primary sources, many of which have been little used or have been misunderstood by recent authors.

1

The Persons-Campion Jesuit Mission of 1580–1581

"The expense is reckoned, the enterprise is begun"

On the morning of June 17, 1580, the customs officer of Dover inspected the passengers off-loading from the bark just arrived from Calais. A fair breeze was blowing and the boat had arrived rather earlier than expected. The seas were untroubled. With full sails the channel crossing had taken but a day and night. It was warm in the sun as he looked over the travelers and their boxes and trunks. Word had been sent from London that Rome had dispatched priests into England. The searcher doubted that any would come his way. Priests landed in small inlets in the dark of night, clad in black robes and clutching their superstitious tokens, their beads and *Agnus Deis* blessed by the Bishop of Rome, which they sold to their co-religionists or exchanged for hidden shelter in the countryside.

A man in military attire introduced himself politely to the Customer of Dover. He was in his mid–30s and had the ruddy complexion of a man who spent his time outdoors. His face was angular, high cheekbones emphasized by a well-trimmed beard and mustache. He wore an officer's suit of leather, laid with gold lace, with jaunty hat and feathers. A captain returning from the Lowlands, he said he was, and he offered his travel papers. With him was a servant he called George.

He needed a horse. Could the gentleman tell him where to find one? He had been out of England for a time, and his superiors had not arranged for his return to London. His voice carried authority. It was full, the voice of a man accustomed to speaking to groups of men without shouting to be heard. Begging the indulgence of the customs official, the captain asked if he would be so kind as to look after a friend of his coming shortly from St. Omers. An English jewel merchant, the friend was, by name a Mr. Edmunds. They had traveled some distance together, and the captain was concerned for the man's safety as he was carrying jewels and diamonds. The government official would be happy to do so, agreeing even to send on the next departing boat a letter to the merchant. Thanking him, the captain and his man George set forth.

The confident swagger, the display of authority over George, the disguise, the dissimulation—all had worked. Robert Persons, S.J., had safely entered England, had navigated his way through the most dangerous moment thus far of this historic journey. Not everything he had said was untrue. He in fact had been out of his native land for six years. As to the military, was he not a member of the church militant? His order, the Society of Jesus, had been founded by a former soldier of the Spanish army, and the Society was infused with military discipline, especially obedience. It was no sin to tell a heretic a fable that was near enough to the truth to avoid a greater evil. The government was denying the Catholics of England their right to observe their ancient religion, and their queen was a Jezebel excommunicated a decade earlier by Pope Pius V. Even the name of his friend was not entirely untrue, Mr. Edmunds's given name was Edmund—Edmund Campion. And they had traveled together, all the way from Rome. So, an element of truth was present. Not that the customer of Dover was owed the truth; the truth is never owed to a person who would use it to harm those doing the Lord's work. The Jesuits had a name for flexibility on truth-telling: *equivocation*. The queen's prosecutors called it: *Jesuitical*.

Early in 1580, Rome decided that a Jesuit mission to England should be undertaken. Two men who had known one another at Oxford's university were chosen to lead the endeavor: Edmund Campion and Robert Persons. Campion was six years older and had been a University Proctor, while Persons was a student when the two had first met. Now their roles were reversed. Campion insisted that Persons be his superior in this mission. Persons was deemed the more prudent, Campion, the man of greater zeal. When he was called to this mission, Campion was in Prague serving as a teacher of philosophy and rhetoric.

The brilliant Campion was made a Fellow of St. John's College at the age of 17. When Queen Elizabeth made a royal visit to Oxford in 1566, Campion, a teacher of rhetoric in his college, was selected to perform before her Court in formal disputation. He was assigned to argue that the tides are caused by the moon's motion. Against him were four "pugnacious youths." Speaking in Latin, he began with a courteous bow to his queen. He could meet the unequal contest, he declared graciously, because he was speaking "in the name of Philosophy, the princess of letters, before Elizabeth, the lettered princess." Campion extended his compliments also to the man next to the queen, the Earl of Leicester, Chancellor of the University. Campion's speech was so well received that he was selected for an extempore debate before the visitation ended. His performances were followed by private meetings of Campion with the queen's two chief counselors: William Cecil and Leicester, who promised the young man their support and patronage. Cecil called Campion "one of the diamonds of England." A few years later he was one of many bright young men of strong religious conviction who fled their homeland for the English College at Douay. In 1573, he became a Jesuit in Rome, and the order had sent him to Prague.

The team leader, Robert Persons, was born in 1546 in Somerset. With the assistance of the vicar of Nether Stowey, he was able to attend school and eventually found his way to Oxford, where he became a fellow of Balliol College. He resigned his position by early 1574 in controversial circumstances and suspect in religion. He left the country to study medicine in Padua. On the way, in Louvain, he was persuaded to make the spiritual exercises of Ignatius Loyola, founder of the Jesuit order. This affected him profoundly. He continued on to Padua and began the study of medicine but abandoned it for the priesthood. He entered the Society of Jesus and was ordained in Rome. Only two years later he was named to lead this dangerous mission into Protestant England. In a nearly unbroken flow until his death three decades later, Persons directed eloquent, learned, and combative pseudonymous publications at English readers, disturbing the government and stirring controversy over the state's religious policies, the succession of the Crown from Elizabeth, and allegiance to her successor. His pen was so effective and at times gracious, that one English Calvinist, Edmund Bunny, edited out Roman Catholic elements and published Persons's *First Booke of the Christian Exercise*, to great success (renamed as *A Book of Christian Exercise*). To dissociate himself from Bunny's corruption, Persons published later editions as *A Christian Directorie*.

The purpose of the 1580 Campion-Persons mission was made clear to the two Jesuits: to minister to those who were already Catholic, not to convert Protestants nor to stir dissent. Their mission was top-down: they were to associate with persons of the higher ranks. A change in English religious policy could come only from the leading families, the nobility and landed gentry, not from the lower classes. Pope Gregory XIII blessed their journey on April 18, 1580, just before they left. A dozen other men accompanied them.

En route from Rome, the small entourage stopped in Bologna after Persons injured his leg. When Campion was asked to preach after dinner, he began with a quotation from Pythagoras and compared the ardors and consolations of Christian life with pagan.[1] In Milan, the small band passed eight days with Cardinal Borromeo, and may well have left with copies of Borromeo's *Last Will and Testament of the Soul*, a spiritual declaration of commitment to the Catholic faith in hard times such as the recent plague in Milan, or the persecution in England. When in Protestant regions, the Jesuit-led missionaries put on disguises. By the end of May, they arrived at the English college at Rheims where they were entertained warmly by Fr. William Allen, formerly of Oxford University as were his guests and many of the seminary students. No English exile was held in higher esteem than Dr. Allen, the founder of the English colleges at Douay (now relocated to Rheims) and at Rome.

The group split to cross the English Channel. Persons' crossing from Calais to Dover was followed two weeks later by Campion and Ralph Emerson, with Campion pretending to be a jewel merchant as Persons had told the searcher of Dover. Dr. Edward Bromburg and Thomas Bruscoe crossed from Dieppe; Ralph Sherwin and John Pascal from Rouen; William Giblet, Thomas Crane and William Kemp from Boulogne; and Humphrey Ely, Edward Rishton, Luke Kirby, John Hart and Thomas Cottam from Dunkirk.

Campion came to London and met with many Catholics while awaiting Persons's return from the countryside. There were wealthy Catholics, particularly George Gilbert, who had sufficient means and influence to hide and protect a missionary and to make introductions to other Catholics who would provide shelter throughout the countryside. Gilbert had been a Puritan but converted to Catholicism while in Paris. In Rome he had met Persons and dedicated himself to the Catholic cause in England. With Gilbert's encouragement, a group of young men came together to assist Persons and Campion. Their names and their families' names would be prominent for many years in the struggles of Catholics with the English government: Vaux, Throckmorton, Fitzherbert, Tichbourne.[2] One important member of the group was Thomas Fitzherbert, who a few years later is a central figure in establishing the intelligence network so important to this story. Another of the mission's supporters was Thomas James, who greeted Campion on his arrival in London. James soon left England, never to return save for a few weeks in mid–1601.

At the end of his year-long mission, Persons recorded its main and exemplary events. He recounted an example of the government's harsh treatment of Catholics that occurred just as he arrived in London in late June and reunited with Edmund Campion. On June 8, 1580, Sir Robert Tyrwhitt, former sheriff of Lincolnshire, was in custody and ordered by the Star Chamber—the Privy Council—to produce his son Goddard, the steward of his home, and a Nicholas Tyrwhitt. The order was prompted by a report from Richard Smith, a disgruntled schoolmaster to Edmund, Lord Sheffield, who was stepson and ward of the Earl of Leicester. Smith was at the Tyrwhitt home in Lincolnshire when Lord Sheffield married Sir Robert's daughter, Ursula. The Tyrwhitt sons, said Smith, were turning Sheffield into a Catholic, and the marriage was blessed by a Catholic priest. Sir Robert had dismissed Smith's complaints, and Smith had ridden down to London to denounce him to the Council.

Now Sir Robert's two eldest sons were thrown into the Tower of London, another was held for questioning in York, and the bride and groom had to post bonds for their appearance. Leicester was able to get his stepson and the new Lady Sheffield to conform to the Church of England and escape further consequences. The other family members were not so ready to conform. On June 27 the Privy Council expressed its displeasure that Sir Robert had not yet produced his son Goddard. Friends of the family tried to set aside the order. Goddard was lying ill in London at Salisbury Place, too ill to be moved. The Council ordered that Goddard be examined, and arrested if the reports of serious illness were false. Within a day or two, Goddard was seized and jailed, where, two days later, he died. Father Persons wrote at length of the death of this son of Sir Robert Tyrwhitt, in a passage that is a good example of Persons's limpid prose[3]:

> A certain young gentleman, of an ancient and right worshipful family, was accused for hearing of a mass celebrated (as it was reported) at the marriage of his sister. Whereupon he fled from his father's house, and kept himself secret in London the year last past. And there by reason of his travail in flying away, and (as I think) through the intemperature of the summer, he fell in to a grievous fever. The adversaries hearing hereof, do run unto him by and by, and in all haste will needs pull him out of the house, and throw him into prison, even as he then was, feeble, faint, and grievously sick. This seemed to the beholders thereof to be a manner of dealing both churlish & detestable. They pray, they entreat, they make intercession, they use all the means they can, to move the adversary to have consideration of the sick, not to heap sorrow upon sorrow, nor affliction upon an extremely afflicted man, not to take away the life of so comely a young gentleman: they proffer as sufficient assurance for his forth coming, as his adversaries would demand, and to undertake for his appearance before the justices immediate upon the recovery of his health: but it will not be accepted. The physicians come, they affirm for certain, that he is utterly undone and cast away, if he should be removed forth of that place into the inconveniences of a prison. All this is nothing regarded: they laid hands on the sick man, haled him away, shut him up in prison, & within two days next after he died, they bury him, and make no bones of the matter, nor scruple, or any regard at all.

The young man at Oxford who later becomes the central figure of Catholic counter-espionage, William Sterrell, surely learned quickly of the sufferings of Sir Robert and his children. Not only was Sir Robert patron of William Sterrell's father (undersheriff of Lincolnshire when Sterrell was born in 1561), but the lands on which the Sterrells had lived at Fillingham probably belonged to Sir Robert. Ursula Tyrwhitt was about Sterrell's age and the deceased Goddard only a few years older. These and others of Sir Robert's sons and daughters were doubtless well known to the young Sterrell. Despite Goddard's death, Sir Robert himself was put in the Fleet Prison. He, too, was in poor health, and the Council allowed him liberty of the prison garden and let his wife remain with him. The following year they let him go home to die. His sons William and Robert remained in the Tower, though William was let out briefly to settle his father's estate.

1. The Persons-Campion Jesuit Mission of 1580–1581

This dreadful treatment of a loyal subject and his family could hardly fail to make a vivid impression on the 19-year old Sterrell. It may have been what set him on the radical course he followed for the rest of his life. Probably at just this time he joined with George Gilbert's secret network of Catholic gentlemen around the Campion and Persons mission.

In early July 1580, just after Goddard Tyrwhitt's death, Persons and Campion met with the small number of secular priests and recent seminarians who were hiding in London to tell them of their mission. One of these was Nicholas Tyrwhitt, seminary priest and probably a close relative to Sir Robert. Laymen, too, were present. This meeting has been named the Synod of Southwark. The two Jesuits had no authority over the secular priests already in England, but they conveyed Rome's position that Catholics could never attend the services of the state Church. English Catholics found themselves in a most difficult position. The state required under pain of serious penalty that they attend services of the state Church, and that records be kept of that attendance. The Catholics' own religion demanded that they disobey these laws.

The English government was aware of the presence of the missionaries and began serious, often brutal, reprisals against Catholics. Numerous arrests of recusants were made, and homes of suspected Catholics were searched. The Tyrwhitts were among the first of a great many.

When Persons and Campion left London, they were joined by Thomas Pounde, who was until recently in prison for his faith. At considerable risk, Persons had visited Pounde in the Marshalsea prison. Pounde was an educated gentleman of wealth and family, and once a lively figure at Queen Elizabeth's Court—until he stumbled in the middle of an intricate dance step requested of him by the young queen. She laughed and kicked him, saying "Arise Sir Ox." He bowed and backed away, murmuring "*Sic transit gloria mundi*," passing is this world's glory. He devoted the rest of his life to austere religious observance. His brother John already was a priest. The Poundes were cousins to the distinguished Catholic families of the Wriothesleys (the Earls of Southampton) and the Brownes (Viscount Montague), and they were close to members of the extended Shelley family.

Soon after being visited in prison by the disguised Fr. Persons, Pounde was released on his own recognizance. He quickly went to the aid of the Campion-Persons mission. With his extensive experience in both Court and prison, Pounde suggested to the priests it would be wise if they left with him a declaration of their purposes, to be used to refute the government should they be arrested on charges of treason. Persons and Campion each quickly composed a statement. Persons's is the more lucid. But Campion drew on his years of teaching rhetoric to produce an address to the queen's Privy Council. He, like Persons, denied any intent to deal with matters of state or policy. But with elated fervor he declared the willingness of the missioners to give their lives to restore the Catholic faith in England, ending:

> Many innocent hands are lifted up to heaven for you daily by those English students, whose posterity shall never die, which beyond seas, gathering virtue and sufficient knowledge for the purpose, are determined never to give you over, but either to win you heaven, or to die upon your pikes. And touching our Society, be it known to you that we have made a league—all the Jesuits in the world, whose succession and multitude must overreach all the practices of England—cheerfully to carry the cross you shall lay

upon us, and never to despair your recovery, while we have a man left to enjoy your Tyburn [the place of execution], or to be racked with your torments, or consumed with your prisons. The expense is reckoned, the enterprise is begun; it is of God, it cannot be withstood. So the faith was planted: so it must be restored.

Thomas Pounde took the statement back to the Marshalsea prison with him. Many copies were made and circulated in London and then the country. *Campion's Brag*, as its enemies soon called it, is a manifesto of the Counter-Reformation, and Campion was quickly regarded as English Catholicism's leading champion. Campion's biographer Evelyn Waugh comments that it was the work of the missionaries, particularly of Campion, to bring hope to a community in a disastrous and seemingly hopeless condition: "They came with gaiety among a people where hope was dead. The past held only regret, and the future apprehension; they brought with them, besides their priestly dignity and the ancient and indestructible creed, an entirely new spirit of which Campion is the type; the chivalry of Lepanto[4] and the poetry of La Mancha, light, tender, generous and ardent."[5] For the English government, Campion was regarded now as a chief conspirator on a mission to destroy the foundations of the state. Elizabeth's officers had state clergy respond to Campion's *Brag*. In December 1580 William Charke, a protestant cleric of puritan inclination, published *An Answere to a Seditious Pamphlet lately cast abroade by a Jesuite with a Discoverie of that Blasphemous Sect* and the following month there appeared from the pen of Meredith Hanmer, another controversialist, *The Great Bragge and Challenge of M. Champion a Jesuite*.

For several more months, in late 1580 and early 1581, Persons and Campion traveled widely in England, finding welcome among Catholics. Nicholas Owen, a carpenter and mason, probably acted as a servant to Campion during this time. Owen's unique service to the preservation of the faith in England was the astonishing art and personal labor with which he built intricately concealed hiding places for priests in many Catholic homes. He will, much later, suffer an excruciating death for his faith and labors.

Persons set up a secret press to respond to the pamphlets of clerics like Hanmer and Charke. A new government proclamation was issued requiring all English citizens to recall from abroad anyone studying in a seminary and to turn over any Jesuits or priests saying mass. Government agents searched everywhere. One by one, priests and seminarians who had accompanied the two Jesuits, and some of those who sheltered them, were apprehended and put to torture on the rack, whose straps and wheels and pulleys could stretch a man until his body was deformed and his innards burst forth. Kirby, Cottam, Sherwin, Johnson, Hart, Orton, Thomson, and Roscarock were racked. Perhaps the most charming and devoted of the seminarists was Ralph Sherwin, arrested in the house of Nicholas Roscarock, a layman in the Gilbert association.

Sherwin was typical of the Oxford scholars who became seminarians. Born in 1550, he was nominated by Sir William Petre in 1568 to one of the eight fellowships which Petre had founded at Exeter College, Oxford. These Petres were the prominent Catholic family originating from the West Country around Exeter, but now based about 20 miles east of London at Ingatestone, Essex. Sherwin proved to be an exceptional scholar. He was awarded the degree of M.A. at age 24, and was accounted "an acute philosopher, and an excellent Grecian and Hebrician." The following year he departed to the English College at Douay. After he was ordained a priest, he stayed at the English College of Rome nearly three years before setting out with the party led by Persons and Campion.

In November 1580, Sherwin was imprisoned in the Marshalsea. Conditions in that prison were rather lax, and Sherwin set about converting fellow prisoners. In December the authorities transferred him to the Tower, where he was severely racked, and afterwards laid out in the snow. The next day he was racked again. After this second torture he lay for five days and nights without any food, or speech with anybody. A year later he was brought to trial on charges of treasonable conspiracy and found guilty.

Campion had continued to visit the homes of Catholics in many parts of England, including prominent families such as the Pierrepoints, the Talbots, the Heskeths, the Worthingtons, the Vavasours. Only a fraction of the families who gave Campion, Persons and others of the mission shelter and support have been identified. As Campion traveled, he wrote, and what he wrote soon appeared as *Decem Rationes*. The full title, translated, gives its purpose: "Ten Reasons, for the confidence with which Edmund Campion offered his adversaries to dispute on behalf of the Faith, set before the famous men of our Universities." It was a challenge to the scholars of the English universities. The manuscript was delivered to Persons for his secret press, now located near Henley, about twenty miles from Oxford, soon after Easter 1581. Because Campion's refutation of Protestantism was directed to a learned audience, Persons thought that all its references (to Cicero, Tertullian, the Bible, Beza, Calvin, Luther, Zwingli, St. Gregory, and many others) should be verified. This scholarly task fell to Thomas Fitzherbert of Swinnerton, later himself the author of a political treatise and a Jesuit. The book's printing took weeks, so limited were the resources for printing, and so great the danger. But it was ready for the special occasion of its distribution: the Commencement ceremonies of Oxford University, Tuesday, June 27, 1581. Copies were clandestinely placed on the benches in St. Mary's Church, the distribution overseen by Fr. William Hartley, formerly a chaplain St. John's, Oxford before his expulsion for religion. It caused an immediate sensation. Particularly notable is its tone in speaking directly to the queen, the same queen before whom he had declaimed 15 years earlier at this same university. Here, Englished, is part of what the scholars of Oxford found in Latin that morning on their benches[6]:

> Listen, Elizabeth, most powerful Queen.... I tell thee; one and the same heaven cannot hold Calvin and the Princes whom I have named [Elizabeth's ancestors, and the great heroes of Christendom]. With these Princes then associate thyself, and so make thee worthy of thy ancestors, worthy of thy genius, worthy of thy excellence in letters, worthy of thy praises, worthy of thy fortune. To this effect alone do I labour about thy person, and will labour, whatever shall become of me, for whom these adversaries so often augur the gallows, as though I were an enemy of thy life. Hail, good Cross. There will come, Elizabeth, the day, that day which will show thee clearly which have loved thee, the Society of Jesus or the offspring of Luther.

Later, another Jesuit, in utterly different circumstances, would again address Elizabeth with similar directness: the poet-priest Robert Southwell. He, too, will suffer the obsequious death on the scaffold at Tyburn.

One young scholar who will not have missed that memorable Oxford Commencement of 1581 was William Sterrell. He was the very sort of young Catholic that Persons and Campion had returned England to strengthen their resolve. He will have read the *Decem Rationes*, and perhaps was one of the young Catholics who distributed them about the benches of the church of St. Mary the Virgin for the masters and students. He had been at Oxford at least three years, and had been a scholar of Magdalen since September 1578. By mid–1579 he had been ready to take his B.A. But on June 30 of that year the President and officers of the college refused their consent to his graduating until he spent the allotted time in study of logic, "*et se de crimine suspectae religionis coram Praeside et aliis purgasset*[7]—"and until he purge himself personally before the President and officers from the offence of suspect religion." In other words, they strongly suspected him of being a Roman Catholic. He must have satisfied them, for he was soon awarded the degree and promptly became a full Fellow (scholar) of Magdalen.

As a very bright student with known Catholic sympathies, Sterrell will have come to Campion's attention about the time when Campion was challenging and energizing the scholars of Oxford with *Decem Rationes*. Like Campion, Sterrell was a young Oxford scholar able enough to become a lecturer despite the whiff of Catholicism, someone to be courted by the Catholics and by the anti-Catholic Earl of Leicester. Sterrell and Campion may well have met during Campion's year in England. Certainly within a few more years Sterrell had come to know many of those who knew and worked closely with Campion, especially Thomas Fitzherbert. Sterrell himself reports in a letter that were he to go to Spain he would find himself in good credit with Fr. Persons, and soon after that he becomes a well-trusted correspondent to Persons. Sterrell will have been greatly interested in the Persons-Campion mission that so directly penetrated Oxford, led by several of its most illustrious sons.

Campion was captured at Lyford, near Oxford, in mid–July 1581. Students had asked him to stay there a second night so that they could ride out from Oxford to hear him, and his decision to do so let the authorities track him down. Persons escaped to the Continent, while Campion was transported to London, and paraded through the streets with a hat placarded with papers denouncing him—the usual punishment of forgers or perjurers. After four days in a tiny cell in the Tower, he was taken out and escorted to Leicester House, the palatial residence later known as Essex House. Campion was led into a large room where he was met by the owner, his former patron the Earl of Leicester, along with the Earl of Bedford, and two Secretaries of State. They questioned the Jesuit at length about his beliefs and his purposes, offering him a great future if only he would reject his church and enter the Protestant ministry. He declined and was returned to the Tower.

Now the government began to torture Campion, to force him to betray his associates and those who had given him shelter, and to confess to a conspiracy to overthrow the queen and her government. He was stretched on the rack. The government was so concerned with the fame that had been given to Campion's *Brag* and his *Ten Reasons* that the Privy Council decided to stage a series of Conferences at which Campion would dispute with Anglican clergy. The format was a bitter parody of the formal disputations at Oxford at which Campion had made such an impression during Elizabeth's 1566 visit. Members of the queen's Court and council gathered to watch the event as two noted clerics, seated at a table and surrounded by theological books and papers and assistants to find passages and mark them, put their chosen criticisms of Catholic faith to the prisoner. Their opponent sat alone upon a stool. He had been in solitary confinement for five weeks, and could barely move his limbs after his rackings. Through four one-day meetings over several weeks Campion was questioned closely on theological doctrine, the first two examiners replaced by fresh pairs as the sessions wore on. Among the matters discussed was the Real Presence of Christ in the Communion, a point that sharply divided the state church from Catholicism. Campion affirmed the Real Presence, and the state clerics said he denied the bodily resurrection of Christ. The clerics quoted from the books on their table. Campion was not allowed a single work or even the opportunity to write.[8]

One of the clerics chosen to dispute with Campion was Lawrence Humphrey, President of Magdalen College. To Humphrey's relief, the disputation was cancelled before it took place, but he wrote a reply to the *Ten Reasons* that appeared in two parts in 1582 and 1584.[9] The unequal debates ended inconclusively, and numerous pamphlets then appeared with government support to refute the *Brag* and the *Ten Reasons*. Campion was returned to prison and in November was given a show trial that convicted him and four others of plotting to overthrow the queen. Among the witnesses to this implausible treason charge was the writer, Anthony Munday, who had been in Rome as a pretended Catholic—a government spy—and now testified as to treasonous activities by Campion and the seminarians at Rheims. Munday wrote pamphlets about Campion's capture, trial, and execution and gave evidence in other trials of the priests on this mission. On December 1, 1581, Campion, Sherwin, and Briant were bound on hurdles and dragged behind horses to the gallows at Tyburn. They were hanged until half-dead, then castrated, disemboweled, and quartered, their sundered parts put up on public display for worms and birds of prey.

Campion was dead, but the martyrdom of a brilliant scholar with a persuasive pen who had undertaken a dangerous mission animated Catholics throughout England. Networks had been formed among them, and dangerous commitments made. Associating with the priests put men and women in severe peril, and heightened their sense of the injustice of a government, their own government, keen to hunt them down for doing no more than participate privately in a sacrament of the religion which, when they were born, had been England's for centuries.

The story of Campion's mission and its extirpation was told immediately by a Catholic priest, Thomas Alfield, in a book secretly printed in Smithfield, just outside London. One of the printers, Stephen Vallenger, was arrested and nailed to a post by the ears, which were then cut off; thus mutilated, he was imprisoned for life. The printer chiefly responsible for running the secret press was a man more like Persons than Campion: a combatant and controversialist for the long haul, rather than a martyr. He was Richard Rowland, better known as Richard Verstegan, another of the close associates in the counter-espionage network established after the failure of the Spanish Armada.

Born about 1548, Richard Verstegan entered Christ Church, Oxford in 1565 but took no degree, probably because even at that early period of the reign, religious tests might be required of students to graduate. In April 1582, shortly after the printing of Alfield's book, Verstegan's printing press was seized, and he fled the country. Setting up in Paris, he continued what was to be a fifty-year career as publisher of religious books and pamphlets, and author of polemical, antiquarian, and poetic works. The English diplomatic mission had the French authorities arrest him, but failed to secure his extradition, and after a period in Rome he settled in Antwerp for the remainder of a long life. His successful *Theatrum crudelitatum haereticorum nostri temporis* (eight editions in 20 years) was richly illustrated with his engravings of events such as the death of Margaret Clitheroe—tortured and executed by *peine forte et dure* (crushed with stones)—and the rackings and executions of martyrs. Verstegan later will become an important contact for William Sterrell in Antwerp, where Verstegan worked with other prominent opponents of the English Protestant regime.

Campion's reference-checker in Oxford in the Spring of 1581, Thomas Fitzherbert, fled to Paris with his wife, Dorothy East. He became a zealous promoter of Mary Queen of Scots, and devoted the remainder of his long life to Catholicism in England, a land he never saw again. His wife will die in 1588. In 1602 he will take holy orders and still later will enter the Society of Jesus, eventually becoming the rector of the English College at Rome.

The Persons/Campion mission was a catalyst, a historic event dramatically affecting the lives of people like Verstegan and Fitzherbert, and others to be named shortly, who were deeply moved by the martyrdoms of Campion, Sherwin, Kirby, Briant, Alfield and others on the mission. The Alfield/Verstegan *True Report*, telling all England the significance of Campion's martyrdom, is accompanied by a poem known by its first line, bitterly echoing the injustice inflicted on Campion by the state scholars in the Tower conferences: "Why do I use my paper, ink and pen?"[10]

One person both grieved and inspired by the example of Campion was the great composer, William Byrd, who even in his own time was called the Father of English Music. His *Psalmes, sonets & songs of sadnes and pietie* published in 1588 included some stanzas of this

Left: Edmund Campion. Artist: Jacobus Neeffs (Neefs) (© National Portrait Gallery, London). *Right*: Robert Persons. Artist: Jacobus Neeffs (Neefs) (© National Portrait Gallery, London).

poem. The following year, Byrd published *Liber primus sacrarum cantionum* (first book of sacred songs), dedicating it to his patron Edward Somerset, now Earl of Worcester. This collection of Latin songs included a setting to music of Psalm 78 (Vulgate/Latin version of the Bible) *Deus venerunt gentes*. This poignant motet alludes to the execution of Edmund Campion and others at Tyburn. Artfully chosen from the Latin Bible, its lines include:

> They have laid out the dead bodies of thy servants as food for the birds of the air, the flesh of thy saints for the beasts of the earth. They have poured out their blood like water round Jerusalem, and there was no one to bury them.

2

Tainted in Blood

The punishment for treason fell not only upon the offenders but also on their families. England in 1580 was not a feudal society but it was stratified. Family was the source of rank, status and wealth. Family was the foundation of one's identity, and most often one's religion. And if treason tainted the head of the family, it tainted the rest of the family, directly or by association. The consequence of attainder is outlined by the Earl of Somerset in Shakespeare's 1 Henry VI:

> Was not thy father, …
> For treason executed in our late king's days?
> And by his treason stand'st not thou attainted,
> Corrupted, and exempt from ancient gentry?
> His trespass yet lives guilty in thy blood;
> And till thou be restor'd thou art a yeoman.

Shakespeare's words applied to the young man who called himself *Callophisus*, for his appearance in the tiltyard of Westminster, London, at 1 o'clock on Sunday, January 22, 1581. He was Philip Howard, eldest son of Thomas Howard who through attainder had forfeited his life and his title as Duke of Norfolk. When his father was stripped of his Dukedom, Philip Howard lost the heirship of his father and also his courtesy title of Earl of Surrey. The sins of the father were suffered by his heirs. As treason's stains were inherited, perhaps, too, rebellion became hereditary. The queen's officers, dedicated to protection of both crown and country, looked with suspicion upon the seed of rebels.

Philip Howard—in mock battle under a romance name that suggested "beautiful face" or a lover of beauty—fought a genuine struggle to ingratiate himself with the queen. For five years he had met with limited success. Though she had executed his father in 1572, Philip Howard was now allowed the honor of being the Challenger in ceremonial combat to demonstrate the superiority of the Challenger's devotion to his mistress, the queen, over seventeen Defenders who appeared at the barriers of Westminster this January afternoon. Parliament was in session and meetings were to resume the next day. It would take a bill in Parliament, with backing by the queen, for restitution in blood of Philip Howard.

Dressed colorfully and often named by color (the White Knight, the Red Knight etc.), the men on horseback were the cream of Elizabeth's courtiers. Among them were the Earl of Oxford, the Lord Windsor, Philip Sidney, and Fulke Greville. Four of the Defenders were drawn from the queen's Gentlemen Pensioners, the monarch's elite bodyguard, her personal companions in arms. Required to attend to the queen at least six months out of each year, the Pensioners each gave an oath of exclusive service and was required to furnish horses and servants for the queen. When attending, they were required to be in her presence by ten o'clock each morning and to bear a "clean and bright axe" for protection of her person.

The tilt-yard of Westminster was constructed by Elizabeth's father, King Henry VIII. Spectators were seated in a double tier of galleries overlooking the long course where the mounted participants rode at one another with wooden lances. In earlier times the field was open and the riders' horses might collide with one another. Now a barrier erected of wood or made of cloth hung on a rope separated the combatants. Jousting demanded courage, strength and skill.

A joust at Westminster conducted by the queen's own guard and noblemen from her chief courtiers was much more than a week-end amusement. It was a visible display of the strength of the Royal Court, a state spectacle of the martial skills and readiness of those who protected the queen. Thus, the presence in combat of distinguished members of her personal body-guard. The ceremonial battles by the young men of the Court were royal entertainment, but politics were always present. While gallants jousted, peers and MPs bargained and schemed in the galleries.

Philip Howard was tall and of dark complexion, but he could not be called handsome. Nor was he prudent. He spent lavishly in his campaign for royal favor and ignored the pious woman to whom he became married when both were only twelve. She was Anne Dacre, a daughter of his father's third wife.

Philip's father, the Duke of Norfolk, had been the wealthiest and highest nobleman of the England when his fortune became entangled with the deposed queen of Scots, Mary Stewart. Three times a widower, Norfolk was eligible as a spouse for Mary, twice a widow (though inconveniently married to Bothwell). A marriage between Scotland's queen and England's pre-eminent noble could revive her fortunes while advancing his. The plan was to restore Mary to the throne of Scotland with Elizabeth's support. Norfolk was a Protestant but the match was associated with Catholic goals. Norfolk reluctantly became leader of a faction at the English court which sought removal of the zealous Protestant William Cecil and better relations with Spain. The match of Norfolk and Mary Queen of Scots would procure Cecil's eclipse. When Queen Elizabeth vetoed the match, it was Norfolk who left the court in disgrace. In October 1569 Norfolk was arrested. His Catholic supporters, the earls of Northumberland and Westmorland, rose against the queen in rebellion. It was Northumberland who (with the Earl of Westmorland) in November 1569 wrote Pope Pius V seeking the excommunication of Queen Elizabeth, resulting in the notorious papal bull *Regnam in excelsis* a few months later. Eventually Norfolk was charged with treason against Elizabeth, principally for his pursuit of a marriage to a queen who herself had a claim to the crown of England and secondarily for support of the English rebels of the northern rising of 1569. In June 1572 the Duke of Norfolk was executed. His eldest son, Philip, was fifteen years old.

Now, eight years later, Norfolk's son proclaimed that his faith and loyalty to his father's executioner was greater than any other of her subjects and that he would prove his goodwill and affection against all challengers in this field of Westminster. Yet only a few more years would pass before his own fate became tied to the woman whose cause had brought down his father.

Who watched the combat in the galleries? The queen, of course. It was her spectacle, in her honor. With her were many of her Court, and surely her principal secretary, Sir

Francis Walsingham. She had taken to calling him her Moor, but whether it was from his slavish devotion or a swarthy complexion cannot be said. After a three year stint in France as England's ambassador, Queen Elizabeth had appointed him Secretary and a Privy Councilor. Trained as a lawyer at Gray's Inn, and having served in Parliament since 1559, Walsingham was first used for espionage by William Cecil, Lord Treasurer, in 1568. For a least a decade, Walsingham had considered Mary Stewart a threat to Elizabeth. In 1569 William Cecil had appointed Walsingham as the guardian of Roberto di Ridolfi (the Ridolphi Plot). Walsingham may have been the anonymous author of a tract at this time attacking the prospective marriage between Mary Stewart and the Duke of Norfolk. He thought it was a mistake that Mary Queen of Scots was not executed in 1572 with the Duke of Norfolk, and Thomas Percy, the Earl of Northumberland. In Paris, where he was English ambassador, he had witnessed the St. Bartholomew Night massacre of Protestants, instigated by Catherine de Medici, the mother-in-law of Mary Queen of Scots. He would make possible Mary Stewart's execution in 1587.

Looking down from the gallery at Norfolk's son, Walsingham will have reflected on the continuing threat from Mary Stewart. If Philip Howard were restored in blood, would he not pose a threat as his father had? Was not treason a hereditary trait of Howards and Percys? The young Howard's Christian name was itself a stigma for Walsingham: born in the reign of Mary Tudor, Philip was christened with the name of his godfather, Queen Mary's royal consort, King Philip II of Spain.

Walsingham well knew that Percy hands had been stained in treason for generations. Henry "Hotspur" Percy and his father, the first Earl of Northumberland, had each rebelled against their king, Henry IV. The third Earl of Northumberland, also named Henry Percy, was posthumously attainted by the first parliament of the King Edward IV. Sir Thomas Percy, the son of Henry Percy, the 5th Earl of Northumberland, was convicted of treason for a Catholic uprising against King Henry VIII in 1537 and hanged, drawn and quartered. Thirty years later, his son, the seventh Earl of Northumberland, rebelled against his monarch. This Thomas Percy had fled in 1569 into Scotland and was subsequently attainted. His younger brother, Henry, had opposed the 1569 rebellion, so Thomas Percy's attainder contained a clause permitting Henry to succeed as 8th Earl of Northumberland, which occurred upon Thomas Percy's execution in 1572, shortly after the Duke of Norfolk's execution. But Henry had himself been sent to the Tower of London for his bad judgment in support of Mary Queen of Scots, and Walsingham distrusted him now. He would be closely watched and imprisoned at the first opportunity.

Walsingham looked around the galleries for members of the Somerset family. He spotted William Somerset, third earl of Worcester, and his son, Edward, Lord Herbert. Father and son were in London while the earl was present in the House of Lords. Both were excellent at the joust and keen observers of the sport. The earl sponsored a touring acting company, and the son oversaw its activities. Both were reputed to be Catholics. They naturally came to mind when Walsingham thought of the Percy clan.

Worcester's sister was Anne Percy, widow of Thomas Percy. As Countess of Northumberland she had been attainted separately from her husband. She had escaped to Flanders while Walsingham was ambassador in France. The countess quickly assumed a leadership role among the English Catholics in exile and was an active supporter of Mary Queen of Scots. Anne and the Earl of Worcester had a brother, Thomas Somerset, who had been jailed several times for his obstinate Catholicism. From his agents, Walsingham knew that Thomas Somerset had helped Fr. William Allen establish the English college and seminary at Douay and had enrolled members of his own family there. He too looked to Mary Queen of Scots as a future queen of England. The sister of William, Anne and Thomas Somerset was Lucy Neville, and she was the mother of Katherine Percy, the wife of Henry Percy, 8th Earl of Northumberland. The Percy and Somerset families were so entwined, Walsingham thought of them as a nest of intercoiled snakes. But Walsingham knew Worcester was cautious, a most circumspect man. Worcester took part in the trial that convicted the Duke of Norfolk. When Queen Elizabeth needed a proxy to represent her at the christening of the daughter of the French king, she sent Worcester as her emissary. He demonstrated his loyalty to his queen by refusing to meet his own sister, the attainted Countess of Northumberland. Walsingham was unsure whether Worcester may have privately met with her, for Walsingham was ill throughout the visit. Worcester, like his close relative Northumberland, and Worcester's son, would be arrested at the first opportunity. This was to occur the following August, none too soon as far as Walsingham was concerned.

Walsingham took special note of one of the Defenders doing battle against Philip Howard. One the Queen's Gentlemen Pensioners, he was George Gifford, a young man from Itchell, Hampshire. Twenty-eight years old, Gifford had just celebrated the first anniversary of his marriage to Eleanor Brydges, daughter of Edmund Brydges, Baron Chandos. Her stepfather was Sir William Knollys, and two of Sir William's brothers (Robert and Henry Knollys) were also participants as Defenders. George Gifford was tied closely to the Court by his position but also by his wife's family. But the young man also had important overseas connections among the Catholic exiles that might prove of value to Walsingham.

Walsingham's vigilant agents in ports and inns searched for dangerous correspondence entering or leaving England. A packet of letters from Rheims where the English seminary was now located was intercepted the previous October. Among the letters of this packet was one from Richard Gifford to his brother "George Gifford of the Court." George Gifford, now a Gentleman Pensioner, was descended from the Throckmortons of Coughton. Walsingham reflected that George Gifford could be a threat or a recruit for Walsingham's emerging plan. Perhaps Gifford was a young man who could be moved to action by ambition as well as patriotism and devotion to his queen, whom he served from an early age. With his martial training and Catholic relatives in exile, he was just the man to accept a dangerous mission into the camp of the Catholic enemy. George Gifford's father died while he was young and when his mother remarried (to William Hodges), he and his brothers were deposited in other nests. While George Gifford was being admitted to the ranks of Elizabeth's Gentlemen Pensioners, his brothers William and Richard Gifford and his half-brother William Hodges all left England to study at Catholic colleges on the Continent. George Gifford was ideally qualified to serve as one of Walsingham's double agents. Other intercepted letters had already identified another of George Gifford's relatives as a potential ally in Walsingham's plan to ensnare the Scots queen in a web from which she could not escape. George Gifford's brother, William Gifford, and their cousin Gilbert Gifford were part of the English religious establishment in Europe, products of the seminaries established by William Allen to keep English Catholicism supplied with ordained priests. Walsingham could play upon the divided loyalties and dissatisfactions of some among the English exiles to bring down Mary Queen of Scots and squelch the rebellious spirits among the Howard, Percy and Somerset families. Pride must have its fall.

Walsingham's duties as Secretary and in Parliament delayed a visit to France that was necessary to put his plan into motion. Summer was soon enough.

The prize for the tilt-yard contest that January afternoon was given to the Earl of Oxford, Edward de Vere, a cousin of Philip Howard. For this occasion, Oxford was styled the "Knight of the Tree of the Sun." Philip Howard's efforts were advanced that January day. Less than two months later he was restored in blood by Parliament and confirmed in his title as Earl of Arundel, which he had inherited through his maternal grandfather. He took his seat in the House of Lords on April 11.

Philip Howard's long, expensive campaign for royal favor, though successful, had not brought him happiness. Resentful of the marriage his father had contracted for him at age twelve, he had neglected his wife Anne. Her father, Thomas Dacre, died when she was only nine and her mother died when she was ten. She was only fifteen when the Duke of Norfolk, her father-in-law (and step-father), was executed and the family into which she had married was disgraced. She filled the void in her life with religion. She converted to Catholicism, perhaps inspired by the fervor of the Campion-Persons mission. She emerged in her early twenties as a woman of strong character, fully capable of independent action. She had the support of her older half-sister, Margaret, who was married to Robert Sackville (son of Lord Buckhurst), and her sister Elizabeth, who was married to her husband's brother, William Howard. These sisters, too, were Catholics and supporters of the Jesuits. All three of these noble sisters will suffer for their strong religious faith. They will remain resolute.

Curiosity about the notoriety surrounding the arrest and trial of Edmund Campion, rather than his wife's associations, drew Philip Howard to the staged disputations on religion between Campion and the government's divines. But the courage and fortitude of the Jesuit martyr made an impression on this supercilious courtier and neglectful husband. The Earl of Arundel's visits to the Tower of London in September 1581 to observe the unequal exchanges between the priest who was denied pen and ink and the forces of her Majesty's government were not to be his last. Walsingham would see to that.

3

A Wolf by the Ears

Sir Francis Walsingham was the Machiavelli of Elizabeth's counselors. He used spies, informants, double agents, provocateurs, and every trick of a secret service. Historians have failed to penetrate fully his labyrinthine designs. His success lay in part in the fact that he kept most of the elements of his schemes in his own fine mind. No others were privy to the interrelations of the players and the parts they played. Walsingham's secrecy was in part to conceal his activities from his own queen and his fellow Council members. His methods were unseemly and he regarded Queen Elizabeth as too squeamish and vacillating to do the things necessary for her own best interest. She recoiled at the blackguards and scoundrels he used to obtain his goals, and hers.

Walsingham conceived a campaign that would turn opinion of English citizens against Catholics. His tactic has been used by politicians throughout history: conjure up a foreign plot or threat of domestic terrorism to unite the populace behind government leaders who promise to keep them secure. While the government issued proclamations and laws against Catholics in public, he implemented a long term plan to identify in the public mind Catholics as assassins bent on killing their queen and overthrowing their legitimate government, acting on behalf of foreign powers.

Walsingham's strategy had two broad purposes. One was to intervene in, and then expose, a European plot against Elizabeth, so as to show that foreign threats were real and justified harsh measures within England against those English citizens who might support foreign enemies. The second purpose was to entrap English Catholics in such plots against Elizabeth, again to show that the Roman-Spanish-French threat to the realm was real and must be suppressed by enforcing adherence to the state Church. Catholics must be tarred with the brush of treason and disloyalty to their own country. Elizabeth's preferred gradualism (letting English Catholicism wither as old priests died) was too uncertain and was threatened by the infusion of fresh young priests ordained abroad.

What the government, and later historians, presented as a series of distinct plots by English Catholics against Elizabeth in the period 1582 to 1586, known variously as the Throckmorton Plot, the Parry Plot and the Babington Plot, all sprouted, in fact, from seeds sown and cultivated by Secretary Walsingham, and all related to a vague plan known in Europe as the *Empresa—The Enterprise*. To vivify the threat to the realm, a person was needed to serve as the object of the conspiracies. The obvious figure was Mary Queen of Scots. Although aging, arthritic, and under house arrest in England for more than a dozen years, Mary Stewart's French background and identification with Catholicism made her the ideal focus for a campaign to inspire fear of foreign intervention. But what Walsingham feared most were time's relentless march and his queen's irresolution.

Walsingham knew the plots against Elizabeth (and her government) would have to appear to originate from abroad: Rome, France, Spain or the Spanish Low Countries. France was the obvious choice. Fluent in French and Italian, Walsingham had many contacts in France. Mary Stewart's conspiratorial relatives, the Guise family, were in France. For a least a decade, Walsingham had considered Mary Queen of Scots as a sovereign threat. In 1569 Cecil had appointed Walsingham as the guardian of Roberto di Ridolfi, the Florentine banker and ardent Catholic associated with the plot bearing his name. Ridolphi's plan called for the Duke of Alba to invade from the Netherlands with 10,000 men. Mary Stewart was to be seated on the English throne, with the Duke of Norfolk at her side.

Time and events reinforced Walsingham's determination to rectify the government's mistake in not executing Mary Stewart in 1572. The Scots queen was 10 years younger than Elizabeth. It required no actuary to predict that unless put to death, Mary would be expected to outlive—and to succeed—her cousin. Each passing year made it ever more clear that no foreign prince would appear to charm Elizabeth Tudor to forsake her unwed state, that no child would issue from her natural body to continue the Tudor line. Mary Stewart had descended from Henry Tudor, Henry VII, the father of Elizabeth's father, Henry VIII, and no one had a superior claim by birth than Mary Stewart. An effort had been made in 1553 to deny Elizabeth's sister, Mary Tudor, her birthright to succeed by installing Jane Grey. So powerful was the notion of legitimacy of rule by consanguinity that "Queen Jane" was ousted before ten days had passed, and she and her consort were eventually beheaded and her supporters executed or imprisoned. Wyatt's Rebellion had failed in its attempt to keep England under Protestant rule. The fact that Mary Stewart's son, James, was King of Scotland and an apparent Protestant made the removal of Mary all the more imperative. Should Mary succeed to the throne, she might return the country to Catholicism before her son could be crowned. She might require his acceptance of her religion or impede his right to succeed her.

Walsingham chose his player-agents with care and moved them about between England, Scotland and France to create the impression of an urgent and imminent threat to the English queen. It was imperative that she have no sense that her own government was a key factor in plots against her life. Thus the deception was two-fold. Walsingham had to deceive not only those who were to be drawn into a plot but also to manipulate the queen who was the object of the plot. As provocateurs, Walsingham's agents had to appear genuine opponents of the English queen and religion, to their own government and to those whom they were trying to incite into action.

Walsingham had no qualms about misleading his monarch. In respect of her natural body, Elizabeth Tudor was a vain and irresolute woman who played her courtiers one against another. Her religious convictions, like her father's, were more opportunistic than deeply felt. She disliked papal pomp but preserved all of the ceremony and hierarchy of her own bishops, and they retained much of their finery. The problem with Roman Catholic bishops was their allegiance to Rome. Bishops loyal to Elizabeth as supreme head of both church and state were not only acceptable but were necessary if she were to preserve and consolidate the powers gained by her father, Henry VIII, in breaking with Rome. Walsingham had little use for bishops, whether English-appointed or Roman, but he could not openly defy his queen on this fundamental. With regard to her second body, the body politic, Elizabeth Tudor was the embodiment of England's Policy and Government, which were constituted for the direction of the English nation and the management of the public good. It was this second Elizabeth Tudor whom Walsingham served. If Walsingham found it necessary to circumvent his queen to fight Rome and promote true religion, it was because the Almighty came before the mighty, and the body politic transcended the interests of Elizabeth's natural self. What he did to preserve the crown was in her interest, and it was better she not know his methods. His actions were warranted for the good of the nation from her own refusal to speak about who would succeed her or even tolerate speech by anyone on the topic of succession. For Elizabeth, to allow Parliament to take up the subject would be to acknowledge that the monarch was subject to Parliament. Her indecision and obstinacy compelled his deeds and his methods.

Five of Walsingham's recruits were central to his machinations that resulted in the execution of the Scots queen. A dozen or so others make their appearances with them. Their actions, and circumstantial evidence, leave little doubt that from 1581 to the execution of Mary Queen of Scots in 1587 their activities were directed by Walsingham.

Three of the five were named Gifford: two brothers and their cousin. Walsingham frequently recruited disaffected seminarians to spy in the English colleges in Rheims and Rome. He insinuated his own agents as students into these institutions. The English government would identify and keep track of English Catholics abroad and their contacts back home, and they could sow dissension among those they infiltrated. It served Walsingham's purpose that by 1578 the scholars and administrators in Rheims and Rome knew they had been penetrated by his agents: it made them deeply suspicious of each other and of newcomers from England. The detailed records of one of his agents, Charles Sledd, note when a student is thought to be a "servant to Mr. Secreterye Walsingham" or "apertayninge to Sir Francis Walsingham."[1]

Gilbert Gifford was one of the many children of John Gifford of Chillington, Staffordshire. In January 1577 Gilbert Gifford arrived at the English College at Douay. There also was his cousin William Gifford, a younger brother of George Gifford, the Gentleman Pensioner who jousts with Philip Howard before Queen Elizabeth. William was a bit younger than Gilbert and had attended Lincoln College, Oxford before taking an MA at Louvain in Flanders. Both Gilbert and William proceeded to the English College at Rome. Gilbert lacked the self-discipline of William and within a year was expelled for misconduct. Walsingham's spy, Charles Sledd, was familiar with Gilbert and William Gifford from his time in Rheims and Rome. Both were included in Sledd's reports of 1579 and 1580 that were given to Walsingham. Sledd briefed Ambassador Cobham in Paris in April 1580 in multiple meetings, and Cobham gave Sledd a secret token to give to Walsingham, together with a written account of the intelligence he had shared; this included details on the Campion-Persons mission group that was making its way from Rome shortly behind the group with which Sledd had been traveling. Sledd met with Walsingham in London on May 17, 1580, and on May 26. Sledd delivered Walsingham a book: "The intelligence of the affairs of Englishmen in Rome, & other places." This report included physical descriptions of a number of priests, including Fr. Persons and several others of the mission that arrived in England a month later. It also included summaries of talks in Rome and Rheims in which Sledd claimed he had heard of plans developed by the Pope and by Spain for an invasion of England and replacement of Elizabeth.

Sledd's reports prepared Walsingham well to receive packets of letters seized as they were smuggled into England. He could link names of students abroad and their families back in England and bring pressure to bear in more places. The name Gifford would have caught his eye immediately. Writing from Paris on August 5, 1580, Gilbert Gifford complained bitterly to his father for forbidding his brother Edward from speaking to Gilbert and for his father's "hard usage" in not supporting him. His harsh language, his sense of entitlement and his effort to instill guilt in his father indicate Gilbert's personality, a character later manifested in the manipulation of many friends and relatives.[2] Gilbert expressed his jealousy at his sisters, who had received more than he, and accused his father of being misled by "whispers" in his ears.[3]

Gilbert Gifford was an angry young man: bitter at his father for lack of support; jealous of his sisters and older brothers; and hostile to the Catholic church for expelling him from the College at Rome. Reading this intercepted letter, Walsingham recognized a soul in turmoil who could be recruited. In his anger, Gilbert Gifford was ripe to betray family and Church while feigning reconciliation. He was exactly the sort of young man Walsingham wanted: corrupt and corruptible. Could one not have predicted in 1580 that a decade later he would be arrested in a foreign brothel, and die in a French prison disgraced in the eyes of all who knew him? Walsingham thought it most fitting that he would turn Rome's English agents into his own operatives and use them against England's enemies in France, Spain and Rome. He would nurse their anger and feed their greed.

Another packet of letters from Rheims was intercepted in October 1580. It confirmed to Walsingham that Gilbert Gifford was a prime candidate for his purposes. A letter in this October packet suggested that Gilbert would be allowed to resume his studies for the priesthood at Rheims.[4] The same packet would have led Walsingham to his cousins, the two brothers George and William Gifford.

When did Walsingham pair George Gifford and Gilbert Gifford together? Perhaps it began on Walsingham's trip to Paris in the mid-summer and early fall of 1581. Although there is no record of Walsingham meeting with Gilbert Gifford, Walsingham did make contact during the embassy with Charles Paget, who had arrived in Paris from England earlier in 1581. Paget now associated with Thomas Morgan, a Welshman who had come to know Mary Queen of Scots while working for the Earl of Shrewsbury, in whose household she was held captive. Morgan had fled England in 1575. A lover of intrigue, he probably became a double agent well before 1581. Walsingham's man, Sledd, encountered Morgan in Paris in 1580, reporting that Morgan had been there about a year after coming from Rome and had recently departed on his way back into England. Walsingham probably drew him into his grand scheme at this time.

By mid–1581 Morgan and Paget had established themselves as agents of Mary Queen of Scots in France. They were perfectly positioned as assets of Walsingham to further his plans. Walsingham will have worked with them through his trusted aide, Thomas Phelippes. A Cambridge graduate, Phelippes had worked for England's ambassador to France and by 1578 served Walsingham. In the summer of 1581 Phelippes was in London deciphering letters for Walsingham and he probably accompanied Walsingham to France in August. Phelippes spent much of 1582–83 in France and became a close friend of Thomas Morgan. Gilbert Gifford later testified that Phelippes "frequently told me that Morgan was a great and intimate friend of his, and also spoke to me of the times they would dine and eat together in Paris."⁵ Should one be surprised that Phelippes will be able to decipher letters to and from Mary Stewart that use Morgan's ciphers? Phelippes had no doubt coached Morgan in encryption techniques while they were together in France.

Soon Morgan and Paget were allied with William Gifford (George's brother) and Gilbert Gifford to stir trouble among the Catholic exiles in France and the Low Countries. Gilbert Gifford moved somewhat freely between Rheims, Paris and Rome in 1582–83, often in the company of his cousin William, and also visited England. He was the probable author in England writing letters in the name of "Henry Fagot," as though he were a French-speaking priest spending brief periods in the French embassy.

William Gifford was a rising star among the English exiles. Walsingham's agent Sledd reported that on October 8, 1579, William Gifford was appointed to debate Natural Philosophy at the English College of Rome, and all the Englishmen of the city were requested to be present. The list of attendees at the disputation and at the dinner afterward with William Allen included most of the men who planned or went on the Campion-Persons mission. Two years later, Gifford was ordained a priest, and by March 1582 Allen made him a professor at Rheims.

Fr. Barrett, himself an Oxford Fellow before becoming a priest in Rheims, described William Gifford, in April 1583, as well-behaved but of an inconstant character and too easily subject to the flattery and favors of some of the factionalists.⁶ The letter points to the influence on William Gifford of Thomas Morgan, and implicitly Charles Paget, who provided some support to the College but who also encouraged dissension between Welsh (Secular) and English (Jesuit-oriented) groups. Barrett observed that "Father William [Gifford] they consider one of their own." Father Persons was back in Paris in May 1583, and he found that the Welsh party had joined with the Morgan-Paget faction that opposed the Jesuits.⁷

Was Walsingham fomenting discord among the Catholic exiles? Perhaps. Another explanation for the behavior of William Gifford is that he sincerely opposed the influence of the Jesuits and was willing to assist his cousin Gilbert and his brother George to that end. That William Gifford would thus cooperate with Walsingham to defeat Jesuit plans did not mean he favored Walsingham's goal to extirpate Catholicism from England. Factionalism in any setting produces odd allies whose shared interests may be limited.

The sluicegate through which communication and information relating to the Scots queen flowed was the French embassy in London. Outwardly, Walsingham cultivated a friendly relationship with the French ambassador, Michel de Castelnau, seigneur de Mauvissière. The ambassador was a central figure in matters involving Mary Stewart. His quarters were in the heart of London, at Salisbury Court. Owned by the Sackville family, Salisbury Court was accessible by Fleet Street and Water Lane and was only yards from White Friar's Church and the Temple, where many lawyers held chambers. Agents of Sir Francis Walsingham lurked in the embassy's shadows, stole into the quarters when the opportunity presented itself, intercepted the embassy mail packets, bribed the employees who could be corrupted, and jailed some of those who could not.

Salisbury Court was a center of political intrigue, with secret comings and goings of supporters of Mary Stewart. The queen of Scots had a French heritage: her mother was

Mary of Guise and her first husband was Francis II, King of France 1559–60, a son of Catherine de Medici. After King Francis II of France died, Mauvissière had accompanied his widow to Scotland, and remained with her a year. So he was well known to the Scots queen when he returned to England as ambassador some years later. The French hoped for continued influence in Scotland, and the French King, Henry III (another son of Catherine de Medici), encouraged Mauvissière to support his sister-in-law and work for her release. Everyone knew that Ambassador Mauvissière was especially concerned for the welfare of the woman most feared by Queen Elizabeth: her own cousin, Mary Stewart. Although held in moderately comfortable captivity in country estates in England since 1568, the Scots queen was a continuing threat to Elizabeth. Mary was next in line to the throne and she was Catholic. The death or overthrow of Elizabeth and the accession of Mary to the crown could lead to the reinstatement of the Roman religion in England, with great significance for France. An assassin's hand could counter the Reformation brought about by Elizabeth's father and advanced by Elizabeth herself. Mauvissière, keenly aware of the difficulties posed to Queen Elizabeth, likened her situation to that of the character in an old fable, who held a wolf by the ears, exposed to equal danger by continuing to hold the animal and by restoring her to freedom. The French called it: *tenir le loup par les oreilles*.

Within the French embassy was a special agent from Catherine de Medici and the Duke of Guise, whose principal function was to arrange communication between Mary Queen of Scots and her supporters in France. His name was Courcelles.

Mauvissière was a convivial man in later middle age: he turned 60 in 1580. His wife was young and pretty, and they had small children. They were Catholic, living in a country where their religion was suppressed. Diplomatic status, however, allowed the presence of a priest and a discreet celebration of the Mass within the French mission. A well-educated man, Mauvissière enjoyed literature, music and the theater. He had a keen interest in history and philosophy. He had translated from Latin the treatise *De Moribus Germanorum* [On German customs] by the French scholar Peter Ramus. Ramus's treatment of Aristotle was fashionable at Oxford. John Case, Oxford's leading teacher of philosophy was cautiously indebted to Ramus's thought. Mauvissière was attracted to the Latin authors: he had put into French verse various sayings of Ovid, Lucretius and Lucan.

The men and women who visited the French embassy at Salisbury Court were some of the most interesting and influential in London. A major attraction of the French embassy during the period 1583–85 was the presence of two Italians residing with Mauvissière: Giovanni "Resolute John" Florio, serving as translator for Mauvissière and as a language tutor to the ambassador's daughter; and Giordano Bruno, the loquacious, peripatetic philosopher, astronomer and seer. The books on which Bruno's reputation rests were written in his two year stay in London.

John Florio was an Anglo-Italian linguist whose *First Fruits* was published in London in 1578. The book was an Italian teaching manual, with parallel dialogues in Italian and English, along with "merry proverbs, witty sentences and golden sayings." He dedicated it to the Earl of Leicester. Born in London in about 1553 to an Italian immigrant Protestant family, Florio had returned to England only a few years before the publication of *First Fruits*. Soon Florio developed a following as a language teacher and translator for affluent Londoners. His father, Michael Angelo Florio, had similarly been established as a teacher of language to the nobility before foreigners had been required to leave London under

Mary Tudor in 1554. One of Michael Angelo Florio's students was Lady Jane Grey, Leicester's sister-in-law, and Leicester doubtless knew the Italian linguist and writer from this connection. The senior Florio had dedicated an Italian catechism to Leicester's father, and published a biography of Lady Jane Grey after he returned to the Continent following her death, with translations of some of Lady Jane Grey's writings. Florio's father also wrote a translation of *Agricola* that he dedicated to Queen Elizabeth. No doubt Leicester was glad to see the return of Michael Angelo Florio's son to London and to find his first literary work dedicated to him. The dedication reminded Leicester that John Florio was "issued from the bowels of him who was your faithful and devoted vassal...."

The fact that Leicester was Chancellor of Oxford University helps explain why John Florio moved to Oxford in the company of one of his pupils. Leicester perhaps arranged introductions for Florio and may have facilitated a stipend for him. The pupil was Emmanuel Barnes, son of Robert Barnes, bishop of Durham. Barnes enrolled as a commoner of Magdalen. Florio, aged 36, himself matriculated in Magdalen in 1581 and was also a teacher to scholars in the University.[8] It was at Magdalen College where Florio most likely first knew William Sterrell. For the next thirty years, wherever one finds Sterrell, one also finds Florio in close association: at Magdalen, at the French embassy, in the circle around the Earl of Essex, and in the Court and household of King James.

At the French Ambassador's, Florio, father of a baby daughter, was employed as a translator for the Ambassador and as tutor of the Ambassador's elder daughter, Catherine Marie. The French Ambassador developed such a trust of Florio that he gave Florio his power of attorney to deal on his behalf when he left England in 1585.

Florio's return to London in 1583 coincided with the visit to Oxford and London of Giordano Bruno, the *Nolano* as he sometimes called himself, for the name of his birthplace in Italy. Bruno was one of history's restless intellectuals, a brilliant man never quite at home in any place or in any system of thought or religion. For a time Bruno was a Dominican monk, but then he took to the life of a wandering teacher, lecturing on Aristotle's errors and propagating Lully's art of memory. He was a magician and philosopher who asserted—though not on Copernican grounds—the earth's daily rotation and annual circling of a stationary sun. In Paris in 1581 Bruno enjoyed great success with Henry III, and the French king sent him on to London in 1583 with a letter of introduction to the French ambassador, Mauvissière. Bruno first went up to Oxford where he hoped to lecture and teach his art of memory. The venture was inauspicious. Not only was Oxford a stronghold of Aristotelianism, but one of its professors soon detected that Bruno's lectures plagiarized from another scholar's treatise. Surely a feat of memory. The lectures were abruptly closed down.[9] Florio befriended Bruno and accompanied him back to London. There, fortified with his letter from King Henry III, Bruno was received by Mauvissière at Salisbury Court, and Florio with him.

During the next two years Giordano Bruno wrote his best known and most successful literary and philosophical works. Among those participating in dinners and social interchange with Bruno and Florio were some of the better known Elizabethan literary figures. These included Sir Philip Sidney (the Earl of Leicester's nephew and husband of Secretary Walsingham's daughter), author of *The Lady of May*, *The Arcadia*, *The Defence of Poesie* and his most beloved work, *Astrophel and Stella*; Fulke Greville, who was author of a number of poems that are collected under the title *Caelica*; Matthew Gwinne, a poet physician who was known as *Il Candido*, and was a close friend and associate of John Case; and perhaps, too, Sir Walter Ralegh. Bruno's *Ash Wednesday Supper* purported to be an account of a dinner at which Greville entertained him, though when later tried for heresy Bruno claimed the dinner was at the French embassy. The Italian writer dedicated his *Expulsion of the Triumphant Beast* to Sidney, memorializing the close friendship between Sidney and Greville. Bruno dedicated books to Ambassador Mauvissière after leaving England on the ambassador's ship, and paid generous tribute to the few English friends he had made. Bruno seems to have had no affection for most of England.

The attention to Bruno given here is necessary to counter assertions, discussed below, that Bruno was subverted within days of his settling in London by Walsingham into a spy in the French embassy against his host, Mauvissière, against Mary Queen of Scots, and against the interests of Henry III who had sponsored Bruno going to England. Bruno had no reason to be a spy for the English government against his friend and host, and the evidence suggested as supporting it is insubstantial.

The close relationship of the French Ambassador and Mary Queen of Scots resumed after he undertook the London post in 1575. The ambassador's older daughter was the godchild of two queens and bore their names, Catherine de Medici (the mother of Kings Francis II, Charles IX, and Henry III) and Mary Queen of Scots (Catherine's daughter-in-law). The captive queen wrote a touching letter to the young girl in 1584, commenting how glad she was to see the proof of her perfections in her letters and sending her a token, given her by the late king, Mary's father-in-law, whereby she could remember her "marreine" (godmother). She asked to be remembered to the girl's mother and that the child continue to love her as a second mother.[10]

But Mary Stewart knew that Walsingham was closing in on her. Shortly before her letter to her godchild, she wrote Mauvissière that she understood he entertained Leicester and Walsingham, yet he should know better than to trust either of them. Both were working to remove her from Sheffield and place her under another guardian. She told Mauvissière that she knew Walsingham would "retain in his hands my packets and yours as long as possible."[11] Prophetically, she warned against naming anyone in such correspondence, "to the end not to fall into danger." Did the poor woman think Walsingham would not have access to even this letter? She will be put to death for naming names in her correspondence that Walsingham was intercepting.

4

The MP from Morpeth
Gentleman Pensioner and Assassin

Between June and August 1583 several conferences were held in Paris in which plans for an invasion of England through Scotland were taken up. The project, called the *Empresa* (the *Enterprise*), was simply the latest of a series of discussions for ousting the English queen. This iteration originated in Scotland by supporters of Mary Queen of Scots and had been carried in 1582 to France. They sought support of the Duke of Guise. Because they were suspected of secret correspondence with some of the Council in England, Thomas Morgan and Charles Paget were initially excluded from the 1582 Paris meetings that included the Duke of Guise, Dr. Allen, Fr. Persons, Fr. Crichton (a Scottish Jesuit), the Spanish agent in France, and others, Nothing came of the plan when King Philip declined to give any military aid.

When the *Enterprise* plans were revisited in the summer of 1583, William Gifford, Thomas Morgan and Charles Paget now took an active role. Walsingham himself had engineered the revival. The new discussions arose from a promise to assassinate Queen Elizabeth made by one of the queen's own guard in exchange for money from the Duke of Guise. The "assassin" had instant credibility because he was the elder brother of the English Catholic theology professor, Dr. William Gifford, who was supported at Rheims by the Duke of Guise.

In an astounding shift of character, the same George Gifford who had jousted with the Earls of Arundel and Oxford, with Windsor, Sidney and Greville, supposedly undertook to aid the escape of a robber named William Nix from prison in the area of London,[1] and then, in April 1583, abruptly fled England for France after approaching Mary Queen of Scots to propose a plot against Queen Elizabeth.

Nix had been caught rummaging around the home of a prominent Catholic family. The intrusion was probably in preparation for George Gifford's plot in France.[2] One Hodgson, the under-jailer, in a deposition on the Nix case, told "That Mr. Gifford promised to pay the forfeiture or fine that should be set upon the Gaoler, were it forty or fifty pounds but if it were over great then would he beg it of the Queen." Why would the queen be called upon to pay the fine of someone aiding a prison escape, if government business were not involved? The family whose home Nix was invading was the daughter of the third Earl of Worcester; she was married to William Windsor, and they lived at Bradenham, Buckinghamshire. Her father wrote a letter against Nix to the judges. Nix denied the charges, "utterly refus[ing] to confess anything as touching any robbery done by himself or anything that may touch Mr. Gifford." Nix is no ordinary robber, for the report states: "That Nix after his escape lay about 7 days in a chamber at Grays Inn...." Gray's Inn was the legal society where many of England's lawyers were trained and maintained offices and living quarters. If Nix were engaging in burglary, it was with the support of powerful friends.

Nix and his backer Gifford were surely seeking information on English supporters of Mary Queen of Scots and efforts to liberate her. Elizabeth Somerset's aunt was the Countess of Northumberland, whose husband had been executed in 1572 for his role in the Rising in the North and his plans on behalf of Mary Queen of Scots. The Countess went into exile on the Continent. She was reported to be plotting to put Mary Queen of Scots on the English throne. Elizabeth Somerset's uncle (another of the Countess's brothers) was Thomas Somerset, a former member of Parliament, who was first committed to prison for a period because of his Catholic faith in June 1562. A benefactor to the English College at Rheims, his own son and a nephew were students at Rheims. He was involved in passing correspondence from Paris to Mary Stewart, on behalf of Thomas Morgan. When Morgan was imprisoned in Paris in 1585 he wrote to Mary and asked that in the event of his death she give some token in gratitude to, *inter alios*, the Earl of Worcester (Elizabeth Somerset's father), and Thomas Somerset. Elizabeth Somerset's brother was Edward Somerset, who was to become the fourth Somerset earl of Worcester in 1589. It appears that he, too, had been arrested in a wave of anti–Catholic prosecutions in 1581. Late in 1583 or early in 1584, William Somerset (the third Somerset earl of Worcester), and probably Edward himself, too, were subjected to house arrest because of the Throckmorton Plot that George Gifford had effectively initiated.

Arriving in France in April 1583 George Gifford contacted the Duke of Guise and promised to kill Elizabeth in exchange for a large sum of money. Guise was the chief figure of the Catholic party and the Holy League in the French Wars of Religion. He was a supporter of his cousin, Mary Stewart, and would have been glad to see her regain her throne or the throne of England. How could a gentleman from the English Court suddenly gain access to the Duke of Guise and win him to a plot? Surely it was through his brother William, who not only was thick with Morgan and Paget but had also gained a close relationship with the Duke of Guise. After William Allen appointed William Gifford as the public lecturer on Thomas Aquinas at Rheims, the Duke of Guise and his brother, Cardinal Louis Guise de Lorraine, granted the new lecturer an annual pension of two hundred pieces of gold. George Gifford's cover story was that, though one of Elizabeth's household for some time, he was secretly Catholic and hated Queen Elizabeth for executing some of his relatives.[3] It was plausible: here were his brother William, who had a special relation with Guise, and his cousin Gilbert, another seminarian exile to vouch for him. The papal nuncio in Paris, Monsignor Castelli, reported that George Gifford had made his proposal known to the Queen of Scots but she had rebuffed him.

Guise—unaware that both William and Gilbert were in touch with Walsingham—supposedly gave George Gifford a bond for 50,000 francs (£5,000) and promised to escrow a like amount for him for when the deed was done. George Gifford thus was offering to step into the role of assassin to carry out a plot that had first been drawn up a year earlier and of which the English government was aware. Walsingham was determined that there would be a plot even if he had to stimulate it himself. The *Empresa* then morphed into the Throckmorton Plot. By the end of June 1583, the immediate plan for George Gifford to kill the queen may have been lost sight of, but it had already stirred the further discussions for the invasion of England that had the support of Guise. George Gifford himself was back at Elizabeth's Court by mid-summer, 1583, and continued to draw his pension of half a crown a day from the government.[4] Indeed, he became a member of Parliament in 1584! But his journey had advanced the discussions for liberating Mary Stewart. Father Persons was sent to Rome to gain the approval of Pope Gregory XIII. Charles Paget volunteered to journey to England in September to obtain for the invasion the support of prominent Catholics.

George Gifford now recedes from view as a conspirator but is brought back again into the action by Walsingham when he is needed. Two years after the Throckmorton Plot, Gilbert Gifford used the story of Guise's dealing with George Gifford to draw Gilbert's acquaintances into the Babington Plot, as they were to reveal in their confessions. And George Gifford continued to encourage an overthrow of Elizabeth in meetings with these Babington conspirators.

Walsingham's use of his provocateurs first bears fruit in the Throckmorton Plot of 1583. Three of the ten children of Sir John and Margery Throckmorton of Feckenham, Worcestershire, were implicated in the Plot: Francis, Thomas, and George. The Throckmortons were close relatives of Sir Francis Englefield,[5] the notorious English fugitive who was an advisor on English matters to King Philip II of Spain. Francis Throckmorton traveled to Europe in 1580, where he and one of his brothers visited or enrolled in the College at Rheims. While in Europe, he met with his uncle, Sir Francis, and other Catholic exiles who sought an alternative to Elizabeth's government. He returned as an agent, it was claimed by the government, for a plan involving France and Spain and the Pope: England was to be invaded by a French force under Henry, Duke of Guise, who would free his cousin Mary Stewart and restore papal authority. In short, this was the *Empresa*, hatched in Paris by George Gifford, William Gifford, Paget and Morgan, among others.

Francis Throckmorton's association with the cause of Mary Queen of Scots can be traced to Courcelles, the man in the French embassy who had the special role of dealing with Mary Stewart's correspondence. He found his contacts among those young men who had supported the Campion-Persons mission. Courcelles came to an arrangement with Francis Throckmorton late in 1581. Soon Courcelles was moving correspondence to Mary through Throckmorton.

As he had promised the Paris group, Paget made a secret trip to England in September 1583. His alias was "Mope." But he did little to further the plan. According to Fr. Persons, Paget used his trip to *thwart* the Guise plan.[6] Upon landing in England, Paget met with Henry Percy, Earl of Northumberland, and with William Shelley of Michelgrove, supposedly to gain their support for an invasion. Soon, Charles Paget's brother, Lord Paget, and another man, Charles Arundell, fled England. Francis Throckmorton and Charles Arundell had both been members of the George Gilbert Association assisting the Campion-Persons mission, and Persons spent his last weeks in England in 1581 at William Shelley's estate at Michelgrove. Throckmorton's London house allegedly served as a center of communication between Mary and foreign agents. But Francis Walsingham, the story goes, uncovered the conspiracy, and Throckmorton was arrested in November 1583.

The Earl of Northumberland, William Shelley, and numerous other suspected Catholics were arrested at about the same time, among them Francis's brother George and their mother, and all were interrogated about disloyal activities. Francis Throckmorton made a confession after torture on the rack. He was tried in May 1584 and executed several months later. The following year the Earl of Northumberland died in the Tower, said to be at his own hand, and in February 1586 William Shelley was sentenced to death for his role in the Throckmorton Plot. But the sentence was not carried out, and Shelley remained in the Tower for years. The Spanish ambassador to England, Bernardino de Mendoza, was expelled for contacts with Francis Throckmorton.

How did Walsingham uncover the Throckmorton Plot so readily? He had monitored the responses to his agent George Gifford's activities in France. Exactly contemporaneous with George Gifford's flight to France and his plotting with the Duke of Guise, a parallel element of the Walsingham plan took shape in London. Dated April 29, 1583, there appeared the first of a series of mysterious letters in non-native French sent to Secretary Walsingham, signed "Henry Fagot."[7] Letters signed with this name eventually gave details suggesting that he was a priest serving Mauvissière. "Fagot's" role complemented the activities of George Gifford in the French and Spanish based plot, the *Empresa*. Walsingham could never reveal to his queen that he had an agent provocateur operating in France, but he could tell her that his stealthy efforts had discovered a plot against her abroad through a source in the French embassy. Moreover, the English government was aware that in 1582 a French-speaking Jesuit priest closely associated with the Duke of Guise had spent months in disguise as Mary Stewart's physician. His name was Henry Samier (Samerie), and he was very active in political matters, to the dissatisfaction of his superiors in the Jesuit order. Using the names LaRue and Hieronymo Martelli, he made other secret visits to Mary Queen of Scots and continued to correspond with her.

As Elizabeth was surely made aware of Henry Samier by Walsingham, there was plausibility to a story that a French priest visiting in the French embassy was won over by Walsingham and brought a clerk with him. Elizabeth herself boasted to the French ambassador that she knew all about the embassy's conduct of secret correspondence for Mary Queen of Scots: "I know all that goes on in my realm; and because I was a prisoner in my sister's reign, I know all the tricks prisoners use to gain servants and to have secret intelligence."[8]

The first significant letter of Fagot related directly to the plot George Gifford was working on with Guise in France, for Fagot reported to Walsingham that on April 24, 1583 (April 14, o.s.) a letter from the Duke of Guise arrived at Mauvissière's embassy, begging Mauvissière to manage the affairs of Mary Queen of Scots in England as secretly as he could and providing money for his doing so. The letter was an intimation of the *Empresa*. This would have alerted Walsingham that George Gifford's initiative was being carried out. In the same letter, Fagot also reported that Francis Throckmorton had dined with the French ambassador and had sent Mary Queen of Scots a sum of money on behalf of the ambassador. The stage was thus set for tying Francis Throckmorton to the plot of the Duke of Guise. The next letter, a week later, also related to the George Gifford/Guise plot: Fagot said there was a letter to Mauvissière from his wife, still in France, saying that Guise had told her he hoped to be in Scotland sooner than Mauvissière or she expected. The implication was that an invasion through Scotland was in the works and that Guise would be there through force. Five days later Fagot reported that he had suborned the ambassador's secretary and could control the mail going to Mary Stewart, a technique later employed by Walsingham and Gilbert Gifford in the unfolding of the Babington Plot. Fagot claimed that Francis Throckmorton and Henry Howard were the chief agents for Mary Stewart. This first group of Fagot letters cease at about the same time that George

Gifford returned to the English Court from France. About this time Gilbert Gifford was back in France.

The use and effectiveness of the "Fagot" letters did not require that there be a real person appearing in the French embassy who called himself Henry Fagot. Gilbert Gifford could easily have come and gone within the embassy in his own name (as he clearly did in 1585–86, while also being known under aliases for correspondence), working with a perfidious member of Mauvissière's own household staff, and sending the letters in idiosyncratic French in the feigned person of "Fagot." Many times over the next twenty years Thomas Phelippes, who in the 1580s was Walsingham's close aide, will create paper characters like Fagot and endow them with personalities and characteristics which have continued to mislead modern historians, as earlier they deceived their recipients and interceptors. Fagot was an early prototype, as was *Emilio*, another Gilbert Gifford/Phelippes/Walsingham collaborative invention. Phelippes learned well from his master, Walsingham. The French ambassador trusted Morgan and Paget, and they sponsored Gilbert Gifford with whom they worked in Paris, along with his cousin Dr. William Gifford. This gave Gilbert easy entrance to the French embassy with Mauvissière, just as it will with ambassador Châteauneuf when he replaces Mauvissière in 1585.

Making use of Mary's copied correspondence and Fagot's intelligence, Walsingham had sent other spies to detect the activities of Francis Throckmorton, whose arrest was soon after Charles Paget's visit into England to advance the Enterprise/*Empresa*, as proposed by George Gifford a few month's earlier. Throckmorton was tortured on the rack and confessed to a plot in which the Duke of Guise was preparing to invade England to liberate Mary Queen of Scots, an Enterprise financed and supported by the Pope and the King of Spain. Guise's venture became the centerpiece of the government's prosecution of Throckmorton, the Earl of Northumberland and William Shelley. In a paper distributed the day of Throckmorton's execution, by "Q. Z. of Lyons Inn," the government set out its case that Throckmorton was the English instrument of the Guise Enterprise.[9] The government's white paper does not, of course, mention Fagot, but it was Fagot's letters that provided the supposed evidence of money being sent to England for the *Empresa*, and it was Fagot's letter that named Francis Throckmorton as the person who became the "convenient Partie in England, to joyne with the forraine Forces." The paper further relates how Charles Paget had secretly come to England to advance the *Empresa* under the aliases of Mope and Spring; his contacts with Northumberland and Shelley had led to their downfall. Indicating the government was not sure what it would do with Shelley, the paper softened Shelley's role.[10]

Supposedly Thomas Throckmorton was working with his brother Francis, but Thomas was now safely in France. Francis Throckmorton's confession implicated the Spanish Ambassador in London, Bernardino de Mendoza. He was called before members of the Privy Council, informed of the queen's knowledge of his dealings, and given a fortnight to leave the country. The Spanish embassy was then closed and not reopened for nearly twenty years. Also arrested and interrogated was Lord Henry Howard, who had been named by Fagot for involvement in the affairs of Mary Queen of Scots. The questions concerned Howard's meetings with Mauvissière and with Throckmorton,[11] which suggests that Fagot's letters were indeed the reason for the government's persecution of Howard.

Lord Henry Howard's nephew, Philip Howard, Earl of Arundel, was also arrested and interrogated in December 1583 about meetings with Throckmorton's associates: Lord Paget,

Charles Arundell, and the Earl of Northumberland. He was asked about any activities he may have had with the French ambassador and with Mary Queen of Scots, who supposedly had referred to him as her son, and about several priests as well as his wife's religious activities. Although not prosecuted at this time, this arrest marked the Earl of Arundel's fate. The government continued to accuse him of involvement in the Throckmorton Plot. His response? He now embraced Catholicism. He was formally received into the Roman church in September 1584 by the Jesuit William Weston. In the next few months, Arundel resolved to go abroad and begin a new life. Aboard a ship bound abroad the following April, the earl's vessel was boarded and he was arrested. He had been betrayed by his own chaplain, Edward Gratley, *alias* Bridges.[12] Gratley had been at Douay and at the English College of Rome with Gilbert Gifford and reportedly was working with Gifford early in 1585 or late 1584 when he ruined Philip Howard. When Sir Christopher Hatton interrogated the earl on May Day 1585 he warned him against lying, inasmuch as Gratley had told Gilbert Gifford of the earl's plans and he in turn had relayed the intelligence to some of the Privy Council. Gratley went over to France before June 1585 and corresponded with Walsingham using the name *Foxley*.[13] At about this time in France, Gilbert Gifford and Gratley colluded in writing a book against the Jesuits, which they sent to Phelippes and Walsingham.[14]

Gilbert Gifford was in all likelihood the writer of some of the letters subscribed by the name "Fagot." A number of the Fagot letters bear Gilbert Gifford's secret symbol, the sign of Jupiter: ♃. This symbol was evidently placed on the Fagot letters by someone within the English government, probably Thomas Phelippes, as a discreet way of identifying who Fagot was, while concealing that identity to outsiders. This same symbol was used by Gilbert Gifford in writing to his controller, Thomas Phelippes.[15] Moreover, Gifford's cousin Thomas Barnes, and Mary Stewart's secretary Curll, each used the same symbol for Gilbert in certain of their own letters.[16] Other circumstances similarly suggest Gilbert Gifford: he knew French well enough from his time in Rheims and in Paris; the Italianisms in the Fagot letters could have grown from his studies—and rowdy living—in Rome. He was reputed an excellent linguist.[17] Letters of Gilbert Gifford in French are similar to the handwriting of certain of the Fagot letters. Though not ordained until 1587, he already had the training of a priest and could easily have been accepted as a man of religion in the Mauvissière household, as well as adopt a priestly pose in letters. His involvement and known movements in the Babington plot coincide roughly with the letters of Fagot from London and later from Paris. The Fagot letters demonstrate a familiarity with Paris that Gilbert Gifford certainly possessed. The infrequency of the letters of Fagot is consistent with the fact that Gilbert Gifford was going back and forth between England and France and Rome. Most importantly, Gilbert Gifford is undeniably complicit with George Gifford, William Gifford, Thomas Morgan, and Charles Paget in 1583 and with Walsingham no later than 1585. A similar fictitious character created in connection with the Babington Plot by Gilbert Gifford with the knowledge and contrivance of Phelippes was *Emilio Russo*.

The secretary at the French embassy who turned over copies of the correspondence of Mary Queen of

The sign of Jupiter was Gilbert Gifford's secret symbol.

Scots was surely Jean Arnault, seigneur de Cherelles.[18] Even when Cherelles was not in England, these copies could well have come back to England via Gilbert Gifford. After leaving England from his first tour of duty at the French embassy in London, Cherelles was a secretary in the King of France's chambers and continued to be involved in English/French politics. It is not unlikely that his duties took him back to London. Cherelles was involved with the same English scoundrels Morgan and Paget with whom Gilbert Gifford schemed, and Cherelles was himself involved with Gilbert Gifford, who a few years later declared that Cherelles was acting for Walsingham.[19] Cherelles was again posted to the French embassy in London when Châteauneuf replaced Mauvissière as ambassador in 1585 but was abruptly recalled early in 1586 for suspicion of treason—of giving intelligence to Walsingham.[20] Knowing he was recalled, Cherelles obtained permission—evidently through Walsingham—to make an extraordinary visit to Chartley to see Mary Stewart. The wily Frenchman conned her out of a substantial sum of money! Through Morgan and through his own government position, Cherelles would have had access to copies of the correspondence of Mary Stewart in Paris, and Gilbert Gifford as "Henry Fagot" would have been the conduit to Walsingham. The matter was easy for Walsingham to manage, and it impressed Queen Elizabeth to think a source in the French embassy produced the documents.

By late 1585 or early 1586, Gilbert Gifford was comfortably ensconced in Thomas Phelippes's own lodgings in London. There is evidence suggesting that Phelippes was providing quarters for priests two years earlier; such priests could well have been Gifford (Fagot) and Fr. John Ballard. A captured Oxford student and seminarian from Rheims named Dodwell reported in late 1583 or early 1584 to Lord Hunsdon that "One Mr. Phillippes, that dwelleth in Doctor Goods his house in Chancery Lane, is the greatest dealer with priests here in London, and by his means they are directed from place to place."[21] This dealer in priests described by Dodwell appears no where else in the records of the period. The observant Dodwell must have stumbled upon Thomas Phelippes.

Why the letters under the name Fagot? Partly this was political theater for the queen of England. The letters were needed to show to the queen and to any member of the Privy Council who might be skeptical of (or troubled by) material coming simply from Walsingham and Phelippes. The creation of a French character named Fagot who was a priest with the ambassador would be convincing, especially since he was occasionally relating details of conspiracy from the confessional. Who would confess treason to their priest if it were not true? The Fagot ruse also hid the involvement of Gilbert Gifford; thus he was able to come forward in the midst of the "discovery" of the Babington Plot to turn informer, as though he had been participating as one of the plotters before a change of sides.

The most important reason for summoning up a "Fagot" was to protect George Gifford, the man of Elizabeth's Court whose flight to France and meetings with the Duke of Guise helped mid-wife the Throckmorton Plot (and then the Babington Plot). Fagot/Gilbert Gifford was able to convey information to Walsingham that related to and probably came from George Gifford's dealings in France with his brother and with Morgan and Paget. The apparent source of intelligence about English connections to the *Empresa* would be "Fagot" rather than the real source, George Gifford, whose role need therefore not be made known to Elizabeth or any other members of her Privy Council. No one need know of Walsingham's dirty hands or George Gifford's participation in a devious device if the information about such a prominent figure as Lord Henry Howard, not to mention Throckmorton and others, were to come from Frenchmen within the embassy. And, in Walsingham's dealings with the Privy Council and the queen, the Fagot mystification strengthened the appearance of ongoing conspiracy.

Yet George Gifford's name would appear in connection with the Babington Plot; it could not be avoided. The way in which Walsingham extricated George Gifford is even more surreal than Gifford's helping the burglar Nix escape from prison. The Throckmorton Plot was only a warm-up, as will be seen shortly. Mary Queen of Scots had turned George Gifford away when he approached her and no evidence could be adduced against her. Though Francis Throckmorton was tried and convicted, Mary Queen of Scots was left with guilt by association despite the lack of evidence against her. In fact, she evidently quashed efforts to rescue her at this time. Fr. Persons later reported to the Spanish that Mary herself wrote to the Earl of Northumberland forbidding him in any way to join either the Duke of Guise or the Spaniards in the proposed enterprise. No doubt she had seen George Gifford for what he was, a Walsingham instrument.

The Throckmorton Plot was the immediate spur for Walsingham and Burghley to circulate a Bond of Association, a pledge transparently directed against a succession of Mary Stewart to the English throne. To discourage any plots for Mary Stewart (and to impress upon all the English the extent of the threat to the queen that Mary posed), the Bond of Association was directed at all conspirators against Queen Elizabeth and most particularly at those who supported the Catholic heir presumptive, Mary Queen of Scots. This "Instrument of Association for the Preservation of Her Majesty's Royal Person" contained a number of solemn undertakings, not least "*to pursue to utter extermination* all that shall attempt by any act, counsel, or consent to anything that shall tend to the harm of Her Majesty's Royal Person." It was first subscribed by the Privy Council and then circulated to the clergy, the nobility and many others for their signatures. While this seemed to promote the security of the queen, its purpose in part was to force the queen's hand in the eventual execution of Mary Queen of Scots, despite her past refusal to put her cousin on trial. A Walsingham biographer (and apologist) has called the Bond a "fraud" which showed "little sign of coherent thought."[22] It was made to appear that it arose from spontaneous support for Queen Elizabeth though it actually emanated from the Court. To give it legislative force, a Parliament was convened that ran from November 1584 through March 1585.

In the middle of this Parliament, another plot emerged that involved another MP. The Parry Plot was centered on Dr. William Parry, a spendthrift and disreputable agent of Burghley and Walsingham. He spent time in prison in 1580–82 for attempted murder of a creditor but was released with a promise to continue spying for the government—a common recruitment ploy. Parry spied in Paris and also traveled to Lyons, Milan and Venice, purporting to be reconciled to the Catholic Church. Back in Paris, Parry drew into discussion various Englishmen on the subject of assassination of the queen. He thus continued the same role that George Gifford had recently played: a provocateur sent by Walsingham to stir up an assassination plot. Thomas Morgan and Charles Paget, Mary Stewart's agents, were among these, and Parry sought also to involve Frs. Allen and Persons, without success. Securing letters from the English Ambassador to France, Sir Edward Stafford, Parry returned to England. He informed the queen that he had been sent by Morgan and the

Jesuits, with the Pope's approval, to assassinate her Majesty as part of a plan to install Mary Stewart as Queen of England. Again, this was a furtherance of the *Empresa*. Parry seemed to have evidence of the plot, because a letter to the Pope seeking indulgence for such a deed had been given a not dismissive reply by a high papal official. All this was to Parry's favor. But then he made a major misstep.

Parry had the temerity to speak in the House of Commons against a bill that would give yet harsher treatment to Catholics. Parry had gone off script. Now another spy, Edmund Neville, came forward to denounce Parry as having discussed the possibility of assassinating the queen. Parry soon admitted that he had made mention to Neville that some Catholics believed that a prince could be killed to advance the faith; however, he had said this, he averred, only to discover plots, as he had already been doing with the government's approval. But the admission was enough to condemn Parry at his trial for treason, and the government reneged on a deal to save him if he made a limited confession. By revealing that he had been working for Walsingham in dealing with the Catholics in Paris and elsewhere, he admitted that he was an *agent provocateur*, that he had tried to procure others to propose assassination of Queen Elizabeth. By executing him, the government made it appear that an assassination plot was real, and that Parry himself was part of it. Parry was acting abroad in the same way that Walsingham was having George Gifford act.

On the scaffold Parry admitted to his Catholicism but denied he had ever done more than he had been authorized to do in uncovering plots. He was executed March 2, 1585, and the government had yet another Catholic plot to decry to the English people and use as justification for still more stringent laws against those of the Old Faith. The next day a new act was introduced for the queen's security, "the Safety of the Queen," that passed before the end of Parliament on the 29th. Sitting in that Parliament, representing Morpeth and voting for a statute to complement the Bond of Association, was George Gifford, the man who had volunteered to the Duke of Guise to kill the queen and thus set in motion the Throckmorton Plot.

5

Persecution of Catholic Gentry

The successive measures taken by the government to stigmatize the Jesuits and make examples of them were expanded. Grimly, the Privy Council and Parliament imposed harsher penalties on anyone who would assist them and then on any professing Catholic. The Privy Council issued a letter in December 1580 calling for making an example of the Jesuits and their confederates "by punishment, to the terror of others." A proclamation ordered the arrest of Jesuits. Soon after the capture of Edmund Campion, a statute made it high treason to convert the queen's subjects to "the Romish religion."[1] A fine of two hundred marks and imprisonment for one year was levied on anyone celebrating the Catholic Mass. The penalty for not attending the Anglican service was increased to the crushing sum of twenty pounds a month, or imprisonment until the fine was paid. The 1584–85 Parliament passed a statute (27 Eliz.1, c. 2) against "Jesuits and Seminarists" that made it an act of treason punishable by death to return to England from a seminary. And leaving England to go to a foreign seminary or college or to assist someone attempting to do so subjected an offender to the penalties of a *praemunire*: the loss of all civil rights, forfeiture of lands, goods and chattels, and imprisonment during the royal pleasure.

The increasing severity reflected the fear of the effectiveness of the Jesuit mission. The holy examples of the martyrs, with courage in the approach of brutal execution, fortified the spirits of lay Catholics and made many converts.

The impact of the government's increased efforts to suppress Catholicism was experienced harshly in the leading families of England. By making examples of them, the lower classes could be more easily controlled. Just as Rome and the Jesuits recognized that their limited mission resources must be devoted to persons of the higher ranks, so too the government concentrated its anti–Catholic campaign on upper-class families known as Catholic. The bonds that tied English family members together were based on inheritances of rank, land, and religious identification.

In August 1580 the English government detained many of the leading Catholics as a prophylactic measure, largely to intimidate these families.[2] Similarly in succeeding years, when local officials and clergy carried out a campaign of harassment and intimidation, it was often against entire families.

Three families will be discussed as examples of the religious persecution. Family members were radicalized as a result. They are noteworthy also because of their close association with the English Jesuits and with the man who became the principal counter-espionage agent of the English Catholics, William Sterrell.

The Skinners of Rowington Manor and Shelfield

The Skinners were a distinguished family of Warwickshire. Anthony Skinner's great-grandfather was of the manor of Shelfield and his grandfather, Anthony of London, was granted additional lands in Warwickshire. Among his ancestors was Sir Thomas Billing, Chief Justice of the King's Bench (d. 1481). Anthony Skinner's father was William Skinner, who in a report of 1577 on lawyers formerly of the Inner Temple was "vehemently to be suspected" for his religion. William increased the Skinner lands by marrying Alice Oldnall of Rowington Manor, Warwickshire.

The Manor of Rowington was a Crown property, a portion of which extended into the limits of Stratford upon Avon. Queen Elizabeth granted it to Ambrose Dudley, Earl of Warwick (brother of Robert Dudley, Earl of Leicester). Warwick and the Countess did not occupy Rowington Manor, but leased it for income. The lessees were John Oldnall, followed by Oldnall's daughter, Alice, and her second husband, William Skinner.

John Oldnall was known as a strong Catholic. His daughter Alice became lessee of Rowington Manor shortly before her father's death in 1558. In December 1562 a fresh lease of the premises was made to Alice, William Skinner, and their son Anthony for their lives. The family made their home at Rowington Manor while retaining the family estate at Shelfield, as well as holding other lands. It was not uncommon for the landed gentry to move about among several homes. A further lease for 30 years, to date from the expiration of the existing lease, was acquired in 1597 by Thomas Audley, who at once sold his rights to Anthony Skinner. Why the convoluted conveyance to Audley then back to Skinner? As will be seen, Skinner was found guilty of treason, and the transaction was a means to preserve the property for Anthony. Such property transactions were often made by Catholics to shield their assets from government seizure.

Anthony Skinner entered Exeter College, Oxford in December 1577, probably meeting William Sterrell at this time. Within a year or two, Skinner entered Clifford's Inn, one of the Inns of Chancery, in preparation of becoming a lawyer. In May 1580, Anthony Skinner was admitted to the Middle Temple. His last entry in the Middle Temple records was in February 1584; he was not expected to return to his chambers. Anthony Skinner had returned to his home. The government's harassment of his family at Rowington Manor became so severe that Skinner decided to quit England.

Many of the parishioners of Rowington were staunch Catholics, and Anthony's father, William Skinner, was well-known as a recusant. Edmund Campion may well have stayed at Rowington Manor on his mission of 1580–81; the Skinners were reputed to harbor priests at the time of the Jesuit mission. In January 1584 William Skinner was arrested for sheltering Catholic priests. A number of witnesses were examined against him; similar scenes were repeated throughout England during this era. The government files on the Skinner family show neighbor testifying against neighbor, servant against employer, rumor reported upon rumor. The government agents sought any sign of disloyalty that could be used to press criminal charges.

The Skinner family's harrier was the fierce Puritan Job Throckmorton of nearby Haseley Manor and the Manor of Preston Bagot. A cousin of the Throckmortons of Feckenham who suffered in the Throckmorton Plot, he was a knight of the shire and had diverse public employments.[3] In January 1584, under a Privy Council order, Job Throckmorton and a group of his followers came to Rowington Manor, seized William Skinner and made a quick search of the buildings. They found little because, as Job Throckmorton reported, "in that the house had been searched once or twice before there was no likelihood at all of any material thing to be had there now." They now examined witnesses. Again, Throckmorton was disappointed because the witnesses produced much less than he had expected. This reluctance of testimony was attributable to "secret laboring underhand & threatening of poor men ... to keep them from deposing their knowledge. Men that promised mountains before hand have when it came to the pinch performed but molehills." The papists were of wondrous cunning; the frail men around them were without grace and easily corrupted, he said. Those who spoke against Skinner did so fearfully. But Throckmorton concluded that there was enough information in the depositions to bring Skinner within the treason statute. It appeared that Skinner had defended the claim of Mary Queen of Scots to be successor and heir apparent of Elizabeth, "besides the great suspicions of harboring the Jesuits" (i.e., Campion or Persons).

Throckmorton advised his correspondent to tell Secretary Walsingham that oaths were of little use in Rowington because the Catholics all had a dispensation from telling the truth to Protestants. The examination of Skinner himself, Throckmorton left to the Privy Council to wring from him what they could: Skinner was "so stubborn & dogged that he altogether refuseth either to enter into recognizance or to be examined by us." Skinner, he said, had great friends and money. Throckmorton assured that Skinner "is as perilous [a] subject as any the Queen hath of his coat (religion)."

Witnesses were brought forth against William Skinner. Each was asked:

> Whether ever they hear Mr. Skynner speak any evil opprobrious slaunderous or reviling words of her Majestie: either touching her life or government: or any evil of Queen Anne her mother or of the unlawfulness of the marriage betwinxt King Henry & her.

This line of questioning related to the legitimacy of Elizabeth's birth and her reign. They might strike the reader today as bizarre: Elizabeth's father himself had put Anne Boleyn to death and had himself de-legitimated Elizabeth so that her younger brother appeared the sole legitimate heir to the Crown. Under Job Throckmorton's accounting, King Henry VIII would have been judged a traitor.

The first witness was Christopher Kirklande, minister at the church at Rowington. He believed that a man named Baker or Birde was at Skinner's and that this man was a priest. Another man had told Kirklande that Baker was seen praying in Latin in Skinner's garden. Beyond this, Kirklande could only say that Anthony Skinner, oldest son to Mr. Skinner, having been sundry times at his father's house since August last, did never yet resort to the parish church and place of prayer, nor did his sister. Roger Richardson, the Summoner of Warwick, also testified that a priest named Baker was at Skinner's house. Baker was said to be a schoolmaster at Cookhill, Mr. Fortescue's house. Richardson knew that Baker was once cited to appear at Worcester but had fled away, and Richardson understood him to be excommunicated.

Thomas Slye, a yeoman of Bushwood, testified that at some point in the past seven or eight years Skinner had been heard to say that the Protestant doctors had said that a woman could not be supreme head, which he must have meant as head of the Church, for he also accused Skinner of defending the Queen of Scots title and saying that she was next heir apparent to the throne of England. Slye also claimed that within these five or six years past there was at Mr. Skinner's house one Wakeman, who being apprehended about the time that Campion was apprehended Mr. Skinner himself did confess to Slye that Wakeman was a priest. At about that time William Whirret, servant to Skinner, told Slye that he "vehemently suspect[ed]" that Wakeman said mass in Skinner's house at the death of Skinner's wife.[4]

Slye went on to say that he did within the year or two see a certain old fellow at dinner at Skinner's house, whom they called Mr. Baker, and was said to be schoolmaster to Mr. Fortescue of Cookhill. But Slye said he looked like a priest, and one thing made him suspect that he was no schoolmaster: Mr. Fortescue sent his children to school to another place.[5]

Three others suspected as papists and confederates of Skinner were also examined. One was Henry Huddlesford, a thirty-seven year old schoolmaster of Solihull who, along with John Cowper and William Saunders, testified that they thought an elderly priest wearing spectacles, named Baker or Roberts, was seen within the past year around the Skinner manor. John Ferfax [Fairfax], the parish clerk of Rowington, testified that William Skinner had called into question the authority of the Protestant Bishops and asked him if a fool made the clerk a lease under a bush, would that be a good lease?: "No more said he are our bishops lawful bishops, whereupon this deponent then gathered he meant the prince's authority was not lawful."

Whether William Skinner suffered a fine for his obstinacy or was sent to prison is not known. His son, however, had had enough of the English persecution. Anthony Skinner left the country.

Thomas Fitzherbert

Thomas Fitzherbert, like Anthony Skinner, was descended from a notable English jurist, Sir Anthony Fitzherbert, Thomas's grandfather. Thomas was the elder son of William Fitzherbert (fourth son of Sir Anthony), a lawyer of the Inner Temple and a member of the Marian Parliament of 1553. Thomas's mother, Elizabeth Swinnerton, brought to the marriage the estate of Swinnerton, Staffordshire. Thomas was born in 1552; before he was six, his father died. This loss was deeply felt, and the already pious Catholic boy remembered years later his first awareness of the paternal death.[6]

Fitzherbert's mother next married Francis Gatacre, another strong Catholic who was frequently subject to government scrutiny and fines. Thomas Fitzherbert referred to himself as Swinnerton for years. Many Catholics who went abroad used their mother's name as an alternate identity. Thomas Fitzherbert was attentive to his Gatacre siblings. At about age 16, Fitzherbert was sent to Oxford for several years. Although an old priest told him it was acceptable to attend the Protestant services, he was discomforted by the experience and left without taking a degree.

Fitzherbert entered the study of law in 1571 in London at the Middle Temple where he was associated with his cousin William Basset and Simon Digby. The following year he was back at Swinnerton but, like Anthony Skinner, refused to attend the local church. He was imprisoned for his recusancy, that is, refusal to attend Protestant services. The effect of this incarceration was to strengthen his resolve. Eventually, like Skinner, he became politicized. On his release he secluded himself and read widely the classical works that would inform his scholarly and polemical writings. He married Dorothy East in 1580, and they soon had a child, a son whom they named Edward. By 1580 Fitzherbert was in London and was now involved in the network of young Catholics who served the Jesuit mission of Campion and Persons. He traveled with the missioners and played a part in the publication of Campion's *Dicem Rationes* that were distributed at Oxford on the benches of St. Mary's Church June 1581. Fitzherbert probably made his acquaintance with William Sterrell at this time. Later he will become Sterrell's principal contact with the English exiles. When Campion was jailed and executed, Fitzherbert was again jailed, this time in the Marshalsea prison. Before the end of 1582 he was out of prison, and he and his wife fled to France.

Within a short time of arriving in France, Thomas Fitzherbert was closely associated with Fr. Persons and was seeking to assist the interests of Mary Queen of Scots in France with the French king and the Guise family. By 1584 Fitzherbert and Mary Stewart were in correspondence with one another. Soon he was employed by the Queen Mother of France, Catherine de Medici (Mary Stewart's mother-in-law), and this relationship extended three or four years.[7] Fitzherbert's correspondence into England was probably handled by Courcelles and William Sterrell, who was very close to the French ambassador, through the French embassy.

Fitzherbert's employment produced some awkwardness for the English government. English relations with Henry III were in a curious state. King Henry and his mother were Catholic, but they were concerned about the power of Spain and the drift of the ambitious Duke of Guise towards Spain. Queen Elizabeth had considered a marriage with the Duke of Anjou, the youngest son of Catherine de Medici. France and England were not hostile to one another, yet an advisor to the Queen Mother of France was an English exile—Fitzherbert. Elizabeth's policy (oft-repeated) was that she was not anti–Catholic and would open no windows into the souls of her subjects, but they must affirm that they were her subjects and not the Pope's. Thomas Fitzherbert's own position was that he loved his country, his sovereign, and his God, and these were not in conflict with one another.

Fitzherbert was in close communication with the English ambassador to France in the mid–1580s, and there was some prospect of his returning to his own lands. The ambassador, Sir Edward Stafford, entreated Secretary Walsingham at the beginning of January 1586 "to procure some favour for Fitzherbert that is here." Stafford assured him "there is not an honester man to his country of his religion than he, the well dealing with him may put courage into many others that have but a prick of conscience and not evil will to the State." Three months later, Stafford forwarded a letter from Fitzherbert to Walsingham, and Stafford again urged favorable treatment of Fitzherbert. Fitzherbert's letter said he had learned that Walsingham was seeking favor for him from Elizabeth. The ambassador had told Fitzherbert that Elizabeth "was not only contented with my present course in the service of Queen Mother [Catherine de Medici], but also otherwise inclined to favour me...." Fitzherbert, however, was concerned that Walsingham's agent, Solomon Aldred (a London tailor turned spy in Rome and France), had told him that Walsingham's favor had been diverted from Fitzherbert, and Fitzherbert was ready to answer any reports that had been made against him.

The correspondence between Fitzherbert and Walsingham was exchanged at the very time Walsingham was closing the door on his trap of Mary Stewart in 1586. Fitzherbert was not aware of the extent to which Walsingham was spying on him and on his friends through Nicholas Berden and Fitzherbert's cousin, Gilbert Gifford (and no doubt others).

During the mid–1580s, Fitzherbert in Paris strengthened his ties with other English fugitives who were later to be important in Sterrell's intelligence activities. In addition to Fr. Robert Persons, these included Hugh Owen and Richard Verstegan, the printer. These were the men who were to establish the English counter-espionage network that functioned effectively in the decade 1594–1603. Hugh Owen, a student of Christ Church College, Oxford, in 1550–53, was Secretary to Henry Fitzalan, 12th Earl of Arundel, grandfather of Philip Howard from whom Philip Howard inherited his title in 1580. Hugh Owen left the service of Henry Fitzalan in 1571 and went to the Continent.

Elizabeth Shelley

The Shelley family of Michelgrove in Sussex was a well-known Catholic family. We have seen that William Shelley of Michelgrove was a supporter of Fr. Persons and Mary Queen of Scots who was sentenced to death in the Throckmorton Plot. Elizabeth Shelley was his sister. She also became active in the Counter-Reformation by supporting priests and seminarians. She seems to have been at the center of an informal network of like-minded Catholics. Her grandfather was Sir William Shelley, judge of the court of common pleas. Her mother Mary Fitzwilliam (whose first husband was John Shelley and second was Sir John Guildford) was the Lady Guildford who was arrested with Lady Morley and Lady Browne for attending a mass in 1574. Elizabeth Shelley had married her stepfather's son, Thomas Guildford, around 1560. Elizabeth and Sir Thomas had at least three children. During this first marriage she had to avoid public display of her religion because of her husband's strong dislike of Catholicism. He was knighted after the queen visited the Guildford estate at Hemsted, Kent, in 1573. Two years later, at his death, Sir Thomas tried to reach from the grave to prevent his widow from influencing their children in religion: he appealed in his will that his wife bring the children up Protestant "as she will answer before the terrible seat of God not to train up any of my children in papistry which if she shall do either secretly or openly" he directed that the Earl of Leicester or Lord Burghley were to take charge of their education.

The strong-willed widow, however, kept a priest in her house at all times. One of these was Fr. Richard Stevens, educated at New College Oxford, who had turned to Catholicism after serving as secretary to John Jewel, bishop of Salisbury, and later Matthew Parker, archbishop of Canterbury. Stevens had gone Douay, was ordained in 1576, and returned to England where he resided with Lady Guildford. She employed a recent Catholic convert named Henry Chadderton as quasi-tutor to her young son, Henry Guildford. Chadderton had been brought to the religion by Thomas Pounde and his brother, Fr. John Pounde. He served in the household for more than two years.

While Henry Chadderton was resident, Elizabeth Lady Guildford married John Gage, a wealthy Catholic who in his household always kept *two* priests. John Gage's brother Edward was married to Elizabeth's sister, Margaret Shelley. Leaving the Guildford-Gage household in 1579, Chadderton went to London and established a connection with another important Catholic family, the Petres. In London he and his sister visited his spiritual father Thomas Pounde, now confined in Marshalsea prison, and his sister embraced Catholicism. Leaving his sister in the care of Lady Petre, Chadderton took Pounde's advice to depart for Douay. Later he became a priest.

Young Henry Guildford soon went up to Christ Church College, Oxford. He will marry one of the daughters of the 4th Earl of Worcester in a double ceremony in 1596 (attended by the queen). At least one of his sisters will marry a Catholic gentleman, Elizabeth marrying Thomas Gage, a younger brother of her step-father John Gage. Other members of the Shelley and Gage families also married with prominent Catholics, including the Skinner family.

Elizabeth Shelley Gage was hard hit in 1580. In the crack-down on Catholics as Campion and Persons traveled on their mission, her husband John and her brother William Shelley were both committed to the Fleet Prison for "obstinacy" in popery. Her brother-in-law Edward Gage was in prison in the Marshalsea. John Gage and his Shelley relatives were in and out of prison during the next decade but persevered in their faith. Another of Elizabeth Shelley Gage's brothers, Richard Shelley, was sent to the Marshalsea prison, in March, for presenting a petition to the queen seeking toleration for English Catholics. He died there in February or March 1586.

Walsingham's spy, Nicholas Berden (*alias* Thomas Rogers), insinuated himself into Catholic circles in London and then in Paris in 1585–86. He provided intelligence on Elizabeth Gage and on her brothers. In April 1585 he reported to his employer that the principal collectors for the seminaries included the priests Blackwell, Hardwick, Hollowell and Willson: "this Willson is for the most part lodged at the lady Gylfords, who is married to Mr. Gage and some times at Mr William Shelley his house in trinity lane." The priest "Willson" is Fr. Thomas Wilson, one of the earliest students to attend Douay. He was surely lodged at Lady Guilford's because among those he was collecting were two of her nephews. And making some of the arrangements for those nephews to leave England for the seminary a few months after Berden's report was William Sterrell.

The experiences of the Skinner, Shelley, Gage and Fitzherbert families are typical of the treatment of Catholic families by the English government. All four families became connected with William Sterrell. The searches, the jailing, and the plundering of the property of these men and women for no other reason than their religion are why many felt it necessary to flee their homes and country. The cruelty and hatred of men like Job Throckmorton and Richard Topcliffe were tolerated or sponsored by the government. Some fled, but others who were appalled by such atrocities bided their time and sought change by other means.

6

Aboard the Ambassador's Boat

Six young men arrived at staggered times on September 13, 1585, at Gravesend, the port on the south bank of the Thames, twenty-five miles downstream from London. The water journey by oar was safer than the London-Dover road that crossed Blackheath. Highwaymen were not their only fear from the land route; government agents were the greater peril. Thieves would merely steal the money and goods that travelers carried on a Channel crossing. If the young men were detected and captured, the English government would fine them heavily and imprison them, perhaps even torture them to learn of their connections. Their destination was four miles further east of Gravesend, where another boat waited. Traveling in pairs, two accompanied the man who was said to have arranged their passage. They called him "Jero," the pronunciation of his Gallic name—Girault (Girault de la Chassaigne).

"Jero" was a servant to the French ambassador, Mauvissière. After a decade in England, Mauvissière was preparing to return home. The Duc de Joyeuse, King Henry III's Grandadmiral de France, sent one of his ships to transport Mauvissière's effects and some of his staff back to France. The ambassador and his family were to follow shortly. Jero was responsible for secreting the lads to the Duke's boat. Should they be searched, the crew were to pretend the young men were servants of the ambassador. In the event, the plan failed.

The six were embarked on an illegal journey. Parliament's law against "Jesuits and Seminarists" made it an act of treason punishable by death to return to England from a seminary. And leaving England to go to a foreign seminary or college, or to assist someone attempting to do so, subjected an offender to the penalties of *praemunire*. The government's purpose was to prevent the very thing these youth were attempting: the attendance at Catholic colleges in Europe. And to punish severely anyone who assisted them.

On the morning of the 14th, the Duke's ship lifted anchor and began to sail towards France. It was soon hailed to by sailors of a boat under Captain Palmer, working for the queen's Searcher of Dover. Was this a routine search looking for merchant goods that were not licensed for export? Or had someone betrayed the young men traveling aboard the ambassador's vessel?

A young Englishman using an alias "haunted" the French embassy in the latter years of Mauvissière's tenure as ambassador. He called himself "Kirby" but the ambassador knew that he was a brilliant scholar from Oxford University. Others using aliases would also come and go from the embassy. As seen already, someone wrote letters under the name "Henri Fagot," relating events as though he were a Catholic priest. Both "Kirby" and "Fagot" would have been well-known to Mauvissière's servant "Jero." "Fagot" certainly knew of Jero and betrayed him to the English government.

Just before the ambassador's boat departed, a letter was sent to Secretary Walsingham bearing the signature of Fagot. After telling of Fagot's discussions with the new French ambassador, Guillaume de l'Aubespine, baron de Châteauneuf (who had been in London for several months) Fagot took up the subject of the butler in the embassy, Girault—"Jero." Several earlier Fagot letters had told of Girault's involvement in bringing Catholic books into England and his taking out church "ornaments" for sale in France (i.e., smuggling). Châteauneuf had expressed interest in the church ornaments and asked where such ornaments could be bought "to give to churches in France." Châteauneuf told Fagot that Girault had made a lot of money in this business. Fagot wrote Walsingham "there are three chests full of them here, and in one of them are books recently written against the religion of England; remember that Girault is the most evil man and the greatest dissimulator in France. He is a perfect plague in this realm."[1] A court order had been secured against Girault to prevent him from leaving London, evidently because of debts. Girault had made the arrangements for the boat for Mauvissière's goods, and was himself traveling on the boat. Thus with Fagot's letter and the possibility of contraband goods being on the boat, it is no surprise that Captain Palmer searched the boat carefully. Perhaps, too, "Fagot" had betrayed the six young men whose voyage was overseen and accompanied by Girault.

The six youths were removed from the boat, which was allowed to continue on its Channel-crossing, and were taken to Dover. They submitted to multiple interrogations and gave written statements. The names given by the youths were: William Byfield, Edward Dodwell, Edmund Denne, William Norton, Arthur Stradlinge, and George Williams. Each was asked to subscribe to the Oath of Supremacy, acknowledging Queen Elizabeth as head of church and state. Three of them had scruples about the Oath.

Only two of the six understood how their passage on the ambassador's boat had been secured. They kept the truth to themselves in their initial statements, sticking to the group story that it was "Jero"/Girault, safely out to sea (so they thought), who arranged it all. Norton remained steadfast, like his uncle who was prisoner in the Tower. Dodwell was the weaker of the two. For the second time in as many years he turned informant. That he waited a week is surprising. He had been captured by the searcher of Dover before. He had given evidence for the state before. His companions on the prior voyage were also seminarians, and they had gone to prison. What accounted for his reluctance now? The new statute? The forceful personality of the man he was now to betray?

When first questioned on the 14th, Dodwell's statement was only to the effect that he "had conference with Monsieur Mauvissière for his passage over and Jero his man, one of the chiefest about him, helped to convey him and the rest." Dodwell immediately swore the Oath of Supremacy. He must have mentioned that he and Norton had talked with the ambassador, for Norton was examined a second time that same day. Norton was asked about his speech with Mauvissière and how he happened to know Dodwell. Though he remained unwilling to take the Oath, Norton expanded upon his earlier statement. He admitted that his uncle Shelley in the Tower had given him support and that he was on his way to Rouen to see his uncle Richard Guilford. His meeting with the French ambassador, he said, came about through his sister, who sometimes served the ambassador's wife. Norton's acquaintance with Dodwell was of long standing, "having lyen in Oxford in his mother's house."

A week passed. Then on the afternoon of September 22 Dodwell told the bailiff that he wished to speak with Edward Stephens, the deputy Searcher of Dover who had captured Dodwell two years before. Dodwell now revealed to Stephens that since their last encounter Dodwell had been maintained by Lord Hunsdon, Lord Chamberlain of England, to whom he had given good intelligence. He promised that he would provide more information on many matters to Stephens, Lord Hunsdon and to Lord Cobham. Dodwell played his information out a bit at a time, to whet Stephens's appetite for more and to obtain entry with Stephens's superiors. Facing prison for years, he was trying to bargain his way out of a difficult spot. His only commodity were the secrets he knew.

It had worked for Dodwell before. Nearly two years earlier he was with a small group of Catholic youth headed to seminary from Gravesend when they were seized off Dover. Dodwell had denounced Raindall, the Searcher of Gravesend, whom they had paid to look away, and his fellow travelers. One of these was John Gerard, whom Dodwell correctly identified as the second son of Sir Thomas Gerard. Sir Thomas was knighted in 1553 and made Sheriff of Lancashire in 1558. The family home was near Tutbury where Mary Queen of Scots was long confined. Sir Thomas in 1571 participated in a failed scheme to rescue Mary. For this, the elder Gerard spent two years in the Tower as close prisoner. His sons were placed in the care of a tutor. Sir Thomas recalled his children upon his release. John Gerard and his brother, Thomas, were sent to Exeter College, Oxford, when John was about twelve, where he had a Catholic tutor. As with Thomas Fitzherbert and Anthony Skinner, the experiences of the family with the heavy hand of government contributed to the zeal of the Catholic boys and led them from their native land. When the University authorities tried to force the Gerard boys to attend Protestant services and receive the Protestant sacrament, they departed Oxford, taking the tutor with them. Gerard enrolled at the English College at Douay and went to Rheims when the College relocated there in 1578. He later studied in Paris and encountered Fr. Persons in Rouen, to whom he announced his intention to join the Jesuit order. Within a short time after Dodwell's betrayal, John Gerard was locked away in the Marshalsea prison. He remained there as Dodwell was again captured and exposed more youths to bargain for his freedom. John Gerard does not gain his release until the following spring, when his bail is purchased for him by a "very dear friend" named Anthony Babington. His father, Sir Thomas, will be swept up in Babington's conspiracy and returned again to prison.

Dodwell introduced the name of a new figure into the narrative of the forbidden journey of September 1585. With Stephens he used only the man's alias, Kirby. But he identified him as a Master of Arts in Oxford. This man Kirby was a major figure in English Catholic circles, alleged Dodwell. From Dodwell's most recent interview, Stephens reported to Lord Cobham that this *Kirby* was "one of the chiefest familiars with Monsieur Mauvissière for all actions of the Scots Queen and also in all matters of weight concerning the papists in England." Mauvissière had showed to *Kirby* many letters that the Scots Queen had sent to him. Instead of attributing the arrangements of the illegal trip to Jero, Dodwell reported that "Kirby was the only dealer for them all unto Mauvissière for their passing over." He even told him where "Kirby" could be found: he commonly stayed at the Sign of the Saracen's Head, Without Newgate, in London. It was not far from the ambassador's quarters.

Stephens sent the six travelers up to Lord Cobham, at Cobham Hall, about midway between Dover and London. Cobham himself interrogated Dodwell and reported to Walsingham additional bits of information that Dodwell volunteered. He was, said Cobham, "a person that can say very much and is acquainted with all the seminarys." Dodwell was still referring to the mysterious man who "haunts Monsieur Mauvissière's house" as *Kirby*. Cobham said *Kirby* "is a person needful presently [immediately] to be looked unto." Having betrayed *Kirby*, Jero, and his five traveling companions, Dodwell now gave Lord Cobham the names of five seminary priests who had lately come over. In accord with the directions of Hunsdon and Walsingham, Cobham sent the six to London.

Hunsdon, however, was fed up with Dodwell. Having breached his trust with Catholics two years earlier, Dodwell had now breached his trust with Hunsdon, and the Lord Chamberlain was unwilling to deal with him directly. The youth was locked up in the Marshalsea prison, hardly the hoped-for welcome. Perhaps here he encountered John Gerard, whom he had betrayed earlier. Dodwell had sought to regain trust among the Catholics and had undertaken this journey without Hunsdon's knowledge. Hunsdon turned Dodwell over to a vigorous agent who often was sent abroad on diplomatic missions and was well-acquainted with Catholic activities and intelligence. He was a clerk of the Privy Council, as his father had been, and later will become Lieutenant of the Tower of London. He was William Wade (Waad). The experienced negotiator Wade insisted on a full confession from Dodwell. No more buying time with teasing and coyness.

Confessing to the illegality of his plans, Dodwell pleaded that would never have taken in hand this journey had he not been driven to great extremity. He could not live by any means nor please his friends by any means, except that he had gone to the seminary. He had left against his will, and was brought back again with his will. He acknowledged that he hoped that discharging his duty would make Hunsdon and Wade more favorable to him, or he would be "undone."

To Wade, Dodwell finally revealed the true identity of the mysterious *Kirby*. He was a Master of Arts now resident in Magdalen College at Oxford. His name was Sterrell.

We hear no more from Dodwell. He had worn out his usefulness. Probably he was dismissed and went on to an obscure life. He had been Hunsdon's man and not a regular spy for Walsingham, and he was not the likely source to tell the government he and his companions were departing on the ambassador's boat. That was surely "Fagot."

The fiction of Fagot and his letter of early September informing on Jero/Girault was necessary to justify a serious breach of diplomatic protocol. The seizure of Ambassador Mauvissière's boat and its passengers was an outrageous act, as offensive as intercepting a diplomatic pouch. Queen Elizabeth will surely have demanded proof of the necessity, a proper cause for stopping the vessel. When informed it was due to a letter of Fagot, she will have recalled the prior letters of Fagot alerting Walsingham and her Council of the Throckmorton Plot. But there was the rub. She might well have wanted to know more about this Fagot. So it was now necessary to usher him off the stage. Thus a letter from an unnamed person, ostensibly from France, was produced about October 1586.[2] It repeated some of the same points as the Fagot letter concerning Girault a short time earlier and gave a farewell to Walsingham, saying that the writer had become an "almoner" (a church officer in charge of distributing money to the poor on behalf of another) for the Duke of Montpensier. Like the previous letter of Fagot, it said Girault had managed to be appointed butler to Châteauneuf and was earning large sums with forbidden books. However, Mauvissière knew that Girault had preceded him in leaving England and on landing in France learned that Girault had probably been killed by pirates. Mauvissière sent a messenger back to London informing Florio and through him Walsingham and the Council. In short, the letter is unlikely to have come from someone actually in the company of Mauvissière.

We hear no more of Fagot—nor of his contemporary, *Emilio* (the latter another conjuration of Walsingham, Phelippes and Gilbert Gifford). Both are like Prokoviev's Lieutenant Kijé, who must be dispatched lest the monarch discover the truth—that he never existed.

7

Mary Stewart and the Theatre of the World

The Babington Plot

A proper plot must have a figurehead, even if he is a scapegoat. The odium had fallen to Ridolfi 15 years earlier, next to Throckmorton and then to Parry. Two decades later it will be an obscure soldier-of-fortune, Guy Fawkes. Walsingham found his proper man in Anthony Babington, the dear friend who had paid bail for John Gerard so he could flee England. Better for him if he had joined Gerard. Central casting could not have found a better conspirator-in-chief for a plot to seat Mary Queen of Scots on the English throne. A member of the landed gentry, from Dethick in Derbyshire, he was attractive in face and form, quick of intelligence, agreeable and facetious. A Jesuit who knew him said he "had a turn for literature unusual among men of the world." Babington's ticket had been punched at each stage to move into the final role.

- Descendant of a traitor, great-grandson of Thomas, Lord Darcy, who was beheaded in 1537? Check.
- Page to the Earl of Shrewsbury and to Mary Stewart while she was held at Shrewsbury's manor at Sheffield? Check.
- Involvement with the George Gilbert association supporting the Persons/Campion mission in 1580–81? Check.
- Paris sojourn to coordinate with the English Catholic exiles? Check.
- Courier of letters to Mary Stewart? Check.

All that remained was for Walsingham to draw the young man into a "mission impossible" plan to rescue his admired mistress from the heretic queen who held her. Walsingham used agents to seduce him into the position of ringleader. Certainly the ubiquitous Gilbert Gifford; and definitely Robert Poley, as vile a spy as ever was; and perhaps, if Mary Stewart was right in her suspicions, Fr. John Ballard (*alias* Captain Foscue, when he wore a gold-laced cape and silver- buttoned hat). Ballard, a mercurial Cambridge Master of Arts with a zest for living large, remains enigmatic. And in the final days, Walsingham will even coax Babington personally, holding out the prospect of his going abroad for her Majesty's secret service.

The principal facts on the Babington Plot are little disputed. Most accounts date the plot from December 1585 to July-August 1586 when the conspirators were arrested. Anthony Babington, whose name bears the shame of the conspiracy, was not brought into a definite plan until about May 1586, and then came reluctantly. Fourteen men were executed in September 1586, and in October Mary Queen of Scots was condemned for authorizing the plan.

The principal members of the Plot have always been recognized as Fr. John Ballard, John Savage, and Gilbert Gifford. It is generally acknowledged that Gilbert Gifford was, from (no later than) December 1585, an instrument of Walsingham, that a priest named Gratley (*alias* Bridges) also served Walsingham, that other agents of Walsingham who infiltrated the plot were Robert Poley, Bernard Maude and Nicholas Berden, and that Gilbert Gifford's collaborators included Thomas Barnes. It is equally accepted that in France Mary Stewart's agents, Thomas Morgan and Charles Paget, were involved in the Plot, along with the priest Dr. William Gifford. But there is disagreement about whether these three were truly part of the plan to free Mary or were in fact linked secretly to Walsingham. The latter is more likely: Morgan, Paget and Dr. Gifford were probably allied with the English government, whether it was for venal reasons or from hostility to Jesuit influence in English affairs.

In prosecuting the conspirators, the government asserted that one group of young men planned to rescue Mary Stewart at Chartley, an estate about 100 miles from London, while another group was to surprise Elizabeth to capture or kill her. When these two elements were accomplished, the Duke of Guise and the Spanish King, it was alleged, were to send a force to provide support for a new government. This Plot was an updated version of the earlier plot, the *Empresa*, with new participants within England, new names in an older narrative.

Secretary Walsingham had the key role in "discovering" the Babington Plot. His assistant, a well-educated man with skill in languages and cryptology, was Thomas Phelippes. In late 1591, the Jesuit poet and martyr Robert Southwell included in his *Humble Supplication to Her Majestie* a discussion of the government's role in the Plot, and referred to "Philips the Decipherer," as he has been known since. Phelippes was the document man in the entrapment of Mary Queen of Scots. He was probably kept ignorant of much of the maneuvering of Walsingham in the Throckmorton Plot and the Parry Plot. A successful spymaster lets his underlings know only what they need to play their limited roles. The master plan was entirely in Walsingham's head and all others in Elizabeth's government left him to his own devices. It was impossible (then and now) to distinguish between what Walsingham discovered and what he himself contrived.

Walsingham implemented his plan in steps. He had laid the foundation through George Gifford's approach to the Duke of Guise that was a catalyst for the Throckmorton plot and then had produced the Bond of Association. Now, Mary Stewart was moved from Sheffield to Tutbury, in Staffordshire, in January 1585. She was placed under the harsh supervision of Sir Amias Paulet. Walsingham's goal was to provoke the Scots queen until she took desperate action that would condemn her. For a year, Walsingham's men cut off all of Mary's letters. Mary Stewart was to have no conference with anyone without Paulet in her presence. Her servants were constantly monitored.[1]

But it was essential to Walsingham's purpose that she communicate agreement to a treasonous conspiracy so that she could be tried and executed. If all outside communication were intermittent, she could not be a participant in a conspiracy against Elizabeth. When her communication was restored, it was through Walsingham's own agents. His instrument in bringing this about was Christopher Blount, gentleman of the horse to the Earl of Leicester. Blount had attended Douay for a time and had met Thomas Morgan in Paris. Already in Walsingham's employ was Robert Poley, a kinsman of Blount. Sometime in the spring of 1585, Poley began cooperating with Thomas Morgan.[2] With the contrivance of Morgan, Christopher Blount had Robert Poley carry letters to Thomas Morgan in Paris in early summer 1585. Morgan then wrote to Mary Stewart that he had secretly met with Poley (Morgan was in the Bastille prison but under lax supervision) and Poley would be a good man through whom correspondence could be carried out. Morgan said they could count on the cooperation of the new French ambassador, M. l'Aubespine de Châteauneuf.

A letter of Poley back to England was intercepted by the English government. Morgan wrote Mary that he expected both Blount and Poley to be in trouble as a result. Far from being in jeopardy, within a short time Poley was employed in the household of Walsingham's daughter and her husband, Sir Philip Sidney—an extraordinary turn for a man known by his intercepted letters to be working for Morgan and Mary Queen of Scots, but unsurprising if both Morgan and Poley were already in the confidence of Walsingham. Morgan boasted to Mary Stewart that he had gotten Poley into Walsingham's own household, for her benefit.[3] Mary Stewart was so isolated from reality that she actually believed that Morgan, a prisoner in Paris, could penetrate the household of the English spymaster and place therein an agent loyal to her.

Another key spy for Walsingham against Mary Stewart was Nicholas Berden, *alias* Thomas Rogers. He was a spy for Walsingham against Catholics within England in 1584–85 and sent many letters reporting on Catholic activities. The intelligence he gathered became a basis for the charges against the Babington plotters: Walsingham instructed Thomas Phelippes on August 2, 1586, to have Berden "set down the names of the principal practisers as well Clergy men as temporal."

Having thoroughly insinuated himself among the Catholics in England, Berden was sent to France in July 1585. Berden was with Fr. Edward Stransham when Stransham was arrested in July 1585. Half a year later, he suffered martyrdom at Tyburn. Berden took Stransham's papers to gain access to the Catholics in Rouen and Paris. By mid–August, Berden had made contact with Thomas Fitzherbert and reported back to his master, Walsingham: "I have delivered the token of Tramsom, *alias* Barber, to Thos. Fitzherbert, who upon sight thereof, received me into his company most willingly, and has given me credit with all the papists at Paris, except Charles Paget, as they are divided in factions...."[4]

According to Berden, Fitzherbert had told Berden of military plans of the Duke of Guise and others (the *Empresa* again). Berden informed Walsingham of Fitzherbert's role as an intelligencer for English Catholics in France and Spain (while pressing Walsingham for more money).[5]

Berden's reports cover Gilbert Gifford's meetings with his cousin Fitzherbert. As the Babington Plot entered its most active phase in May 1586, Berden returned to London, smugly noting that he had been so effective that Fitzherbert and others had employed him to be their correspondent. By this time Gilbert Gifford and Berden were cooperating closely to entrap Catholics. But both Gifford and Berden were playing both sides.

In his book on the Babington Plot, Fr. Pollen remarked on the fact that Walsingham had *not* ordered Berden to return from Paris and that Walsingham would not thereafter meet with Berden: "he would neither write to the man, nor give him an interview. The Secretary of State was evidently not going to supply such a creature with news, on which to trade at will."[6] The explanation is that Berden, like Gilbert Gifford, was betraying all parties. For it was surely Berden whom the Spanish Ambassador sent back into England. Mendoza informed King Philip on May 11/1, 1586, saying[7]:

> I have decided to obtain intelligence about [English armaments] by means of sending an Englishman to London, a man who is recommended to me by Paget as being thoroughly trustworthy. He has already left, and takes with him credences for friends of mine in London, and also other letters from Charles Paget....

Pollen noted that Berden was observed in Paris on April 24, 1586, and was in London by early May. Berden's letter to Walsingham upon arriving in London matches the description of the Englishman Mendoza dispatched, for Berden wrote[8]:

> I have been thought mete to be employed by Charles Padgett, Charles Arundell, Stephen Brinkley from Allen & Persons, Godfrey Foulgiam & Thomas Fitzherbert to be their correspondent here for the receiving and delivery of such letters as they shall send unto me, and to give them Intelligence from England.

Though very suspicious of Berden, Walsingham still found him useful and dealt with him through Phelippes and others.

The relationship between Mary's jailer, Paulet, and Phelippes was close. Paulet had been the English Ambassador to France in 1577. Phelippes, a recent recipient of an M.A. from Cambridge, accompanied Paulet as his secretary. Also with them on this journey to France was Francis Bacon, aged 15 and fresh from Cambridge and Gray's Inn. Bacon spent the next several years in Paulet's household, where he came to know well Phelippes and Phelippes' younger brother. Bacon returned to England on the death of his father in 1579. After Paulet left, Phelippes continued in France in the service of Sir Henry Brooke (Cobham), the new ambassador. Phelippes was acting as decipherer for Walsingham as early as July 1581; a letter of Walsingham spoke of Walsingham's having committed "to my servant Philips" a message in cipher that was intercepted with a letter of Mary Queen of Scots.

Mary Stewart's move to Chartley House in December 1585 after less than a year at Tutbury was part of a calculated effort to again increase her discomfort and the likelihood of her seeking freedom, a tightening of the screws. With Mary secured tightly under Paulet at Chartley, Walsingham's agents now simply had to recruit some Catholic lads, stirred by romantic notions of freeing an unjustly imprisoned queen and wresting the land from heresy—a chivalric adventure. As with the Throckmorton and Parry Plots, they were to be persons closely associated with Morgan and Paget in Paris.

Early in 1586 letters going to and from Mary at Chartley and her supporters were passing through Phelippes's hands. The communication was by beer barrels with a secret compartment. The brewer who delivered the barrels was bribed, and government officials referred to him as the "honest fellow," the merry brewer of Burton. Gilbert Gifford and Robert Poley both had a hand in the setting up of the communication system for Walsingham and served as couriers.

Where her intercepted letters did not themselves sufficiently show Mary's knowledge of a plot, Phelippes would emend them to establish her guilt, before sending them on their way. Some years later, another Walsingham agent, Thomas Harrison, will confess that he and Phelippes had forged the letters used to convict the Babington plotters and Mary Queen of Scots, and that he, Walsingham, Phelippes and Bernard Maude had drawn up the plot.[9] Phelippes will offer his own *mea culpa* to her son when he becomes the English monarch. Originals of the allegedly damning letters were all lost or destroyed. The only evidence used by the government were copies of deciphered, translated texts of an unverifiable nature. At the so-called trial, nothing could be done by Mary Stewart to impeach such unreliable evidence.

Like Francis Throckmorton, Anthony Babington had been recruited to be a courier/correspondent by Courcelles, the agent in the French embassy for the affairs of Mary Queen of Scots. Babington confessed he was recruited by Courcelles in mid-1580, after Babington had returned from six months in France. Courcelles appeared at Babington's London lodgings, bringing him letters from Thomas Morgan. These and subsequent packets of letters Babington sent on to Mary Stewart through Anthony Rolston and a Mistress Bray. He handled about five packets in the space of two years, ending this role about spring 1583. Courcelles's involvement with William Parry and Thomas Morgan led to his expulsion from England in March 1585.

Thomas Morgan wrote to Mary and vouched for Babington's character. Because Morgan knew Walsingham read his messages, such letters to Mary conveyed intelligence to Walsingham about the persons he might use to entrap Mary. Among the group of young men attached to Babington were Charles Tilney, a playwright whose uncle was the Master of Revels; Thomas Salusbury, a young Welshman whose brother was a poet and courtier; and Chidiock Tichbourne, a gentleman and poet. All four were members of the Gilbert association that aided Campion and Persons in 1580–81.

When Babington was drawn in, there was already a "plot" under way involving Fr. John Ballard and John Savage, both of whom had been at the English College at Rheims. Savage later confessed that he had come to Rheims from the camp of the Duke of Parma and was talking with Christopher Hodgson when Dr. Gifford overheard them and suggested the murder of Queen Elizabeth. Most likely, this first suggestion was at the time of George Gifford's visit to his brother in the spring of 1583.

Ballard *alias* Foscue was a tall, dark-eyed, dark-bearded Cambridge graduate. According to a companion, Fr. Anthony Tyrell—a far from reliable witness—Ballard had for several years talked of a willingness to kill Queen Elizabeth. He became known to Morgan and Paget by the end of 1584, and by early 1585 he was reporting to them on political conditions in England and Scotland, where he was circulating among the Catholic nobility and gentry.

After a trip into Scotland looking for support for an invasion project, Ballard was back in London by February 1586 and had linked up with John Savage and Gilbert Gifford. Ballard was soon meeting with Edward Windsor and Charles Tilney and became acquainted with Babington. By the middle of March 1586, a group had been assembled; they dined together at a tavern called the Plough. They included Ballard, Babington, Robert Barnwell, Chidiock Tichbourne, Henry Dunn, and Bernard Maude (another Walsingham operative). The occasion was to see Ballard off, for the next day he left for France. In Paris, meetings in mid-April took place among Ballard, Morgan, Paget, Solomon Aldred (yet another spy working for Walsingham), Gratley and Dr. William Gifford, though not necessarily all together, and Ballard met with Bernardino Mendoza, the Spanish ambassador to Paris.

Dr. Gifford had sneaked away from his teaching post at Rheims and met secretly in

Paris with Aldred, Gratley and Sir Edward Stafford, the English ambassador. After this meeting, he wrote to Walsingham, offering to "serve Her Majesty [Queen Elizabeth] ... not only for the natural duty and allegiance I bear unto Her Highness before all princes christened, but also somewhat the rather for the ingenuous and most bountiful actions your honour has shewn diverse and sundry ways to me and mine...."[10] He said he had sought "to return home and to join with Her Majesty goods, lands and life for the defence of her sacred person and the welfare of my dear country against all ambitious foreign practices...." Walsingham, he said, could give him particular directions "by my kinsman Gilbert Gifford." He finished by acknowledging that he was bound to Walsingham "for my eldest brother [George Gifford] and divers other my friends, as also for my own particular...." Thus does Dr. Gifford implicitly establish in writing that he knew his brother George had been working for Walsingham when George had visited him in April 1583. Equally clear is his knowledge that Gilbert Gifford is colluding with Walsingham, for Walsingham is to communicate with Dr. Gifford through his cousin.

Historians have struggled to reconcile Dr. Gifford's encouragement of a plot against Queen Elizabeth with his exchanges with Walsingham. The answer is simple: Dr. Gifford knew that Walsingham was the prime mover of a fictitious plot that would never reach fruition because Walsingham entirely managed it. For Dr. Gifford, the greatest hope for toleration of Catholicism in England was to remove the influence of the English Jesuits. Walsingham and Dr. Gifford had common cause against the Jesuits. He accepted uncritically the claims of Soloman Aldred, who was employed by Walsingham to hold out the hope of accommodation of Catholicism. Two decades later, the Jesuit faction through Sterrell will exact revenge on Dr. Gifford.

Ballard returned to London in May with a project for rescuing Mary Stewart from Chartley and with indefinite promises for support of an invasion, which Ballard amplified to a planned assault by the Catholic League, fixed for the following September. All of this was reminiscent of the Throckmorton Plot, with some of the same participants.

Also in early May 1586, Gilbert Gifford made a quick trip to France. The interception of Mary Stewart's correspondence had been under way for some time. Gilbert Gifford was the courier who took the packets of letters from the Brewer of Burton and carried them to Thomas Phelippes, either near Chartley or in London. After Phelippes deciphered and copied the documents, the letters were resealed and carried by Gifford to the French embassy. In May, Gilbert Gifford drew in a new figure to assist him while he was off to France. This man, who had the minor role of a substitute bearer of letters, later becomes important in the activities of William Sterrell's network. Historians have known almost nothing about him, and have assumed that his statements at the time of the Babington Plot were lies to deceive Mary Stewart. They were not. He was Thomas Barnes, another cousin of Gilbert Gifford.[11]

Thomas Barnes was in Rome with George Gilbert and William Allen in about 1581, and was arrested in London in the company of Fr. Stephen Rowsham in May 1582. He was apparently released about 1585. When Barnes wrote to Mary Queen of Scots in June 1586 after his cousin Gilbert Gifford asked him to carry correspondence to Mary, he spoke truthfully of his "long imprisonment." In a confession, Barnes described making his way to Chartley and said he had encountered Rowsham, a priest, at Stratford upon Avon. Barnes said he asked Rowsham to pray for him "because I had divers things about me with the which, if I should be apprehended, would turn me to as great trouble as I had sustained afore, if not more." The "divers things" were letters to Mary Stewart. While at Chartley, Barnes was interrogated by Sir Amias Paulet. Subsequent correspondence in the name of Barnes or Barneby was written by Thomas Phelippes.[12]

Another courier under the name "Emilio" was supposed to be carrying letters as a relative of Barnes. He has confused some historians, just as he was intended to confuse anyone inquiring closely into the activities of Gilbert Gifford. This "Emilio" was invented to cover the paper tracks of Gifford, when it was in fact Gifford himself carrying such letters. Gifford wanted to plausibly deny later that he had betrayed Mary Queen of Scots. Gilbert Curll, Mary Stewart's secretary, testified that a cipher had been prepared for "Emilio" for corresponding with Charles Paget, and one of Curll's enciphered letters was addressed to "Emilio." Châteauneuf, the French ambassador was also led to believe such a person as "Emilio" was in the service of Mary Queen of Scots. When Phelippes and Gifford wanted to insinuate Nicholas Berden into the confidence of Châteauneuf, they proposed that someone should be disguised as "Emilio Russo" to introduce Berden to Châteauneuf.[13] Some such introduction must have been made, for Berden soon wrote to Phelippes that he had been at the French Ambassador's residence on the previous Thursday and he gave names of the Catholics whom he had encountered there.

Gifford later explained to Phelippes that "Emilio" was needed to disguise from Paget in Paris the identity of one of the duplicitous couriers:

> [W]hen Morgan examined me secretly touching the parties that conveyed letters I was forced to name two, whereof Barnes was one. And for that purpose I dealt with Barnes, never thinking, as Christ Jesus save me, but to make him a colour for Emilio and his writing once or twice would cause all blame to be removed from myself when things should be opened, which I knew must needs be shortly.

In this same letter, Gifford said he needed Barnes to write to Paget concerning the conveying of letters. If Barnes was not in hand, Gifford told Phelippes that he should feign Barnes's hand and direct the letter to Gifford, using Barnes's alias of "*Pietro* Maria." It was necessary that "Emilio" be gotten rid of to avoid scrutiny of Gifford: "And I pray you use Emilio no more. Let him be one of them that were hanged, for, before God, they will suspect." This is exactly what Phelippes thereafter did. He wrote to Gifford that "Emilio" was one of those who was hanged.[14] An unexplained disappearance of a character in the carriage of letters to Mary Stewart would have caused more suspicion of Gilbert Gifford. Similarly, it had been necessary to invent an end to "Fagot" lest Queen Elizabeth suspect that the supposed priest, whose letters she had been shown, was an invention of Walsingham to mislead her.

Phelippes and Gilbert Gifford together created multiple fictitious characters, and here we have seen three—Henry Fagot, Emilio Russo, and Pietro Maria. Once created, Phelippes or Gifford could write in their names or pretend such a person existed. Thomas Phelippes and William Sterrell will do the same numerous times in the next two decades.

The letters carried by Thomas Barnes in June 1586 included Mary's correspondence with Babington. Babington outlined to her a plan for her rescue, with himself at the head of a group of ten, to be followed by a hundred more men waiting nearby. The "usurping Competitor," Queen Elizabeth, was to be dispatched by six gentlemen. With Babington's plan in Mary's hands, Phelippes now moved his deciphering activities closer to the source, waiting for the trap to close. Phelippes had been at Chartley around Christmas 1585 when Mary Stewart first was placed at Essex's estate. He was there again for two weeks or more in July 1586, finally leaving Chartley on July 17, 1586. He perhaps carried the letter of that date that would led to Mary's death sentence. Mary Stewart wrote to Morgan telling him of Phelippes's presence. She remembered that "one named Phillippes" who worked for Walsingham had been recommended to her long ago by Morgan. This was probably when Morgan and Phelippes were collaborating in France in 1581–82. Mary's verbal portrait of Phelippes is the only record of Phelippes's characteristics: "this Phillippes is of low stature, slender every way, dark yellow haired on the head and clear yellow bearded, eated in the face with small pockes, of short sight, thirty years of age by appearance and as is said secretary Walsingham's man...."[15] The poor woman thought she might hear back from Morgan whether this Phelippes was the one who might be turned to her service. But another letter of this same date, to Anthony Babington, condemned her.

On July 17, 1586, Mary replied to Babington's proposal, concurring with his plan and giving specific instructions about her rescue. When Thomas Phelippes passed this letter on to Walsingham he drew a gallows, to show that Mary had just assured her own execution. Walsingham waited until Babington responded to Mary's letter. He was monitoring Babington's activities by Robert Poley, who had now insinuated himself into the company of Babington. In the case of Poley, as with Gilbert Gifford, the English government gave the impression that Poley was drawn into some activity in the Babington Plot in 1586, when in fact he had been begun his double-dealing a year earlier.

Poley has earned infamy for his duplicitous role in seducing the confidence of Anthony Babington. He arranged three or four meetings between Babington and Walsingham himself in late June and early July 1586. Poley purported to be an insider with Walsingham and could help Babington receive a passport to travel in Catholic lands. Babington would do service for Walsingham and the queen in his travels, i.e., become a spy himself. Walsingham even promised to procure Babington's access to her majesty over his proposed service. Walsingham had Poley tell Babington of Jesuits and other Catholic conspirators recently entering England from Rome via Boulogne and asked Poley to learn what he could of this plan to kill the queen. Babington sent word to Walsingham that indeed two Jesuits were among the Catholics secretly brought into England from Boulogne. These were Robert Southwell and Henry Garnet. Also arriving were Roger Yardley (who was soon arrested) and Walsingham's man from Rome and Paris, the quondam tailor of London, Soloman Aldred.

In early August, the arrests of the plotters began. Babington's hurried final note before his capture was to Poley: "Farewell sweet Robyn, if as I take thee true to me. If not, *adieu omnium bipedum nequissimus*." Goodbye, of all two footed creatures the worst.[16] After his involvement in securing the execution of Babington and others, Poley goes on to participate in the death—perhaps an unofficial execution—of Christopher Marlowe in May 1593. Shortly after Marlowe's death, William Sterrell will call Poley the "vilest spy that ever was," and Ben Jonson, will compose a poem—*Inviting a Friend to Supper*—similarly vilifying Poley's name. Robert Poley, and other alumni of the Walsingham College of Advanced Espionage Studies, such as Anthony Munday, Richard Baines, Michael Moody, Thomas Harrison, and Bernard Maude, will circulate on the fringes of state affairs for the next two decades, and those associated with the English Jesuits will work to counteract them. Phelippes will take the most extraordinary path of all of Walsingham's recruits when he is drawn into the Jesuit network and counters his former associates.

When Babington was captured he confessed all. He was taken at the Bellamy estate of Uxendon Manor at Harrow-on-the-Hill. The Bellamys suffered much for helping Babington and friends and for sheltering priests over the years: the execution of young Jeremy (Jerome) Bellamy with the Babington Plotters; the later rape of one of the Bellamy daughters by England's most notorious official sadist, Richard Topcliffe; and the ruin of the entire family within a few years. Uxendon is where Fr. Robert Southwell is captured in 1592.

Mary was informed of the government's knowledge of the conspiracy on August 11, 1586. She was now confined in a new place, Tixall, while Chartley was searched by Waad. She was deprived of her servants, her money, and what little dignity was still allowed her.

The trials of the plotters were conducted in mid–September, 1586, and all tried were convicted. They were executed in two groups, the first (September 20) suffering the full treatment of hanging, castration, disemboweling, and the heart hacked out still beating. Babington was one of this first group. Another was Chidiock Tichbourne who, the night before he died, composed a haunting elegy.[17] The butchery produced revulsion in the crowds, and the second group were merely hanged the following day.

George Gifford

What of the plotter George Gifford, whose fanciful flight to France in 1583 and whose bargain with the Duke of Guise were used to encourage the Babington Plotters? Despite testimony from various Babington Plot participants as to George Gifford's involvement, he simply denied all.[18] But to allay suspicions about the government using him to trap his relatives and friends, he was placed in prison in August when the other conspirators were arrested. As George Gifford is accused in the Babington Plot, he is charged with another crime in a scheme that seems surreal. The charges were evidently to inculpate another of Francis Throckmorton's brothers, and to justify delaying action on George Gifford while the Babington Plotters and Mary Stewart were being tried.

On December 13, 1586, charges against George Gifford were sent to Walsingham. They related to events of some months earlier, and we again see George Gifford as a provocateur among English Catholics. These charges again involved burglary, as the allegation of April 1583 had, and again the burglar Nix appears, this time identified as William Nix, a "notable" thief. Gifford allegedly "had an instrument or engine used and employed in the robbery of divers houses in and about the cities of London and Westminster & in other places, viz. at Mr. Mackwilliams his house at Charing Cross & the Bishop of London his house...." The charge is that Gifford's "engine" was used but Gifford himself was not present, though it "is supposed that Mr. Gifford had his share in the said robberies." As in 1583, Gifford's horses supposedly were used. It was also alleged that a trunk of Gifford's was taken that contained a press for stamping out foreign coins, and that he was examined concerning this by some members of the Privy Council. Christopher Denny and Clement Owffield (Offield) testified that Gifford had conference and dealings with them about coining foreign money. The real object of the charges appears, however, in the allegations that Gifford's engine was used by Gifford's man William Haynes *and George Throckmorton*, cousin of George Gifford and brother of the executed Francis Throckmorton, to rob a goldsmith of London of plate and jewels worth 200 pounds or more "which goods were carried to Throgmorton house in London." One Elizabeth Johnson testified that Gifford and Throckmorton went secretly to where the stolen goods were, evidently to divide up the booty.

George Throckmorton had been taken again into custody back in August. On August 17, 1586, he testified that George Gifford had informed him of Mr. Offield, who could make the philosopher's stone (called the Great Elixir).[19] He had also been interrogated about Anthony Babington. The government had no case against George Throckmorton and could not prosecute him in the Babington Plot conspiracy. They had failed to find any evidence against him at the time his brother Francis had been tried and executed, and they had to release him from prison at that time. Hence the government now resorted to the bizarre claims of burglaries by means of a special engine. George Throckmorton, like his brother Thomas, saw that he would only find safety by fleeing abroad. Soon he was in Brussels.

George Gifford—a principal to the escape of a robber, a plotter for the assassination of the queen in cooperation with the Duke of Guise and later with Anthony Babington, a robber of homes and businesses in London and Westminster, and owner of a stamp press for counterfeiting money—was imprisoned in Beauchamp Tower (of the Tower of London) for about three years but then released.[20] There, he had the time to carve elegant Latin epigrams that still remain: *Dolor patientia vincitur* (sorrow is conquered by patience) and *Mala conscientia facit ut tuta timeantur* (a bad conscience makes what is safe seem fearful).[21]

He apparently continued to draw his daily pension from the government while in the Tower. The Privy Council wrote a letter in June 1590 to the Lord Mayor of London to give Gifford his liberty "considering there is no direct proof of the fact committed."[22] He soon returned to the merry life of the Court of Elizabeth, married into the Cecil family (something that never could have happened had he ever been a traitor and common burglar), became an admiral on voyages with Sir Walter Ralegh (husband of another of George Gifford's Throckmorton cousins), and was presented eventually with a knighthood. Moreover, Gifford was a dutiful son. A letter of the Privy Council to George Gifford of May 23, 1593, identified him still as a Gentleman Pensioner and informed him that he could continue to keep his mother in his own care.[23] Like other recusants, she was supposed to be confined to her own home, but she was unable to live by herself because of age and sickness.

In March 1611 George Gifford wrote to Robert Cecil recalling that he had "served 39 years without reward" and seeking a favor of Cecil as a kinsman of Cecil's wife.[24] He could hardly have written that to the Lord Treasurer, his own kinsman, and the Secretary of State (who had records of all the intrigues of the past half-century) had he not been acting on the government's behalf in 1583–86 when he peddled a plan in France to kill the queen of England. He was a good son, a loyal subject, and a Walsingham double agent.

George Gifford's inscriptions in the Tower of London.

Gilbert Gifford

And Gilbert Gifford? He fled England just as the arrests were about to begin in the Babington Plot.[25] Why would he flee if he had been acting with Walsingham all along? He was a very bright lad, and doubtless saw that he was likely to be executed (as happened to William Parry) or imprisoned like other Walsingham agents. Men such as Walsingham use sweet words for a time to induce others to confess and cooperate, but they hold their subject then in the utmost contempt. The English ambassador to France, Edward Stafford, reflected this when he declared to Walsingham of turncoat spies that "if there were no knaves, honest men should hardly come by the truth of any enterprise against them."[26] William Sterrell himself warned Dodwell, another Catholic turned informer, that his master would "at the last despise you" and gave him a Latin aphorism, as a Walsingham or Lord Hunsdon would say: *amo proditionem sed non amo proditorem*, I love the treason but not the traitor.[27]

Gilbert Gifford had incited the plot all along, and the conspirators would inevitably raise his name at trial as having drawn them on. If he were not tried and was released, the government would be acknowledging that he—and the government—was in fact the provoker of the Plot. The government could not acknowledge that the chief inciter of the Plot was a government agent. People would have reacted as the English ambassador to France did when he learned the truth of Gilbert Gifford's—and Walsingham's—duplicity. After capturing Gilbert in Paris, Stafford wrote angrily to Walsingham that Gifford's "examination and confession may give subject to Her Majesty's enemies to procure a scandalous opinion to be conceived of her and her Council, as they mean to turn a letter or two, and especially one of Phelippes to him, so as to prove that he was the setter on of the gentlemen who were executed for that enterprize of the Queen of Scots, and then to discover them, and that he was practised to this by you and Phelippes, and they would fain have it with Her Majesty's knowledge."[28] Stafford knew that the Babington Plot was a Walsingham contrivance, and Stafford himself had played a part in Paris meetings with the men named as conspirators.

Gilbert Gifford lived on in Rheims and Paris, continuing to send intelligence back to Phelippes and writing to his cousin Barnes, using aliases of Mr. Colerdin, Nicholas Cornellis, Thomas Willsdon and maybe others. He was ordained a priest in March 1587 and was arrested in a brothel in December. He was confined to the Archbishop of Paris's prison in deference to his clerical status and died by 1591.

Gratley, too, made an ignoble end. He embezzled for his own use three thousand crowns entrusted to him by the Countess of Arundel that was supposed to be carried to Cardinal Allen. For his many misdeeds, he spent five years in prison in Rome.

Phelippes seems to have been unsure about the true relationship between Gilbert Gifford and George Gifford. He was probably unaware of the full extent of the duplicity of his employer, Walsingham. Clearly puzzled by the treatment of George Gifford, Phelippes asked Gilbert Gifford. His response is enigmatic: "And as for George Gifford it were a long circumstance to declare how cunningly I was brought into the matter … which I knew nothing but by mere conjectures at my first coming over, and I brought him only this message from D. Gifford [Dr. Gifford, George's brother]." He then gained a further light on the matter and had thought George Gifford "a man unresolved and unfit of whom to build of. But since I have understood the matter a thousand ways. It is certain that such a devise there was in hand: Nau [secretary to Mary Queen of Scots] had the handling of it, and delivered money for the purpose in Throgmorton's time, and Ch. Arundel laid it forth. This is the sum and substance and is most sure. Now give me leave to insinuate how you may salve all sores; which you may do either in laying the discovery of matters past upon him [George Gifford], for all men think he uttered it *a principio* [from the beginning]. Or in laying it upon Nau, or else that Heywood uttered it, for he hath spoken it to divers in these parts. Guise would give nothing beforehand…. Look not for mathematical satisfaction at my hands."[29]

This Gilbert Gifford statement seems to say George Gifford was the principal figure all along. Though Gilbert Gifford had at first thought George was unresolved, he learned that he was quite the contrary: a thousand ways. That is to say, if George Gifford had sought a plot against Elizabeth, he had soon abandoned it and returned to Court (and thus was a man "unresolved," as Gilbert had first thought); but if he were a provocateur for Walsingham, he was quite resolute and extraordinarily effective. The source of money going to George Gifford was not Guise directly but Nau, for Guise would not pay any money before the *Empresa* was carried out. All this had occurred in 1583: Nau had "*delivered money for the purpose in Throgmorton's time*," i.e., April 1583, when "Fagot" reported on Francis Throckmorton's presence at the French embassy, up to the arrest of Throckmorton in November 1583. Ch. Arundel "laid it [the money] forth": this was Charles Arundell who fled England in November 1583 with Charles Paget's brother, Lord Paget. Recall that "Fagot" had reported that Guise had sent money to the French embassy for managing the correspondence of Mary Queen of Scots; this could well be the money of Nau, Mary's secretary, of which Gilbert Gifford wrote. Nau may have delivered the money to George Gifford or have given it to Charles Arundell who gave it to George Gifford. Gilbert Gifford probably did not know for certain. It is likely that Charles Arundell was an instrument of the English government when he "laid it [the money] forth" based on the evidence of his subsequent behavior in Paris.[30]

Further evidence of the work of George Gifford with the Babington plotters comes from another government official who, like Phelippes, was not privy to the full story. Justice Richard Young was given the task in December 1586 of drawing up charges against George Gifford—as though the government were actually going to proceed against him. After writing up the bizarre charges of the robbery engine he added a postscript based on his earlier examination of John Ballard, who had been executed September 20. What Young wrote was quite different from the supposed confession of John Ballard before John Puckering, Thomas Egerton, Francis Bacon and Edward Barker of August 16 and 18, 1586, wherein Ballard had confessed to knowledge of a letter to Mary Stewart from Babington seeking her authorization for the plot and of her response authorizing it, as well as Ballard receiving money of Charles Paget and Edward Windsor. No, Young remembered Ballard talking of George Gifford. After going over the charges against Gifford from the supposed robberies, evidently thinking that the postscript was to call attention to a matter he thought more important than the robbery charges he had been instructed to write up, Richard Young wrote:

> Item: it was confessed by Ballard that he talked with Mr. Gifford and told him that he had been in France and brought him letters from his brother William wherein the said Gifford was entreated and persuaded to leave the Court and to go over into France where order was taken for his maintenance, nay said he sith that I have consumed and spent myself in the Court I will take another course and Ballard did also confess that divers times he had speech and conference with him [George Gifford].

William Gifford seems to have arranged maintenance for George Gifford after the latter had been in France in April to June 1583, and, moreover, that Ballard and George Gifford had met "divers times" during the period when Ballard was plotting to kill Elizabeth (which might indicate an active role for George Gifford in the plot in 1586 as well as back in 1583). Ballard seems to confess to bringing letters to George Gifford from his brother William Gifford, letters that persuaded him to come over to France in April 1583. Justice Young must have been perplexed that the government was not taking stronger action against George Gifford, brother of an exiled priest and co-conspirator with Ballard.

Morgan and Paget were deeply involved with Gilbert Gifford and with George Gifford's brother, William. Their contemporaries suspected that they were in fact English spies. Walsingham's agent Berden reported in August 1585 that Paget had been blamed for not dealing in the new conspiracy as he was directed, and for discovering it to the Council in England.[31] He had overthrown two great persons, the earl of Northumberland and William Shelley, so that they accounted him a spy. The great suit which he made for the release of Thomas Morgan, who was also "accounted a spy by all the papists here" brought him further into suspicion, so that they excluded him from their practices, and labored to discredit him with the Duke of Guise, the Pope, King of Spain, and others, as also to keep Morgan in prison.

Some historians also have suspected that Paget and Morgan played a deep and treacherous game that may well have involved their coming under fire from the English government to increase their credibility among Catholics and to reassure Mary Queen of Scots of their loyalty to her while she was yet alive. At Morgan's trial in the Low Countries a few years later, considerable evidence was given that pointed to Morgan being an English agent all along, as Fr. Persons and others had suspected.

Perhaps the best judgment on Gilbert Gifford's role was that given by Robert Southwell, the Jesuit poet. In late 1591 he wrote knowingly about Gilbert Gifford's secret role in his *Humble Supplication to Her Majestie*. He described the Babington Plot as "rather a snare to entrap them, than any devise of their own." Walsingham and his accomplices had "plotted, furthered and finished" the treason. Robert Poley, "Sir Francis Walsingham's man, and thoroughly seasoned to his Masters tooth," was the chief instrument to contrive the Plot. Southwell's knowledge came in part from letters of Phelippes to Gilbert Gifford that were discovered among Gifford's effects in Paris and from examinations of Gifford. He continued that "all the letters that fed them [the Babington conspirators] with foreign hopes, all the devices that wrought them into home-bred Imaginations, sprang all out of the same fountain of Sir Francis's fine head. *For Gilbert Gifford having some years before been Master Secretary's Intelligencer (as the date of Philips letters unto him discovered) when the matter was once on foot in England was made the mean to follow it in France among certain of the Scottish Queen's Friends....*"[32] Gifford was plotting with the government long before the Babington Plot. And Southwell gives an account of the dating of letters of Gifford to Phelippes that preceded by "some years" Gifford's supposedly having been caught by Walsingham in December 1585.

The Trial and Execution of Mary Queen of Scots

What was to be done with Mary Queen of Scots? For Walsingham, it was a simple: she must be executed. So long as she lived, she was a potential successor to the crown of

England and thus a continuing threat. Walsingham knew well the mind of Elizabeth. She would be extremely reluctant to take action. She would vacillate. She would temporize. She would be persuaded on one course and then waver.

The Bond of Association drawn up by Walsingham and Burghley was clear on this point. All who signed had agreed that "if any such wicked attempt against her most royal person shall be taken in hand ... we are most bound, and that in the Presence of the eternal and everlasting God, to prosecute such person or persons to death...." Now it had to be done. Walsingham and other Councilors pushed the queen step by step. When it seemed she would decline to execute her cousin, Walsingham created an entirely new and novel plot against her life, supposedly instigated by the French ambassador himself.

Mary was removed from Chartley to Tixal for a few weeks, while all her jewels and papers were seized. Before September was out she was immured at Fotheringhay Castle, in Northamptonshire. An ad hoc commission of peers and members of the Privy Council was appointed to try Mary. Thirty-six commissioners assembled at Fotheringhay and held their meetings, with their pre-ordained outcome, on October 12–13. Walsingham, a commissioner, confronted for the first time the queen for whose death he had so long planned and had worked so diligently (if underhandedly) to bring about. She knew that Walsingham was her chief enemy. Mary's trial turned on the letters that had been conveyed via the beer casks. Mary denied the charges against her and suggested the letter to Babington used to establish her guilt was a forgery. Walsingham took that as a false charge against him and replied with indignation.

Queen Elizabeth sent a letter demanding that the commission make no sentence before meeting again in London. On October 25, after sessions in Westminster, the commission pronounced the sentence of death against the Scots queen, which the Parliament quickly confirmed. Two weeks later, Elizabeth's officials informed Mary of the sentence and she began to compose her final letters.

Henry III of France sent an envoy who tried to persuade Elizabeth not to execute a sovereign queen. His efforts failed as Elizabeth signed the death sentence on December 4. When this was published in London, bonfires were made, and bells rang out the news the whole day. The French envoy and the French ambassador continued to plead for the life of Mary Stewart.

Yet Elizabeth wavered. Walsingham grew increasingly frustrated with her. He wrote a brief listing many reasons she should quickly carry out the execution, mostly for her own safety. Delay encouraged more plotting against her, he argued. To Burghley he expressed his exasperation, and complained of the queen's ingratitude in terms that sound of self-pity. He explained his determination to leave the court:

> Her Majesty's unkind dealing towards me hath so wounded me as I could take no comfort to stay there. And yet if I saw any hope that my continuance there might either breed any good to the church or furtherance to the service of her Majesty or of the realm, the regard of my particular should not cause me to withdraw myself. But seeing the declining state we are running into, and that men of best desert are least esteemed, I hold them happiest in this government that may be rather lookers-on than actors.

The letter reveals much about Walsingham and his priorities: his office as Secretary and Privy Councilor was first to *breed good to the church* and secondly to serve her Majesty and the realm. He had said much the same thing in a letter to Burghley sixteen years earlier from Paris: "Above all things, I wish God's glory and next the queen's safety."[33] It was religious zeal that motivated his actions throughout his public life, and he saw the execution of Mary as a godly enterprise. His own queen did not share his zeal for reform of the church nor did she see that the killing of the Catholic queen Mary was essential to ridding England of the vestiges of Roman Catholicism.

So Walsingham conspired once again to push his queen into action by contriving yet another plot against her life, to convince her by events where his brief had failed, that he was right in claiming delay encouraged plotting against her life. Walsingham now manufactured the Stafford Plot.

Walsingham's instrument this time was William Stafford, the brother of the English ambassador to France, Edward Stafford. No love was lost between Edward Stafford and Walsingham, but Walsingham had cultivated the ne'er do well younger brother. William Stafford was willing to do Walsingham's bidding to repay him.

William Stafford came forward in mid–January 1587 to allege that the French ambassador to England, Châteauneuf, and his secretary, named "des Trappes," had drawn Stafford into a plan to kill Elizabeth. Stafford said that he had introduced des Trappes to Michael Moody, a prisoner in Newgate for debt. Moody was to murder the queen by placing a bag of gunpowder under her bed and touching it off. Seized suddenly by repentance, Stafford confessed he had gone to Walsingham's house at Barn Elms and revealed the whole matter to him, and Walsingham had taken the story of the plot to his queen. Queen Elizabeth had des Trappes arrested as he was traveling to Dover to reach Henri III with news of Mary Stewart's planned execution. She appointed four of her Councilors to interview the French ambassador. Châteauneuf appeared and accused Stafford of having invented the whole plot himself. He admitted that Stafford had made some such murderous proposals to him, but said that he had rejected them altogether and had threatened to expose the young man to Elizabeth. For more than the next month, the French ambassador was kept a virtual prisoner in his own house, and his communication with France was interdicted.

The William Stafford Plot was one more demonstration to Elizabeth of the necessity to go through with Mary's execution. It also had the effect of isolating the French ambassador from communication with his own king or others within England. Pleading his own illness, Walsingham remained absent from further duties at Court.

Once Mary was executed (February 8, 1587), Elizabeth sent Walsingham to confer with Châteauneuf. Walsingham now expressed regret about the Stafford episode. The queen and her Council had concluded that des Trappes was entirely innocent. Stafford, Walsingham said, was only trying to extort money. Not long after, Elizabeth received Châteauneuf, treated him cordially, and apologized. All charges against des Trappes were dropped, no action was taken against William Stafford, and Michael Moody continued for years to serve as a spy for Walsingham and Lord Burghley. The Stafford plot of 1587 was just as phony as the George Gifford Plot of 1583.

Walsingham's monomaniacal plotting against Mary Stewart for the better part of a decade was successful but came at high cost. By the time it was over, Walsingham's health was almost ruined, as were his finances. His personal circumstances were mirrored in the government for which he was Principal Secretary: Walsingham's methods had corrupted the English judicial system through its increasing reliance on spies and torturers.[34]

Essential to Walsingham's goal of transforming a weak, captive woman into the greatest threat to the English government was to make her the living symbol of the Roman Catholic

Church. Gradually, over nearly two decades of imprisonment, Mary Queen of Scots came to accept the role Walsingham had scripted for her. She came to see herself as a martyr to her faith and played it out in her final days and hours. With a slight change for gender, Duncan's pronouncement on Cawdor can be applied to Mary Stewart's acceptance of death at Fotheringhay [*Macbeth*, 1.4]:

> Nothing in her life
> Became her like the leaving it; she died
> As one that had been studied in her death,

When the commissioners appointed for her trial arrived at Fotheringhay, Mary knew that everything was stacked against her. The laws and statutes of England were to her unknown, she said, though she knew that the statute passed under the Bond of Association was expressly framed for her destruction. She was destitute of counselors, and a queen has no peers for jurors. Her papers and notes were all confiscate, and no man dared speak in her justification. She told Lord Burghley and Lord Chancellor Hatton that there was a wider significance to her fate than the outcome of the immediate, tainted proceeding[35]:

> As for this assembly, it may be, for aught I know, devised against me, to give some colour of a just and legal proceeding, though I be already fore judged, and condemned to die, yet I adjure ye to look to your consciences in this matter, for remember the theatre of the world is wider than the realm of England.

For her trial she dressed the part of the martyr, wearing a black velvet robe, with a long white lawn veil thrown over her pointed widow's cap. Weak, she walked with difficulty but with measured dignity. She passed through a double row of halberdiers, armed with two-edged pole axes, who were entirely unnecessary to protect the commissioners from this feeble woman or prevent her escape. The halberdiers were part of a force of 2,000 men brought to shock and awe any who might think to side with Mary. The double-moated castle of Fotheringhay already insured against outside penetration or departure from within. She took her seat before the assembled nobility and jurists with a composure and self-possession that surprised them.

The principal evidence against Mary Stewart was written in one hand: Thomas Phelippes. Her letter to Babington with its supposed approval of the design against the life of Queen Elizabeth was only Phelippes's decipherment. The prosecutors produced the sworn statements of her secretaries Nau and Curll who had written on the copy of this alleged letter to Babington, stating that it was the "same letter sent from her to him, or like it." How could the copy of Phelippes's decipherment be either the same or like the original cipher? Nau and Curll had separately deposed that Mary wrote the minutes in French and gave them to Curll, by whom they were translated into English, after which they were put into cipher by Nau. Thus, there should have been three separate documents to verify each letter: Mary's minutes in French, Curll's translation into English, and Nau's cipher. These were not produced and there is no record of them. Thus Mary Stewart was convicted on Phelippes's version of the decipherment. The government had already executed Babington rather than wait to have him testify at Marty's trial. For his work against the defendant, Phelippes was allowed to play a special role at the trial. But Phelippes was not produced as a witness to tell how the letters had come about, only to read them.[36] Mary was given no chance to expose the deception that was practiced upon her.

At one point in the trial Mary Stewart spoke to the central fact of her religion as her principal basis for guilt, saying "My innocence is well known to God. My crimes consist in my birth, the injuries that have been inflicted on me, and my religion."

Conscious that she was playing to the "theatre of the world," Mary Stewart wrapped herself in religious symbolism, When offered the ministrations of an Anglican bishop, she responded that she had both heard and read much on the subject of Protestantism, especially since her detention in England, but her mind was fully made up "that she would die in the religion in which she had been baptised, and would willingly give ten thousand lives if she had them, and not only shed her blood, but endure the severest tortures in its cause." Exasperated, the Earl of Kent stated most clearly what the prosecution of Mary had been about all along: "Madam, your life would be the death of our religion, and your death will be its preservation."

The morning of her execution arrived, Mary dressed in modest attire, a widow's gown of black satin and petticoat skirts of crimson velvet. That it was a sacramental occasion was seen in the *Agnus Dei* about her neck and rosary beads with a cross at her waist. In the oratory where she prayed, kneeling at a small portable altar, she administered Holy Eucharist to herself.

Returning to the company of her ladies, she reflected on the fact that she had been queen of two countries, of Scotland by birth and of France by marriage. Now she was to die as few, if any, monarchs had ever died: at the hands of a foreign executioner.

After the castle clock struck eight, she was escorted by her keepers to Fotherghay's great banqueting hall. A twelve foot square platform had been erected to serve as a scaffold for her decapitation. A rail surrounded it and the floor of the scaffold was covered in black cloth. As she entered, Mary's eyes beheld the chair, also covered in black, that was her place. Before it were the block where she was to place her head and the axe that was to sever her neck. A large fire burned in the nearby fireplace on this cold winter morning. She mounted the two steep steps onto the temporary scaffold and seated herself in the sable covered chair. Again she refused Protestant rites. She said her own choice of prayers in Latin, French and English. She forgave her two executioners when they knelt before her. Two of her ladies came forward to help her remove her mantle but became too distraught to perform this final office for their mistress. She calmed them. She removed a rosary that she had instructed a servant to give to Philip Howard's long-suffering wife, the Countess of Arundel, but one of the executioners interfered even with this last gesture of a gracious queen. When the names of the Howard brothers had come up in a Babington letter at her trial, Mary had exclaimed: "Woe is me, that the noble house of Howard should suffer so much for my sake!"

Mary's eyes were covered with a sanctified cloth that had held the Holy Eucharist. She knelt on a cushion and placed her head on the block. Her final words were a heavenly invocation—"*In manus tuas*. Into thy hands, O Lord, I commend my spirit." Now the axe descended. The executioner bungled his sole function and three blows were required. "God save Queen Elizabeth!" he cried out as he held up the bloody head. A few minutes later, it was placed on a black velvet cushion in front of a window opening into the castle's courtyard. Uncovered now, as the curious looked in upon a conquered queen, her royal eyes looked out. Perhaps they had already seen the next act that would, in consequence of her death, be played out in the theatre of the world.

8

The Spanish Armada and English Catholics

The execution of the Scots Queen was the catalyst that launched the Spanish Armada. Before, talk of invasion often arose from Walsingham's operatives. That is what provocateurs do—they provoke, they stir up, they create plots and *projets* that they blame upon others.

Consider the three plots discussed so far: Throckmorton, Parry and Babington. All three apparently proceeded from the efforts of Mary Stewart's two agents in France—Morgan and Paget, together with Dr. William Gifford, who sought favorable treatment from Walsingham. Communications involving the Duke of Guise, the Spanish ambassador (Mendoza), and other English exiles in France were initiated by Morgan, Paget or a Walsingham agent. Gilbert Gifford and Berden tried to draw Mendoza into an assassination attempt. A firm plan to invade England came after the Babington Plot executions. A war to restore Catholicism in England had little appeal to the governments of France or Spain.[1] Pope Sixtus V was ambitious to advance the church but was suspicious of the Jesuits and apprehensive about expansion of Spanish power. He was willing to renew the excommunication of Queen Elizabeth, but such was his skepticism he conditioned a papal subsidy for a Spanish invasion upon an actual landing on English soil.

March 1587 was the crucial month, when the news of the execution of Mary Stewart reached Madrid and Rome after the English ambassador in Paris, Stafford, confirmed to Mendoza the truth of the reports. For the Duke of Parma in Flanders, the execution made him amenable to invading England; but he urged caution and preparation. For Philip II, vengeance for the state-murder of a sovereign was an easier decision than an attempt at rescuing a captive queen. The killing of a head-of-state threatened all the crowns of Europe. Philip II had once been king of England by his marriage to Mary Tudor. Elizabeth, his sister-in-law, dismantled Mary Tudor's restoration of the ancient religion in England and was bent on destroying Catholicism and Spain's dominion on the Continent, backing both the Dutch revolt against the Spanish and the French Huguenots with their German sponsors. Philip II felt he had special obligations to the Catholics of England.

The English government could not triangulate with France against the Spaniard. Whatever Henry III of France may have thought of his sister-in-law Mary Stewart, there was grief and anger throughout France over her execution. Moreover, France was preoccupied throughout 1587–88 with the War of Three Henrys—King Henry III; Henry of Navarre; and Henry, Duke of Guise.

English security lay not in caution but in a series of preemptive strikes along the Spanish coast, to diminish the capacity of the Spanish to invade England. The task was given to the aggressive anti–Spanish naval commander, Sir Francis Drake. This fervent follower of Walsingham had proven himself repeatedly. After attacking Vigo in Spain in late 1585 Drake had sailed to the Americas where he humiliated the Spanish by sacking the port of Santo Domingo and capturing the city of Cartagena de Indias.

Drake set sail in April 1587. The queen's authorization was to distress the Spanish fleet in its havens. Just as Drake sent farewell to Walsingham, Elizabeth again wavered. She sent a courier to Plymouth recalling Drake, establishing a record she did not wish to engage in war with Spain while simultaneously initiating war. The message arrived a day late, yet still it was something that could give her plausible deniability—just as she had done with the execution of the Scots queen.

Drake "singed the beard of the King of Spain" in May 1587 when he occupied the harbors of two of Spain's main ports, Cadiz and Corunna, destroying 37 naval and merchant ships in relative leisure. But Drake's actions through to July were far more than pirating of a few prize vessels bearing wealth from the New World or cornering Spanish vessels in their home ports. Rather, it was a campaign of destruction against the people of Spain and anyone trading with them. His unopposed cannon waged war on weaponless fishing folk and their villages, cutting up even their nets so they could not soon return to their trade. Drake bragged to Walsingham of destroying hoops and pipe staves that could be used to make barrels and casks, on the rationale that they might be used for provisions of the Spanish navy.[2] He remained on the Spanish coast for about two months, plundering what he could without undue risk. Suddenly he departed for the Azores. He must have gotten intelligence of the return voyage of the great Portuguese carrack, the *San Felipe*. It carried enormous wealth: spices, silks, ivory, gold, silver and jewels. With it in escort, he returned in triumph to London on July 6. Spain could not let the English depredations go unanswered. Any doubts about sending a massive fleet were dismissed.

The Armada was to be an invasion of England. A massive fleet assembled at Lisbon was to meet up with the Duke of Parma a thousand miles to the north, and his forces would be transported by barge across the channel. Once landed, the Spanish army would march to London and install a new, Catholic government. English Catholics were expected to welcome the invasion. King Philip appointed the Marquis of Santa Cruz, an experienced and capable admiral, as commander. However, he died in February 1588 and was replaced by the Duke of Medina Sidonia. An able leader, he lacked naval experience.

The King of Spain's plan was not doomed to failure at the outset. It was flawed, but it might have succeeded had weather conditions been more favorable and had the English naval operations been less adept. The fundamental problem was the difficulty of supplying vessels and transporting significant numbers of soldiers on a slow, lengthy voyage. It sailed on May 28 but was not ready to engage the English navy until July 21, 1588. By the time of the first skirmishes, the Spanish crew members were malnourished and ill, their supplies of powder and shot inadequate for sustained sea battles.

The launch, and failure, of the Armada caused significant suffering among Catholics in England and changed the assumptions among English Catholic exiles. As word spread of Spain's preparations, many English Catholics opposed an invasion on their behalf. They offered support to their queen. The records of the tense events of the 12 months prior to the sailing of the Spanish fleet are spotty. Lord Burghley had begun drawing up lists of Catholics to be restrained as the head of Mary Queen of Scots rolled to the floor at Fotheringhay.³ Government agents soon were searching homes of known Catholics and finding forbidden religious goods, beads, relics and books. For example, revisited was Lyford Grange, the residence of Francis Yates where Campion was captured in 1581. To Walsingham, Edward Unton reported turning up not only popish items but also the arrest of two servants who confessed they had been reconciled to Rome when Campion had visited.⁴ The government made plans to round up others who might favor the Spanish because of religion. The Privy Council had the country's sheriffs catalog the names of recusants in their jurisdictions.⁵ By the summer of 1588 numerous Catholics were rounded up and confined in the Tower and other places, including Quinborough, Hartford, Maidstone, Leedes Castle, as well as various episcopal residences.

The government felt justified in the suspicion cast on all English Catholics by pointing to the example of Sir William Stanley. He had distinguished himself in service with English forces in Ireland 1570–85, where he was knighted. After a brief period in London, he accompanied the Earl of Leicester to the Low Countries, leading an Irish regiment. Leicester appointed Stanley governor of Deventer in October 1586. Three months later Stanley transferred the town, and his regiment, to the Spanish. The exiles used the example of Stanley to encourage Catholics in England to revolt.

Intelligence pertaining to England provided to King Philip and his Council was inadequate and often ill-informed. They had a few sources within England but these were poorly situated to provide sound information. Before he had been expelled from London, Ambassador Mendoza was able to report to his Spanish masters from first hand observation and local contacts. Relocated to Paris, he tried to continue the same role. King Philip was acutely aware of the inadequacy of intelligence. He wrote Mendoza in April 1586⁶:

> I can well believe the difficulty you will find in obtaining trustworthy reports from England...; it is a matter of such great importance at present that reports should be obtained, that I must again enjoin you expressly not to be satisfied with the news you may be able to glean from the French embassy in England....

The Spanish king was especially interested in English naval activities. Mendoza used sources in England and in France that were often unreliable. As discussed earlier, Mendoza apparently trusted several of Walsingham's key agents, specifically sending into England Nicholas Berden to gather intelligence on armaments as demanded by King Philip. Mendoza also met multiple times with Gilbert Gifford about the Babington Plot.⁷ When Gilbert Gifford reported to Mendoza in early August 1586, he convinced the Spaniard that he represented many of the English Catholics who were ready to assist in an overthrow of the English government. Nearly all that he told Mendoza was fabrication, but he was correct in asserting that Sir William Stanley would defect to Parma once he was in the Netherlands. Gifford's passage was facilitated by the French ambassador in England, Châteauneuf, in the belief that Gifford was bringing money for the Catholics. Gifford continued to try to supply intelligence to the Catholics in Paris while attempting likewise to maintain his ties to Walsingham and Phelippes. Mendoza was also misled by a priest he had sent into England to gather intelligence.

Several men can illustrate Mendoza's difficulties; they were linked to a claimant to the crown of Portugal, António, Prior of Crato, whom the English government supported. He arrived in England late in 1585 and was hosted for a time by Queen Elizabeth's personal physician, a Portuguese named Roderigo Lopez (later to be executed). Two of the claimant's followers were recruited to supply news for Spain, through Mendoza. One was referred to in correspondence as "Sampson." Living in Paris but in communication with Portuguese in London, he was Antonio de Escobar.[8] Mendoza's letters to the Spanish king often refer to what Sampson has told him, and a number of memos survive that are styled: "Sampson's Advices from England."

Mendoza also received letters from London from Antonio de Vega. King Philip instructed Mendoza that de Vega would write to him under the name of "Luis Fernandez Marchone."[9] Mendoza would have been skeptical about de Vega. He seems to be identical to the Antonio de Vega whom Mendoza was reporting in 1581 as issuing letters of marque to English privateers on behalf of the Portuguese pretender for attacks on the Spanish.[10] De Vega reported on developments in England from the trial of Mary Queen of Scots until he fled to Flanders in danger of his life by early 1589.[11] He claimed that the French ambassador was his brother-in-law to enhance his credibility but this seems doubtful.

Neither de Vega's letters nor Sampson's advices have much information on the state of the English Catholics. They seem to have had no contacts among them.

Mendoza cultivated other sources in Paris that did provide some good information. The English ambassador to France, Sir Edward Stafford, was an informant in the pay of Spain. Stafford and Walsingham were generally hostile to one another and each distrusted the other. The ambassador may have been using the connection with Mendoza to serve the interests of England—as well as his own purse. In his letters to the king of Spain, Mendoza calls Stafford "Julius." "Julius" passed on good information on English naval activities, as well as other information, received from Lord Burghley.[12] Stafford's intermediaries with Mendoza were two English Catholic fugitives: Sir Charles Arundell (a relative of Stafford's wife) and then on his death Thomas Fitzherbert.[13] Arundell's actual loyalties are unclear. Stafford repeatedly asserted that Arundell's devotion to England was extraordinary, while Mendoza was equally certain that Arundell served only his Spanish masters.

With the round-up of the Catholics accused in the Babington Plot in August 1586 and the execution of Mary Queen of Scots, Fitzherbert came to realize that he had been spied upon by Walsingham. He was not however, fully aware of the duplicity of his cousin Gilbert Gifford. He seems to have accepted Gilbert's protestations of innocence, for Fitzherbert wrote letters on Gilbert's behalf. Just after the execution of Mary Stewart, a series of events occurred that shaped Fitzherbert's life thereafter. In 1588 he lost his wife, the Armada was defeated, and Henry III had the Duke of Guise and Guise's brother, the Cardinal, assassinated while Fitzherbert was still employed by the Queen Mother.[14] France was embroiled in civil war, and Fitzherbert had become an intelligencer for the Spanish. He was assigned to Rouen. His reports were expected to be sent to Bernardino de Mendoza, but the arrangement was unsatisfactory. In 1591 Fitzherbert told the Spanish Secretary of State Juan de Idiaquez he could not as yet establish his connections with England "where before now there would have been set up a fine system of corresponding if the lack of money and my referring the plan to Don Bernardino ... had not prevented the execution of my hopes."[15] It was at just this time, 1591, that Thomas Phelippes became aware of William Sterrell's correspondence with Anthony Skinner and with Thomas Fitzherbert and drew Sterrell into the service of the Earl of Essex. Fitzherbert and Sterrell may well have been corresponding occasionally during the Armada period, but no such letters have surfaced.

Persons, Englefield and Allen

The three key English figures influencing the Spanish king and the Pope had not been in England for some years. Fr. Robert Persons and Sir Francis Englefield were in Madrid urging King Philip to return England to Catholicism and advising him how best to accomplish this. Persons had spent less than 18 months in England, in hiding, 1580–81, and Englefield had not returned since he fled the island nearly three decades earlier. Fr. Allen had departed England more than two decades before the execution of Mary Queen of Scots and the Armada. These three had no regular sources of intelligence on England and largely relied on second-hand reports from Paris or Brussels from people with little access to English government internal information.[16]

Persons and Allen saw the need for planning for governance of England after a Spanish invasion. A spiritual leader in England was essential. They lobbied for a cardinal's hat for Fr. Allen, pressing first in Spain for the support of King Philip and then to the Pope. The effort was orchestrated in part by Robert Persons. Count Olivares, the Spanish ambassador to Rome, wrote King Philip concerning Allen's elevation. As execution approached for Mary Stewart, it was the more necessary for the English Catholics "to have some great personage upon whom they may fix their eyes and hopes, and who may console them and prevent them from giving way to despair."[17] King Philip concurred. An appeal to the Pope for the appointment in March 1587 noted: "So many [of Allen's pupils] have suffered martyrdom that it may be said that the purple of the cardinalate was dyed in the blood of the martyrs he has instituted."[18] Sixtus V acceded to Spanish pressure and created Allen cardinal-priest on August 7, 1587, with the title of San Martino ai Monti. It was anticipated that after the success of an invasion Allen would hold the office of lord chancellor as well as that of archbishop of Canterbury.

Allen and Persons coordinated in publishing pamphlets that would justify a Spanish invasion and prepare English Catholics for a new government. Dated as April 23, 1587, at Rome, Cardinal Allen published a defense of Stanley's action in turning over Deventer and his regiment to the Spanish.[19] In response to a letter from "R. A." asking his opinion, Allen asserted that the English involvement in a war against Philip was sinful and unjust. Stanley's actions were from an informed conscience. Allen argued that any English Catholic should do the same.

If one of Elizabeth's knights, a distinguished soldier, could turn over his men and arms to the Spanish, how could any English Catholic be trusted to defend his country? How many of the seminarians Allen had sent into England from Douay, Rheims and Rome would urge sedition as Allen now did? But there was more that would incite the English government, both from Allen and from the Pope.

The English exiles persuaded Pope Sixtus V to issue a bull renewing the excommunication of Queen Elizabeth to justify the invasion. It declared her to be a heretic and schismatic, a bastard, a usurper to the crown. It charged her with stirring up sedition and rebellion among the subjects of other nations, with bringing in the Turk against Christians, and with persecution of bishops, priests and other Catholics. The broadside condemned

Elizabeth for imprisoning Mary Queen of Scots, for abolishing the true Catholic religion, and for profaning the sacraments. The Pope absolved all of her subjects from obedience to her and commanded them not to yield to her authority. English Catholics were told to unite behind the Duke of Parma and the Spanish King. The invasion, said the document, was only for the purpose of restoring England to the true religion.

As the Armada prepared to sail, Cardinal Allen published in Antwerp an "Admonition to the Nobility and People of England." Like the papal bull, it made many accusations, in greater detail, against the English queen. Allen also urged English Catholics not to fight for the queen against the Spaniards[20]:

> Fight not, for God's love, fight not, in that quarrel, in which if you die, you are sure to be damned: fight not against all your ancestors souls, and faith, nor against the salvation of all your dearest, wives, children, and what so ever you would well to, either now or in the time to come. Match not yourselves against the highest: this is the day no doubt of her fall, this is the hour of God's wrath towards her and all her partakers: Forsake her therefore betime, that you be not inwrapped in her sins, punishment and damnation.

Also printed was "A Declaration of the sentence and deposition of Elizabeth, the usurper and pretended Queene of England," a summary of the "Admonition," which was a broadside to be distributed on the success of the Armada. Few English Catholics saw these calls. Like the Spanish fleet, they failed to make landfall on the island. But copies did reach members of the Privy Council.

In June Lord Burghley sent Walsingham a "vile book" written by a Cardinal in favor of the invasion.[21] He sought that Walsingham suppress the book under pain of treason. He also wanted an answer to it be written "as if it were from the Catholics of England." Burghley said that the Cardinal was deceived if he thought any nobleman or gentleman of possession would favor an invasion, adding that the book would cause danger to all Catholics. The papal bull and the Cardinal's pamphlet reinforced the government's determination to keep known English Catholics from engaging in any action. Proffered support from some English Catholics was declined. Others, as we have seen, were imprisoned or confined to their homes.

Two weeks later, Burghley informed Walsingham that he had received a "roaring hellish bull" of which 12,000 copies had been printed in Antwerp.[22] This was the broadside summary of Cardinal Allen's book. Burghley sent Walsingham a draft proclamation for suppression of the bull. The proclamation described Allen's book as "but a blast or puff of a beggarly scholar and traitor" that was intended as a "traitorous trumpet to wake up all robbers and Catholics in England against their sovereign."

Jesuits in England

Only a few Jesuit priests were in England at the time of the Armada. William Weston (*alias* Edmunds) was their senior. An Oxford contemporary and friend of Edmund Campion, Weston had been ordained in 1579 and returned to England in 1584. Among his notable acts were the conversion of Philip Howard and his exorcisms of spirits in Dedham.[23] Weston was arrested in August 1586 at the time of the Babington Plot, when Berden and another chanced upon him at Bishopsgate, in London. Walsingham's spy Berden had cultivated and then betrayed him. In January 1588 Weston was removed from the Clink to the castle of Wisbech, where the government placed many Catholic clergy to isolate them. Weston was put into solitary confinement.

Four of the most notable English Jesuits arrived in England between July 1586 and October 1588. Their youthfulness led to their prosecutors' label of contempt: "boy priests." Three would be executed for their religion.

Southwell and Garnet

Henry Garnet and Robert Southwell left Rome together, May 8th, and landed in England, July 7, 1586. They met with Weston shortly before his arrest.

Born in 1555, Garnet was the son of a schoolmaster who passed on his scholarly inclinations to his son. As a young man, Garnet conformed to the Church of England. For two years he worked as an editor at the press of Richard Tottel, a law printer. Perhaps he learned the craft of printing as well. Here he came to know a young lawyer named John Popham, later the Lord Chief Justice who will sentence Garnet to death. At the age of twenty, Garnet was called to the life of a priest. He moved to Rome, attended the university there and took orders, becoming a priest and Jesuit. A brilliant scholar, he taught Hebrew and mathematics, even writing a treatise on physics. With Weston in prison, Garnet became the Jesuit Superior, which he remained until his execution in 1606. As Superior, Garnet was responsible for the direction of other Jesuits in England.

Garnet's junior companion was twenty-five year old Robert Southwell from Norfolk. At fourteen, Southwell was received into the Jesuit college at Douay and was associated with the English College, founded in 1568 by William Allen, in the same town.[24] His studies took him to Paris and Rome. He came under the influence of his philosophy teacher, the Jesuit Leonard Lessius. Not immediately accepted as a Jesuit, his first verses lamented this rejection. In 1578, however, he was admitted to the Society of Jesus at Rome and was ordained in 1584. For two years he was prefect of studies in the English College. A priest-government informer, John Cecil (*alias* John Snowden), provided a description of Southwell: an auburn-haired young man of medium height and beardless.[25]

The first safe-houses of Garnet and Southwell were provided by Lord Vaux of Harrowden. Southwell soon located his activities in London, where he served as a contact for priests arriving in England, furnishing them with money, clothing and food.[26] With a press and secure housing now available to him, Southwell undertook his "apostolate of letters."[27] His writings, both prose and poetry, were part of his mission. The instructions given to Garnet and Southwell as they left for England included provision for "pamphlets to be printed for the defence of the faith and the edification of Catholics...."[28] What contacts he made among writers and poets in London cannot be established, but Southwell certainly had an intense interest in the poetry then being written and had access to published and unpublished works that he drew upon. He found a patroness who enabled him to publish clandestinely in the midst of hardship and hiding.

John Gerard and Edward Oldcorne

John Gerard was imprisoned in 1583 but escaped England in 1586 after Anthony Babington had made bail for him. He spent the next two years in Europe. He was ordained a priest and entered the Jesuits in the summer of the Armada. The failure of the Spanish fleet was not fully appreciated when he and Fr. Edward Oldcorne were sent from Rome into England. Oldcorne was the same age as Fr. Southwell (27) and Gerard would turn twenty-four before landing in England.

When Oldcorne and Gerard arrived in Eu, France, in September, conditions had become very bad for the Catholics in England. From other priests, he learned of the dangers[29]:

> The Spanish Fleet had exasperated the people against the Catholics; everywhere a hunt was being organized for Catholics and their houses searched in every village and along all the roads and lanes very close watches were kept to catch them. The Earl of Leicester, then at the height of his power, had sworn that by the end of the year there would be no Catholic left in the country....

After a short wait, they received instructions from Fr. Persons in Rome: they were free either to go ahead with the enterprise or stay back until things in England had quieted. Without hesitation, they seized the opportunity to work among the English. Once they had secured a boat to carry them across the Channel, two priests from Rheims joined them, Christopher Bales and George Beesley. The two Jesuits landed on the inhospitable East Anglia coast while their companions sailed a bit farther before disembarking. Bales and Beesley were not long at liberty: they were captured and executed. Gerard and Oldcorne proved more elusive. Oldcorne quickly went to London and connected with Fr. Henry Garnet.

Notwithstanding the great dangers, it is amazing that Oldcorne was able to conceal himself as a priest. Gerard describes him as a man who had difficulty hiding his strong feelings that today would be called prudery. As he made his way to London, Oldcorne fell in "with a party of sailors and men of that sort." Gerard says that Oldcorne felt he "was forced to reprimand them when they started to blaspheme or drop into filthy conversation. It was a dangerous thing to do."[30] Taking refuge in the house of a London Catholic, Oldcorne could not keep himself from smashing a painted pane of glass depicting Mars and Venus: it was too indecent to be allowed to stand. Within two years, Oldcorne was able to settle in at Hindlip House near Worcester, supported by the Habington family.

Gerard more easily adapted. His background as an educated man, the son of a knight, aided him as he made his way through the countryside. Government agents stopped strangers along the road to determine their religion, but Gerard assumed the cover of a sportsman in search of his lost falcon. In an encounter, he would ask whether the people he met knew anything about a stray hawk: "perhaps they had heard its bell tinkling as it was flying around. I wanted them to believe I had lost my bird and was wandering about the countryside in search of it. This is what falconers do."[31] Like all others whose lives depend on stealth and wariness, Gerard learned to equivocate, to convey a misimpression.

Intelligence for Walsingham

The intelligence provided to Walsingham at the time of the Armada is difficult to ascertain. His papers from this period were evidently seized shortly after his death.[32] Some survive. Some information can be gleaned from other sources, such as the many files maintained by his aide, Phelippes, that were seized in 1605.

One indication of Walsingham's methods is a paper he drew up in the spring of 1587: "A Plot for Intelligence out of Spain."[33] England's ambassador in France, Stafford, was to obtain what he could from the Venetian ambassador. He sought to make use of the French ambassador in Spain. Agents in Rouen were to send news from travelers arriving from Spain. Two men— French, Flemish or Italian—were to go along the coast to observe Spanish preparations. Intelligence was to be obtained at the Court of Spain, from Italy, from Brussels and from Leyden but with no indication of how. He expected to employ an Irishman, Lord Dunsany. Around this time, he was provided £3,300 by the queen to obtain intelligence. Some of this money may have gone to Gilbert Gifford in Paris.[34] Gifford continued to correspond into England, probably trying to reach Walsingham through Phelippes, who instructed him to "practise" with the agents of foreign princes, including the papal nucio, the Bishop of Glasgow, Paget, Morgan, Arundell, Fitzherbert and others. Gifford offered to do good service, though he was detested by Stafford, the English ambassador, and distrusted by the Catholic exiles. His communiques continued even after he was arrested and thrown into the bishop's prison in Paris.

Monsieur Châteaumartin

A French agent of Walsingham was named Pierre d'Or who delivered intelligence as Monsieur Châteaumartin.[35] Born in Lyons, he became a merchant in Spain and Portugal and supported the Portuguese claimant, Dom Antonio. Châteaumartin began work for Walsingham sometime before the Armada. Settling at Bayonne, he displayed the trait of many double agents, drawing pay from each of his masters but giving loyalty to none. Both Elizabeth and Philip II paid handsome sums to him. Châteaumartin was one of the few Walsingham agents whom Burghley continued to employ after 1590. He became the English consul for Bayonne and St. Jean de Luz, which gave him a good vantage point for gathering intelligence. In 1592, he made a trip into England on behalf of the Spanish turncoat, Antonio Perez, who followed into England a year later. But he also turned on Perez for the Spanish. Caught in his own intrigues to betray Bayonne to the Spanish, Châteaumartin was deprived of his head in July 1595.

Nicholas Ousley and Anthony Standen

Two of the Englishmen abroad who provided useful service to Walsingham were Nicholas Ousley and Anthony Standen. Ousley was a merchant settled in Malaga, Spain. Mendoza was aware of his activities for Walsingham and reported to the Spanish king in July 1587 that Walsingham regarded Ousley as one of the cleverest men he knew. The queen, he said, was indebted to him for his "regular and trustworthy information."[36] Later, Ousley reportedly was imprisoned by the Spanish for his spying but bribed his way out. He made his way back to England and served in the English navy aboard Drake's ship.[37] For his services, he was rewarded with the income of the parsonage of St. Helen's in London.

Anthony Standen's contributions were greater.[38] Although born in England, he had gone into Scotland in the service of Lord Darnley, by whom he was supposedly knighted (hence the title "Sir"). Standen was in France when Darnley was murdered, and he decided to go into exile. He soon assumed the role of an independent intelligence agent, providing information to the English and the Spanish as he migrated from France to Flanders to Florence. A recommendation from Mary, Queen of Scots, led to his service to the wife of Francesco de' Medici, grand duke of Tuscany. He maintained contact with Walsingham over the years and cultivated the English Secretary with much intelligence after Mary Stewart's execution and the deaths of his Florence patrons. Standen proved his worth in 1587–88 with his reports on Spanish military preparations under the pseudonym of "Pompeio Pellegrini." His worth proved to be valued at a pension of 100 pounds a year from Elizabeth's government, the same as promised to Gilbert Gifford for his betrayal of Mary Stewart and English Catholics.

Standen provided hard military intelligence about Spain's resources and capabilities. The historian Conyers Read attributes to Standen the copy that Walsingham obtained of a detailed report of the grand admiral of the Spanish fleet. The report listed ships and their locations, and gave details of sailors, soldiers, wages, naval stores and the like. Such information was invaluable in making English preparations. To better assess conditions, Standen went into Spain in the months immediately before the Armada and sent Walsingham reports on Spanish movements, evidently from Madrid and from Lisbon.[39] Although serving as a Walsingham agent, Standen was able to preserve his relations with the Catholics in Europe and remained in contact with Fr. Persons.

A Wave of Executions

The Armada's defeat was followed by an increase of persecution; a number of Catholics, especially priests and seminarians, were put to death. None of these victims had done anything to threaten the realm. Whereas some six priests were executed in all of 1587, the number of executions jumped to twenty-one priests and ten lay people, all after the failure of the Armada. One historian has written of "the holocaust of August."[40] On August 28, 1588, eight Catholics were hanged, drawn and quartered in locations scattered over London so as to spread fear among the Catholics. These killings were followed by another six brutal executions two days later.

Among those six hanged at Tyburn on August 30 was Margaret Ward. She had helped Fr. William Watson escape from prison. After her capture, she was flogged and hung up by the wrists, the tips of her toes only touching the ground, for so long a time that she was crippled and paralyzed. The torture was to force her to tell the location of the priest she had aided, but she refused. At her trial, she was offered her liberty if she would attend Protestant worship. Again, she refused. Another layperson who was executed that day was Edward Shelley, who had been betrayed by Walsingham's spy, Berden. Shelley's only crime was "aiding and comforting" Fr. William Deane who was executed two days before Shelley. In October Fr. William Hartley, who had distributed Campion's *Decem Rationes* at Oxford, was executed at the Theatre in Shoreditch.[41]

The Earl and His Countess

Philip Howard, Earl of Arundel, was already in the Tower, but now the government used him to put on a show trial that would tie him with Cardinal Allen, Fr. Persons and the Pope to expose their villainies against England with the Armada. On April 18, 1589, he was tried for treason. The trial was conducted at the Court of the King's Bench with a great many participants and a sizeable audience. In addition to four prosecutors, there were 14 commissioners and a jury of 23 noblemen and peers. Since the previous summer, the government had been putting together its case by getting statements from informers and by repeatedly interrogating Arundel's fellow prisoners. The confessions and testimony of three men in particular were relied on: Sir Thomas Gerard (father of Fr. John Gerard), William Shelley, and Fr. William Bennet. The gist of their statements, used at the trial along with the live testimony of Gerard and Bennet and others, was that on learning of the approach of the Spanish fleet, the earl had mass said for its success and had organized a 24 hour prayer session by a group of prisoners, including Catholic priests. Much was made of a letter he had sent much earlier to Cardinal Allen offering to help him to advance the Catholic cause. The earl was alleged to have told Fr. Bennet that Cardinal Allen would "direct the crown of England." The prosecution even produced and read from Allen's "Admonition to the Nobility and People of England" and from the bull of Pope Sixtus V; Arundel was accused of helping procure the bull and the invasion.[42] Admitting to holding prayer sessions, he said they were to ward off a rumored massacre of Catholics. The prosecutors denied that the earl acted for religious conviction, producing a letter from years earlier in which he had complained of the proceedings against his grandfather and his father: "Whereby it is apparent, said Mr. [Attorney General] Popham, it was Discontentment moved my lord, and not Religion ... being discontented he became a Catholic...."[43]

The outcome of the deliberations was never in doubt. All his honors became forfeit and he was condemned to death (as had been his father). The earl submitted himself to the nobles and peers and asked that they be his mediators that he might talk with his wife and see his infant son, born after his imprisonment, whom he had never seen. Though he lived until death in prison in October 1595 (perhaps by poisoning), he never saw his wife again or his heir.

As Philip Howard suffered in prison, and then after his death, his wife/widow showed extraordinary strength of character and devotion to her religion. After the death of the Duke of Norfolk in 1572, his heirs were engrossed for nearly thirty years in efforts to reverse the seizure of the lands to which they were entitled in their own or their wives' right (the Dacre properties). One set of seizures was of the northern Dacre estates, the inheritance of the wives of Philip and William Howard. Another was the Crown's seizure of Philip's own lands on his attainder for treason in 1589; the portion to which his wife became entitled on his death was not surrendered by the queen without further litigation.

Early in 1587, Robert Southwell became the spiritual adviser to Anne, Countess of Arundel. Through letters, Southwell fulfilled the same role for the imprisoned earl; these became the basis for Southwell's *An Epistle of Comfort*, which was printed on a press in one of the countess's houses. For the countess, Southwell composed *A Short Rule of Good Life*, which circulated in manuscript until published in 1597. It was an adaptation of the Ignatian Spiritual Exercises to the needs of laypersons. The countess was close to her sister-in-law, Margaret Howard, wife of Robert Sackville (son of Lord Buckhurst). Southwell played a part in Margaret's spiritual life. When she died at the age of twenty-nine, Southwell composed a prose elegy, *Triumphs over Death*, that was addressed to Philip Howard, to console him for his sister's death. It was published in 1596 under Sackville patronage.[44]

The Countess of Arundel continued to support other Jesuits. Her steward, Robert Spiller, becomes a courier for the secret intelligence network that will operate in the last dozen years of Queen Elizabeth's reign. When James becomes king of England, she will gain influence as do her brother-in-law, Thomas Howard (Earl of Suffolk) and her uncle, Henry Howard (Earl of Northampton).

Cardinal Allen and Fr. Persons had far overestimated the support that Catholics in England would give to the invasion. Persons's "credit in Rome suffered after the failure of the Armada" from this misjudgment.[45] The failure of the Armada was in part a failure of intelligence: Spain (and Rome) had no reliable and regular sources of information on which they could rely. Persons, Fitzherbert and Jesuits in England began looking for well-placed advisors.

9

The Essex, Phelippes and Bacon Intelligence Initiative

Walsingham's death in April 1590 left a void in Elizabeth's government and in the purses of his aides, spies and informers. Lord Burghley lost a trusted colleague, and he felt the years on his own weary soul. Burghley was not the man to take over Walsingham's network. Robert Cecil, Burghley's son, would fill the role of principal secretary soon enough.

If Robert Cecil's portrait pose looks as aloof and imperious as Walsingham's, it is in part because both paintings are by John De Critz the Elder. However, the similarities are more than brush strokes on canvas. Elizabeth saw in young Cecil the qualities and abilities that led her to repose confidence in Walsingham. Like Walsingham, young Cecil worked prodigiously. Perhaps he felt he had to prove himself: he was small, and nature had not graced him with attractive features. He was no more inclined to the court entertainments—dances, masques and plays—than Walsingham, impeded in part by his weak constitution and his twisted, slightly humped back. Both men were good managers, attracting talented

Left: Sir Francis Walsingham. Artist: John De Critz the Elder (© National Portrait Gallery, London). Right: Robert Cecil, 1st Earl of Salisbury. Artist: John De Critz the Elder (© National Portrait Gallery, London).

aides who effectively carried out assigned tasks that kept the English government functioning. But Walsingham, Burghley and Cecil kept their servants in their place, not suffering any to rise to a level where they might displace their master or think they had merit independent of their station. Each man was in tight control of his own personality and passions, enduring the indignities imposed by the queen they served. Robert Cecil would bow submissively when Elizabeth called him her dwarf.

Robert Cecil's motto is shown on his portrait—*sero, sed serio*: late but in earnest. Late is certainly apt as his parents had been married nearly twenty years when they had Robert in June 1563. Little Robert was spoon-fed earnest pieties by his parents. He was raised by his father's written precepts for his sons that Shakespeare mocks in *Hamlet*:

Polonius	Lord Burghley
Neither a borrower nor a lender be; For loan oft loses both itself and friend, And borrowing dulls the edge of husbandry.	Neither borrow money of a neighbor or a friend, but of a stranger; where paying for it thou shalt hear no more of it. Otherwise thou shalt eclipse thy credit, lose thy freedom, and yet pay as dear to another.

Robert Cecil followed his father's admonition in choosing and relating to those who worked for him: "Be not served with kinsmen or friends, or men intreated to stay; for they expect much and do little: nor with such as are amorous, for their heads are intoxicated. And keep rather two too few, than one too many." Lord Burghley had taught his son caution in trusting others. And in this counseling we can find Robert Cecil's unwillingness to take up Walsingham's network: "Trust not any man with thy life, credit, or estate. For it is mere folly for a man to enthrall himself to his friend, as though, occasion being offered, he should dare not to become the enemy."

Thomas Wilson, whose patrons were Lord Burghley and Robert Cecil, was a Cambridge scholar and an intelligencer whose shrewd observations on those who governed England reveal much. In his "State of England anno dom. 1600," unpublished until 1936, Wilson commented that the governing elite "suffer very few to be acquainted with matters of state for fear of divulging it, whereby their practices are subject to be revealed, and therefor they will suffer few to rise to places of reputation that are skillful or studious of matters of policy, but hold them low and far off so that the greatest politicians that rule most will not have about them other than base pen clerks, that can do nothing but write as they are bidden, or some mechanical dunce that cannot conceive his Master's drifts and policies." Wilson attributed this to Burghley and said it was continued by his son Robert Cecil: of the "old Treasurer ... it was written that he was like an aged tree that lets none grow which near him planted be, and it is well followed by his son at this day."

Thomas Phelippes aspired to be more than a base pen clerk or mechanical dunce. Thomas Morgan had pegged him as "glorious and greedy of honour and profit."[1] After his success entrapping Mary Queen of Scots, Phelippes was rewarded with a post as customs officer of London, the same post his father, William, had held. But he wanted more. When Thomas Phelippes offered his services to Cecil after Walsingham's death, Cecil politely declined. Phelippes turned to the man who would prove to be Robert Cecil's chief rival for power, the husband of Walsingham's daughter, the Earl of Essex, Robert Devereaux. Essex and Cecil were fire and ice, passion against prudence, courage against cunning. They were

Plato's two horses, with Elizabeth the charioteer reining them together. Burghley had warned his son of two men he should not emulate: "Seek not to be Essex; shun to be Ralegh."[2] With Robert Cecil as their nemesis, both Essex and Ralegh will be sentenced to death.

After the Armada, a state of war continued between Spain and England, intermittently fought on the high seas and in brief raids. At times, the English joined forces with the protestant French king, Henry IV, to fight Spanish-backed factions within France itself. Control of the Low Countries was of continuing concern to Spain and England, and so, too, was France's allegiance. Both countries would send troops to the Low Countries or to France to support their proxies. The execution of Mary Stewart did nothing to diminish the rumors of plots from abroad to kill Queen Elizabeth. A spy network was needed to gather intelligence on Spanish activities in the Low Countries, intrigues in the French civil strife, and plots among the English exiles. Invasion or assassination attempts were to be anticipated and countered. Essex's participation in fighting in the Low Countries and in France convinced him of the great need for reliable foreign intelligence. He saw it as essential for his statesman's role. The development of the Essex intelligence network began in 1591–92. Essex sought an independent source of foreign information so he could be useful to the Queen.

Essex's spy network was run primarily by Anthony Bacon and by Thomas Phelippes, but Francis Bacon had a more prominent role than his brother Anthony at the beginning. When Phelippes and Bacon recruited Sterrell into the service of the Earl of Essex in 1591, they had long known one another. When Phelippes accompanied Sir Amias Paulet to France in 1577, with them was young Francis Bacon. In Paulet's household Bacon came to know Phelippes and Phelippes' younger brother very well. Bacon returned to England on the death of his father in March 1579.

The queen began looking to Essex for her foreign intelligence. By the end of 1593, Francis Bacon, Anthony Bacon and the Earl of Essex "together formed a kind of small Foreign Office" and "all matters of intelligence were reported to be wholly in the Earl's hands."[3]

The spying relationship among Phelippes, Sterrell, Francis Bacon and Essex developed in the spring of 1591. The need for intelligence was intensified by the fact that Spain had landed troops on the northwest coast of France in aid of the Catholic League fighting against Henry IV, who had recently become king of France. The English feared another Spanish fleet. With the Spanish occupying French soil and coastal strongholds just opposite the English coast, intelligence about Spanish plans was extraordinarily important. The French situation was a continuing threat to the English. French Catholics considered Henry IV's kingship illegitimate. The Duke of Parma, Alessandro Farnese—Spain's governor in the Low Countries—invaded France in league with the Spanish forces. Henry IV appealed to Elizabeth. She sent over 600 men under Sir Roger Williams, followed shortly by 3000 more under Sir John Norris.

The Earl of Essex was eager to fight in France. He saw himself as a warrior by birth, a Coriolanus. He had already fought in the Low Countries in 1587, where his friend Sir Philip Sidney had died. Essex knew that success in war and statecraft required good intelligence. Francis Bacon urged him develop reliable sources. Bacon probably approached Phelippes with the possibility of bringing his talents to the use of Essex.[4] Bacon would have known of Cecil's rebuff to Phelippes. Robert Cecil had no fondness for his cousin Bacon. Francis Bacon and Thomas Phelippes thus allied themselves with Essex. The consequences proved harsh for both.

Phelippes Negotiates with Sterrell

Phelippes will have first learned of William Sterrell from the government's surveillance of the embassy of Mauvissière in 1585 and may have had further information from Thomas Barnes, who was working for Phelippes among the English Catholics in France and the Low Countries just after the Armada. Phelippes discovered that Master Sterrell of Magdalen College was maintaining a secret correspondence with Catholics in the Low Countries. He approached Sterrell, offering Sterrell an opportunity to advance the Catholic cause as well as to show his patriotism. Phelippes's technique was to ingratiate himself with Catholics torn between loyalties. The argument ran thus: The queen is not herself anti–Catholic; she seeks no windows on the soul. But she is justifiably concerned about plots against her person. The harsh measures against the Catholics are temporary measures, and they can be discarded after the perpetrators of Catholic plots are thwarted. You may help Catholicism in England by spying on the radical faction and Jesuits who are causing the turmoil and are threatening the queen. You may help bring toleration by sounding out the reasonable Catholics and communicating with them and letting us know their intentions.

Phelippes surely knew little of his quarry other than that he was an Oxford lecturer. The thirty year old scholar came from a respected Lincolnshire family. His father, Henry Sterrell, was a country lawyer who served a term as Undersheriff to Sir Robert Tyrwhitt. His mother was Katherine Southwell (spellings include Southill, Sutill, Sotehill), whose Lincolnshire family seat was the manor of Redbourne, a short distance north of Lincoln, acquired by Sir Gerard Sotehill nearly two centuries earlier. Her family tree is adorned with knights and sheriffs of Lincolnshire, and another branch of the same family furnished an Attorney General for Edward IV or Henry VII. Henry Sotehill fought in the snow with the Yorkists on Palm Sunday 1461 in the Battle of Towton, a battle reenacted grimly by Shakespeare in *3 Henry VI*. Katherine's great-grandmother was daughter to Sir John Bussy/Bushy of Hougham (20 miles south of Lincoln). Bushy had been Sheriff of Lincolnshire three times and thrice Speaker of the House of Commons. His dismissal to summary execution by order of the usurping Bolingbroke in 1399 is staged in *Richard II*. When Sterrell's father died, his mother remarried and young Sterrell and his little brother were sent away to be raised elsewhere. William was soon at Oxford and little Henry Sterrell was at the home of their uncle, Anthony Meres. As he entered the service of the Earl of Essex in 1591, Sterrell poignantly reflected "I … have been ever brought up in the University...."

At Magdalen College, Sterrell was early identified as "suspect in religion." Both his BA and MA degrees were delayed as a result. His Master of Arts was awarded only after the direct intercession of the University's Chancellor, the powerful Earl of Leicester.

Despite being hindered in his degrees and the enmity of some of the other Fellows of Magdalen, Sterrell did not hesitate to risk trouble with the university authorities. In the middle of June 1587 a Convocation (all qualified members of the degree of M.A.) was called to consider new statutes for the University. Since November 1581 newly entering students were required to subscribe their names to the Oath of Supremacy, recognizing Elizabeth as head of both state and church, the University's response to the distribution the previous June of Campion's *Rationes decem* at graduation ceremonies. However, the statute did not apply to those already matriculated within the University. Now, the Masters took up a proposal for a statute requiring the Oath of Supremacy of all who had not been covered by the statute of 1581. Speaking in favor of the proposal was Richard Coxe, a minister new to Oxford. The youthful preacher expressed contempt for two Oxford Masters of Arts who were Catholics: Thomas Warren and George Errington, both of Trinity College. Errington had been released from prison only a few months before. Angered by the speech of this Cambridge divine against Errington, who had suffered in prison for the very crimes of which Sterrell himself was guilty, Sterrell spoke up. In a stage whisper, Sterrell said someone such as Coxe should not be speaking against Masters of nine or ten years standing. As their exchanged barbs grew more heated, Sterrell said that Coxe was not fit to be a witness: Coxe himself might be suspected of *felony*.

The confrontation was so serious that Dr. William James, the Dean of Christ Church College and Vice-Chancellor of the University, intervened. Dr. James warned Sterrell that he should take heed of what he said. These were, said the Vice-Chancellor, grievous words and would bear an action in slander. Sterrell remained adamant and coolly extended his accusations in some detail. Soon Coxe sued Sterrell in the University's court and Sterrell replied with a counter-suit, asserting Coxe had damaged his reputation grievously by "thou-ing" him. Coxe had told Sterrell: "Thou carest not what thou swearest against any honest man." The *Oxford English Dictionary* examines the changing usage of "Thou": "*Thou* and its cases *thee, thine, thy*, were in Old English used in ordinary speech; in Middle English, they were gradually superseded by the plural *ye, you, your, yours*, in addressing a superior and (later) an equal, but were long retained in addressing an inferior."[5]

In *Coxe v. Sterrell v. Coxe*, the litigants, after preliminaries, followed the custom that most civil disputants took: they referred the case to arbitration in December 1587.[6] The final entry in the Oxford records for the suits is dated January 19, 1588: "Commissa est ca."

The litigation of Sterrell with Richard Coxe is a revealing snapshot of Sterrell. He is a man of brooding passion, unwilling to stand by quietly when a brave friend's reputation is attacked. Yet even in the heat of the moment, his words are carefully chosen; he goes right up to the edge of slander, understanding the elements of the offence, but does not cross the line. Even with the Vice-Chancellor himself warning against slander, Sterrell holds firmly to his position and expects to be vindicated. He is courageous and forceful, but also a troublemaker, who favors an unpopular cause. These are qualities that had brought him to the attention of others, not only the French ambassador, but powerful English Catholics.

Phelippes surely did not appreciate the intelligence and resourcefulness of the man he was recruiting—through guile and intimidation—in 1591. Sterrell turned the offer of spying into a device for furthering the well-being of English Catholics, especially the Jesuits. It was not Sterrell but Thomas Phelippes who swung from one side to the other. Phelippes lacked religious principle. He needed money and his own government pushed him aside and imposed crippling debt on him. Sterrell required time to bring about the turning of Phelippes. In the meantime, there was danger for Sterrell from all directions.

Phelippes later described how Sterrell entered the service of Essex as a spy. In 1591 he had found "an old decayed intelligence between Sterrell and the fugitive traitors on the other side."[7] For the service of the queen, Phelippes had accepted an offer made to him "of restoring the same, knowing much good might be wrought thereon." Phelippes thus indicated that Sterrell already knew the "fugitive traitors" and had long been in correspondence with them, though Phelippes implied this correspondence had ceased.

Was the "decayed intelligence" really Sterrell's? Or was it through Sterrell on behalf of another man? It slowly came out that Sterrell had a noble acquaintance, a patron, a man who was coming to his own at Court after the death of his father not long before. Sterrell described himself to Phelippes as being "towards a nobleman whose fortune I may follow," employing "towards" as defined in the *Oxford English Dictionary* as "beside, near, in attendance on, about; in the possession of; with." This was Edward Somerset, 4th Earl of Worcester.

The relationship of Worcester and Sterrell was extraordinary, one that echoes the Roman statesman Cicero's bond with his secretary, M. Tullius Tiro. The two most likely came together in 1585 or earlier. Sterrell often stayed at Raglan, Worcester's castle in Wales. Throughout the time that he served Worcester, Sterrell wrote intelligence letters to Catholic fugitives and foreign agents. Sterrell was caught several times, but there is not the slightest hint that any accusation was ever made that Worcester himself sponsored Sterrell's intelligence activities or was tainted by them. Worcester cannot have been unaware of what Sterrell was doing under his own roof. Worcester reposed the greatest trust in Sterrell, and Sterrell carried out purposes that Court life and Crown service proscribed for Worcester. Worcester did not have to direct any activities by Sterrell, for Sterrell was capable of acting as Worcester's agent—in the several senses of the term's synonyms: deputy, steward, factor, substitute, representative or emissary. The correspondence that Phelippes had discovered may have been carried on by Sterrell as a proxy for Worcester.

Edward Somerset's uncle, Thomas Somerset, was involved with the correspondence of Mary Queen of Scots as was William Sterrell; the informant Dodwell reported this of Sterrell in 1585. Thomas Somerset was an important benefactor of the English College at Rheims and had a son and a nephew enrolled there while Sterrell as "Kirby" facilitated transactions across the Channel. Both Thomas Somerset and William Shelley were in the Tower when Sterrell obtained passage for Shelley's nephew on Mauvissière's vessel, and in 1595 Sterrell will shepherd Worcester's nephew, Thomas's son George, back across the channel from Europe.

When Sterrell was likely in trouble with the government and with his university in 1585, Edward Somerset may have taken him under his protection. At the time when Sterrell as "Kirby" was assisting Catholic youth to go abroad to William Allen's seminaries, Allen was reporting to the King of Spain on the devotion of Worcester's family to the Catholic cause.[8] The nobleman and his wife had need of a tutor for their growing number of children. The Somersets lived in the great castle of Raglan, one of the most magnificent in Wales. The Somerset children numbered more than half a dozen by mid–1580s and were undoubtedly schooled by a visiting tutor. Eventually six Somerset daughters and five sons reached adulthood. Sterrell was probably brought to Raglan to provide an education that would prepare the sons to attend Oxford and the daughters to be ornaments of their future husbands' households. Two of Worcester's sons and Sterrell's half-brother matriculated from Magdalen College on June 26–27, 1591. Worcester also needed a secretary to attend to correspondence and the administrative responsibilities of a large household, one which sponsored an acting company. Sterrell's association with Worcester would have brought him into intimate contact with an acting company that in 1585 included actors who later achieved prominence on the London stage, such as Edward Alleyn, Edward Browne, Richard Jones and James Tunstall. Coupled with experience in Oxford academic plays, Sterrell had the opportunity for a strong foundation in both popular and classical (i.e., Latin) theater; his later letters are sprinkled with allusions to Roman plays and literary works.

In the late 1590s another young Catholic of Magdalen College was employed by Worcester as both secretary and tutor (to two daughters), William Taylor (Tayler or Tailer). In 1597, after receiving BA degrees from both Oxford and Cambridge but being refused a fellowship because of his religious inclinations, Taylor was "invited to live with the Earl of Worcester, whose two sons at Magdalen were friends of his, along with their schismatic tutor."[9] A "schismatic" was a Catholic who was willing to take the Oath of Supremacy and to attend Protestant services as required by law. This "schismatic tutor" was William Sterrell. Taylor's statement confirms that Worcester employed young men in the dual capacity of tutor and personal secretary. While occupied with Court business for Worcester, Taylor was able to meet with the Archpriest Blackwell and corresponded with Jesuits. The Archpriest and Jesuits assisted Taylor in leaving England secretly to become a priest in Rome. Sterrell at the time of Taylor's departure was working closely with Blackwell and the Jesuits, and he surely would have been Taylor's point of contact with them.

"Lay your plots and I will supply all things"

Phelippes had approached Sterrell with a proposal while also telling his old friend Francis Bacon that he had just the man for intelligence work in the Low Countries, and perhaps in Spain as well, for the Earl of Essex. The mission of an intelligence operative would be to discover the plans of Spain for another attempt at invasion of England, the preparations for such an attempt in the Low Countries or in France or in Spain, and plotting that might be taking place to assassinate the queen.

The intelligence mission would be an honorable undertaking. Sterrell was not to be a *provocateur* like Poley or Gilbert Gifford. He would move among the English Catholic exiles who would be privy to information and to plotting by the Spanish and their allies. Quite a few English exiles were in the pay of the Spaniards, and the Spanish often coordinated their plans with these exiles.

William Sterrell had the intelligence, the education, the language skills, and the experience that would allow him to pull off an intelligence mission. He was unencumbered by wife and children. He had no property that would suffer neglect. From his study of Roman and Greek political history and philosophy, he had an intense interest in political issues, and he could see the parallels between the struggles of Roman times and those of the Elizabethan era. Most importantly, Phelippes had in his hands correspondence between Sterrell and an English Catholic, Anthony Skinner, who was overseas working with the pro–Spanish exiles. Phelippes could use this correspondence to destroy Sterrell, or to draw him into service that would ingratiate Phelippes with the rising figure of Essex and with the queen. Essex, who was married to Walsingham's daughter, was enthusiastic about securing Phelippes's service. The young earl assured him continuing financial support, telling Phelippes to spend whatever was required: "Take no pity of my purse"[10] and "lay your plots and I will supply all things."[11]

Worcester gave his blessing to Sterrell's joining Essex's team and continued a stipend to Sterrell. Worcester was entering fully into the social life of the Court after his father's death in 1589. As soon as Edward Somerset succeeded to the earlship, he received honors worthy of his station and his abilities. The queen sent him as ambassador to Scotland in

1590 to congratulate James on his marriage to Anne of Denmark and to invest James with the Order of the Garter. Within a year she made Worcester Councilor of Wales. In 1591 Worcester was admitted to the Middle Temple and was created Master of Arts at Oxford in 1592. The Order of the Garter was conferred in 1593.

Edward Somerset was esteemed a man of the utmost integrity, held in high regard by all who knew him. Throughout his public career, he avoided controversy and was protective of his reputation. He enjoyed life at Court, and took a leading part in the hunts, tilts, dances, concerts, masques and theater that were the social life of the nobility, yet he was diligent in fulfilling the duties of his public offices. The Somerset household was both literary and musical. Inventories of books and musical instruments from the family show a wide range of interests. Worcester's patronage of the prolific playwright and author Thomas Heywood was reflected in a number of dedications by the writer to Worcester, whom he called "my Mecaenas," him who "gave my Muse first wing, and from [whose] bounty she had voice to sing."[12] Worcester was a long-time patron and friend of the "Father of English music," William Byrd, the well-known Catholic musician and composer. In 1589, Byrd published and dedicated his *Liber primus sacrarum cantionum* (first book of sacred songs) to Edward Somerset.[13] Edward Somerset and his wife were guests at Ingatestone Hall, the home of the Petre family who were also patrons of Byrd, at Christmas 1589, where Byrd was staying for the Christmas season and playing for the families.[14] The relationship continued until Byrd died in 1623, in his retirement apartment in Worcester's house in the Strand.

Sterrell's Targets: Stanley, Jaques et al.

The undertaking that Sterrell was offered was a mission to go into the Low Countries camp of Sir William Stanley, the notorious turn-coat. Stanley's distinguished family included his cousin, Ferdinando Stanley (Lord Strange, the Earl of Derby).

Sterrell may have encountered Stanley in London around the time of the Babington Plot or perhaps Stanley's lieutenant, the infamous Captain Jaques, a black-clad Anglo-Italian soldier whose name was Giacomo de Franceschi. Jaques was born in Antwerp of a Venetian father and raised in England. At one time he worked for the Lord Chancellor, Sir Christopher Hatton, a fact often raised with his name. After serving as Stanley's lieutenant in Ireland, he had a peripheral role in the Babington Plot, possibly for the English government.[15] Stanley later will rescue Sterrell from arrest by the Spanish Governor at Antwerp, and Sterrell will maintain close relations with Jaques. These suggest Sterrell already knew Stanley and probably his lieutenant, which would be among the reasons why Sterrell was chosen for a mission to the Low Countries.

After Stanley switched allegiance to the service of Spain in 1587 he served then under the Duke of Parma, Spain's governor in the Low Countries. Stanley's camp became the seat of numerous alleged plots to invade England or to assassinate the queen. Some of the interesting men associated with Sir William Stanley were the English exiles Fr. William Holt, Fr. Richard Sherwood (alias Carleton), Hugh Owen, Thomas Fitzherbert, the Earl of Westmorland and the notorious Captain Jaques. At some point, Sterrell had developed a correspondence with several of them and provided services, such as relaying correspondence and money to relatives. Most likely, these ties to the English fugitives went back to the time of the Campion/Parsons mission. Because of his connections, Sterrell was perfect for the tasks conceived by Francis Bacon, the Earl of Essex and Thomas Phelippes: if he could be persuaded—or coerced.

About March 1591 William Sterrell responded to proposals made by Thomas Phelippes. They arose from several letters of Sterrell with Anthony Skinner. Sterrell informed Phelippes that he had spoken to his employer, the Earl of Worcester, about Phelippes. Worcester knew enough of what was going on to ask Sterrell what the relationship between Phelippes and Lord Burghley was.[16] Sterrell answered "none at all." Worcester appears to have distrusted Burghley and did not want to become involved with any activity on Burghley's behalf, through Sterrell, in foreign intelligence. Burghley and Walsingham were probably responsible for Edward Somerset's arrest in a wave of anti–Catholic prosecutions in 1581. William Somerset (Edward's father the third Somerset earl of Worcester), and probably Edward himself were subjected to house arrest, again by Burghley and Walsingham, because of the Throckmorton Plot.[17] Yet Worcester was willing to associate with the Cecil family for purposes of advancing those causes dear to Worcester, his family and his faith.

Francis Bacon wrote to Thomas Phelippes concerning an intelligence operation, apparently with Sterrell in mind. Bacon advised Phelippes how to handle the relationship with Essex, the sort of guidance that Bacon was fond of delivering to his friends. Bacon had set up an appointment between Essex and Phelippes so that they could advance the proposal. He wrote to Phelippes[18]:

> The more plainly and frankly you shall deal with my Lord, not only in disclosing particulars, but in giving him caveats and admonishing him of any error which in this action he may commit, (such is his Lordship's nature) the better he will take it. I send you also his letter which appointeth this afternoon to repair to him; although if you are not fully resolved of any circumstance, you may take a second day for the rest and show his Lordship the party's letter.

The "party's letter" which Phelippes is to show Essex is probably an extraordinary letter that William Sterrell had just written to Thomas Phelippes.[19] It provides an example of the man's intelligence, his command of language, his ability to turn a phrase, and his gravity:

> Good Sir, I have thought upon such things as I motioned to you yesternight and therefore think good to let you understand my resolution. I came at your sending for seven score miles. I have been there ten days in town myself, my man, and my horse, ready to attend when time served, and to adventure myself for others' good, as much and more for mine own. I have proposed three things and neither of them is effected.

Sterrell asked first that the number of the parties knowing of his proposed service be enlarged. Secondly, he wanted written evidence that he was serving the queen and Essex: "to show that I go over for her Majesty or the Earl of Essex's service that at my return I be not reputed a fugitive. You may die in the meantime, then what shall be thought of me? When I have practised among such markable persons and so inwardly as I must, it will not be sufficient to say that you employed me. They may ask, where is your warrant or what have you to show? And so I shall be well rewarded if I live. I am not ignorant how little service is esteemed when it is past, and what light occasions are taken to shift men off." Third, he wanted to meet Essex face-to-face, "that I may press him with his words at my return." If these were done, he would accept the offer of service. He asked for return of his Skinner letters and his exchanges with Phelippes.

Sterrell recognized that the employment as a spy in the circumstances presented to him must be kept secret from others in the government. He fully understood that Essex was going outside the regular channels of government. Though Essex had a close relationship with the queen, he was not yet a member of the Privy Council. The Council would have been concerned if they had known of the intelligence network that Essex was beginning to build. Moreover, secrecy was needed so that word would not reach those who were the objects of the spying. The English Catholic exiles continued to have family and supporters within England, some in prominent positions. One could never be sure what household servant was a Catholic who might pass on information overheard from some careless official. Secrecy was lax in Essex's group of retainers and attendants who were notable more for enthusiasm and talent than for organization and discipline.

Sterrell's motivation for entering spying with Phelippes and Essex was not monetary. Although he prudently expressed hope for "condign reward" from the queen and for his "due deserts" from Essex, there was no arrangement for him to be paid.[20] Rather, he was to receive his regular stipend from Worcester. Financially, he was fairly well off and had no reason to endanger himself on the slender possibility of reward. Worcester was one of the wealthier noblemen of England, ambitious for himself and his large family, and he would never have endangered his own reputation by employing a man of low character whose actions could ruin Worcester. Sterrell refers in the correspondence with Phelippes to "my man." He was a gentleman and had a servant or servants in his own employ.

The young philosophy lecturer and follower of a nobleman (Worcester) had no desire to embark on a spying role. A condition of the negotiations was that if Sterrell were not employed by Essex as Phelippes proposed, Sterrell's letters would be returned. What Skinner's letters concerned is not known, but as Skinner was in the Low Countries in mid-1591 and attempting to return to England, it seems likely he was trying to gain Sterrell's assistance in re-entering the country. When Skinner did come in a few months later, he and Richard Ayliffe (a contemporary of Sterrell from Magdalen College) were immediately arrested. Sterrell could have been tried and condemned with them. Instead, Sterrell's agreeing to serve Essex on a mission may have saved not only Sterrell himself but perhaps also Skinner.

The mission to the Low Countries went forward with Sterrell operating from London and from Raglan Castle. Sterrell continued his work for Worcester, who was aware of Sterrell's intelligence activities and approved of them, though perhaps not with knowledge of the details. But Sterrell could not juggle service to Worcester, spying, and his praelectorship at the same time, so he resigned from the position at Magdalen College, March 24, 1591. This must have been difficult as he loved the College and he loved learning. His move also shows the great danger in which he found himself.

The State of Catholics in England

Phelippes and Essex requested Sterrell to inform them of the outlook of the Catholics in England on Spain and the prospects of peace. What Sterrell was asked to do was not to spy on the Catholics in England but to sound their views on Spain. Sterrell visited with a number of the leading Catholics, and sent to Phelippes in August 1591 a thoughtful discussion of Catholic political sentiments. It provides an unsentimental assessment of the Catholic condition in this period. Sterrell has an extraordinary grasp on political issues and a historical awareness. He uses the first person plural, as though he were speaking collectively for the English and then for the English Catholics.

Sterrell saw himself less as a spy than as an intermediary in a peace effort. The English Catholics do not favor a Spanish invasion but see little other possibility of gaining toleration for their religion. Sterrell is willing "to cause Thomas Fitzherbert to go to Rome about" seeking a peace. He was preparing to go to see Fitzherbert soon and the rest of the same letter concerns plans for the trip.

The preparation for a trip to the Low Countries in 1591 involved steps to establish Sterrell's credit with the exiles whom he was to visit. He was already well-known to some of the exiles, such as Anthony Skinner and Thomas Fitzherbert. But he still had reasons for taking current steps to maintain his credit and establish that he could accomplish things in England for the exiles. One means of doing this was to secure relief for recusants who were known to the exiles. This may also have been a way of raising funds for his activities. Sterrell told Phelippes, "it remains that you provide for my expenses, provide my license for me and my man because I may happen to bring some with me, set at liberty those two recusants whom I must employ who have little to give or nothing. The money that I shall have I will cause some Catholic to make over if I can."[21] The two recusants were named Bullock and Cole.[22] A third was Robert Bellamy. Sterrell was to meet with Phelippes the next day at a garden and in a week was going to Gravesend, the port for leaving England. He was also going into Oxfordshire before his departure. Perhaps he had unfinished business at the university or was seeing his brother Clare or Worcester's sons.

Sterrell adopted aliases for his correspondence: Robert Robinson and Henry Saint Main. As with other names that Sterrell adopted in writing, the aliases show a lively mind. "Robert, son of Robin" reflects the fact that Sterrell's mission was on behalf of Robert Devereux, who was called "Robin" by his family. "Saint Main" is the French for Saint Hand or Holy Hand, and its symbolism is suggested in several lines in Shakespeare's *King John*, where the papal legate, Pandulph, tells the king:

> And meritorious shall that **hand** be call'd,
> Canonized, and worshipp'd as a **saint**,
> That takes away by any secret course
> Thy hateful life

This *alias* is a sly reference to Pius V's bull of 1570 that allegedly would have allowed a good Catholic to assassinate Queen Elizabeth.

Calais and Lille, August–September 1591

In late summer 1591 Sterrell made a preliminary trip across the English Channel to meet with his friends Thomas Fitzherbert and Fr. Sherwood, to establish their intelligence procedures. Thus was launched, without the understanding of Essex and Phelippes, the Jesuit-linked network that would soon operate from Elizabeth's Court for the remainder of her reign. Sterrell took a ferry down the Thames to Gravesend about August 10. Soon, he arrived in Calais.[23] Lodging there for a few days, Sterrell/Saintmain let it be known that he was an Englishman come abroad for religion.

An Italian named Angelo, learning of his presence, made contact with Sterrell. Telling

Sterrell his ship would not be leaving for Spain for more than three weeks, Angelo inquired how he might visit the English Court. Although Angelo said he was Venetian, Sterrell "replied that his tongue was Roman, and he was for [going to] Spain, wherefore his welcome thither would be correspondent." The two men spoke together over a couple of days. Angelo found Sterrell "cunning in the state of England" and invited him to go into Spain with him where Sterrell could speak with the Spanish King. The Italian was eager to convert England, and all that was wanting was a resolute man, that is to say, an executioner to kill the queen. Such a man was already in France, he said, a servant of the Pope's French nuncio (representative). The assassin, later described as a "desperate Italian," had been prepared to kill Henry of Navarre (Henry IV) but could not get near him.

Sterrell suggested to Angelo that it would not be expedient to kill the English queen while the King of Scots was living, the implication being that James would be as bad as Elizabeth for Catholics. To facilitate the executioner's journey into England and Scotland, Sterrell sent for letters to be procured from Sir Walter Ralegh. But before these arrived Angelo departed. Sterrell had directed that the ship be stayed, but someone else was negligent in effecting it.[24] The failure to apprehend Angelo or the desperate Italian caused his credit to come into question, and Sterrell had to defend his actions.[25] Proceeding to Lille, Sterrell made contact with Sherwood and Fitzherbert. Lille was a short distance from Calais and would have been a convenient location between Rouen, where Fitzherbert now resided, and Antwerp, where Sherwood had settled.

Upon his return to London, Sterrell informed Phelippes that he was expecting letters from Fitzherbert and Sherwood. He sent a cipher to Phelippes to use. Sterrell had provided them with a London address to which they should write. At Lille, codewords, ciphers and instructions had been exchanged by the intelligencers.[26] Phelippes needed a key from Sterrell to decipher the letters. The same *modus operandi* was employed by Sterrell and Phelippes for the next dozen years in correspondence with the Catholic exiles: Sterrell would meet with the exiles in the Low Countries, they would write to the name or names he supplied them, and the letters would come then to Phelippes. Phelippes and Sterrell would together prepare the letters under an alias and these would be sent to the Low Countries by courier. Aliases were frequently changed. When one alias was used for receiving letters in England and another for sending correspondence from England, any one intercepting letters would be unable to match them up. Even handwriting was disguised. "Alias" does not fully convey what Sterrell and Phelippes did. Rather, they created fictitious persons and became increasingly skillful at it. The precedents included Fagot, Emilio Russo and Pietro Maria. More would follow.

As he prepared for another trip to the Continent, Sterrell used Phelippes to settle accounts with a couple of rascals who had cheated him. He sought to have a Mr. Cut and a Mr. Phillipson "committed," i.e., arrested. He playfully told Phelippes: "Cut is an iron monger, whom I would wish you to turn to silver." Sterrell urged Phelippes not to neglect this, for it would return him some money that he needed for furnishing out a second voyage. The two men owed a debt to Sterrell or to a friend. Sterrell later asked Phelippes for "continuance of my credit til I had gotten something by those knaves that so often have cozened me."[27] The knavish Cutt was Robert Cutt, a London ironmonger and money lender who had frequent business dealings with Ireland.[28]

Cutt's transaction had involved Sherwood, *alias* Carleton, as Sterrell adds: "It is apparent that the money was lent to Carelton [Carleton, i.e., Sherwood] by his own name, the scrivener that dwells without Newgate amongst the Sadlers near to the tavern hath the presedentes [originals] of the bonds." Sterrell himself was a witness to the transactions.

Richard Sherwood—Carleton—was a London merchant before he became a Catholic priest in the early 1580s. He was in London while Sterrell was haunting Mauvissière's embassy, and Fr. Persons had recommended Sherwood/Carleton as priest for Mary Queen of Scots. Sterrell must have signed as surety a debt of Sherwood/Carleton's, and when Sherwood was banished in 1586 Sterrell had to answer for it, even though Carleton may have in fact paid but could not return to England to testify.[29] That Carleton/Sherwood looked to Sterrell for money on occasion is evidenced by another letter of Sterrell some months later in which he says (with bemusement): "Sherwood's letter is after his old cozening way to draw money from me, but I know him."[30] That Sterrell was standing surety to Sherwood in the mid–1580s confirms that Sterrell was closely associated with the Catholic network, and Dodwell's report of 1585 was accurate. Because Sherwood was very close to William Higham and Roger and Anne Line in the mid–1580s, we may surmise that Sterrell's association with them likewise dates from this period. The Lines and Higham will be again associated in a matter involving Sterrell and Sherwood in 1594, when a curious object—a diamond stick-pin—is assigned by Sherwood to Sterrell.

Liberty for Recusants—Cole, Bullock and Bellamy

Sterrell also used Phelippes to gain the liberty of Catholics in England. He asked Phelippes "let Cole and Bullock have their liberty otherwise my credit will be in question with them."[31] This ploy became a favorite of Sterrell's. He gains the release of Catholic prisoners on the assertion that this is necessary for him to retain influence with the Catholics upon whom he is ostensibly spying. Using his alias of Robert Robinson, Sterrell did the same for Robert Bellamy, whose family (which owned Uxendon Manor at Harrow-on-the-Hill, a frequent refuge of Catholic priests) suffered greatly for their faith. His brother Jerome Bellamy was executed in the Babington Plot. Their mother, imprisoned for religion, died in custody. Robert Bellamy had preceded his mother and brother into prison, committed in early 1585 for hearing of mass. After six years he escaped but was captured and recommitted by Walsingham. Bellamy reported to Lord Keeper John Puckering that he was again set at liberty by the Privy Council "*by the means of Robert Robinson, who had twenty marks for his labour, being a suitor to the privy-council....*"[32] The confession of Bellamy as to who got him out of prison underscores why William Sterrell would use aliases, and why it was unwise to use one's own name even when helping Catholics; it was impossible to know who would confess once in custody. Numerous captured Catholics turned informant, often under torture.

In early October 1591, Sterrell again wrote Phelippes concerning his upcoming trip to the Low Countries. He had not heard from a certain Italian (probably the elusive Angelo), so he believed that the man may have taken other directions. He urged Phelippes again to deal with Cutt and Philipson. Something might be wrested out of them so that with it, added to what he already had, would serve to furnish him out again. He recommended that Cutt be charged suddenly: "Let Andrew Smith [Smythe] the porter to the Carrier of

Oxford be examined, Staveley knows him."³³ Ezekiel Staveley was a courier and tailor whose shop Phelippes used for receipt of letters. Sterrell suggested that Phelippes might seek to get Lord Burghley to pick up the cost of the intelligence gathering.³⁴ A recurring concern of Sterrell's from the outset was to enlarge the circle of people in the government knowing of his involvement as a means of protecting himself should he be discovered. He did not wish to be charged with spying on the English government. He urged Phelippes to bring the Lord Treasurer into that loop of people privy to his efforts.³⁵

Sterrell told Phelippes that he had conceived a "plot how to deal with the Spaniards myself without the credit of any English, and that I will compass by Don Pedro who is prisoner here." He planned to leave right after Christmas, traveling first to Antwerp and then to Brussels. By April he would return for other employment or remain in the Low Countries. He warned of danger to the queen, as there were others employed to like purpose as the Italian. This "Don Pedro" was Don Pedro de Valdés, a knight of the Order of Santiago and captain general of the kingdom of Andalucia. He was the most famous of the Spanish prisoners taken by the English from the Armada. The surrender of his flagship, the *Nuestra Señora del Rosario,* to Sir Francis Drake, was a celebrated event of the English victory. In English custody for five years, his ransom was finally arranged in February 1593, the very last man of the Armada to be released. Custody in England was more than comfortable for the courtly Don Pedro. He was a guest of Drake's relative, Richard Drake, and Francis Drake's wife Elizabeth was a frequent visitor to Don Pedro.³⁶ The Spaniard was allowed to hunt and attend parties because of his status, and he developed friendships with Englishmen who helped him maintain contact with his family in Cadiz. The historian Gustav Ungerer observes that after Don Pedro's release, "he repaired to the Low Countries and every ten days he received news-letters from London which he forwarded to Madrid. His informants must be sought among the English recusants at the Elizabethan Court. Some of them are bound to have been identical with those who provided R. Verstegan with intelligence."³⁷ Ungerer sensed the presence of Sterrell though not his identity. The relationship with Don Pedro must have preceded Sterrell's recruitment by Phelippes in 1591 if Sterrell already knew Don Pedro well enough to "compass" a plot with him.³⁸ After Don Pedro went to the Low Countries, someone back in England was supplying information to him and to Richard Verstegan, particularly about the Spanish refugee to France and England, Don Antonio Perez. To recount Sterrell's close encounter with the flamboyant Antonio Perez would be to get ahead of the 1591–92 mission. Essex will soon encourage Sterrell to send intelligence to Verstegan, Don Pedro Valdés and others.

Anthony Skinner's Treason

Sterrell was again placed in danger when Skinner and Ayliffe were arrested. On December 28, 1591, the Privy Council authorized a warrant to the keeper of the Marshalsea prison to receive into his custody Anthony Skinner and "Richard Acliffe" (Ailiffe/Ayliffe).³⁹ They were apprehended at Gravesend coming up the river in a small boat from Calais. While incarcerated, the two men made confessions as to their activities. Richard Ayliffe, "pleb. of Hants" (Hampshire) entered Magdalen College only a few months before William Sterrell.⁴⁰ Skinner and Ayliffe had been out of the realm for about eight years and had remained for the most part at Rome, the one (Skinner) in service for a time with Cardinal Allen and the other (Ayliffe) with the Bishop of Cassano. Just as Cardinal Allen had been a Fellow of Oriel College Oxford, the Bishop of Cassano (Owen Lewis) had been a Fellow of New College, Oxford, from which College he led twenty others into exile.[41]

After reporting the activities of Skinner and Ayliffe and forwarding their preliminary confessions, the Privy Council instructed the government's attorneys to determine if the two men had committed treason, and if so to proceed against them. Skinner's conviction and sentencing was reported by Richard Verstegan, the English fugitive publisher living in Antwerp, who wrote to Fr. Persons August 3, 1592[42]:

> Mr. Anthony Skinner is condemned, but not executed. Neither is it thought he shall be, for that some kind of offer of his pardon has been made to some of his friends for the sum of 500 pounds; and it is thought less will be taken. The Vicechamberlaine, as I hear, has undertaken to get it. When he was on the torture, they urged him to confess that he was sent to kill the Queen, to which he confessed; but so soon as he was released, he forthwith denied it, saying that their tortures were such as might make him to say whatsoever they pleased.

Word spread of Skinner's harsh treatment. Anthony Rolston, a double agent associated sometimes with Thomas Fitzherbert, was unwilling to return to England after learning that "Anthony Skinner, who was so well affected [to Queen Elizabeth], hath been so hardly dealt with."[43]

Had Skinner turned informant for the English government?[44] The Vicechamberlain mentioned by Verstegan as saving Skinner was Sir Thomas Heneage, who had a role in anti–Catholic spying. But the story is more complicated. Within a short time of saving Skinner, Sir Thomas Heneage married a devout Catholic who maintained priests in her home—the Countess of Southampton—and the couple associated with other Catholics who were close to the Earl of Worcester and William Sterrell. The part played by the Countess of Southampton in securing the release of Anthony Skinner is uncertain but likely very significant: her cousin and financial superintendent was Edward Gage, who was soon father-in-law to Anthony Skinner. For years after escaping death as a traitor, Anthony Skinner continued to be fined and persecuted for his faith; two of his sons attended Douay and were ordained Catholic priests.[45] In 1603 he will be instrumental in diplomatic relations between England and the Low Countries.

Sterrell's Instructions

The preparation for Sterrell's second trip continued over the Christmas season, which Sterrell spent at Raglan, Worcester's magnificent Welsh castle built upon a hill, called *Twyn-y-Ciros*, Welsh for Cherry Hill. In a January 1592 letter, Sterrell again offered heroic gestures on behalf of the queen: "If you can persuade her Majesty to address some plot to entrap Sir William Stanley, I hope to effectuate it, at leastwise I will venture, although I went to Spain where *I would think to find no small credit with Persons the Jesuit*. I may easily go there [thither] from Calais in one of Guerdon's ships." Such a proposal for a single-handed endeavor by a 31 year old scholar in the midst of an enemy camp would seem sheer folly. Again Sterrell showed his concern about not being labeled a traitor, as he requested that his license be signed by two members of the Privy Council.

Finally, in early February, Thomas Phelippes issued Sterrell, in the name of Mr. Saintmain, instructions as he was dispatched into the Low Countries. A draft provides that Sterrell was first to go into the Low Countries to see Fathers Holt and Carleton [Sherwood] and "the rest of the faction." He was to seek their recommendations for a journey into Spain. In both places he was "to learn certainly and assuredly what present plot or design for England is afoot." The instructions named Angelo as responsible for the failure of Sterrell's earlier mission. Sir Walter Ralegh's name was mentioned as providing letters for the executioner discussed earlier. Sterrell was to learn if there were other plans against the queen. He was authorized: "To take upon himself the conduct or execution of anything that shall be thought fit to be done at home for furtherance of these designs except attempt against the Queen's life." The purposes for such instructions was no doubt to provide a written justification for Sterrell's mission should he be arrested by the English for treason.

The instructions mention Staveley, the tailor who was to accompany Sterrell for part of the mission and serve as a courier. Staveley was to be given credit so that he could convey letters and for this purpose he was to "put into a show of traffic and ordinary passage to disguise his employment." The mission was dangerous and eventful.

10

In Spanish Lands
The Bisley-Moody Plot

The Route to Liège

Sterrell's Low Countries' mission lasted from March to August 1592. The scholar/spy encountered danger and suspicion at every turn—at home and abroad. "Robert Robinson" passed himself as a London merchant, a dealer in textiles and goods. His companion was Ezekiel Staveley, a tailor and pub keeper. Staveley and wife maintained an alehouse, "without Bishopsgate," under the sign of the White Goat. Staveley doubled as a courier, and his tavern was a convenient place for letters to be sent. Mistress Staveley served as hostess in her husband's absence and tended to the mail and visitors from overseas looking for "Robinson"/Sterrell. Mail was also received at the Sign of the Swan, Bishopsgate Street. Mail sent to "Mr. John Morice [Morris]" would be picked up by Thomas Phelippes.

Sterrell and Staveley probably left by boat from Gravesend and proceeded to Calais. Moving northward along the coast they made their way to the English-controlled town of Flushing (Vlissingen) on the southern coast of Walcheren Island, at the mouth of the western Schelde (Scheldt) estuary. England had gained control of the town as security for the queen's loan to the Netherlands in 1578. The port was a gateway for sea traffic going to Antwerp, which in 1585 had returned to Spanish control. The town's governor was Sir Robert Sidney, younger brother of Sir Philip Sidney. His sister-in-law, widow of Sir Philip, was now the wife of the Earl of Essex. More than once, Sterrell will invoke the name of Essex to escape arrest by the English. He was more fortunate than his contemporary, Christopher Marlowe. Sterrell and Staveley passed through Flushing only a few weeks after Marlowe was taken into custody there and deported back to England.[1] Within a year, Marlowe and Sterrell will be both sought by the Privy Council.

A short distance from Flushing was Middelburg, a trading center and headquarters for the Merchant Adventurers, a company of English merchants who exported finished woolens from England. From the late 15th century to 1564, its fleets traded with the company's market at Antwerp. As much as three-fourths of English foreign trade was controlled by the company by the mid–16th century, and the company's officers were financiers and advisors to the Tudor monarchs. In 1564 the company lost its market in the Spanish Netherlands and sought new markets. Although the company had resumed trade with Antwerp 1573–1582, its continuing political difficulties led to its abandonment by the Merchant Adventurers in favor of Middelburg.

Middelburg was a pleasant Dutch city, with a substantial English community inclined to puritanism. Merchants, religious refugees, soldiers, adventurers, traveling musicians and others passed through Middelburg. All came under the watchful eyes of English agents who would question travelers. They inspected baggage for contraband and examined the travelers' letters. Thomas Ferrers, deputy governor of the Merchant Adventurers in Middelburg, was a diligent agent who was suspicious of "Robinson" and Staveley.

In Middelburg, Sterrell and Staveley parted company. Staveley remained in the city, awaiting directions from Sterrell. The apparent reason for the separation was that Sterrell's traveling papers were inadequate for the two to pass together. However, it is likely that Sterrell wanted temporarily to dump Stavely. There is no reason to believe that Staveley was anything other than a stout protestant who was loyal to Phelippes and his queen. For Sterrell to work with his Catholic associates and let them know what his real game was, Staveley would have been a great hindrance. Once his Catholic friends knew what Sterrell was up to, Stavely could re-join him. Sterrell probably took a route similar to that he later instructed Stavely to follow. If so, he circled north and east through Dutch-held territory until he could make his way southward to Antwerp. He rapidly exhausted his money through payments for papers to cross borders and to escape inquisitive officials. He went to Dort, Breda, and then Antwerp. The city was bounded on one side by the river Scheldt and surrounded for the rest by inter-connected ditches and canals (the "Ruien") that would empty and fill with the ebb and flood of the tide. Landward access was by bridges.

Sterrell's entrance to Antwerp in early April was dramatic: he was captured and confined at the city's citadel by the Spanish governor of Antwerp, Don Christoval—Count Mondragon—a fierce old warrior of ninety.[2] Sterrell's alias of "Robinson" was unfortunate as the authorities were seeking another Englishman named Robinson who reportedly was planning to poison Sir William Stanley.[3] Sterrell maintained his composure, and his release was effected by the very people he was coming to spy upon: Sir William Stanley, Hugh Owen and a certain unnamed friend, probably Fr. Richard Sherwood. Sterrell's own brief account to Staveley in Middelburg begins dramatically[4]:

> Kneel down and thank God that you came not, for if you had, assure yourself you had died for it although you were the best Catholic in England, not having any body to give their word for you. I have had much ado and was like to have lain in the Castle. Sir Will. Stanley and Mr. Owen with my friend [Sherwood?] could scarce get me forth. I have been greatly accused by secret enemies, but now have answered all.

The deputy governor of the Merchant Adventurers, in Middelburg, received word of the seizure of Robinson and intercepted some of the letters of Sterrell written in the name of Robinson.[5]

After Stanley, Owen and Sherwood obtained his release in Antwerp from Mondragon's castle prison, Sterrell spent some time with them there or in Brussels, a couple of days journey to the south. Fitzherbert and Sherwood had done good work in preparation for Sterrell's coming for him to have been met by these three influential Catholic exiles. Much later, Sterrell said this was the first time that he had met Owen. The fact that a few months after his return to England Sterrell was sending letters to other exiles in Brussels suggests that he spent some time in this city before resuming his journey eastward.

Leaving Brussels, Sterrell fell in with a group of about 800 soldiers marching east to Namur. Under the command of Count Berlaymount, a Walloon nobleman, they were to join up with the forces under the Governor General of the Low Countries, Alexander Farnese (Duke of Parma). Parma was in ill health. King Philip of Spain was attempting to remove him from his post, but he was a seasoned commander and was needed in Spain's war against the French King, Henry IV. The French and English (with a force under the Earl of Essex) had been holding the city of Rouen, on the northwest of France, under siege for the better part of a year. Essex was proud of his role but had returned to England shortly before Sterrell's mission. One of the first items of intelligence that Sterrell sent home was that Catholic forces against Henry had been successful in raising the siege and relieving the town.[6] Parma had been on his way to relieve Rouen but now turned northward again. Sterrell said the rumor—"whispering"—was that Count Berlaymount's men had gone to Namur to escort the daughter of the King of Spain into the Low Countries; so, too, had Count Arenberg.[7] This daughter, Isabella Clara Eugenia, had a claim to be heir to the crown of France.[8] She is an important figure in Sterrell's life for the next 35 years.

From Namur, Sterrell traveled to Liège, the capital city of the Bishopric of Liège. The region was independent of Spanish or Dutch control. Citizens from feuding countries could travel to Liège and have commerce. It was a good place for gathering intelligence and gossip and it was near Spa, whose curative waters have given a name to healthful resorts everywhere. It was a lovely city on the Meuse River, a pleasant place to pass a summer. Sterrell arrived there by the first of May. He spent about three months in Liège and Spa, using Liège as a base from which to travel and make contacts. Familiarity with the terrain and the people was important in establishing a successful network.

Sterrell sent instructions to Staveley in Middelburg. Staveley was to return home to Phelippes and then come to Liège with money for him. Staveley was directed to bring Anthony Skinner with him. Sterrell specified a route that was supposed to be safe for Staveley, but it proved to be life-threatening. Staveley carried a letter to deliver to "Morice"/Phelippes.[9] As instructed, Staveley returned to London and was again dispatched by Phelippes and Essex to catch up to Sterrell in Liège.

Sterrell instructed Staveley to inquire for him at "Mr. Stanihurst's house near Saint Paul's Church or else at Mr. Birbecks an English priest and chaplain in St. Martin's Church." Shortly, however, he took up rooms at the sign of the Lance Courone in Saint Hubert Street, near St. Martins. Sterrell's quarters were on the hill looking down on the main part of the city. Sterrell now mentioned Thomas Cloudsley.[10] He wrote Phelippes that Cloudsley would be a messenger, but Sterrell warned that Cloudsley must know Phelippes only as Morris. Sterrell did not tell Phelippes that Cloudsley's brother was an English priest who had recently been arrested near York. Thomas Cloudsley was a layman, born at Wakefield in Yorkshire, 40 years old. Richard Ayliffe knew him in Brussels and described him as of "a mean stature, face a high colour, black beard cut in point in the middle of his neather lip, a little tusset of whitish hairs."[11] He was a little bald in forehead and had "a little crookedness in one of his legs about the knee."

The "Stanihurst house" belonged to Walter Stanihurst, brother of Richard Stanihurst, an influential exile. The Stanihurst father, James, had been Recorder of Dublin and was three times Speaker of the Irish House of Commons. Both Richard and Walter had known Edmund Campion well. Campion lived with the Stanihurst family in Dublin for 7 months, and the two brothers escorted Campion away from Dublin in March 1571 when English authorities sought to arrest him.[12] After the death of his first wife at the age of 19, Richard Stanihurst was in England in 1580–81. He assisted the Campion-Persons mission, and Sterrell probably made the acquaintance of Richard at that time. After a brief imprisonment,[13] Richard went to live in the Low Countries, and his brother Walter joined him.

Richard's second wife was Helen Copley, a daughter of Sir Thomas Copley of Gatton, Surrey, who went into exile for religion in 1570. Sir Thomas died in the Spanish military camp near Antwerp in 1584, leaving in his will 500 marks to Helen, to be paid to her at the day of her marriage. The bequest was subject to the condition that she marry in accordance with the wishes of her mother and her aunt, Mrs. Mary Shelley, who lived at Rouen.[14] This aunt was Mary Fitzwilliam, twice widowed, by the deaths of her first husband John Shelley and her second, John Guildford. Thomas Copley spoke of her as Mary Shelley (rather than as Lady Guildford) because Sir Thomas's own mother was a sister of John Shelley. There were close family ties between the Gage family, the Shelley family and the Guildfords, and this same Aunt Mary was the grandmother of William Norton, whom William Sterrell aided in 1585 as Norton sought to go to Rouen to his uncle Richard Guildford, son of "Aunt Mary." Sterrell had natural entree into the Stanihurst/Copley families. Moreover, the Earl of Worcester had a sister, Elizabeth, whose husband William Windsor was a close relative of the Copleys of Gatton.

When Sterrell arrived in Liège in 1592, Richard Stanihurst had recently departed for Rome and Spain (where he remained until 1595) and had stopped in Liège en route.[15] Walter later joined Richard in Spain.[16] Although biographical data on Walter Stanihurst is sketchy, he was in Liège around this time, for a later letter to Sterrell (as Hallins) from Liège refers to "Richard Stanihurst brother to the said Water [Walter] who you knew in this town…."[17]

The other friend in Liège mentioned by Sterrell was "Mr. Berbeck," William Birkbeck, a Cambridge graduate who entered the English College at Rheims in 1581. After ordination he was sent into England in April 1583. By 1585 he was in prison in York Castle and was banished from England in September of that year. In about October 1590 he returned to England briefly before becoming chaplain at St. Martin's, Liège, shortly before Sterrell arrived there. In 1598 he will again be in prison in England.

Sterrell was readily accepted into the several circles of English exiles. One group favored the Jesuits and the Spanish, the "Spanish faction" who hoped King Philip's daughter would succeed Elizabeth as queen of England. The "Scottish faction," were more inclined to the "secular" priests and sought a Scottish successor to Queen Elizabeth. That Sterrell so quickly was taken into the confidence of different groups evidences his own remarkable abilities and suggests he knew some of them from prior associations. He overcame the suspicions of exiles who knew that spies were often sent to work among them. Sterrell could not have gained credit with them in a matter of a few weeks without extensive prior contact and strong endorsements.

Sterrell repeatedly asked that Anthony Skinner be sent over to join him.[18] The English exiles were aware that Skinner and Ayliffe had been imprisoned.[19] Sterrell undoubtedly knew of their arrest before he went over. He urged Phelippes to see to Skinner's release on the basis that he would be a spy against the exiles.

A concern that troubled Sterrell (with good reason) was the effect of his mission on his relationship with the Earl of Worcester: "Forget not to do my duty to my own Lord [Worcester] I pray you as opportunity serves. I hope there is firm amity between him and the other [Essex] which I wish to continue."[20]

Sterrell's 1592 letters provide an interesting picture of the conditions he found and the persons with whom he visited. He writes of such men who "in England were tailors and are here for gentlemen, such as charge the King to no end, which I mean not to do and therefore my credit is the more."[21] Sterrell slipped in intelligence about the state of the Catholic exiles and the strength of Spain's forces in the Low countries and the morale of the Spanish supporters, while sounding as though he was writing to a Catholic gentleman ("Morice") in London, in the guise of a Catholic who was very much opposed to the Protestant "hereticks."

The need for money was repeatedly raised by Sterrell in May and June. The money could have purchased access to letters of people that Sterrell was to spy upon. A letter of June 13 from Liège has several messages in code telling where priests were leaving Europe and entering England and indicating that the Governor of Bergen-op-Zoom was false to the queen.[22] The information was far too general to be useful: Sterrell said no more than that priests were going into Lancashire from Flushing, Calais and Dunkirk and landing far from any town. Several of the letters refer to clothing. The terms were likely code words. "If I had money I would *intercept the cardinals packet.* I can assure you that there is no better taffety [taffeta] to be had in any of these parts, as for the velvet I promised and am in bargain for without money and that out of hand it will be bought up of others." Taffeta and velvet are used here to mean intelligence.[23]

The mailing of letters between hostile countries was expensive and dangerous. So, too, was the transfer of money. A letter might take twenty days or more to make its way between London and Antwerp or Liège. A spy could not easily find carriage for correspondence overseas. The destination or even the name of the sender was an open invitation to interception by government agents or crafty entrepreneurs. And there was equal peril in trying to send letters into England. As Sterrell put it: "there is no letter can pass under any known name but will be filched by one or other."[24] Reporting that he had not received a letter that Phelippes had sent, he could not imagine that "a letter by the post in any man's own name being an Englishman could pass without interception."[25] This is why he (and priests) frequently changed aliases in correspondence. Lacking an established network or system, Sterrell tried to cobble together a method of transmission in 1592, instructing Phelippes how to reach him: Phelippes was to send his letters to one Quentin Pertry in Middelburg who would then send them to his brother Simon Pertry in Antwerp who would then send them on to Sterrell in Liège.[26] His own letters were to move in the opposite direction back to Morice/Phelippes. The Pertry connection failed Sterrell almost immediately.

Sterrell also tried to set up a method for receiving money. Initially he told Phelippes to send money to Antwerp "by one of these merchants—Jan Tear or Haunce Pike, they be in London and have factors here."[27] However, Sterrell did not soon receive any, and by the end of the month he changed his instructions for routing so that he could receive money in Liège. He sent multiple instructions to Phelippes to use an Italian factor in London, Signor Oratio Franchotti Lucois, who would address his bill to Père Galle, a merchant in Lumbert Street in Liège.[28] Galle had written to Signor Lucois that "if one Mr. John Morris do deliver any money to him for Robert Robinson in Liège he should receive it and address his bill of exchange to him, and he will repay it." At the same time Sterrell speculated that his letters sent through Quentin Pertry of Middelburg had gone astray.[29] He was so right!

The vigilant Thomas Ferrers[30] of the Merchant Adventurers in Middelburg took immediate action when an alert soldier brought him a suspicious Englishman who was carrying letters addressed to "Ezekiel Stavely in London without Bishopsgate at the sign of the White Goat."[31] He opened the letters and sent them on to Lord Burghley with a report. The man with the letters was John Townshend, who said he had been given letters to carry to England by a Walloon named Quentin Pertry. Townshend had "her majesty's warrant to travel out of England two years." He was allowed to depart and Ferrers "procured" to speak with Pertry who had given them to Townshend; the procurement was surely by means of a soldier sent to bring him to Ferrers. Pertry related that he knew Staveley from five years earlier when Pertry was living in England and visited at Staveley's alehouse. The sender was Robinson (then lying in Antwerp), who had given the letters to Quentin's brother Simon. Staveley was expected in Middelburg shortly and Ferrers would have him sent on to Burghley. He would do the same with Robinson, who was now in Liège, if he were able. Ferrers knew that Robinson was to be greatly suspected: "Robinson coming to Antwerp Mondragon did imprison him but forthwith the chief of the Jesuits there did cause him to be released, and as I hear he is now a pensioner to the King of Spain and hath 20 crowns per month."

How was John Townshend selected to carry Robinson's letters? He would seem merely to be a passing stranger, as was probably intended. Scrutiny reveals the close connections that linked families and their followers in cross-Channel relations. John Townshend matriculated from Magdalen College in 1581, age 13 of Raynham, Norfolk,[32] son of Roger Townshend, a servant of Thomas, 4th Duke of Norfolk and then of Philip Howard, Earl of Arundel. Roger Townshend would surely have been acquainted with Hugh Owen (who had served Thomas Howard's father-in-law and knew Philip Howard) just as John Townshend would have been well-acquainted with William Sterrell, his contemporary at Magdalen College. Roger seems to have been in trouble for being committed abroad to diverse persons in 1585. And the available biographical data on John indicates he was in the Low Countries in 1592.[33] Townshend was closely associated with the family of Francis and Anthony Bacon, who were privy to Sterrell's mission. In about 1592 or 1593, Townshend married a daughter of Nathaniel Bacon, half-brother of Francis and Anthony.

A few weeks after Ferrers had seized Sterrell's letters, Staveley returned to Middelburg after encountering many dangers. Poor Stavely! His summer as a courier for Sterrell was rough.[34] By early June, Phelippes and Essex had dispatched Stavely from London to meet Sterrell in Liège. Passing through Middleburg again he was sighted but not detained. He followed the route that Sterrell had laid out for him in a letter. On the way from Breda to Liège he was robbed. The robbers nearly took him prisoner to Geertruidenberg but let him go. He returned to Dort and then traveled with the post into Brabant (Brussels) and on to Liège, where he found Sterrell, at the *Lance Courone*. Stavely spent about 6 days with Sterrell and then set out from Liège back to Dort to await further word from Sterrell. On the way a company of freebooters (land pirates) carried him into the woods and stripped him naked and took all he had. Learning he was an Englishman, they decided to let him go. He found his way back to Middelburg.

Within an hour of Staveley's arrival, deputy governor Ferrers was calling at the house where he stayed. He demanded answers to questions about the letters addressed to Staveley that Ferrers had sent on to Lord Burghley. Robinson, Ferrers told Staveley, accompanied Jesuits and enemies of England. When Staveley was given a chance to speak, he explained that he and Robinson were working for the Earl of Essex. The invocation of Essex worked an immediate change in Ferrers, as Essex was his relative. Ferrers asked what Staveley had to show from Essex. Staveley had nothing—the freebooters had taken all—but Ferrers was willing to write Essex a letter explaining what had happened, and so too did Staveley to

Phelippes.³⁵ As he languished in custody, Staveley may have regretted setting aside his needles and tavern-keeping for this adventure.

Phelippes and Essex must have been quite upset about Ferrers's report to Burghley. As soon as Phelippes learned of it (apparently through the report Ferrers had sent to Burghley), he took Ferrers to task in a letter of July 19. Ferrers responded with an apology to Phelippes.³⁶ He said that he was not to blame for what he did but wished it had not been done. Ferrers promised not to deal further to the prejudice of the activities and that he would furnish Staveley as he needed. He offered whatever service he might provide and delivered two letters to Staveley, who was still in Middelburg, that Phelippes sent. Ferrers was thus brought into the support of Sterrell's mission. Ferrers asked that he and his wife be remembered to Phelippes' mother and his brothers and sisters.³⁷ This aside indicates that Phelippes—Customs officer of London—had good personal relations with merchants trading in the Low Countries or Netherlands. Such relations in part stemmed from the fact that Phelippes's father had been a prominent wool merchant before becoming customs officer in London. Phelippes must have done many favors for the merchants with whom Ferrers was associated, favors that may explain why he is soon in prison on account of deficiencies in customs collections. In mid–August Ferrers reported that he was providing money to Robinson and Staveley and would provide more if need be.³⁸

Sterrell Encounters English Provocateurs: Reinold Bisley and Michael Moody

Sterrell's 1592 mission was to make contact with the Catholic exiles and they were to assist him then in proceeding on to Spain. Although he did not at this time go to Spain, his instructions were in "both places to learn certainly and assuredly what present plot or design for England is afoot."³⁹ The initial concern seems to have been for the "executioner" that Angelo had described. But Sterrell was expected to ferret out other plots, and in this Sterrell was engaged in a curious competition. He was a principal in one of two rival spy networks. An Essex biographer observed that a "rivalry appears to have arisen between Essex and Burghley, which of them should be the bearer to Elizabeth of the earliest foreign intelligence; which, by means of foreign agents and spies, should soonest detect the practices and plans of her enemies."⁴⁰ Sterrell purported to detect plots but he really seems to have been intent on exposing the spying efforts of the rival agents of the Cecils. This is the likely reason that Sterrell's name became distasteful to the queen. The intelligence Sterrell gathered on this mission went to Essex and the queen.

The most dramatic assassination plot against the queen that Sterrell reported from the Low Countries concerned Reinold Bisley, some time a soldier of Flushing. He was "a short black fellow, with a red face," whose father had an office in York.⁴¹ Also sent into England for furthering the plot was William Whip, sometimes a tailor in Gray's Inn Lane in London; he had a pension of 30 crowns a month. Whip's wife kept an alehouse there, where the parties "convented to kill the Queen." Michael Moody, he reported, had been sent into England in Lent with the same purpose.⁴² This was the same Michael Moody who was used by Walsingham in an ersatz "plot" at the time of Mary Queen of Scots's execution.

Sterrell reported that these plotters had been sent by Sir William Stanley. Was Sterrell actually betraying Stanley and some of the English? Only if there were a plot to kill the queen and only if Bisley and Whip were English Catholics associated with Stanley. Upon receiving Sterrell's intelligence (about the end of May), Phelippes promptly took steps to isolate Bisley. Interrogatories were drawn up by Phelippes to be administered to Bisley and two others "if they be taken" inquiring of his acquaintance with Sir William Stanley and Owen.[43] On May 30 Phelippes wrote a note[44] to the Earl of Essex discussing a man whose name is not given but was probably Bisley: "It may please your Lo: [Lordship] the Q. [queen] resolved that the party should be stayed here under color of an intended employment some fortnight or three weeks because he should not start, but in the mean while be questioned withal by my Lo: Buckhurst & Mr. Vicechamberlain of the grounds of his credit on that side." The mention of Lord Buckhurst aids in identifying the man as Bisley. Phelippes told Essex that the man's answers could be compared with "that advertisement we should receive from our man [Sterrell] for which purpose St [Stavely] shall be dispatched this night with full directions." At just about this time Stavely was sent again from England.[45]

A short time later, Phelippes examined Bisley.[46] He told Phelippes that he was acting for the English government. Phelippes asked whether Bisley "undertook not to pretend service to the Q[ueen] the better to color that employment." Bisley declared that he knew Owen, Fr. Holt and one "Thwing" who was his kinsman.[47] Thwing had given him credit with Owen and the others, but Owen at first distrusted him. Bisley satisfied Owen by establishing that he had come over on business for the daughter of the Countess of Northumberland, that he had a pass from Lord Buckhurst, and that he had directions to give news of the Low Countries on his return. Bisley said he had been working with Michael Moody, and Bisley's work for Owen was a trial of what he could do. He said further that Owen willed him to visit Sir William Courtney to see what part he would take if an army were sent to England. Phelippes' notes show there were other persons to be dealt with by Bisley, including a "Mr. Somerset."[48] Supposedly, Bisley had brought letters in his buttons from Stanley and Owen.

The appearance that Sterrell turned over a Catholic ally of Stanley and Owen to the English authorities is dispelled when it is confirmed that Bisley was in fact acting for the queen's government, as a Cecil double agent on a trial basis.[49] The effect of William Sterrell's allegation against Bisley was to uncover Bisley as a spy for the English government *against* the Catholics, rather than revealing a Catholic plot against the queen.[50] Historians have mistakenly believed that Sterrell betrayed a Catholic agent and that Phelippes had then turned Bisley into a spy for the English.[51] Rather, Sterrell cleverly unmasked a man already working for Robert Cecil. A letter by "Reinold Boseley" evidently written to Cecil was dated April 7, 1592—well before Sterrell's intelligence from the Low Countries. It reports on the same Whipp that Sterrell reports on in May.[52] "Boseley" was "employed beyond the seas in Her Majesty's service" and he reported that Stanley and Hugh Owen wanted William Whipp, who had been a servant to Sir Robert Sidney, to come to England and again serve Sidney. The plan was for Whipp to copy the keys to Flushing where Sidney was governor. The same report stated that Michael Moody was to try to promote a marriage between Arabella Stuart and the son of the Duke of Parma.

Once Bisley was arrested and questioned by Phelippes and not tried and executed, it could only mean that Bisley was a government spy. Later, Phelippes received two letters from Lord Buckhurst saying that Buckhurst had obtained the queen's consent that Bisley should be delivered and have £10 towards his charges.⁵³ Buckhurst told Phelippes that her Majesty "is not yet well satisfied with him (Phelippes)" and that a "great impression has entered into her heart against him." The queen desired that Bisley should be employed in some service. The queen was unhappy that Bisley had been locked up and questioned by Phelippes. Phelippes later related to Essex that Sterrell had made the queen quite upset with Phelippes. The Bisley affair was a major reason for her displeasure.

Bisley was to cause Sterrell problems shortly, but there was an additional element to Sterrell's desire to undo Bisley. Phelippes, it will be recalled, was told by Bisley that he had come over to the Low Countries on business for the *daughter of the Countess of Northumberland*, and that the examination notes disclose that Bisley was dealing with matters of "*Mr. Somerset*." Thus if Bisley was doing secret duties for the English government, he was betraying the daughter of the Countess of Northumberland and Mr. Somerset, who were both Catholic. The Countess of Northumberland was the sister of William Somerset, 3rd Earl of Worcester and aunt of Edward Somerset, William Sterrell's patron. Her husband had been executed in 1572 for his support of Mary Stewart. Their daughter was Mary Percy, first cousin to the 4th Earl of Worcester. She was a devout Catholic who sheltered priests in London, priests with whom Sterrell had dealings. In 1598 Mary Percy will found a Benedictine Convent in Brussels. Her business matters in the Low Countries in 1590 arose from her mother's property there from her long years in exile and Mary's own plans to settle there. The "Mr. Somerset" was George Somerset, son of Thomas Somerset (Worcester's uncle), who died in government custody in 1586. George Somerset was nephew to the Countess of Northumberland and first cousin to both Mary Percy and Edward Somerset. Thomas Somerset was owed substantial sums by Cardinal Allen that still had not been paid when Allen died in 1594, and George Somerset was Thomas Somerset's heir. In 1595 William Sterrell will help George to return to England after years in the Low Countries. Sterrell's turning Bisley in as a potential assassin of Queen Elizabeth prevented Bisley from doing harm to the cousins of Sterrell's employer, Mary Percy and George Somerset.

With Bisley one again sees the lengths to which the English government, whether Walsingham or Lord Burghley or others, would go to harass the Percy and Somerset families and other Catholic families. Sterrell became an effective agent to undermine those efforts.

Bisley's work with Michael Moody confirms that Moody was working for the English government.⁵⁴ Moody had suffered little for his supposed 1587 assassination scheme, indicating quite clearly it was all a sham. Moody was naturally suspected of spying by the Catholics in the Low Countries. Several of Sterrell's reports on Moody suggest that he was doing to Moody the same thing that he did to Bisley. One said that Moody "doth nothing without the consent of the best and of Mondragon himself whatsoever slanderous tongues report of him."⁵⁵ Another said that Moody had been sent into England at Lent to kill the queen.⁵⁶ Knowing that Moody was an agent for the English government, Sterrell probably sought to call him into question when he added that Moody "coseneth [fools] the Queen notably." Such a report simultaneously reveals Moody to be working under the authority of the English government and puts his loyalty to that government into doubt.

Moody's activities as a provocateur soon got him into serious trouble in the Low Countries, and an effort was made by the English government to extricate him.⁵⁷ Edmund Yorke, a prisoner soon to be executed, confessed that Moody was coming over to England to kill the queen, and another prisoner, Richard Williams, confessed that he thought Moody was already in England.⁵⁸ The government knew just where Moody was, probably because he was in constant communication with a government contact. Moody in 1595 is imprisoned by Count Mondragon.⁵⁹

The Bisley and Moody episodes are examples of the counter-espionage technique that William Sterrell used to brilliant effect. The key to being a credible, successful double agent is to provide intelligence that is perfectly true, yet harmless to your true master. Learning of Bisley's and Moody's spying against the Catholics, Sterrell revealed their role to Phelippes and thus also to Essex and Bacon. This exposed Bisley and Moody and made them less useful to Cecil and Burghley. Moreover, knowing that Bisley had already reported on Whipp the tailor, Sterrell also reported on Whipp—thus demonstrating that he was gathering good intelligence of spying activities by Catholics (assuming Whipp actually was doing such). Whipp may have been aware of Sterrell's reporting; in any event, he was in no more danger than before. Repeatedly, Sterrell gave intelligence to Essex and later to the government about priests and spies that was slightly outdated, and it was always ineffective. Discovering where someone has been hiding shows you have good information, but reporting this after they have left renders the information harmless.

Besides Bisley and Moody, there were other *agents provocateur* who served Robert Cecil and Lord Burghley in the Low Countries. The two most colorful ones, both well known to William Sterrell, were Anthony Munday, a hack writer who had vilified Edmund Campion, and Robert Poley, "sweet Robyn," one of the provocateurs of the Babington Plot. Another was John Daniell, whose name figures prominently in confessions in 1594 of several men who admitted to involvement in treasonous practices.

Return to London, September 1592

By mid–August, 1592, Sterrell and Stavely were together again in Middelburg. Stavely borrowed £3 from Thomas Ferrers and Sterrell borrowed £10.⁶⁰ Sterrell's return to London in early September 1592 was marked by confusion and miscommunication. Thomas Phelippes was away from London when Sterrell arrived, days earlier than expected. Owing to Phelippes's absence, Sterrell did not report to anyone right away. Upon receiving word from Phelippes, Sterrell communicated directly with Essex about the mission, and the two of them had difficulty establishing a rapport. Part of the problem was that Sterrell brought with him Cloudsley, who had been in the service of Hugh Owen and Sir William Stanley, and this courier may have believed that Sterrell was actually working with Owen and Stanley (which in fact he was) rather than spying on them. Another part of the problem was that Sterrell was not candid with Essex. Secrecy was so lax around Essex that Sterrell feared betrayal.⁶¹ So Sterrell was sent to Francis Bacon to get matters straightened out. Bacon smoothed the difficulties, and Sterrell evidently again met with Essex to greater satisfaction if not contentment. Three letters, all directed to Thomas Phelippes, give a sense of the relations among the parties.

The first is an undated letter of Essex to Phelippes⁶²:

> Mr. Phelippes: Your absence has put both the Q[ueen] and me to pain. First that we heard by my Lord Treasurer that the party [Sterrell] was come to London two days before we heard anything from him. Next that when I had received his first letters he gave us no satisfaction in anything of worth. Whereupon I

10. In Spanish Lands

wrote to him and urged him to set down to me the reasons of his coming over and the means he had to do service, to both which demands he has answered me. His means are two, one by a letter carrier [Cloudsley] whom he has brought over to have opportunity to take Burkett[63] a priest to whom all or the most of the fugitives' messages are directed and by an other the credit he has gotten with Father Holt, Owen and Fitzherbert to discover all their practices, they being like to send over onto him and commit to him their greatest secrets and also this messenger who is by them used, being at his [Sterrell's] devotion. This carries some good probability of good service. The other [the carrier, Cloudsley] must be tried by the event. Now you are come I lay all my cares upon you. Sound him, this Cloudsley, who is their messenger, to the bottom and for service present or future lay your plots and I will supply all things. I pray you let me hear presently from you. Send your letters to my wife[64] to Barn Elms and she shall send them on to me. I commit you to God and the Q[ueen].

Your very assured friend
Essex

[p.s.]: I have sent you a warrant for Cloudsley which you may use at your discretion.

Next is a letter from Francis Bacon to Phelippes concerning the arrival of Sterrell. Dated September 15, 1592, it reveals that there is some suspicion of Sterrell, apparently by the queen herself.[65]

Sir, I congratulate you on your returning, hoping that all is passed on your side. Your Mercury [Sterrell] is returned; whose return alarmed as upon some great matter, which I fear he will not satisfy. News of his coming came before his own letter, and to other than his proper servant, which maketh me desirous to satisfy or to salve. My Lord [Essex] hath required him to repair to me; which upon his Lordship's and mine own letters received I doubt not but he will with all speed perform; where I pray you to meet him if you may, that laying our heads together we may maintain his credit, satisfy my Lord's expectation, and procure some good service. I pray the rather spare not your travail, because I think the Queen is already party to the advertisement of his coming over, and in some suspect which you may not disclose to him. So I wish you as myself, this 15th of September, 1592.

Yours ever assured,
Fr. Bacon

Finally, William Sterrell can be heard on these events. They made him "in my dumps" and malcontent. Under the name Robert Robinson he wrote to Phelippes[66]:

Good Sir, I was not so glad of your coming home as I was sorry to think you should send me to another [Bacon? Essex?][67] to be examined, the very concept whereof so grieved me that I have not been quiet since. I went as you sent word I should, but I could hardly make him understand me, but I have not communicated onto him the chief point which concerns Fitzherbert and of old service. Neither shall any man know it but yourself, for I find by Mr. Bacon that there is small secrecy used. Being thus in my dumps and malcontent Stavely came to me and told me that you were not willing to have had me go to Mr. Bacon and that his man deceived me, which if it be true I am glad, for then I hope you are affected towards me as before. Had I known so much there is neither Lord nor Lady should have made me ago to him and so I signified to Mr. Bacon himself, who then assured me that it was your mind. His man came to me with the letters saying you had seen them and wished me to do according to your direction. Whether I win or lose, and if they will do things without your privity, they shall do them without me, but if it so happens by reason of your business you please to refer me over to another, let it be to such a one as knows what is what. I sent that day my man to your house 3 times but your man would neither go nor send to you, and so my man can justify to their faces. Let me know by Stavely whether I shall come, and I am at your command.

Yours most assuredly,
R. Robinson

Subsequent developments confirm that Sterrell is in some difficulty for spying on behalf of Essex. Sterrell and Bacon have come to a relationship of confidence after initial problems of communication, but Sterrell does not at this stage have a close relationship with Essex. Essex and Bacon are not aware of Sterrell's "old service" which involved Fitzherbert, and he is unwilling to reveal it under any circumstances. Evidently Sterrell felt that he had compromised himself with some of his intelligence against the English Catholics abroad but was certainly not willing to betray Fitzherbert and others. Phelippes's knew of the old correspondence with Fitzherbert but no one else around Essex knew. The information that Sterrell did reveal was partial and unsatisfactory, especially to Queen Elizabeth herself. The months that Sterrell had spent overseas in the company of Stanley, Owen, Holt, Fitzherbert, Sherwood and others produced only the result that Sterrell was in good credit with them and might do good service in the future. This was hardly what they had expected. It was exposure of assassination plots they wanted, and Sterrell was not delivering. Sterrell's difficulties were such that he was soon casting about for another means of earning a living.

Two documents in the State Papers do look as though Sterrell and Phelippes tried to use the intelligence Sterrell had developed to satisfy the thirst for conspiracy at the Court.[68] These "informations" have no date but must have been before December 1592, for they mention the Duke of Parma as though he were still alive. "Saint Main" was written on one of these, indicating that it was the result of Sterrell's activities. They spoke of a design to kill the queen to be followed by an invasion by Sir William Stanley and the King of Spain. The assassination was to be accomplished by "the desperate Italian" whom the Pope had diverted from an attempt against the King of France to Queen Elizabeth—the mysterious Angelo whom Sterrell had encountered in Calais. Probably the document here was a list of "talking points" used by Phelippes to gain Essex's support for Sterrell's overseas mission. Angelo and "the desperate Italian" showed that Sterrell and Phelippes were able to detect plots and to provide intelligence. The "information" continued by saying that many priests had been sent into England, as Sterrell had reported in his letter of June 13, 1592.[69] "Angelo" was probably a fiction of Sterrell (and Phelippes) to justify his activities.

The second document took up the taboo topic of domestic politics. It stated that the uncertainty about the succession would push the ambition of competitors. The realm, it observed, was divided into three factions: Catholic, Protestant and Puritan. Two of these factions were persecuted. All three would want protection of the Crown and this would hinder the peaceable decision of titles. The Council was condemned or hated, the nobility weak and the common people weary of exactions from them. Whether Phelippes submitted either of these to Essex or to the queen is not known. A frank discussion of the succession such as they contained would have landed Phelippes and Sterrell in prison. So, these views were probably never made public, but they reveal Sterrell's reflections on the government around him.

Trouble Ahead

Repercussions from Sterrell's overseas mission were inevitable. The exposure of Bisley and Moody could not help but offend Lord Burghley. The Lord Treasurer was ready to rein in Phelippes (and Essex) for intruding into Burghley's activities. But he could not move too abruptly, as Elizabeth favored the gallant young Essex who was risking his life in battle for her. For many years she had played her courtiers against one another, and she welcomed Essex's efforts to provide her with useful intelligence. Sterrell was undermined over a period of six months; it reached a crisis for him in March and April 1593. Thomas Phelippes, too, will find himself in great trouble with the Crown and will be dismissed from his position as "customer" of London in actions overseen by Burghley.

11

The Parliament of 1593
Sterrell and Marlowe

Raglan—November 1592–February 1593

For five months after his return, Sterrell put up a good show that he was working at developing intelligence against the Catholic exiles. He had few results for his previous year's work, but much promise. Cloudsley was with him off and on, and it seemed he had matters afoot. Three other regular messengers were at work: Ezekiel Stavely and James and Robert Paynter, father and son.[1]

In mid–September 1592 Thomas Ferrers informed Phelippes that an Englishman whom "Robinson" (Sterrell) had told him to expect had appeared at Middelburg.[2] He was "a man of 27 or 28 years of age with whitely hair, both head and beard." The man slipped away before he could be questioned. Sterrell returned Ferrers's letter to Phelippes with the comment that it was his hard hap never to have anything done accordingly.[3] Ferrers had let the man escape. The white-haired man fits the description of Roger Walton, a provocateur against the Catholics reporting occasionally to Robert Cecil. Sir Edward Stafford in 1588 described him as a little above 20, slender, tall, with sallow complexion.

Sterrell was operating now from Worcester's castle, Raglan. The letters from abroad came through Phelippes's hands, for they were sent to a location in London that he controlled. Sterrell's outbound letters were carried by Stavely, by Cloudsley, by the Paynters, and by some of the merchants from whom Phelippes collected customs. Sterrell, however, directed Phelippes not to make further use of merchants but instead to send to old Paynter, and this would be safest.[4] Sterrell was writing to Fitzherbert,[5] Hugh Owen, Fr. William Holt, the Earl of Westmorland, Fr. Richard Sherwood, and others. He would send letters to one destination by several routes in the hope that one would get through. Each letter would reference the last letter that was received. Hugh Owen and Thomas Fitzherbert were fully aware that Sterrell served Worcester and was writing from Raglan.[6]

In October and November 1592 Sterrell had Phelippes send letters to Fitzherbert by Calais, Dieppe and Flanders. There was some difficulty over coordinating cipher-keys for messages. Sterrell and Fitzherbert had code words or *tokens*[7] that alerted one another to problems or gave directions to take action. Sterrell related to Phelippes that he had sent a letter to Fitzherbert without a cipher and so "sent him this word *cupio* to use for fear he should not have his copy ready."[8] Upon receipt of this word (Latin for "I desire"), Fitzherbert responded that he understood the full import of the message.[9]

Sterrell warned Phelippes against writing to Fitzherbert independently of Sterrell:

"There are so many privy tokens between us as you cannot possibly write correspondently."[10] Fitzherbert would know they were not Sterrell's own letters.[11] This prevented Phelippes from working around Sterrell. The person to whom Fitzherbert had forwarded the message of "*cupio*" was probably Fr. Richard Sherwood. Sterrell's intelligence was sent on to Spain for Fr. Persons and Sir Francis Englefield, but any payments that were made would have been transacted through Brussels or Antwerp because of their proximity to England and the comparative ease of payment from there. Until 1594–95, Sherwood remained Sterrell's primary contact in Brussels and Antwerp.[12]

In December 1592, Fitzherbert encouraged Sterrell to come to Dieppe.[13] He was eager to undertake weekly correspondence. As an intelligencer for the King and Council of Spain, he sorely needed intelligence from England. Reestablishing relations with Sterrell was a godsend to Fitzherbert and probably was the principal factor in his being chosen to succeed Sir Francis Englefield as English Secretary to King Philip in 1596. Fitzherbert urged Sterrell to write all he could learn of the Jesuit society and the English Catholics "for the satisfaction of Parsons."[14] Persons knew him as Sterrell, not under an alias. The elements of a network are now is place, but it remains tentative until Phelippes is fully turned by Sterrell.

Suspicions continued in the Essex circle about Cloudsley, and this increased distrust of Sterrell. Sterrell encouraged Phelippes to put Cloudsley to the test, as Essex himself had instructed.[15] He gave Phelippes stage directions how to proceed. Phelippes must first seem discontent with Cloudsley, but not threatening, and then should be encouraging. Cloudsley would be used to find an elusive priest, Birket (the future Archpriest), and to carry letters over to the Low Countries.

By the end of November 1592, there was some problem lurking, something that could ruin all. Sterrell asked Phelippes whether there were any letters for him. He would come to London if necessary, but otherwise he would wait and travel with Worcester. The journey would be slow, he commented, as Worcester was bringing four marriageable daughters with him. Worcester's position at Court was rising. He had just been in Oxford in September to receive an honorary degree on Queen Elizabeth's visit to the University, only the second of her long reign. Now two of his daughters were to be received as ladies in waiting to the queen. Around this same time, Worcester was admitted to the Middle Temple, the legal society that was also a gathering place for London's influential. Worcester, said Sterrell, had a good opinion of Phelippes's discretion and a friendly relation with Essex. Sterrell then sounded a somber note: "But that I hope upon Cloudsley's coming and Fitzherbert's letters I should be in no ordinary melancholy, there is some thing that doth hinder all what somever it is." What accounted for Sterrell's melancholy?

At the beginning of January 1593, Sterrell informed Phelippes that their journey to London had been delayed by the Christmas visit of young Lord William Compton, nephew of Worcester's wife.[16] Although Sterrell tried to sound upbeat, his recitation of problems makes clear that he was worried. There had been complications in the correspondence with the English exiles. Cloudsley returned, somewhat reviving Sterrell's spirits, but Cloudsley delivered his letters to the wrong people. He had given Owen's letter to Westmorland and Westmorland's to Holt, they being of diverse factions. Sterrell had received letters from Holt and Sherwood. Sterrell thought his credit with the English exiles might be in doubt, "having written such great gudgings [lies] to them as I did." There were problems arising from Bisley, who apparently was still locked up in London from Sterrell's earlier report that

Bisley was an assassin sent by Sir William Stanley, and possibly trouble from John Daniell.[17] Sterrell seems to have been under suspicion all around. Richard Ayliffe reported to the government's agents of sighting Cloudsley in London in December 1592 as Cloudsley was going to see Sterrell; this would have contributed to mistrust of Sterrell.

Sterrell was right to suspect Daniell as employed by the queen, and again one sees Sterrell's work bearing counter-espionage fruit, exposing anti–Catholic agents of the English government who were working among the exiles. Daniell had been in Brussels at about the same time as Sterrell and had come into England in September 1592—just at the time Sterrell did. Daniell had immediately told Lord Burghley of supposed plots in the Low Countries by Sterrell's friends, Sir William Stanley and Hugh Owen. He probably made allegations against Sterrell at the same time, hence Sterrell's problems with some of the Privy Council. One of Daniell's associates in the Low Countries will soon name Sterrell as the man at the English Court to whom they were to turn for help in escaping after assassinating the queen of England.

On a brighter note, Sterrell told Phelippes that Worcester continued to support him. Phelippes need only "signify that I must be used in her majesty's service he [Worcester] will not only be content with my absence but pay me my stipend as if I were resident with him." Worcester would even "grant me a lodging in his house in London." Sterrell hoped that Phelippes could find some basis for sending Sterrell over to Dieppe to meet with Fitzherbert. Yet Sterrell was worried that "some of the Council" would not deal with him "roundly," (openly, without concealment). What alerted Sterrell that some members of the Privy Council were distrustful? Perhaps Phelippes revealed to Sterrell that Bacon in September had warned that the queen was "in some suspect" of Sterrell, though Phelippes was forbidden to disclose this. Sterrell's closing carried his sense of difficulty: "Yours ever most assuredly *against all the world* to his poor power, Wm. Sterrell." Falling into mistrust by all sides, Sterrell felt that Phelippes was his only friend. But Sterrell was misleading Phelippes too, so he must have truly felt alone.[18]

Soon Sterrell's Welsh courier returned with a letter from Phelippes, and Sterrell quickly wrote again.[19] Cloudsley, he said, was being true to Phelippes but false to Sterrell, which was as Sterrell desired. Sterrell was glad that Phelippes had not tried writing to Owen for it would have given away the role they were playing with Cloudsley. Sterrell said that when he wrote to Owen he was using the name "Mr. Jonnes" and not that given in Owen's cipher, which was Thomas Cutbert. Sterrell was sowing confusion so that any suspicious correspondence with the Catholic exiles could be explained away.

Despite the problems Sterrell was having, he received good intelligence while at Raglan. The Duke of Parma had died only a few weeks before Sterrell's January 15, 1593, letter. Sterrell knew of Parma's death and its implications for Spain and the Low Countries. He also knew that Parma was temporarily succeeded by his deputy, Count Mansfeld.[20] Sterrell's grasp of the factions at Brussels was based on first hand experience among the Flemish and Walloon locals, the Spaniard officials and soldiers and the exiles. His understandings of the factions and the relations of the Low Countries with Spain showed considerable political acumen.

Cloudsley met with Sterrell and then left. Supposedly he was in search of the elusive priest Birket. In reality, he was undoubtedly doing what had enticed him into England with Sterrell—visiting his brother who was a priest, Peter Cloudsley. Sterrell wrote Phelippes to obtain a letter that would protect Cloudsley from arrest.[21] Cloudsley had first joined with Sterrell in about May 1592, shortly after he would have learned of his brother's arrest. Working with Sterrell and pretending to search for the priest Birket provided Cloudsley with a reason for being in England where he could try to help his brother. Sterrell and his friends repeatedly used such crafty devices to advance their own ends.

Sterrell and Phelippes collaborated on a letter in which Sterrell informed Fitzherbert that he had been at Raglan to avoid the plague in London.[22] He wrote Fitzherbert that he had been "greatly injured by Low Country merchants," probably meaning Daniell or Bisley, provocateurs operating in the Low Countries at the same time as Sterrell. Sterrell intended to go to Dieppe to meet with Fitzherbert. The Parliament, he said, was for the queen to raise money for the troops in Brittany who were fighting for the French King. Using codes, he discussed the troops being sent to Normandy. Sterrell provided lengthy news of the "great carrack" that had been captured earlier in 1592: the *Madre de Dios,* which bore an immensely rich cargo from the Indies. Many of its riches and jewels were pilfered by the English captors' crews, and disputes continued for several years over the respective shares of the queen and the investors in the ships that captured the carrack. Fitzherbert will have passed the information on to Antwerp and to Madrid.

Sterrell's last letter to Phelippes before leaving Raglan for London was on February 2, 1593. It reflects some suspicions of Sterrell from Phelippes that Sterrell sought to negate: "Let me find you as I expect—my unfeigned friend and leave I pray you all suspicion. I trust you find by Fitz'r':s [Fitzherbert] letter that I have proceeded upon good ground and I doubt not that you will be careful to satisfy the greatest in my behalf." Sterrell was counting on Phelippes to satisfy unnamed powerful people. Sterrell went on to reveal problems developing with Worcester: Sterrell was having to let his foot-boy go, as Worcester had commanded that "none of us shall keep any boys." This was prelude to a greater disruption of Sterrell's relation with Worcester. Shortly before Parliament convened on February 19, Sterrell and Worcester arrived in London. The customary procession for the Parliament was cancelled because of the plague. Sterrell's world, so precariously balanced as it was, soon began to tumble.

Among the Lords and Lordings

Despite foreboding signs, the opening of Parliament in February 1593 was a festive occasion for Worcester and Sterrell. Old friends and new celebrated with parties and music as members gathered from around England. Sterrell wrote Phelippes a note expressing regret that he had not been a party where he was expected: "We had many lords and lordings at dinner, who spent all the day in music, and you might have done well to come among them. Here was Sir Harry Gray, Mr. Vavasour, and young Mr. Dudley, the great Lord's son, men well known to you."[23] Sterrell will have praised Dudley's father, the late Earl of Leicester, who had written letters on behalf of Sterrell at one or more crucial times to permit Sterrell to receive his degrees from Oxford.

Although Phelippes had missed the dinner, Sterrell planned for Phelippes to meet with Worcester later. The manner in which Sterrell and Phelippes worked together seen in the same letter: "I will write to Owen if you will send me some brief notes by Painter, and will send the letter to you." The drafts of letters in the State Papers in Phelippes handwriting have given the impression that Phelippes was the letter-writer and Sterrell merely transcribed them. This impression arises from the fact that most of the Sterrell correspondence from this period consists of letters seized from Phelippes's own files, many only drafts. The relationship was more complex. Phelippes's "brief notes" were simply the starting point for Sterrell's letters. Sterrell and his recipients had their own "privy tokens" that Phelippes did not know and would not have understood in the final letters that Sterrell sent overseas. The large number of letters of Sterrell in his own hand in the period 1616–1626 show him to be a master at conveying political and military intelligence in a highly economical writing style.

The Privilege of Parliament Controversy: Topcliffian Terror

During the Parliament of 1593 Sterrell was called upon to gather information secretly to help one of Thomas Fitzherbert's cousins. The events described here show how pervasive (and perverse) were the effects of anti–Catholicism and how torture could be used for criminal ends. Queen Elizabeth's master of torture, Richard Topcliffe, entered an infamous compact with another Thomas Fitzherbert, a cousin to Sterrell's correspondent of the same name.[24] Topcliffe had promised to secure the death of the man's uncle, also named Sir Thomas Fitzherbert, his father John Fitzherbert, and his cousin William Bassett.

In the Parliament of 1593 the murderous nephew, Thomas Fitzherbert, became a *cause celebre*. On the day of his election to Parliament he was arrested. He was outlawed after twenty-two judgments for debts that included one for £1400 to the queen, and £4000 to others. The man who arrested him was Sheriff William Bassett of Blore, his cousin as well as cousin of the exile Thomas Fitzherbert. Should Thomas Fitzherbert be allowed to take his seat in Parliament despite his being outlawed and jailed for debt? Members of Parliament enjoyed a privilege of freedom from arrest, but did the privilege extend to one who was not in Parliament or on his way to or from Parliament at the time of the arrest?

When Parliament opened, Topcliffe, a former member, brought Fitzherbert's case before the Committee on Privileges. The Committee concluded, on March 1, that Fitzherbert should not be seated; a member of Parliament had to be a "fit" man, not an outlaw.

Sir Edward Hoby challenged the ruling, and urged that "outlaw" in this instance was personal rather than criminal and the privilege should apply. The debate continued for more than the next month. The Speaker, Edward Coke, suggested bringing both Bassett and Fitzherbert before the House by means of a writ of habeas corpus. On March 17 Bassett appeared before the House, as did Richard Topcliffe, representing Fitzherbert. Topcliffe spoke of the "ancient cause of malice" between Fitzherbert and Bassett and began accusing Sheriff Bassett of being a receiver of priests and having intelligence with Catholic refugees. He raised alarms concerning the safety of Fitzherbert at Bassett's hands and "what traitors and bad people resorted now of late to Bassett's house."[25] Before resolving whether the Commons had power of to issue a *habeas* writ, Sheriff Bassett brought Fitzherbert before the Commons. Fitzherbert was heard and the privilege was denied him.

In the middle of the privilege debate, William Bassett discreetly contacted William Sterrell to try to learn what might be said about him. Bassett will have known of Sterrell through his cousin, the exiled Thomas Fitzherbert who had entered the Middle Temple with Bassett. Bassett had contacted Sterrell to find out what Fr. Thomas Clark had said about him.[26] Clark had attended Rheims, was ordained in 1590, and was immediately sent back into England. A big man of 37 with a short black beard, he wore a leather jacket and carried a big sword. In January 1593 Clark was captured and at Canterbury confessed at length about his background and where he had been hiding.[27] He betrayed some of the people who had sheltered him over the previous two years but not all. His confession does not mention Bassett. Bassett could not know that except by collecting rumor.

The records do not disclose whether Fr. Clark was sent to the Marshalsea Prison, but it is likely he was sent to London and underwent further examination from Topcliffe. In April and July Clark preached recantation sermons to establish that he abjured the Roman faith and was rewarded with a special pardon. His pardon coincides roughly with the arrest of Fr. Robert Gray in early August by Topcliffe.[28] Gray had been a tutor of William Bassett, and Gray's confessions implicated Bassett for having helped Gray. He confessed that he had sundry times been to Bassett's house and that Bassett had given him a purse and two nags. Bassett was evidently examined.[29]

Topcliffe's information about Bassett probably came from Clark (arrested January 1593) and not from Gray (arrested August 1593). Clark would have told of Bassett receiving Gray. Because Clark was in government custody and was continuing to give evidence to the government, Topcliffe would not have announced to Parliament that his source of information was the apostate priest Clark. Subsequently Clark betrayed another priest, Edward Osbaldeston, who was executed at York in November 1594.

Topcliffe was so callous that he brought a claim against the conniving nephew asserting that Fitzherbert had breached his agreement under bond to give Topcliffe £5,000 to persecute the man's father and uncle to death, as well as Bassett. Fitzherbert's defense was that the conditions had not been fulfilled: Even though the father and the uncle had been put into prison, they had died of natural causes, and Bassett was still alive. The matter was committed to a secret hearing. Topcliffe's rash tongue there brought him into prison for contempt of court (making accusations against the judges), but not for conspiring to kill men to force an inheritance. Topcliffe prevailed on his claim for payment: His final days were spent at Padley Hall, which he acquired (though not permanently) through his Fitzherbert persecution.

The news of Bassett and Fitzherbert was recounted to the exiles.[30] The treacherous Fitzherbert was in the Fleet prison. Topcliffe openly gave out speeches in Parliament deeply touching Bassett "as if he were a receiver of priests and had intelligence with some on the other side of the sea, whereupon he [Bassett] has made complaint to some of the Lords but Topcliffe says he will prove it." The letter also reported the executions of two Separatists (Puritans) at the insistence of the Anglican bishops to show their displeasure at the House of Commons for not supporting a strong anti-recusant bill.

A New Lesson

From about mid–March to early June 1593 Sterrell was in great need of money and support. Sterrell wrote Phelippes "I hoped to have heard from you with some supply where

I stand in need, and this plague has driven all my friends from London that I cannot receive my own."[31] Another told Phelippes that it was necessary that order be taken for a certain stipend in order for them to continue.[32] Sterrell mysteriously added that he was planning some new course of action, telling Phelippes: "I must turn to a new lesson, which I will make known to you at meeting...." Sterrell must have met with Phelippes and told him what he meant by "a new lesson." Phelippes promised Sterrell that Essex would provide regular support for Sterrell. Sterrell thanks Phelippes "for the hope you put me in because my expenses are great and my money little."[33]

The "new lesson" was that Sterrell intended to study law. He had "provided a chamber in New Inn, the fine for my chamber for 2i years and for such things as are in it comes to 14£ and 4 marks by the year." New Inn was the Inn of Chancery under the control of the Middle Temple. Sterrell's younger brother had read law at New Inn and had just been admitted to the Middle Temple, on January 23, 1593.[34] Sterrell made no references to his brother in his surviving letters until after his brother's death many years later. The absence of his brother—with whom he had a warm and loving relationship—from his letters is another indication of Sterrell's passion for secrecy.

Sterrell renewed the invitation to Phelippes to dine with Worcester and Sterrell. Worcester, he said, wanted to make acquaintance with Francis Bacon through Phelippes. Whether the dinner of Phelippes, Sterrell, Bacon and Worcester occurred cannot be determined, but it is interesting to contemplate the first meeting of Worcester who would rise to Privy Councilor, Master of the Horse and later Lord Privy Seal and Bacon who would rise to Attorney General, Privy Councillor, Lord Chancellor, Baron Verulam and Viscount St. Alban. Yet tensions were growing between Sterrell and Worcester. The fact that Sterrell was enrolling at New Inn indicated this. Sterrell complained to Phelippes that Worcester "continues towards me all one; the Earl [of Essex] has not countenanced me with his good word to him, wherein he shows me small favor." The sense of this is that Worcester's treatment of him has not improved and the failure of Essex to send Worcester good word of Sterrell has not helped matters.

Exime Me Hisce Malis—*Sterrell and Marlowe*

Sterrell's relationship with Worcester was ruptured in March 1593.[35] Sterrell was growing desperate that Essex take some order for his well-being, "for every hour with me here is worse than other, *coniectum oculorum ferre non possum*" ("I cannot bear the gaze of [people's] eyes).[36] Something had happened to make Worcester and his household treat Sterrell with suspicion or as shameful. A stream of turgid English and Latin phrases poured from Sterrell reflecting his hurt and indignation:

> And to assure me of their good will I am not allowed Whitbred. Such a jest in an ale house were very pretty. It is a world to see how men's minds can vary not long since I was trusted with the very secrets of the inward man, now I am not worthy a half-penny whitt loaf. In lent last he would not leave [me?] for never any a child he had, this lent he is with child with my absence. *Tanti casua humana rotant*.[37] ["So fast revolve the accidents of human affairs"] This unkind fickleness hath in it neither wit nor good nature, but I will deal honestly, even *propter honestum* ["for the sake of uprightness"]. What so ever I know I have forgotten. I promised faith and faithfully I have dealt and ever will. Let god requite the wrong. In the meantime good sir as you ever have favored me, as I intend all faith to you even such as my Lord hath found and is not worthy of, even so endeavor I beseech you to help, *exime me hisce malis* ["deliver me

from these evils"], a more grateful man shall never be, although more able to show it then. I thus *me totum tibi committo* ["I commit my whole self to you."]

    Yours ever for I have nothing but myself to give. W: Sterrell.

More letters rapidly follow in which Sterrell makes clear that he and Worcester are maintaining an uneasy cordiality but that Sterrell is definitely parting from Worcester at the end of Parliament. He pleads with Phelippes to secure some definite allowance from Essex. He vents his unhappiness at his treatment from Worcester, but he does not want Worcester to learn of this.[38]

Within a short time Sterrell again wrote: "If the Earl [Essex] would make me some allowance then I might stay in London. If he do not I must shift for my Lord is resolute in his opinion. I may stay with him but I am like to have nothing."[39] Phelippes must have informed Sterrell that he had spoken on his behalf with Essex, for another letter thanks Phelippes and again complains of Worcester's treatment.[40] He was now, he said, as a voluntary follower with Worcester, "neither in wages nor at command." The small employments wherein the Earl of Essex had used him had saved Worcester £20 which Sterrell should have had for the whole year but now had nothing. Although Worcester had promised to provide feed for Sterrell's horse, Sterrell now had to provide for himself and also had to dismiss his man servant: "these indignities I bear, perforce, *quia dominus opus habet* [like a slave who is made free owes service to his master]." He expected that when Essex sent him support he would be revived, but in the meantime he was "out of heart...."

The day of paying for his chamber at New Inn arrived, and Sterrell seems never to have gotten the money he needed. He hoped that Phelippes would fulfill his promise to provide some money and he also hoped "to take such a course to live as I will not grow much chargeable to the Earl [of Essex]. When my chamber is taken and furnished, I will endeavor to live of my self, because I may make some suit to the Earl hereafter for some things of worth."[41] The refusal of Worcester to pay Sterrell the stipend he had promised to pay only three months earlier also upset Sterrell. He complained that Worcester "has made leap year[42] with me, accounting me as none of his, but he has sent me no discharge—only this much he signified, that he was resolved to go into the country, which he thought was no good course for me, but yet if I would come at any time I should be welcome."[43]

As the day of Worcester's departure from London approached, Sterrell pleaded to Phelippes for money and attributed his loss of employment with Worcester to Essex's failure to speak to Worcester on Sterrell's behalf. On Tuesday, probably the Tuesday the Parliament ended, April 10, 1593, Sterrell wrote that Worcester was leaving on Friday and planned to follow the Court (i.e., accompany the queen on her progresses).[44] Worcester had no use for Sterrell "so we part for certain which had the Earl [of Essex] vouchsafed his good word in my behalf I verily think we should not have done." Sterrell was now alienated from both Worcester and Essex. He began looking for work with some other nobleman as a secretary.[45] Sterrell was reluctant to make claim directly to Essex. He knew well the need for a powerful patron, as Lord Burghley had counseled his own son in his "Precepts": "Be sure ever to keep some great man thy friend ... for otherwise in this ambitious age thou mayest remain like a hop without a pole, live in obscurity, and be made a football for every insulting companion to spurn at."

When Friday arrived, Worcester had delayed his departure one more day and Sterrell wrote another desperate letter to Phelippes.[46] He had to leave now and was "driven to stick to myself." He was in immediate want of money and prayed for Phelippes to give him what was due. Even the courier Paynter refused to come.

Sterrell must have been in personal peril for a time, suspected of treason. His letter of January 2 to Phelippes indicated some members of the Privy Council had apparently called his activities into question. The *provocateur* John Daniell is the likely source of the suspicions. Cloudsley thought that Sterrell was working for the fugitives and spying upon the English. Sterrell admitted to the Catholics overseas what his role for Essex was.[47] This in turn called into question his loyalty to the queen. Sterrell had taken steps to counteract this impression that Cloudsley had conveyed to others.

A report from Richard Verstegan to Robert Persons, dated April 30, 1593, recounted Sterrell's troubles: "I send herewith also a letter sent unto me from my cousin [close friend], Thomas Fitzherbert, whose case seems unto me to be very hard. I perceive by intelligence from a friend in 25 [England] who is of this country [Flanders] that my cousin has employed one there [in England] about some special service, and has been at charges for the same; but the party is taken for being 225 [Catholic] yet hopes for liberty, and (as I am informed) does hold on his resolution, and will do his business so soon as he shall be free; and by sundry letters that I have seen I do deem him to be an honest man, and that he will be as good as his word."[48] Verstegan's letter surely concerns Sterrell, and it would indicate that Sterrell had been charged and deprived of his liberty. Verstegan's assessment of William Sterrell is all the more remarkable as Sterrell had been over to the Low Countries ostensibly as a spy for the Earl of Essex. It demonstrates that the Catholic exiles placed a great deal of trust in Sterrell.

Sterrell's difficulties were such that he was "like a man out of my senses, for that I hear nothing."[49] He was deeply troubled that he has not heard from two men: Thomas Ferrers of the Merchant Adventurers in Middelburg and Francis Harvey, a merchant in Middelburg and a member of the Parliament of 1593 (and four earlier Parliaments). Francis Harvey lived in Middelburg for several years and Sterrell told one of his Antwerp correspondents to send mail to Sterrell through Francis Harvey "who knows me to be the Earl of Essex's man."[50] Sterrell must have looked to Harvey and Ferrers to support assertions concerning his activities in Middelburg in the spring and summer of 1592.[51]

Another figure who was "at charges" for spying in the Low Countries in April 1593, who was in trouble with the Privy Council, and who had been deprived of his liberty was the poet and playwright Christopher Marlowe. A Cambridge MA, his background was similar to Sterrell's. It has been suggested that Marlowe may well have been working for the Catholic cause in the early 1590s.[52] His *Massacre at Paris* and *Edward II* are described as "Catholic propaganda."[53] But there is no reason to think he had any connection to Thomas Fitzherbert or was the subject of Verstegan's letter. Marlowe had been arrested in Flushing in January 1592 and sent back to London. He was up again on charges early in 1593 and was interrogated before members of the Privy Council May 20, 1593. On May 30, 1593, he was stabbed to death at an inn at Deptford in the company of three men: Robert Poley, Ingram Frizer and Nicholas Skeres. Poley was an agent of Robert Cecil at this time and later. Poley was one of the chief *provocateurs* against Anthony Babington in 1586.[54]

Both Sterrell and Marlowe were subjects of the Privy Council's scrutiny in April and May 1593 and for the same reasons: their activities in the Low Countries. The two men— so close in age and background and experiences—were surely not ignorant of one another and their mutual plights. When Sterrell, a year after Marlowe's homicide, called Poley the "vilest spy that ever was," he perhaps had Marlowe's death in mind. Worcester, Sterrell's patron, was not a member of the Privy Council until 1601. He was in no position to protect Sterrell, and it was prudent to distance himself from Sterrell. The man for whom Sterrell had been working, the Earl of Essex, was promoted to the Council only on February 25, 1593, after Sterrell's problems with the Council had begun. Essex was preoccupied with the Parliament until its end in April and with his promotion of the candidacy of Francis Bacon for Attorney General. He had ignored Sterrell's pleas for help through Phelippes up to that time, and Sterrell was reluctant to contact Essex directly. But Essex could be fiercely loyal to the people who worked with him, and he admired the well-educated. So he may well have intervened for Sterrell at the crucial time around May or early June 1593 when Sterrell was most desperate. And Essex had need of Sterrell's talents.

Exactly how Sterrell's and Marlowe's fates were connected in May 1593 is probably unknowable. Poley is probably the key figure, and the rivalry between Cecil and Essex is at the heart of the matter. Despite Skeres' employment with Essex, Poley was a Cecil agent and he may well have gotten Skeres to work with him to expose Marlowe's activities. Perhaps Marlowe was being importuned to give evidence against Sterrell and his refusal resulted in the outburst at Deptford. Though conjectural, this is as good an explanation as any other that has been advanced, and it becomes more persuasive when we examine a possible mutual connection to Arbella Stuart shortly.

Despite the queen's distaste and the general suspicion of Sterrell in the spring, 1593, within a short time after the killing of Marlowe, Sterrell was again working for Essex on intelligence and for Worcester. This was a dramatic turn-around, involving the confidence of two of the most influential earls of England. A Spanish exile was the instrument of Sterrell's rehabilitation.

The Spanish Defector, Don Antonio Perez, aka Raphael Peregrino

Sterrell continued to importune Phelippes in early June 1593.[55] He feared that a courier had lost some important letters. Sterrell complains he no longer has a horse but will buy one as soon as he can. He cannot come to see Phelippes without a horse because he is not in London. He is at Gains Park, Epping, and this same location is the address of a letter a month later from Phelippes to Sterrell. Then the letters and the complaints stop. Only a year later Sterrell reported his worth as being more than £800, quite a substantial sum of money in 1594 when a successful professor was paid no more than £40 per year. Why the great turn in fortune?

Gains Park, Epping is the answer to Sterrell's return to grace. In early June 1593 Essex was taking under his protection a Spanish fugitive, Don Antonio Perez. Essex was to meet with him and the French envoys coming from Essex's friend, the French King, Henry IV. Sterrell's presence at Gains Park in June 1593 allowed him to interact with the "peregrinate" Don Antonio. The estate belonged to Sir William Fitzwilliam, Lord Lieutenant or Deputy of Ireland.[56] That Essex received Antonio Perez at Gains Park in June and July 1593 may have been due to associations of Sir William Fitzwilliam with the Bacon family or with

Essex's wife. Sir William was cousin to Ann Bacon, the mother of Anthony and Francis Bacon.[57] Francis or Anthony Bacon could have arranged for Sterrell to stay at Gains Park while awaiting more favorable financial circumstances. Sterrell no doubt importuned Bacon for support, just as he sought assistance from Phelippes and Essex. Bacon had nearly as great a role in recruiting Sterrell as Phelippes. Bacon had smoothed over difficulties between Sterrell and Essex when Sterrell returned from the Low Countries eight months earlier.

The diplomatic undertaking in June and July 1593 was at an exceptionally important time for Essex and Francis Bacon. Essex had just been made a member of the Privy Council. He was pressing the queen to have Francis Bacon appointed Attorney General of England, while Essex's principal rival, Robert Cecil, was striving to have Edward Coke named to that powerful office. Essex and Cecil knew that control of the Attorney General position and of an intelligence network were twin components of political power. Upon becoming a Privy Councillor, Essex wrote Anthony Bacon how important their young intelligence service, especially as it concerned Catholic affairs overseas, was for Essex's future and their relations with the queen.[58]

The project of Anthony Bacon and Essex for the recruitment of Don Antonio Perez was bearing fruit. Formerly Secretary of State for King Philip II, Perez was an intriguer of the first order. But when he engineered the assassination of a rival who might expose his misdeeds he was arrested by King Philip and imprisoned. After eleven years, Perez escaped Madrid, eventually attaching himself to the French King, Henry IV. The flamboyant Perez had a way of making a nuisance of himself, and Henry thought it good for Perez to go to England for matters of state. Henry appointed Perez as a special envoy to make known his planned conversion from Protestant to Catholic for reasons of national unity (Paris is worth a mass, in his famous declaration of July 1593). For Elizabeth to welcome Perez into London was most awkward. A traitor to his own sovereign, Perez was not supposed to be protected by another sovereign. Lest she encourage treason to sovereigns, Elizabeth could not personally take in Perez. Yet if Essex were to welcome Don Antonio, this would be acceptable. It would be a private reception, not an act of the state. Such formalism is the stuff of diplomacy. And for the frugal Elizabeth, Essex would bear Perez's extravagant expenses!

The value of Perez to the English was two-fold. He knew the Spanish governmental apparatus and the personalities to give guidance to the English policy makers—such as Essex, whom the queen was tapping for increased intelligence work. His second value was for propaganda. He could paint the Spanish in an unfavorable light.

The use of Perez for propaganda had begun in 1591 or 1592. Just as the Catholic exiles made use of false imprints to hide the place of printing, so, too, did the English engage in misleading publications. Lord Burghley first employed this device in the 1580s. Now Essex assumed the role of sponsoring deceptive imprinting. He (or his agent) arranged for the second edition of Don Antonio Perez's *Pedaços de Historia, ô Relaçiones*. The book was first printed at Pau, France, in 1591, paid for by Princess Catherine de Bourbon, King Henry's sister. The second edition, sponsored by Essex, was enlarged and identified itself as made at the end of September 1592. The printer was Richard Field of London. The book was printed in London but the title page said it was impressed in Leon. It was dedicated to the Earl of Essex. The date at which the book was actually printed is uncertain, no later than 1594, but it appears likely that arrangements were already made with Richard Field for Perez's book when Field registered Shakespeare's *Venus and Adonis*.[59] Richard Field had other Spanish books that were surreptitious, i.e., gave no place of publication but they included a Spanish version of his name, Ricardo del Campo.[60]

On June 1, 1593, the Earl of Essex entertained the French Ambassador, Prégent de La Fin, Vidâme of Chartres, and his father Jean de La Fin, at Gains Park Hall, Epping. Antonio Perez was with them, and he remained at Gains Park while the Frenchmen went on to the Court.[61] Phelippes sent Sterrell a proposed letter of intelligence to the Low Countries, in which Sterrell was to describe the information arising from Perez as Perez awaited the Ambassador's return. Sterrell was at Gains Park to work with Antonio Perez. An undated (calendared as "June? 1593") set of notes by Essex to Thomas Phelippes most likely describe the function that William Sterrell was to serve with Perez for Essex[62]:

> The informer [Sterrell] must be extraordinarily careful in getting all the news he can of Antonio Perez, what is the end of his coming hither and how he has been dealt with. He may advertise that Perez did not come the first or second time when the Vidame had audience, and that when he did, he came privately, and kissed the Queen's hand, but had no great speech with her; and that he has had two private conferences with her since....

These notes show that Sterrell was (1) to get information from (i.e., debrief) Perez, and (2) pass on intelligence (advertise) about Perez for foreign consumption. This was an important intelligence role for Sterrell. There was a hint of this role in Sterrell's letter to Phelippes in late April 1593: "When the Earl sends me as you promise, I shall be revived." Phelippes and Essex must have decided to use Sterrell to work with Antonio Perez when Perez first arrived in London in April 1593, and Essex, the Bacon brothers, and Phelippes arranged for the undertaking to take place in Gains Park. William Sterrell was indeed "revived."

Why would Essex want Sterrell and Phelippes to pass on information about Perez? Sterrell was Essex's principal source of information about the English fugitives in the Low Countries. Essex understood that to receive intelligence, one must give intelligence. As he wrote to an agent, possibly William Sterrell himself[63]:

> I would wish you to make use of your acquaintance and conversation in the places where you live, which you shall easily do if you choose such company as do know much, and have advertisements from many parts. And, also, if you can enter into a cause of traffique with them, giving the news of these parts of England, Ireland, and Scotland, *for payment of those of all parts of France and the frontiers*. For the manner of writing your advertisements, I will leave you to yourself, only advertising you, *that at the first you strive rather to write all than to be scant*, for upon new directions you may every day cut off when I have made you know what I think superfluous. Also strive to know *res gesta magis quam consilia* [the thing done rather than the counsels]; not but that I think the latter of greater use, but that I think the former falls better into your course, and will be to be gotten, where, if you show yourself so curious of the other, you shall be paid with smoke.

In keeping with Essex's instructions that encouraged Sterrell to advertise abroad, Phelippes and Sterrell wrote Thomas Fitzherbert of recent developments in early July 1593.[64] Antonio Perez was awaiting the French Ambassador's return from the queen. From Perez they were thoroughly informed of the King of Spain's estate (i.e., condition) and find he is "weakest at home." Sterrell also informed Fitzherbert that Anthony Standen, who had long known Fitzherbert, had been drawn over by Anthony Bacon and was now being maintained by the Earl of Essex. As recounted earlier, Standen had become a double agent for Walsingham after the execution of Mary Queen of Scots. Walsingham's death left him in a quandary, and for a time he was lodged in a French prison until Anthony Bacon arranged for his extrication.

Perez's book was brought out in Spanish and shipped overseas for propaganda. The book purported to be written by "Raphael Peregrino" about Antonio Perez, but "Raphael

Peregrino" was simply the *nom-de-plume* of Perez. "Peregrino" signifies a traveler or wanderer. The collector of Perez's many letters concluded that "The customs clearance of the London edition of the *Relaciones*, which Field printed for exportation, is likely to have been effected by Phelippes."[65] Certainly Sterrell and Phelippes was sending the books abroad, for one of his secret correspondents, "William Nicols," directed him in late 1594: "Fail not to send me those books when they come forth against the King of Spain, written by Antonio Perez...."[66] A few weeks later, "Nicols" urged: "I pray you use all diligent means to get so many as you can of those Spanish books that Anthony Perez hath made. They shall be well paid for and distributed here in good sort to the disgrace of whom it toucheth. If you can send them by the hundreds they shall be well spread abroad and paid for. Mr. Gynger's man doth desire it; I mean his secretary. Therefore I am the more earnest to trouble you in this matter."[67] These two letters were sent to Peter Hallins, one of the personas created by Sterrell and Phelippes. "Nicols" was Hugh Owen (in collaboration with Richard Verstegan). The name "Mr. Gynger" is deciphered (by Phelippes) as the King of Spain. The second letter indicates that Mr. Gynger's man—the Spanish King's man—wants hundreds of the Perez books, perhaps to demonstrate the perfidy of Perez and to expose those whom the book revealed to be friends of Perez.

12

Who Can Protect the Queen?
A Rivalry over Assassins

Dr. Lopez, John Daniell et al.

Sterrell survived the perils of his Low Countries mission but 1594 held further troubles for him and even more for Phelippes, soon a prisoner. Sterrell's name was raised in treason prosecutions that riveted the English Court and London. The prosecutions grew out of the rivalry between the Essex and Cecil factions as they tried to outdo one another in saving the queen from foreign assassination plots. The immediate prize each sought was the post of Attorney General. The candidate of Essex was Francis Bacon, of the Cecils, Edward Coke.[1]

Bacon, a younger son of Elizabeth's Lord Keeper, was a trusted advisor of Essex, and Francis's brother Anthony headed Essex's intelligence network. Essex did his best to advance Bacon, declaring to Robert Cecil that "it is the Attorneyship that I must have for Francis, and in that I will spend all my power, mine authority, and amity, and with tooth and nails defend and procure the same for him against whomsoever...."[2] The "tooth and nails" (and heads) were those of alleged assassins as Essex and Cecil each sought to demonstrate he was the better man to ferret out and prosecute plots, preferably involving the dreaded Jesuits, against Queen Elizabeth.

Essex managed an intelligence coup when he charged the queen's physician, Dr. Roderigo Lopez, in January 1594 with a plot to assassinate his royal patient. Lopez was a Jew of Portuguese background and is speculated to be the inspiration for Marlowe's *Jew of Malta* and Shakespeare's Shylock in *Merchant of Venice*. Initially, the Cecils ridiculed Essex's claim and Queen Elizabeth was furious at the "rash and temerarious" Essex.[3] Two days after the queen's scolding, Essex came forth claiming new evidence of Lopez's plotting.[4] There followed a full scale investigation, a "sweet moment" for Essex.[5]

Not to be outdone, the Cecil faction produced another plot originating in Brussels to kill the queen. A key role was played by one *provocateur*, John Daniell, whom the Cecil side brought forward. His tales of treachery emanating from English fugitives were seemingly confirmed by another informer, William Polwhele, and two of Daniell's followers, John Annias and Hugh Cahill, as well as Patrick Collen.[6] The Cecilians produced a meta-plot that advanced through a series of plots employing various actors. The principal parties to the conspiracy were alleged to be King Philip's Secretary in Brussels, Stephano Ibarra, in league with English Catholic exiles: Sir William Stanley, Jaques Franceschi, Fr. William Holt, Hugh Owen, Thomas Throckmorton, Dr. William Gifford, Dr. Thomas Worthington, Charles Paget, Edward Garret, and Michael Moody.[7] Out of all this flurry of accusations only Collen was tried and executed. Three others later were interrogated as conspirators, Edmund Yorke, Richard Williams and Henry Young and the first two of these were executed. The initial allegations of this Ibarra meta-plot were from the Cecil informant, John Daniell.

Curiously, however, Daniell's evidence of a conspiracy related back to May 1592 when (he claimed) two priests (Frs. Archer and Holt) along with Sir William Stanley and Hugh Owen had recruited him to find an Irishman to kill the queen. Stanley and Owen had rescued Sterrell from the custody of Count Mondragon in Antwerp that same month. Daniell had sought out Hugh Cahill, with the understanding that Cahill was not actually to follow through on a promise to murder the queen. Daniell had then written letters to the Earl of Ormond and to Burghley which were dispatched from Calais by an English agent there, Thomas Jeffrey.[8] Six weeks later a passport from Burghley came to Daniell, and Daniell arrived in England August 24, 1592. In September Daniell reported to the Lord Treasurer. He provided Burghley with a list of names of Englishmen and Irishmen in the Low Countries, with their descriptions, that could be used to capture them upon entering England. Perhaps Sterrell was among them. Cahill came to Calais to await his passport and met with the priests Archer, Henry Walpole, and John Scudamore/Skidmore. Cahill entered England with Skidmore. Daniell informed Burghley of Cahill's arrival, and took Cahill to Burghley's house in the Strand but he was ill. Three or four days later Justice Young examined Cahill and placed him in Daniell's charge, rather than in prison. Cahill stated that on "arriving in London, [he] did his duty, as the Lord Treasurer knows." His "duty" meant that he had denounced Fr. Scudamore as seeking the queen's death.[9] Cahill had remained in Daniell's charge from that time (about November 1592) to the time of their later examinations and statements, in February 1594. Thus Daniell's and Cahill's initial allegations of a plot, made to the Cecil faction, long preceded the use made of the reports in 1594.

The statements of William Polwhele and John Annias begin a few weeks before the 1594 statements of Cahill and Daniell.[10] Polwhele's initial confession of his own promise to kill the queen attributed the plan to Jaques Franceschi (with approval by Fr. Sherwood). He also implied a Richard Hesketh had been sent into England with such a purpose. Only later did he name a William Tompson and Patrick Collen (also spelled Cullen, O'Collen and Guillone) who were to be assassins.[11] Like John Daniell, Polwhele reported to Thomas Jeffrey at Calais to get a passport to enter England to confes a conspiracy. That is to say, William Polwhele was ostensibly a voluntary informer, using the report of a plot to gain passage back into England, rather than a fugitive who was captured and then confessed.

John Annias's return to England was the assistance of John Daniell was more pressing, for he had just killed a Spaniard.[12] Daniell was in a position to aid Annias with the government's attorneys. Annias's memory improves through successive confessions and he brings Polewhele back into conspiracy against the queen. In one statement Annias apparently said he knew Collen but not Polwhele[13] but in another he says that six weeks earlier he had been with Polwhele at Calais.[14] Still later he confesses that he was "told by Polwhele that Collen was gone over to kill the queen."[15] Patrick Collen's confessions in February admitted to a plot, directed by Jaques Franceschi and approved by Fr. Holt, to kill Antonio Perez.[16] He was executed, however, for plotting to kill the queen.

The statements of Polwhele and Annias subtly called the Earl of Essex into question, noting for example that "Annias had a jewel which he was to have presented to the Earl of Essex at his coming into England, meaning to have become his Lordship's man."[17] When Polwhele invoked the name of Sterrell in his confession, Sterrell was thought of as Essex's man. Jaques, Polwhele alleged, had told Polwhele how to murder the queen.[18] Jaques asked him if he had friends at Court to help him escape; Polwhele said he had two: "Mr. Fortescue and Mr. Sterrell." Jaques gave further instructions as to what Polwhele should do if Fortescue or Sterrell would do not help him. It is notable that Polwhele knew Sterrell was "at Court" and that he, not Jaques, advanced Sterrell's name.

On February 21, 1594, Hugh Cahill confessed that in May 1592 he was in Brussels with John Daniell and that Daniell, under a pledge of secrecy, had told him that Sir William Stanley, Fr. Holt, and Hugh Owen wanted him to kill the queen.[19] He was then taken by Daniell to meet with each of these three, and they had told him he would be a saint if he killed the queen and had promised him money. John Daniell afterwards brought money to Cahill and told him that it was from a priest. He also said that he met with a Jesuit, Fr. Archer. It was always important to implicate a Jesuit in a plot.

The day of Cahill's confession, John Daniell made a similar "declaration."[20] He had brought Cahill to England on Lord Burghley's passport, obtained through Thomas Jeffrey. Daniell gave a more complete declaration a few days later, describing a series of meetings in May 1592 with Fr. Archer, Fr. Holt, and then with Stanley and Owen.[21] He gave very precise dates, quite surprising for a statement made nineteen months after the meetings, and precise descriptions of conversations. Daniell persuaded Hugh Cahill to undertake the murder of the queen on behalf of the others but also got Cahill to promise never to put the plan into execution. He received money from the priests and then went to Calais, where he made contact with Thomas Jeffrey.

These two statements were not the first declaration of Daniell in this month. On February 6, John Daniell went to Justice Richard Young and reported a plot to burn the Tower of London. Another plot alleged by Daniell was that someone was to burn the ships at Billingates. Yet another was to set the inns and woodstocks in London on fire.[22] Daniell evidently made this report to Justice Young the day after Annias had similarly described plans for setting fire the queen's ships.[23] Two days after Daniell's declaration, Annias's memory again improved.[24] His new testimony matched Daniell's February 6 declaration. Why had he not stated this in his earlier confessions? He continued: "When before Council, had no memory, and never having been examined before, was afraid; the same when before the Lord Admiral and Lord Treasurer, and when he delivered his answer to the articles; it is hard to deal with princes, except a man be well assured in what he says."[25] More likely, the statements of Daniell and Annias were being coordinated by the queen's prosecutors.

Although it is clear that Polwhele knew Annias and Collen, it seems unlikely he was initially acting in concert with Annias, Daniell and Cahill. Rather, the timing of his return to England coincided usefully with the desire of the Cecil faction to seize upon a threat to the queen. Statements from these five individuals (Polwhele, Annias, Collen, Daniell and Cahill) against various Englishmen in the Low Countries were rolled into a blurred conspiracy that Secretary Ibarra was said to head; later Yorke, Williams and Young were subsumed into this conspiracy and Polwhele, Annias, Daniell and Cahill could all be displaced from public view; no severe action was to be taken against them for capital crimes.

Doubts about Polwhele arise from the fact that he initially went to Rheims to study and only became a soldier under Stanley and Jaques after some months as a student.[26] Daniell and Cahill evidently had already departed from the Low Countries by the time Polwhele joined with Sir William Stanley. Annias, Collen, Daniell and Cahill all appear to have been Irish soldiers of a different class. Polwhele surely was already an agent of the English, cut from the same cloth as George Gifford a decade earlier.

The confessions together suggest that there was in fact an assassination planned from Spain and the Low Countries. However, the target was not Queen Elizabeth but the Spanish turncoat, Antonio Perez. Patrick Collen confessed to an assassination plot against Perez.[27] Polwhele seems to have given evidence that Tompson or Collen was to have killed the Spaniard.[28] In one of his examinations Annias testified that Captain Oliver Eustace [another Irishman under Stanley] had received a request from Richard Stanihurst in Spain, to attend Ibarra, who could acquaint him with an intended enterprise for killing Antonio Perez in England.[29] Marginal notes made by the government interrogators were to the effect that Collen's goal was really to kill the queen and the pretence that he was to kill Perez was only a "shadow." Annias's testimony came to conform to this line, based (he said) on what Oliver Eustace had told him, that the plot "could not be upon Ant. Perez, who had already done his worst."[30] Polwhele reinforced this by reporting that he "often heard Jaques say that he did not esteem the killing of Perez, who has done all the hurt he can…."[31] A captured priest named Robert Barrowes (Barwise), who was to serve as an informant off and on for the government for years, gave testimony in March 1594 that John Annias had told him as recently as the past Christmas at St. Omer that he was going into England to kill Antonio Perez.[32] It was far more useful to the Cecil faction to treat Collen as having the queen as his target, not Perez. He was executed almost immediately after arraignment, months before Dr. Lopez.

Essex used the Lopez trial to try to advance Bacon by commissioning Bacon to prepare the government's case for proceeding against Lopez. Bacon drew up an account of the trial. The case against Dr. Lopez developed through the examinations by the government prosecutors of Estevan Ferrera de Gama, Emanuel Louis Tinoco, and Lopez himself. However, at the same time, Polwhele, Collen, Annias Daniell, and Cahill were all making their declarations. Coke as Solicitor-General was able to gain control of the Lopez proceedings. His sponsor, Robert Cecil, wrote the queen (through Thomas Windebank) on the afternoon of the Lopez trial, apparently with reference to Attorney General Egerton and Coke, that "never was prince's cause so triumphantly handled by such a couple of servants as gave the evidence."[33]

The role of Essex as a primary source of intelligence about plots against the queen was subtly undermined by the rash of confessions that did not derive from Essex's network. In fact, the evidence seemed to indicate that Essex was being used to advance the plots. Even from Brussels, Hugh Owen could discern that the evidence given in January and February 1594 was being used to taint Essex. The appointment of Edward Coke as Attorney General was made on April 10, 1594. Coke and Cecil cemented an alliance that would last until Cecil's death. Coke would marry Cecil's wealthy niece (26 years his junior) and be promoted to Chief Justice of the Court of Common Pleas with the support of Cecil.

The multiple investigations of 1594 were linked together in a letter of August 1595 from John Daniell to Robert Cecil.[34] Pleading for money, Daniell wrote Cecil that after obtaining a passport from Lord Burghley, "I came hither and discovered my intelligences, which appear true by the coming over of Polwhele, Guillone [Irish spelling of Collen], York, and Williams." He continued:

> Upon the arraignment of Guillone [Collen] both I and Hugh Cahill came, by command of the queen's attorney and solicitor [Edward Coke], to discover the wicked practices attempted against her person and country, by her foreign enemies and unnatural subjects beyond seas, and were ready to avouch the like at the arraignment of Dr. Lopez, if occasion had served. I have forsaken a pension of 5 s. a day beyond the seas, besides the loss of 800 crowns and hazarding my life. At the arraignment of York, Williams, and Southwell, the Jesuit, I was nominated the first discoverer of the late practices intended against Her Majesty and her dominions.

Daniell said that for three years he had pressed his suit for reward (i.e., since coming over in August 1592) and was near to perishing for lack of food. He offered his continued service and added that he, his wife and their nine children prayed for Cecil. Evidently Cecil finally secured a pension to Daniell; he wrote another letter to thank Cecil for his aid in getting the queen to grant him a pension of 40 pounds.[35]

Annias continued as a prisoner in the Tower for a time. While in the Tower, he volunteered to spy on Catholics and to steal the Spanish King's books in Brussels that contained the names of all Englishmen who might be of service to the Spanish.[36] He reported to the Council that the "cause of my faults was concerning religion," not mentioning that he had confessed multiple times to knowledge of plots against the queen. Eventually he was freed to spy for Robert Cecil. According to his own story, he was required to try to poison Florence MacCarthy in Ireland. For so stating, Robert Cecil demanded that Annias be hanged, which was carried out in November 1602.[37]

As for Polwhele, he is surely the Captain William Polwhele who entered the service of Sir Richard Leveson and obligingly married Sir Richard's notorious mistress, Mary Fitton, in 1606. Mary Fitton, sometimes alleged to be the "dark lady" of Shakespeare's sonnets, had borne an illegitimate son to William Herbert, Earl of Pembroke, and two illegitimate children to Sir Richard Leveson. It is most likely that Polwhele was a government agent when he went over to Rheims in 1592 and was serving the ends of Attorney General Thomas Egerton when he came forward in 1594 and testified. When Polwhele was examined on February 25, 1594, it was only by Egerton and Coke. A biographer of Mary Fitton has noted that she married Polwhele against "her parents' wishes, but with the powerful encouragement of the Egerton family...."[38]

Sterrell and the Prosecutions of 1594

It is notable that Polwhele and Daniell, not Sterrell, were the source of intelligence on conspiracies supposedly planned by Stanley, Holt, Jaques Franceschi, Sherwood and Owen. Sterrell had been among this group in the Low Countries at the same time as John Daniell and William Polwhele, yet he gave no evidence in the government's proceedings. This helps explain why the queen was very dissatisfied with Sterrell during this period, even after he had assisted Essex with Antonio Perez. These plottings were almost certainly fabrications by Polwhele, Daniell and Cahill. This is important in assessing whether there really were a number of plans to kill the queen emanating from the Catholic exiles in the Low Countries—as Robert Cecil and Edward Coke maintained.

The reference to Southwell by Daniell is especially telling. Fr. Robert Southwell had arrived in England in mid–1586 and had not left the country before his arrest in July 1592. Daniell had been out of the country for years prior to his coming back later in 1592. Daniell simply could not have had any direct evidence concerning Southwell, and yet the government of Cecil and Coke was using the allegations against Jesuits in the Low Countries to taint Southwell. As a Jesuit he was part of the meta-plot, they alleged.

Coke was in his first prosecutions as the newly appointed Attorney General and was determined to prove his mettle. His tactic in these trials, and for years thereafter, was to associate all Catholics he tried with a vast overseas conspiracy (usually involving Jesuits) to bring down the Protestant government of England by assassination of its temporal and spiritual head.[39]

Although John Daniell had come forward in mid–1592 with intelligence, and Cahill by December 1592, nothing was made of these until more than a year later. Sterrell was aware of Daniell's presence in London in late 1592 and 1593 and knew that Daniell was up to some mischief. On January 2, 1593, Sterrell had written to Phelippes about Daniell.[40] From the statements and confessions, it is clear that Daniell himself had initiated the plans to kill the queen, and perhaps this was done to provide himself with a basis for returning to England. Had he not come forward claiming to be a foil to a conspiracy, he himself would have been subject to prosecution for treason upon reentry into England, as had been Anthony Skinner and Richard Ayliffe. Daniell's 1595 statements concerning his role in the arraignment of Collen and readiness to give testimony in the proceedings of Lopez and Southwell would suggest that Cecil and Coke had Daniell ready as a witness in the meta-plot that they had conjured.

To her credit, the queen had her doubts about Daniell. Just as Dr. Lopez (of whom the queen was fond) was being tried, Thomas Windebank had approached the queen about providing money for certain Irishmen. She seemed willing to sign, he reported to Cecil, but then told him to write to Cecil "that no part of the money should be given to Daniell and another, whose name she had forgotten [most probably Cahill]...."[41]

The proceedings involving Polwhele, Annias, Daniell, Cahill, and Young, and the prosecutions/executions of Lopez, Tinoco, de Gama, Collen, Yorke, and Williams,[42] were part of an intense rivalry between Essex and Cecil for influence with Elizabeth and to advance their respective candidates for Attorney General, Francis Bacon and Edward Coke. Convictions were to be gotten at any cost, and the greatest cost seems to have been subornation of perjury through torture. The use of torture and perjured informers against Catholics during the reigns of Elizabeth and James are a sad chapter of English legal history and are indelible stains on the reputations of Bacon and Coke.

Richard Hesketh's Plot

The final word on the Polwhele, Annias, Collen, Daniell and Cahill investigations will come from Hugh Owen. But first must be recounted the recent execution of a man mentioned by Polwhele: Richard Hesketh, hanged on November 29, 1593. On his 1592 mission, Sterrell may have encountered Hesketh, then a soldier in Stanley's regiment. An enciphered message of June 13, 1592, by Sterrell ("Robinson") reported on activity in Lancashire. There was intelligence "between Strange and the Cardinal [Allen]," said the letter. Strange was Ferdinando Stanley, Lord Strange, soon to become the Fifth Earl of Derby upon the death of his father. Lord Strange, a patron of the arts and master of a company of actors, was a cousin of Sir William Stanley, and for Sir William, Strange was the leading candidate to replace Queen Elizabeth if she were to die. Strange's mother had descended from King Henry VII (as had Arbella Stuart). In 1591 Sir William Stanley had made a trip to Rome to confer with Cardinal Allen and others, and he promoted to them the possibility of replacing the queen with Lord Strange.[43]

Ferdinando Stanley's father (the 4th Earl of Derby) died, on September 25, 1593. That same day, Richard Hesketh appeared at the family estate of Lathom. He brought a letter with him that was then delivered to Lord Strange, now Earl. It was an invitation for Strange to be successor to Queen Elizabeth. No fool, Strange immediately suspected that he was being set up in the same way that Mary Stewart had been. He took Hesketh into his custody and rode to Queen Elizabeth to report the proposal. Within weeks Hesketh was executed.

The May 1594 Letter of Owen to Sterrell

What we know often cannot be separated from how we know it. A well-known intelligence device is the creation of documents that are placed carefully for "accidental discovery" by one's adversaries.[44] Although the letters of William Sterrell discussed for the period 1591–93 mostly came from the files of Phelippes seized in 1605, one letter—to Sterrell from Hugh Owen in May 1594—apparently fell into the government's hands by a carefully contrived "accident." The purpose of the letter was to counter statements and confessions of John Daniell, Hugh Cahill, Richard Hesketh, John Annias and William Polwhele that had touched upon Owen, "Robinson," and the Earl of Essex. The letter reached the government on a "mistaken" delivery to the wrong person.

The letter was contained in a packet addressed to "Mr Robinson in London" and delivered to the son of one John Robinson of St. Helen's parish in Cheapside. This Robinson took it to the Lord Mayor of London who, finding the letter inside addressed to "Mr Sterrell, London" and signed by "Hu: Owen," and aware that Hugh Owen was known as a practicer against the English state, took the packet to Burghley.[45] This is what Owen and Sterrell doubtless intended: for the letter itself says, with artful understatement, that the writer (Owen) has but "small acquaintance" with the recipient (Sterrell), they having met "but twice," once in Antwerp and the other time at the Spa. It proceeds to a series of protestations of Owen's innocence of recent plots against the state which had resulted in the execution of men (Hesketh and Collen) who were officially said to have implicated Owen in their crimes. But though the letter was clearly intended to reach and influence the queen's government, it was equally clearly written by Owen himself, whose acquaintance with Sterrell was by no means as small as he stated. Sterrell himself could safely be made a part of this ruse because he had been known for two years as an agent (often under the alias Robinson) of Essex in dealings with the Catholic exiles in the Low Countries.

In denying the statements of Hesketh, Annias, and Polwhele, and those of John Daniell and Hugh Cahill, Owen sought to clear his name and the names of Essex and "Robinson." Owen alludes to the fact that accusations in the proceedings have touched Essex's name and he is writing in part to clear Essex. He says that he knows Sterrell "wholly depend[s] on him" and he authorizes Sterrell to show his letter if it will give any contentment to Essex. Owen had learned that Hesketh had been asked if Essex would have taken part with the Earl of Derby (Lord Stanley) in a revolt. Hesketh had evidently answered that "one Robinson" had told Owen "that the said Earl of Essex meant to have the crown himself if he could." This would have implicated Sterrell ("Robinson") in promoting Essex as a potential claimant to the throne. Owen swore that such a conversation had never taken place. Owen acknowledged knowing John Daniell but asserted that Daniell's claims of Owen and Stanley seeking to have Daniell and Cahill kill the queen were entirely false. Daniell, he said, had accused him in the Low Countries of being a correspondent with the Privy Council in England. Owen noted that Daniell and Polwhele were brought to give testimony at the arraignment of Patrick Collen that Sir William Stanley, Owen and others had sent Collen to kill the queen. This, too, was false. The Council was being abused by "perjured Jacks." Daniell, he went on to say, had given to Burghley a list of men's names together with their descriptions, one of whom was John Annias, a great friend of Daniell. So, when Annias fled into England "for murdering & robbing a Spaniard who of trust had put himself into his hands" he was arrested because of Daniell's list.

Owen concluded his letter by saying that the Duke of Parma had frequently received similar information of plots against him but made no account of them. In a message clearly intended for the queen and her Council, Owen added that if the queen and Council similarly made no account of such fables and inventions, they would never unquiet themselves as they do, nor so easily permit false juries to cast away so many innocent men.

How would one get such a message to the queen and Council in a credible manner and at the same time make it appear that Owen and Sterrell had not been in correspondence with one another over the previous year? If Sterrell were to deliver such a letter to Essex to pass to the queen and Council, it would have been dismissed as self-serving. But what if Sterrell could arrange to have the letter go to the Council as if by accident? The probable identity of John Robinson suggests the connection.

The Lord Mayor's letter to Burghley identifies John Robinson as a "stapler" dwelling in St. Ellins—i.e., St. Helens, a parish within Bishopsgate Ward. A clue is found in Polwhele's statement that the friends of the Catholics at Court to whom he was to turn for escape and refuge were Mr. Fortescue and Mr. Sterrell. Sir John Fortescue was Master of the Wardrobe, and his nephew[46] was a Catholic assistant of his,[47] resident in the Blackfriar's Gatehouse[48] that served as a refuge for Catholic priests and laymen in London. Sir John Fortescue's steward was John Robinson, also an active Catholic who sent a son or sons to the Jesuit school at St. Omers, France.[49] The Catholic identity of this steward of Sir John Fortescue, his clandestine help to Catholics in hiding and his use of the Blackfriars' house as a refuge are nicely encapsulated in a letter of May 1599[50]:

> I am told that Dudley the priest (lately escaped out of the Marshalsea, as you have heard) doth yet remain in London. I hear he is in the Blackfriars in one Mr. Robinson's house who is steward to Sir John Foskewe [Fortescue]; his house is over against Sir John's door.

A steward of the Wardrobe may well have had a background as a stapler, a merchant in woolens.[51] Sterrell surely had the letter delivered to the son of John Robinson with the understanding it would be passed on to the Lord Mayor.

Sterrell again was brought into play to counter the fabricated claims of assassination plots. His counter-espionage role is delicate. Owen's trust of William Sterrell continues to grow in 1594 and soon Sterrell becomes the "general factor" of the Catholic English fugitives. Yet Sterrell was also trusted by some who were close to the English Privy Council and he was able at times to act as a go-between when it served the purposes of the English government. Others, such as Anthony Standen, engaged in similar functions. That Sterrell survived the prosecutions of 1594 is testament to his consummate skills as an intelligence operative.

Phelippes's Difficulties

Walsingham's expenses as English spymaster had left him heavily in debt. Phelippes no doubt aspired to the role played by his mentor and master, and his financial difficulties quickly pushed him into deep trouble with Lord Burghley, the Treasurer. The circumstances suggest that Phelippes failed to account for customs that were owed to the Crown. He landed in prison for his offences.

Richard Carmarthen was the Surveyor of the Port of London and in 1594 was undertaking reforms of the collection of customs. There was dissatisfaction with the way Phelippes handled his post. Carmarthen wrote Sir Robert Cecil that the queen had had a "hard accompt" of one prior customer and that "we find little better of Phillips [Phelippes]."[52] The Lord Treasurer, said Carmarthen, had taken order "that no more money shall come into his [Phelippes] hands." Carmarthen had dealt with Phelippes "to offer satisfaction in payment to her Majesty for this debt, which is 10,000*l*, which he hath promised me yesternight to do." Robert Cecil's father was much disquieted by this matter, according to Carmarthen, and it contributed to Lord Burghley's ill health. For years to come, Phelippes was to be financially crippled by the debt he incurred from Carmarthen's review of his Customs office accountings, and it probably embittered him towards the government and Robert Cecil. Though Phelippes pretended to pass intelligence to Cecil for many more years, Phelippes shifted his allegiance to the Catholics and the Low Countries, and they rewarded him generously, sometimes through Sterrell and sometimes through diplomatic officials.

13

The General Factor and Arbella Stewart

The General Factor

In the last two decades of Elizabeth's reign, the Catholic intelligencers abroad included Thomas Fitzherbert, Fr. Robert Persons, Hugh Owen, Richard Verstegan, Fr. William Baldwin, Richard Bayley, Richard Stanihurst, Sir Francis Englefield, Fr. Richard Sherwood and Cardinal Allen. Nearly all were Oxford men, and most of them had excellent, even exceptional, language skills. At various times they operated from the Low Countries: Brussels, Antwerp (Anvers) and nearby Liège; from France: Paris and Rouen; from Spain: Madrid and Vallodolid; and from Rome, Milan and Venice. In the 1590s and early 1600s, one important source of intelligence from England was the Jesuit Superior, Father Henry Garnet. The other was William Sterrell, together with his Protestant associate, Thomas Phelippes.

The Jesuit Superior in England, Garnet, commented on the difficulties of correspondence in September 1594. After expressing hope of hearing from Persons, Garnet warned: "Yet this I desire you to consider, that the safety of sending letters from hence as it now falleth out is greater than of receiving; and therefore it behooveth you to send with great wariness, for it were no small prejudice unto us if any letter of yours should miscarry, as I hear I know not what rumour one hath of late…."[1] Garnet was able to get some letters out safely, but had lately been constrained. Even so, Garnet was afraid even to tell Persons of the means of moving letters, out of fear the letter itself would be intercepted, thereby divulging their methods.[2]

The intense interest of the English government in the Jesuit packets of letters is underscored by the repeated torture of Fr. John Gerard to learn the details of conveyance. He was examined in April 1597 by commissioners from the queen who were among the most important law officials in England: William Waad (Secretary of the Privy Council), Edward Coke (Attorney General); Francis Bacon (Queen's counsel); Sir Richard Berkeley (Lieutenant of the Tower); and Thomas Fleming (Solicitor-General). Waad demanded: "Didn't you receive a packet [of letters] a short time ago and hand it over to so and so to give to Henry Garnet?"[3] Gerard would only acknowledge that if he had received letters, they dealt only with the dispatch of money to religious officials and students on the Continent. He received letters as "Standish," and he wrote with a feigned hand because he would bring no man to trouble.[4] When he refused to give more information on intelligence and the location of Fr. Henry Garnet, they produced a warrant authorizing his torture. He was obstinate, so the group conducted him to the torture chamber, and he was hung from the wall by manacles.

After a time, the commissioners left the torture to three or four robust men to attempt to break him. They could not.

The government's special interest in the movement of letters is also reflected in a report by Garnet of Gerard's torture. He wrote to the General of the Jesuits in June 1597 that Gerard "hath been thrice hanged up by the hands until he was almost dead and that in one day twice. The cause was (as I now understand perfectly) for to tell where his Superior was, and *by whom he had sent him letters which were delivered him from Fr. Persons*."[5] Gerard was surely protecting Sterrell. Yet Sterrell was so deep an agent that even Waad entrusted him to meet with Gerard in the hope of greater gains.

Establishing and maintaining communications channels was immensely important to the English Catholics, especially the Jesuits. If they could gain intelligence of government actions and the activities of their opponents, even better. How did Sterrell earn the trust and confidence of the group of Jesuits and lay Catholic exiles who came together as a successful intelligence network in the last decade of Elizabeth's reign? Thomas Fitzherbert was his most important means. In a letter from Dieppe, France, of April 1593 to "Robinson" (Sterrell), Fitzherbert promised to make Sterrell's ability known so that that Sterrell might take the part "of general factor if not for all in those parts yet at least for some of the principal as the Cardinall [Allen, in Rome] and father Parsons [then in Madrid]."[6] Sterrell's role would be to write "of those points he mentioned in his last as anything wanting advertisement for the special satisfaction of Parsons that he can learn of the Society [Jesuit] & Catholics." The developments from this initial proposal can be traced in Sterrell's letters and activities of 1593–94.

The Wicham–Derrick Correspondence

Sterrell used the alias of "Harry Wicham" as he and the exiles set up a regular intelligence correspondence. Fr. Richard Sherwood facilitated the establishment of a network, writing to Sterrell under the alias now of "Francis Derrick," rather than "Carleton."[7] Living in Antwerp, Sherwood worked closely with Hugh Owen, Richard Verstegan, and Thomas Fitzherbert. Sterrell's first contacts with Sherwood dated from the mid-1580s. When Persons was trying to get Sherwood to become a chaplain to Mary Queen of Scots, Sterrell acted as surety for Sherwood on a debt. Two brothers of Sherwood were priests, and one of these was in a London prison in the early 1580s, as were Sherwood and their mother. Intercepted and stolen letters from 1594 reveal that Sterrell worked on behalf of Sherwood's dear friends Roger and Anne Line and her brother William Heigham, that he had close connections to Arbella Stuart (niece of Mary, Queen of Scots and a potential successor to Queen Elizabeth), that he was moving into a new relationship with Hugh Owen, and that his wealth had increased dramatically in a year's time.

Sherwood asked Sterrell to obtain a "warrant" for Roger Line from the Earl of Essex.[8] Roger Line was in Flanders but his wife Anne and her brother, William Heigham, remained in England. All three were devout Catholics who had suffered imprisonment. Sterrell dared not move the Earl of Essex for a man so notorious as Line, but with money it might be procured from one of the Lord Treasurer's Secretaries. Sterrell promised to do what he could. The bribe money was evidently to come from a diamond stick-pin that Sherwood signed over to Sterrell.⁹ A few months later Sherwood urged Sterrell: "I pray you to get over Mr. Higham by [any] means you can. I pray you find means to redeem the jewell which I fear will else be +++++ [torn]." Money from redemption of the jewel may have gone to William Waad, a follower of Lord Burghley and secretary of the Privy Council. With Waad, Sterrell linked his association with William Heigham to a project that involved Arbella, a potential heir to the English crown.

Sterrell provided services as an intermediary for the exiles and their families. He transmitted letters and money between a mother in Godstowe, near Oxford, and her son in Antwerp, Francis Owen, who was serving in the Spanish army.¹⁰ For a Throckmorton friend, Sterrell was to obtain in London a musical instrument and a youth who could play the lute.¹¹

Sterrell ("Wicham") provided news of interest to overseas members of other families. He reported that "the young Lord Mountague [was] commited for Christening his own child, because no heretic should christen it as he terms them."¹² News of the family of Lord Montague would be important to many of the Catholic exiles. Lord Montague was the son of Mary Dormer, half-sister of the Duchess of Feria. His wife was Jane Sackville, daughter of Lord Buckhurst; her sister-in-law had been close to Fr. Robert Southwell before her death and his imprisonment. Lord Montague's mother was remarried at this time, and her new husband—Sir Edmund Uvedall—was posted to the Low Countries and took William Sterrell into custody not long after this letter but quickly released him.

Sherwood (Derrick) warned Sterrell (Wicham) to be secret or he would "lose his credit with [Cardinal] Allen, Throkmor, James, who have so good opinion of him as they mean to use him in their affairs, whereby he may rise to great wealth and estimation." "Throckmor" could be Thomas Throckmorton or George Throckmorton, brothers of Francis who was executed for the Throckmorton Plot of 1584.¹³ They were cousins of Sir Francis Englefield. The two surviving Throckmorton brothers were often in the Low Countries, as testified to in 1594 by prisoners who confessed to a plan of killing the queen, allegedly through Throckmorton's encouragement.¹⁴ "James" was Thomas James, an Englishman functioning as a consul in Spain. He was a friend and correspondent of Fr. Persons, and was influential in Spain and with Archduke Albert.¹⁵

Sherwood also told Sterrell that he would hear from Hugh Owen, Sherwood or their "old friend" Thomas Fitzherbert. The latter stood ready to help and was now in great credit with the Duke of Feria: "You have friends, if you use fidelity, secrecy and discretion, able and willing to advance you when time shall serve." Although Sherwood had raised the hope that through service Sterrell "may rise to great wealth and estimation," Sterrell had already informed his correspondent that money was not his object¹⁶: "I am worth 800£ yet if all were gold, I would not care to spend one half if I were employed so as I might be hereafter, *in aliquo numero*, but when I so deal as I neither get *in hoc seculo, neque in futuro*, I must save my money to live upon myself."¹⁷ Sterrell had come into a substantial sum of money between May 1593, when he was virtually unemployed and could not afford a horse, and August 1594.

Sterrell seems to have been working out a new relationship with Hugh Owen through Sherwood. Perhaps Owen was not quite prepared to place heavy reliance on Sterrell. Owen was frequently the target of duplicitous agents from England, such as Michael Moody and Robert Poley. Sterrell complained to Sherwood that Owen has been pleased with intelligence he sent Owen but Owen was not making sufficient use of Sterrell. He said Owen "promised me far greater matters but performed them not...." As he told "Derrick," "they must allow me for a counseller, if I do deal for them. I know many matters are ill-handled by their too much overweening." He wanted not to be used "in minimis" and wished to "palter no longer" in sending news. No man could please them more that he can "by reason of my mr [master, Essex]." Their old friend of "Roan [Rouen]"—i.e., Fitzherbert—had moved, so Sterrell was temporarily out of contact with him. Sterrell sent a letter to Owen through Sherwood, and told Sherwood to write back to him by sending letters to Francis Harvey in Middelburg. Harvey, he said, was his friend and knew him to work for Essex. Harvey would assume that "Derrick" likewise worked for Essex. Thus did Sterrell have a member of the English Parliament serving as a conduit of information from a Catholic priest.

As a stronger relationship with Owen ensued, Sterrell went from providing news of developments within England to working with Owen and the Jesuits on matters of greater importance. If there had been friction (genuine or feigned) between Sterrell and Owen for a period in 1594, it was gone by the time the two met with others of the network in Antwerp at year's end. The complexities of the letters and the developments of the relationships make them perplexing. The players were all highly sophisticated and linguistically gifted—all were fluent in multiple languages. Wily survivors, they were involved with intelligence and intrigue for many years. All of the ones under discussion died of old age, not one by execution for spying: Sterrell, Fitzherbert, Owen, Verstegan, Phelippes, Persons and Sherwood.

"The traffick of Arbella [Stuart] is accepted"

The matter of the greatest importance to English Catholics was the succession to the crown of England. The preference was for a Catholic or at least a person who would tolerate Catholicism. Necessarily, they had to look among those who had a hereditary claim to the throne. Hereditary monarchy was the long-standing norm for political rule in England and much of Europe. The relative claims to the English crown were explored in "R. Doleman's" *Conference about the Next Succession to the Crowne of Ingland*, published in 1594 by Sterrell's associates in Flanders. High on the list of potential successors was Arbella Stuart. Sterrell was selected for a role in exploring her succession possibilities, a part earlier played by Thomas Barnes.

Arbella Stuart was a descendant of Margaret, eldest daughter of Henry VII. Thus she was niece of Queen Mary Stewart and was first cousin of James VI of Scotland. Little Arbella was well-acquainted with her doomed aunt. Arbella's parents died young, and she was raised by her grandmother, Bess of Hardwick, whose husband, George Talbot, 6th Earl of Shrewsbury, was keeper of Mary, Queen of Scots.

Arbella's potential as a successor to Elizabeth was first suggested by the English Catholic fugitives in the Low Countries even before Mary Queen of Scots was executed. Mendoza reported the interest of the Catholic exiles in an Arbella match with Parma's son in a letter to the Spanish king late in 1586.[18]

The death of Mary Stewart elevated the candidacy of Arbella. A marriage of Arbella to Parma's son had attractions for some in the English government as well as for the

Catholics abroad. Parma, who was Italian, was commander of the Spanish forces in Flanders. Walsingham had Phelippes direct Thomas Barnes to explore the Arbella marriage project no later than 1589. If Arbella married Parma's son, Prince Rainutio, Parma might be split off from the Spanish, thereby strengthening English policy in the Netherlands. Rumor of such a marriage could increase the disaffection of the King of Spain and Parma. And Walsingham may have concluded that if Arbella married Parma's son, the likelihood of her becoming Queen of England might be diminished—and the way clearer for her cousin James VI of Scotland to assume the English crown. Moreover, having an agent pursue in Flanders an Arbella marriage would allow Walsingham to gain better intelligence on the English fugitives and their activities and on Spanish forces.

Barnes's years at Douay, Rheims and Rome had given him close relations with the English exiles, and he was able to move among several factions. He was a cousin of Dr. William Gifford, who was influential at the Brussels Court for years.[19] Dr. Gifford was closely allied with Charles Paget, and Barnes worked with both. Rather like Sterrell, the exiles understood that Barnes was associated in some fashion with figures in the English government. Dr. Gifford and Paget were part of the "Scots" faction of the exiles, favoring James VI.

Barnes reported to Phelippes and Walsingham in May 1589 about the sentiments of the anti–James faction: "they harp much on Lady Arabella, despairing of the King of Scots, whom Father Holt calls the cunningest young man ever bred."[20] With ties to both factions, Barnes discussed the Arbella prospect separately with both Hugh Owen and Charles Paget, the two leaders of the rival "consorts" (as called in Barnes's report) among the English. The Duke of Parma's Secretary encouraged Barnes: he was acting "with the privity of Cosmo the Duke's Secretary who useth those two consorts of English fugitives severally." Parma himself probably was seeking to forward the marriage of Arbella to his son and was using both camps of the English fugitives to explore the subject. Parma must have been satisfied with Barnes's progress and intelligence, for after returning to the Low Countries Barnes reported that Parma had granted him a pension of 35 crowns.[21]

For each "consort," Barnes reported on the prospects of Arbella's cause at the English Court.[22] James's supporters were strong and none was forwarder for James than Secretary Walsingham, notwithstanding the hatred he bore James's mother. Barnes said James did not need to marry Arabella to further his title, "though he has been scared with her to keep him in order." Who was using Arbella's claim to the English succession to keep James in line? The answer is unclear but the rumor was such that Burghley instructed Robert Bowes, the English ambassador in Scotland, to deny a report made to James VI from Spanish sources that Elizabeth had "moved and offered marriage betwixt the Duke of Parma and the Lady Arabella (Stuart)."[23] Burghley declared that neither the queen nor he had ever thought of such a thing. Of course, the denial confirmed that the thought was not unthinkable.

Burghley would have approved an effort to disaffect Parma from Spain, for Burghley, in August 1590, sent Parma (through Carlo Lanfranchi, an Italian banker at Antwerp), the decipher of a Spanish letter to show Parma the malice of the Spaniards towards him.[24] A year later Burghley again sent Parma a packet of intercepted letters that Sir Robert Sidney, the English agent at Flushing, noted were "practices to stir the Duke of Parma against the King of Spain."[25] Yet Burghley was not behind Phelippes and Barnes.[26] He and his son,

Robert Cecil, were gaining intelligence on the Arbella matter from another of Walsingham's former agents, Michael Moody, who was handled through other veterans of the intelligence trade, Sir Thomas Heneage and Robert Poley.

Both "consorts" in Flanders were suspicious of Barnes and dubious as to his motives and authority. Fr. William Clitherow (ally of Paget) wrote to Barnes in cipher that "You are said to practise a marriage for the son of the Duke of Parma with Arbella, and it is written so into Italy and Spain for to disgrace and plague you, and one of the counsel [Privy Council] of England gave out this matter of you as it is said."[27] Paget wrote to Barnes two days later, not mentioning, however, anything of Parma's son and Arbella.[28] But he did discuss the presence of "one Morley that playeth on the organ in [St.] Poules that was with me in my house; he seemed to be a good Catholic and was reconciled, but notwithstanding suspecting his behaviour I intercepted letters that Mr Nowell wrote him whereby I discovered enough to have hanged him; nevertheless he showing with tears great repentance and asking on his knees forgiveness I was content to let him go." Paget was no doubt aware of the Arbella project of Barnes and was alluding to it indirectly by reference to Morley's letters, expecting this to draw a response from Barnes, which it did.

Phelippes drafted a letter for Barnes to send back to Paget and Clitherow.[29] Barnes was to write that his adversaries were trying to trap him; he was sought for as the practicer of a marriage between Arbella and the Duke of Parma's son, which was given out to be his errand to England. He continued: "It is true that Morley, the singing man, employs himself in that kind of service [i.e., the marriage practice], and has brought divers into danger." Morley, who had just visited with Charles Paget, was Thomas Morley, and may have been one source (against his wishes) of the information on Barnes. That Barnes had not kept Paget and Clitherow informed about Arbella matters suggests that Hugh Owen's group was the primary sponsor of an Arbella project, not the Paget/Gifford Scottish faction. This is supported by the fact that the priest James Younger (*alias* George Dingley, *alias* Thomas Christopher), after capture in London in 1592, confessed that while in Spain a year or more earlier he learned of a plan of Hugh Owen's ally, Sir William Stanley, who also was then in Spain, to have Arbella conveyed out of England by stealth.[30] Owen and Thomas Fitzherbert had come to Spain with Stanley a short time before Stanley had disclosed the plan. Another captured priest, the Jesuit Henry Walpole, confessed in 1594 that he had heard of Owen and Fr. Holt laboring to advance the cause of the Prince of Parma, whenever her Majesty died. And he was told of Barnes, "who came from the Council here into Flanders about 4 years ago, did treat a marriage betwixt the prince of Parma and a lady called Arbella."[31]

The confirmation from Phelippes/Barnes that Morley of St. Paul's was engaged in the Arbella matter suggests he is most likely the Morley who was tutor to Arbella at this time. Nearly a year after this, Arbella's guardian wrote to Lord Burghley (in response to a warning that Arbella was in jeopardy of being kidnapped) concerning "one Morley," who had "attended on Arbell, and read to her for the space of three year and a half," but had now been dismissed and was "much discontented."[32] The countess wrote that she had "some cause to be doubtful of his forwardness in religion, though I cannot charge him with papistry," a description that could well have fit Thomas Morley. The Countess noted that Morley was very importunate to serve without pay, which made her suspicious.[33] In order to have credibility as a promoter of a match between Arbella and Parma's son, Barnes would have had to have someone close to Arbella who could establish that a match was indeed possible. The tutor of Arbella was exactly such a person, and this would explain Morley's eagerness to continue as her tutor even without payment.

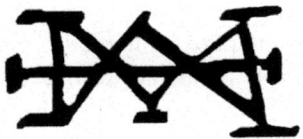

Michael Moody's letter symbol.

Aware of Barnes's effort for a match for Arbella was the self-seeking and not-so-secret agent of the English government in the Low Countries, Michael Moody. He wrote his handlers, Sir Thomas Heneage and Robert Poley, from Flushing: "I beseech you send me word, whether you be not acquainted with matters that one Barnes hath in handling, touching the Lady Arabella."[34] Moody's intelligences were passed on to Burghley and the queen. They were not satisfied with Moody's incompetent service. Nevertheless, Heneage and Poley were authorized to write back to Moody that neither the queen nor Burghley and Heneage had knowledge of Barnes, "either touching La[dy] Arabella, or any other matter"; therefore, Moody should look after Barnes and signify what he found of him.[35] Moody was chastised for his indiscretions in his dealings in Flanders and in his letters into England.

Moody had been at work on the Arbella project for a few months for Burghley and Robert Cecil.[36] Distrustful of Moody, Cecil had another agent, named as John Ricroft in his letters, reporting on Moody's behavior.[37] Before leaving for the Low Countries in August 1591, Moody was seeking to obtain, with the assistance of Sir Thomas Heneage, a portrait of Arbella by the painter Nicholas Hilliard. A letter from "John Ricroft" to Robert Cecil said Moody was busy in getting a picture of Arabella to carry to the Duke of Parma and "has Mr. V's [Thomas Heneage, the Vice-Chamberlain] letter to aid him therein to Hildyard."[38] It was probably Robert Cecil to whom Reinold Bisley wrote that "Michael Moody, Sir Edward Stafford's servant, is employed from beyond sea, to practise with Arabella about a marriage between her and the Duke of Parma's son; he was sent once before for her picture, and has been thrice in England this year."[39] Moody was likely seeking the portrait for the Duke of Parma's secretary Cosmo, the same man who had set Barnes at work between the two "consorts" of English fugitives. "Ricroft" reported to Cecil that Moody got into the favor of Cosmo by revealing all he knew about England.[40] Cosmo had set Moody to work as well as Barnes.

The seriousness of the Parma/Arbella project was indicated by the appearance of Parma's son in the Low Countries in the latter part of 1591, as reported by Cardinal Allen to the King of Spain. This, in itself, would suggest that Parma was a promoter of the Arbella match. Allen, in Rome, was kept informed of the Arbella proceedings of Barnes. Allen informed the Spanish king that it may have been a year since the negotiations were started, though very secretly, for the marriage of Arabella and the Prince of Parma.[41] The unexpected journey of the Prince to Flanders had "increased the rumours and suspicion about it, and in the last months these have grown, owing to the continual goings and comings of certain Englishmen from England to the Prince." Allen was aware that Queen Elizabeth had knowledge of the negotiation. Although he was very suspicious of the motives and sincerity of the English, he concluded that it should be pursued if the project had the consent of the Pope and the Spanish crown.

Sterrell was in Flanders when the Arbella project unraveled for Barnes in 1592. In May, Sterrell wrote to Phelippes warning about both Barnes and Moody.[42] Take "heed how you trust Barnes for I know he cosens [tricks, betrays] you, and you are cast off for your labor."

At the same time, he wrote that Michael Moody had been sent into England with letters to prepare for the Queen's assassination and that he "cosens the Queen notably." However, these letters are so obscure in their meaning one cannot even guess whether the letters were to indicate that either Barnes or Moody was an unfaithful spy or to strengthen standing of one or the other among the Catholic exiles.

Charles Paget informed Barnes in July 1592 that Barnes's pension from the Duke of Parma had been terminated the previous October by special order of Cosmo. The reason, said Paget, was because Barnes "gave intelligence that were nothing worth and therefore merited not a pension but by a friend I understand that Father Holt had told Cosmo that one had sent him word out of England that you treated a marriage between the Lady Arbella and the D[uke] of Parma his son and that yourself told it to some there, whereof I marvel much for that I never heard you had any such commission. The Earl of Westmorland sayeth you told him as much."[43]

Paget said the termination had occurred "since October last" (i.e., 1591). Paget was already aware of Barnes's interest in the Arbella marriage project well before this July 1592 letter. What Paget seems to be saying here is that he marveled that he never heard Barnes had "any such commission," i.e., from the English government. Paget had been in communication with agents of Burghley, and from them he had heard nothing of Barnes having a commission. Paget had asked Barnes directly about his role in the marriage project in October and Barnes's draft reply had only acknowledged Morley's role.

What likely happened then is that in October 1591 Moody got word from Heneage and Poley that Burghley and the queen knew nothing of Barnes's involvement in a marriage project. Moody passed this on to Owen and to Cosmo as well as to Paget. Walsingham, Phelippes and Barnes had entertained the Arbella project when Walsingham was alive. Phelippes, through Barnes, had tried to press on with the project despite the fact that he no longer had support (or even knowledge) of anyone in the English government. In a pattern he was to repeat later, Phelippes thought he could continue an intelligence effort and turn it to his advantage when an opportunity presented itself. But when Cosmo realized no one in the English government was sustaining Barnes, he was right to conclude that the intelligence that Barnes provided was now "nothing worth" and merited no pension. It was a temporary setback for Barnes and Phelippes.

Moody, too, had tried to work the possibility of an Arebella/Parma match to his advantage. Although Moody had tried obtain a portrait of Arbella for Cosmo, he was never authorized by his sponsors in the English government to seek a marriage between Arbella and Parma's son. The project collapsed.

Barnes was likely working with the Owen faction for the Arbella marriage prior to his dismissal by Cosmo, and Paget and Burghley's agents Poley and Moody were initially seeking to undermine the match, or more accurately a Barnes role in a match. Once Barnes had been undercut, Paget and Moody warmed to an Arbella match and sought to advance it with Burghley's encouragement. Several documents support this understanding of the facts.

After being discovered as one who had recently been among the Catholic fugitives in the Low Countries, Nicholas Williamson (a servant of Shrewsbury, and thus specially acquainted with Arbella's circumstances) was questioned about his knowledge of a "plot or practice for the Succession." He responded by saying that the Prince of Parma had a claim to the crowns of England and of Portugal by descent from Edmund Crookback (Earl of Lancaster and younger son of Henry III) and would offer unto Queen Elizabeth to marry with Arbella and to become enemy to Spain. Williamson said Hugh Owen and Thomas Fitzherbert were thought to be the contrivers of this device in the days of the Duke of Parma but they now considered Arbella's father to have been a bastard, diminishing her claim.[44] Williamson thought that in mid– to late 1594, when an embassy was planned for Sir Thomas Wilkes to the Low Countries, Charles Paget had "revived this motion again, hoping that, in regard of a common peace and to have quietly enjoyed Portugal and the Low Countries, the King of Spain would have consented thereunto. And this was said to have been Cardinal Allen's device before his death, for the present tolerating of Catholics in England. Others said that if Sir Tho. Wilkes had come there had been an offer made of the King of Spain's own son to the Lady Arbella." In short, Williamson indicated the practice began with Owen and Fitzherbert but with the death of Parma, they had cooled to the notion. Paget then had sought to advance the practice and that Arbella was to have been a topic of discussion of the Wilkes embassy. But this planned embassy collapses.

Members of the Owen faction prepared a special report to Archduke Ernest when he assumed the role of governor of the Low Countries in 1594. They were disturbed by the continuing influence of Charles Paget and Thomas Morgan, who (while living off Spanish pensions) had long been working against the interests of the King of Spain, and who undermined the work of Cardinal Allen and the Owen faction. After Morgan's banishment, the report said, Paget was acting in concert with the double agents Robert Poley and Michael Moody. One (Poley) had been responsible for the capture and execution of Fr. Ballard and this also had led to the execution of Mary Queen of Scots and the fourteen gentlemen of the Babington Plot. The report continued that these two spies came and went between England and Flanders with passports of both parts, and dealt freely with Charles Paget. One of them had thirty ducats entertainment each month from the Spanish king. They always brought hopes of peace and return to England with intelligence on Flanders, which is what the English Privy Council wanted. They deceived the ministers of the Spanish king with false hopes because the English had no thought of making peace.

Taking up the role of Paget, Poley and Moody on the Arbella project, the report continued: "Yet Charles Paget with these hopes have entertained their negotiations with these two spies for a long time; and in the time of the Duke of Parma dealing with the [proposed] marriage of Lady Arbella in England with the duke's son, *to soften him by these means*, and after the death of the Duke they have given hope of peace to the Counts of Mansfield and Fuentes, and all are deceptions…."[45] "Soften" here probably means that Paget and the double agents were trying to encourage the marriage so as to soften the Duke of Parma in his fighting against the English in the Spanish Low Countries; i.e., to lose his zeal to defeat the English and the Hollanders. The death of the Duke of Parma on December 3, 1592, and his replacement first by Count Mansfield and then by Archduke Ernest probably affected the positions of the Catholic factions, as Nicholas Williamson indicated.

In 1594–95, the Catholic exiles continued to be interested in Arbella. Sterrell's immediate circle of intelligencers—Persons, Owen, Fitzherbert and Verstegan—were "the chief advancers, and the setters forth" of the *Conference about the Next Succession* that was completed in 1594 (as reported by the Williamson).[46] In the *Conference*, Arbella's title was considered just after James of Scotland. The *Conference* authors observed "in that she is a young Lady, she is thereby fit ... to procure good wills and affections, and in that she is unmarried, she may perhaps by her Marriage join some other Title with her own, and thereby also Friends."[47] The authors recognized she had a strong claim to the throne but they did not warm to her, preferring the succession of the Infanta of Spain ("a Princess of rare parts both for Beauty, Wisdom and Piety") or perhaps a son of the Earl of Hartford or one of the children of the Earl of Derby.[48] Prudence dictated that the exiles proceed as though Arbella might become queen. As they had observed, her title might be strengthened by marriage to another claimant. But it was not spelled out that she might marry the Duke of Parma (Rainutio had succeeded to the title of his father), who was discussed just after the Infanta of Spain.[49]

There is one striking observation about Arbella's candidacy in the *Conference*. Commenting on the candidate favored by the protestants, the purported speaker says that "though the house of Hartford was wont to be much favored by them, but of latter years little speech hath been thereof, but rather of Arbella, *whom the Lord Treasurer is said especially to favor at this present*."[50] If Arbella was the choice of Burghley, it would be enough to cool the zeal of Owen's circle. The *Conference on the Next Succession* was likely the product of the same hands that wrote the 1594 report to Archduke Ernest. They were surely relying on the same information about the English government's role on the Arbella match carried out through Paget, Poley and Moody. That report to Ernest indicated that these English agents were giving false hopes of an Arbella match to Flanders. The *Conference* seems to take Burghley's candidacy of Arbella as serious and sincere (without regard to whom she might marry). This indicates the subtle politics the sophisticated authors of the *Conference* were playing: as we will see repeatedly done in future intelligence originating from the Owen group and transmitted through Sterrell, the *Conference* authors were sowing discord between the English Court and James of Scotland. James, they knew, would read the *Conference* and see it reported as well-known fact that the Burghley/Cecil faction preferred the candidacy of his cousin Arbella over his own claims, returning to the matter that Burghley had instructed Robert Bowes to counter a bit earlier. Burghley, of course, may have favored Arbella and the report was accurate, yet was still useful to divide London and Edinburgh.

The Catholics in exile were faced with the fact that Arbella had as good a claim to the throne as James of Scotland and perhaps was favored by one of the most powerful political figures in the kingdom, Lord Burghley. If she could be married to the right man, the state of the English Catholics might be greatly improved. This prospect was attractive enough to keep alive the exiles' interest in Arbella and her marriage potential, even though the elder Parma was gone and his son no longer a factor in the equation. To whom would they turn for continuing intelligence on Arbella? William Sterrell.

In October 1594, Sherwood informed Sterrell: "I am to advertise you that the traffick of Arbella is so far entertained and accepted."[51] Sherwood said he and Sterrell would confer together for "better utterance of that commodity. Allen is the principal merchant." Cardinal Allen in December 1591 had concluded that the marriage of Arbella had potential for the English Catholics. Exactly what Sterrell was to do in the "traffick of Arbella" is not articulated, but Sterrell was cooperating with some in the English government on the matter and doing so through William Waad.

Sterrell's association with the cause of Mary Queen of Scots, aunt of Arbella, may have brought him into acquaintance with the young Arbella around 1581–82. Sterrell had associations with the Talbot family in which Arbella was raised, the same family that had custody of Mary Queen of Scots. George Talbot, 6th Earl of Shrewsbury and custodian of Arbella, had two sons who entered Magdalen College when William Sterrell was completing his Bachelor's degree: Edward age 18 (as was Sterrell), and Henry, age 16. Both remained at Magdalen for three years, where they must have known Sterrell very well. It is not difficult to imagine Sterrell visiting them at their estate as a cover to call upon Mary Queen of Scots. Their older brother, Gilbert, had been a student at St. John's College, Oxford. By the time that their father died in 1590 and Gilbert became the 7th Earl of Shrewsbury, the younger brothers were estranged from Gilbert, but Sterrell may well have already become associated with the family. Gilbert was close to his niece Arbella; he was married to Mary Cavendish, the younger sister of Arbella's mother, Elizabeth.

Gilbert Talbot and Sterrell's patron, Worcester, were closely associated with one another at Court and evidently were good friends. Worcester's genial letters to Shrewsbury are witty and convivial. Shrewsbury and Worcester were made Knights of Order of the Garter in 1592 and 1593 respectively, and shared responsibilities in the Order's rituals.[52] A report to the Privy Council in 1592 said that Shrewsbury maintained a household of "notorious papists and dangerous recusants."[53] In 1603 Worcester has "my Lady Arbella" convey a letter from Worcester to Shrewsbury.[54] And Worcester's wife and Lady Arbella are both ladies in service to Queen Anne in 1603.[55]

Sterrell may well have had a connection to Thomas Morley, who likely was tutor to Arbella as well as an agent in the Low Countries at about the time Sterrell was there. Morley received an Oxford degree in 1588 while Sterrell was a praelector. Morley was associated closely with the composer William Byrd. Sterrell's employer Worcester was a patron to Byrd, with Byrd dedicating music to Worcester as well as playing for him at Christmas 1589, at a time when Morley was probably a tutor to Arbella. Thus Sterrell had multiple connections to Morley and to Arbella Stuart.

Sterrell was expected to accompany Sir Thomas Wilkes on his diplomatic mission to the new governor of the Low Countries, the Archduke Ernest who was a cousin to the king of Spain. Sterrell was to be the man to explore the possibility of an Arbella marriage. Burghley and Robert Cecil would have wanted to know what was being done to advance a Catholic marriage for Arbella. The Catholic exiles would have been interested in anything pertaining to the succession and Arbella's claim, especially if Burghley favored Arbella. Sterrell positions himself as a confidante to both English authorities and to the exiles on Arbella. But multiple events intercede to limit what he can accomplish.

14

Co-opting the Privy Council

John Gerard and Nicholas Owen

How was Sterrell able establish his credit and trustworthiness to the Catholic exiles? Officials of the English government permitted him to operate and assisted his efforts so that they, too, might gain good intelligence. Sterrell's letter to William Waad, dated October 15, 1594 (just after Sherwood beseeched Sterrell to "get over Mr. Higham by [any] means you can") shows the double agent at work. Essex had been made a member of the Privy Council in 1593, and Sterrell was communicating with the Privy Council through its clerk, William Waad. Sterrell asked for directions from Waad so as to respond to inquiries from the Duke of Feria (Thomas Fitzherbert's employer), to whom Sterrell was providing intelligence. Sterrell informs Waad that he has already satisfied the Duke of Feria on some points. The Duke (who served the Spanish king) wanted to know the Queen's thoughts on the French King's intentions of a general peace. Sterrell's poured cold water on a Spanish peace initiative, saying that "the inward drift of the Spaniard in this negociation of peace is but to breed jealousy between the three states, and thereby to induce them to disjoin and so to ruin themselves." Waad, like Essex, understood that to maintain intelligence with those of the other side, Sterrell would need to show his use to them. Sterrell asked Waad for "a warrant for the release of Nicolas Owen, a prisoner in the Gatehouse, who was taken with Gerard the Jesuit," from whom [i.e., Gerard] Sterrell hoped to obtain some service.[1] He wanted the warrant to be given to Sterrell himself so that he could gain intelligence from Owen before he got him out. There was urgency in obtaining the warrant for Justice Young's man was trying for the same thing, "but if he get him out then I shall have no more use of him [Owen]." At this time, Owen was not known to the government to be the builder of priest hiding holes on Catholic estates.[2]

Gerard moved among various homes in England for six years after arriving in November 1588, using aliases and hiding in priest-holes—some constructed by Nicholas Owen—when pursuivants came in search of priests. The turncoat priest John Cecil (*alias* John Snowden), had helped the government to identify him as "John Garret" whom he supposed was the son of "Sir Thomas Garret" when John Cecil lent his anti–Jesuit talents to Robert Cecil and Lord Burghley, in 1591.[3] While Gerard was in London in April 1594 securing a new apartment, a government spy informed on Gerard. He and Nicholas Owen were arrested together. By this time, Gerard was notorious for his activities throughout England, and he was taken for questioning by Sir Thomas Egerton, who was just leaving his position as Attorney General.

Gerard was shuttled among prisons over the next few years. While he was in the Clink prison, summer 1594 through spring 1597, Sterrell had easy access to Gerard. Thus Sterrell was able to carry messages from Gerard to Fr. Persons in Spain in 1595.

Gerard was frequently put to the "bloody question" and tortured, sometimes by the Court sadist, Richard Topcliffe. The "Bloody Question" was first used for propaganda effects in 1581 in the trials of Campion, Sherwin and Briant.[4] It was a trap that depended on the proposition that it was impossible to be both a good Catholic and a good subject of the queen: "If the Pope should send an army to England, for whom would you fight—the Pope or the Queen?" Topcliffe would put the Question to the prisoners before or during torture. What could one respond to such a question? To say you would follow the pope was to confess to treason. To say you would support the queen was to deny your religion. To refuse to answer the question was itself punishable, a penalty known as *peine forte et dure*. For her silence, Margaret Clitheroe was pressed to death on March 25, 1586. Refusing to plead to the charge of having harbored Catholic priests in her house, she thereby avoided a trial in which her own children would be obliged to give evidence against her.

Jesuits developed a method of dealing with the Bloody Question and with interrogations concerning their supporters who sheltered them and who had them say Mass in their homes. This method was "equivocation," a technique of avoiding the answer to a question by responding with indirection or with an inward reservation as to meaning. The word is now synonymous with "Jesuitical." The *Oxford English Dictionary* says a "Jesuit" is a "dissembling person, a prevaricator." *Jesuitical* is "Having the characters ascribed to the Jesuits; deceitful, dissembling; practising equivocation, prevarication, or mental reservation of

Martyrdom of Saint Margaret Clitheroe from *Verstegan's Theatrum Crudelitatum Haereticorum*.

truth." Gerard and two Jesuits who were executed, Robert Southwell and Henry Garnet, were notorious for equivocation. On one occasion Topcliffe posed Gerard the Bloody Question, and he responded with an excellent example of the technique. Gerard described their exchange:

> I saw [Topcliffe's] subtlety and wicked cunning. He had so framed his question that whatever I answered I would be sure to suffer for it, either in body or soul. I picked the words of my reply.
> "I am a loyal Catholic and I am a loyal subject of the Queen. If this were to happen, and I do not think it at all likely, I would behave as a loyal Catholic and as a loyal subject."
> "Oh, no," he said. "I want a plain and straight answer. What would you do?"
> I answered:
> "I have told you what I think and I will not give you any other answer."
> Then he flew into a most violent rage and spat a torrent of oaths at me.[5]

Sterrell's efforts with Waad in 1594 were successful in obtaining Owen's release from the Gatehouse and gained Sterrell access to Gerard. In his autobiography, Gerard relates that "some Catholic gentlemen had paid down a sum of money and had him [Owen] released."[6] Owen could not be released from prison without high-level government intervention, and one can be sure that Justice Young's man would not have been described by Gerard as a Catholic gentleman. William Sterrell as "Robert Robinson" had secured a similar release for Fr. Robert Southwell's friend Robert Bellamy in 1591.

Sir Thomas Gerard was a dear friend of Essex who had Essex's complete trust.[7] Neither Essex, nor his sometime agent William Sterrell, would seek to bring harm to a son of Sir Thomas Gerard. It was understood at the time that Gerard was among those priests to be executed, but no priests were executed from February 21, 1595, when Fr. Robert Southwell was put to death, to July 12, 1598, when John Jones was executed. This was the period when Essex was at the height of his popularity and influence in England, and it is likely that he (and Sterrell) played a part in the hiatus in executions. Sterrell may have been partly responsible for the sympathy Essex expressed for Gerard. On June 11, 1595, Henry Garnet wrote to Father Parsons: "We have also lately heard for certain that the Earl of Essex praised his [Gerard's] constancy, declaring that he could not help honouring and admiring the man. A secretary of the Royal Council [probably Waad, with whom Sterrell had interceded] denies that the queen wished to have him executed. To John this will be a great trouble."[8] The reason Garnet would say it would be a "trouble" is that Gerard wished for martyrdom; instead, he received many weeks of brutal torture. The government seemed determined to execute Gerard, but William Sterrell's strategy in dealing with Waad and through Essex is clear: "Let the priest live, and when I gain credit with him, (i.e., his trust), he will lead us to others, including the Jesuit Superior Garnet." Through such a stratagem, Sterrell bought time for Gerard, and this eventually enabled his escape. But a failure to deliver Garnet would damage Sterrell's credibility.

A few months after Garnet's letter to Persons on Gerard, Persons was able to receive a note in Gerard's own hand. It was surely a moment of great joy to Persons. In October 1595 Persons was visited in Spain by a man from London, conveying secret messages: "a man of 35 years who has spent many of them in attending prisons and being of service to prisoners who are suffering for the Catholic religion; and so he brings me, concealed in buttons, shoes and other more secret places, a number of notes from different prisons, and one of them is from Fr. John Gerard written when he was in expectation of martyrdom."[9]

This can be no one other than William Sterrell: he was in his 35th year, a long-time visitor of prisons,[10] in communication with Gerard in 1594–95 (with access granted by the Council!), and in the midst of establishing a communications network to serve Persons and his associates.

When it came time for Sterrell to deliver on Garnet—well, that just failed from someone else's fault, specifically Mr. Waad's. Sterrell paid a price for his failure to deliver Garnet. Waad let it be known that Sterrell had promised to take Garnet, and when this got over to Sterrell's associates in the Low Countries, his enemies there used it to sow distrust of him. Owen, however, understood Sterrell's methods.[11]

How many times could William Sterrell work this strategy on the English government? Not more than three or four, but the evidence of the effectiveness of such a strategy comes from the most unexpected of sources, the odious Topcliffe himself. About two months after Gerard escaped from the Tower, Topcliffe wrote to Sir Robert Cecil of a scheme to let one priest out of prison to facilitate the capture of a more notorious one: "It may seem strange that I should sue to have a traitorous friar delivered out of prison to a better lodging or friend. It is to take a traitor ten times weightier than himself. I do not name the party for secrecy.... The Lord Keeper liketh the scheme."[12] Had Sterrell again worked his magic, now on Richard Topcliffe who was from a Lincolnshire town only a few miles from Sterrell's own?

Another connection of Essex and Fr. Gerard was Essex's sister. A short time before he was arrested, Gerard was staying at Broad Oaks (Braddocks), the home of William Wiseman. Gerard was attempting to convert Penelope Rich, Essex's sister as well as one of his advisors. Lord Rich, her husband, was Wiseman's neighbor. Gerard went openly to the Rich house, pretending to bring a message to her from a relative of hers. He dined with Penelope and talked with her for more than three hours. Gerard's autobiography reports that she wrote to her lover, Lord Mountjoy, that she planned to convert to Catholicism. Mountjoy rushed to her side (she was carrying his child at the time) and gave her a long letter of reasons against a conversion. She passed the letter on to Gerard for him to answer, which he did. While Penelope did not convert, Gerard reports that "frequently she would talk about me to one of her maids of honour who was a Catholic."[13] No doubt Penelope would have intervened with Essex on Gerard's behalf, as she intervened on behalf of John Bolt, a Catholic musician who had been arrested at Broad Oaks in March 1594, just before Owen and Gerard were taken.[14]

Bolt was a singer, virginalist and organist who lived at Court for three years; it was said that Queen Elizabeth thought highly of him for his voice and skill in music. He lived with Catholic families where he taught music and practiced his religion. He had recently served in Thorndon Hall, the home of Sir John Petre, whose son will marry the daughter of Sterrell's patron, the Earl of Worcester, two years later.[15] The marriage of Sir William Petre and Catherine Somerset (Sterrell's former pupil) will take place in the London home of the Earl of Essex. Four prosecutors examined Bolt and extracted Bolt's confession that he had upon him a poem entitled "St. Peter's Complaint." This was written by Robert Southwell who was confined in the Tower even as Bolt was being examined; the book was not openly published for another year.[16] Edward Coke examined Bolt, and Bolt confessed to having upon him pages of verse beginning "Why do I use my paper pen and ink...."[17] This poem, written to commemorate the interrogation and execution of Edmund Campion, had also appeared in print in a book of music published by William Byrd in 1588. Bolt admitted to being a Catholic, but he refused to name the person who had reconciled him to the Catholic Church and obstinately refused to answer the Bloody Question. But he did not meet the same fate as Robert Southwell. Penelope Rich secured his release and he escaped to the Continent. After leaving England, Bolt became a priest.

William Higham and His Sister Anne Line

A second letter to Waad from Sterrell in October 1594 repeated his earlier request regarding Nicholas Owen. This letter, like the previous, also referred to William Higham, whom "Derrick" (Fr. Sherwood) had wanted to get to Antwerp by any means. Sterrell wrote to Waad:

> I am constrained to importune you to have resolution in these four points. First to have some directions to answer Fitzherbert his letter: secondly, William Higham is come to town who hath been so often writ for; I must know whether I shall send him over or not: I do not think he shall be messenger in the matter of Arbella between us; it is best no doubt I send him: thirdly, let me understand whether I shall have Nicholas Owen out of the Gatehouse or not: lastly, whether I shall have any money this quarter. In good faith, I have none.—This Friday morning.[18]

Sterrell's communications to the Duke of Feria were being carried out through Thomas Fitzherbert. Waad and probably one or more members of the Privy Council knew Sterrell was involved in the "traffick of Arbella." He was using this activity to justify seeking a warrant for William Higham to go abroad, with their complicity. Sherwood had written to William Higham of London a letter of 16 August 1594 pressing him to come over to Antwerp with his sister to join her husband.[19] Sterrell's demand for money increased his credibility with the government; a man who acts for money is not likely to be governed by religious sentiment.

The sister of William Higham was Anne Line, the refuge-keeper for John Gerard, and her husband was Roger Line, who was already in Flanders. The same month—October—that Sterrell was writing his notes to Waad that he wanted to send Higham "over" and telling Waad "it is best no doubt I send him." Sherwood had implored Sterrell "to get over Mr. Higham by [any] means you can." It will be recalled that Sterrell and Sherwood had corresponded in July 1594 on a "warrant" sought by Roger Line (no doubt a passport for his wife and her brother to come to the Low Countries) but Sterrell had indicated that because of the man's notoriety, he could not move Essex, yet he might be able to obtain the warrant by payment of money to one of the Lord Treasurer's secretaries. Sherwood had provided the money in the form of the assignment of a jewel over to Sterrell. As a clerk of the Privy Council and follower of Lord Burghley, William Waad fit the description of one of the Lord Treasurer's secretaries. Phelippes knew Waad well, for both had served with Cobham and Walsingham in France in 1580–81, both were members of the Parliament of 1584, and both were involved in the examination of the papers of Mary Queen of Scots that led to her execution. Waad has been described as the "English counterpart to the Spanish grand inquisitor."[20]

Anne Line was among the forty martyrs of England and Wales canonized by Pope Paul VI in 1970. For most of the time from the death of her husband in 1595 in the Low Countries and her execution in 1601, Anne Line maintained a safe house or houses in London for John Gerard and those whom he assisted. An example of the latter is William Alabaster, an Anglican minister and poet who was chaplain to Essex on the Cadiz expedition of 1596. Alabaster was converted by Fr. Thomas Wright to Catholicism, and both were imprisoned. When Alabaster escaped, Anne Line and John Gerard sheltered him in her London house for two or three months before Gerard slipped him out of the country.[21] Suspected of assisting in John Gerard's escape from the Tower in 1597, she moved repeatedly to avoid arrest. As will be related below, she is captured early in 1601 and then executed by hanging. Her crime: a priest was seen at mass in a house she maintained.

Anne Line and her brother, William Higham, were disinherited by their father for professing the Catholic faith. Her husband had been disinherited by both his father and his uncle for his Catholicism. Gerard's autobiography relates the stories of their families at length. He had met Roger and Richard Line (who inherited in place of the Catholic Roger) in Roger's room, and contrasted the two brothers: Richard was "dressed in silk and finery, while [Roger] wore plain and cheap clothes."[22]

Anne Line's association with William Sterrell is reflected in another reliable report. In the *State Papers* is a list sent by the Earl of Huntington to Lord Burghley of Jesuits, seminarists and old priests, along with notes of the places in London where mass was said and the names of those who were present.[23] There is a single line under masses in London: "Mrs. Lyne and her acquaintance, Mr. Shelly and others, in the Earl of Worcester's house." The date given is January 20, 1593. Sterrell was arriving in London with Worcester at this time, just before the Parliament of 1593, and this was well before the request had come for him to aid Roger and Anne Line in helping William Higham to leave England. From the spy's report it is obvious that Worcester was anything but a fallen-away Catholic. Mass was secretly being said in his own house in London, and other notorious Catholics were present. The "Mr. Shelly" is one of the uncles of Sir Henry Guildford, who was soon to marry Worcester's daughter, Elizabeth. The entry is all the more remarkable when one realizes that the Earl of Huntington who made this report was the brother of Worcester's wife.

Thus we see Sterrell at work, getting the Catholic William Higham out of England on a passport with the full cooperation of the clerk of the Privy Council, on the supposition that this would further an intelligence scheme. Sterrell's ability to get Higham safely away, his securing Nicholas Owens's release from prison, and his exchange of communication with the English government for the Duke of Feria were more than enough to establish in Brussels and Madrid that he was a trustworthy man able to get information at the fountainhead of the Privy Council. These traces of the man's activities are found in a few of letters and papers that have survived 400 years. How many more of his deeds went unrecorded or have been lost? How many more lives were touched by this man who years later sought anonymity even in his funeral, asking only that heaven shelter his remains?

Robert Southwell

Southwell was close to the Bellamy family of Uxendon Manor at Harrow-on-the-Hill. The Bellamy estate was one of the great refuges of Catholic priests. Edmund Campion had found shelter there for a time during the mission of 1580–81, and it was the first household to take in the Jesuit Fr. William Weston.[24] This Catholic family were a natural target for the government and suffered for their hospitality. Richard Topcliffe, "*homo sordidissimus*" (most vile man), arranged for the arrest of the youngest Bellamy daughter and used her to betray her family and Robert Southwell.[25] With a gang of men in attendance, Topcliffe arrested Southwell in June 1592. His letter to the queen gloated: "I never did take so weighty a man."[26] He even described to the queen what tortures he would use in getting Southwell to answer questions pertaining to the Countess of Arundel and Fr. Persons.

For nearly three years Southwell remained in prison. His trial was held on February 20, 1595, Sir John Popham presiding. The result was foregone. Southwell's execution the next day was an emotional event. A group of the supporters of the Earl of Essex attended. In the face of death, Southwell showed great courage, and he prayed for his queen that she would so use those gifts and graces which God, nature and fortune had bestowed upon her that she would please and glorify God and advance the happiness of their country. The first stage of execution was to be hanging, followed by the ignominious castration, disemboweling and ripping out of the heart that were the fate of traitors. Southwell spoke courteously to the Protestant minister, and as the noose tightened he prayed in Latin: *In manus tuas, Domine, commendo animam meam*: Into your hands O Lord, I commend my spirit.

Normally, the person to be executed was cut down before he passed out so that castration and disemboweling would be accomplished upon a live victim. Now from the crowd stepped Charles Blount, Lord Mountjoy, and he stood beneath the gallows. He was a close companion to the Earl of Essex and now the lover of Essex's sister Penelope. His brother (or cousin) Christopher Blount was the (third) husband of Essex's mother. Less than a year earlier, Penelope had nearly been converted to Catholicism by Southwell's friend, Father John Gerard. Others of the Essex group were with Mountjoy. Mountjoy and the others prevented the sheriff's men from cutting the rope, thereby permitting Southwell to die without further pain and humiliation. It was an act of kindness and respect. "I cannot answer for his religion," Mountjoy cried out with emotion, "but I wish to God that my soul may be with his."[27] It is reported Queen Elizabeth showed signs of grief for his death.

15

Trustworthy Men at the Fountainhead in the Council

When Sterrell told Waad that Higham was not to be the messenger in the Arbella matter but that Higham should nevertheless be sent, it is likely that Sterrell meant to go himself and to take Higham with him. Within a very short time Sterrell was in Antwerp meeting with his correspondents. His trip to Antwerp in January 1595 was in planning for some five or six months. Originally he expected to go to Brussels with the English diplomat Sir Thomas Wilkes.[1] A protégé of Walsingham, Wilkes was a veteran diplomat who had undertaken repeated missions to the Low Countries.

Francis Bacon, with whom Sterrell worked on intelligence matters, had urged Queen Elizabeth to send someone to negotiate with Archduke Ernest, now governor of the Spanish Netherlands, concerning English conspirators.[2] An overture to Ernest was delayed for months as the Lopez trial and executions took place and the public revelations of the Yorke, Williams and Young conspiracy. The queen wrote to Brussels for a passport for Sir Thomas Wilkes in September 1594. Wilkes would take up the proof of conspiracies and seek action against seven fugitives who were participants in alleged conspiracies against the queen: Sir William Stanley, Holt, Owen, Throckmorton, Paget, Dr. Gifford, and Dr. Worthington. Perhaps while attempting the extradition of these fugitives, Wilkes (or Sterrell) was to sweeten the negotiations by raising the prospect of a marriage of state between the Lady Arbella and the son of the Spanish King, as Nicholas Williamson had heard. However, the Wilkes mission was cancelled by the queen in late October 1594.[3] A Spanish report originating from London said that Thomas Wilkes was not going to Flanders, the pretended reason being the unseeming familiarity which the Archduke Ernest used in his letter to the queen.[4]

Sterrell, however, made good on his promise to appear in Antwerp. First, he and Owen put themselves on a new footing, with new aliases. Letters to Sterrell were addressed to "Peter Hallins," a *coopman* (merchant) of London.[5] Thus began a correspondence to Sterrell as "Hallins" for the period 1595 to 1601 from "J. B.," who was sometimes identified as "John Petit." More than 40 of these letters survive and all are from Hugh Owen.[6] There are no letters from "Peter Hallins" to anyone.

The *modus operandi* of Sterrell and Phelippes during the period they worked together (1591–1604) was to have foreign correspondence sent to a fictitious person at a specified location in London, often through a third person.[7] Instead of writing as "Hallins" Sterrell used other outgoing aliases: Fenner, Cordale, Rivers, Orwell, and Renzo. Letters left London under one alias and return mail came to a different alias. Such correspondence was much less susceptible of being detected as to the true identities of the correspondents. When abruptly confronted by Robert Cecil in January 1605 Phelippes acknowledged that he was receiving correspondence from Hugh Owen through the "ordinary Duch post of Antwerpe under a direction to Peter Hallyns he writeth." Phelippes told Cecil that Owen probably did not think "Hallins" was Phelippes but that Owen thought his correspondent was with "a friend of Mr. Sterrells who was the first that set it afoot being employed by my Lord of Essex."

In fact, Owen knew from the outset that Sterrell was "Hallins." In a December 1594 letter, Owen makes several references to prior correspondence between them under other names and to Sterrell's "old friend Fitsher," Thomas Fitzherbert, as well as indicating they had met in person.[8] Recalling that Sterrell had complained in a letter of September 1594[9] about being too open with Paget because Paget was close to Robert Poley, Owen responded "if I had been acquainted with Pistol's man [Robert Poley] or that matter by him or Paget, I would never have written to you about it...."[10] Owen's letter also makes reference to the trip that had been planned for Thomas Wilkes. In doing so, he shows how well he understood Paget's activities: "The said Paget laboured hard of late to have permission for Pistol's man [Poley] to come hither, assuring he would find means to discover much of Wilks' secrets if he came to these quarters...."[11]

Owen ("Nicols") went on to inform Sterrell that "I am not employed to be a factor for any since my master died...."[12] This is a reference to Cardinal Allen's recent death, which is confirmed when a few lines later he says "You must understand, moreover, that Paget doth not draw in one line with Fa. Holt and Persons, nor Mr. Cloves (*Car:*)[13] when he lived, with whom I kept correspondence." At his death, Allen had left Owen "in the lurch above 700 crowns" for unrecouped intelligence expenses. Owen related that some letters of Sterrell had been seen by the wrong parties because of the routing of the letters through Richard Verstegan in Antwerp; Owen and Verstegan shared their mail. Mishandled letters are an occupational hazard, sometimes fatal, in espionage.

The death of Owen's patron Cardinal Allen and the rivalry from the Charles Paget faction at the Court of Archduke Ernest left Owen in need of support. He especially needed a well-placed English correspondent if he were to continue his intelligence function. Archduke Ernest told the Spanish King of the great need for reliable political intelligence from England. In December 1594 Ernest sent the King a copy of the queen's Council's letter to Richardot explaining why the Wilkes's embassy was cancelled. He commented that "Every effort is made to learn what passes there [in England]; but there is no person of substance engaged in this; the advices are of less value than they should be."[14] He sought better communications. The Jesuits provided some information but they could only report rumor because of their precarious, hidden existence. Ernest said he made use of William Holt and Hugh Owen "but more sources of information are necessary." He found Paget had been used by Parma and Mansfield but Cardinal Allen had warned against him, as had Owen and Frs. Holt and Creighton.

Owen invited "Hallins" (Sterrell) to come see him. After alluding to a letter of October 1594 in which Sterrell had said he was coming to Middleburg, Owen wrote: "If you have to trade for St. Thomas Onions (Middleburg), and do continue in your former opinion to come to Bottels (Antwerp), I shall be most glad of it, and will procure such means for your safety as shall give you contentment; and so you shall come and return safe or not come at all, always provided you give me some notice aforehand...." Sterrell and his correspondents meet in Antwerp just a month later. Within a matter of only days of receipt of the December 2 letter, William Sterrell was on his way from London to Antwerp. Upon arrival, he was joined by a young man who gave a vivid account of the events.

The Conclave at Antwerp, January 1595

Present at the initial meetings of the new Sterrell-Owen intelligence network in Antwerp was a reluctant young witness, John Gatacre. He was brought to Antwerp by his half-brother, Thomas Fitzherbert, the "old friend" to both Sterrell and Owen. Nine years earlier John Gatacre, then aged 15, enrolled at Oxford. John was the offspring of Thomas Fitzherbert's mother's second marriage, to Francis Gatacre.[15] In 1593 or 1594 John Gatacre enrolled at Douay[16] and left after a year. To arrange his return to England, he joined up with his half-brother Thomas Fitzherbert in Brussels and, together with Hugh Owen, they went to Antwerp where they met with Verstegan and Sterrell.

The group were joined by another intriguing figure, clad in black satin—the black-bearded, strange-oathed Captain Jaques. Dining at Verstegan's residence near the bridge of the tapestry makers, and lodging at a Dutchman's place, the associates spent some days conferring together in January 1595. Sterrell took Gatacre under his care. He gave him the alias of John Fenne, and had "Fenne" pretend to be his servant, just as he and the French ambassador had done with the group of Catholic lads who boarded his ship in 1585. Sterrell and Gatacre made their way back to Middelburg and spent several days there. Gatacre seems not to have understood the reason for remaining in Middelburg until they were joined by another man, who also had studied at Rheims and elsewhere in Europe for some years. This was George Somerset, son of Thomas Somerset who had died in prison for his religion in 1586. George was first cousin to Edward Somerset, the Earl of Worcester—Sterrell's patron. Gatacre now suspected double-dealing by Sterrell. Probably Sterrell had made arrangements for this rendezvous with George Somerset well in advance, and, as he normally did, he had kept the planned meeting entirely secret from those around him. Gatacre was "jealous," meaning dubious or suspicious. Sterrell's liaison in Middelburg, Francis Harvey, provided support services. The return of George Somerset to England had been in the works for some time. In August 1594, Richard Williams—lately come from Flanders and being examined for treason—had told Essex and Cobham that Somerset, kinsman to the Earl of Worcester, was coming to England by way of Calais.[17] Sterrell was now to shepherd George back, just as he had probably seen to his going over in the early 1580s.

The little group coming from the Catholic Low Countries obviously invited suspicion; they were stopped by English soldiers after leaving Middelburg. Taken to the English "cautionary town" of Flushing, they were detained by Captain (Sir) Edmund Uvedall, governor of Flushing. Sterrell had been similarly detained and questioned three years earlier by Thomas Ferrers. Sterrell must have had an interesting discussion with Sir Edmund Uvedall, for within a short time Uvedall sent him on his way into England. Sterrell told Uvedall that he was working for Essex, and Uvedall then checked out his story with merchants of Middelburg, doubtless Francis Harvey.

At first, Uvedall's release of Sterrell seems inexplicable in light of the deposition given by young Gatacre. The former seminarian told in detail of Sterrell's meetings with three of the most notorious English fugitives, men accused of seeking the assassination of the queen of England. The Wilkes mission had planned to seek the extradition Hugh Owen, among others. The story Gatacre told would have led to the arrest and execution of almost any Englishman who had acted as Sterrell had. Yet Sterrell was allowed to leave, and soon Gatacre, too, was released. Uvedall wrote to Lord Treasurer Burghley's secretary, Maynard, that he had questioned Sterrell and detained Somerset and Gatacre. He informed Maynard (and Burghley) that he had sent Gatacre's examination on to Essex "because they do appertain to him" and glibly stated that in the examination there was "*no matter of any purpose.*"[18] Gatacre had in fact told Uvedall an incredible story; the details he gives provide the clues as to why Sterrell and Gatacre were given treatment by Uvedall that preserved their lives. Gatacre testified[19]:

> From Douay I went to Brussels, where I had a half-brother, pensioner to the king of Spain, called Thomas Fitzherbert, who, coming for the king of France with the Duke of Feria, remained with the Duke at Brussels. I moved him concerning my passage into England, but was delayed 10 or 11 weeks by the frost.... When the frost broke my brother went with me to Antwerp, and in our company went Mr. Owen, as I think, a pensioner to the king of Spain. At our arrival we had our diet together at one Verstegan's, and lodged at a Dutchman's house. Within three or four days came this Mr. Sterrell, upon what occasion I know not, but I confess that from the time of Sterrell's coming, after every dinner and supper incontinent [immediately], I departed the chamber and left them to their talk. One day a Mr. Jaques came to dinner whom I never saw before that time. He was attired in black satin, with a man attending on him. He uttered these or like words at the table: "By God, they say in England I would have killed the Queen, but, by God, belie me." What he was I am unable to say; he was slender and reasonable tall of stature, and had a black beard; and had been, as he said, a follower to the deceased Lord Chancellor [Hatton]. These parties be all that had any speech with Sterrell. To come to myself, my brother committed me to him, who promised he would be a means for my passage. I departed from Antwerp with him under colour of his "serviteur."

Captain Uvedall would have instantly recognized the names of Owen and Jaques. For years Robert Cecil sought Owen's extradition for crimes against the state and later even tried to have him kidnapped. Jaques was infamous as Sir William Stanley's lieutenant, chief of the English regiment serving the Spanish in the Low Countries against the Hollanders and the English. Stanley was another whose capture was sought by the English government.

What was it that Sterrell said that kept Uvedall from sending Sterrell and his companions to a treason trial? The initial sentence in Gatacre's statement above provides the necessary information. Gatacre's brother Fitzherbert served *the Duke of Feria*. The importance of this to Uvedall lay in another fact which Sterrell undoubtedly knew: Uvedall's wife of two years, Mary Dormer, was the half-sister of Jane Dormer, the Duchess of Feria and mother of this Duke of Feria. Jane Dormer, daughter of Sir William Dormer, had been a lady serving Queen Mary Tudor, and she had married King Philip of Spain's representative in England, Don Gomez Suarez de Figueroa de Cordoba, the Count of Feria.[20] By the 1590s, her son, the Duke of Feria, was a highly trusted Spanish official with activities in Spain, Paris and the Low Countries, and Sterrell's correspondent Thomas Fitzherbert was the Duke's close advisor on all things English. Uvedall's wife, Mary, was half-sister of the Duchess of Feria and aunt to the current Duke of Feria, and she was Catholic. Her brother Robert had sheltered Fr. Campion in 1580–81 at the family estate of Wing, Buckinghamshire. Her first husband was Sir Anthony Browne, eldest son of Viscount Montague, who was the only lord to speak against Elizabeth's Act of Uniformity. One of her sons became a Jesuit lay brother. Sir Anthony Browne's only sister was Mary Browne, the Countess Southampton, mother of Henry Wriothesley, third Earl of Southampton. No wonder then that Edmund Uvedall sent the statement of Gatacre on to the Earl of Essex and not to Lord Burghley. It touched deeply on Uvedall's immediate family. The larger Uvedall family were Catholic and connected to other Catholic families; a historian of the Jesuits notes that some of the family retired to Antwerp.[21] After Sir Edmund Uvedall died, his widow Mary took as her third husband Sir Thomas Gerard, brother of the Jesuit Fr. John Gerard.

Uvedall also took the confession of George Somerset, and this he sent on to Lord Treasurer Burghley, along with a mention of the fact he had apprehended Gatacre and Sterrell.[22] The confession said that George had been sent to Bruges by his father fifteen or sixteen years earlier.[23] A month later Uvedall wrote to Burghley again asking whether he should send George Somerset on to England or set him free. Gatacre and Somerset were detained but eventually released.[24] No doubt Uvedall instructed Gatacre not to repeat to anyone else what he had written in his statement to Uvedall. Because Gatacre's deposition was sent to Essex by Uvedall with the discussion of whom Sterrell was meeting—Owen, Fitzherbert, Verstegan, and Jaques—it must be assumed that Sterrell's actions were approved by Essex.[25] Meanwhile, Hugh Owen remained with Verstegan for a few months, and they were joined by Jaques's commander, Sir William Stanley.[26] One suspects that Stanley had met with Sterrell and the others as well, but that Gatacre had understood that he should not confess to meeting with the most infamous turncoat in English history.

By early 1595 Sterrell was in a solid relationship with the members of the Low Countries intelligence group who were associated with the Jesuits, with the Brussels government, with the king of Spain, and with Rome. The meeting with Sterrell in Antwerp had required advance planning: their purpose was the establishment of a long-term intelligence relationship conducted under carefully established procedures. It operated successfully until 1603, when the accession of James to the English crown removed the concern that was the focus of the intelligence network, the succession question.

After Antwerp

Subsequent to the meetings in Antwerp, the Sterrell-Owen-Fitzherbert group went back to their principals to secure support for the intelligence enterprise. Owen and Verstegan had to get backing in Brussels. Fitzherbert had to look to the Duke of Feria and to Madrid, where Sir Francis Englefield and Father Persons were the chief influences with the King of Spain on English matters. Sterrell (and Phelippes) had to turn to Essex. The Jesuits were to be an important element in the plan, as they were the principal beneficiaries of much of the intelligence. They were an international organization, well-disciplined, composed of educated and highly motivated men, unburdened by families and unconcerned with personal wealth. Jesuit counselors were adjuncts at the Courts of Brussels, Madrid, Rome, Vienna and Florence. Sterrell was to be, as Fitzherbert had promised, their "general factor" at the English Court for the next eight years.

A week or so after Sterrell left Antwerp, "Nicols" (Owen, with Verstegan) again wrote to "Hallins" (Sterrell with Phelippes), using commercial language to disguise their intelligence. The proposals discussed with Sterrell for an intelligence operation had met with approval but Owen's principals needed to be provided some additional proof of the bona fides of the correspondence.[27] They wanted to be informed as to the persons on whose behalf Sterrell was operating. The second half of the letter, in a different hand, again uses merchant language to convey the idea that Sterrell will be well paid for his commodities. "Nicols"(Owen) understands that Essex is the man behind Sterrell. He says: "Please to signify unto my good Lord of Essex how ready I am to serve him." The developing relationship is proceeding under the wing of Essex, though probably without Essex's full knowledge. "Nicols" purports to be willing to engage in intelligence service for Essex, and he—Nicols/Owen—believes rightly that "Hallins" is in the employ of Essex. Sterrell and Phelippes waited for the proper moment to approach Essex about a new intelligence undertaking. It would take more than a year to complete the arrangements for the network.

Sterrell in Madrid, October 1595

In the fall and winter of 1595–96 Sterrell undertook two trips into Flanders and went on to Spain on one of these to cement relations with Persons. To become "general factor … for … father Parsons" as Fitzherbert sought, a face to face meeting with Persons would be necessary.[28] Sterrell visited Persons about October 1595.[29] The timing was significant. It is less than a year after Sterrell's meetings in Antwerp with Persons's close associates, Fitzherbert, Owen and Verstegan, and was probably a visit to further the plans they all had made in Antwerp in January. This was also about five months after Fr. Thomas Wright had gone to London under the protection of Essex. Wright had given some intelligence concerning Spain to Essex. Sterrell was in a very good position to know what Wright had passed on to Essex and to the English government. This would have been of considerable concern to Persons and his supporters.

Through much of 1595 and into 1596 political change was taking place in Brussels, Madrid and Rome that affected the Sterrell-Owen-Fitzherbert network. Archduke Ernest died within a matter of days after Sterrell had left Antwerp, in February 1595. A temporary governor was named as King Philip decided on the future of the Spanish Netherlands. Philip chose two people to rule in Brussels who were to be central to Sterrell's life for the next 30 years, one a Catholic Cardinal, the other a princess. Philip was the father of the princess, the Infanta Isabella, who was soon to be the bride of Albert, the Cardinal Archduke whom Philip appointed governor in Brussels in early 1596. Nearing the end of his reign, the Spanish King arranged for Albert and Isabella to assume a limited sovereignty over the Spanish Netherlands. Philip II also had to replace his two trusted English advisors in Madrid: Sir Francis Englefield and Fr. Robert Persons.

For many years Sir Francis Englefield had been the principal English intelligencer for the court of King Philip II, and Fr. Persons in recent years had assumed an even more influential role with King Philip. By late summer 1596 Sir Francis was dying, and his replacement was to be Sterrell's long-time correspondent Thomas Fitzherbert. Fr. Persons was preparing to leave Madrid permanently for Rome, and he strongly urged King Philip to support an English intelligence operation in Brussels to be handled by Hugh Owen and Richard Verstegan. William Sterrell was to be the English base of an intelligence line that extended from London to Brussels/Antwerp (Owen and Verstegan), and then to Madrid (Fitzherbert) and Rome (Persons).

Sir Francis Englefield and Fr. Persons and the Intelligence Network

Sir Francis Englefield was a Catholic who befriended Mary Tudor. When she became queen in 1553, Englefield was made a Privy Councilor. Mary's death and the crowning of a Protestant queen in 1558 caused Englefield to remove to Europe. When Elizabeth's government became more anti–Catholic, Sir Francis became an active opponent of Queen Elizabeth. A property of Sir Francis is germane to this narrative.

As he departed England on account of religion in 1559, Englefield executed a deed for the benefit of Margaret Fitton, the wife of his brother John Englefield.[30] The deed contained a provision that if Sir Francis should die without issue his lands should descend to John Englefield, or if he were not living then to the heirs of John. After Sir Francis stayed abroad beyond the time he was licensed, his property was sequestered, with certain of the revenues then going to the Exchequer. In 1571 an Act of Parliament was passed for seizing property of fugitives. A year later it was followed by another Act, which allowed the queen to grant leases of property thus seized by the Crown. Sir Francis sought to put his lands beyond the reach of the government by making a further conveyance early in 1576. He executed a deed to his nephew, Francis Englefield (son of John, now deceased), with use in Sir Francis for his life. However, Sir Francis included two provisos: (1) if he had lawful male issue, then the grant to his nephew was void; and (2) if Sir Francis should deliver or have delivered to his nephew a gold ring with the intent to void the grant to the nephew, then the grant was to be of no effect. In 1584, Sir Francis was implicated in the Throckmorton Plot and was attainted for high treason with the attendant forfeiture of his lands.[31] Were it not for the questions about title to these properties, we would not know of the odd sojourn in Spain of the young printer who would later publish Shakespeare's *Sonnets*.

As an advisor to King Philip II of Spain, Englefield had urged the dispatch of the Armada to England in 1588. Through Englefield intelligence from England was passed to the Spanish King and his Council. A letter of January 1595 from one of Spain's English servants, Anthony Rolston (who for a time sent intelligence back to England), related to Anthony Bacon the special role of Sir Francis Englefield: "All the affairs relating to England and Englishmen, which were to be transacted in the councils or the court, were to pass through the hands of Sir Francis Englefield, to whose report credit was given."[32] Fr. Persons's status in Madrid in 1595–96 was perhaps even greater than that of Sir Francis Englefield.[33]

Nearing death, Sir Francis on September 8, 1596, dictated a final letter of advice to the Spanish king whom he had served for four decades.[34] Among other items, he discussed the support the king should give to Fr. Persons. He encouraged the project Persons was proposing for Flanders for a special conference on the affairs of England to be held under their newly-appointed governor, Archduke Albert. He urged the king to appoint Thomas Fitzherbert as Englefield's successor in providing intelligence and advice on England. Sir Francis even recommended knighthood for Fitzherbert, who had provided intelligence in English matters to Philip from Rouen, Paris, and the Low Countries. Conveniently, Fitzherbert had just arrived in Spain in the company of the Duke of Feria. Englefield's recommendation and the move of Fitzherbert to Madrid were in furtherance of the plans Sterrell, Owen, Fitzherbert, Verstegan and Sherwood had made in Antwerp in January 1595 (also advanced by two more trips of Sterrell to Flanders in 1595–96) and Sterrell and Persons in October 1595.

Thomas Fitzherbert fit into Persons's plans as the Jesuit made ready to depart Spain at the end of 1596 for the troubled English College of Rome: he was to look after Persons's interests in Spain. The relationship between Persons and Fitzherbert is indicated by the fact that in 1600 Fitzherbert took the extraordinary step of requesting the Spanish Council of State to obtain the support of King Philip III for a Cardinal's hat for Fr. Persons.[35] Persons's last contacts with the Spanish Privy Council were directed to setting long-term policies for England. William Sterrell was a key element of those plans and was mentioned by name to the Spanish crown.

A special document to understanding the unfolding events of 1596 and several years thereafter is an undated memorandum of Persons to Martin de Idiaquez, one of Persons's contacts for King Philip II's Council of State. Entitled "Principal points to facilitate the English Enterprise," it reflected the state of affairs in August 1596, as a new armada was preparing to sail from Spain.[36] The "principal points" were Persons's (and Englefield's) plan just when Fitzherbert arrived in Madrid.

Persons sought commitments from the Spanish King for restoring England to Catholicism, Persons's lifelong goal. The king should make a vow to God to seek this end. The king should allay concerns about joining the English Crown to the Spanish by indicating, through a "little tract" by some reputable Englishman, that Philip did not claim the English crown for himself. Persons suggested Sir Francis Englefield as the author, but Persons surely was to be the writer. Persons's memorandum urged support of Catholics in Scotland and of little raids upon England by English exiles in Flanders. Persons sought the establishment of a special Board to advise Archduke Albert on English affairs. Its main purpose was to undercut the influence of an anti–Jesuit group that was influenced by Persons's long-time opponent Charles Paget.[37] Persons spoke directly of the possibility of the Spanish King sending another Armada in the near future, which Persons said should include an English Catholic ecclesiastic to provide reassurance to Catholics in England of the honorable intentions of the king.

The Jesuit urged the king to support intelligence activities in England: "the great point which ought to be considered first is to obtain very good information from England of everything that is being done or said by the enemy." Garnet—the Jesuit Superior in England—had informed Persons that "*trustworthy men may be obtained in London, who will get their information at the fountainhead in the Council*, and they themselves will provide correspondents in the principal ports, who will keep advising as to the warlike preparations." He urged that this support could be handled through Flanders with the use of the English exiles Owen and Verstegan, who had long worked with Fitzherbert. Persons was clearly describing the Sterrell-Owen-Fitzherbert network that would soon work with Persons in Rome.

The final paragraph of the "Principal points" mentioned Sterrell by name and this point was clearly tied to the previous regarding English intelligence. Persons wrote: "It would be well for some fitting person also to go to England to treat with those earls who twice sent their agent Sterrell to Flanders last winter."³⁸ Thus, Sterrell was one of the trustworthy men in London, who could get information at the fountainhead in the Council.

Sterrell's two visits to Flanders in the winter of 1595–96 were in addition to his trip to Antwerp in January 1595. The first of these must have been the time of Sterrell's October 1595 trip to see Persons in Spain. Probably Sterrell used the possibility of some negotiations for the return of the English cautionary towns of Flushing and Briel as an excuse to go abroad. The status of these towns was frequently a subject for negotiation in this period. Persons had apparently made King Philip aware of prior work of Sterrell.

With Persons leaving Spain, Owen in 1596 needed to shore up his role as an intelligencer on a new basis in Brussels, and with a new Governor over the Spanish Netherlands. The influence of Owen in Brussels is indicated in a 1596 confession of Anthony Copley to the English Privy Council in which he said that Fr. Holt and Hugh Owen "have the sovereign dealing for all Englishmen's matters in the Flander court. None can be preferred in that court without their favour, nor obtain any pension there without the liberality of their good word: the one being in credit with the prince's secretary, none more…."³⁹

Persons's Guest in Madrid: Thomas Thorpe

Arriving in Madrid at the about same time as Sterrell's associate Thomas Fitzherbert, most likely with Fitzherbert, was a man from London, newly admitted to the Stationers Company. He was greeted warmly by Sir Francis and Fr. Persons and was established in Sir Francis's own ample quarters, in the company of several of Persons' seminary students. The man was almost certainly connected with the efforts of Persons, Englefield and Fitzherbert to gain support for an English intelligence service. He probably was sent to Spain by Sterrell and his later career as publisher would suggest a long-time association with Sterrell. He was Thomas Thorpe, publisher in 1609 of *Shakespeare's Sonnets*.

Thomas Thorpe was the son of Thomas Thorpe, innkeeper of Barnet, Middlesex, and was apprenticed in 1584 to Richard Watkins, a printer and stationer of London. On February 4, 1594 "Thomas Throp" was admitted a freeman of the Stationers company.⁴⁰ Little is known of Thorpe's activities between 1594 and 1600.

On 19 March 1597 Thomas Thorpe was part of an inquisition in the Court of the Exchequer in London.⁴¹ Thorpe was asked whether Sir Francis Englefield was dead, how Thorpe knew he was dead, how he came to the knowledge of Sir Francis's death, where he died and how he died. Thorpe responded that he had met with Sir Francis in Madrid a few weeks before Sir Francis's death and spoke with him three or four times before Sir Francis rode to Vallodolid, where he died. Thorpe stayed in the Madrid house of Sir Francis after his death.

The purpose of this inquisition was to establish the right of Sir Francis's nephew, also named Francis Englefield, to a certain property. Queen Mary had granted the manor of Wootton Bassett in Wiltshire in 1555 to Sir Francis Englefield in tail for life with remainder in tail to his brother John.⁴² Sir Francis thus had only a life estate (if he had no male issue) that was forfeited to Queen Elizabeth, and this property had been granted in 1589 to parties who held title for the Earl of Essex. But because all Sir Francis had was a life estate, this property would pass on his death to the heir male of Sir Francis's brother, John, who was

Francis Englefield. Until the death of Sir Francis, a 1589 Crown grant to Thomas Crompton, Robert Wright, and Gelly Meyrick, for the benefit of the Earl of Essex, had lawfully placed them in possession of the manor. But on the death of Sir Francis, his nephew was entitled to possession as holder of the remainder interest under the 1555 grant. The Exchequer proceeding to establish the death of Sir Francis Englefield was to determine that the rights under the 1589 grant to Essex's nominees had terminated, and Francis Englefield was entitled to enter upon the property. In 1597, Francis Englefield took up his residence at Wootton Basset.[43] The Thorpe deposition (with another) enabled Francis Englefield to occupy Wootton Basset, and this is the reason why the copy of the Exchequer document now in the Bodleian Library was made for him.[44]

Thorpe's first-hand account of seeing Sir Francis Englefield and his notorious associate Fr. Persons and staying in Englefield's Madrid residence after his death was more than sufficient to establish the death of Sir Francis. But why should Thomas Thorpe, a young member of the Stationers Company who had recently completed his apprenticeship, be in a position to meet with Sir Francis Englefield and Fr. Persons? By his own account, Thorpe had been in Madrid for some weeks before Sir Francis went to Valladolid, where he died in mid-September 1596. He was still there some three weeks or more after the death. Persons put considerable trust in Thorpe in providing lodgings and sharing information with him. How was Thorpe able to leave England for Spain? What was he doing meeting with Englefield and Persons? Why would Persons trust him? Why was Thorpe not imprisoned upon his return?

Thorpe's Journey: How and Why

Travel from England to Spain was strictly controlled. No person could leave England without a passport, and one had to have powerful friends at the English Court to gain a passport. Returning, Thorpe would have faced treason charges, just as had Anthony Skinner in 1592. He was surely given assistance by someone with influence at Court and trusted by the government. There is nothing to indicate that Thorpe suffered any negative repercussions from his visit to Spain and his association with Sir Francis Englefield and Fr. Persons. Yet there is also nothing to indicate that he was working as an agent for the English government at any time.

Nor could Thorpe have entered Spain without safe conduct from Spanish authorities. Fr. Persons, Thorpe's host, would easily have obtained clearance for the young Englishman, and no Englishman could enter Madrid without his knowledge. But Persons had last walked on English soil when Thorpe was no more than eleven years old. Why would Persons entertain and house Thorpe, expose him to the young seminarians, and reveal to Thorpe a secret (Englefield's death) that he was keeping quiet even from the Spanish authorities? The only plausible explanation is that Thorpe was sent by someone well trusted by Persons. William Sterrell is one of the few men who can be identified with such influence in London and with Persons and with Persons's intelligence associates in Antwerp and Brussels.

The family who most immediately benefited from Thorpe's inquisition testimony was Francis Englefield's, the nephew of Sir Francis. And that family was closely connected to Thomas Fitzherbert's patron, the Duke of Feria. The mother of the Duke of Feria was the

Englishwoman Jane Dormer. Francis Englefield's wife was Jane Browne, daughter of Anthony Browne and Mary Dormer, half-sister of Jane Dormer. Jane Browne may well have been named for her illustrious aunt Jane Dormer.[45] The Duke of Feria and Francis Englefield's wife thus were first cousins. In fact, the family relationship was dual: Jane Browne Englefield's aunt Elizabeth (sister of Anthony Browne) was married to Sir Robert Dormer, half-brother of the Countess of Feria, Jane Dormer.[46] Both the Dormer and Browne families were very strongly Catholic, and the Continental Dormer branch sought to assist their family who remained in England. It is likely that Thomas Fitzherbert would have facilitated communication between the Dormer family in Europe and the Dormer/Browne connections in England through his correspondent William Sterrell. Multiple instances have been cited in which Sterrell served as the go-between for Catholic families who had relatives on the Continent and how Sterrell helped Fitzherbert's cousin William Bassett and his half-brother John Gatacre. Another of Jane (Browne) Englefield's relatives who would have Court ties to the Essex circle and William Sterrell was her aunt Mary (Browne) Wriothesley, Countess of Southampton, full sister of Anthony Browne. And Sterrell's patron, Worcester, was himself closely related to these Catholic Brownes.

It is, of course, unlikely that Thorpe went into Spain to benefit the nephew of Sir Francis: he could not have known that Sir Francis would die soon after Thorpe's arrival. The family background helps us understand that Thorpe was sent by someone with entree to Sir Francis and Fr. Persons. It also makes understandable that Thorpe could testify in London in a property title proceeding for Francis Englefield about his stay in Spain without the consequence of a treason trial. The Browne-Worcester connection was an influential one.

Why would Sterrell select Thorpe? He was a printer-stationer, and the Catholic network needed someone to facilitate the propagation of religious and political material into England. Persons wanted to send forth books and pamphlets. Thorpe's business practices—a middleman without the burdens of a shop and fixed press—were congenial to the needs of Persons and other Catholic writers who would have found him most useful to arrange printing and distribution of Catholic works. In fact, Persons wanted a printing press and presumably an English printer to accompany the armada that was assembled for an invasion to take place soon after Thorpe arrived in Madrid. Persons's "principal points" for the king said that to avoid doubt and division among the friends of the Catholic cause, "it will [be] necessary to write many letters; and declarations will have to be printed." To provide for these, a printing press should be sent in the fleet for the printing of such letters and declarations. The excommunication of Queen Elizabeth should be renewed and printed and distributed in England. Printing declarations and bulls in Antwerp in 1588 had been unproductive. Perhaps Thorpe was groomed for this role. The 1596 armada suffered the fate of bad weather that had helped defeat the Spanish fleet in 1588.[47]

Upon his return to England, Thorpe facilitated the printing of Catholic works. Most had to be in secret. He was clearly associated with printers of Catholic works and Catholic writers.[48] One of these was Valentine Simmes, a well-known printer who secretly published Catholic works and was jailed for such activity in 1607, where he was joined with another printer, Henry Owen, brother of Nicholas Owen whose freedom from prison Sterrell had earlier secured. Thorpe and Valentine Simmes were openly associated with the publication in 1604 of Fr. Thomas Wright's *The Passions of the Mind*, which had introductory verse by the Catholic writers Ben Jonson and Hugh Holland. Wright was a former Jesuit and associate of Fr. Persons in Spain. He had returned to England in 1595, seeking the protection of the Earl of Essex.

Gaining Access Through Essex

The final step in completing the Sterrell-Owen network was to secure a safe sponsor so that if the exchange of intelligence were discovered by government agents hostile to the Catholics, the English intelligencers would be seen as working in support of the queen. That is, Phelippes and Sterrell needed a sponsor. The Earl of Essex was again to be their cover. Essex was probably aware of Sterrell's efforts to establish a continuing correspondence with the English Catholic fugitives during 1595 but Phelippes and Sterrell sought express support for an expanded program in late 1596. Phelippes informed Essex of the most recent correspondence that Sterrell had been receiving for two years in the name of Hallins.[49] Phelippes abstracted some of the Nicols/Hallins correspondence, with a running commentary addressed to Essex.[50] Although he does not specifically identify "Nicols," the excerpts leave no doubt that Owen is the source of some or most of the intelligence in the excerpts. Phelippes lets slip Owen's name to Essex in a postscript: "Touching the truth of this negotiation your lordship is best able to judge by your other intelligences. But *Owens* meaning is apparent to make debate and mistrust by publishing thereof in this manner."[51] In marginal identifications, the letter deciphers the name *Guillamme de Boys* as Owen and the excerpt urges that Owen not be named as the source, adding: "you must use your discretion as Guillam de Boys be made no author who trusteth you much as you may perceave."

Phelippes reminded Essex that five years earlier Phelippes had learned of Sterrell's intelligence connections with the exiles and had restored the exchange of information. Problems arose with Sterrell's mission, and Sterrell was suspected without cause; the queen had become "distasted with the man and the matter." Phelippes himself had difficulties and was imprisoned for a year, and now was in great debt to the queen. Despite his troubles, Phelippes told Essex, "with carriage and care, together with the party's [Sterrell's] patience and travail" he had recovered a port where he hoped Essex would find the traffic in intelligence could be both safely and profitably exercised. If it were so, Phelippes hoped that Essex would recommend his industry and devotion to the queen in disproof of the "slanderous and false" allegations made against him. Phelippes followed up with two more letters attaching documents to buttress his case.[52]

The timing of this December 1596 proposal by Phelippes (and Sterrell) to Essex is in close proximity to Persons's memorandum to the Spanish King seeking support for an Owen/Verstegan intelligence operation connected to "trustworthy men ... in London, who will get their information at the fountainhead in the Council." The King and Spanish Council doubtless did give Persons the support he sought. From Thorpe's deposition, this was about the time he and Fr. Persons parted company. Was Thorpe the messenger to Sterrell and Phelippes who brought them word that Persons's English enterprise was going forward, signaling them to approach Essex? Perhaps. No doubt Thorpe was well paid for the risks he assumed by traveling into the land of the arch-enemy of England and conferring at length with notorious and attainted fugitives. He will have earned the gratitude of Francis

Englefield and his wife. Too, he will have deserved great credit with Sterrell and Sterrell's employer, the Earl of Worcester, who by 1603 was well-positioned at Court to reward a publisher with patronage.

Phelippes made a proposal to Essex to reopen Sterrell's old correspondence with new support and a new tack. Sterrell had fallen into suspicion by the other side, and Phelippes had to work hard to restore confidence in him.[53] The way to proceed was to have Sterrell claim he had again turned against the English government and had brought someone with him to advise the fugitives. Phelippes proposed that he and Sterrell create an imaginary correspondent at the English court who would provide intelligence to Owen. Phelippes pretended that Sterrell was not aware of this proposal, for Sterrell had just left for Wales with his lord (Worcester). Phelippes could continue the intelligence on his own until Sterrell returned. He prayed that Essex not inform William Waad of this employment, "or that any mention was made of him [Waad]; for though he be my good friend and an honest faithful gentleman, I know he lies too open to these crafty fences and was kindly overtaken in this action, as when time serves I will more particularly inform you." To show that Phelippes's loyalties were with Essex against the Cecils, Phelippes included extracts from a letter between two Catholic exiles that the Lord Treasurer had gotten Phelippes to decipher a year before.[54]

The Queen Is Drawn In: "her majesty had advertisements that pleased her"

Phelippes later testified that Essex approved the proposal and secured the cooperation of Queen Elizabeth. Subsequent events indicate that the correspondence thus initiated flourished for the next seven years and that Essex was aware of some portion of it, albeit only such as Sterrell and Phelippes chose to share with Essex. When the long-term correspondence was finally discovered after James became king, both Sterrell and Phelippes asserted that Essex and the queen had authorized the correspondence between Sterrell and Hugh Owen, and she had gained much from it.[55] Just after Cecil arrested him in January 1605, Phelippes wrote Cecil a long explanation of the 1596 proposal to Essex[56]:

[margin: Adresse to Sterrill from Owen]
Whereupon against the time of the Adelantado his enterprise [i.e., the October-November 1596 armada] as I take it being on that side as it seemed resolved to broach an Intelligence. There was a letter addressed unto Sterrill [i.e., Hallins] from Owen [i.e., Nicols] as he said showing all confidence and for that there would be special use, urging him to enter into a Course of Intelligence for the which he should have an honest entertainment which other such matter of moment as I thought fit being brought to me to recommend to my Lord.

His Lo: [Essex] communicating the whole with the Queen by her commandment Sterrell had order to proceed as was required. And so by many things which passed to and fro much light was gotten. I was then a prisoner in the Fleet yet managed it wholye to her Highness contentment sometime by the entremise [entremise—mediation or intervention] of my Lord of Essex sometime by Mr. Carmarthen.

Phelippes went on to tell Cecil that Phelippes himself took up the correspondence, despite his continuing in prison for a time. He and Sterrell hit upon a stratagem whereby Phelippes "came in as a man in a Cloud by the name of Vincent...." When Sterrell was pressed by the Court of the Archduke as to the identity of the secret correspondent, they used the story of Spirit Orthon, who would disappear if his identity were revealed. The correspondence coming from the Low Countries "came as from a Chanon [canon, monk] of Liège." This "monk" was assigned the name of John Petit by Sterrell, Phelippes, and their correspondent.[57] The queen enjoyed the correspondence that ensued, said Phelippes: "her majesty had advertisements that pleased her." In the months after his initial statements, Phelippes's story evolved. He deliberately down-played the role of Sterrell in the correspondence to protect him. Sterrell had the powerful protection of the Earl of Worcester, and Phelippes desperately needed some backing at James's Court if he were to hope ever to be free or. "Vincent" was only one name used by the Sterrell/Phelippes team in writing intelligence letters to the Low Countries.

Fr. Henry Garnet

Thomas Phelippes's letter to Essex of December 9, 1596, and the abstracts of "Nicols's" correspondence mentioned one more person who is important to the ensuing correspondence. This was Henry Garnet, Jesuit Superior for England. His name is linked forever with the Gunpowder Treason of 1605.

The excerpts from one of the letters from "Nicols"/Owen to "Hallins" (Sterrell) states: "Some your ill willers have given out that Wade should say how you had promised to find father Garnet and deliver him to Wade's hands but let not that trouble you." Thomas Phelippes then alluded to this statement in his letter to Essex[58]:

> You may see how Mr. Waad was overtaken in discovering the promise of taking Garnet. It set Garnet and his crew against our man [Sterrell], so as it cost six months writing to and fro to salve that suspicion though they never charged him [Sterrell] with it, or wrote of it, but that by some letters from hence, shewed me by Mr. Waad, I found they accused our man as a dealer with the state, which in some sort at his first going over he did not deny; whereupon your lordship may see the letter from Petit [the "monk" of Liège][59] is grounded.

Evidently Sterrell had promised he could take Garnet, but then word got out of the effort, and Garnet "and his crew" avoided Sterrell. The supposed effort to find Garnet was all theater with Sterrell. It was part of the tactic that Sterrell had used with Waad to justify the release of Nicholas Owen from prison. Garnet and Sterrell no doubt conferred on an occasional basis, and it was through Garnet's hands that the Sterrell/Phelippes secret intelligence passed, endorsed by his signature "H" [for Henry] on many of the letters to show that they had come through him. Though much sought after, Garnet eluded the government's pursuivants until the massive manhunt after the Gunpowder Plot. Sterrell was one of those who was set to finding Garnet. True to his pattern, Sterrell just could not quite find him, though he was close to capturing him, and would have if someone else had not tripped him up. Or so he maintained. He survived his failures by serving up intelligence that amused the queen, "advertisements that pleased her."

16

The Network at Work
Tricks of Strong Imagination

> And as imagination bodies forth
> The forms of things unknown, the poet's pen
> Turns them to shapes, and gives to airy nothing
> A local habitation and a name.
> Such tricks hath strong imagination
> —*A Midsummer Nights Dream* 5.1

The Crafting of Letters

Sterrell and his associates eluded the English government (and historians) by the complexity of their communications. Think of the Sterrell-Phelippes-Owen intelligence enterprise as a workshop in which names, identities and roles were imagined and crafted into life. The enterprise had offices in London, Brussels and Antwerp. The epistolary characters that they bodied forth performed roles in those cities and other venues, including Madrid, Paris and Rome. What the men did is breathtaking in its audacity. Everything depended on the ingenuity of the three principal men, using letters to achieve their ends. They held no arms, led no troops, lacked financial resources and remained hidden behind assumed names. Yet they were significant players in international developments. They took great risks and were eventually discovered. Only Phelippes seems to have suffered punishment. Robert Cecil imprisoned Phelippes for years without affording him a trial. And Cecil sent agents to Flanders to kidnap Owen and return him to England for execution for treason. The Archduke who governed the Low Countries protected Owen. And Sterrell? He continued an active role in Court life, managing royal entertainments, arranging visits of foreign dignitaries, and receiving gifts from King James himself.

The intelligence correspondence can be divided into:

1. the J. B./Hallins letters, in which "J. B." or "John Petit"—a canon of Liège—wrote to "Peter Hallins"—a *coopman* (merchant) of London;
2. the Robinson/Boulant letters;
3. the Rivers letters: Anthony Rivers—imagined as a *socius* or executive assistant to Fr. Henry Garnet—is the nominal writer in most; and
4. the Orwell-Vincent letters.

From these and related letters can be traced the intelligencers' efforts to influence the English Court, their handling of several major controversies touching upon the Jesuits in

England, and their appearances in diplomatic relations between England and the Low Countries in the period 1597 to 1605.

The Hallins Letters—Fishing in Troubled Water

Hugh Owen and his associates in Flanders were writing to Sterrell as though he were a merchant named Hallins by 1594.[1] The person writing to Hallins generally purports to be a monk (canon) of Liège. The monk is supposedly an Englishman who remains devoted to Queen Elizabeth, and Liège is given as his place of residence as it is a neutral territory. "JB" says he is writing in her Majesty's service.[2]

The Hallins identity was created for letters coming into England and were meant to be seen by English officials. Phelippes, in a document probably given to Robert Cecil in April 1600, stated that "the Advertisements from Liége ... *were meant should come to view* and *were to possess the state with conceits [ideas] for their purposes....*"[3] They were instigated, he indicated, by the Archduke Albert himself to "vent [disperse] his Liége merchandise [information, intelligence]." Queen Elizabeth probably read them; they were "advertisements that pleased her" as Phelippes told Robert Cecil in 1605.[4] The intelligence to "Hallins" was designed to produce in the queen and members of her Council a favorable impression of the Archdukes, Albert and Isabella, and an unfavorable impression of the Kings of France and of Scotland. Sterrell was in a position to pass these letters at Court after his patron Worcester became Deputy Master of the Horse in January 1598. Worcester, and with him Sterrell, would be present at Court almost constantly after this appointment, especially with Essex (Master of the Horse) occupied abroad. Phelippes, too, had his connections at Court and passed intelligence (including "Hallins" and "Boulant" letters) to Cecil, to Lord Treasurer Buckhurst, and to Lord Cobham.

An example of the "conceits" intended for the queen's reading will serve to illustrate the tenor of the correspondence—witty, learned and gossipy, designed to appeal to and flatter a witty, gossipy queen. At a time when the Low Countries intelligencers wanted to breed distrust of the French king in Elizabeth's policy, Owen/"J. B." wrote to Sterrell/"Peter Hallins"[5]:

> I am sorry to see Frenchmen speed so well and the more for that their greatness is set up and upheld by England whereby they make a rod for their own tail.[6] [the English have made a whip to be used against themselves].... I pray God her Majesty with her Council have no cause to repent then for making strong ancient enemies and others that will never be true friends. Now that he [Henry IV] be King of France absolute he mocketh her Majestie saying he had rather be bitten by a dog [Spain] than scratched by a cat [Elizabeth] which words he useth always to say upon all occasions when her Majestie or her ministers for her have demanded some towns in France [in return for loans].

Similarly, in June 1600 "JB" wrote to "Halyns" words that were sure to upset the queen; the Hollanders she had so long supported were indifferent to the approach of her death and were to throw immediately their support to James of Scotland[7]:

> One in Holland wrote these words following to a friend of his in this town [Liège] who showed me the letter & is a very honest man & giveth the like relation of his friend that writeth unto him from Holland. The States are informed that the Queen's weak state of body is such as not like to continue long & that they care not if she were dead tomorrow, being resolved in private council that so soon as they shall understand decease they will presently ship a competent number of men with other necessaries & pass them over to aid the King of Scotland. I know this to be their intention but whether they have been dealt with by the king of Scotland or not I cannot tell.

"J. B." reports often that the Scots king is not to be trusted. The "monk of Liège" vividly warns in March 1598 that James "made open speeches to his nobles demanding money to make wars against England for revenging his mother's death & hath sent ambassadors to divers foreign princes his friends praying their assistance for that cause and to attain the succession of the crown of England."[8] Intelligence was sent that James had dispatched men to Germany to buy guns for war with England.

The J.B. letters frequently provide details of contacts between Scots emissaries and the Spanish court, with a goal of promoting distrust of James by Queen Elizabeth. Thomas Fitzherbert, the member of the group in Spain in 1599, explained to an advisor to the Spanish king why the Spanish Court should maintain the contacts with James, particularly if the young Spanish king should decide to attempt an invasion of England[9]:

> The communications with the Scots ... will arouse the suspicion of the queen of England against the king of Scotland, and she will not trust him to help her when his Majesty attacks England, and may perhaps in the meanwhile try to disturb Scotland (which she can easily do by means of her many connections there), the effect of which might be to upset both countries to such an extent as to prevent the Queen from injuring Spain, as she usually does. His Majesty will thus fish in troubled water to his own benefit and her disadvantage.

Of course, the queen of England had to be informed of such communications between the Scots and the Spanish; Fitzherbert's role was to pass intelligence of Scot/Spanish contacts on to Owen *et al* and they sent it on to the English Court in the guise of the letters of the "monk of Liège" to "Hallins"—Sterrell. When one of Cecil's men went through Phelippes's store of letters in 1605 he encountered a number of the letters of "J.B." and scrawled on the back of one: "this found among Tho. Phelippes papers wherein are many untruths of Scotland and of the King."[10]

On occasions when the intelligencers wanted to convey information to Elizabeth and Cecil that was unlikely to be available to a "monk at Liège," they pretended that the monk received news from a friend who traveled with Archduke Albert. The friend would write from Brussels or the army camp to the "monk at Liège" and these letters would be forwarded to "Hallins" in London. Phelippes would pass these to Robert Cecil. The friend, for example, could comment in detail on each of the English treaty negotiators at Boulogne in June 1600, information that a monk residing in Liège would not be directly privy to. The same friend could send to "Liège" from the camp outside of Ostend details of the siege as it progressed, as he did in a letter of September 1601, together with details of the negotiations of the Duke of Lennox for the Scottish King with the King of France.[11] This letter Phelippes passed on to Robert Cecil on October 3, 1601, saying it pertained to "proceedings at Ostend and of the D. of Lennox negotiation in France."[12] The siege at Ostend was a matter of special interest to Cecil as his own nephew had taken a thousand men to participate in the defense against the Archduke's siege.[13]

Throughout 1597 to 1605, Hugh Owen was the principal English intelligencer to Archduke Albert and Isabella, the governors of the Low Countries. The couple held Owen in high esteem and credited him with several intelligence successes that owed much to information supplied by Sterrell and Phelippes. Albert and Isabella sought amicable relations between their newly sovereign country and England. Several times they used Owen and Sterrell and their associates to promote peace.

The Robinson/Boulant Letters

A canon of Liège was no fit person through whom diplomatic correspondence could pass, so a new personality was conjured up who was said to be a mutual friend of the canon and of Hallins and Robinson (both were alter egos of Sterrell). "Jaques Boulant" was brought on stage in 1598 and again in 1600 to be a conduit of diplomacy for the Archdukes and the English government.

"Boulant" was created to counter intrigues of Charles Paget in 1597 and then "Boulant" took on a life of his own as one who could serve as a peace intermediary. Paget was working secretly with Robert Poley (reporting to Sir Thomas Heneage) and Michael Moody in the Low Countries in 1594. Sterrell had outed Poley as a spy to Owen. Sir Thomas had died in October 1595 and Moody had been imprisoned and died late in 1596, so Paget's go-betweens were gone. When Paget tried to re-establish contacts and influence in England, "Boulant" was created to undermine Paget.

The Anthony Rivers Letters—Spirit Orthon

Just as Queen Elizabeth was given letters from abroad, the Archdukes Albert and Isabella were fed intelligence from Elizabeth's Court that originated from Sterrell and Phelippes. The purpose was not to manipulate but to inform, to shore up the position of Hugh Owen, and to retain the support of the royal couple for the English Catholics. There was more reason to hope for sympathy for the plight of the English Catholics from the Archdukes than from Spain. At the same time in 1605 that Phelippes confessed to Robert Cecil the identity of Hallins, he informed Cecil that the Archduke Albert had been told the story of Spirit Orthon, lest the identity of the writer of letters that Albert read be disclosed[14]:

> After a time Sterrell was pressed to acquaint them with the true name of Vincent and he being much troubled therewith I found this expedient: that he should refer them to the tale of Spirit Orthon in such a place of Frossard—which wrought so well as answer was returned they were not wary of their friend yet alluding to the circumstances of the same tale. And Benson [Owen], as he wrote after, was forced to content the Archduke himself with the same payment, who laughed heartily thereat.

The letters outward from England from Sterrell and Phelippes went under a series of aliases. "Vincent" was the one that Phelippes confessed to in 1605 because Cecil had just intercepted several letters under that name, but other names included George Fenner, Francis Cordale, Ortelio Renzo, Thomas Nevell and, most importantly, Anthony Rivers.[15] The outward Rivers letters went to multiple recipients in Flanders and Rome, generally with about the same information.

The Rivers letters date from 1599 to 1604. They are addressed via assumed names to several English Catholics overseas. The recipients were Fr. Persons, other Jesuits, and Hugh Owen and his associates. The letters are all in the same handwriting and reflect the same voice of the writer. Some were intercepted by the English government and are found in the State Papers, and the remainder of the letters reached their destinations and thus some found their way into repositories of the Catholic Church.

The letters under all five names provide news from the English Court. They touch on current political, social, and religious topics. The Rivers letters especially track the events of the Archpriest Controversy, a religious-political dispute explored below. This "broile" was between a group of dissident secular Catholic priests and adherents of the English Jesuits. It reached a crisis in 1601–02 though it had long simmered. The letter-writer was closely associated with Fr. Henry Garnet and was someone well-known to Fr. Persons. The intercepted letters were captured in the packets that also contained Garnet's letters to the same assumed names in "Venegia"—Venice—as well as letters to persons in Antwerp. The routing of the letters was almost certainly through Antwerp and probably were meant to be read there first and then shared at the Archdukes' Court. The Rivers letters and the Garnet letters refer to one another.

Three intercepted Jesuit packets in the period 1599 to 1603 allow us to understand the operation of the intelligence network and the purpose of the newsletters.[16] The fact that the letters were sent together reveals a good bit about the intelligence methods of the Jesuit-Sterrell/Phelippes group and their relationships.

The Orwell-Vincent Letters

The third level of correspondence out of England from Sterrell and Phelippes was in the names of Orwell and Vincent or Vincent Hussey. These were working letters in the period up to James's accession in 1603. Such letters contained hard intelligence and were most likely used for taking up the business aspects of the intelligence network. These names were used in some letters back to Sterrell and Phelippes but others were sent to "Monsieur Robinson" or to Halyns. Few letters under the names of Orwell and Vincent survive. Sterrell seems to have pulled back from much of the intelligence activities around the time of James's accession, and Phelippes continued doing business after the change in government as "Vincent." The correspondents of "Orwell/Robinson" and "Vincent" were "Jacob Samander" or "J. Sauf" (who was almost certainly Richard Verstegan)[17] and "Nicols" (Hugh Owen). Because Verstegan was a printer and publisher he was in a position to send monies through commercial transactions across borders.

An example of the third level correspondence is a letter of "Jo. Nicols" of June 21, 1599, in Owen's italic hand, and a companion "J. S." letter of June 30, 1599.[18] This Nicols letter (addressed from Middelburg) was doubtless sent with a "J.B." letter of 20 June. The "Nicols" letter includes the following: "My host hath the cheese for my cousins Hussey and Orwell. So all those reckonings are even to the end of June. He stayeth to ship it until A.L.'s ship goeth to London...."[19] "My host" is often used by Owen for Verstegan, and the allusion to A.L.'s ship establishes a clear link with the "J.S." letter of June 30.[20] This letter is from Verstegan,[21] and includes the following: "I hope A.L. will fraught his ship for London about some fourteen days hence, and then I will not fail to give order about the sending of the cheese...." From Phelippes's explanations alongside his extracts of "Petit/Nicols" letters, made for Essex in December 1596, we know that for these linked correspondents, "cheese" was code for money.[22] So each of these two lower-level letters confirms that Verstegan has money to send by A.L.'s ship, money which will settle accounts up to the end of June.[23] This is only readily explicable as money payable by way of pension—for "Hussey" and "Orwell" have not yet had time to submit accounts for *expenses* up to the end of June. Who then are the pensioners in England, "Hussey" and "Orwell"?

Interrogations in late January 1605 provide the answer. On January 26, Cecil administered interrogatories, in his own hand, to Stephen Phelippes, brother and assistant of Thomas. In answer to Cecil's ambiguous question "By what name do the persons beyond seas write unto him [Thomas Phelippes]?," Stephen replied that he did not remember, "other than Vincent *Hussey* and, in former time, Sterrell was *Orwell* and Robinson."[24] His statement also gave a rough indication of the (substantial) sums coming in for this purpose, and made it clear that it was Sterrell who arranged for the final delivery of Thomas Phelippes's portion.

The "Seepage"

The multiple names and levels of correspondence are confusing. And it was intended to be confusing to anyone who was not intimately connected with the correspondence. The exchange of intelligence was extremely dangerous. All had to be deniable if the letters were intercepted. The flow of letters could only be linked together through great effort. No one at the time of the correspondence could have aggregated the letters to identify and compare them. By assembling many letters from several sources and comparing them, some "seepage" across the identities appears. Through confidence of anonymity or carelessness the parties occasionally exchanged information across the identities that allow the writers to be linked. An order for gloves furnishes an example of the "seepage."

"J.B.," purporting to be in Liége, wrote to "Peter Halyns" in London, dated June 10 (31 May, o.s.) 1599. He transmitted an order for two dozen bespoke [custom-made] English gloves.[25] Exactly four weeks later a letter from "Fenner" [one name in the "Rivers" series] of June 30, 1599, o.s., was addressed to "Giulio Piccioli or Bernardo Edlyno." It responded to the letter that had been sent by J.B. to Halyns, stating: "*I have bespoken your gloves*, but they are not yet ready."[26] And three weeks later a "Cordale" letter [the next name in the "Rivers" series] to Antwerp again referred to the gloves bespoken for Edlyn[27]: "I wrote to you and Edlyn for a Bruxells tike [tick] for a bed, and I shall expect it and by the next opportunity I hope to *send Edlyn 2 dozen paire of gloves according to his patterne*." After delivery of the gloves (almost certainly gifts for the newly arrived Archdukes Albert and Isabella), "J.B." wrote to "Halyns" thanking him for the gloves yet grumbling "but you swerved much from the pattern."[28] Aggregating the many letters in these names that survive, it can be seen that Hugh Owen is the person referred to as "J.B." and as "Edlyn," while Sterrell is the person who is the referent for "Halyns," "Fenner," "Cordale" and "Rivers." Other examples of "seepage" occur. At the time, it would have been impossible to link such "seepages."

17

Charles Paget, Meet Monsieur Boulant

"this letter will make a contemplative idiot of him"[1]

The Peace Overture

The inventive intelligence team leaped into action when Charles Paget undertook an intrigue late in 1597. Although known for double-dealing, he still possessed influence among some at the Brussels court. Archduke Ernest was suspicious of him,[2] and his status at the Archduke Albert's coming in 1596 was uncertain. Hugh Owen and Robert Persons were determined to end any role of Paget in the affairs of English Catholics, urging the Spanish king to take a hand.[3]

Paget's gambit to gain influence was to write a letter into England in December 1597 to open negotiations for a treaty between the Archduke and England.[4] The Archduke apparently thought that Paget could open a channel of communication with the English Court. Paget noted that when Thomas Barnes was last in Brussels, he sought by Paget's means to see if Albert was inclined to peace but had returned to England without answer. Paget said that the Archduke was now inclined to amity with all, including France and England.[5] He purported to speak on behalf of the Archduke to seek peace and alluded to the negotiations that were to take place between the French and the Spanish.

Did Archduke Albert authorize Paget to make an overture to the English? Perhaps. But there is no evidence that Cecil received Paget's letter nor that it prompted Cecil to go to France to negotiate a short time later. An Anglo-French treaty of May 1596 provided neither country would negotiate with Spain without apprising the other, so Cecil would have known of the pending discussions regardless of the letter of Paget. In February 1598 Robert Cecil and several other English envoys set forth to France to confer with King Henry IV about his negotiations with the Spanish. Cecil met with King Henry and representatives of the Hollanders in March and April. The Spanish side was represented by envoys from Archduke Albert. During the negotiations, by early April the Archduke was given authority by Spain to negotiate also with the queen of England.[6]

In the middle of these negotiations came a new overture from the Court of the Archdukes. "J. P."/Owen wrote to "Hallins," enclosing a letter of March 7, 1598, from "Monsieur de Boulant," whose role implicitly was to supplant Paget.[7] It was "an overture of further intelligence" pertaining to peace to restore "the ancient amity between England and the house of Burgundy."[8] A second "Boulant" letter was sent, dated April 2, 1598, in which "Boulant" set down reasons why the queen "should not stand to the French" but should instead consider an alliance with the Archduke, wherein Boulant offered his services.[9] Queen Elizabeth responded that Phelippes should make an answer to "Boulant" through instructions she gave to Richard Carmarthen, who had been responsible for oversight of Phelippes in his Customs office.[10]

"Monsieur Boulant" (like "Robinson") was a creation of Sterrell and Phelippes. After Cecil arrested Phelippes in 1605, Phelippes confessed as much to Cecil. He and Sterrell had "possess[ed] the Q[ueen] of a letter written to Sterill by the name of Robinson from one Mons Boulant, an old familiar of his at Liège, for broaching of peace long before the Treaty of Bolen [Boulogne–1600] by the Archd[uke's] own direction."[11]

Both Sterrell and Phelippes told Cecil in 1605 that Sterrell was used by the Archduke in seeking a peace with England. Sterrell and Phelippes were countering Paget's 1597 initiative. If Paget had become a mediator between England and the Low Countries it would have been a disaster for Owen, Fitzherbert, Verstegan, Persons, and the English Jesuits. Paget was seeking to promote a treaty with the backing of France that would have expelled the Jesuits from England as a condition for limited tolerance for English Catholics. By interposing themselves in the peace process, Sterrell and Phelippes (and those with whom they worked) gained the upper hand. They supplanted Paget in the Archduke's retinue. "Monsieur Boulant" proved useful and the intelligencers would again bring his persona into diplomacy when the opportunity was presented later. For now, they had to finish off Paget lest he return to influence with the Archdukes. Though no further use of "Boulant" was made at this time, the intelligencers had succeeded in displacing Paget's influence, and Archduke Albert was "firmly persuaded" of Sterrell's "fidelity and dexterity."[12] Unaware that "Boulant" had dislodged him as a mediator for the Archduke, Paget continued to correspond through Barnes, staking his future on an unidentified figure whom he thought was restoring him with the queen.[13]

The Undoing of Charles Paget

Paget's eagerness to return to England was turned to his downfall. Using letter-tricks to obtain incriminating documents from Paget, the intelligencers provided Robert Persons with the instruments to end the influence of Charles Paget. Robert Persons in August 1598 described the role played by "two Catholics" in England operating under the greatest secrecy.

The troubles between Persons and Paget arose well before the execution of Mary Queen of Scots. In June 1597 Persons traced their enmity back to the year 1582 when Paget was excluded from a meeting of Persons in Paris with the Spanish Ambassador, the Duke of Guise, the Archbishop of Glasgow and others over the future of Catholicism in England and Scotland.[14] The group decided that the only course was through the support of the king of Spain. Paget and Morgan thereupon aroused distrust between Mary Stewart and Persons. Persons said he tried taking Paget and Morgan into trust but they continued to oppose him at every turn. They were responsible for William Parry going to Queen Elizabeth, for Ballard's plot to kill the queen the Babington/Ballard Plot, for Gilbert Gifford's deceit and for strong opposition to the *Succession Book*. Dr. William Gifford, now Dean of Lille, was Paget's ally and worked against Persons and the Jesuits, Persons said. Persons sought to have the king of Spain remove some of the ringleaders of the Paget faction from Flanders or to deprive them of their pensions.

The Spanish Council and the Catholic hierarchy in Flanders were reluctant to take any action against Paget.[15] But then Persons learned that Paget was secretly negotiating to return to England with the blessing of Queen Elizabeth (i.e., the Barnes/Paget correspondence). And he had verbatim copies of the actual letters Paget had written that showed Paget's loyalties and his willingness to betray others. Persons sent these on to his superiors. Within a short time Paget was cut off from his pension. Ousted from the Low Countries, he fled to Paris where he sought the favor of the English ambassador by betraying the English serving the Archdukes or the Spanish. Where did Persons get these extraordinary documents? From Phelippes, Thomas Barnes and William Sterrell.

Barnes's contacts with Paget were coordinated with Phelippes. The relationship is seen in a draft letter of February 1593: on the outside is Phelippes's notation of the purpose of the letter: "For Barnes to be written to Paget."[16] Barnes had been a Phelippes's operative since the Babington Plot. A Catholic gentleman of independent means, Barnes was periodically in the Low Countries and maintained cordial relations with the faction of Paget and Dr. William Gifford. Unaware that Barnes communicated with Phelippes, Paget thought that Barnes was an agent of the Earl of Essex.

Paget's "bold" overture for peace for the Archdukes in late December 1597 produced no favorable response from Cecil. As Paget complained, "Secretary Cecil does not show himself willing to pleasure me." Secretary Cecil probably was unaware that Paget sought to obtain Cecil's pleasure. Phelippes and Sterrell seized the moment to trap Paget and to benefit Persons. Barnes was dispatched to Brussels and met with Paget at the Capello, the great Chapel in the Palace of the Archdukes.[17] Barnes convinced Paget that he was sent on behalf of the Earl of Essex to draw Paget into service for Essex. Paget rose to the bait and declared himself ready to serve Essex and the queen and to betray the Catholics in the Low Countries. What Paget had said in the Capello became disputed.[18]

Barnes returned to London and wrote back to Paget that the queen was open to Paget returning to England and restoring his lands. Paget was thrilled and responded with letters back to Barnes (*alias* "M. Gerard Burghert") of April 27 and May 8, 1598.[19] These were his undoing. The April 27 letter said the greater his offence has been, "the greater is the Queen's mercy" in pardoning him. Showing the liberality which makes her famous, she would oblige him to spend his life at her feet. He showed how greatly he had been fooled, by Sterrell and Phelippes. Noting that the English Commissioners were in France at that moment, Paget sought an appointment to the English contingent: "I do not doubt but my presence would be profitable for some respects that be not thought of, so as I might be there afor treaty were concluded … and besides though I say it I should be no ill instrument perhaps to further the treaty itself…." Such was Paget's delusion, that he thought he could go immediately from attainted fugitive to English negotiator! More likely, it reflected that Paget had proved himself as a loyal subject to the queen for his service to Walsingham in the Babington Plot and to Lord Burghley through Poley and Moody. Paget said he had removed to Liège and could be written to in the name of "Robert Tissue."

The May 8 letter of "Tissue" to Barnes compromised Paget still further. He again identified the lands he wished restored. He discussed the peace accord that had just been completed between France and Spain and gave advice. Paget instructed Barnes to burn his letters. Barnes burned not the letters but Paget himself by turning the letters over to Paget's enemies.

Now that Paget was hooked, Barnes (prompted by Phelippes and Sterrell) informed Paget that the queen's generosity was subject to a condition, as indicated by Barnes's patron (whom Paget now thought to be Essex).[20] Paget must betray the Jesuits. Paget expressed his great gratitude and hoped "to make good by deed what I protest by words." He understood what was expected of him and promised to discover Jesuit plots and to lessen their credit everywhere.[21]

Paget provided military and political intelligence in the letter, and asked for Barnes's greatest secrecy, "because Holt and Owen brag that they have intelligence from some that are in credit with the Earl of Essex [i.e., Sterrell] and Secretary Cecil [i.e., Phelippes]." Foolish Paget did not know he was writing directly to those very men.

Within a short time Paget fulfilled his promise to betray the Jesuits.[22] He called his essay: "A brief note of the practices that divers Jesuits have had for killing princes and changing of states." This diatribe was directed primarily against Persons. According to Paget, Persons had been behind the book "Leicester's Commonwealth," the Parry Plot, the Babington Plot ["Parry's and Savage's practices"], the plot of the Duke of Guise [the *Empresa*/Enterprise], the *Book of the Succession*, and the plots of John Daniell and Polwhele and others. Persons had made all priests entering England swear loyalty to the Infanta (Isabella) as successor to Elizabeth. The Jesuits, he said, had collected money for the poor but then used it on their own books and plots. Paget urged that when the queen sends an ambassador to meet with the king of France, she should use the occasion to discover all the practices of the Jesuits and to force them all out of England. The queen could get the king of France to intercede with the Pope to retire all the Jesuits out of England during the life of the queen.

Sterrell and Phelippes gave copies of Paget's letters and his anti-Jesuit tract to Persons to destroy Paget's reputation. Persons translated them into Latin and sent them on to his superiors in the utmost secrecy and urged strong measures against Paget's treachery. His fifteen year struggle against Paget now met with vanquishment of his foe.

Persons wrote to Cardinal Cajetan, the Cardinal Protector, from Naples August 22, 1598, concerning English Catholic affairs.[23] The English Catholics, he said, were concerned that some of the English in Flanders and France were giving hope to Queen Elizabeth that she could have peace without concessions on religion. Of course, he was speaking of Paget's efforts to influence the peace negotiations. Persons sought Cajetan's support of the Jesuits remaining in England and that this be a condition of peace, the opposite of what Paget sought. He then continued with enclosures of 3 papers relating to the affairs of Charles Paget. He explained:

> The first two come from England, having been sent very secretly by Catholics who have had the means to read the originals and copy them word for word. Two persons of credit write under oath that they have done so and I am in possession of the said copies in English. The same persons on other occasions have sent the originals themselves of letters on affairs of the same sort, but with the obligation of our sending them back immediately to the Secretariate in England for fear that they should be found out. And so now they are very insistent that these letters be read with great secrecy at this time; and on that account I doubt very much if it would be safe for your Eminence to send these papers relating to Paget to the Curia....

Persons assigned the items the letters A, B and C. Item A consisted of copies of two letters of Paget, dated April 27, 1598, and May 8, 1598; these were the letters Paget had sent to Thomas Barnes (*alias* "Burghert"), the originals of which are now in the State Papers and abstracts of which were in Phelippes's letter files. The existence of these originals and copies and their locations leave no doubt that it was Phelippes, Barnes and Sterrell who were the sources for Persons. The letters were identified as from Paget to his agent in London and were intended to be shown to the queen. Persons preserved (if he knew it) the identity of the recipient of the two letters (Barnes). Both letters, of course, showed Paget eager to return to England. They also showed his willingness to give intelligence to the queen. Item B was "A Proposition of Charles Paget for calling the Jesuits out of England, by means of the French king, during the treaty." This was the document Barnes had tricked Paget into writing as a condition of gaining the queen's favor. Item C was Persons's own "Answer to Charles Paget's principal calumnies against the Fathers of the Society of Jesus."[24]

Persons sent a similar letter to Monsignor Peña. The latter was another papal official and a confidant of the Duke of Sessa, the Spanish envoy to Rome.[25] Thus, Persons's letter was sure to gain the attention of the Pope and the Spanish authorities. Persons said he was anxious for the Duke of Sessa to see everything from Paget "so that at all events his Holiness [the Pope] may be made aware of the kind of treaty they are aiming at with the help of the king of France...." He wanted Peña to make strong recommendations for action against Paget and to prevent the Pope from supporting a treaty that would lead to the Jesuits being recalled from England. To Peña he provided a bit more information about the background of the documents than he had told Cajetan. The papers, he wrote (italics indicate the additional information):

> have been sent over from England with great secrecy by two Catholics who have found means over there to see his [Paget's] letters. They have already sent us others previously of much the same import, *relating to the secret negotiations with the Queen*; and the *Archduke has seen some of the originals*, which were sent and afterwards returned to the Secretariate in England, in order that the senders might not be discovered; for that would mean complete ruin for them and be *an obstacle to other matters of greater importance*. However two men write from there under oath that they are copies taken word for word from Paget's originals.

This and Persons's letter to Cajetan show that the two Catholics had previously sent secret information of "secret negotiations with the Queen," that these were shared with Archduke Albert, and that the "two Catholics" had some continuing relationship with the Jesuits because they were important to "other matters of greater importance." Barnes's correspondence with Paget was passed to Phelippes and thus it was Phelippes (and Sterrell) who had the originals of Paget's letters. All of this demonstrates Sterrell and Phelippes having a continuing intelligence relationship with the exiles in the Low Countries and with Fr. Persons. Less emphasis is given Barnes because Phelippes's and Sterrell's statements to Cecil in 1605 did not indicate Barnes had any significant role in the intelligence correspondence, and Cecil himself did not treat Barnes as a significant actor in matters even when he had Barnes in his custody in 1606. Barnes was more a messenger than a player.

Paget's Spanish pension was terminated. He departed hastily for France, where he began currying favor with the English ambassador.[26] Within a few months after Persons's letters were written, Paget learned that he had been betrayed. He did not suspect Barnes. In November 1598 Paget wrote to Barnes that he had thought Barnes dead for he had only now received letters of September and October from Barnes. Desperation shows in four anxious letters back to Barnes that Paget wrote November 20–30, all preserved in Phelippes's copies. Paget reported that a tall young man named Turner, who was son to one of the queen's huntsmen, had appeared in Brussels in September, claiming that Essex had sent him to kill Sir William Stanley.[27] The man had told Owen that Paget was wholly at the devotion of the queen of England. Paget urged Barnes to get the Earl of Essex to look to the man for he would bring trouble.[28] A couple of days later, Paget was more definite: "Owen has informed the Cardinal Governor [Archduke Albert] that Paget has intelligence with the Earl of Essex and is wholly at the devotion of the Queen."[29] Paget said they pretended not to know, perhaps to learn further news. He was retiring to France with all diligence and hoped to see Barnes at Paris with a pardon for him from the queen and a passport. Barnes was instructed to send letters for Paget through William Clitheroe, a priest allied with Paget and Dr. William Gifford. Paget knew "there is somebody plays false there" and he would write more of it when he got to France.

On November 30, Paget again wrote Barnes saying "how desirous I am that the business which you have so long given me hope of is near ended."[30] Paget expressed some wonder that he had never received certain letters that Barnes mentioned, and suggested that Barnes might try sending "by Jaques's means." Jaques, as seen above, was allied with Owen, Verstegan and Sterrell. Paget was being duped by the very people he was counting on for delivery back into England. Paget repeated his message of gratitude to the Earl in a letter of January 23, 1599; he reported again that his problems stemmed from the actions of Baldwin the Jesuit and Hugh Owen.[31]

By April 1599 Paget was settled again in Paris and resumed his letters to Barnes. One of April 24, 1599, was sent through Thomas Edmondes, the English agent at Paris, together with a letter of the same date to Secretary Robert Cecil.[32] Paget sought Cecil's assistance in obtaining the hoped-for pardon from Queen Elizabeth. This certainly would have surprised Cecil and Essex, as Phelippes, Sterrell, and Barnes had been acting without the knowledge of either in playing Paget. As soon as Phelippes learned of the letter to Cecil and the communication through Edmondes, he wrote to Paget,[33] Phelippes revealing himself as the one who was trying to help Paget with the queen. He denounced Paget for his presumption in addressing Edmondes and Cecil directly before the matter was ripe. It was "madness of you [Paget] to think that even the greatest personage in England dared move Her Majesty for such a grace to be showed to one attainted by the highest Court in the land, of the highest treasons." Phelippes admitted that "it was I who set the matter abroach, intending to have done it by my Lord of Essex, but his Lordship never heard of it." Barnes, he said, had told him of their speech together in the Capello at Brussels, and Phelippes attempted to move the queen about Paget and had made progress on his suit. But Paget had mishandled the matter and had given offence in London and placed himself in danger where he was. Now Phelippes was concerned, he said, that Paget's errors would turn to Phelippes's disgrace.

Paget still did not understand the trick that had been played on him, for he had no reason to think that Phelippes (and Sterrell) would have been in contact with Owen and Persons. His response to Phelippes's letter was apologetic.[34] The original of the letter is extant, together with Phelippes's marginal comments in response to each of Paget's remarks. These comments were surely ironic observations he passed on to Sterrell (or Cecil). Paget thanks Phelippes for his troubles in Paget's cause. He had understood from Barnes that his pardon was absolute and regrets that it is conditional on some notable service. Alluding to the paper he wrote denouncing the actions of the Jesuits, which he now realizes went to Phelippes, Paget said: "If I had any such stuff in store, by what is past I am warned to become heedful, and mean not hereafter to take as an excuse for revealing a thing, which ought by the rules of discretion to be secret, that I did not advise you to keep it secret, when the publishing would be dangerous to me, and disappoint the Queen's service." To this, Phelippes commented marginally: "What the Queen did with his paper I know not. It was an accusation of the Jesuits." Phelippes, of course, knew exactly what had happened to the paper against the Jesuits: he and Sterrell had immediately sent it to Fr. Persons.

Paget continued to hold out hope that the queen would give her pardon and that Phelippes would be of assistance. He wrote: "Princes have often granted such favours to persons who have become more serviceable than those who have never been disgraced." He said that Phelippes had made errors "but it is I that will feel the smart." To this, Phelippes commented: "He is too wise in his own conceit." Paget finished by imploring that since Phelippes "embark[ed] in my affairs without my privity, for the desire you have to do the Queen service, and your care of my welldoing, end what you have so well begun, and advise me what is fit to do."³⁵

Paget, Phelippes and Barnes exchanged a few more letters. Paget seems to have grasped part of what had happened to him, for he wrote to Barnes that he verified the old proverb, to take heed of trusting a friend.³⁶

Phelippes and Sterrell, however, were not yet done with Paget. They knew he was still seeking the queen's pardon and was now using other channels. They called Paget into question with Cecil. They remained in touch with their "monk at Liège." In a letter to "Hallins" from Liège, June 30, 1599, the "monk" wrote his opinion of Charles Paget: "Besides he is an inconstant fellow, full of practices and true to no side whereof I will ere long send you some particulars to prove his falsehood in friendship to sundry he professed friendship to."³⁷ The particulars he promised followed, as a report called: "A Letter from a Catholic at Brussels to his friend, a Monk at Liège."³⁸ The "Letter" was a scathing indictment of Charles Paget and gave the reasons why he had suddenly left the Low Countries (and the service of the king of Spain) for France. The writer, almost certainly William Sterrell, pretended that the letter should go no further than the recipient: "let whatsoever I write may die with you." Of course, this was to grab the intended reader who was surely Secretary Cecil—and Queen Elizabeth. The writer portrayed Paget as a man continually in "broils and practices" from his earliest days, a restless spirit unable to be quiet in any estate:

> It is a wonderful thing amongst the diversities of nature to see and consider the restless spirits and busy brains of some that can never be quiet nor repose in any estate, but be continually hammering new devices to the hurt many times of others and overthrow in the end of themselves: of this humour is Mr Charles Paget, who from the first hour that his years permitted him to converse with men hath evermore been tampering in broils and practices betwixt the bark and the tree, friend and friend, man and wife, and as his credit and craft increased betwixt Prince and Prince. And this being as natural unto him as to eat drink or sleep, it is as impossible to leave it as to forbear any one of the other.

For many years, he continued, Paget had been against Queen Elizabeth, employing Gilbert Gifford and then Ballard in the Babington Plot. Some thought he was actually both for and against Mary Queen of Scots. Sterrell catalogued Paget's intrigues on behalf of the King of Scots, whom he played against Elizabeth, and said that Paget sought for James to become reconciled with the Pope and to obtain the Pope's aid in displacing Queen Elizabeth. Despite his actions against Elizabeth, Paget "as though he walked in clouds or danced in a mist" now offered his service to Elizabeth—she should "trust him as she listeth [pleases]." The writer said that he had read a piece written by Paget against the Jesuits to gain favor with Elizabeth, and that it was filled with falsehoods: "If his intentions be as treacherous as his slanders are false, he deserves rather a halter than pardon." The "Catholic at Brussels" then countered the false accusations that Paget had made against Persons and the Jesuits. Paget, he said, had himself intended to land in England with the Armada. He concluded then by giving the real reasons for Paget's sudden departure from the Low Countries:

> The reason of his leaving the King of Spain's service and sudden departure into France I take to be for that being charged with some points of this note and but coldly denying them, finding his conscience guilty, he feared some after-claps, and for that cause and the more freely to practise in matters of Scotland he made his retreat thither.

The apparent original of this letter to "a monk at Liège" is among the English State Papers together with a copy of it in the handwriting of Thomas Phelippes. Only a year before this letter Phelippes had informed Cecil that he had a contact at Liège who was willing to assist with a peace effort. Phelippes doubtless passed on to Cecil this "Letter from the Catholic at Brussels to the Monk at Liège" as to Paget's true character, as he did others in the coming months. Cecil, of course, had been informed by Paget himself that Phelippes and Barnes had been involved with seeking a pardon from the queen. Cecil would have asked Phelippes about Paget, and Phelippes would have said that he had bad reports on him from Brussels and "Liège" and that Paget was escaping his misfortunes within the Catholic community. He would have passed on to Cecil the letter from "Liège." Cecil echoed the "Letter from the Catholic at Brussels to the Monk at Liège" in his discussion of Paget only weeks after the letter would have arrived in London in early August 1599. On September 25, 1599, Cecil wrote the English ambassador in Paris instructing him to give no comfort to Paget. In ascribing Paget's motives for his new support of the queen, Cecil tracked the final paragraph of the July letter from Liège[39]:

> I see the Queen is not minded to pardon him [Paget] and restore him upon such merit as giving intelligences, which may be true and may be false. *For we do know that he is out with the Jesuits' faction not out of love to the English, but out of other private ends,* which do divide most of these fugitives only in proportion, to emulate and supplant each other, but ever to *convenire in tertium* [come into fractions].

Phelippes and Sterrell engaged in letter tricks several times more with Cecil. Another occasion presented itself in the spring of 1600.

18

Treaty Negotiations and Burgundian Jewels

A Double Treachery Thwarted

The mysterious "monk of Liège" (Hugh Owen) and his associate, "Monsieur de Boulant" had checked the influence of Charles Paget in Brussels and interjected themselves in diplomatic affairs. France and Spain successfully negotiated the Treaty of Vervins in April 1598, while Robert Cecil and other English Commissioners were lookers-on. The English declined an invitation to join the Franco-Spanish treaty without the participation of the Dutch. Elizabeth's government felt Henry IV of France had betrayed them and was divided about making peace with Spain. The landscape was significantly changed by the near simultaneous deaths of Lord Burghley (August 4) and King Philip (September 3/13), who had each dominated their governments for four decades, and an alteration in governance of the Low Countries. Sterrell (and Phelippes) played a substantial part in helping Hugh Owen navigate the impact of these events and shape the diplomatic relations between London and Brussels. Sterrell further proved his worth to the Archduke, perhaps even saving his nascent kingdom from a palace coup while Albert was out of the country.

Archduke Albert had been appointed governor of the Low Countries in February 1596, as part of the arrangement in which he was to marry King Philip's daughter. In May 1598 she was made sovereign by her father as her dowry. She promptly gave authority to Albert. The couple were proclaimed sovereigns by the States-General in Brussels in August 1598. Following King Philip's death, Albert departed from Brussels, installing his cousin, Cardinal Andrew of Austria, as temporary governor. Almost immediately, Cardinal Andrew sought a settlement of issues between the Low Countries and England. He tapped Jerome Coemans, an Antwerp merchant, to go secretly to England to open negotiations with Robert Cecil and the queen. Arriving in London in mid–January 1599, Coemans met with Cecil and two weeks later with the queen. The skeptical English told Coemans that Cardinal Andrew needed to establish that he had power from Spain to treat upon peace. Six weeks later Coemans returned to London bringing assurances that the king of Spain and the Archduke had authorized negotiations. However, there was inadequate showing of the authority.

Traveling with Coemans was Carlos Lanfranchi, another Antwerp businessman who was an informer to Burghley and Cecil.[1] Lanfranchi now served as the agent of some Low Countries nobility who sought a separate peace with England. This had the potential to undermine Archduke Albert and to split the Low Countries off from Spain, as had been an aim of Burghley and others earlier. The historian Albert Loomie explained Lanfranchi's treachery and how Hugh Owen countered it[2]:

> Unknown to Coemans, Lanfranchi carried special letters to the English Court purporting to be on behalf of the nobility of Flanders and Brabant. They offered a general pacification in the Low Countries by a league of the Walloon nobles, the Dutch Estates, and England, towards reuniting the provinces and excluding Spain. Hardly had the letters been delivered at the English Court when they were summarized and reported to Hugh Owen ... [who] reported to Spain that Cardinal Andrew [temporary Governor] was still unaware of the intrigue. At frequent intervals [Owen's] *avisos* on English affairs gave new details of the secret discussions.

Owen noted a "double treachery" was involved. One was against Cardinal Andrew, "under whose shadow they play this comedy" and the second against the Spanish control of the Low Countries. By the end of May, Owen concluded that the Lanfranchi intrigue had failed: the "discontented nobles" had discontinued their efforts, and "he reported a growing belief in the English court that it had all been a snare." Loomie's final reflection is that "the coup of Hugh Owen in penetrating the intrigue so rapidly should not be underestimated.... His unmasking of the activities of nobles still prominent at the Court in Brussels was of great importance to the Archduke Albert," and consequently to the long-term position of Owen.

Owen's sources in the English court were Sterrell and Phelippes. They fed information to Owen who passed it on to the Archduke Albert and the Spanish. Owen, as "Nicols," in turn wrote letters back to Sterrell and Phelippes seeking more information. Then, as "J. B." Owen sent them information on Coemans and Lanfranchi in Flanders that was designed to undercut the two as such information was passed on to Cecil and the queen. Perhaps Sterrell or Phelippes gained access to Lanfranchi's secret correspondence with Robert Cecil. Some of Lanfranchi's letters to Cecil ("Horatio Scali") are preserved in the Cecil letters.[3] A letter of "Jo. Nicols" in "Middleburgh" establishes that it was Sterrell and Phelippes who supplied the Lanfranchi intelligence to Owen.[4] It mentions "Hussey" and "Orwell," the names used by Phelippes and Sterrell in the more direct correspondence with Owen and his group. "Nicols" tells them: "You send me (although it be promised) no more stuff that came from Lanfrank who I presume is not idle." He refers to Lanfranchi as a "proud puppy withal full of envy and malice" and discusses his "cozenage" (treachery). A short time earlier, Owen, as "J. B." had written to "Halins," in a letter intended to be seen by Cecil and the queen, that he was aware of Coeman's movements and actions, as Coemans had come to Brussels and Antwerp before hastily traveling to Spain.[5] Thus Owen, as "J. B.," was supplying information about Coemans's movements that was as fresh and detailed as Coemans's own associate Carlo Lanfranchi supplied to Cecil. Later, Coemans expressed amazement at Cecil's knowledge of his secret dealings.[6]

In the same letter, "J. B." complained of England's insincerity about peace discussions. It was thought, he said, that England delayed to see how their campaign against the Irish fared.

The next month, "J. B." again wrote of Coemans and of another man who worked with Coemans as a messenger for Robert Cecil, Jehan (Jean/John) Leroy. He is probably the same John Leroy who had earlier brought messages for Thomas Edmondes to Burghley.[7] The purpose of providing this to "Halins" (Sterrell), who passed it on to members of the English Court, was to make clear to Cecil that he was not able to act in secret; this had the effect of limiting or neutralizing any English effort to divide the people of the Archdukes' lands. He wrote[8]:

One John Leroy is returned from England who carried letters to Robert Cecil from the Marquis de Havre & others under pretence of treating a peace but many deem it is a color to cover other devises to make a great[er] revolt in the Low Countries than is already. The said Leroy brought letters (as himself did report) from Sir Robert Cecil in answer to the said Marquis which he delivered at Brussels & thence is gone to the Cardinal [Andrew]. His companion Coeman is also returned from Spain to Brussels who was at Barcelona with the King from whence he went to Milan and parted with the Archduke at Barcelona.

Over the next six months Coemans was to travel to Spain and again to England several times. "J. B." (Owen) continued to write to Sterrell of Coemans and his companion Jean Leroy, sometimes in less than flattering terms. The effect was to let any reader, including the queen and Cecil, know that in the Low Countries it was well understood what game the English were playing in the peace discussions. On August 18 "J. B." wrote that Coeman and Leroy were gone into England, claiming that peace was assured; others, however, made merry of this claim as they "had thoroughly discovered that you there had more intention to *broullier les cartes de nouveau* [mix up the cards anew]" and thrust the new lords (the Archdukes) out of the country rather than making a firm peace.[9]

A month later Coemans was again in London—his fourth trip—and "J. B." (Owen) again doubted the sincerity of the English on the subject of peace[10]:

> Divers do think that if you had intention to come to a true peace that you would treat by the means of a man of more worth than a surgeon's son who otherwise was never advanced to any dignity or office that might credit him But all is well that endeth so. *Hagase el milagro y hegalo el diablo.* [Let the miracle be done, though the devil do it]

Though Cardinal Andrew and Coemans had secured letters that indicated Philip III and Albert and Isabella approved of negotiations it was obvious that the English should not seriously discuss peace terms until the Archdukes returned to Brussels and began their joint rule. Their grand entrance into the city was on September 5, n.s., 1599. "J. B." (Owen) said he had come from Liège for the occasion.[11] He recounted the color and pomp of the occasion and remarked "The Court Seer [Overseer] carried a stick before them ... longer than the Swert [sword] that I have seen carried before her Majesty when I was in England & a scholar of Oxford." Owen will, no doubt, have presented the Archdukes each with a dozen pair of high quality leather English gloves, custom made in London and sent over by William Sterrell.

The Coemans–Lanfranchi episode shows Sterrell and Phelippes working closely with Hugh Owen to affect the relationship between the governments in London and Brussels. They are doing this to aid the Owen faction in Brussels, using fictitious identities in correspondence passed on to Cecil, the queen and probably others. The longer range goal was to establish optimum conditions for the Archdukes to rule. Their successful reign held the best hopes for favorable conditions for Catholics in England.

Boulant and Boulogne, 1600

With the Archdukes installed in Brussels, a new and awkward dance of negotiations could begin. The stage-managed character of "Mon. Boulant," re-appears, a supposed friend of Sterrell.

In January 1600 Thomas Edmondes arrived in Brussels to pursue an agreement with the Archdukes. Contrary to English desires, Archduke Albert said that his side would not meet for treaty negotiations in England. Working then with Jean Richardot (President of the Archduke's Council) and Louis Verreyken (Audiencier—an officer of the Chancerie) Edmondes reached an understanding that a preliminary meeting would be held in England with Verreyken, followed by formal negotiations in France, at Boulogne. Albert wrote Elizabeth agreeing to a meeting to take place there March 6 or 7.

On February 18, 1600, Verreyken arrived in London for preliminary discussions. He was warmly received by the Treasurer, Lord Buckhurst. The following day he was guest of the Lord Chamberlain, whose acting company performed "Sir John Oldcastle" for the visitor.[12] Verreyken's host for a time was Sir Walter Ralegh.[13]

Verreyken was received by the queen on February 23 and then spent three days with the Privy Council. Both sides raised areas of concern for negotiations. The Archdukes wanted to renew the treaty formerly existing with Burgundy, to cut off trade of England with Holland and Zealand, and to have the queen restore to the Low Countries the cautionary towns possessed by England. The English wanted free trade with the Indies; English merchants should not be subject to the Inquisition when trading in Spanish regions. A commission was appointed by the queen to consider proposals and investigate the issues raised. Verreyken had no authority to make agreement upon any point, so no further progress could be made prior to the Boulogne meeting. A new date for negotiations had to be established.

Verreyken left London March 11 for Brussels. He was immediately followed by Thomas Edmondes, whom the queen sent to meet with the Archdukes. The only progress Edmondes could make in discussions with Albert and Richardot was to set a new date for a Boulogne conference: May 16. Edmondes returned to London.[14] Sterrell and Phelippes at just this moment become more deeply involved in the treaty process, within a day or two of Edmondes returning. They received communications from Owen or a visit from Owen's close associate Richard Bayley.

The Boulogne Peace Overture

Someone close to the Archduke made an overture concerning the peace negotiations through Sterrell or Phelippes. A note of Phelippes dated April 17, 1600, reflected that the queen was encroaching upon the Archduke, requiring free traffic in the Indies, and that she wanted to be repaid the money she had lent the Dutch, "for 28,000£ whereof she had the jewels of Burgundie in pawn. It seemeth they would ripen matters before they assemble to conclude."[15] The note states that "He" (unidentified) "prays some confident [secret] person to be sent to Bullen [Boulogne] at the meeting and direction how to find him by such a French man as shall be sent hither for the purpose." It asserts: "The advertisements written from Liège are certain and not feigned," surely referring to the "J.B." letters that Phelippes from time to time shared with Cecil. The note showed a readiness to have private negotiations to smooth the public negotiations at Boulogne.

Two letters of Phelippes to Cecil relate to the April 17 note.[16] Phelippes sought to perform a matter of intelligence service "at this time of treaty for advancement whereof if I durst I would have adventured to address myself unto your Ho[nor] sooner." Commenting that it would take too long to explain how it came about, he assured Cecil of the certainty of doing good service. As he explained: "the principal point in matter of intelligence is to procure confidence with those parties that one will work upon or for those parties a man would work by, I have found the way to have both...." He promised to employ his dexterity to the utmost of his power. His purpose, he urged, was to do the queen service and improve his own estate.

Phelippes explained the device of intelligence and service offered. The English trade with the Indies was a principal concern for the negotiations; the debt for the jewels less so. The latter was perhaps only a cover—to justify payments to some Englishmen at Court to win their allegiance and support. Sterrell was involved: he used the peace negotiations and jewels to justify his correspondence with Owen and receipt of money from the Low Countries when Cecil interrogated him five years later. On that occasion, Sterrell avoided giving specific dates to Cecil but said that "they" (unidentified) wrote that if Sterrell could find them some persons in good position that could negotiate the "matter of peace and deal for the redeeming for the Arch Duke jewells" there would be provided £200 yearly for him. He continued: "At that time Mr. Phelippes was appointed again to be my overseer by the Earl of Essex. He took hold of it, and handled the matter of peace and jewells in such sort as they paid it and continued it till the Christmas before the queen died...."[17]

Sterrell must have intended to go to Boulogne, just as he had expected to go to a conference at Brussels with the English diplomat Thomas Wilkes in 1594. But just about the time the Boulogne dates were being set, another, more important date was being finalized that took precedence. This was the for the most important wedding of 1600 and the most significant wedding for the family of the Earl of Worcester. The Earl's eldest surviving son was to wed Robert Cecil's niece. As of early May 1600, the marriage was in preparation but the final date was yet to be set by the queen.[18] Under the circumstances, Sterrell could not leave his patron.

The peace conference was opened at Boulogne on May 20. An English commission met with representatives from the Archdukes, the Spanish and the French.[19] The two principal sides wrangled for days over trivial matters. Nothing of substance was accomplished.

Phelippes informed Cecil that "our man" was unable to go to Boulogne and that the other side was upset with "our man."[20] He even produced a letter in French from a "Jean Leclerque" to "Vincent Orwell."[21] "Leclerque" wrote that his cousin and "Jacob Samander" had waited for 8 days for him to appear, warning that his credit is in jeopardy.[22] Phelippes gave no explanation for "our man" not going to Boulogne. Never had Phelippes told Cecil that Sterrell was "our man," so he could hardly say that "our man" was deeply occupied with the wedding now taking place June 16–18, 1600 for Cecil's own niece.

Sterrell had been expected in Boulogne by Owen and his associates as a clandestine observer. But Sterrell would have informed Owen and Verstegan that he was not coming. Unofficial observers were at work on the fringes of the negotiations. Among them was Robert Taylor, an English lawyer who lectured at Douay and who worked for the Archdukes. He will soon be an important agent from them to London. Taylor was sent to Boulogne as an observer by Ottavio Frangipani, the papal nuncio to Brussels. There for the English was Thomas Harrison, sent as a spy by Cecil.[23] He was disclosed as such by "J. B.'s" friend in Brussels.[24]

The "Leclerque" letter obscured the fact that Phelippes (and Sterrell) apparently had found someone to go to Boulogne on behalf of the jewels and the peace. Two other Englishmen showed up at Boulogne during the negotiations likely meeting with the Archdukes' representatives. Ostensibly visiting the summer campaign of the United Provinces, they were Lord Cobham and Sir Walter Ralegh. Neville noted their presence and wrote to his secretary, Ralph Winwood, in Paris: "I cannot think but they have some other end."[25] He later added, "they carried some message." Cecil's biographer concluded that "it would seem that they made contact with the Count d'Arenberg...."[26] Arenberg was the Archduke's representative. Cobham and Ralegh are likely "confident persons" sought by Phelippes's correspondent for private negotiations at Boulogne; Cobham is soon working with Phelippes to negotiate for the Archduke's jewels and for "other service." It was for receiving a pension from Arenberg that Cobham and Ralegh are convicted of treason a bit later.

Lord Cobham's visit to the Boulogne area was brief. He too had to be in London for the wedding of Worcester's son. It was the social event of the season, and Lord Cobham was related by marriage to the bride. He played hostess for the queen on the occasion. Perhaps the wedding was when he first raised the matter of the Burgundian jewels with her Majesty.

Boulant Returns: Redeeming the Archduke's Jewels

The Boulogne negotiations had fizzled into nothing but had prompted side-developments that kept diplomacy alive. By November 1600, Phelippes and Cobham were firmly at work on the Burgundian jewels, and instructions came from "Monsieur Boulant" in Flanders, which Phelippes passed on to Cobham.[27] "Monsieur Boulant" was the fiction of Sterrell, Phelippes and Hugh Owen, whose letters were used for back-channel negotiations with the queen of England. Phelippes informed Cobham: "if the Q[ueen] Majesty would set down with herself what should content her to be abated out of the whole recovering principal and interest being put together (whereof the executors of Sir Horatio Palavicino [who had died a few months earlier] are to expect their portion as he majesty shall advise) it should quickly be put into practice." Phelippes explained that the complexity of the transaction arose from the unwillingness of the Archduke to appear to be seeking them directly. He noted the incongruity that the money had been borrowed against the Archduke himself by the Hollanders who were yet against him in arms, and the Archduke expected the towns that had borrowed the money to repay the debt.

Essex had no knowledge of these negotiations, which Sterrell and Phelippes later claimed were begun on his behalf. When Essex attempted a revolt against the queen only a few months later, Essex blamed Cobham and Ralegh for his downfall and said that England was being sold to the Infanta! Essex did not know that Phelippes had put Cobham and Ralegh into exploring the issue of peace and the Burgundian jewels. Many prudent men had cut off or distanced themselves from Essex as his control, wealth and influence rapidly diminished.

"A mean and color to do other service"

After Essex's execution in February 1601, the clandestine negotiations for the Burgundian jewels resumed. Phelippes now sought from Cobham an inventory and valuation of the jewels. A foreigner was to view them to report to the Archduke. Phelippes asked Cobham to learn how much the queen wanted for them, bluntly adding he would "augment it so as to serve your Lordship's turn and my own."[28] Cecil's secretary, Levinus Munck, had told Phelippes that, if the queen would be satisfied with the principal and small interest, "I would make it a good match for you and myself." A good match indeed, for Palavicino's biographer states that by 1598, "the debt of £28,000 of twenty years before had now risen to close on £90,000, due on the accumulated arrears of interest at 10 per cent."[29] Phelippes brought another letter about the jewels to Cobham at the end of June.[30]

The jewels were merely the opening to something larger, Phelippes suggested to Cobham: "I am bold to put your Lo[rdship] in mind of the matter of the jewels, whereof besides that there will come money to the Queen and some benefit to ourselves, *it may be made a mean and color to do other service, which may turn your Lo[rdship] to honor if it please you make use of it.*"[31] The other business with the Archdukes in which Phelippes and Sterrell were agents was negotiation about peace. Cobham was sought as an agent of the Archdukes, if he had not already embarked on such a course at Boulogne (or earlier).

A letter to "Boulant" was sent by "Robinson"/Sterrell (written by Phelippes)[32] in April 1601. "Robinson" informed "Boulant" of the progress of the nobleman who had the queen's ear on the jewels and the possibility of peace.[33] "Robinson" discussed further details on the handling of the debt and said that the nobleman (the French draft identifies him as "my Lord Cobham guardien des cinq portes"): "hath been above all others a persuader and furtherer of the peace and reviving the ancient amity and alliance between this Crown and the house of Burgundy so in this affair he will be most ready to do any honorable office which shall be in his power."

The Lord Treasurer Buckhurst was also involved with so large a royal transaction. He was associated with both Cobham and Phelippes, as reflected both in correspondence and rumor. The French ambassador recorded in 1597 that Cobham and Buckhurst were known to maintain intelligence with the Low Countries through Catholic refugees.[34] Buckhurst apparently employed Phelippes in financial transactions. Writing from prison in 1596, Sir Anthony Ashley complained to Robert Cecil that his fellow prisoner, Phelippes, had secretly represented Buckhurst in property transactions.[35] Buckhurst also helped Phelippes in the transaction in which Phelippes' debt to the queen became joined with the queen's debt to Palavicino.[36] Phelippes's cousin worked closely with the Lord Treasurer, and Phelippes passed intelligence to Buckhurst through him.[37]

"Boulant" responded to "Robinson's" letter in June 1601 with instructions on handling the redemption of the silver vessels and jewels. "Robinson" was to communicate with the "canon of Liége," the common friend he purportedly shared with Boulant.[38] Phelippes notified Cobham on June 28, 1601, and promised to bring the letter to Cobham.[39] Cobham may have taken the matter up with the queen, but a decision was made, perhaps by Cecil, not to respond to the overture.

With the latest "Boulant" letter unanswered, the Archdukes dispatched Jerome Coemans on another mission to London. Traveling as "Antonio Vittore," Coemans arrived in London in early September. He met with Levinus Munck and sought to speak with Cecil.[40] While Coemans was waiting, the English heard of the Spanish dispatch of a force into Ireland to aid the Irish rebels. Coemans was dismissed, on the suspicion that the Archduke had been fully aware of the Spanish plans for Ireland.

The English Initiative to Boulant: Two Shafts from One Quiver

The English defeated the Spanish force at Kinsale, Ireland at Christmas 1601. No sooner did the news of this victory reach London than Elizabeth's government opened a peace initiative to the Archdukes through Phelippes by having "Robinson"/Sterrell solicit a fresh overture from "Boulant." Sterrell again was being used in the shadows of diplomacy by the English and the Archdukes as he had been used in 1594 in contacts with the Duke of Feria, through William Waad. A letter of January 9, 1602, was sent into the Low Countries discussing the English victory, the failure of the negotiations at Boulogne, and the suspicion of the latest Coemans mission.[41] It invited "Boulant" to revive his earlier overture "provided that we be not pressed in the matter of religion to any inconvenience or touching the Cautionary towns wherein there are many points of necessary jealousy which cannot sodenly be accommodated...." The invitation to the Archdukes to make a peace overture was more explicit in a "Robinson" letter two weeks later.[42]

The January 9, 1602, solicitation was answered by "Boulant," re-urging a peace negotiation.[43] Purporting to write from Nieuport, near the siege of Ostend, "Boulant" took up two points of contention between Brussels and London: religion and the towns in the Low Countries held by the queen. On the first, "Boulant" assured "Robinson" that the Archduke's representatives would not ask anything unacceptable to the queen. As to the second, "Boulant" assured that satisfaction could be given to the queen and the Hollanders by a truce for a term of years and free trade.

The Archdukes also dispatched another communication to London, containing essentially the same terms, by President Richardot via a Portuguese named Fortado.[44] The back channel of "Robinson" and "Boulant" was reinforced by a more official communication, one that appeared to be initiated by the Archdukes, not the English who had solicited it. The Richardot overture sought to renew the negotiations, with the same two points "Boulant" had made: Nothing would be demanded that should "disgust" England or be prejudicial to the service of the queen. As to the places the queen held in the Netherlands and the confederation she had with the Hollanders, a course would be taken "with the Queen's liking as would draw quietness on all hands and that security that might be pretended."[45]

While the "Boulant/Robinson" letters were exchanged, Sterrell continued to write his overseas associates as "Rivers" (and related names). In one, he reflects that a policy debate of the Privy Council about a peace with the Archdukes had preceded receipt of the "Boulant" and the Fortado responses/overtures of early February. On February 12, 1602, Sterrell wrote to Robert Persons (and doubtless to Owen and Verstegan), of the debate within the English government.[46] Sterrell said that overtures had been solicited by the English, alluding to the letters of January 9 and 23 for "Boulant."[47] Moreover, he indicated that, while encouraging an overture, Cecil was skeptical that it would take place.[48] With Worcester now on the Privy Council, Sterrell was the best source of intelligence on English policy possible.

Sterrell informed Owen that there was disagreement in London on the goals of the Archduke and of Spain. Did the Archduke affect peace for the establishment of himself in the quiet possession of the Low Countries and so that he would not be forced to depend upon Spain? Or was Spain's alienation of the Low Countries into the sovereignty of the

Archdukes only a stratagem from the beginning to trick the Hollanders, with the Archduke and the Infanta only a "stalking horse … to catch this wild fowl" whereby they would gain income and she be made the queen of Portugal?[49] By mid–March, a few weeks before the government's responses to "Boulant" and Fortado, Sterrell was reporting that the peace initiative was unlikely to bear fruit.[50] A week later Sterrell ("Rivers") reported to his friends that the peace effort was failing.[51]

Despite Sterrell's pessimism, the English government decided to keep the negotiations alive, though posturing as to which party had been at fault for the impasse in negotiations at Boulogne. Cecil directed that two letters be sent: one to "Boulant" by "Robinson" via Phelippes,[52] and a second to be signed by Thomas Edmondes and given to Fortado.[53] Although both letters were critical of Spain and reiterated Elizabeth's policies, each offered some encouragement of a peace if the Archdukes and Spain together were willing.

The "Robinson" letter to "Boulant" (March 27) acknowledged that the Fortado overture originated from Boulant's efforts. Alluding to Cecil as his friend, "Robinson" wrote to Boulant that the "friend" confirmed that Richardot's Fortado memorial conformed so closely to Boulant's letter "as none that saw them but would judge them to be shafts taken both out of one quiver as he [Cecil] said…."[54] The "friend" also said that Fortado was shortly to be dispatched with an answer signed by Edmondes. "Boulant's" help was solicited to bring the parties "to come to accord happily by our private hastier supply…." Peace, however, required the participation not only of the Archduke but also Spain: "the King of Spain and the Archduke having different ends in regard of their several affairs we cannot build upon anything that proceeds from the Archduke alone."

A day later, Thomas Edmondes responded to Fortado for the overture from Richardot.[55] Although it contained words of readiness to pursue peace, they were so qualified and conditioned, and accompanied by such unconciliatory remarks, as to convey the opposite sentiment. The queen was ready to pursue peace but only if the king of Spain were fully ready, and this appeared very doubtful. Edmondes's letter said that if her Majesty should entangle herself again in negotiations for a treaty upon such generalities only from the Archdukes' side she may be accused of too much credulity. Whenever her Majesty saw in the king of Spain, as well as in the Archduke, grounds that would incline her to believe that he really intended to come to an honorable and safe peace, she would be most ready to fall into a course that would "return to that ancient amity which hath heretofore long continued between the two Crowns and States." However, he continued, it seemed most strange to her majesty that if the king of Spain wished peace that he would aid the Irish rebels and try to conquer one of her kingdoms.

Sterrell seems not to have seen the specific wording of the Edmondes letter given to Fortado. Thus he did not realize that its tone could readily be taken as insulting to the Archdukes. In a "Rivers" letter to Persons in Rome dated two days after the Edmondes letter, Sterrell reported there was still hope for peace from the Fortado overture.[56] A week later Sterrell again expressed hope for peace, reporting that the "overture made of Peace is in good forwardness…."[57] Three weeks later, however, Sterrell reported that the peace effort was dead, "clean quashed" by the decision of the queen to send more aid to the States to preserve Ostend.[58]

The prickly reply to Fortado soon reached the Brussels Court, while the milder letter of "Robinson" to "Boulant" was delayed or lost. The canon of Liége (i.e., Owen), reported that the Archdukes' government regarded the English reply as an "impertinent and insolent answer."[59] The reply to "Boulant" still had not been delivered as of May 19/29 when "J. B." (Owen) wrote to "Robinson" of "Boulant's" displeasure at not receiving a letter.[60] He expressed concern that there had been no response regarding the Burgundian jewels "about the which he had written often afore." Shortly afterwards, the Brussels court did receive an explanation.

Cobham's Withdrawal from the Jewel and Peace Negotiations

The Edmondes letter to Fortado had mentioned nothing of the Burgundian jewels and silver. Their redemption remained a back-channel topic about which "Boulant" and the Archduke remained in suspense until "Robinson's" response of March 27 to Boulant finally turned up (in the original or a copy), not long after May 29/19.[61] They then learned that the nobleman at work on the Burgundian jewels (i.e., Cobham) had dropped out of the picture. "Robinson" explained the long delay in answering the June 22, 1601, overture by saying that nothing had taken place with regard to the Burgundian jewels because "the Lord that had dealt therein was from Court far off in a voyage almost to the furtherest part of the Realm."[62] Indeed Cobham was in the realm's westernmost part, Cornwall, in August 1601, shortly after the June 22 overture.[63]

"Robinson" said that there were subsequent problems in entertaining the negotiations over the jewels. His abstruse explanation demands close attention and parsing:

> And since besides that we thought the Archduke being engaged in that chargeable [costly] siege of Ostend it was no fit time to deal in such matters, there happened a strangeness [estrangement] between that lord and my friend whom I had employed to him in that business.

"And since" means that even after the Lord that had dealt on the jewels [Cobham] was returned there were two reasons why the matter had not been pursued. One was the siege of Ostend. Cecil strongly disliked the Archduke's relentless assault on this outpost of the Hollanders.[64] Thus the comment (ostensibly by "Robinson" but dictated by Cecil) is sarcastic (though less than insolent): as the siege was so costly to the Archduke, surely it was not a fit time to deal in repatriating jewels in return for large payments by him. The second reason was that there had happened "a strangeness between that lord and my friend whom I had employed to him in that business." As this purports to be "Robinson"/Sterrell writing this statement, it means that an estrangement has taken place between Lord Cobham and Phelippes (the "friend" whom Robinson had entrusted with dealing with Cobham in the matter). So, sometime in the latter part of 1601 or early in 1602 there was supposedly a falling out between Cobham and Phelippes.

But was the estrangement between Phelippes and Cobham? In reality, the coldness was between Cobham and his brother-in-law Robert Cecil. As Cecil himself put it, outwardly with Ralegh and Cobham he was all friendship. He wrote to Sir George Carew: "in show we are great"; but "all my revenge shall be to heap coals on their [Ralegh and Cobham] heads."[65] Cecil was quietly undermining both Cobham and Ralegh from 1601 on. Cutting Cobham off from the negotiation over the jewels and peace would serve to accomplish this, even as Cecil worked with Cobham and Ralegh in financing a privateer against Spanish shipping ("in show we are great"). A Cecil biographer observes that if by 1601–02 "Cobham had been detected in intrigues with Spanish agents, then he became a serious threat to the Principal Secretary, the official responsible for the conduct of foreign affairs."[66] If Cobham had succeeded as a peace-maker before the death of Elizabeth, he would have been better placed to become a king-maker. Because Cobham's identity is alluded to in the March 27, 1602, letter to Boulant (dictated by Cecil), it is clear that Cecil knew of Cobham's employment as go-between for the Archdukes. In fact, Cecil took over for himself the authority for the Burgundian jewels.

In July 1602, Cecil sought and obtained from William Davison the background on the Burgundian jewels and the debt they secured.[67] Davison had negotiated the loans 25 years earlier and was now clerk of the treasury. Davison's opinion was that the jewels had been over-valued in the books.[68] An inventory of the jewels held in the Queen's Treasury a Westminster soon followed.[69]

Count Arenberg wrote to Cobham in November 1602 seeking a conference on matters pertaining to peace.[70] A few months later, as James was approaching London, Cobham passed on to the new king certain correspondence from Arenberg, taking care to note that he had held intelligence with Arenberg for some time, with Queen Elizabeth's appointment.[71] Six weeks later Cobham met with Arenberg in London, and only a few weeks later—after the Bye Plotters' arrest—he was detained on suspicion of treason. Cobham then implicated Ralegh. Both were charged with plotting the king's murder—"the Main Plot."

Cecil explained the charges against Cobham to his ambassador in France, Sir Thomas Parry: "If now you will ask whether the Count of Arenberg had any hand in the matter, I must answer you truly, that the Lord Cobham privily resorted to him; first to confirm former intelligence concerning the peace...."[72] Cecil must mean either the very "Boulant" negotiations which he had instigated, or the multiple involvements of Cobham in peace intelligence (including the Boulant matter). Phelippes and Sterrell had evidently disclosed to the Archdukes' government that the nobleman through whom they were working was Cobham, and Arenberg's contacts with Cobham will therefore have been with awareness that this was the noble conduit of "Boulant's" overtures.

19

Essex's Dismal Tumult

Did Worcester merely tolerate Sterrell's intelligence work or was Sterrell acting for Worcester? Sterrell's initial work among the English Catholics probably developed around the time of the Campion-Persons mission. He and Edward Somerset's uncle were both concerned with the affairs of Mary Stewart in 1583–5. By 1591, Sterrell and Worcester were closely associated. Worcester approved of Sterrell's work for Essex, Phelippes, and Francis Bacon until Worcester dismissed Sterrell for a brief period. But the bond was soon restored and continued to Worcester's death in 1628.

Sterrell's two sponsors, Worcester and Essex, were close allies at Court. For Essex, Sterrell's intelligence on the Catholic exiles could be passed on to the queen, thereby confirming his command of foreign affairs. For Worcester, Sterrell's activities served to protect the Catholics in England and Flanders, especially the Jesuits whom Worcester secretly supported. The alliance between Worcester and Essex was reflected by the fact that Worcester was, by May 1596, expected to become deputy Master of the Horse to Essex.[1] Worcester's eldest son William Somerset (Lord Herbert) accompanied Essex on his expedition to Cadiz that summer, where Essex knighted him.

The strong ties between Worcester and Essex were made most visible in November 1596, when Essex was host for the dual weddings of two of Worcester's daughters. The grooms were from two strongly Catholic families, and one of these long had ties to Sterrell. Sir Henry Guildford married Elizabeth Somerset and William Petre married her younger sister, Katherine.

Henry Guildford's mother, Elizabeth Shelley, raised her children Catholic over the objections of her first husband, and when she remarried, she wed a devout Catholic, John Gage. Henry Guildford's first cousin was William Norton, the young man whom William Sterrell spirited aboard the French ambassador's boat in 1585.

William Petre's godfather was Lord Burghley, but he had Catholic tutors. William's father John Petre conformed to the state church to the extent of attendance, but he would not receive the Anglican communion. He served in the Parliaments of 1584 and 1586. William received his Oxford BA in February 1591, and in 1593 joined the Middle Temple, a few months after William Sterrell's brother, Henry. At the age of 22 he was elected a member of Parliament. The Petre and Somerset families had long been friends. Both families were patrons of the great musician and composer William Byrd, and the Shelleys, too, had associations with Byrd.[2]

At the time of the great dual wedding, Essex was at a turning point in his quest for political power. The queen was upset with him for having squandered his successful raid on Cadiz. He had created too many knights, and was negligent in securing wealth from the voyage. Francis Bacon warned Essex that he would become estranged from Elizabeth unless he sought to "win the Queen," above all by turning aside from any further military office or repute. He suggested pursuing other offices (such as Lord Privy Seal).³ Instead, Essex sought military glory. An expedition to the Azores in 1597 brought more criticism. Lord Charles Howard was made Earl of Nottingham and was given precedency over Essex. To re-establish Essex's status, the queen made Essex Earl Marshal.⁴ When Robert Cecil departed for France in February 1598 Essex also became acting Secretary of State. Essex needed Worcester's assistance. Worcester's role of Deputy Master of the Horse gave him substantial responsibilities requiring his presence around the queen, particularly as Essex was heavily occupied with other matters. He oversaw all the queen's movements outside the Court. Worcester had these duties almost continuously after Essex began his Irish debacle.⁵

Despite the fact that Essex's father was wrecked over Ireland, Essex volunteered to pacify the Irish rebel Hugh O'Neill, Earl of Tyrone. As he prepared to leave, Essex wrote to the queen to look to Worcester to serve her and urged her to show him favor despite his religion.⁶ Fortune may have been kinder to Essex's memory had he died in Ireland as his father had.

William Sterrell kept his exile correspondents—Owen, Verstegan and Persons— informed of Essex's run of bad luck in Ireland. He knew well the dangers of his letters: immediately before retailing detailed news about Essex's campaign in Ireland, a June 1599 letter said, "As for Irish affairs, all writing and relating of news is there prohibited upon pain of death."⁷ Essex, he reported, had fortified Waterford with a garrison before pacifying part of Munster and marching to Diveling.⁸ Three thousand fresh soldiers were sent to Essex against Tyrone. Sterrell clarified the orders of the queen and Privy Council to Essex concerning Southampton. Rumors in London were that Southampton, whom Essex had placed in charge of the cavalry (contrary to Elizabeth's directions), had been recalled home. Instead, Sterrell said, the "Earl of Southampton is not commanded to return but only to leave his office and place which is general of the horsemen…."⁹ He also sent information (gained through Worcester) on the quarrel between Southampton and Lord Grey over the control of the horsemen.

As to Essex's state of mind, Sterrell wrote: "It is thought certain true that the Earl of Essex is very much discontent, and I can assure you that at Court it is muttered that her Mat^{ie} and the Earl have to their sure friends each threatened the others head, and undoubtedly all kindness is forgotten between them."¹⁰ Perhaps Sterrell had read Essex's Hamlet-like letter to the queen of June 25, 1599, expressing his unhappiness, with eloquence and grace¹¹:

> Is it not known from England that I receive nothing but discomforts and soul's wounds? Is it not spoken in the army, that your Majesty's favor is diverted from me, and that already you do bode ill both to me and it? Is it not believed by the rebels that those whom you favor most, do more hate me out of faction, than them out of duty and conscience? …
> Let me honestly and zealously end a wearisome life. Let others live in deceitful and inconstant pleasures. Let me bear the brunt, and die meritoriously. Let others achieve and finish the work, and live to erect trophies.…

Letters of Sterrell were intercepted by the English government in a Jesuit packet in July 1599.¹² These demonstrate his excellent understanding of the characters of the principal figures in this Court drama. His analysis is superior to other accounts on the state of mind of Essex and his status in Court intrigue from the period:

> The Earl of Essex here in court has little or no grace at all. Her Majesty altogether averted from him and wholly directed in all business by Mr. Secretary [Robert Cecil], who now rules as his father did and who albeit he pretend love and friendship to the Earl of Essex yet in heart is thought his greatest enemy, envying his former greatness with the Queen and intending his utter overthrow if Irish affairs take not better effect as they are not like.
>
> My Lord of Essex, albeit he know this much and be still thought discontented in the highest degree yet does he dissemble it and shows so dejected a mind as there he dares not attempt anything without direction from hence and labors by letters and all other means to soothe and flatter Mr. Secretary, that he and her Majesty may conceive and retain good opinions of him and his proceedings.

Sterrell also described how Essex stood among the English people. Here, Sterrell revealed his own awareness of the fickleness of the crowd, comparing him to the late Duke of Norfolk.[13]

The parallel with the Duke of Norfolk is striking. Like Essex, Norfolk was earl marshal and had a large, popular following. Like Essex, Norfolk anticipated a Scottish successor to Elizabeth. Like Essex, Norfolk was opposed by a Cecil (Lord Burghley, Robert Cecil's father). Norfolk was found guilty of treason on evidence that was developed by William Cecil and was executed in 1572. Did Sterrell foresee the likelihood of Essex being executed on the strength of evidence of treasonous intent produced by Robert Cecil? Perhaps. He certainly placed Cecil's Iago-like malice towards Essex in envy of Essex's former greatness with the queen.

Essex Agonistes

With his men diminishing and supplies exhausting, his motives and judgment impugned by his opponents back at Court, Essex met with Tyrone and negotiated a truce on September 8, 1599, without consent of the queen or Council. Returning to England, he rode directly to the queen at Nonsuch and strode into her bedroom unannounced in early morning. He, damp and dirty in his riding clothes; she, wigless, unprepared for a visitor. She received him cordially, but Essex's affront was menacing. Soon he was facing charges. Like the Duke of Norfolk.

The Privy Council recommended later that the queen release Essex but she declined. Kept in restraint of Lord Keeper Egerton at York House, he was not allowed visits from his wife despite a serious illness. When Essex was brought to London in October 1599, it was in Worcester's carriage.[14] The Star Chamber issued a declaration of Essex's offences. In March Essex was allowed to return to Essex House, after the queen required all of his friends living there to quit the place. His wife could visit but not reside with him.

On June 5, 1600, Essex was tried at York House by an ad hoc tribunal of privy councilors, peers, and judges for offences against Her Majesty. Among them were the promotion of Southampton, the treaty with Tyrone, making too many knights in Ireland, and returning from Ireland without leave. As the long day became evening, the lords and judges each gave judgment. Their speeches were elaborately critical of Essex—all except Worcester's. His consisted of just thirteen words, in two diplomatically poised lines, quoted from Ovid's *Tristia*, the poet's laments in exile among the Getes. They are from the passage in which Ovid points to the mysterious reason why the emperor banished him—he had seen something he was not meant to—and compares himself with Acteon the hunter who was turned into a stag and torn to pieces by his own hounds because he came upon the unclad Diana. Worcester thus obliquely recalled Essex's precipitate return from Ireland in late September

1599 when he rushed unannounced into the queen's bedchamber.[15] Picking up the two lines of Ovid immediately after the two about Acteon's "offence," and the two about Ovid's, Worcester gave his "judgment" on his friend Essex's offence[16]:

> Scilicet in superis etiam fortuna luenda est,
> Nec veniam, laeso numine, casus habet.

That is, if one offends a divinity (such as Diana) *even by accident*, one must pay for it. So Worcester is saying that Essex, though scarcely guilty of wrongdoing, must—like heroes, and the Roman poet—accept that he now has to "pay" for giving offence, and suffer the unforgiving reaction to those unlucky stumbles in Ireland and at court which have offended his godlike queen. Worcester's Ovidian allusion was worked out in advance, no doubt in consultation with his secretary, Sterrell, who quoted Ovid multiple times in his intelligence letters over the years.

News of the York House proceeding travelled quickly to Flanders. Hugh Owen immediately tried to influence the queen by sending a letter to Sterrell (as Peter Halins) that praised Essex's handling of himself before the commissioners and expressed hope that Elizabeth would show him benevolence. Robert Cecil, whom Thomas Phelippes showed such "advertisements" from Holland from time to time, was commended for his temperance in the hearing.[17] The J.B./Hallins letters sought to affect policy by adroit and timely flattery, as will Fr. Persons through letters that Sterrell will pass to Cecil via Phelippes.

Worcester worked on behalf of Essex to reconcile with the queen. According to at least one report, Queen Elizabeth secretly visited Essex during this period of disgrace at court in 1600, and she was accompanied by Essex's friend, Worcester.[18]

Another Worcester Wedding

Essex's tribulations took place as Worcester prepared for another wedding, a wedding nearly as magical as the 1596 dual wedding that Essex hosted. Worcester's eldest surviving son Henry was to marry Anne Russell, daughter and heir to John lord Russell and Elizabeth Cooke-Hoby-Russell. She was maid of honour to the queen and niece of Robert Cecil. The queen personally determined the wedding date.[19] The couple were married at her mother's house in Blackfriars June 16, 1600.

A vivid memorial of that June wedding and Queen Elizabeth's participation is the *Procession Portrait*, surely commissioned by Worcester. He is in the center foreground. The background alludes to his two Welsh castles, one on the river Wye, the other against the Black Mountains. The wedding couple are in white; the bridegroom helps bear the canopy for Elizabeth, who is just above Worcester. To the left, leading the Procession are members of the Order of the Garter, their emblems prominently portrayed by the artist. Absent is Essex.

Essex's Trial and Execution

A letter from London to Fr. Persons, surely from Sterrell, observed[20]:

> At the celebrations of the marriage of the eldest son of the Earl of Worcester to a lady at the court, she [the queen] had waltzed day after day. Indeed people marvelled how much she had danced and walked and how pleased she appeared with the decision she had taken as regards the Earl of Essex. From all this some gathered that he was to be restored to his former familiarity with the queen.

The Procession Picture of Elizabeth I (Queen Elizabeth I; Edmund Sheffield, 1st Earl of Mulgrave; Charles Howard, 1st Earl of Nottingham; George Clifford, 3rd Earl of Cumberland; George Carey, 2nd Baron of Hunsdon; Gilbert Talbot, 7th Earl of Shrewsbury; Edward Somerset, 4th Earl of Worcester). Artist: George Vertue (© National Portrait Gallery, London).

Sterrell's intelligence, once again, was accurate. Two days later, the lord-keeper explained in a charge to the commissioners that Essex had been treated by the queen with exceptional clemency; Essex "shall have the liberty of Barnelms [his house, formerly Walsingham's]...."[21] Essex was allowed to leave York House for Grafton, Oxfordshire, the seat of his uncle, Sir William Knollys. Essex was finally granted his liberty in August 1600. He did not use it wisely.

Essex worked to restore his former position at Court through his friends and pleadings to the queen. Yet his circumstances continued to deteriorate as his debts mounted. Especially hurtful was the loss of the "farm of Sweet wines," the right to collect for ten years customs duties on wine imports.[22] He grew desperate, convinced that his complete destruction could only be avoided by gaining the presence of the queen and ousting his opponents from her counsel. If only she would see him face to face!

Essex still had many supporters and he thought the people would take his side. Sterrell wrote to Fr. Persons shortly before Essex's downfall[23]:

> The Earl of Essex is now altogether at his house neare Temple Bar, and out of favour as yet with her Majesty but growing again to wonted popularity, by being often visited, by many of the nobility, as the earls of Worcester, Southampton, Sussex, Rutland, Bedford and others, wth many captaines and cavaliers, and the whole pack of Puritans, insomuch as now it is thought both the Queen and Mr Secretary stand in some awe of him....

Groups of Essex's followers congregated at Essex House. Some had their own discontents with the queen. A plan developed by which Essex and a band would march upon Whitehall and present themselves to Her Majesty.[24] By Saturday February 7, 1600, some 300 Essex supporters were gathered at Essex House, an ominous massing of men that caused alarm. Early the next morning, the queen's councilors sent four men to meet with Essex: Sir Thomas Egerton (Lord Keeper of the Great Seal), Sir John Popham (Lord Chief Justice), Sir William Knollys (Comptroller, uncle of Essex), and Essex's friend—Worcester. The four, with one servant to carry the Great Seal, were admitted into the Essex House courtyard. The rest were excluded. Amidst cries for rebellion, at least two of the deputation were locked away in a study by Essex before his march towards the queen's chambers. In the street outside was a witness to the dire events: William Sterrell.

An account by Sterrell was written three days after the dramatic events of Sunday.[25] Its description of events corresponds to the recitations given at Essex's trial on February 19. Sterrell names a number of the Earls and Lords and gallant gentlemen who went forth "in their doubletts and hose with naked rapiers only in their hands" who "carried with hope to draw the citizens to follow and join with them." He vividly describes the strange bustling, the people seeming to pity Essex's case but afraid to join him, the Bishop of London assailing Essex, the wounding of Essex's step-father, Sir Christopher Blount. He turns to events at Elizabeth's Court where weapons were put to defence, a barricade of coaches was set up to close the passage that ran to Charing Cross, companies of foot and horse were assembled and marched by 3 p.m. He then describes the denouement at Essex House, with Sir Robert Sidney giving safe passage out to the women. He quotes Sidney as asking Essex: "And yourself my Lord, what mean you to do? for the house is to be blown up with gunpowder unless you will yield." The men inside yielded and were taken into custody, and as Sterrell put it, "this dismal tumult like the fit of Ephemera, or one-days ague" ceased.

Yet Sterrell's account glaringly omits one of the significant figures from the day's events: no where is Worcester mentioned. All accounts tell that Egerton, Popham, Knollys and Worcester were sent to Essex and that all four entered into Essex House. But Sterrell's account only speaks of Egerton (the Lord Keeper) and Popham (Lord Chief Justice) as being locked up in Essex's inner chamber. It appears likely that Worcester and Knollys were initially separated from the two other men sent by the queen and were to be treated more favorably. The omission of Worcester may reflect Sterrell's understanding that Worcester was given more cordial treatment by Essex and his men.

The trial of Essex and Southampton was on February 19. The outcome was foregone. Worcester was among the peers of the jury and concurred in the declaration of Lord Keeper Egerton, attested to by Chief Justice Popham who presided over the trial. Sterrell was likely present at Essex's trial and heard him condemned to death. Essex bared his neck to the executioner's axe on February 25, 1601. Southampton, Rutland and many of the rest were spared their lives.

Blaming Catholics; Execution of Anne Line

Essex was popular among the people, and his many followers included leading members figures. How was the government to explain away a rebellion by a subject who had received such bounty from the queen? To mask the regime's bitter internal divisions that underlay Essex's tumult, the government put it about that the insurrection was Catholic in nature. The prosecution's opening statement at Essex's trial by Sarjeant Yelverton put Catholic conspiracy center front: "as Cataline entertained the most seditious persons about all Rome to join with him in his Conspiracy, so the Earl of Essex had none but Papists, Recusants, and Atheists for his adjutors and abettors in their capital Rebellion against the whole estate of England."[26] Attorney General Coke taunted Essex to explain the actions of his counselors John Davis and Sir Christopher Blount (Essex's step-father), both papists, implying that they acted for religion.[27] Prime Minister Cecil similarly declared to Essex that "we know you, for indeed your religion appears by Blount, Davis and Tresham [Francis Tresham, another Catholic], your chiefest counselors for the present, and by promising liberty of conscience hereafter."[28]

To confirm this narrative, some Catholics already under arrest were show-tried and publicly executed within a couple of days after Essex himself. One was a gentlewoman who some years earlier was reported attending mass in Worcester's London house: Anne Line. Her close connection to William Sterrell was described earlier, when Sterrell was asked by their mutual friend Fr. Richard Sherwood to secure passage for her and her brother to Flanders where she could join Roger, her exiled husband. Sterrell had tried to work some arrangement with the secretary of the Privy Council, William Waad, in 1594, and perhaps was successful gaining leave for her brother, William Higham. A short time later, however, Roger Line died in Flanders.

Moving about London in secret, Anne Line assisted lay Catholics and worked with priests, including Fr. John Gerard, Fr. Henry Garnet (the Jesuit Superior), and Fr. Francis Page, a London law clerk brought to the church by Gerard. The week before Essex's outbreak, she was arrested as a priest conducted Catholic ceremonies in her house. The pursuivants were sent by Chief Justice Popham; he overbore the jury at her trial and condemned her to death.

This frail widow's hanging on a snowy February morning, and the casting of her corpse into a roadway pit, under common criminals, was starkly affecting. But those who knew of the loving constancy with which she and her husband had borne his exile for religion in the late 1580s, and of her fidelity and courage after his death, were even more moved by the ending of a saintly life. The Countess of Arundel, herself widowed by religion, sent her coach to recover the body that night, and doubtless sponsored a requiem for Anne Line's proper burial in some secret place. Not many months after her death, Shakespeare's poem usually called "Phoenix and Turtle" was published in an anthology dedicated to Sir John Salisbury.

20

The War between the Priests

"a good quarrel to draw emulous factions and bleed to death upon"
—Troilus and Cressida, 2.3

With Essex dead, so too was the Essex faction. His followers were dead, imprisoned or removed from influence. Yet the status of his close associate Worcester was enhanced. Already Worcester, and through him Sterrell, had near continuous access to the queen as Deputy Master of the Horse while Essex was abroad and then suspended while confined. In April 1601 Worcester became Master and was appointed to the Privy Council in June. Sterrell, through Worcester, was now privy to all political developments at the seat of government. Sterrell had a position that few spies in history have occupied.

Sterrell (and Worcester?) became deeply involved in a religious-political struggle in which the government engaged in a cynical scheme to divide the English Catholics and undermine the Jesuits. Walsingham had pursued this strategy vigorously for a decade. His agents in Douay, Rheims, Paris and Rome had cultivated the divisions and resentments in the seminaries. Walsingham had sponsored an anti-Jesuit pamphlet written by Gilbert Gifford and Gratley, and Phelippes had been privy to Walsingham's efforts in the 1580s. In 1599, Robert Cecil and Richard Bancroft, the Bishop of London (soon-to-be Archbishop of Canterbury), took up where Walsingham left off, using some of the same anti-Jesuit crowd and other long-time enemies of Fr. Persons. Through dissident priests, Cecil and Bancroft, with the cooperation of the French government, were able to reach into the Vatican to exploit the jealousies among priests in hiding in England and theological differences among Catholic clerics in Rome. Bishop Bancroft took a smoldering ember of emulation among priest-prisoners and fanned it into a flame that consumed Catholic efforts at unity for the English succession as Elizabeth's reign was ending.

Sterrell, through Phelippes, sought to influence the government through astute use of letters, much as he had with the "Boulant" letters and the other letters he received as "Hallins" and "Robinson." Had Sterrell's role been discovered, it surely would have meant his head. Although Phelippes was a key component of Walsingham's anti-Jesuit program, he was now a central player assisting the Jesuits, especially Fr. Persons. Just as Sterrell and Phelippes used Thomas Barnes to ruin Persons's enemy Charles Paget, so, too, will they soon use Barnes to ruin Dr. William Gifford.

Extensive documentation records the clash of spies, government agents versus the Jesuits' supporters. Old antagonists appear, Persons still haunted by Christopher Bagshaw who had been an opponent at Balliol College, Oxford, and Charles Paget, now operating from Paris and seeking to revenge himself on both Persons and Sterrell. Robert Poley shuffles on and off the stage once more. Dr. Gifford lingers before his dispatch.

The Archpriest/Appellant Controversy of 1598–1602 was religious, political, and international. A small group of secular Catholic priests (many imprisoned at Wisbech Castle) allied themselves against both Archpriest Fr. George Blackwell and the English Jesuits. The queen's government and church intervened to support the dissident priests. The French government, too, assisted the dissidents. The French and English governments were trying to drive the Jesuits out of England by exploiting internal divisions in the Roman church.

Sterrell gave a succinct statement of the origins of the Appellant controversy and the personal involvement of the queen, Secretary Cecil and the Bishop Bancroft of London in July 1602, tracing it back to Walsingham[1]:

> All these stirres have had original from Wisbech, and the Queen herself is said to have been the first motive of this division, remembering how Walsingham thought to have set a faction amongst the Cardinals, and afterwards to have nourished the like in the Seminaries. She, finding now fit matter to work upon at home, thought it good policy to set it forward, and so advised Mr Secretary [Robert Cecil] and he posted it over to my Lord [Bishop] of London, who hath no less bestired him in this, than he did in Cambridge with his quarter staff, when any broiles were on foot.

The Controversy Before 1601

The Roman Catholic church lacked formal organization within England. From the mid-1570s to his death in 1594, Cardinal William Allen was recognized as the informal head of the English Catholics. The Appellants controversy grew in the vacuum left by his death. Its first disruption was the Wisbech stirs of 1595–98. The government was holding about three dozen priests at Wisbech castle in Cambridgeshire. When in 1595 the Jesuit William Weston sought to bring about a voluntary discipline among them, he was bitterly opposed by about a third of them, led by Frs. Thomas Bluet and Christopher Bagshaw. Bluet was an older priest who was arrested in 1578 and confined at Wisbech from 1580 to 1601.[2] Bagshaw had been head of Gloucester Hall, Oxford, after being a bitter opponent of Robert Persons within the fellowship at Balliol College, Oxford. Imprisoned in 1585 immediately upon return to England after becoming a Douay-trained priest, he proved to be a cooperative prisoner.[3] Both Bluet and Bagshaw maintained contacts with the anti-Jesuit factions in Europe and collaborated with dissident English Catholics in Flanders and Rome to oppose alleged Jesuit misdeeds in Flanders.

The Archpriest crisis erupted in March 1598 when George Blackwell was appointed to the new office of Archpriest to serve as head for the 300 secular priests living clandestinely in England. His letter of appointment by Cardinal Cajetan appealed for unity and expressed a fear that some Catholics might greet the appointment with *aemulatio* (envious rivalry) against the Jesuits. The cardinal instructed the Archpriest to act in consultation with the Jesuit superior in England, Henry Garnet.[4] The Jesuits had only about a dozen priests in England. But they were an elite group, well-disciplined and supported by patrons. They had a superior system of communication within England and effective methods of sending and receiving letters and money overseas.[5]

Close to the Jesuits, Blackwell had been an Oxford scholar. Ordained priest in 1575, he was sent to England in late 1576. He was imprisoned but released by the influence of his brother, who worked for John Aylmer, Bishop of London.

The First Appeal (1598)—The Archpriest's appointment was opposed by some secular priests. Claiming that Cardinal Cajetan's document did not sufficiently show itself to have been papally authorized, the dissidents sent two of their number to Rome, to appeal against the new arrangements as inappropriate to English conditions and covertly designed to give the Jesuits in England unconscionable influence over the secular priests and their finances.[6] Their petition of thirty priests was rejected.

A brief reconciliation in 1599 broke down in protests against (i) the treatment in Rome of the priests during the first appeal, (ii) the allegation that priests who had denied the Archpriest's authority had been in schism, and (iii) Blackwell's suspension of the priestly functions of some of the dissidents.[7] One of the dissidents, William Watson, presented Attorney General Coke in April 1599 with a denunciation of the Jesuits.[8] The government soon used Watson to encourage dissension.

Second Appeal (1600)—In November 1600 an appeal to Rome against Blackwell was signed by thirty-three priests. Blackwell forwarded it to Rome.[9] The queen and Cecil now made their first major intervention, and the whole matter was assigned to Bishop Richard Bancroft. He was long experienced in troublesome religious groups[10] and familiar with many details of the Wisbech Stirs.[11] A letter and pamphlet war followed. Fr. Persons was the primary focus of the hostility of the dissident clergy.

Around the end of 1600, Bancroft secretly set out forty-five articles of enquiry, to which Bagshaw responded, first in brief answers in a paper for Bancroft, and then at book length in his *A True Relation of the Faction begun at Wisbech*.[12] Bagshaw had for twenty-five years been a personal enemy of Persons. Able but disorderly, he was described as a man "with a windmill in his head."[13] Long associated with Charles Paget and other English anti-Jesuits in France,[14] Bagshaw was collaborating with the English government by 1598. He probably contributed substantially to the government's awareness of the anti-Jesuit sentiments and of the opportunity to ruin the missionary efforts and political hopes of English Catholics. Bancroft prepared the articles for a dossier,[15] a strategy of active disruption, and a possible book. The government fostered a third appeal.

Third Appeal (1601–02)—A third appeal to Rome had strong backing of the queen and Council. The Council directed that Fr. Thomas Bluet (who had been in close contact with Bancroft) and three others, including Bagshaw, be released and allowed to raise funds to proceed to Rome.[16] The Appellants who journeyed to Rome included John Cecil, Thomas Bluet, John Mush, and Anthony Champney. The dominant figure became Cecil, *alias* Snowden, a relative of Robert Cecil and a long-term informer.[17]

Bishop Bancroft's leading role in exploiting the dissidents included giving them *de facto* liberty, housing, assistance in the publication of their anti-Jesuit tracts, which began appearing early in 1601. His aims were described by Sir Roger Wilbraham, a government official, who wrote in his private journal what Bancroft told him[18]:

> [T]he Bishop of London, on the advice of the Council, and, as he told me, especially the Secretary's [Cecil] advice, has worked to bring about discord between the Jesuits and secular priests, whereby they have written divers railing quodlibets and pamphlets against one another, so that the treacherous purpose of the Jesuits to depose the Queen as unlawful has appeared from their very writings.

Although most of the pamphlets purported to be published in Europe, scholars have confirmed Sterrell's 1602 reports to Fr. Persons that the books and pamphlets were printed in London by publishers favored by the government.[19]

Pitted against each other were two master controversialists: Bancroft, the state's energetically political Bishop of London, and Persons, Prefect of the English Jesuits, who for two decades had sought to reverse the English government's anti-Catholic policies. Though he wrote sermons and provocative pamphlets himself,[20] Bancroft excelled in sponsoring others' wits in religious frays. He was leader of the state church's response to the Martin Marprelate tracts, the pseudonymous Puritan pamphlets attacking the bishops.[21] In polemics of 1597–1603 concerning witchcraft and exorcism, the official pamphleteers were sponsored by Bancroft, and some of them were his employees.[22]

Persons was an astonishingly prolific writer. His limpid prose is a model of lucidity and persuasiveness. None of Bancroft's pamphleteers could approach his skills. But to participate in the fervid polemics with Bancroft's Catholic protégés, Persons needed copies of their works, and he needed information about their authorship, and the circumstances surrounding their composition. From the middle of 1601 until October 1602, the aim of Persons' unremitting work was to head off the threats to the Archpriest and the English Jesuits.[23] Throughout, Persons was ably assisted by Sterrell in London. The network that Persons had helped create five years earlier was indeed able to obtain "*information at the fountainhead in the Council....*" Sterrell was now "general factor" of Persons in London.[24]

The Appellants threatened the English Jesuits' mission. Persons could not acquiesce in the charge made by their pamphlets that the Jesuits were fomenters of rebellion and plots against the queen. The Pope could end the English mission more completely than the queen ever could: by ordering them out of England. The Jesuits were expelled from France in 1595, and the papacy itself was open to French influence, and resistant to Spanish, to an extent unprecedented for generations. Moreover, theological opponents of Jesuit teachings on divine grace and human freedom had taken deep into the papal curia their campaign for a condemnation of Jesuit theology. An opportune moment to petition Rome for the withdrawal of the English Jesuits had arrived.

In a forceful memorandum for the Pope written before the Appellants had stated their case, Persons asserted that they were going to say that the queen would grant Catholics liberty of conscience on condition that "the office of Archpriest be abolished and done away with, and that the fathers of the Society be expelled from England."[25] The Appellants did hold out the prospect of toleration for Catholics in return for the Pope "initiating some scheme"[26] for relieving the persecution of Catholics. Reports in Rome[27] and abroad[28] took the "scheme" to include the withdrawal of the Jesuits. Withdrawal of the Jesuits was high in the Privy Council's objectives in mid–1601 when it authorized the expedition of the Appellant priests.[29] A letter to Persons in late January 1603 reports[30]:

> [T]hree of the Appellant priests, thought to have been Mush, Champney and Bishop, have by means of the bishop of London had a secret meeting with some councillors, that is, Popham the Chief Justice, Secretary Cecil and one other. [Buckhurst, the Lord Treasurer]. The Secretary, in the name of all the others, said to these priests rather disapprovingly that it is true that you were at Rome as you promised, but you returned without carrying out anything that you promised to do, that is *that the Jesuits would be recalled,* the Archpriest deposed, no more papal Bulls or Briefs sent into England, and that the Pope would call on other leaders to make no further assaults on the Queen's state.

Sterrell as "Anthony Rivers": Purpose and Practices

The methods Sterrell and Phelippes employed to assist the English Jesuits and to counter the government efforts were three-fold. As "Anthony Rivers" Sterrell passed information to Fr. Persons about the discontented priests and their publications and about government actions against the Catholics. He rapidly dispatched multiple copies of the books and pamphlets so that Persons could distribute them in Rome. Phelippes' experience as collector of outward customs facilitated the transportation. Nothing was of greater help to Persons in opposing the Appellants. Persons probably shared, selectively, the Rivers letters in Rome: The information relayed to him almost weekly, direct from Sterrell's immediate access to the Privy Council, enabled Persons' vigorous intra-curial diplomacy to preserve the Jesuit mission to England and counter the threat that the government of Catholics in England might devolve to priests close to the state church and to Bancroft.

A second method employed by the intelligencers was even more audacious than dispatching intelligence to Brussels, Antwerp and Rome. Sterrell, through Phelippes, passed reports of the Appellants' reception in Rome directly to Robert Cecil to influence him to withdraw support of the Appellants and quell their anti–Jesuit campaign. The reports originated from Persons himself. Thirdly, the intelligencers probably had a hand in the importation and distribution of Persons' massive rejoinders to the anti–Jesuit books.[31]

"Johnson": Richard Fulwood—The transfer of Jesuit correspondence and packages such as books, from and into England was often carried out by two laymen, Richard Fulwood, *alias* Johnson, and Robert Spiller, *alias* Freeman. Fulwood was an administrator for Garnet who arranged the movement of correspondence, cash, and Catholic priests and students back and forth to the Continent.

A "waterman" using the name "Thomas Johnson" who was captured carrying young men overseas to seminaries on May 16, 1601, was probably Fulwood.[32] In October, as the Appellants were setting out for Rome, Phelippes sought "Johnson's" release through Secretary Cecil and Lord Cobham, saying to Cecil (with double meaning) that Johnson's liberty was "of much moment for the consequence of these [intelligence] services."[33] Phelippes pressed Cobham (with whom Phelippes was working on the repatriation of the Burgundian jewels) to get the Bishop of London to go along with the release.[34] What Cecil, Cobham and Bancroft did not know was that Phelippes needed Johnson/Fulwood released to pursue the business of the state's prime opponents in the religious controversy.

Some months after Phelippes' efforts to obtain release for "Johnson," statements by a captured priest were passed on to Cecil, telling him of Fulwood's role in carrying letters and persons overseas. In July 1602, Robert Poley (whom Walsingham and then Cecil used for nearly two decades) forwarded to Cecil a long statement of Fr. Robert Barwise, who was negotiating information for release from prison and better treatment.[35] Barwise had confided in Poley "the secret in and out passages of the Jesuits, the conveyance of their closest affairs, and in what places they chiefly remain here within." Barwise named couriers and routes used for the passage of people and communications, reporting: "For the conveyance of their packets, they seldom commit them to any shipper, but send in these aforesaid 'passenges' some special agent of theirs with charge of the businesses. The chief for that purpose are, as yet I can learn, Robert Spiller, Richard and John Fulwood, etc."[36]

Robert Spiller—Barwise's "Robert Spiller" was steward for the Countess of Arundel, who long supported the Jesuits.³⁷ His brother was a high official of the Exchequer.³⁸ He was a correspondent of Verstegan and one of Fr. Garnet's assistants. Unknown to Cecil until much later, Spiller was assisting Sterrell and Phelippes with Garnet.³⁹ Cecil and Bancroft not only knew from Barwise of Spiller's work with the Jesuits, but were also aware that his employer, the Countess, had close relations with the Jesuits. In December 1602, Bishop Bancroft wrote to Cecil that he had learned of a draft of a Jesuit "treatise" sent to Persons, who had revised it. The treatise had then been sent into England to the Archpriest and now was with Garnet "or with the Countess of Arundel. It is high time," he urged, "to look to that lady."⁴⁰

Rivers's Intelligences to Persons

Some of the information about the Council conveyed to Persons by letters from Garnet probably came from Sterrell.⁴¹ A fragment from a "Rivers" letter to Persons dated September 1 indicates that much has already been revealed to Persons regarding Thomas Bluet and his traveling companions who set forth for Paris.⁴² Sterrell probably supplied Persons with a letter from Bluet to Mush dated July 1, which Persons transcribed into his *Briefe Apologie*. The obtaining of the letter was a coup, for amazingly it recounted how Bluet had just arranged with the queen and Council for the expedition to Rome to prosecute the third appeal.⁴³

As Sterrell reported, the Appellants journeyed to Paris. Here, with the help of Charles Paget, Thomas Morgan and other Catholic exiles,⁴⁴ and perhaps of Robert Cecil, they gained the backing of the king of France. He gave them letters of support and sent instructions to his Ambassador at Rome, Philippe de Béthune, to further their cause. Ambassador Béthune and the French representative to the Pope, Cardinal d'Ossat, were to become the strongest supporters of the Appellants, and Rome was now more inclined to the French than the Spanish.

While the Appellants were in Paris, Sterrell sent four new books to Persons. He promised to send two more, an English version of Watson's *Quodlibettes* and a book of Anthony Copley.⁴⁵ The books supplied speedily by Sterrell became Persons' primary evidence against the Appellants.

Cecil and some privy councilors sought to give Bancroft protection from criticisms directed both from within the Council and from the Puritans. Bancroft had asked Cecil to provide him with such a letter, signed by "some three or four of your Lordships," so that he could then approach the Lord Keeper, the Chief Justice, and the Archbishop of Canterbury.⁴⁶ Such a letter was forthcoming, affirming that it was with the approval of the queen that Bancroft had "been driven sometime to restrain and sometime to relieve" sundry Romish priests in the cause of "laying open the malicious practices of the Jesuits."⁴⁷ Nevertheless, open opposition to aspects of Bancroft's policy seems to have continued within the Council.

At the beginning of March 1602 Sterrell sent on more pamphlets of the dissidents to Rome. Persons must have communicated some impatience with delay, as Sterrell spoke of problems of finding "good means for the transporting, whereof many times we have great difficulty, and that may be the cause that you had not the *Quodlibettes*, and such like with so great celerity as you desired, whereof notwithstanding both my cousin [Henry Garnet] and my self had special care and omitted no industry till we had remitted of each sort 4 to the end you and other friends might have full notice of the contents." Persons may have been flattered to learn that the Bishop of London had caused 50 copies of Persons' *Briefe Apology* to be printed by the queen's printer, to be presented to the Privy Council and his friends. Volleys were being exchanged rapid-fire in a war of pamphlets.

The *Briefe Apologie* is characteristic of one phase of Persons' efforts: it seeks to discredit the Appellants' cause by emphasizing their shady dealings with the queen and Council. His audience here is the Roman curia, and English Catholics. The work emphasizes the malign efforts of the "Council of England" against English Catholics over the years. The Council were leaders of the common enemy. Such was Persons' first line of defence.

But soon Persons shifted to a different tactic, focused on London. Its centerpiece: anonymous letters delivered to the English government through Sterrell and Phelippes. And he issued a new work aimed at limiting government support of the Appellants. This coincided with growing public discontent that the government was supporting Catholic priests, some of whom were flaunting their liberty. In March Sterrell reported on an address to the assize judges by Lord Keeper Egerton: Jesuits, priests, and Puritans all labored for the subversion of the state; the Jesuits were worst, but the priests who had written against them were nourished in their contentious humors by pride and ambition. "He [Egerton] spake also much against the liberty that some priests enjoyed, affirming all such as relieved or received them to be within the compass of law, willing the Justices to have regard thereunto." Sterrell emphasized this disarray within the government.[48]

A week later Sterrell said that Bancroft's principal sponsor, Cecil, was showing signs of queasiness about the policy.[49] Persons and Sterrell cooperated (long distance) to increase that queasiness. Sterrell's next regular letter reported that Cecil "disavoweth all good conceit of any priest whatsoever...." However, there was encouragement for Persons: "for learning, gravity, and modesty, he [Cecil] attributes much more to the Archpriest's party, the other, in their books, discovering too apparent levity."[50] Sterrell said that the queen herself commanded the faction to be still nourished, with the intent that the college of cardinals would be divided in opinions and the Pope would be distracted from determining the controversy or soliciting the king of Spain to endanger England.[51]

Events in Rome

The Appellant priests arrived in Rome in mid–February. The four began their round of curial visits on February 20, 1602, n.s., finding the cardinals friendly. Though disobedient to the Archpriest, they were not judged schismatic by these cardinals. However, they soon had to deal with the books sent by Sterrell. The Vice-Protector and the Inquisition had been supplied with "certain English books printed in England ... containing much bad matter." These had been dispatched by Sterrell to Persons in December, possibly supplemented by the *Quodlibets*. Mush's diary records that at the Inquisition "we disclaimed from them as in truth we were not privy to the making or divulging of them, nor did we know the author or what they contained."[52] The books kept the Appellants in Rome on the defensive throughout the appeal. The Commissarie of the Inquisition was very friendly, Mush reported, but "found great fault with certain English books printed in England which had been delivered him containing much bad matter."⁵³ On February 24, the French ambassador told them that the Pope found fault with the books and that the Pope had heard the dissidents were "contentious and troublesome."⁵⁴ The Appellant delegation must have marveled that the books reached Rome before they did.

At their first audience with the Pope the Appellants were roundly berated. He committed the cause to two cardinals in whom they had no faith. The Pope had heard many evil things about them, that they were sent by heretics [Bancroft and the Council] at their cost, and that they had set out books containing heresies. Sounding dejected, Mush wrote: "Our protestation of obedience to him [the Archpriest] he called *verba & parole* [words and yet more words]. All we proposed seemed to dislike him."⁵⁵ Sterrell's letters to Persons and the books had their desired effects. The fierce invective of the books, hostile to decades-old Papal policy as well as to Jesuits, could not be explained away by the subtle Dr. Cecil nor by earnest Fr. Mush. Even the French ambassador began to back off his support. He told the appellants that he was not in a position to show himself to stand for them.⁵⁶

"Intelligence" to Cecil

Phelippes insinuated himself with Cecil on the Appellant controversy early in 1602. Records survive of five, perhaps six, transmissions to Cecil of relations from Rome which were composed by Persons to influence Cecil and passed to him through Sterrell and Phelippes.⁵⁷ A letter of May 4 from Phelippes to Cecil enclosed a letter from Rome dated April 27, 1602.⁵⁸ This relation travelled from Rome to London astonishingly fast: sixteen days. Persons's aims and methods can be understood from this first surviving transmission to Cecil. The relation begins, in all four versions: "—to—. I have written to you before what was past" about the Appellant priests. They had a courteous audience [March 5, n.s.] of His Holiness, "but yet he gave them a sound reprehension." The purpose of supplying this relation to Cecil, emerges plainly in the succeeding sentences:

> They making great instance to be delivered from the note of schism and rebellion before the coming of the first brief [April 1599], His Holiness remitted himself [on April 10/11, 1602, n.s.] to his second brief [August 1601], and imposed silence upon all that passed before the first brief, adding that he would have his two briefs [of 1599 and 1601] exactly observed. Upon this followed the examination of eleven books, published in Latin or English, out of which thirty-nine propositions were exhibited as erroneous and scandalous, together with the form of a certain oath taken therefrom.

The relation is calculated to minimize an event which the Appellants were trumpeting as a stunning victory: the ruling on April 10/11, n.s., by the two cardinals, with papal approval, that the original non-acceptance of the Archpriest had not been schismatic and confessions heard by them since then need not be repeated. The relation forwarded by Phelippes to Cecil was accurate: the Pope and cardinals meant their ruling to be no more than a repetition of points settled in the *Brief* of August 1601, and strongly willed that there be no further publicity about the matter.⁵⁹ Yet the Appellants' victory cries⁶⁰ were echoing throughout Europe; the Appellants' boasts about the April ruling are mentioned in six successive Sterrell/"Rivers" letters.⁶¹ The purpose of the relation was to provide Cecil with a sobering view from Rome. The Pope had taken no new stand. The Appellants in Rome were disowning all the Appellant books save the two Latin ones of May 1601 and were denouncing Watson (the editor of all the books issued in late 1601) as someone just as fit for hanging. Persons wrote that "seeing that these men here do detest those propositions already that were written in favour of Protestants, I marvel what [Bancroft] will gain by them at the last." The relation noted that harsh Puritan criticism of Bancroft "about the Praemunire, for favouring an appeal to Rome," really strikes at "some more potent [i.e., Cecil] than he [i.e., Bancroft]."

Cecil could not have missed the point. The proposals being promoted by the Appellants in Rome would backfire. Catholic bishops might replace the Archpriest. Can this, or their alternative of six archpriests, really be more satisfactory for "their patron Bancroft" or for the State, "than one poor quiet archpriest who troubles no man"? Romans were laughing at the Appellants' political ambitions.[62] In short, the Appellants should be regarded by Cecil as fractious losers. Bancroft's sponsoring their polemical publications was backfiring.

The letter of April 27/17 is skillful advocacy; it contains no detectable misinformation, but brings forward much that might be likely to chill the English government's enthusiasm for its Roman project. Bancroft was Persons's principal antagonist, and Persons was fighting him by passing letters to Cecil. Very shortly Phelippes will pass on to Cecil a copy of the *Manifestation* itself, a book that marks Persons' strategy of direct diplomacy.

Sterrell now provided more information that could be used against the Appellants in Rome. They denied involvement in most of the pamphlets. The pamphlets that Sterrell/ "Rivers" sent and his letters provided confirmation from London that it was well known that the tracts emanated from the Appellants.[63] Bluet, Champney and Mush were the very priests in Rome denying knowledge of the books, and Bagshaw was supporting them from Paris. Sterrell attributed specific pamphlets to Bagshaw, Bluett and Mush respectively. Persons could use this to accuse the Appellants of lying, hypocrisy and schism. The four in Rome purported to represent the other secular priests in England and could not simply disavow the books.[64]

Sterrell related to Persons that Watson's behavior was becoming scandalous.[65] His ostentatious appearance in public, wearing a plumed cap and leading an entourage of two men and a page, was unseemly for a priest. He was displaying the instability that will within a year bring his execution for a genuine plot against the Crown. For this mad priest's prison escape earlier, Margaret Ward was executed in 1588.

More Roman News for Cecil

In a letter of June 4, 1602, Phelippes enclosed a relation headed "A note about the proceedings of the English priests at Rome that call themselves Appellants."[66] Dated May 25, 1602, n.s., it shows fast transit from Rome. This relation is acknowledged in due course by Rivers/Sterrell.[67] Four copies exist: (i) a corrected draft preserved in Persons' Roman papers,[68] (ii) a fair copy, kept in the same papers,[69] (iii) another fair version, preserved in the State Papers along with Phelippes' note to Cecil, and (iv) a version, also preserved in the State Papers, in the same hand as the surviving relation of April 27, probably William Sterrell's.[70] When these versions are collated, the entire system is laid out: Persons' draft and fair copy in Rome (each addressed simply "Good Sir," without identification of writer or addressee), the copy sent in the Jesuit packet to London, and the copy made and filed by Phelippes and Sterrell—one or other of the last-mentioned two being the version transmitted to Cecil.[71] The true recipient addressed by Persons was always meant to be the very man whom it thus reached.

This relation of May 25/15 tells a story much like Persons's anonymous relation of April 27/17. It refers to "my last of 27 April," and into its account of the Appellants' difficulties is inserted the news that "Fr. Persons has been forth from Rome, for the most part, since I wrote my last." Not meant to be genuine correspondence, the letter of May 25, n.s., like each other in the series, names no one as writer or as the recipient it addresses as "Good Sir." Each was written or dictated, by Persons himself, as an imaginary English bystander in Rome writing for the benefit of an imaginary correspondent, with the purpose that it be given to Robert Cecil in London to provide him with a downbeat assessment of the Appellants in Rome, who are not faring well. The Pope had commanded the Appellants' books to be censured by the inquisition. The writer recounts a presentation of two Appellants to the Pope's representative, Cardinal Borghese, who did "wonder to see such spirits among us." Yet the Appellants in Rome were denying that they sought to remove the Jesuits from England.[72] The message was clear: the four Appellants were not keeping their promises to Bancroft, Cecil, and the Privy Council. Persons and Sterrell were driving a wedge of distrust between Cecil and the Appellants.

A Book Is Delivered to Cecil—Persons' Manifestation

The news "letters" from Persons to Cecil were soon complemented by delivery of a book to Cecil with an approach like the letters. Phelippes sent Cecil an undated note and a book "whereby you will see that our seculars are miserably overmatched when it comes to writing. I must crave leave, so soon as I can be at fit leisure for it, to publish somewhat for the clearing of that point, page 43, which I have folded down; being myself also by name most spitefully and falsely touched in that pamphlet of Southwell's about that matter."[73] The book "now come abroad" was the *Manifestation*, which on p. 43 recalls that Southwell in his supplication to Her Majesty "did also signify that Mr Walsingham had entertained for divers months the knowledge and notice of that [Babington's] association as it is most certainly known that he did by the confession of divers that dealt with him therein, and thereby also most probable that the poor gentlemen were drawn thereunto [the Plot] by his [Walsingham's] malice and craft." The "pamphlet," Southwell's *An Humble Supplication to Her Majestie*, was written in late 1591 and was critical of Phelippes's role in the Babington Plot, but was published only in late 1600 by the arrangement of the dissidents as part of their struggle with the Jesuits.[74] Phelippes' show of self-interested indignation in delivering Persons' appeal to the Privy Council seems calculated to arouse Cecil's interest in the book's wider concerns.

In *A Manifestation of the Great Folly*, Persons shifts tactics radically. For English audiences, Persons now represented Cecil and others with whom the tumultuous priests are dealing as "very wise and discreet men, and of no evil nature or condition."[75] Indeed, he wrote of "the great wisdom and most honourable disposition" of the Council. Persons' audience shifted so as to include Cecil and other councillors. Persons flattered them with his confidence that, being wise and discreet, "they will easily discover the great and strange passion of these men together with their intemperate spirit, and that they do not this they do or say for any love towards them, but for revenge towards us; not of judgment or affection, but of envy and precipitation...."[76]

The speed with which the *Manifestation* was written and sent from Rome into England is extraordinary. Persons did not have Copley's book *An Answer* and the Englished version of Watson's *Quodlibets* before mid-January 1602. Yet the *Manifestation* discusses them in considerable detail and contains information supplied by the Sterrell/"Rivers" letters. Portions of the *Manifestation* were written in late January or in February 1602. Persons refers to "the four priests which are said to be in Paris" and identifies three of them by name[77]; he speaks of the time "when they shall have spent in Paris the good sommes of money which they carried out of England with them...."[78] By April 27 it appears that the book has been set in type, apparently in Antwerp, and it is in the hands of Cecil in London in June.

More "Intelligence" to Cecil

On July 30 Phelippes sent Cecil two separate packages, one from Rome, the other Antwerp.[79] Both showed that the Appellants' claim that Elizabeth was inclined to toleration were discredited overseas by the executions of three priests. Sterrell on April 28, 1602, had written to Persons of the martyrdom of three priests, Francis Page, Thomas Tichborn and Robert Watkinson. The queen's personal approval of these executions was sufficient to dispel any notion that the Appellants represented a move to English toleration. Sterrell's letter said that men of good knowledge gave two reasons why the government undertook the sudden persecution. First, the State wished to show the falseness of the Appellants' assertions that the government was inclined to toleration, and to demonstrate that the Appellants were not employed to this end by the government. The second reason was that the Puritans were disturbed by the closeness of the Bishop of London to Watson "and others," and so to prevent "actual rebellion" by the Puritans the priests were executed. Sterrell carefully laid responsibility upon the queen.[80] Sterrell's account of the executions deprived the Appellants of their claim to be a vanguard of toleration.

The July 30 papers given to Cecil provided details on the expected judgment of the Holy Office against the Appellants' books[81]:

> In the end either they and their fellows will be found to have had part in these books, or this all will fall upon Mr Bancroft of London to have feigned them of himself—and then will both Catholics and Puritans have just cause to write against him, the first for forgery, the second for apostasy....

By placing the expected opprobrium for the Appellants' failures upon Bancroft, Persons again invites Cecil to dissociate himself from the Lord Bishop.

The Roman papers in Phelippes' transmission of July 30 are acknowledged in a Sterrell letter to Persons just two days earlier: "I think it will be to good purpose, that their [Appellants'] Protector [Bancroft] have a cooling card, he is grown to[o] to[o] insolent, railing at Jesuits beyond truth or modesty."[82] Playing or dealing a "cooling card" dashes the hopes of one's opponent, and one object of the Persons-Sterrell enterprise was to detach Cecil from Bancroft, and discredit Bancroft's anti-Jesuit project. Perhaps the "cooling card" was effective; in a letter of September 1, Sterrell said, "it is observed that my Lord of London is of late much altered from his wonted vein of railing at the Jesuits, and would seem indifferent to them; whatsoever the matter is, it may be the touch of forgery and apostasy that sticks in his stomach...."[83] Sterrell's reference to "forgery and apostasy" tracks closely the use of "first for forgery, the second for apostasy" by Persons in the document passed by Sterrell and Phelippes to Cecil. Sterrell let Persons know the "cooling card" served its purpose.

The Pope's Breve

A transmission to Cecil on August 21 consisted of the usual apparently hasty note from Phelippes, covering another account of the Roman affair.[84] But this time there was nothing in Sterrell's hand, and no comprehensive "note" or "relation," but rather, in Phelippes' own hand, "an extract of such letters as came by the last post," namely letters dated 3 and 10 August, n.s. This was the climactic period in the proceedings in Rome, and Persons had stepped up his letters to one a week.[85]

The extracts were brief. The first letter had recounted a recent minor but telling discomfiture of the Appellants in Rome. The August 10 letter reported what would prove to be the essential resolution of the whole appeal, a "copy" (draft) of a "decree," given out by the Holy Office to the parties (recording the provisional decision of the cardinals on July 20, n.s., approved by the Pope).[86]

Although Sterrell wrote frequently, there were no letters between July 7 and 21 or between July 28 and August 25 because duty to Worcester intervened. On July 28 Sterrell reported that "this day the Queen appoints to begin her long progress to Bristol ... not to return to these parts before October," but on August 25 he recorded that "the progress of Her Majesty was soon at a stay...."[87] As Persons would well understand, Sterrell, as aide to the Master of the Horse, would presumably be required to accompany the queen's progress away from London, and this is doubtless the reason why after the mid-year many if not all Persons's relations of affairs at Rome were directed to Garnet rather than Sterrell, and why the Roman news forwarded to Cecil on August 21 was in Phelippes' hand. Sterrell could not safely transmit his dangerous letters from the queen's traveling entourage.

A September 22 Sterrell/"Rivers" letter implicitly acknowledged that the main battle in Rome was over, with the Archpriest "extreme melancholy."[88] Both in Rome and London little more remained to be done but publish the edicts which would dispose of the case—first the papal brief, dated October 5, n.s., and then the royal proclamation of November 5/15. The proclamation's terms had already, more than seven weeks earlier, come to the detailed knowledge of Sterrell and was communicated by him to Persons on September 16 using the "Rivers" hand and methods but a new pseudonym.

A transmission to Cecil by Phelippes of November 3 may have been a trigger for the issuing of the queen's Proclamation two days later. Phelippes explained the long gap between August 21 and November 3 by saying he has been "abroad" on vacation. His note said: "The Breve is looked for daily in authoritative form." Enclosed was a relation from Rome, transcribed in Sterrell's hand, and dated September 14, n.s., bringing the account up to date.[89] The relation reported the cardinals' provisional decision of July, 20, n.s. and the arguments presented by each side for modifications; an estimate was given of which arguments are likely to succeed. Knowing that the definitive *Brief* was imminently expected to reach England, Cecil may have judged its account sufficiently trustworthy a basis for his final assessment and decision to issue the Proclamation of November 5, before any copy of the *Brief* had reached England.

Elizabeth's (Cecil's) Proclamation

The Proclamation of November 5, 1602, withdrew the government's support of the dissident priests. It condemned both them and the Jesuits and made clear that there would be no toleration for papists.[90] Based on Phelippes' note indicating that the Pope's breve was not available on November 3, it seems most likely that Cecil's part in the queen's Proclamation was based in significant measure on the intelligence passed to him by Phelippes and that the proclamation was issued so promptly so as not to appear a response to the *breve*, which by November 5 had still not arrived.[91]

A letter by Sterrell of September 16, using the name "Thomas Neevell," had foretold for Persons the coming endgame in England:

> I hear of a proclamation penned, and ready for the press, against Jesuits and all sorts of priests, that whereas by their own books and writings, each against others, it appears manifestly that they are of turbulent spirits, and practisers against the State, abusing moreover her Majesty's clemency by false and sinister reports, as well at home as in other countries, that she inclined to toleration and to mediate with the Pope for revoking of censures, and the like, with a large preamble to this effect, therefore all such are straightly charged, and commanded, by a certain day to depart the Realm, whereof if they fail, whosoever may be found, with their receivers and abettors, to be presently proceeded against with all severity; and for the discovery and apprehension of such, all Justices of Peace in their circuits are commanded to make diligent and often searches in places suspect, and to authorize other petty officers to do the like; and in this Mr Secretary is thought the chief agent.[92]

This is, in fact, the substance of the English government's long *Proclamation* issued six weeks later.[93] The summary by Sterrell omits only the distinction which the eventual document draws between Jesuits (and secular priests supporting them), and on the other hand "certain of the secular priests dissenting from them in divers points." The Appellants were attacked with fervor only a little less than that directed at Jesuits, and the liberty given the Appellants in London was denounced.

Priests of the Appellant party were given just a month longer than the Jesuits and their supporters to leave the realm. To all appearances, the queen, Cecil, and Bancroft were reeling in the line on which they had played the dissidents for eighteen months and more. But it was all in considerable part for show, specifically for calming the Puritans. On December 15 Sterrell reported to Persons that "nothing is yet done for the execution of the late Proclamation."[94] Bancroft, moreover, was printing more Appellant books, and Bagshaw was in correspondence with Cecil. Five weeks after the last of the Proclamation's four deadlines for departure from England, Sterrell reported to Persons: "Our Appellants are no changelings; they follow the Bishop of London as heretofore."[95]

Perspectives

From the outset, William Sterrell knew that the government would never extend religious toleration to the Roman religion.[96] The government needed a visible external enemy, to limit internal dissent and faction. The old Marian priests were almost all in their graves.

Though generally courageous and dedicated, the seminarians were often young, disorganized and ineffectual. The Jesuits were disciplined and making progress with gentry and nobility; the government wanted them eliminated. The government exploited and deceived a group of captive priests, hoping to unravel Rome's efforts to organize the Catholic priesthood in England more effectively. Sterrell's actions—some of them aimed at influencing events in Rome, others at influencing decisions at the highest level in England—were all designed to counter the government's manipulation of the dissidents. As close to the Council table as any non-councilor could be, meeting daily with the likes of Cecil, Popham and Coke, Sterrell knew first-hand of the cynicism of the government officials who sponsored this remarkable excursion into Catholic internal affairs.

In the end, both Bancroft and Persons could mark successes. Withdrawal of the Jesuits was a long shot, a possible bonus for a course of policy whose aims were always (i) to disrupt and demoralize the Catholics of England, (ii) to make public a full-blooded Catholic critique of aspirations, plans, and efforts by Jesuits and other Catholics to change the religious policy of the state, and (iii) to neutralize Catholics during the imminent succession. In these the government was successful. As James was arriving in London, Bishop Bancroft recorded those three aims and described their accomplishment: most notably, the Infanta Isabella might even have become queen of England had it not been for the bitter internal feud of the Catholics that he had exploited. It was because the Catholics were divided that "there could be no opposition against [Elizabeth's] successor.... If ... the Jesuits without this interruption [six years of struggles with the dissident priests] had held on their course as they had began, out of all question the Infanta would have been grown exceeding strong in this realm by the time that her Majesty died."[97] The two antagonists, Bancroft and Persons, came to parallel judgments. In his final known letter to his ally "Rivers," in mid–1603, Persons, too, attributed James' successful accession to the Appellants.[98]

The aim of Persons and his English associates (Garnet, Blackwell, and Sterrell) was that the Jesuit mission and the Archpriest be preserved, and both the government and the Holy See dissuaded from granting to dissident priests any status that would make them the leaders of an English Catholic community. These aims were attained. Persons could justifiably have judged that his campaign of persuasion, in Rome and London alike, had achieved all that could reasonably be hoped for, and Sterrell could equally have judged that his own feats, in providing speedily to Persons intelligence and the dissidents' books in Rome as well as enabling Persons to communicate directly with Cecil, had played their part.

When Persons wrote his July 1603 letter to "Rivers" he was responding to a June "Rivers" letter, the first such since the accession of James. Persons said he could deal more confidently with "Rivers" for now "Rivers" was "on this side of the brooke." Thus, Sterrell was in Flanders. What was he doing there? Persons's letter suggests clues.

Anthony Rivers's Metamorphosis as Ortelio Renzo

After the issuance of the Papal *Breve*, Anthony Rivers' role in the Archpriest controversy was at an end. With the queen's death approaching and James's succession virtually certain, Sterrell could easily believe the purposes to be served by a Court intelligencer were diminishing. But several other important developments were at work.

Sterrell probably got word that Ralph Winwood had sent Robert Cecil a letter of April 10, 1602, informing Cecil of Sterrell's correspondence with Fitzherbert, Owen and Fr. Sherwood. A short time later, Cecil had also learned of how the Jesuit correspondence was being carried out. As recounted earlier, Robert Poley had brought to Cecil details of correspondence (using Spiller and Fulwood as couriers) in July 1602 through the report of the priest/informant Fr. Robert Barwise. The collapse of such weak vessels was an ever-present peril to Sterrell.

If Sterrell were to continue in the same role after the arrival of a new sovereign, the risks might very well be greater. Sterrell began to withdraw from the correspondence. On November 17, 1602, Sterrell wrote Persons telling him that he had seen Person's last relation on the close of the Appellants case and the Pope's *Breve*. He said he had sent Persons the queen's proclamation on November 10, and also said he was well satisfied by the "letter to Perugia." Sterrell said he had not heard directly from Persons for a time and said perhaps "my impertinent manner of writing hinders you from more serious affairs." So, he announces that he has spoken with Garnet of some important matters that Garnet will relate "by his close manner of writing [presumably cipher], of what he thinks necessary," evidently Sterrell's discontinuance of correspondence.[99]

That the extraordinary intelligence efforts were winding down is seen in a letter of Sterrell to Verstegan indicating that expenses would now be less. The activities relating to the Appellants involved considerable expense, particularly for couriers, for books, for services (such as copying documents) and probably for bribes for customs inspectors. "Rivers" wrote Verstegan that his cousin, Garnet, hoped that the allowance he received from Persons would now suffice because Garnet would "not be pressed to send wares of so great bulk, nor so often...."[100]

Persons, Baldwin and others must have encouraged Sterrell to continue. He agreed reluctantly and offered as excuse for not writing more in the future that he may be "scant of time."[101] The same letter signaled a shift to a new alias, Ortelio.[102]

Correspondence did go forward with at least one or more letters in the name of Ortelio Renzo by Sterrell. But the nature of the correspondence shifted. The multiple newsletters seem to have ceased, and Sterrell reduced the amount of letters that he sent. He apparently stopped writing directly to Persons until he went to Flanders in June 1603. Phelippes appears to have tried to continue a level of intelligence drawing upon discussions with Sterrell. Before turning to the accession of James to the English throne, it will be useful to relate some other aspects of Sterrell's intelligence dispersed to the Jesuit network.

21

Scenes of a Dying Queen

Elizabeth's Decline in the Sterrell Rivers Letters

The biographer Michael Holroyd has commented that he learned how to make himself invisible because "it is the invisible person who tells the visible world's stories."[1] William Sterrell practiced his craft by cloaking himself in secrecy, appearing to all the Court as a silent cipher, always in the shadow of his master, the Earl of Worcester. His name itself, like its homophone, suggests barrenness—sterility. Few courtiers or Councilors even noticed his presence. Quietly, he would take notes, observe the people around him, and then he wrote.

Sterrell provided shrewd observations to his overseas correspondents on the final years of Elizabeth's reign. Such intelligence gave substantial guidance to the overseas Catholics in assessing a course of action for a regime change. Sterrell was exceptionally well-positioned. Worcester was to be a member of the Privy Council for more than two decades. As Master of the Horse (1601–1616) or Lord Privy Seal (1616–1628) he seems always to have been accompanied by his faithful and faceless confidante. Sterrell's letters describe the decline of Elizabeth, the shoring up of power by Robert Cecil, and the transition to the reign of James I.

Diplomatic Visitors

Gloriana's final years shone even as the queen decayed, bright paint covering a worn visage. Foreign visitors still came and praised the old woman, danced with her, complimented her beauty and grace with words as hollow as a courtier's smile. Her courtiers all awaited the end of her reign—and jockeyed for position in the next. Elizabeth struggled against her mortality, denied its inevitability and inevitably lost. Sterrell reported the shine and the decay of the queen's dying years.

Early in January 1601, there arrived in London a special envoy—an Italian who came to Elizabeth bearing goodwill from the new bride of Henry IV of France. He was Don Virginio Orsino, Duke of Bracciano, cousin to Maria de Medici who by virtue of her favorable marriage was the fresh queen of France. Don Virginio accompanied the young bride from Florence to meet her husband in Lyons, and then continued on England. Duke Orsino was received in London by Italian merchants, particularly Filippo Corsini,[2] and given a nobleman's welcome by the queen and her Court. Like the French king and his new wife, Orsino was Roman Catholic. In the midst of the activities was the Earl of Worcester, perhaps chosen for a special role because of his known Catholicism. The queen wanted Orsino to take favorable accounts of England to the Archdukes in Brussels, to which Orsino was traveling after London, and to Orsino's relatives, including the French king and queen. Worcester and his family appear prominently in the list of participants in the Court events. His secretary was close by.

Also in London in early January 1601 was the Russian ambassador, Grigori Ivanovich Mikulin, present to ratify a treaty of friendship between England and Czar Boris Godunov. Mikulin and his retinue were feted along with the Florentine Duke. Both Orsino and Mikulin gave written accounts of their entertainment that are consistent with Sterrell's report to Fr. Persons in Rome, indicating that Sterrell's observations are first hand.

On January 6, 1601, Elizabeth celebrated a day of festivities with the foreign visitors. Each was brought separately to Whitehall by men of high rank. Diplomatic protocol required that the envoys not eat in the same chamber, and Orsino was conducted by the Lord Admiral to a banquet hall adjacent to the room where Ambassador Mikulin and the queen ate. After this, Orsino returned to the presence of Elizabeth, who conversed alternately with Orsino and Mikulin. When the queen retired, Orsino was taken to Worcester's lodgings in Whitehall to rest before the remaining activities. Supper for Orsino was prepared in Worcester's quarters, and Worcester and the Earl of Cumberland came to sup with Orsino. Afterwards, Orsino rejoined the queen for the evening's entertainments, noting in his letter that now it was without the presence of the Russian.[3] Among the guests named were not only Worcester but also his wife, the Countess of Worcester, and his son and daughter-in-law, the newly-wed Lord and Lady Herbert.[4] Sterrell recounted at length details of Orsino's visit suggesting the Duke, who was on his way to Brussels, might be engaged on a peace mission.[5]

Religious significance was attached to the actions and gestures of the Protestant queen and the Catholic envoy. Orsino described the events of the day when the queen greeted him and took him with her as she went to chapel[6]:

> [A]ll the Court set forward in order toward the chapel. The order is such that I am having the whole noted in writing; nor do I believe I shall ever see a court which, for order, surpasses this one. I attended her Majesty to a room next the chapel, where I stayed, in company with many gentlemen; and as we stood in excellent conversation, we heard a wondrous music. At the end of half an hour her Majesty returned, with all the Court two by two according to their quality and degrees before her, and all the countesses and ladies after; and while I accompanied her she was ever discoursing with me, as she had also done before.

The Duke omitted that he was perhaps a little too much in attendance on the queen as she participated in a Protestant ceremony. Sterrell as "Rivers" gave this description of the same event to Fr. Persons[7]:

> She invited him to go with her to her closet over the chapel, having before given order that the Communion table should be adorned with basin and ewer of gold burning tapers and other ornaments, some say also a crucifix, and that all the ministry should be in rich copes. The Duke of curiosity accompanied her, and she was very pleasant thereat, saying she would write to the Pope not to chide him for that fact, with other like discourses, and so, service ended, they returned. But herewithal many Papists are much scandalized....

Ever conscious of symbolic acts, the queen had directed, just at the time of Orsino's visit, the restoration of an ancient sign of England's Catholic heritage and her ties to Spain, the Eleanor Cross at Cheapside. This monument dated from c. 1294, erected as one of a dozen similar crosses commemorating the progress of the remains of Eleanor of Castile, wife of Edward I, from Lincolnshire to her burial in Westminster Abbey. The purpose for the Cross's restoration was to impress upon the Catholic visitor that the English government was not so harsh in attitude to Catholicism as might be thought overseas. Sterrell related this undertaking in civic improvement[8]:

> At this time six of the Council have written to our Lord Mayor of London commanding him in her Majesty's name, with all speed to cause the cross in Cheapside to be repaired, and the figure to be set up as perfectly and precisely in all respects as it was before. The like command was sent by Mr Secretary some years since, but our Mayor and Aldermen refused to obey, pretending it was superstitious, and willing to set in place thereof the picture of Justice. Now no more delays will be allowed, an all diligence is used that it may be finished before the Duke's departure, that he might make relation therof in foreign parts, as though we were not so ill affected in religion, or the same so much persecuted here, as abroad is supposed.

The Cross's symbolism for England's Catholic heritage continued to rancor militant Protestants, and the lovely monument will be violently destroyed in 1643, near in time to the destruction of Worcester's castle, Raglan.

The Russian envoy gave an account of his dinner with the queen:

> And as we sat at dinner, the Queen sent by the Carver *[Lord Sussex]* a gift to Grigori—a white loaf on a dish covered with a napkin, and he spake to Grigori: "Our great Lady," quoth he, "Elizabeth the Queen, of her grace bestows on you this loaf. And moreover," quoth he, "she graces you with this napkin." And Grigori prostrated himself to the Queen's favour in the gift and the napkin.[9]

Sterrell gave an observer's account that was much like the Ambassador's own report[10]:

> The Ambassador of Muscovia that is residing here, was this Christmas very honorably feasted at the court. He one day dined in the presence at a side table with the Queen, her Majesty drinking to him did send him divers dishes, and particularly bread, salt and water as the custom of his country is, at the receipt of which he always rose and prostrated himself on the ground.

In the same letter, Sterrell commented on the queen's appearance: "It was commonly observed this Christmas, that her Majesty when she came to be seen was continually painted not only all over her face but her very neck and breast also, and that the same was in some places well near half an inch thick."

Another Catholic visitor arrived from France in April 1602, the Duke of Nevers. Sterrell reported that he "was honorably entertained by her Majesty. She danced with and courted him in the best manner. He, on the other side, used many compliments, as kissing her hand, yea and foot when she showed him her leg. He behaved himself courteously to all."[11] Unlike Orsino's venturing to attend Anglican religious ceremonies with the queen, Nevers "would not be present with her Majesty in her closet at our service time, but retired and met her as she returned. He went religiously to the French Ambassadors to Mass."

Cecil's Support of James

By the end of 1601, it was clear to Sterrell that Robert Cecil was now preparing the way for James of Scotland to succeed Elizabeth on the throne. Just before Christmas, he wrote to Persons that Secretary Cecil "is now thought to work cunningly by all covert means to advance the Scott when time shall serve."[12] A month later Sterrell reported that "all our greatest men here make great show of affection to the Scots king, the most part as it is thought rather for fear than love."[13] A Scot had told one of Sterrell's friends that James had no doubts that he would be king and that he would "pull down our English pride and insolency." This had displeased many. Sterrell's comment on James was *ex ungue leonem*: By his claws is the lion known.

A year before her death, Sterrell provided a vivid portrait of the queen in her decline. The court has been at Richmond some twelve days but was to move to Greenwich because of an ache in the queen's arm. She expected more ease by a change of air.[14]

> A cunning bonesetter or Surgeon had lately a sight therof; he said it was a wind with a cold rheumatic humour settled there [in her arm], and to be removed by rubbing and applying of whott [hot] oils and ointments. Her Majesty told him he was mistaken for that her blood and constitution was of its nature very whotte [hot], he replied that neither flesh nor blood in that part made any show thereof, but much more the contrary, wherat she was exceedingly displeased, commanding him from her presence, she being most impatient to hear of any decay in her self, and thereupon will admit no help of physick or surgery, fretting and storming when she feels any little pain, and sometimes retiring her self from all access for 3 or 4 hours together.

The courtiers were more than annoyed at the old woman's "humours": "All the nobility seem weary of her passionate humours, and withdraw themselves from the court by all devises possible." The queen's aches in her arm continued into March, so she was "much out of tune."[15] The pain, wrote Sterrell, had fallen into her side but she continued to be "frolic and merry." Her face, however, showed decay and "to conceal when she comes in public she puts many fine clothes into her mouth to bear out her cheeks, and sometime as she is walking she will put off her petticoat as seeming too hot, when others shake with cold."[16]

Though Cecil often absented himself from the Court at Richmond to remain in London, he continued to "sway all of import"; he daily sent Elizabeth some "revel or toy" to maintain her favor.[17] Others of the Council estranged themselves from Court by all occasions. Remaining with the queen regularly were only the Master of the Horse (Worcester), the Vice Chamberlain (Sir John Stanhope) and the Comptroller (Sir William Knollys). Sterrell captured the circumstances with a phrase he may have picked up from Dr. John Case's *Sphaera Civitatis* (1588), an Aristotleian treatise on government: *Mens hominum novitatis avida*—the human mind is eager for newness/ change /revolution.

An attempt was made on the life of James early in 1602, by an English Papist. The English government purged itself from all suspicion, Sterrell reported when the news first arrived, "attributing such attempts and advises to the Papists, and for confirmation, we have sent the king certain letters of advises from Italy, in which intelligence was given that some such matter was in plotting." Cecil, he continued, "seeks by all means to insinuate himself into the Kings good opinion, but all is but policy, it being certain that he loves him as little as others."[18]

The attempt on James was soon clarified.[19] The sequel, Sterrell wrote, showed it to have been a frantic passion in the man rather than any sinister intention against the king. The mans name was Dethick, once an apprentice in London with one "Mr. Heckes," a mercer.[20] After apprenticeship, Dethick became a factor for Hicks and others in Florence, and there did also service for the state, in being the means for conveyance of intelligence by letters from Italy. After a time in Paris, Dethick had gone into Scotland. He lodged at a barber's house near the Scottish court, and he suddenly came down with his rapier drawn, and killed one great "Jeamye" in the shop. Upon being apprehended and examined, he said he had not killed the right Jeamye. Sterrell informed Persons that some said Dethick confessed that he meant to have killed the king, others that being come again to his wits he denied it. The English, Sterrell wrote, say he was sent by the Pope and king of Spain "to perpetrate so wicked a fact." Some that stood ill affected to Mr Secretary, "make (I know not what) surmises, for that Mr Heckes' brother, is most inward wth Mr Secretary and this Dethick directed all letters to him. The Scots King dissembles as though all were nothing, and has now sent Aston his Agent to receive his pension."[21]

The succession was of great interest to Persons, and Sterrell described the efforts on both sides of the English/Scots border to have James succeed Elizabeth: "All our great persons seek by all means to have the Scottes King well conceited of them, and he on the other side labours by many Agents to entertain affections here, dissembling if he have any mislike, and I hear he has in every part of the Realm certain principal persons appointed immediately upon notice of the death of her Majesty to proclaim him, and to make what party they can for him, all this notwithstanding I hear some have an intention to match the Earl of Hartford's younger son with Arbella [Stuart], and to carry it that way but those *supra nos nihil ad nos*." This Latin adage (attributable to Socrates and included in a work of Erasmus), "what is above us concerns us not," is perhaps ironic, as Sterrell's master Worcester was in a position to influence the outcome of the succession.[22]

At the end of June, Sterrell related that Elizabeth intended a journey to Oxford and Bristow but the ache in her arm was increasing and extending now to her hip; accordingly, it was thought she could not perform such a trip. Instead, she might go to Bath, where the Lord Chamberlain, Hunsdon, was convalescing. As he had written before, Cecil continued to be the power in the state: "Mr Secretary rules all affairs of State, and holds still in special favour with her Majesty."[23]

Sterrell continued to comment on the queen's progress to Bristow and how the planning was affected by her health. A letter of 21 July said the plan was for the journey to begin the next Tuesday (27 July) but the Privy Council was trying to delay the trip "both for that they would not be far from London in these troublesome times, as also for her Majesty's ache continuing in her arm, and beginning in her thigh or hip, they doubt she will hardly be able patiently to endure so long travel."[24] Despite the growing infirmities, he reported that the queen "hunted on Monday last in Eltham Park on horseback with good show of vigour and ability."

The queen's summer progress of 1602 finally got underway only a day late, on Wednesday, 28 July. Sterrell's letter, sent as he left with the queen, included a marginal comment of special interest to an all-Oxford team of recipients—Persons, Owen, Verstegan, and Baldwin: "We have had here much rain, lightning, thunder, tempest, and hail of admirable bigness, 5 inches and more about, which brake many of the windows of the colleges at Oxford but hath done much more hurt in the fields by blasting and beating down the corn."[25]

Almost a month passed before Sterrell wrote again to his overseas correspondents.[26] This was no doubt due to his accompanying Worcester and the queen, which limited his ability to pass his letters by secure route. The queen's entourage soon arrived at Harefield Place, a short distance west of London. The estate recently became a residence of the Lord Keeper, Thomas Egerton, with his marriage in 1600 to Alice Spencer, widow of Ferdinando Stanley, 5th Earl of Derby.

As the queen's health and her glory faded, the members of the Court were increasingly reluctant to travel, particularly as her ability to undertake the hardships of a journey made planning very uncertain. Sterrell expressed his resignation and weariness in Latin: *Sic ut quimus quando ut volumus non licet*—we do what we can.[27]

One of the purposes over the many years of Elizabeth's reign of the "progresses" through the countryside was to reinforce the image of the strength of the government in the person of the queen and the majesty of the Court with its color and noble attendants. The goal was significantly impaired when the queen's health and infirmities showed her old and weak. On such an occasion Sterrell repeated his Latin invocation of "we do what we can" in mid–November: "The Queen came to Whitehall from Richmond on Monday last but whereas she meant to have come in great pomp she was taken with some sudden distemper by the way, and so went in her close barge, whereby our Lord Mayor and Citizens that rode out in great state to meet her lost their labour."[28] At this time it was clear that the Archpriest controversy had come to an end and that the queen's reign was nearly over. The time neared for Sterrell to end his intelligence to Persons. He signaled this and said he hoped Persons would not "think that I surcease upon any disgust or other dislike," and he assured the Jesuit that he "will ever be ready to serve you…." After he and Phelippes had labored to undermine the candidacy of James, it was painfully obvious that the Scot would ascend.

Sterrell passed a few more letters to Persons in the final months of Elizabeth's life. In mid–December he reported of the queen's dining at Robert Cecil's new house in Strand by Ivy Bridge. Cecil "gave her 10 several gifts, the most part very rich Jewels."[29] The dinner and presents were valued at £3000. Although the queen was merry and well pleased as she departed, her weakness again betrayed her: she refused help to enter the barge, whereby stumbling she fell and a little bruised her shins. She recovered in time to dine at the Lord Admiral's a short time later. In the same letter Sterrell reported on James's activities in England as he prepared to become king: James had "many solicitors in England that labour to make all principal men for his party against her Majesty's decease, offering all present security under the King's own hand, for liberty of conscience, confirmation of privileges and liberties, restitutions of wrongs, honours, titles and dignities, wth increase according to desert etc."

The last letters, dated 9 March, of Sterrell to Persons and his other correspondents before the death of Elizabeth never reached their destinations. They were intercepted by the English government. Perhaps Sterrell dispatched replacements for the seized letters. Even if the letters never reached their intended recipients the last Rivers' letters of Elizabeth's reign are fascinating on several grounds.

Sterrell's letter to Persons is especially long, with much news on the decay of the queen. The Countess of Nottingham, the wife of Lord Admiral Howard, had recently died and Elizabeth "hath seemed to take her death very heavily, remaining ever since in a deep melancholy, wth conceipt of her own death." The queen "complains of many infirmities, suddenly to have overtaken her, as impostumacion in her head, aches in her bones, and continual cold in her legs, besides notable decay in judgement, and memory, insomuch as she cannot attend to any discourses of government and State." She took for her delight listening to "some of the 100 merry tales, and such like, and to such is very attentive, at other times very impatient and testy."[30] One of the reasons Sterrell gave for the queen's melancholy was her sadness over the execution of the Earl of Essex. What prompted the queen's sadness was Robert Cecil's persuading her to authorize a pardon for the Irish rebel, Tyrone. As he relates this, Sterrell implies that it was Cecil who had secured the death of Essex by opposing a pardon for Essex: "Mr Secretary was very earnest to effect this [pardon of Tyrone], and prevailed not wthout many difficulties, her Majesty pretending it to be a most dishonorable act, to pardon a notorious Rebel that had made 7 years war with her, whereas she could not be permitted to spare Essex's head, for one day's delict, and whensoever now she reflects upon this, she falls into great passion, and this also thought a principal cause of her sickness."[31]

None of the Council but Secretary Cecil dared come in her presence, wrote Sterrell; all at Court were "in the dumps." Because it was clear that Elizabeth was likely not to last beyond May, the matter of the succession was "now ordinary discourse both in Court and country." There were many rumors over Arbella Stuart, including some that she might be contracted to marry Secretary Cecil, who was now inward with Arbella's relative, the Earl of Shrewsbury.

Sterrell reviewed issues of foreign affairs as well as domestic problems in his long missive. On both fronts money was a big problem. The treasury was essentially bare, adding to the queen's health problems. For want of money, the ambassador to France was unable to follow the French king. Geneva was beseeching £20,000 of the queen for military purposes. The queen owed the city of London £60,000 and the city was pressing hard for payment. Sterrell reported that Attorney General Coke (a superb property lawyer) had found a "quirk" to overthrow the conveyance of the City's charter land.

From the 1603 intercepted letter of Sterrell to his "very dear and loving Partner" Richard Verstegan (as "Gio. Battista Galfredi") we have a glimpse that suggests fascinating possibilities. The letter to Verstegan touches on business matters and the settling of accounts, couched in obscure terminology, but also relates news of mutual friends and letters forwarded. Then Sterrell comes to something else that has passed between them—the manuscript or description of a book[32]:

> I acquainted such friends as I thought fittest, with the intended discourse of antiquities, and both the matter and method seemed to please; the book itself will be grateful [pleasing] to many. The caution I gave for the dedication, was not upon any conceipt that the Author intended such a course, but only to utter my private opinion, and in such cases *nimia cautela non nocet*.

The intended book is certainly Verstegan's *Restitution of Decayed Intelligence in Antiquuities, concerning the most noble and Renowned English Nation* printed in Amsterdam in1605 by Robert Bruney, to be sold in St. Paul's Churchyard by John Norton and John Bill. The Latin proverb means abundant or excessive caution is not a fault. In context, it appears that Sterrell cautioned the author concerning the dedication. To whom was it dedicated when it appeared something more than a year, perhaps two, later? King James himself.

Verstegan's book treats upon the early invasion of Britain, the formation of the Anglo-Saxon language and the etymologies of ancient Saxon proper names and early surnames, as well as of titles of honour and offices. Reflecting his own family background, he rejected the British contribution to England's history and languages in favor of Germanic elements.

Who were the friends Sterrell "thought fittest" to acquaint with this intended discourse of antiquities? Perhaps Sterrell was instrumental in arranging for Norton and Bill to represent Verstegan in the sale of the book. We have already suggested the close ties of Sterrell with Thomas Thorpe. We believe that Sterrell and Phelippes cultivated the London printers and references to several appear in Sterrell's letters. In 1604 Sir Thomas Bodley, founder of Oxford's Bodleian Library, appointed John Bill his agent in acquiring books printed abroad, and Bill made a trip to the Continent to acquire books, including many religious works. Sterrell could well have steered Bill to Verstegan or assisted Bill in going into Spain, just as he apparently did with Thorpe in 1596.

Sterrell's 9 March 1603 letters intended for Hugh Owen and Robert Persons both contained intelligence of military and political significance. If Spain were interested in intervening in the English succession, the preparations of James and of the Cecil government for possible conflict would affect planning in Madrid or Brussels. To Owen and Persons, Sterrell wrote that there was no "prevalent Competitor to the K: of Scots, upon whom the greater part of the Realm seem to have" fixed their hopes. Many English, however, had an aversion to James "and would be opposite were there any to pretend as potent." Between England and Scotland there was much interaction, "the better to hold that King in good terms." Elizabeth sent James £2000 sterling as a gift, and had since augmented his pension £2000 per annum. For his part, James was reported to "omit no diligence, to have all things in a readiness." He could put 14,000 cavalry into the field. Military preparations were underway in England as well, but their purpose was a matter of some conjecture:

> In our North parts, new and trusty Captains are appointed over all the trained Companies, and view made that all things may be in readiness, troupes are ordered for supplies, the Lord Burleigh president [Robert Cecil's brother] has the charge of this, and this thought purposely to make head against the Scot but so subtle is the Secretary [Robert Cecil], who rules all, that hardly can it be judged, which way he levels. Certain it is his inward man is averted from the Scot, and withal it is most certain that he is altogether opposite to the Spaniard, and now also in no very good terms with the French King, upon, surmise and jealousies, that he also is tampering to establish this crown upon himself or some of his. In fine we begin to be afraid of every shadow and many stand at gaze desirous to see Secretary take a certain course some way."

Worcester, Sterrell and the Funeral Ceremonies

Worcester and Sterrell would have learned of the queen's death on 24 March 1603 immediately. Worcester's daughter, Elizabeth Guilford, was a lady in waiting for the queen in her final days. She related to another of the queen's maids that she had encountered an apparition of the queen walking about on the night of Elizabeth's death and had then found her sleeping in the chamber where she had left her.[33]

Upon Elizabeth's death, the Privy Council immediately chose two men to represent them to take the news to James that he was to be king of England: Sir Charles Percy and Thomas Somerset, Worcester's son and William Sterrell's former student. Sterrell had tutored Thomas at Raglan to prepare him for Magdalen College. A day or so later the Council dispatched several others, including Sir Thomas Lake, Clerk of the Signet and friend of William Sterrell.

Worcester was well-known to the new king. The Earl of Worcester was first associated with James from the celebration of the Scots king's marriage to Anne of Denmark and her coronation in Edinburgh in May 1590. Worcester was Elizabeth's special ambassador for the events and to inform James that he had been nominated a Knight of the Garter. James's new Queen Consort particularly noted Worcester's presence in her letter of thanks to the queen of England.[34] It was an auspicious beginning, and Worcester was to flourish at James's English Court. Worcester's smooth transition from the Elizabethan to the Jacobean reign was exemplified by his being placed in charge of the ceremonies for Elizabeth's funeral. The new king also named Worcester as Earl Marshal to conduct the ceremonies for James's own coronation in London 20–28 July 1603 and for his delayed procession as king the following March. He will also be charged as Earl Marshal for the 3–6 May 1605 christening of Princess Mary. As Worcester's Secretary and aide, William Sterrell undoubtedly participated in the planning and made many of the arrangements for these events.

The funeral ceremonies for Elizabeth were an affair of state that marked the end of one era and the beginning of a new. The English nation both mourned and celebrated. Worcester (and no doubt Sterrell) used his theatrical knowledge and experience to stage a solemn event, one that was to strike just the right note for a people who grieved but were prepared for a future without their queen. Worcester arranged a magnificent procession that took place on 28 April 1603. The cost of the final pageantry was enormous: well over £11,000. He organized a march of a thousand or so of the queen's Court, government and retainers who took her body from Whitehall, where it had lain in state for a month, to Westminster Hall, where it was to be entombed. Prominent among the marchers from beginning to end were members of Worcester's immediate family.

The orders of the Proceeding show that the knight marshal's men were to lead, to make a way for 15 "poor men of Westminster" who were followed immediately by "260 poor women 4 and 4 in a rank." Next were servants of Gentlemen, Esquires and of Knights, then two Porters, four Trumpeters and two grooms leading a horse. A dozen of the banners that symbolized England were interspersed with the queen's household servants. Worcester's son Thomas bore the Standard of the Lion and was followed by two more grooms leading a horse fitted out with black velvet, followed by yet more servants and the children of the Chapel in surplices. The Banner of Cornwall was borne by Worcester's son, Henry, Lord Herbert, leading the Aldermen of London, the queen's Solicitor and Attorney General Coke, the Sergeants at Law and the Master of Revels, among others. Eventually the onlookers saw approach the four horses, with trapping of black velvet, which drew the chariot that carried the coffin of the queen. It was overlaid with purple velvet and upon it was a lifelike representation of the late monarch, in robes of state and with crown and sceptre. Her canopy was borne by six knights, one of whom was Sir Edward Winter, Worcester's son-in-law. Just behind the funeral chariot was the queen's horse, the "Palfrey of Estate," led by the queen's Master of the Horse, the Earl of Worcester. Just after Worcester was the Chief Mourner, Helena, Marchioness of Northampton, supported by Lord Treasurer Buckhurst and the Earl of Nottingham. Bearing the chief mourner's train were countesses, baronesses, earls' daughters and other ladies of the queen's household; among these women were Worcester's wife, his daughters and his daughters-in-law. Closing out the procession were Sir Walter Ralegh as captain of the guard, with the guard—five deep in rank—pointing their halberds downward. Carrying the queen's "representation" (effigy) into the church were eight knights and gentlemen, one of whom was Worcester's son-in-law, Sir Henry Guilford.

More than a few of the many thousands of the audience along the route would have noted the predominance of the Somerset family. Had an artist painted the queen's Funeral Procession, it would have closely resembled the Procession Portrait from the 1600 wedding of Henry Somerset, with as many of Worcester's family appearing as before. The symbolism of both occasions was the same: the family of the Earl of Worcester occupied a central position in the reign of Queen Elizabeth. Because this funeral ceremony was the first state event of the new regime, it augured well that Worcester was to continue in high estate. And with him, William Sterrell, who was about to undertake the most important mission of his career.

22

Transitions and Treasons, 1603

For four decades England's Catholics subjects had endured oppression. A continuation seemed insufferable. Realists among them knew that James of Scotland was unlikely to be more tolerant than Elizabeth. How could Catholics ease their plight? Their eyes turned to Brussels (Archduke Albert and Isabella) and Valladolid (Philip III). Would either support an uprising against James? Or could they encourage James to be lenient through negotiations?

Rebellion against James could not be considered without knowing the intentions of the Archdukes and the Spanish king. Seeking foreign influence on a domestic religious policy question would require coordination between English Catholics and the diplomats of Flanders and Spain. Both courses were seriously explored, and William Sterrell appears to have been a figure in both aspects, one tending toward war and the other to peace. This appears initially inconsistent, but the goal was the same, toleration; the question was one of means. Which might succeed? Sterrell was a fit man to gauge the Archduke's intentions and to gather intelligence as to the inclinations of the young and untested Spanish monarch. Within weeks of receiving a magnificent grant from James, Sterrell traveled to Brussels to sound Archduke Albert on support for an uprising and dispatched an envoy, the infamous Guy Fawkes, for like purpose to Madrid. At the same time, he (with Phelippes and other associates) was apparently coordinating with English Catholics for peace negotiations among England, Flanders and Spain.

Is rebellion always treason or can it be morally justified? Confiscation of property, imprisonment and execution of persons who seek the free exercise of their religion rank high as violations of natural rights or human rights. What constitutes the legitimacy of a sovereign? How does one human being have a hereditary birth-right to control the lives of an entire people? Through much of Queen Elizabeth's reign, the English government took the position that Mary Queen of Scots had no legitimate claim to the English throne. Why would her son have a greater claim than she? Rather than face another 45 years of oppression, an English Catholic might well consider opposition to the investiture of James and seek outside intervention. But a realist might conclude that prudence dictated yet more patience and pursuit of efforts to ameliorate the condition of the Catholics.

Although Elizabeth's government (led by Robert Cecil) immediately hailed James as the new monarch, there was a three month window of opportunity to seek change. Four developments between May 7, 1603, when James arrived in London, and his July 25 coronation at Whitehall relate to the plight of English Catholics accepting James as their new monarch. Occurring nearly simultaneously were: (1) The Main and Bye Plots; (2) the Spanish Treason—a plot in progress that was a prelude to the Gunpowder Plot; (3) a new

"Boulant" overture; and (4) the mission of Dr. Robert Taylor. The window closes with a letter of Fr. Persons to Sterrell that marks the end of any serious, coordinated effort to prevent the coronation of James as king of England.

The Main and Bye Plots

Two efforts to deprive James of the English crown were detected by mid-summer 1603. They have been called the Bye Plot (the priests plot) and the Main Plot (the Cobham/Ralegh plot). It suited the tactics of Attorney General Coke to link the two; all that they had in common was that George Brooke of the Bye Plot was the brother of Lord Cobham of the Main Plot.

In the Bye Plot the conspirators were catholic priests and laymen who planned to kidnap James. They intended to seize him and hold him hostage to obtain a pledge of religious toleration and to gain the removal of unsympathetic councilors. Learning of the plan, Fr. Henry Garnet informed the government through a third party. In addition to George Brooke (Cobham's brother), the Bye Plotters included Fr. William Watson (the plumed priest of the Archpriest/Appellant Controversy), Sir Griffin Markham, Anthony Copley, Sir Edward Parham, and Fr. William Clark. Arrests and confessions of the conspirators took place in mid–July. Brooke, Clark and Watson soon were executed and others were exiled.

The Main plot has been described aptly as "an obscure affair ... a scheme to replace James with his cousin Arbella Stuart, involving Sir Walter Ralegh, Henry Brooke Lord Cobham, and the Archduke's ambassador Count Arenberg."[1] Because there was less evidence of a conspiracy in the Main than in the Bye Plot, Attorney General Coke linked the two to enhance the appearance of guilt in the Main Plot, arguing that the conspiracies were "joined in the Ends, like Sampson's Foxes in the Tails, howsoever sever'd in their Heads." Cobham and Ralegh were convicted and sentenced to death but their lives were spared by the king. The weakness of the evidence is suggested by the fact that no action was taken towards Ambassador Arenberg (unlike Ambassador Mendoza who in 1584 was expelled in connection with the Throckmorton Plot) nor the woman allegedly meant to replace the king, Arbella Stuart (unlike Mary Stewart who was executed in 1587 in connection with the Babington Plot).

Did the Cobham/Ralegh "treason" arise overseas? If so, doubtless Count Arenberg initiated the intrigue with Cobham. The prosecution hinted at this in the trials of Cobham and Ralegh. Cobham did go to Arenberg's London lodgings and did meet with the diplomat, as testified to by Arenberg's associate, Mattias la Renzi, a businessman from Antwerp.[2] But who prompted the meeting? One of the most compelling pieces of evidence against treating Arenberg as the initiator has been largely ignored by historians. Matthew Questor was a man who did some work for Cobham. He gave a statement in 1603, stating that he tried to arrange a meeting at Cobham's behest but that Arenberg turned him away, saying it should be arranged through Cecil.[3] Questor returned to Cobham with Arenberg's reply and Cobham angrily rejected Arenberg's recommendation. Ralegh was in the outer chamber and Cobham and Ralegh thereupon left in a chafe. No dates are given for this event but Questor states that it "happened not long after the Count's first arrival." Most likely, Cobham went to Arenberg's immediately after Questor had told Cobham that he should make his contacts through Cecil. Cobham left Ralegh at Durham House, Ralegh's leased town house that the king had ordered Ralegh to vacate by June 25.[4] There seems to have been only the one meeting between Arenberg and Cobham. If so, it hardly has the appearance of a conspiracy. Arenberg wanted to avoid meeting with Cobham unless it were done with the knowledge and blessing of the English government. Arenberg surely was not initiating a conspiracy with Cobham and Ralegh.

Did Lord Cobham have a plot in mind to propose to Arenberg when he insisted on meeting him? There was no evidence of a plot. Cobham's brother accused him of being privy to the Bye Plot and of trying to raise money from Spain to furnish a second action to surprise the king. On being confronted with his brother's statement, Cobham is supposed to have admitted dealing with Arenberg for money, that he had planned to travel to Flanders and Spain, and that he had intended to return to England by way of Jersey to discuss with Ralegh distribution of the money.[5] He admitted soliciting 300,000 crowns (£75,000) of Arenberg to distribute as he saw fit and thereby save Arenberg's master millions. Arenberg (said Cobham) wanted some discussion about the distribution of the money. Cobham's confession hints at his thinking: he told Arenberg that the king was well affected for the peace but he "feared that some of our principal councilors would hinder it." Cobham also indicated to Arenberg that the French were encouraging the king to assist the Hollanders with 2000 soldiers in their opposition to the Archduke and would be providing money to support the Hollanders. But before specifics could be given, Cobham's brother was made prisoner and Cobham feared writing further.

Evidence from Ralegh, too, suggests that someone (perhaps Phelippes?) was in contact with Lord Cobham about peace before the arrival of Arenberg. Ralegh testified that Cobham had offered him 8000 crowns (£2,000) for the furtherance of the peace between England and Spain and that he would have the money within three days; this offer had been made *before* Arenberg came.[6] If this was true, then Cobham had been launched on a participation in a peace effort *before* Arenberg had come to London.

With James's accession to the throne of England, Lord Cobham and Sir Walter Ralegh had good reason to assume that their prospects under the new regime were poor. Both had depended upon the favor of Elizabeth. Neither had cultivated James. But Cobham did have a relationship with the Court of the Archdukes, a relationship he may have thought could be put to his advantage. He was involved in a 1600 effort to gain support for the candidacy of the Infanta (the Archduchess Isabella), and his participation in a 1600–01 negotiation for peace and for the redemption of the Burgundian jewels, marked him as potentially in league with the Archdukes. It is likely that Cobham was aware of the Brussels-originated overtures of Dr. Robert Taylor and Thomas Phelippes in 1603 (discussed below), and sought an enhanced role for himself from Arenberg. Cobham's great misjudgment was that he insisted on meeting personally with Arenberg, and sought to be put in control of the distribution of the money to buy influence with the Privy Council and the king's advisers. Ralegh understood that the Archdukes and the Spanish were prepared to pay substantial sums to purchase influence, and he wanted a share. Cobham and Ralegh were meddling in foreign affairs and were prepared to provide intelligence, but they were hardly guilty of any intent to overthrow the king. Meddle, yes; rebel, no. Learning of Cobham's contact with Arenberg, and aware of his earlier activities with the Archdukes, Cobham's detractors saw an opportunity to ruin both Cobham and Ralegh, despite the flimsy evidence of a plot.

The Spanish Treason—Sterrell in Brussels, June–July 1603

A real effort to oppose James in 1603 was not detected by the English government until two years after the Bye and Main Plots. Several threads of activity by English Catholics in Rome, Brussels, Spain and England came together in 1603 and became known as the Spanish Treason. These were efforts of a few English fugitives and their allies to propound a forceful policy towards the English succession. This Spanish Treason has been seen as a prelude to the Gunpowder Plot of 1605. It was old wine in a new cask, an effort to revive the Enterprise that had been fermenting since 1582.

The principal participants in the effort to resurrect the *Empresa* were Thomas James, Thomas Wintour, Anthony Dutton (probably the alias of Christopher Wright), Oswald Tesimond (alias William Greenwell or Greenway), Guy Fawkes, and William Sterrell. Fawkes, Tesimond, Christopher Wright and his brother John Wright were all once students at the free school of St. Peters in York, known as "Le Horse Fayre." Lesser roles were played by Persons, Owen, Fr. Creswell, and several Catholic gentlemen in England. Most of these will be implicated in the Gunpowder Plot.

Thomas James was active in the English Catholic cause from the time he aided Campion and Persons in 1580/81. He was a successful merchant who moved to Spain after leaving England for religion; a brother remained in London. James had a trusted relationship with Persons, and in March 1601 Persons and the Spanish ambassador at Rome, the Duke of Sessa, recommended to the Pope that James be sent to Brussels and England for the best information about the possibility of Isabella's succession to the English crown.[7] After conferring with the Archdukes and the Spanish ambassador in Brussels in June, James spent three weeks in England sometime in July/August 1601. He met with Frs. Garnet and Blackwell and with Catholic families. In January 1602 he returned to Madrid by way of Brussels and Paris and soon took up the post of English Secretary to the Spanish king, in succession to Thomas Fitzherbert and Sir Francis Englefield.[8]

In the early part of 1602 Thomas Wintour (alias Timothy Browne) joined Thomas James in Madrid. Three Wintour/Winter brothers will be executed in the Gunpowder Plot. On November 10, 1590, Thomas (age 18) and his older brother Robert (age 20) entered the Middle Temple and were bound with Richard Moore.[9] Thomas left for the Low Countries, fighting with the English against the Spanish forces. He was soon in the employ of William Parker, fourth Lord Monteagle. He became more devout in religion and was a close companion to Robert Catesby, who will be the principal figure in the Gunpowder Plot.

According to Wintour's statement after capture in 1605, his 1602 journey to Spain was to carry a message from Lord Monteagle, Robert Catesby and Francis Tresham to King Philip III.[10] The message was that they (and others) had suffered as a result of their treatment after the Essex rebellion; their devotion to the Spanish king could be obtained by bestowing pensions. They could supply 1000 to 1500 horse if needed in a Spanish attempt against England.[11]

With the assistance of Fr. Joseph Creswell, an English Jesuit who was the agent in

Spain for the colleges for English students, Thomas Wintour met with Philip III and was soon advised by the President of the Spanish Treasury that he would receive 100,000 escudos for his purposes and that a Spanish *empresa* was forthcoming within a year.[12] Accompanying Wintour was Fr. Tesimond.[13]

Letters of Fr. Creswell indicate that Catholics in England and Flanders were making plans for participation in a Spanish invasion.[14] Creswell had served as rector of the English College at Rome before relocating to Spain in 1592 at the request of Fr. Persons, where he eventually headed the College of St. Albans at Valladolid. While in Rome he apparently developed close ties to the Count de Olivares, then the Spanish ambassador to the papacy. Persons had Creswell named head of the English Jesuits in Iberia. The Spanish soon looked to Creswell for intelligence on England. An English spy reported to London in 1599 that "the Jesuit Creswell hath so good intelligence that there wags not a straw in the English court but he hears of it … this Creswell has weekly a porter's burden of letters of intelligence from all places which is the cause of his estimation in this land."[15] Creswell's intelligence on England probably owed much to Sterrell's "Rivers" letters to Baldwin, Owen, Verstegan and Persons.

Around 1600, Creswell at the encouragement of the Spanish (probably through Juan de Velasco, the Constable of Castile) entered into relations with two persons in London to obtain news from England and promised them 30 ducats a month.[16] These surely were William Sterrell and Thomas Phelippes; by 1605 Phelippes was complaining that he was denied rewards from the Constable he had expected for services.[17] Creswell's letters said Sir William Stanley was expected to lead a force. Thomas Sackville, a son of the Lord Treasurer, was in Ghent meeting with Stanley in late 1602, apparently sent by some of the leading English Catholics who had learned of the Spanish promises to Wintour, and he went on to confer with Sessa, now the Spanish envoy at the Papal Court, who with Persons had originally dispatched Thomas James. Sackville told Sessa:

> It is of the greatest importance that a commission be given at once in Flanders that, at the moment of the Queen's death, Col. Stanley should cross over to England … to give assistance in the place to which he will be called. This will encourage the councilors greatly to make a decision and the Catholics to be united in their defence. The arrival of the Colonel with such a small force will not cause much unrest, yet it will clear the way for all the rest.[18]

Several times in the period of late 1602 and early 1603 Creswell sent correspondence mentioning "the person who keeps the correspondence between the Catholics of England and Spain in secret"[19] or the person "though whom he corresponds with the English Catholics."[20] This correspondence related the disappointment of the English Catholics that nothing was coming of the *empresa* and urging the need for timely action.[21]

The Spanish Council considered the Creswell papers in February 1603 and decided that there should be no support for making Archduchess Isabella the successor to Elizabeth. Instead, Spain should support someone born in England to be nominated by the English Catholics and granted the rights of succession that belonged to King Philip.[22] Count Olivares, the former envoy to Rome (1582–92) who had encouraged the Armada of 1588 and was a supporter of Frs. Creswell and Persons, suggested supporting an Englishman who had characteristics like those of the Earl of Worcester. He urged the king of Spain "to influence the English Catholics to select an Englishman of their own faith, possessing if possible, some claims to the crown … the person chosen should not be very shy of the heretics, and should grant them toleration."²³ It should be someone who could "reconcile the Catholics with those who are not Catholics, or with the Queen's ministers...." Once the queen's ministers saw they would not be injured they would bring peace with Spain, and "it might be possible to make some arrangement for the recover of the ports held by the Queen in the islands (Zeeland &c)[Flushing and Brill]."²⁴ The description fit Worcester more than any other. Olivares, who worked closely with Persons, was probably recalling Persons's memorandum of 1596 in which Sterrell represented unnamed "earls who twice sent their agent [Sterrell] to Flanders ... to see what foundation there was for the new offer about Flushing."

However, the English Catholics had no candidate. In early March 1603 the Spanish Council again took up the issue of the English succession and focused on a proposal of Count de Olivares.²⁵ Among the points the Council considered was encouraging the English Catholics to assert that as good Englishmen they sought a native king. The report stated that it might be arranged for Fr. Persons to go to Flanders where he could unite with the Archduke to carry out the Spanish goal. The Pope could strengthen Persons with a Cardinal's hat, as the Pope had done with Fr. Allen. Persons and Creswell could be told that Philip III would treat the person selected by the English Catholics as if he were Philip's own son. Olivares proposed that the Spanish king could support the Catholics' candidate by landing a "good large body of men" from Flanders at a port of the candidate's choosing or they might be sent up the Thames to London.²⁶ The costs would be limited because the soldiers would come from the Spanish forces in Flanders and the English king-elect would see to provisions for the soldiers. In return for Spanish assistance, the English might repay the expenses and cede to Spain the Isle of Wight. The Council as a whole agreed with most of Olivares's proposals but deferred further consideration of plans to send troops.

When Elizabeth died a short time after the March Council debate, the Spanish were not prepared to intervene. English Catholics who hoped for a Catholic succession sought to impress upon Brussels and Valladolid that it was necessary to act immediately if the reign of James were to be thwarted. Several men went to those capitals to press the case for immediate action. The first was "Anthony Dutton," i.e., Christopher Wright. On c. April 7/17, 1603, Anthony Dutton/Christopher Wright²⁷ was detained by the French at Fontainebleu, on his way to Spain from the same Catholic circle as sent Wintour and Thomas James in Spring 1602. On May 5/15 he arrived in Valladolid. He told the Spanish that another person in his circle had been selected to see the Archduke to seek help with troops "or at least with arms and munitions" against King James.²⁸ He probably was referring to the Englishman who later met with Archduke Albert on July 3, 1603, surely William Sterrell. Wright reported that the English Catholics "have a large number of horses, more than 2,000 at hand, and if they had the money they would have in their grip all the good horses in the kingdom." But the English Catholics needed to know what they could expect from Spain before they could determine to act. A week later, Wright elaborated upon the plans and capabilities for opposing James in a thirty-three point paper.²⁹ The Spanish Council was unpersuaded and responded with skepticism, to which Wright replied that with work, speed, secrecy and good weather "we will have won the game in six days."³⁰

By mid–May 1603, information about the new king's policies and plans were circulating in London and among the Catholics who had been hopeful that James would bring a greater toleration to religion. The reports were negative, and now Fr. Blount and the Archpriest

Blackwell concluded that James would show no clemency for Catholics; they wrote of this to their superiors on the Continent. At about this time they and Fr. Garnet were meeting with the Archduke's special agent into England, Dr. Robert Taylor.

While Wright pressed for support in Valladolid, another Englishman sounded Archduke Albert in Brussels. On the evening of July 3, 1603, n.s., Archduke Albert received an Englishman whose name was kept secret from the Spanish Ambassador who was then in Brussels. Nor would the Archduke disclose the name even to his brother-in-law, the Spanish king, when he wrote to him the next day of the private meeting and forwarded a long report.[31] Albert described him only as "a very intelligent man who has been corresponding in England with the Fathers of the Society of Jesus in matters of religion." This description fits William Sterrell, the Oxford praelector in philosophy who had been corresponding regularly with the Jesuits. Moreover, Archduke Albert was aware of this special correspondence and probably the identity of William Sterrell as the correspondent, the "Spirit Orthon" who sent regular intelligence. Archduke Albert and Sterrell probably first met when Albert was in Brussels in February and March 1596 as he began his governance of the Spanish Low Countries, when Sterrell was sent into Flanders twice to take up the possibility of English relinquishment of Flushing.[32] This would explain the willingness of Albert to receive this mysterious figure. The Archduke said the man carried a written report of a meeting between Dr. Robert Taylor (Albert's own agent), the Archpriest Blackwell, and Fr. Henry Garnet.

William Sterrell was almost certainly in Brussels during part of June and July 1603. On July 6, 1603, n.s., Persons wrote to "Anthony Rivers" noting that he (Rivers/Sterrell) is unusually "on this side of the brook" and had not written to Persons since the accession until June 14, n.s.[33] Everything in Persons' letter would fittingly be a response to a suggestion of renewed miseries of Catholics in England and at least hinted-at thoughts of forcible action to overthrow James. The letter assumes the recipient's knowledge of the mission of Thomas Wintour ("Tymothy his journey") and Thomas James's mission, but suggests in undeciphered code that Persons does not know X [?Wright] and would like to know more about him. The Persons letter is to an Englishman with whom Persons has long shared political correspondence and who normally is not in Europe. No other person than Sterrell can be identified who had such correspondence with Persons.

The Archduke's visitor asserted he spoke for Dr. Taylor and Catholic priests in London. He gave a report of what Blackwell, Garnet, and others said in response to Taylor's offer of the Archdukes' assistance. While Taylor was still in England to see if the laws against Catholics could be modified when Parliament next sits, "it has meanwhile seemed appropriate to the said Father Superior and the others to send *una persona espresso y confidente* to inform His Highness of the present state of things."[34] The Archduke's visitor told him that under James there was no hope of obtaining any form of toleration. He suggested preparation for war; there was no greater opportunity for rebellion than the present as the English treasury was empty. This report paralleled what Sterrell had written to his correspondents a couple of weeks before the queen's death: that many in England had "utter aversion" to James, that they would oppose him had they any potent competitor, that the queen's "coffers are empty" and that there were "no means for supply" for the fighting in Ireland.[35] The Archduke's informant had intimate knowledge of the 1602 visit to Spain of Thomas Wintour and Oswald Tesimond.[36] The Catholics, he said, had prepared arms and horses and that their "party" had increased to 30,000 men and that 8,000 were ready "under arms."

As the intelligent Englishman was meeting with the Archduke, a quartet of Englishmen were meeting the Spanish envoy, Juan de Tassis. On July 4, 1603, Tassis wrote King Philip a letter describing his meeting the previous evening with Robert Spiller, Sir William Stanley, Hugh Owen and Fr. Baldwin.[37] These four were the closest advisors to Archduke Albert on English policy. The fact that their meeting with Tassis away from Albert's Court exactly coincided with the English visitor's meeting with Albert indicates that the two meetings were timed to prevent the Spanish envoy from learning the identity of Albert's visitor. Albert would not have met with a messenger from the English Catholics without his trusted advisors' knowledge. All four were key figures in Sterrell's secret correspondence.

Two weeks earlier, on June 16, 1603, an Englishman who had recently crossed to the Low Countries wrote a letter of introduction for Guy Fawkes to take to Spain. Fawkes, from Yorkshire, was a soldier in the Low Countries. The unnamed Englishman was almost certainly the same man who met with the Archduke Albert on July 3, William Sterrell. He dictated to Fawkes a long letter not to be written out until Fawkes arrived in Spain. When reduced to writing by Fawkes, it proved to be quite similar in structure, sequence of thought, and content to the informant's Report sent to Spain by the Archduke on July 4.[38] Three of the associates of Sterrell who met with Tassis while Sterrell was with the Archduke are said to have sent Fawkes into Spain: Stanley, Owen and Fr. Baldwin.[39] This would further indicate that Sterrell was the man dealing with both Fawkes and with the Archduke.

Although the Spanish Council of State debated seriously the reports made by Wright, Fawkes and Albert's visitor (Sterrell) in meetings of July 22, 26 and 31, they concluded that the project for intervention was too rash. The transition to James had been peaceful, and no action would be taken. James's years of seeding stories through emissaries to Catholic capitals about his future tolerance had their intended effect at the necessary moment. Too, the Catholicism of his Danish wife brought James a measure of trust from Rome and the Spanish.[40] Wright/Dutton and Fawkes were kept under close watch by Fr. Creswell (at the direction of the Council) as the Council was concerned that the two Englishmen might jeopardize the embassy of peace of Juan de Tassis. On August 12, 1603, the Council confirmed that there would be no action.[41] Wright and Fawkes were not allowed to leave Spain until early 1604.

The Spanish reluctance to support overthrowing James was surely reinforced with the news, beginning in July 1603, of the arrests and prosecutions in the Main and the Bye Plots in which the Spanish were accused of involvement. Moreover, Persons's views on the infeasibility of an overthrow were probably known to the Spanish Court at this time.

The Preparations of 1603

Was there a readiness for a rebellion in 1603 as Wintour and Fawkes reported to Spain and Sterrell to the Archduke? Probably. If William Sterrell were associated with the raising of men, we would look to two areas in particular, Wales and Lincolnshire. And evidence there is. A 1605 report on Jesuit activities in Herefordshire related that just after the queen's death, the Catholics of the region were in arms:

When the Queen was dead North the priest came out of Monmouthshire in all haste into Herefordshire, signifying that the catholics were up in arms there and stirred as earnestly as he could the catholics of

Herefordshire to do the like. And Lister one of the Jesuits with his companions were as busy in Worcestershire, telling them that the catholics in Herefordshire were in arms.[42]

This Fr. North was *alias* Reginald Eaton.[43] He and Fr. Robert Jones, S. J. worked closely with William Morgan, Worcester's son-in-law. William Morgan was a leader of the Catholic "stirs" of May-June 1605, discussed below. The report makes clear that Worcester's son-in-law was a leader in taking up arms in the period *immediately after Queen Elizabeth's death*.[44] Sterrell then would have certainly been in contact with his employer's immediate family in Wales and could reliably report to the Archduke on the ability of Catholics to raise men to arms.

The confession of Thomas Wintour about his meetings in Spain in 1602 implicated an invasion in Wales.[45] He heard this also to be Sir William Stanley's opinion. The Earl of Worcester was made lord lieutenant of Monmouthshire and Glamorgan in 1602 and was in the very position needed to stay "the Queen's powers" while English Catholics joined a Spanish force.

In Lincolnshire, another Catholic leader close to the Jesuits apparently made military preparations in 1603 just after the queen's death. He had family connections with Sterrell, was a strong supporter of Fr. John Gerard, and was a close friend of Robert Catesby (involved in the Spanish Treason and the Gunpowder Plot) and other Gunpowder Plotters. Robert Tyrwhitt was grandson of Sir Robert Tyrwhitt for whom William Sterrell's father was undersheriff. In November 1599 Robert Tyrwhitt was appointed Sheriff of Lincolnshire.[46] Tyrwhitt was married to Bridget Manners, sister of Roger Manners, the Earl of Rutland. He and Bridget and several of her brothers came under the influence of Fr. John Gerard. In Robert's case Gerard's personal influence had its beginning in 1600, while Robert was sheriff, and from then on Robert was one of Gerard's principal supporters, supplying him regularly with substantial funds and horses.[47] The evidence that Tyrwhitt was in readiness to take action at the queen's death comes from a confession of August 1603 by Anthony Copley, the Catholic poet who was among those convicted in the November trials for the Bye Plot against King James. Copley accused the Jesuits of plotting insurrection against the king:

> Sir Griffith Markham's telling me that a special friend of theirs [the Jesuits] in Lincolnshire one Mr Terwitt did lately nothing but ride up and down that shire among his friends making show of instant action....[48]

Though the "Spanish Treason" and the Bye Plot overlapped chronologically, there was no connection between them, so it is not surprising that Copley could say no more about Tyrwhitt's preparations. The authorities in Lincolnshire would not have pursued his report on Robert Tyrwhitt: Tyrwhitt's brother-in-law Roger Manners was appointed Lord Lieutenant of Lincolnshire in September 1603 just after returning from a special mission to Denmark to present Christian IV (Queen Anne's brother) with the Order of the Garter. Tyrwhitt was close friends to several of the men whose names are tied to the Spanish Treason of 1602–03 and with the Gunpowder Plot of 1605. Recall that Robert Catesby had sent Thomas Wintour into Spain in 1602 to explore Spanish support for a Catholic successor to Elizabeth.[49] Tyrwhitt was personally associated with conspirators Ambrose Rookwood and Robert Catesby, for in 1602 the three men were pledged together to borrow £3000 from one Thomas Sutton.[50] Catesby and Tyrwhitt were associated closely with one another at the time of the Gunpowder Plot and Tyrwhitt himself was suspected of being a plotter.[51]

The Gunpowder conspirators evidently had meetings at a lodging sometimes owned by Tyrwitt.

It is likely that in the months shortly before and immediately after James's accession, arms and men were ready or could be quickly raised in case it was decided to oppose the coronation of James I. But the project, which in mid–May seemed urgently desirable to Sterrell, the leading Jesuits, and the Archpriest and doubtless many other bitterly disillusioned Catholics, dissolved in the face of European indifference, temporising, and resistance, and the inability to point to a viable Catholic candidate for the crown. Worcester himself was too cautious and too tied by personal bonds to English Protestants to lead an opposition. He likely would have gladly served Isabella had she become queen or was prepared to accept the crown himself if the Spanish had intervened. Sterrell probably hoped for and even sought the latter (without openly speaking for his employer). The moment, however, passed. Failing to take the current when it served, they lost their venture. By early or mid–July, when Persons' lengthy letter counseling his long-time correspondent (and those whom he represented) against action, the possibility of a rebellion was effectively over.

A Boulant Overture of 1603

While Sterrell tested the interest of the Archdukes and the Spanish on support for an armed opposition to James, Phelippes worked with the Archdukes' representatives. He explored the means of achieving peace and influencing the government of James. During the transition, the government of the Archdukes, the "chanon of Liége," and Thomas Phelippes attempted to revive "Monsieur Boulant" as an instrument of peace. An undated paper by Phelippes, identified by Phelippes as describing "The proceedings with M. Boulant about peace—1602," set forth details of how the Boulant-Robinson correspondence had been used as a diplomatic device in the late queen's time, including during the Fortado mission of early 1602. The paper, written shortly after the queen's death, was an overture to make use of "Boulant" for new negotiations between England and the Archdukes. After describing the former Boulant proceedings, Phelippes stated that just after Elizabeth's death, the canon wanted "Robinson" (*alias* Sterrell) to resume negotiations. Phelippes said that if he had "warrant or direction" he would be at the king's service and "at your Lo: commandment."[52]

To whom was this overture for further service directed? The references in the memo to "Mr. Secretary" in the third person indicate that second person references to "your Lo": are not to Secretary Cecil. Phelippes later described his working through three men close to the new king in 1603: Sir David Foulis, Sir Thomas Lake, and Edward Bruce, Lord Kinloss.[53] In 1605, Phelippes told Cecil that he had not worked through Cecil on this further "Boulant" matter because he, Cecil, was involved in a dispute between Sir Arthur Ashley and Phelippes. In a 1606 letter, intended for the king, Phelippes told the same story: Shortly after the queen's death "an address was newly made to the imaginary correspondent ['Robinson'] in Mancicidor's name [Don Juan de Mancicidor, the Archduke's Secretary of State and War]" to set awork a new peace effort.[54] But he, Phelippes (as he recounts), had run into a problem with Cecil, and so at the king's first coming did not follow Cecil "as he had done before til the Queen's death" but "gave proof to others of his devotion to the King's service." Phelippes wrote of "Discovering to Sir Thomas Lake the vanity of Dr. Taylor's first negotiation [as informal emissary of the Archdukes] and acquainting my Lo. of Kinloss with the opportunity and means he had to serve the State upon that ground of the former correspondence."[55] Lord Kinloss, then, was his "Lordship" through whom a Boulant overture was to be undertaken.

Phelippes was never fully forthcoming in his series of confessions and pleadings in 1605 and 1606. But from them it emerges that he was contacted by the Archduke's government, both through the "chanon of Liége" (the false identity used by Hugh Owen for correspondence with "Hallins"/Sterrell) and the Archduke's Secretary of State and War, Mancicidor.[56] This Spaniard had been with Archduke Albert since Albert moved to Brussels as governor in 1596. Mancicidor, a great friend to Owen, was familiar with Owen's correspondence with the London agents since at least 1599 and no doubt earlier.[57]

The Intriguing Dr. Taylor

Phelippes's "Boulant" memorandum of 1603 was coordinated from Brussels with the activities of an English agent of the Archduke, Dr. Robert Taylor, who had entered England and was making contact with English Catholics and members of the English Court.[58] Doctor Taylor, lecturer on canon law at Douay, was now a special envoy of the Archdukes. His brother was a steward for the Earl of Cumberland,[59] long a close friend of Worcester.

Sterrell likely had known Taylor well before the first appearance of "Monsieur Boulant" as a diplomatist in 1598. Like Sterrell, Taylor had assisted the transit of Catholic lads overseas.[60]

Cecil's interrogations of Phelippes, Sterrell, and their associates in 1605 revealed bit by bit that Dr. Taylor had been working for some time with an Englishman whose alias was (sometimes) "Freeman." A servant of Phelippes, Abraham Ferkin, testified in late January 1605 he had recently taken an unsigned letter from Phelippes to Doctor Taylor, and some three or four others at "sundry times." Cecil asked him also about "Mr. Freeman" but Ferkin could only say that about a month ago "Freeman" was at Phelippes's house.

Thomas Phelippes's brother Stephen was also questioned about "Freeman," whom Cecil thought had the alias of "Needam."[61] Stephen Phelippes knew of "Freeman" and "heard Freeman lay sometime at my lady of Arundells," the Countess of Arundel, widow of Philip Howard. Cecil then asked about money received by Phelippes and Sterrell from abroad.

Stephen described an extraordinary, close and continuing relationship between his brother Thomas, William Sterrell and "Freeman":

> I received at one time my brother being in the Fleet [a London prison] of Mr. Sterrell 18*l* for my brother after which I received quarterly 80*l* by the space of a year and a half or more till my brother came out of the Fleet with money with a greater sum. I did by Mr. Sterrell's commandment or direction fetch some time at one merchants some time at another till Sterrell have found some means to have it some other way it should come. From whom or from what body I did not inquire only it seemed it came from beyond seas. After which time I never received any of Sterrell but I did imagine he fetched it himself. If since the K[ing] came to the crown they received any I am not privy to it for that if any man paid my brother it was Sterrell or Freeman. The sums I received at several times for my brother of Sterrell came not above to four hundred or five hundred pounds at most and what since I know not. The uttermost that ever I know my brother received in a year was two hundred pounds and whether he continued it or not at that rate I know not but I heard him complain that he was not well dealt with that he had nothing given him when the Constable [Constable of Castile] was here.

Thus, Sterrell and "Freeman" were alternate conduits of payments from Flanders to Phelippes. Both were servants of Catholic nobles, both worked with Fr. Garnet and with the English Catholics of Flanders, and they must have coordinated their activities closely. Connecting the dots surely infuriated the English Secretary of State when he realized that "Freeman" was not Needam but Robert Spiller, about whose role as a courier for Catholics Poley had informed Cecil in 1602. Only after the Gunpowder Plot will Phelippes confess to long involvement with "Freeman," whom he admitted was Robert Spiller.[62] Spiller's activities were an extension of the Countess of Arundel's support of the Catholic church, just as Sterrell's own work should be seen as the work of his employer, Worcester.

At the very moment that Spiller was providing intelligence in early to mid-1603 for the Archduke and the Spanish envoy, there was also in the household of the Countess of Arundel Fr. Oswald Tesimond, S.J. An informer to Chief Justice Popham reported in July 1603: "My Lady Arundell keeps two Jesuits daily in her house. I am now acquainted with one of them called Tesymonde [Tesimond], a Yorkshire man...."[63] Tesimond, it will be recalled, accompanied Thomas Wintour to Spain in 1602 as part of the "Spanish Treason." Spiller was surely privy to the mission of Tesimond and Wintour. Spiller was well-acquainted with the soldier whom Sterrell dispatched into Spain in 1603 in furtherance of the "Spanish Treason": Guy Fawkes.[64]

Spiller/Freeman, Dr. Taylor, and Sterrell's friend Anthony Skinner were all working on the Catholic cause at about the time King James arrived in London in early May 1603.[65] Dr. Taylor was sent on a special mission to England for the Archduke within a short time of James's ascendancy; he probably arrived in England in late April or early May. Hugh Owen was influential in the selection of Taylor for this mission. Archduke Albert did not consult with the Spanish about the undertaking. Under the non-public proviso of Philip II's conferral of sovereignty on his daughter Isabella, Spain continued to have primacy on military and foreign affairs for the Low Countries. Taylor was not a diplomat with credentials to present to the new government. The diplomat was Count Arenberg, who did not arrive in London until June 7, 1603, and even then absented himself from Court saying he had the gout. Only after Taylor returned to report to the Archduke in Brussels in July did the Spanish learn of Taylor's mission.

Taylor's outreach to English Catholics and members of the Court was aided by Anthony Skinner, Sterrell's old friend. Although convicted of treason in 1592, Skinner moved among the upper-class Catholic families, such as the Plowdens and Gages. A summary of Taylor's report makes clear that one of Skinner's attributes is that he is well known to Hugh Owen.[66] The common denominators of Taylor and Skinner are that the two are well-known to both Sterrell and Hugh Owen. Taylor and Skinner were examining the prospects for peace and religious toleration and seeking to determine what pensions would have to be paid to members of the English Court to obtain peace and toleration.

Taylor's interviews with the Earl of Cumberland, the Countess of Suffolk and Sir Thomas Lake were facilitated by Taylor's brother and by Skinner.[67] These talks generated estimates of the cost to incline certain of the Privy Councilors to peace.[68]

Sterrell (and Phelippes) were probably behind meetings with members of the Court, just as Sterrell may have been instrumental when Lake assisted Skinner in gaining a license to travel abroad shortly after the Gunpowder Plot.[69] Sterrell could not take part directly because of his position at Court. His employer, Worcester, was very protective of his reputation and wanted to avoid even the appearance of an improper relationship with the Spanish. In 1605 Phelippes confessed to his role in Dr. Taylor's meetings while distancing Sterrell from correspondence and activities after the death of Queen Elizabeth. Phelippes sent Cecil a long letter in which he described a correspondence under an alias after the queen's death. He did "nothing to the prejudice of his majesty's service but rather the furtherance in respect of the Peace ... with D. Taylor's Negociations having been the only subject thereof."[70] Letters Cecil had intercepted were for Doctor Taylor's negotiations. He admitted to involvement with the Spanish ambassador (Tassis) and playing a part under the name of Boorman. Phelippes said he had communicated matters in the negotiations with Thomas Lake and urged Cecil to verify his good intentions by consulting Lake.

The Countess of Suffolk, with whom Skinner and Dr. Taylor negotiated, was the wife of Thomas Howard, Earl of Suffolk, who was King James's new Lord Chamberlain and a Privy Councilor (appointments of April 6–7, 1603). He was a brother of Philip, Earl of Arundel (who died in prison), and William. While Thomas Howard was not an active Catholic, his brother William was. Their uncle, Henry Howard, (made Earl of Northampton in 1604), was also a Privy Councilor and very influential with the new king and was sympathetic to Catholics. The Countess of Suffolk purported to speak with authority on the views of the English Catholics. Her sister-in-law, the Countess of Arundel, was the employer of Robert Spiller who was working with Dr. Taylor and Anthony Skinner, as well as with Sterrell, Phelippes and Fr. Garnet. As will be seen in the next chapter, the Earl and Countess of Suffolk were well positioned, along with Worcester and Sterrell, to influence the Court through control of the royal entertainments.

Dr. Taylor conferred with the Countess of Suffolk about the views of the members of the Privy Council towards the English Catholics. Would it be sufficient for the Catholics to be allowed to celebrate the mass in their homes? She said that if the Archduke could provide 200,000 escudos (about £50,000), members of the Privy Council would be amenable.[71] The Countess of Suffolk served as intermediary for Robert Cecil in receiving monies from the Spanish on later occasions and was likely fronting for him in discussions with Dr. Taylor. The Spanish ambassador to England, Don Pedro de Zúñiga, informed his king in 1606 that half of the money paid to the countess was actually for Cecil.[72] Lady Suffolk remained for a long time in the service of the Spanish. It was rumored that she was Robert Cecil's mistress. She will report to the Spanish of Cecil's statements to her. She dominated her husband, and a French diplomat captured her well when he described her as "witty, scheming, ambitious and indiscreet."[73]

Lake told Dr. Taylor that there were three factions at Council. A minority favored peace. Another group was for war but would take money instead. A third wanted war but were already being paid for their position by the Hollanders. After reviewing Taylor's goals, Lake said peace could be accomplished for about £40,000; tolerance could be put toward achievement. On June 30, 1603, Taylor and Skinner left England for Brussels to confer with the Archduke; after a short stay, they returned into England for further discussions with persons influential with the Council.

Taylor was already on his way back to Brussels when the mystery man of the Spanish Treason met with Archduke Albert on the evening of July 3. This man, surely Sterrell, told Albert he was bringing a report from Taylor, the Archpriest Blackwell and Fr. Garnet. As related earlier, the foursome of Spiller, Owen, Stanley and Baldwin met with the Spanish envoy who was in Brussels on his way to England, Juan de Tassis. The four Englishmen gave to Tassis information on conditions in England. Most of the information necessarily came from Spiller as the other three had spent little or no time in England in many years; Spiller had probably been with Taylor and had returned to Brussels ahead of him, probably with Sterrell. The four compiled a list of names, which Tassis sent the next day to Spain in cipher.[74] It characterized the thirteen members of the Privy Council who had served during the reign of Queen Elizabeth, as well as the seven new English members and five Scottish additions. The group told Tassis of Worcester:

> The Earl of Worcester. He is the King's Master of the Horse and has been a Catholic and is believed to remain one within his heart. He has always favored a peace but is timid by character and anxious to protect his prestige. With him [try] his secretary, Sterrell, and it is suspected that gifts will gain his favour.

The Englishmen were preparing Tassis for his embassy into London but they were not entirely forthcoming with the Spaniard. All four knew much more about Sterrell than they revealed to Tassis. The same is true Robert Taylor. The report says that in dealing with the Earl of Cumberland (George Clifford) "it helps to rely on a person named Robert Taylor with whom one can plan how to win him over." Tassis was unaware that Taylor was serving at that moment as a special envoy of Archduke Albert to the English Catholics. Indeed, Tassis was not to learn of Robert Taylor's secret diplomacy until a few days later.[75]

What did Taylor and Skinner report to Archduke Albert shortly after Sterrell's meeting of July 3? There are three different summaries of Taylor's statements, all in Spanish.[76] Two are from the decoded dispatches sent by the Archduke, and the third is a report by Tassis. The first is what Taylor learned in his stay in England. The second is on what Taylor informed his friends in England about the intentions of the Archduke. The substance of these concerned the discussions Taylor and Skinner had with English Catholics and Court figures and included the suggestions for payments made by the Countess of Suffolk and Sir Thomas Lake. But the report of Taylor in all three versions also included a statement from the Jesuit Superior, Fr. Garnet. The most complete of the three makes a remarkable statement that the moment was ripe for reforming England through force[77]:

> The aforesaid Fathers have entrusted him [Taylor] with saying further to His Highness that there was never a time more suitable for reforming that kingdom by way of force than at present, by reason of the general disgust against the King and his Scotsmen, through which the party of the Catholics is stronger by more than 30,000 men than it was before the death of the Queen, and in the event that His Highness considered it appropriate to assist them with 12,000 men they held as many other Catholics ready, not counting other friends, and with that they would do whatever they wanted to, in that Kingdom as those who came in from outside would publish that they were coming in order to make a King native to the same Kingdom or one whom those of [the kingdom] would elect being a Catholic, and the said Fathers were of the opinion that they would appoint the Infanta because there is no one of royal blood who was a claimant[.] His Majesty being pleased to proceed by this route the said [Fathers] request that they be given notice in time, for certain respects and reasons that are declared to His Highness.

Taylor then was carrying the same message in favor of "the Spanish Treason" as the Englishman of the July 3 meeting. The Archduke, however, declined the call for intervention. It is doubtful that he gave any indication of his intentions to Sterrell or Taylor. Archduke Albert always had a reputation as a man of few words, and then a dissembler.[78]

Dr. Taylor's discussions with the figures at the English Court about peace and toleration are not inconsistent with the report of favor for force among certain of the Catholic priests and laymen. His function was to gather information about the state of the English Catholics and the politics of the Court. He was not in England to forward a rebellion or an invasion yet neither was he there to impede a program of action. He reported information to the Archduke that could be used whatever course Albert should decide upon.

Taylor and Skinner returned to England shortly after reporting to Archduke Albert. Skinner arrived in time to participate in a meeting of July 17, 1603, of a substantial group of prominent English Catholics with the Privy Council in the presence of King James. Partly in response to a petition of "Supplication for Toleration of Catholic Religion," King James had called Sir Thomas Tresham and other lay Catholics to Hampton Court to confer.[79] The deputation was greeted with courtesy and given an assurance that recusancy fines would be abated. But there was no writing and no assurance that the harsh laws would not be enforced.

Before the month of July was out, Skinner was suddenly called back to the Court from a visit to the country estates of his friend Francis Plowden and Plowden's uncle Ralph Sheldon.[80] The meeting to which Skinner was summoned must have been one at which he and Dr. Taylor conferred with five members of the Privy Council. The only record that survives of this meeting appears to a report that they made to Fr. Garnet, which was then related to the Spanish.[81] Among the Councilors were Robert Cecil, Thomas Howard (Earl of Suffolk) and Henry Howard (Earl of Northampton). Although Taylor tried to tell the Councilors that Fr. Baldwin and Hugh Owen were proponents of peace, the Councilors spoke very badly of them and of Colonel Stanley. Taylor and Skinner reported that 18 out of 24 Councilors were opposed to peace. Garnet was evidently disappointed with the gist of the meeting for he concluded that toleration of Catholics could only come from armed intervention from overseas. The report ends:

> The father superior of the Society writes this report with his own hand, received from the mouth of the aforesaid Taylor and his companion and, notwithstanding what is said in it, he [Garnet] says that he and others are of the opinion that everything is impostures and inventions to gain time, because they have not a real [Spanish coin] with which to wage war, and *if the King of Spain were to come sword in hand, the conditions of peace that he desires could be obtained without having a big war* [alcançara las condiçiones de paz que el quisiera, sin habar gran guerra].

This report is consistent with what Sterrell asserted to the Archduke Albert in his meeting of July 3, about six weeks earlier, about the views of Garnet, Taylor and Baldwin.

With the arrival of Tassis in England (August 21, 1603), Taylor's role diminished, but he remained in England to assist Tassis and to provide intelligence to the Archduke. Spain insisted on the primacy of its own representatives, and Taylor was no ambassador. Taylor's ability, however, to serve the Archduke and to work with Tassis was no doubt enhanced considerably by the fact that his wife's brother was on Tassis's staff.[82] He remained in communication with Fr. Henry Garnet.[83]

Dr. Taylor was noted dining with some of the Gunpowder plotters shortly before the Plot was revealed in November 1605.[84] After the Gunpowder Plot, Dr. Taylor continued to meet with Cecil to resolve differences between the English and the Spanish and the Low Countries.[85] The Spanish ambassador had Dr. Taylor report to him on the trial of Henry Garnet.[86] It was in Dr. Taylor's London house that Fr. John Gerard hid for a time just after the Gunpowder Plot was uncovered.[87] How close were William Sterrell and Dr. Taylor? It is no mere coincidence that when Sterrell retired in 1626 from many years of service as an intelligencer to the Archduke and then his widow Isabella, Sterrell's successor in that role in London was the son of Robert Taylor and Mary Fowler.[88]

The Taylor/Skinner activities were surely linked to Sterrell and Phelippes. When Sterrell met with Archduke Albert on July 3, he said he had recently met with Taylor and Garnet. Phelippes in 1605–06 described the connection of his activities with Taylor. "Boulant" was floated as a possible intermediary in peace negotiations in 1603 who would again work with "Robinson"/Sterrell. Phelippes also asserted that he was contacted by Brussels to perform tasks parallel to those of Dr. Taylor but added that Sterrell had no involvement in this activity. Phelippes said his correspondence with Hugh Owen had been broken off shortly before the queen's death, and now was resumed without Sterrell's knowledge. He continued:

> But within a while after [the queen's death] as D. Taylor was sent upon one errand so Vincent [Phelippes's alias] another way was earnestly required by a letter on the behalf of the Archduke by Benson [Owen].[89]

If Phelippes, too, had been sent on an errand by the Archduke, what was his errand? Phelippes never reveals this in his confessions, saying only that he "gave such satisfaction for his part to the said Mancicidor as he was thought to deserve great thanks."[90] He suggests that it "may be specially for helping to save a great deal of money wherewith *they were made believe at first by others peace was to have been brought*." Who were these "others" who had overestimated the price of peace? It appears that he was not speaking of Taylor and Skinner and the courtiers with whom they initially spoke (Cumberland, the Countess of Suffolk and Sir Thomas Lake). The "others" were likely Cobham and Ralegh. That is to say, Cobham may have been employed by the Archduke (through Count Arenberg or through Phelippes) to perform tasks similar to those assigned to Taylor and Phelippes.

If "Boulant" were being revived just as King James was coming in, it is likely that Phelippes would have looked to Cobham for assistance in "Boulant's" overtures. This would better explain why Phelippes circumvented Cecil in 1603 than the lame excuse Phelippes offered Cecil in 1605 (that Cecil had sided with Sir Anthony Ashley in an earlier dispute). In 1605 and 1606 Phelippes could hardly have told Cecil that he and Cobham had been involved together in a matter proceeding from the Archduke, for this is precisely what had earned Cobham and Ralegh their death sentences in late November 1603. The confessions of Cobham and the statements of Arenberg are consistent with the hypothesis that Cobham, in May–June 1603, was drawn into a new peace effort that was a continuation of his earlier involvement through Phelippes and "Boulant" in 1600–1602 and similar to the parallel contacts being made by Dr. Taylor with members of the Court in May 1603.

Cobham's actions have striking parallels to the contemporaneous mission of Dr. Taylor at Court and to Phelippes's attempted renewal of "Boulant." Taylor (aided by Anthony Skinner) was seeking to determine what sums of money might be necessary to obtain support for peace. As recounted earlier, Taylor, Skinner and Robert Spiller reported to the Archduke and to the Spanish envoy in Brussels about each of the people around the king and what might be necessary to induce support for peace. When peace was obtained the following year, very substantial gifts and pensions were provided by the Spanish. Discreet discussions pertaining to the same had preceded the peace settlements. Phelippes, like Cobham, said he was saving the Archdukes and Spanish much money by the intelligence he provided about the costs of peace.

Now to the Matter Itself—The Letter of Fr. Persons to "Rivers"[91]

Persons's letter to his English associate, surely "Anthony Rivers," includes the thoughtful ruminations of one old friend to another on political changes in England and conditions in Europe as of July 6, 1603, n.s. But it is this and more: it is counsel to the Catholics of England not to undertake present action against King James but rather to wait until conditions are more propitious for strong action. Persons expected the letter to be communicated to a larger circle and to serve as a signal that armed rebellion against the new king would not find support in Europe. Coming from a man long identified as a champion for armed intervention in England, it was certain to throw cold water on any plan of arms.

Persons begins with an acknowledgment of a "Rivers" letter of June 14, probably sent by Sterrell from St. Omers. Persons says he may deal more securely while Sterrell remains in Europe. He comments that the handwriting is not his own but is another hand known to Sterrell, that of John Lilly: "your old acquaintance who salutes you heartily."[92] Persons continued, "Now to the matter itself," indicating that the letter was directed to consideration of a particular issue in which Persons and Sterrell were mutually interested. Persons reviewed twenty plus years of omissions and failures that led to the present impasse, to his frustration and disappointment. Since his 1580 mission into England, a special care of Persons was the conversion of James to Catholicism "by request and order" of his own mother, Mary Queen of Scots, and a particular concern also of Cardinal Allen, Sir Francis Englefield, Hugh Owen, and others. After a dozen years, it was clear that those hopes and efforts were in vain.

Realizing that James would not change, around 1592 Persons and others turned to consideration of Philip II's daughter Isabella as a successor to Elizabeth. But now she was out of question: she had married, France had grown stronger, Spain was unwilling to prosecute her candidacy, her husband the Archduke was preoccupied with problems in Flanders and many Spanish did not wish to see the Archduke grow great by the joining of Flanders with England. The king of Spain had shown his willingness to support any Catholic whom the English Catholics thought fit for the crown, but Queen Elizabeth died before action was taken. James entered with such applause, it was "as if he had been the greatest Catholic in the world." Now, however, men begin to "droop again," that is, to conclude against James.

In recent years Persons was of the opinion it was not secure "to adventure upon any forcible attempt in the said Queen's days." Rather, he thought Flanders and Spain should be ready to act upon her death. But they did not do so, "no more than they would have done the other [against Elizabeth] if we had relied on them for it, nor than they have done in Ireland etc." And for the past two or three years, Persons continued (alluding to the "Spanish Treason" that had developed from Thomas James's trip into England in 1601), some of their friends in England had not made him privy to the particulars of their plans, "neither concerning Timothy his journey [Thomas Wintour] nor his companion [Tesimond? Thomas James?]." Here part of the letter is in undeciphered code.

Persons describes "notable omissions" that would have made a difference. Philip II could have acted easily against Elizabeth soon after she came to the throne. He could have advanced Isabella's candidacy before the French came to oppose her. He could have sought more effectively to win over James while still a child. And the king of Spain could have been ready at the queen's death to intervene "as he was often forewarned." Persons laid part of the blame on the timidity of the Catholics in England: "And on the Catholics part ... there was a great omission in not making some show of union among themselves and of their numbers and forces at the Queen's death, not so much to oppose themselves to the present king ... they would now know with what conditions his Majesty would receive them." Having made no demonstration, few in Europe believe "that either their number, quality, or disposition of mind is such as has been given out." So all the princes of Europe seek the friendship of James: "certain it is that none will stir against him for the present until new occasions bring new dispositions of mind." The English Catholics could not look to Europe for intervention. Thus Persons came to "the matter itself"—what the English Catholics should do:

> I do not see possibly here what may be counselled in the present case of our country (supposing that no help may be hoped for the present from any foreign prince until matters be better tried) but only to have patience and to expect the event of things, and to deal effectively with the Archduke, and the King of Spain, and with Ambassadors in England, that if they make peace with him, they make it not without some condition of toleration for Catholics....

So there it was. The great advocate of rebellion against religious tyranny in England admits there will be no foreign intervention for the English Catholics and they must refrain from action. Their course should be to seek to influence James through the ambassadors of Spain and of the Archduke. Persons continued his counsel: "Let our friends there be diligent in soliciting them [the Ambassadors] and advertise often hither how it goes forward, and let fit men be appointed to deal with them confidently and secretly there, and if then nothing be done and the national disgust do grow in the mean space, it will make some way for remedy afterward." Persons warned that Catholics had to take heed that passion not cause some to break out, i.e., revolt, which would lead to more severity. The Pope had ordained, Persons said, that "all such rash attempts be avoided."

Persons' counsel carried weight with the English Catholics and could not be dismissed by Sterrell and those whom he represented. The date of the letter is July 6, 1603, n.s. If it took two to three weeks to travel from Rome to Flanders or England, then it would have been in London about July 26/16. Persons's letter would have added urgency to the summoning of Anthony Skinner to London so that he and Dr. Taylor could confer with the Privy Councilors. The disappointment of Garnet and Baldwin in the turn of events can be sensed in the report of Garnet to Spain of early August 1603 that indicated the time was propitious for the king of Spain to come "sword in hand" into England.

It was not to be. As Persons had written, an invasion of England for the benefit of English Catholics had no appeal to the leaders of Catholic Europe. The Archdukes were engaged in the siege of Ostend and still in war with the rebellious Netherlands. Spain yet smarted from its failed expeditions against England and Ireland. Philip III had no wish to compound the failures of his father. Pope Clement VIII found James's accession acceptable: he had corresponded with James and had been led to believe that James would be more tolerant than Elizabeth. The Archpriest controversy made clear to Rome that the English Catholics were hopelessly divided and leaderless. Henry IV of France was an uneasy ally with Protestant England even before the accession of James, and he had no desire to see Spain strengthened by an English partner who owed his or her authority to Spanish assistance. The entry to the English crown of James, the son of a French queen consort, was not threatening to France.

When a Treaty was concluded in August 1604 among England, Spain and the Spanish Netherlands, it confirmed what Sterrell and Persons had concluded a year earlier. The Archdukes were persuaded by their chief minister, Jean Richardot, that negotiation over English toleration for Catholics was futile. The Spanish king held out hope for such a goal somewhat longer but his special envoy, the Constable of Castile, concluded that the peace treaty should be accomplished first and the question of toleration deferred until later.[93] Accordingly, the Somerset House Treaty ended hostilities between England and Spain and largely abandoned English support of the Dutch Revolt. English merchants would be able to trade with the Low Countries and with Spain, and English traders would not be subject to the Inquisition if they behaved discreetly. Europe, it was clear, was indifferent to the plight of English Catholics, and there was no possibility of successful opposition to James I. All one could do was hope he could be persuaded, directly or more subtly, to temper the enforcement of the recusant laws.

The Somerset House Conference, 1604 (Juan de Velasco Frias; Juan de Tassis, Count of Villa Mediana; Alessandro Robida; Charles de Ligne, Count of Arenberg; Jean Richardot; Louis Vereyken; Thomas Sackville, Earl of Dorset; Charles Howard, Earl of Nottingham; Charles Blount, Earl of Devonshire; Henry Howard, Earl of Northampton; Robert Cecil, Viscount Cranborne) (© National Portrait Gallery, London).

22. Transitions and Treasons, 1603

In the high summer of 1603, Sterrell and his master will have set themselves definitively, perhaps with strong feelings both of regret and relief, on the alternative course: compromise and collaboration, to preserve what could be retained and protected until such time as a Catholic marriage of the king's heir might restore the prospect of Catholic religious practice in England and Wales. The moment for which Sterrell had worked for more than two decades had come and then resolved into the kingship he had feared. The intelligence network had lost much of its reason to continue. Now in his forty-third year, what course would his remaining years take?

23

From Intelligence to Entertainment

The Grants of May 1603

With the new king accepted by the Catholic rulers of Europe and the Pope, how was a conscientious Catholic to bring about religious change in England? Elizabeth's (Cecil's) government was left largely intact by James. For the right persons, influence could be exercised in the Court entertainments and in the queen's household where the royal children and their secretly Catholic mother were susceptible to subtle guidance. These two venues were little controlled by the Privy Council and the Parliament. Court entertainments allowed influence through the adroit handling of invitations and seating of diplomats and through artful presentation of themes to affect perspectives of the sovereign and his government. Plays and masques could be instruments of policy and diplomacy. Entertainments were stories that could serve as lessons for the Court audience, affecting their thought. Now that English Catholics could not expect direct intervention from abroad, Worcester and Sterrell changed tactics. Phelippes was no longer needed. Shifting for himself, his negligence will prove nearly disastrous for Sterrell.

Worcester already had great advantages from his triple roles in the governance of England at the end of Elizabeth's reign. As an earl, he was a member of the House of Lords. As a Privy Councilor, he was part of the principal governing body. As Master of the Horse, he was one of the highest officers of the monarch's household. By December 1601, Worcester had also been made joint commissioner of Essex's former office of Earl Marshal. Worcester used his new positions aggressively to advance his acting company. For decades he had sponsored actors, even before he inherited Worcester's Men from his father. Although the Privy Council had limited the number of acting companies in London to two, on March 31, 1602, it allowed a third company to perform: Worcester's company (after absorbing Oxford's Men), subject to the restriction that it perform only at the Boar's Head, an inn-yard theater that could hold a small audience.[1] Worcester's Men sealed an agreement with the Elizabethan theatre entrepreneur Philip Henslowe in a meeting at the Mermaid Tavern in August.[2] This allowed Worcester's Men to use Henslowe's Rose Theater, a larger, multi-level theater in Bankside, Southwark. As James settled into his new kingdom, he appointed Worcester and Sterrell to positions from which they could influence English religion in indirect ways.

The king gave Worcester a special role in approving and financing court masques and entertainments. As Shakespeare scholar E. K. Chambers explains: "the organization of the masks, in which Jacobean Court extravagance centered, was not entrusted to the Revels at all, but to some nominated officer, under the direct supervision of the Lord Chamberlain and the Master of the Horse, who received funds direct from the Treasury for any expenditure which did not fall within the provinces of the Wardrobe or the Office of Works."[3] Chambers inferred the special role of Suffolk and Worcester from the financial accounts of the masques. It is no stretch to suggest these two Earls were similarly responsible for management of Court plays. Worcester was Earl Marshal for Elizabeth's funeral ceremonies and was likewise responsible for King James's coronation. Worcester was the king's constant hunting companion and the natural choice for oversight of court plays as well as masques.

Worcester's substantial influence in the new King's entertainments is seen in actions that James took almost as soon as he arrived in London about May 7, 1603. Although the staging of plays was halted with Queen Elizabeth's death, by May 9, James granted Worcester's company a license to perform.[4] Worcester arranged (with the king's authority) for his company to become Queen Anne's Company, placing it officially as the second Court company.[5] Worcester's son Thomas was appointed Queen Anne's Master of the Horse and thus her frequent companion.

Worcester arranged for William Sterrell to be appointed landlord of the palace housing the Office of Revels by King James on the same date that the Lord Chamberlain's Men (Shakespeare's company) were made the King's Men.[6] This was where the Office of Revels had its seat and where the King's Men spent much of their rehearsal and preparation time.[7] Sterrell was one of the "nominated officers" who can be identified who was under the direct supervision of Suffolk and Worcester. The grant to Sterrell was surely made so that he (and through him his master Worcester) could be in close proximity to the activities about the Court entertainments. His role in Court entertainments is shadowy but doubtless substantial.[8]

Worcester and Sterrell would have necessarily interacted with others with substantial influence on Court plays and masques. Several of the most important were directly associated with persecuted English Catholics. Edmund Tilney remained Master of Revels under James, but George Buc was appointed to his position in the summer of 1603 to take effect upon Tilney's retirement (about 1610). Buc in the meantime apparently assumed substantial responsibility for the office as deputy Master of Revels. Buc's brother Robert, described by Buc as his "beloved brother," was a seminary student, ordained in 1600, and later a Jesuit. He may have been a priest (in hiding) in England when Buc was appointed in 1603. Tilney's nephew (or cousin) Charles Tilney was executed in the Babington Plot in 1586. Charles Tilney was also a cousin of George Buc.

The Lord Chamberlain was Thomas Howard, Earl of Suffolk, whose wife, Katherine Howard, Countess of Suffolk, was a lively figure in Court entertainments, a Catholic, and a Spanish agent, *alias Roldan*. Thomas Howard's father was the Duke of Norfolk, executed in 1572 as a traitor. His brother, Philip Howard, died in prison for his Catholicism. Thomas's sister-in-law, the Countess of Arundel, was a very strong Catholic whose servant Robert Spiller did much work for the Jesuits and was a courier for Garnet's and Sterrell's secret intelligences to the Archdukes' court. Thomas's other brother, Lord William Howard, was imprisoned for his religion in the 1580s and remained an ardent Catholic throughout his life. During the negotiations for the August 1604 peace treaty, the Spanish ambassador, Tassis, corresponded with Suffolk and his wife through Dr. Robert Taylor, the English lawyer who was a servant of the Archdukes and who taught at the Catholic university of Douay, where so many of the seminary priests had been trained.[9]

Thus, the Lord Chamberlain, his wife, Edmund Tilney, and George Buc, had experienced sufferings of the English Catholics in their own immediate families. Suffolk and his uncle, the Earl of Northampton (brother of the executed Duke of Norfolk), were advising King James to be lenient to the Catholics in the period immediately before the performance of *Measure for Measure* in 1604. In a meeting at Hampton Court on September 14, 1604, called by James to discuss a complaint by Catholics over the illegal imprisonment of recusants after they had paid their fines, Northampton opened the discussion by begging the King to follow his merciful inclination "and not to wash your hands in the blood of Catholics."[10] Suffolk joined his uncle and several others in advising moderation in the Catholic question. This theme can be seen in Shakespeare's *Measure for Measure*.

The acting companies attached to the Court were called upon to perform diplomatic functions. At the negotiation of the Somerset House Treaty (August 1604, among England, Spain and the Hapsburg Netherlands), a group from the King's Men were assigned to "waiting and attending ... upon the Spanish Ambassador at Somerset House" for 18 days.[11] The same chamber accounts include:

> To Thomas Greene [leading actor and manager of the Queen's Men] for allowance of himself and ten of his fellows grooms of the chamber and the Queen's Players for waiting and attending upon Count Arenberg and the rest of the commissioners at Durham House....

So, Worcester's former company (still controlled by persons close to him) was attending upon the ambassador from the Archdukes. This would have allowed Worcester, Sterrell and others of Worcester's followers full opportunity to further their own diplomacy and entrench their close relationships with the Archdukes' representatives. Recall Persons's advice to "Rivers"/Sterrell: "Let our friends there be diligent in soliciting them [the Ambassadors] and advertise often hither how it goes forward, and let fit men be appointed to deal with them confidently and secretly there...."

The Queen's Household

Queen Anne did not travel to London with her husband. She remained in Scotland to arrange the transition and was particularly concerned with the raising of her children. Sent to accompany her as she made her way from Edinburgh was a group of ladies that included the Countess of Worcester. The new queen was secretly Catholic, just as the Countess of Worcester was known to be discreetly Catholic. Their religious outlook seems to have made a common bond. On going into her own chapel, the queen is reported once to have embraced the Countess of Worcester and remarked "You do well to guard carefully your religion."[12]

Worcester himself described to the Earl of Shrewsbury the "feminine commonwealth" of the newly arrived queen in which the ladies were "of divers degrees of favour."[13] They were divided into three groups: the private chamber, the drawing chamber, and the bedchamber. His own wife and Arabella Stuart, he said, were not of one certain chamber. Because he was keenly in touch with the functioning of the queen's household through his wife and their son (the queen's Master of the Horse) and other of their relatives, little could escape Worcester's attention nor his influence. The Somerset presence extended widely in the Court of James.

By 1604, the queen's principal secretary was John Florio, who was also a tutor to the royal children. Florio had been at Magdalen College when Sterrell was there, had been in the French Ambassador's house in London when Sterrell was there under the cover name of Kirby, and had been with Southampton when Sterrell was working for Essex, whose constant companion was Southampton. Samuel Daniel was brought into the queen's employ (a Groom of the Privy Chamber) by the same influence and was given the authority to license plays performed by the Children of the Queen's Revels. Worcester, and Sterrell, probably had a large hand in bringing Florio and Daniel under the queen's patronage. Moreover, they had a common patron in Lucy, Countess of Bedford, Worcester's relation by marriage; Lucy was also of the queen's bed chamber.[14]

The guardian of the king's elder son was another man from Sterrell's old Oxford college, Magdalen—Sir Thomas Chaloner. Phelippes will soon confess that he had shared with Chaloner some of Owen's secret correspondence.[15]

Some Catholics sought to have the monarch's children taught by teachers favorable to Catholicism. This was a goal for Fr. Persons, which he conveyed to Sir Anthony Standen, the English Catholic James sent to the Italian States in 1603. The gist of three letters to Standen from Persons while Standen was in Italy was: "I share your opinion that neither is the king a Catholic nor will he allow the Catholics liberty of conscience and so we must make it our aim, with the help of the queen, to have the children, who are now of tender age, instructed in the Catholic faith. This will be very easy for the queen, because she can give them, as teachers, whom she likes, and it will not be difficult for you to give her the names of some who are not reputed as Catholics, but yet have obtained their Doctor's degrees here with us with great distinction."[16]

A letter of Standen to Persons was intercepted and caused great embarrassment as well as jail time to Standen.[17] This may have prevented him from seeking to implement Persons's plan, especially since the letter discussed the queen's Catholicism. Whom did Persons have in mind? Prince Henry's principal tutor or protector was Sir Thomas Chaloner. He had been abroad in Italy for several years after leaving Oxford. There is no evidence that Chaloner was Catholic. John Florio was a tutor to the royal children; his education in Europe is unknown. Other Catholics had entrusted their children to Florio for education, including the French ambassador in 1583–85.

Worcester's Position at Court

Worcester's position as Master of the Horse gave him unparalleled access to King James. He became a close companion in the sports that James enjoyed much more than affairs of state. The new queen enjoyed the Court entertainments as much as the old queen. So, the English now had a hunting king and a dancing queen, and Worcester was well positioned to please both of them.[18]

While Worcester and the king hunted, Robert Cecil served as a faithful drudge on the king's staff. James referred to Cecil as his little beagle "that lies at home by the fire when all the good hounds are daily running on the fields."[19] Worcester was one of the best hounds. To Shrewsbury, Worcester commented on the pace set by the king; his remarks reveal how close he was to the king and how that proximity was accompanied by influence in the Court[20]:

> [S]ince my departure from London I think I have not had two hours of twenty four of rest but Sundays, for in the morning we are on horseback by eight, and so continue in full career from the death of one hare to another, until four at night; then, for the most part, we are five miles from home; by that time I find at my lodging sometimes one, most commonly two packets of letters, all which must be answered before I sleep, for here is none of the Council but myself, no, not a Clerk of the Council nor Privy Signet, so that an ordinary warrant for post horse must pass my own hand, my own secretary being sick at London. And yet, I thank God, never better in health; but wish heartily to be back at London, as you think I have cause, being far from my humour to turn penman at these years.

The very day of this letter William Sterrell, Worcester's absent secretary, was commencing a lease for the tenements in which he would live for most of the rest of his life, in fashionable Westminster.[21]

The Coronation and Entertainments

Worcester's preeminent role in Court pageantry is seen in his selection by the king to act as Earl Marshal. He supervised the formal crowning of James as king, on March 15, 1604, a grander celebration than the limited ceremonies of July 25, 1603, when the plague prevented substantial gatherings. Six weeks ahead of the event, Worcester gave his friend Shrewsbury a preview of the coronation; most people in the royal procession would "ride upon footclothes, some of one colour, some of another, as they like, but the most that I hear are of purple velvet embroidered, as far as their purse will afford means."[22]

Sterrell described the day[23]:

> The next day being the 15 of March, his Majesty with the Queen, and Prince, attended by all the nobility of both sexes, and the principal officers of his household, passed in most triumphant manner, through London, where 8 arches or Pageants were made in the way, and all the streets railed and adorned on both sides, and the companies of the city standing on one side, all in order, from the tower to Temple Bar. The Earl of Worcester was earl Marshal, the Lord Mayor carried the scepter, all the Aldermen attended at the cross, and presented King, Queen, and Prince with 3 fair standing cups of gold. The Earl of Arundel had his place as *primus comes*.[Principal Count] The Queen rode in an open chariot, and gave good contentment, by pleasing countenance, and affability to the people, the King kept greater state, saluting by moving his cap, the Embassadors of France and Spain, placed in several houses in Cheapside, the like he did to the Aldermen. The lady Arbella, and the old Countess of Arundel followed the Queen in caroche, all the rest of the Ladies on horseback, both Lords and Ladies were richly, and gallantly attired, and so they passed to Whitehall.

The description extends the length of the procession; it is not from a point along the route. Sterrell perhaps rode on horseback with his patron or walked as an attendant in the parade. Participating also was Ben Jonson, a Catholic whom Worcester probably selected as a speaker. Jonson appeared at the last triumphal arch, his part memorialized in a book on the Coronation Entertainment almost immediately, which included ceremonial speeches given on the king's entrance to Parliament on March 19.[24] Sterrell was present of the latter occasion as well and sent on to his correspondent a copy of the king's speech.[25]

Masques and Plays

Masques and plays were different forms of Court entertainment. A play was performed by professional actors before a passive audience. A masque combined dance and performance by amateurs, members of the Court who were themselves part of the "audience"; all were guests at a grand party.

Typically the masquers would enter the performance hall walking behind costumed torchbearers. The scenery would resonate with the theme of the masque. Musicians and singers performed; the masquers gave speeches, danced, and then drew members of the audience into dances. Masques were written for special occasions, with roles designed for particular members of the Court. A masque's writer was commissioned. In Elizabeth's reign, the "masque simple" was preferred to the "masque spectacular." In the Stewart Court, the "masque spectacular" was ascendant. Published records of some of these richly splendid entertainments are available. Commissioning a masque was patronage, and the choice of publisher was surely also patronage. Worcester and Sterrell were in a position to influence both.

Worcester's aims were as much political as artistic in arranging Court entertainments. These performances were associations that strengthened political relationships. David Lindley, in the introduction to a collection of masques, commented[26]:

> Masques were major political events, often inordinately costly, where the court displayed itself not only to itself, but also to foreign ambassadors and diplomats who eagerly sought invitation (and frequently caused problems in quarrels over precedence, or because of the refusal of an ambassador from one country to appear with another).

The Court entertainments offered an opportunity to influence policy as to France, Spain and the Low Countries. After James's accession, the heart of loyalist Catholic strategy was the marrying of King James's heir to a Catholic who would raise her children as Catholics and whose terms of marriage would meantime win for English Catholics "rights of conscience." Worcester and his allies at court attempted a Catholic marriage (Spanish, not French), first for Prince Henry before his early death in 1612, and then for Prince Charles.

Worcester's family often had prominent parts in the masques, no doubt due both to Worcester's rank and to his role as overseer and purser for these extravaganzas. One of the first of the "masques spectacular" was written for the new queen by Samuel Daniel. *The Vision of the Twelve Goddesses* was performed on Sunday evening, January 8, 1604, at Hampton Court by the queen and her Ladies. Prominent roles were played by Worcester and his wife's niece, Dorothy Hastings.[27] The wardrobe of the late queen was ransacked to provide sumptuous fabrics for the costumes. The performers were preceded by torchbearers—pages in white satin gowns, with stars of gold, and torches of white gilded wax. The masquers entered by a staircase, walking three abreast. At a temple's altar, they presented offerings, songs and speeches. The ladies drew the lords (including Worcester) and two of the ambassadors out for dances. The Spanish envoy "showed himself a lusty old reveller."[28] The masque ended at midnight and was followed by a banquet with the king and the ambassadors.

The international political character of the staging of the *Vision of the Twelve Goddesses* was described by Sterrell ("Ortelio Renzo"). Worcester's faction at Court worked to bring about a peace treaty among England, Spain and the Archdukes in Brussels. Worcester and the English Catholics hoped that some toleration of Catholicism would result from the negotiations. The French were opposed to the possibility of closer relations between England and France's neighbors on both its northern and southern borders. Favor was shown to the Spanish by inviting the Spanish Ambassador to the queen's masque, rather than the less grand masque by men of the Court on New Year's day, to which the French Ambassador had been invited. Sterrell explained the political dynamic[29]:

> The Court is yet at Hampton court.... The holy days were passed over with accustomed Christmas recreations as playing, dancing, masking, and the like. 2 masks were famous, the one acted by noble and principal men on New Year's day, the other by the Queen and 11 honorable Ladies the Sunday after twelfth day. The French Ambassador was present at the first and the Spanish solemnly [formally, ceremoniously] invited [to] come to the second, albeit much against the Frenchman's will, who labored all he could to have crossed him. All the Ambassadors were feasted at Court this Christmas, first the Spanish and Savoyan, 2nd the French and Florentine, 3rd the Poloman and Venetian, and all highly pleased but the French who is made content to see the Spaniard so kindly used and it is plainly perceived that he and the Florentine and in some sort the Venetian labour all they can underhand to divert us from making Peace with Spain, and for that purpose the Duke of Florence maketh overture of a marriage for our Prince with his daughter and a million in dowry. But if money may suffice it is deemed the King of Spain will double or treble the million with a daughter of Savoy so as other good conditions may be concluded for reducing the Hollanders to obedience and ease of the Catholics at home, upon which points it is supposed the Constable [the Spanish envoy] will peremptorily stand. The Ambassadors of Savoy and Florence were here at great contention for precedence and our King could not accommodate it or at least would not, and by that occasion I suppose the Savoyan made less stay, being gone from hence about 16 days past or rather more.

The marriage of Prince Henry to a Spanish-connected Catholic is unquestionably an important consideration in Sterrell's letter. The reference to "a daughter of Savoy" is to two marriageable daughters of the Duke of Savoy and his late wife; the mother of those daughters was sister to King Philip III of Spain and the Archduchess Isabella in Brussels. France, he observes, is working with Florence and the Venetians to hinder an English-Spanish peace treaty. The Court entertainments were being used to promote Anglo/Spanish/Low Countries harmony, no doubt by Worcester, to influence the course of diplomacy. Sterrell's letter shows how conscious he (and Worcester) were of the power of the Court entertainments on politics.

A year later (six months after the signing of the Spanish treaty) another "masque spectacular" was performed. Authorship was granted to the Catholic Ben Jonson. The event was the first of a series of collaborations of Jonson with the brilliant set designer Inigo Jones. The queen requested an African theme, so the author produced *The Masque of Blackness*, performed January 6, 1605.[30] To defray the costs of the *Masque of Blackness*, £3000 was drawn from the Exchequer.[31] The Ladies appeared as the twelve daughters of the River Niger, dressed in strange costumes, and their faces, necks and arms were painted black. The masquers were placed in a great concave shell, and hidden engines moved them up and down on the waters. By their sides swam six sea monsters, bearing twelve torch-bearers. The queen (about seven months pregnant) and her ladies were searching for a far-off country whose sun (i.e., the English king) turned Blackness into Beauty. Among the Ladies was Anne, Lady Herbert, Worcester's daughter-in-law who had married Henry Somerset in the great wedding of June 1600.[32] Earlier in the day Worcester's younger son Thomas, the queen's Master of the Horse, was created a Knight of the Bath.

As with the masque of the previous year, there was considerable diplomatic gamesmanship in providing an invitation to the Spanish ambassador while not inviting the French ambassador. Again it was engineered by someone at Court that the Spanish Ambassador would attend but not the Frenchman. Beaumont, the French ambassador, blamed Sir Lewis Lewknor, accusing him of being corrupted by bribes from the Spanish. He should have suspected Worcester and the Lord Chamberlain's wife, both of whom favored the Spanish.[33] "Vincent" (Phelippes, informed by Sterrell) reported to "Benson" (Hugh Owen) that the

Frenchman "very vainly and insolently troubled the King and the Lords" over this affront to Beaumont and his master, the king of France; this no doubt damaged the French standing at Court. Perhaps similar gamesmanship occurred ten days earlier with invitations to the performance at Court of Shakespeare's *Measure for Measure*.

Kemp the Jester and Shirley the Adventurer

The entertainments at Court could provide employment (at government expense), access and cover for people serving the Catholic intelligencers. Actors and performers traveled abroad. Their presence in a foreign country was readily explicable on non-religious grounds, and their costumes and equipment easily concealed letters, religious items and books.[34]

One of the most famous actors of the period was Will Kemp. He served with Leicester's Men, the Lord Chamberlain's Men, and with Worcester's company; he was also an investor in the Globe Theater. Will Kemp has been identified as the "jesting player" who carried dispatches from the Low Countries to Walsingham.[35] The name Kemp was common; nothing is known of the family origins of Will Kemp. A Roman Catholic Kemp family was closely related to the adventurer Sir Anthony Shirley, and if Will Kemp were related this might explain why Will Kemp the jester would be chosen as a courier to Sir Anthony at a crucial time.[36] In service in the Low Countries with the Earl of Leicester when Will Kemp was a jester and courier for Leicester was Sir Thomas Shirley, together with two of his sons, Anthony and Thomas.[37] There was likely at this time close contact between the actor and the Shirleys (as well as the possible family connection) that will play an important role later when Kemp undertakes a strange journey to Rome and seeks out Sir Anthony Shirley.

Although a successful actor in London, Kemp seems to have sold his share in the Globe to Shakespeare in 1599 preparatory to leaving England. Perhaps to raise money for his European trip, Kemp made a celebrated "Morris dance" from London to Norwich, a distance of 114 miles in February/March 1600. The third day of his journey he stayed at Ingatestone, the estate of the Petre family, Worcester's son-in-law.[38] Once abroad, Kemp met with the adventurer and Essex follower Sir Anthony Shirley, whose good reception at the Vatican had been assured by "frequent displays of zeal for Roman catholicism...."[39] Their meeting(s) took place about April 1601. At this time Fr. Persons met with and supported Anthony Shirley as a claimant to the office of Persian envoy at the Vatican; Shirley also became an agent of the Spanish king.

Anthony Shirley's Persian adventure (accompanied by his brother Robert), was undertaken initially for the Earl of Essex, who was related to Shirley's wife. The news of Essex's reversals at Court surely contributed to his shift from anti–Spanish adventurer to Spanish agent, as well as learning that the queen would not receive him back into England.

The activities of the Shirley brothers were of great interest to the English Catholic intelligencers. A copy of a letter apparently sent to Sterrell from Liège dated April 13, 1601, reported: "Shirley that came from the Persian is now in Italy, (in Florence I take it) and from there to depart towards Rome."[40] Shirley entered Rome and almost immediately was meeting with the Spanish Ambassador, Sessa, and Fr. Robert Persons. Shirley, one of the most experienced seamen of the English navy, gave Sessa and Persons detailed information about the best places for the landing of men to invade England.[41] Hugh Owen reported on developments to Sterrell with remarkable speed: "Strife & contention grow in Rome for precedencie between Sir Anthony Shirley & his persian companion. Father Persons made an accord between them & Shirley was preferred. The pope dispatched them thence with a viaticum [travel funds] to pass forward to other countries. Sir Anthony declared himself to be a Catholic in Prague & at Rome...."[42] After scarcely a month in Rome, Shirley unexpectedly left.

Kemp's meeting with Anthony Shirley was widely noted. A diarist commented that Kemp traveled in Germany and Italy and made many reports of Shirley after meeting him in Rome.[43] A play by John Day and others, *The Travailes of the three English Brothers*, on the foreign adventures of the brothers Shirley, represents Kemp meeting Anthony Shirley, though transposing the venue to Venice. Echoing Sidney's 1587 reference to his courier, the play has Sir Anthony call Kemp: "Jesting Will." Kemp has sought audience with Shirley, and the knight's greeting would indicate the two already knew each other well[44]:

> Servant: Sir here's an Englishman desires access to you.
> Sir Anthony: An Englishman. What's his name?
> Servant: He calls himself Kempe. *Enter Kempe*
> Sir Anthony: Kemp, bid him come in. Welcome honest Will....

The play also has Sir Anthony meeting with and praising the Pope in highly favorable terms.[45] Did Kemp pass information from Persons's associates in England to Sir Anthony and to Persons? Perhaps so. The priest largely responsible for converting Sir Anthony and probably helping arrange his visit to the Pope and Persons was the Jesuit Fr. Joseph Creswell, who in 1580 had assisted Campion and Persons when they were in London and was in Spain when Sterrell visited Persons in 1595; in fact, the letter by Persons describing Sterrell was to inform Creswell of the visit. Creswell, as discussed above, was one of the recipients of the Sterrell-Phelippes intelligence. On his return to England in 1601 Kemp was in the service of the Earl of Worcester.[46]

A trip to the court of the Emperor of Germany and to Rome, both seats of Catholicism, was a curious journey indeed for an impecunious English actor no longer associated with a company and with no known purpose for his undertaking. Kemp's well-publicized meeting with Shirley, a man denied permission by the queen to return into England,[47] a man now in the service of Spain and with 1000 escudos from the Pope and another 400 from Cardinal Aldobrini,[48] is likewise very curious. Perhaps Will Kemp was pursuing the same goal as Anthony Shirley: a settlement of sorts of religious issues among Scotland, and Rome and Spain. If this is so, then it is not at all curious that Will Kemp would find employment with the Earl of Worcester upon his return into England; Worcester perhaps was his employer (via Sterrell) from the outset of the curious journey.

Hassenet the Vaulter

A secret courier would leave no letters of his own, but his role may be manifested in the confessions and letters of others. Evidence establishes the existence of one such entertainer who was nourished at Court and worked in the same circles as Sterrell: John Hassenet, a celebrated "vaulter" or gymnast.

Hassenet's record as an international messenger is described by the Jesuit Henry Walpole in confessions of 1594. Tortured multiple times, Walpole provided the government with a bonanza of information. Coke's notes say that Walpole received "diverse letters beyond sea by the hands of John Hassenet to be delivered in England without any express direction contained within or upon these letters."[49] This indicates Hassenet knew to whom to direct the letters. Several Walpole confessions discussed the movement of intelligence and the activities of the English exiles: "Verstegan sends up and down letters and intelligences and books betwinxt the Cardinal [William Allen], Parsons, Holt, O[w]en and England." He named Hassenet as a courier.[50] Walpole said that Hassenet was supposed to travel into England with him but Fr. Holt asked Walpole to let Hassenet remain with him.[51] Fr. Holt was one of Sterrell's correspondents at this time, and Hassenet may well have been courier to Sterrell.

Walpole revealed that Hassenet was well-informed on the Jesuit Superior in London. He stated: "Touching Garnet I have heard of Hasnett that he kept at Mris Vaux her house in London."[52] Hassenet must have been one of Garnet's courier. Sterrell's letters under aliases traveled in Garnet's packets, and Hassenet probably carried letters written by Sterrell. John Hassenet was still active in intelligence circles a decade later when a spy in Brussels learned of Hassnet. This was Thomas Allison, a man who provided information to Robert Cecil for years in hopes of preferment. The report was given to Sir Thomas Chaloner to convey to Cecil[53]:

> There is one Hasett als. Hashett a vaulter who having been lately beyond the Seas, kept in the company of one Browne, Grene & Leadbeater & other Englishmen players that go up and down the Country. A little before his coming from them, he told those three, that either he was to have or should have procured for him to have the teaching of the young Prince [Henry, age 10] to vault, and then the whole hope of England should lie in his hands and at his pleasure to break the neck of him with a trick and it was no great matter, for he was brought up according to his father's religion of whom there was no hope for him to become a Catholic, and such a piece of fortune which might be as it were by mischance would deserve to be well rewarded, and every man must raise his own fortunes as so would he….

Browne, Grene & Leadbeater mentioned also by Allison are identifiable with Robert Browne and Thomas Greene who were associated at one time or another with Worcester's company or its successor.[54] Allison said Browne and others were prepared to be witnesses against Hassenet. Although Allison does not state that Hassenet is involved in intelligence, the report is in the immediate context of Allison undertaking intelligence for Hugh Owen; Allison's contact with Hassenet arose through Owen. Browne carried letters for the Earl of Essex from Germany in 1595.[55]

Philip Henslowe, the theater entrepreneur, recorded loans in his diary for John Hassenet's vaulting performances in 1598 and 1599.[56] On July 29, 1603, a warrant was issued for payment of £10 for a performance by John Hassenet: "for presenting and making show before his Highness of his skill in vaulting which he performed with his Majesty's good liking."[57] Hassenet again performed on August 11, 1604, at Whitehall before King James and the Spanish ambassador, who arrived in London the day before to conclude the Treaty of Peace with Spain.[58] At the same time, members of Worcester's acting company (now the Queen's Men) were entertaining and attending upon Count Arenberg, the Ambassador from Brussels.[59]

1605—Prince Henry at Oxford

The powerful influence of Worcester is reflected in the college the King and Queen chose for their older son; it was the one most closely associated with Worcester's five sons and with Sterrell: Magdalen. The royal family made a visit to Oxford at the end of August 1605 to enroll the eleven year old Prince Henry. From start to finish, the visit appears a production of Worcester and people associated with his Secretary, Sterrell. On August 27, 1605, James's heir apparent was led into Magdalen College by a procession headed by Worcester, and there greeted by the President and Fellows. The college's welcoming speech was delivered by James Mabbe (verses by whom would later appear in the First Folio of Shakespeare). Mabbe undoubtedly knew Sterrell well. He had enrolled at Magdalen in 1586 when Sterrell was lecturing on Moral Philosophy and, like Sterrell, was a Demy. A principal in the disputation held later that day in the President's lodgings, where Henry was to live, was Worcester's son, Charles.[60] The King took a large part in the disputations and they "pleased the King exceedingly."[61] The two youngest sons of Worcester had just entered the college, Charles (17) and Edward (14) on April 16.[62]

24

Measure for Measure
A Sermon to a King

Of "government the properties to unfold"

The ultimate potential for influencing political policy through the Court entertainments was to perform works directly to the royal Court calculated to foster a particular view and agenda. An example is Shakespeare's *Measure for Measure,* which was staged by the playwright and his sponsors to influence their king and government. The play sought to create an atmosphere favorable to those who, like the play's Isabella, refuse, even at great loss, to compromise religious principle. The Catholic Isabella of the play is identifiable with the Catholic recusants who for conscience-sake refused to participate in the ceremonies of the state church even at the loss of property and life at a time when the English government had harshly renewed the anti-recusant laws. Secondly, the play portrays sympathetically a Catholic Duke and Isabella that draws heavily upon the royal Catholic couple across the channel: the Archduke and Isabella. A few months earlier King James had signed the Somerset House Treaty with them and with Spain. The playwright and his sponsors sought to advance favorable relations between the two countries and their reigning couple, who were sympathetic to English Catholics.

The state's application of law is pervasive in *Measure for Measure*. The Duke opens the drama, informing that his purpose is of "government the properties to unfold." The play is the Duke's "discourse" on governance. It has been described as a "skeptical meditation on the nature, limits, and prerogative of legal power as well as on the ethics of justice."[1] It was an explicit lesson on proper governance when it was performed for King James and his court at Whitehall Palace on December 26, 1604.

Court, State-Imposed Morality and Religion in 1604

The setting of *Measure* is Catholic Vienna. Claudio has been arrested and sentenced to death for fornication, evidenced by the swelling pregnancy of Juliet before formal marriage. The sex was not entirely illicit, for they have entered a contract of marriage, known as *sponsalia per verba de præsenti*, in anticipation of more formal ceremonies. The acting sovereign in Vienna in much of the play is Angelo, Deputy to Duke Vicentio, who has placed Angelo in charge during his absence, while the Duke is supposedly "travelled to Poland" to compound with other dukes concerning the King of Hungary. The Duke, however, assumes the habit of a friar from Friar Thomas and says he will visit both prince and people, "as 'twere a brother of your order, like a true friar." He will observe Angelo, and shall see, "If power change purpose, what our seemers be." Claudio's sister, Isabella, seeks to save Claudio from death by pleading to Angelo, who now holds the state's power of life and death.

We first meet Isabella as a novice in a convent about to take vows. Her strong impression upon Angelo leads him to offer to trade Claudio's freedom for her virtue. She refuses adamantly. The Duke, still in the guise of a friar, engineers a solution. Angelo had once made a pre-contract, a promise to marry with Mariana but had repudiated her when she lost her dowry. The Duke has Isabella return to Angelo with the promise that she will submit herself in exchange for her brother's life. The Duke has Mariana substitute for Isabella at the appointed hour (the *bed trick*). Angelo beds the woman but breaches his promise; he does not suspend the execution of Claudio. The Duke again intervenes and a dead man's head, that can appear to be Claudio's, is taken to Angelo as proof of the execution (the *head trick*). Soon, the Duke reappears as himself: he rewards the good and punishes the wicked (but sparing the lives of all), with justice and wisdom. As the play ends, it appears that the erstwhile friar, the Duke, and the novice of the convent, Isabella, may wed.

The surface of the story is similar to its sources[2]: a legal system, maintained by hypocritical officials, treating harshly sexual acts out of state-approved wedlock. For the audience at Whitehall, the play may have appeared audacious, as though it were shining a critical light upon the harshness of the late queen on two members of the nobility who were now favored by the new king, James I. The audience would have recognized parallels of the play to the punishments by Elizabeth of two earls, Southampton[3] and Pembroke,[4] who were likely in the audience.

An unmistakable religious theme runs through *Measure*. The female protagonist is in a convent, not yet an avowed nun. The principal male character assumes the habit of a friar. Isabella invokes God as the saviour of all forfeit souls, saving all from original sin through His mercy. The title itself is taken from the Bible, from the Sermon on the Mount, a passage that is a call for humility in dispensing justice, tempered by mercy.[5]

A New King and the English Catholic Question

The king for whom the play was written had been on the English throne for only a year-and-a-half, and the gravest question of the kingdom was the treatment to be given to Catholic "recusants." The August 1604 treaty settled the state of war that had existed since before the 1588 Armada, but it failed to address the status of English Catholics, the "ease of the Catholics at home" that Sterrell had hoped for in January 1604. Like Isabella, the English Catholic leaders pleaded for relief for their brethren from the letter of the strict laws. The state demanded that the Catholic recusants violate their consciences, as Angelo demands of Isabella, and engage in grave sin that would condemn their souls in eternity—a demand they refused, as does Isabella. Twice in the year before the play, Catholics of England submitted supplications to the king seeking relief and toleration. Their supplications are re-presented in *Measure for Measure*'s plea for toleration for conscience-sake. A more specifically political aspect of the play, consistent with the Catholic goal of toleration, is the author's careful delineation of the principal characters. King James and his Court could not have failed to see the parallels between the Duke and Isabella and the Archduke and Isabella just across the English Channel, whom James and his wife had sought to cultivate while they were yet in Scotland.

Shakespeare's *Hamlet*, written before James came to the English throne, is splendid precedent that a courtier might use a play to influence a king and compel him to confront his own actions. Hamlet arranges for a performance of *The Murder of Gonzago,* a play with parallels to Claudius's murder of Hamlet's father. Hamlet tells the audience:

> The play's the thing
> Wherein I'll catch the conscience of the King. [*Hamlet*, 2.2]

The play within a play has the desired effect on Claudius.

With *Measure for Measure*, Shakespeare staged a play to catch the conscience of King James. In portraying the plight of the Catholics who refused to consent to the demands of the state that they commit the mortal sin of abandoning their faith, he expected the play to catch the conscience of the king, and to open James to conclude that wisdom and justice lay in relaxing the strict enforcement of the recusant laws.[6]

Isabella's Recusancy

The central conflict of *Measure for Measure* is Isabella's refusal to consent to have sex with Angelo. Without this refusal to submit to the sovereign, this recusancy, the story would not hold together. Claudio has already been condemned to death when Isabella goes to Angelo at Lucio's request. Before proposing an explicit exchange of sex for Claudio's life, Angelo poses a hypothetical choice to Isabella. The question is framed so that whatever she answers she will be sure to suffer for it, either in body or in soul:

> [If] there were
> No earthly mean to save him but that either
> You must lay down the treasures of your body
> To this supposed, or else to let him suffer–
> What would you do? [*Measure*, 2.4]

Many in the audience would recognize Angelo as posing a variant of the "bloody questions" demanded of Catholic prisoners by their prosecutors.[7] Like them, she's asked to do a thing she is forbidden by conscience and religion to do, and she refuses. She responds: "As much for my poor brother as myself." She would take death. It is a choice between this life and eternity, as she soon relates to her brother.

Critics who speak of "Angelo's attempted rape of Isabella" distort the play's presentation of the issue of sex. The ethical issue is always one of consent, not force. Angelo seeks an exchange in which Isabella must be complicit. If he physically forced sex upon her, her soul would not risk damnation. Only voluntary participation would damn her; only refusal would prevent loss of her soul in eternity.[8]

Angelo and Isabella exchange views on forced consent and sin. She tells him: "I had rather give my body than my soul." Angelo argues that compelled sins do not count as do those entered without compulsion: She would be performing an act of charity.[9] She rejects Angelo's offer: "Better it were a brother died at once, Than that a sister, by redeeming him,

Should die forever." Isabella assumes her brother would prefer death to her dishonor, but she is mistaken. When she informs Claudio that if she would yield Angelo her virginity, "Thou mightst be freed!" he urges her to take the deal. He suggests, alluding to Angelo's wisdom, that the "momentary trick," the trifle of sex, would not be a mortal sin resulting in damnation. Claudio tries to persuade Isabella of innocence in compelled consent, echoing Angelo himself.[10] She insists she would give her life but not her honor.

Critics have found Isabella harsh, selfish, even hypocritical. Modern critics do not take seriously Isabella's concern over mortal sin. They do not like her for her unwillingness to submit her virginity to Angelo to save her brother. They must discount Isabella's other words to Claudio, "were it but my life! I'd throw it down for your deliverance." Her choice is not between "love for her brother" and her "personal integrity"; rather it is a choice between love for her brother and her love of God.

Isabella's choice reflects the dilemma facing England's Catholic recusants in 1604. Her refusal to give in to the demand of the state that she commit a mortal sin reflected Roman Catholic teaching to its English Catholics. They were prohibited from attending Protestant worship and partaking Protestant communion even at the risk of capital crime. They were expected to hear Mass even if it meant death should they be captured. Numerous English Catholics gave their lives rather than renounce their faith, including Margaret Ward, Anne Line and Margaret Clitheroe. The priests who were executed were generally given the choice to live by converting to the state religion, as were many laity; but, in the view of their church this would be apostasy and they would lose eternal life.[11] English men and women were not executed for fornication, but they were for recusancy.

The question of recusancy had been taken up early in the Persons-Campion mission of 1580–81. The most important point taken up by the group of English Catholics at the Synod of Southwark in 1580 at the beginning of the Persons-Campion mission determined that nothing could ever justify a Catholic in attending Protestant worship in England.[12] A number of the English missionaries (not all) ordained on the Continent instructed their followers that they must abjure the protestant ceremonies on pain of mortal sin. This refusal to attend those services became a dividing line among the English Catholics.[13] Many wavered, as did Claudio regarding Isabella. Some English Catholics, "church-papists," compromised and outwardly conformed, reasoning much like Claudio (and as urged by Angelo) that nature dispenses with the deed (outward consent/conformity) so far that it becomes a virtue.

The entire setting of *Measure for Measure* can be seen as Catholic. Doctrines of the Roman church rejected by the state church are alluded to. The sacrament of confession is shown when the Duke/Friar tells Juliet he will teach her how to arraign her conscience and try her penitence and when Angelo instructs the Provost: "Bring [Claudio] his confessor; let him be prepared."[14] The state church generally regarded "the Romish doctrine concerning Purgatory.... [as] repugnant to the word of God."[15] Yet Claudio in *Measure* speaks recognizably of purgatory after death when the spirit goes to:

> bathe in fiery floods or to reside
> In thrilling region of thick-ribbed ice. [*Measure*, 3.1]

The same Protestant article against Purgatory provided that "Invocation of Saint, is a fond thing vainly invented, and grounded upon no warranty of Scripture" and also was "repugnant to the word of God." The Duke invokes his own patron saint upon a matter: "If anything fall to you upon this more than thanks and good fortune, *by the saint whom I profess*, I will plead against it with my life." The friars Thomas and Peter are presented favorably as they help the Duke expose the misdeeds of Angelo, and the nun Francisca is a model of modesty and virtue. The villain of the play, the hypocritical Angelo is described by the Duke and Claudio by the term used as a synonym of Puritan: *precise*.

Several characters in the play suggest that Isabella is a saint, a term that would draw on Catholicism rather than Protestant doctrine.[16] Significantly, Angelo describes Isabella as a saint who has been sent to tempt him.[17] A common charge against Catholics by the magistrates was that they were "seducers." This identification of Catholics as *seducers* was well-established in Elizabeth's reign.[18] The accusation of "seducer" continued into the reign of James I, and often struck at people close to the Court.

Four months before the performance of *Measure*, a commission to banish priests and Jesuits was set up. James himself wrote to his Council on September 1, lamenting that, despite his hopes that clemency might induce the reformation of the Catholics, still Jesuits and seminary priests were continuing into England. A government document of September 5, 1604, declared[19]:

> many of these jesuits, seminary priests, and other priests and persons abovesaid, being at large, but also divers of them, being so in prison, desist not, as much as in them lieth, from the *seducing* of divers of our subjects....

Seduction language was used against both William Byrd, the great composer, and his wife in May 1605 as part of the crackdown on Catholics. His well-known Catholicism was largely ignored by Queen Elizabeth and King James. A document from the Court of Archdeaconry of Essex from May 1605 reflects the charges of seduction against the couple.[20] Similar allegations were made against the Court favorite in masques, Ben Jonson. The Consistory Court of London for the Parish of St. Anne's, Blackfriars, for January 10, 1606, cited Ben Jonson and his wife for failures to attend services. The complaint stated that "as far as we can learn ever since the King came in [1603] he is a poet and is by fame a *seducer* of youth to the popish religion."[21]

The proceedings by lower level Protestants against Catholic figures who were prominent in Court entertainments suggests a fear that the "seducers" at Court might be targeting the king and queen themselves. Both complaints call attention to the king's apparent tolerance of Byrd and Jonson. That *Measure for Measure* is a play presenting sympathetically the plight of Catholic recusants indicates that such contemporary fears were not without foundation.

Scholars have found the Duke/Friar to use equivocation, as did the Jesuits. The Jesuit practice and defence of equivocation, particularly in response to the government's "bloody questions," was well known and figured prominently in the trials of priests. Shakespeare gives examples of equivocation in plays, and expressly defends it in *Measure for Measure* when the Duke says: "So disguise shall, by the disguis'd/Pay with falsehood false exacting."[22] The Duke/Friar pretends to have heard Isabella's confession and says she is virtuous. Peter Milward, Shakespeare scholar and Jesuit, suggests that he either lies or commits sacrilege.[23] Milward believes that the Duke-as-Friar was practising acceptable equivocation in relating a confessional role. Thus, too, does Milward note that the Duke-as-Friar "seems to excuse his plan (the bed trick) by the notorious Jesuit doctrine of equivocation."[24] Fr. Henry Garnet's use of a marriage vow to discuss equivocation in his *Treatise on Equivocation* finds an echo in *Measure for Measure*[25]: Garnet's example roughly corresponds to Angelo's denial of a marriage contract with Mariana, a matter on which the Duke must judge. *Othello*, performed at Court shortly before *Measure for Measure*, similarly appears to draw directly upon Garnet's unpublished *Treatise on Equivocation*.[26]

The Recusants' Supplications

Isabella's pleas to Angelo for mercy are the artistic presentation of the Catholic recusants' supplications to King James for toleration in the months between his accession and the performance of *Measure for Measure*. The state demanded they commit mortal sin in exchange for self-preservation, similar to the demands made on Isabella. The Catholic recusants' petition of 1604 underscored their dilemma, which was found in[27]:

> the undissembled profession of our inward faith, in refusing to go to the protestant church; a necessity which, under guilt of deadly sin and breach of our church's unity, all are bound unto, that believe the verity of the catholic religion, and purpose still to keep themselves her children.

The supplicants in this, and in a 1603 petition, complained that other dissenters in religion were treated less severely.[28] As Isabella puts it:

> Who is it that hath died for this offense?
> There's many have committed it. [*Measure*, 2.2]

How should a wise sovereign respond to a plea such as Isabella's, or to the supplications of the Popish recusants? What would a clement sovereign do?

The Character of the Duke

The play's early scenes mark the Duke as a thoughtful, well-intentioned ruler, "a gentleman of all temperance," who is concerned that his realm has become disordered. His leniency has resulted in laxity in the law and corruption. He sees a need for stern measures: "strict statutes and most biting laws, The needful bits and curbs to headstrong steeds." Unwilling to undertake these actions himself, he takes leave of his office and has Angelo act in his place. He loves the people but not their applause. Reforms coming from the Duke would have seemed more dreadful than coming from Angelo. A series of deceptions shows him to be a dissembler. He is not actually leaving Vienna but instead takes up the habit of a brother.

Many of the English Catholics in 1604 would have identified James as a Duke transformed into an Angelo. James had come to his majority of 18 in 1584 and assumed his responsibilities as King of Scotland. For the 19 years between then and 1603 (corresponding to the 19 zodiacs of laxity by the Duke, *Measure*, 1.2) when he acceded to the crown of England, he led many to believe he was inclined to tolerance in religion, that he might even profess Catholicism. James described himself in *Basilikon Doron* as lax in enforcement from the beginning of his reign in Scotland.[29]

James's relaxed attitude towards enforcement of laws against Catholics changed shortly after entering England: "Na, na, gud fayth, wee's not need the Papists now."[30] To their great disappointment, the "recusants still believed that James had promised them toleration...."[31] By 1604, the stringent recusancy laws were more strictly enforced and were expanded by additional measures. With concern over potential obstacles to the treaty of August 1604 out of the way, the government further increased enforcement. The Tierney/Dodd *Church History of England* observed that James "proceeded at once to let loose the whole fury of the persecution" and includes a catalog of actions (with supporting evidence).[32] A new proclamation was published, instructing judges and magistrates to be more rigorous. A commission was appointed for the banishment of the missionaries. Clergymen were required to collect the names of all recusants within their parishes. Fines were levied with increased vigor. On July 16, Fr. John Sugar and Robert Grissold, a layman, were executed at Warwick. In September, another layman, named Bailey, shared the same fate at Lancaster. Twenty-one priests and three laics were sent into perpetual banishment.

Fr. Sugar and Robert Grissold were both offered the opportunity to live if they would only conform to the outward signs of the state religion. Both refused.[33] On the scaffold, Fr. Sugar declared he was being executed for conscience-sake, not treason.[34] Like Fr. Sugar, whose bloody drawing and quartering he witnessed, Grissold told the spectators that he died for conscience.[35] The Catholic intelligencers in London, particularly Sterrell, Anthony Skinner and Robert Spiller would have known Grissold, for his brother, John Grissold, was caretaker of White Webbs, a home of Anne Vaux where Fr. Henry Garnet generally resided.[36] The Grissold family was very close friends to the Skinner family, neighbors at Rowington.[37]

Did Shakespeare have such martyrs in mind with *Measure for Measure*? A likely allusion may be found in Act 4 scene 2 to the execution of a priest three years earlier. Fr. Mark Barkworth was executed in 1601 with Anne Line, for whose memory Shakespeare composed *Phoenix and Turtle*.[38] The Friar/Duke wills that one prisoner's head be substituted for Claudio's. When the Provost objects that the substitution will be discovered by Angelo, the Friar/Duke responds:

> Duke: Oh, death's a great disguiser, and you may add to it. Shave the head, and tie the beard, and say it was the desire of the penitent to be so bared before his death. You know the course is common.

It was an *uncommon* course for men in England or Vienna about to be executed to have their heads shaved—unless the "penitent" were a Catholic priest. Fr. Barkworth had his head shaved before he was hauled to Tyburn. A letter of Fr. Garnet reported: "Father Mark had shorn his head after the manner of a monk, with a crown, because the Order of the Benedictines in Flanders used to receive the tonsure when the moment of death was near at hand...."[39] The reference in *Measure* seems likely to be directed at Mark Barkworth by a poet/playwright who was so moved by the execution of Barkworth's fellow martyr Anne Line that he dared write and publish a poem about her shortly after her death. An earlier martyr who shaved his head as a mark of his religion was Alexander Briant, executed with Campion in 1581.

Another reference to a martyred priest perhaps is found in Angelo's retort to Isabella's plea for Claudio:

> It were as good
> To pardon him that hath from nature stolen
> A man already made, as to remit
> Their saucy sweetness that do *coin heaven's image*
> In stamps that are forbid. [*Measure*, 2.4]

This is best seen as Angelo drawing a moral equivalence between murder and the Elizabethan crime of distributing an *Agnus Dei*: a wax disk, blessed by the Pope, stamped with a cross and the figure of a lamb. It symbolizes Christ, the Lamb of the New Testament. Elizabethan statute made it an act of treason to bring into England or give to others an *Agnus Dei* or other articles blessed by the pope.[40] The first Catholic seminarian priest executed, in 1577, was Cuthbert Mayne, "who was wearing the waxen *Agnus Dei*, prohibited under Elizabethan law."[41] The charges for which he was executed included his delivering *Agnus Deis* to Catholic recusants. The records are silent as to whether the charges against Fr. John Sugar in 1604 included the forbidden *Agnus Deis*; many of the seminary priests wore them.[42] But the quote above can be identified with Fr. Sugar: his name is synonymous with "sweetness" and the alias he adopted was "Sweet."[43] In dealing with the magistrates, he appears to have been very "saucy" in the same sense that term is almost uniformly used in Shakespeare's plays, viz. *insolent*.[44] In 1604 English statute treated coining heaven's image in an *Agnus Dei* as the equivalent of murder but did not so equate bastardy. Was Shakespeare not questioning an actual state of law rather than a fictive one?

In another exchange, Isabella tells Angelo:

> were I under the terms of death,
> Th'impression of keen whips I'd wear as rubies,
> And strip myself to death as to a bed. [*Measure*, 2.4]

Critics of Isabella have seen these lines as infused with sexuality, as a beating fantasy growing from her repressed sexuality. A better reading would be that Shakespeare alludes to the whippings that were actually administered to the Catholic recusants, often when they were stripped naked. The executed Jesuit, Robert Southwell, wrote a petition to Queen Elizabeth attesting to the torture of many priests, who are "*whipped naked* so long and with such excess that our enemies, unwilling to give constancy the right name, said that no man without the help of the devil could with such undauntedness suffer so much."[45]

Viewing *Measure for Measure*, would James have seen himself in the role of the Duke or as Angelo (or as unleashing Angelo)? Critics have often written of similarities of James to the Duke. As mentioned above, James himself had stayed the execution of Cobham and Ralegh at the last minute, no less theatrically than the Duke does for Angelo.[46] Yet, the Duke and Angelo are two aspects of the same figure of Authority. It is the Duke who sets up Angelo to enforce the law; as Friar Thomas tells him, it is he who "unloose[d] this tied-up justice." Angelo is the agent of the Duke and thus an extension of him.[47]

The play asks the king, "Would you prefer to be seen as Angelo, or as the Duke?" If James sees himself as Angelo, his portrayal is harsh and unmerciful, and he has been given a public reproof. If James sees himself as the Duke, he can gain a distance from the laws of his land being strictly enforced; he can see that the harsh justice of the magistrate is excessive and tainted by corruption. A king observing a play about a sovereign's exercise of his God-given authority cannot avoid reflecting on his own exercise of power. King James himself described a king as an actor on a stage in *Basilikon Doron*.[48]

The soliloquy of the actor playing the Duke on the stage can be seen as an instruction, a cautionary sermon to a king on wise governance. James will have beheld a sovereign declaim:

> He who the sword of heaven will bear
> Should be as holy as severe;
> Pattern in himself to know,

> Grace to stand, and virtue go;
> More nor less to others paying
> Than by self-offenses weighing.
> Shame to him whose cruel striking
> Kills for faults of his own liking!
> Twice treble shame on Angelo,
> To weed my vice and let his grow! [*Measure*, 3.2]

What sovereign would not prefer to be the Duke rather than Angelo? In subsequent acts, the Duke applies craft against vice, to bring both justice and mercy to the parties to the drama. Wrongs are righted, the afflicted are comforted, the mighty are afflicted, and punishment is meted but with a more gentle hand than the law provides expressly. The play ends with four marriages or potential marriages. Left enigmatic is whether Isabella will accept the Duke's proposal, which has been made twice. The playwright seems to ask, Will the King and the Catholic recusants be joined in spouse-like union?

The Hapsburg Duke and Isabella of Brussels

James could well have imagined himself sharing characteristics of the Duke, but he and his queen must have been struck by the close parallels between the Duke and Isabella and another couple well known to both King James and Queen Anne. The play can be taken as a graceful portrayal of the couple who were the new rulers of the Hapsburg Netherlands. The Duke can be identified clearly with Lucio's comment: "If the Duke, with the other dukes, come not to composition with the King of Hungary, why then all the dukes fall upon the King." This accurately described a controversy among the Hapsburgs at the time of the play. Archduke Albert, a younger son of the Holy Roman emperor Maximilian II, was a Hapsburg. Albert's brothers in 1604 were Rudolf II, Matthias and Maximilian. Rudolf was Holy Roman Emperor and King of Hungary but was mentally unstable. Rudolf's brothers were struggling to remove him from control of Hungary, and they succeeded in having the authority granted to Matthias in 1605.[49] Thus the play was correct in assessing Hapsburg political circumstances that if the Archduke Albert did not reach agreement with Rudolf (the King of Hungary) then all the dukes would fall upon the King. By setting the play in Vienna, Austria, by using the Archduchess's own Spanish name and by identifying others in the Archduke's family, the author left little question that he intended the play to identify the Archdukes to anyone aware of dynastic affairs.

Just as the law had slipped in *Measure*'s Vienna and the Duke wishes to restore order, so, too, did Albert and Isabella bring good order to the Hapsburg Netherlands.[50] The absolute authority of Archduke Albert was essentially as depicted for the Duke and Angelo.[51] Other details of Albert's background and authority offer striking similarities to the Duke. When Lucio refers to the Duke in disguise, he calls him "Goodman Baldpate," even though the friar seems to be hooded, as noted by editors of the play. Baldpate refers to the tonsure given upon taking of minor orders. As Albert had taken lower orders, he was tonsured by the papal nuncio in May 1577. Three months later he became a subdeacon and the next year a deacon. Although his ordination was planned, he was never ordained a priest. However, he was elevated to status of "cardinal priest," rather than cardinal-deacon.[52]

Although he could not hear confessions as an ordained priest, Albert had strong powers of the church and heard confessions in another sense. Albert was appointed by his uncle, King Philip II, as first viceroy of Portugal in 1583. Also in 1583, the Pope made Albert papal legate for Portugal. He "was almost as much the alter ego of the pope as he was the alter-ego of the king."[53] He was invested with a vast share of the spiritual jurisdiction of the papacy; he could *inter alia* "judge a wide range of cases, hand out or remit penalties, give dispensations and indulgences…."[54] Significantly, in 1586, the new Pope, Sixtus V, named Albert inquisitor-general, giving him control of the Portuguese Inquisition. The portrayal of Duke Vincentio by Shakespeare has led one critic to describe him as a "grand inquisitor."[55]

Other markers identifying Isabella with the Archduchess Isabella are equally strong. Isabella is a Spanish name.[56] The Isabella of the play is an especially pious woman who is visiting in a nunnery, but not yet a member. She is "in probation of a sisterhood," among the votarists of the order of Saint Clare. To remove any doubt that the Franciscan order of Poor Clares is intended, the playwright gives the nun who accompanies Isabella the name *Francisca*. Is the playwright's choice of the order of the Clares a gracious allusion to the name of Isabella *Clara* Eugenia, the Archduchess? Or is it more? The playwright's knowledge of Isabella, the Infanta, was apparently such that he knew she had ties to the Franciscan order of Poor Clares all her life. She had close contact with the order as a girl, in the Poor Clares' convent of the Descalzas Reales—the Royal Convent of the Unshod at Madrid. It was within the curtilage of the royal palace in which she grew up. The church of the Descalzas functioned like a court chapel. In the 1580s, two of Isabella's close relations became members of the community, Empress Maria, who was sister of Philip II, widow of the Emperor Maximilian II, and mother of Archduke Albert; and her daughter Margarita, sister of Archduke Albert, who in 1584 took her vows in the convent church, escorted to the altar by Philip and the Infanta Isabella. After her father's death in 1598, Isabella stayed eight months at the Descalzas, with Maria and Margarita, until her marriage to Albert was consummated at Valencia in April 1599. Thus, just as the play's Isabella is at a nunnery of Saint Clare in the period immediately before her anticipated marriage to the Duke, so, too, was Isabella in a nunnery of Saint Clare in the period just before her marriage to the Archduke.[57]

As the marriage plans for Albert and Isabella were made in 1596, the Spanish Court (including Isabella) was at Toledo, the seat for which Cardinal Albert had been appointed. *Measure for Measure* makes allusion to the shift of the Duke from religious leader in Spain to spouse of Isabella as they prepare for marriage in a way that would be perfectly applicable to Cardinal priest Albert and his intended spouse:

> Duke: Come hither, Isabel.
>   Your friar is now your prince. As I was then
>   Advertising and holy to your business,
>   Not changing heart with habit, I am still
>   Attorney'd at your service. [*Measure*, 5.1]

The Cardinal Archduke was given dispensation by the Pope to wed Isabella, so that the two could rule the Hapsburg Netherlands. It would be accurate for Archduke Albert coming to his quasi-sovereignty of the Hapsburg Netherlands to say of himself as the Duke of *Measure for Measure* says of himself:

> Escalus: Of whence are you?
> Duke: Not of this country, though my chance is now
>   To use it for my time. I am a brother
>   Of gracious order, late come from the See
>   In special business from his Holiness [the Pope]. [*Measure*, 3.2]

The "special business" from the Pope is doubly true for Archduke Albert, for he had remained the papal legate and inquisitor-general for Portugal after he left Lisbon in 1593.[58]

Albert shared certain other characteristics with Duke Vicentio. Just as the latter was shy of crowds, secretive, and a dissimulator, so, too, was Archduke Albert. As described by the most recent historian of the Archdukes' reign, "Albert spoke little and in a soft voice. His demeanour was grave and composed. In fact his studied appearance hid a very shy man, who hated crowds and found it difficult not to blush in the presence of women." The papal nuncio, Guido Cardinal Bentivoglio, observed: "he is a prince of impenetrable secrecy, and no less with his face than with his words."[59] Bentivoglio compared him to Trajanus, the first Roman emperor born in Spain, "of all his good faculties, there is none in which the two are as alike as in dissimulation."[60]

King James and Relations with the Hapsburg Netherlands

James, as King of Scotland, was acutely aware of the change in government in the Hapsburg Netherlands. Perhaps he saw it in the light of recent historians who have described it "a supreme gesture of conciliation" by King Philip II.[61] James, still in Scotland, sent an envoy in November 1600 to congratulate the Archdukes upon their accession. Cordial relations followed between the two royal couples.[62] Queen Anne was known to be inwardly Catholic,[63] and she admired her pious sister sovereign, Isabella. Queen Anne had multiple reasons to identify closely with the Infanta Isabella. Both were daughters of European kings who had been disappointed initially by the birth of female offspring. For reasons of dynastic politics, both were transplanted from the land of their birth to a distant capital where their native tongue was foreign. Each had a younger brother who had recently become king of the country of their birth.[64]

James was aware that Isabella had a claim to the throne of England. As related earlier, Catholic exiles had put forth Isabella's candidacy in *The Conference on the Next Succession*. The Spanish Council of Philip III toyed with the possibility of her installation in London and removal from Brussels. But all such possibilities were rejected as improbable by realists. Thomas Wilson (one of the Cecil Secretariat), for example, ranked her twelfth among candidates, her number "may well be the last because it is the least to be reckned of and furthest of[f]."[65] Most importantly, the Archdukes had no desire to challenge James or rule England. When James became King of England early in 1603, the Archdukes immediately showed their acceptance of his legitimacy. They sent Charles de Ligne, Count Arenberg, to London with letters of credence recognizing James's lawful status.[66] Without Spanish approval, Albert allowed English ships into the ports he controlled and released English prisoners of war. In response, James unilaterally declared a ceasefire between England and the Low Countries.[67]

Charles della Faille, Secretary to Count Arenberg at the Archdukes' legation in London, was entrusted with a large parcel to carry from Brussels to England.[68] It held large portraits of Archduke Albert and Isabella. These were presented to Queen Anne by Count Arenberg at Woodstock Palace late in September 1603. When Queen Anne asked how she could reciprocate, Arenberg expressed hope she would promote peace with the Hapsburgs and help to diminish the aid that was being sent to the Dutch who were fighting against the Archdukes.[69]

Meeting with representatives of the Archdukes in 1604, Queen Anne once again expressed her high regard for Isabella. She promised she would never cease wearing a miniature portrait of the Infanta Isabella she had received, "until she died, being convinced that Her Highness was wearing hers and that their friendship was as indissoluble as a knot and as strong as a rock." And knowing that Isabella's livery was red, white and blue, England's queen continued that "the colours red and white are mine and for the love I bear to the Infanta I shall add blue."[70]

At the time of the performance of *Measure for Measure*, the Court of the Archdukes in Brussels was one of the chief diplomatic centers of Europe.[71] But there were also dynastic reasons for the strong cordiality between the Stewart royalty and the Archdukes. James and Anne were parents and were expecting another child as *Measure for Measure* was performed. They were thinking about to whom their children should be married. The sovereignty of the Archdukes would become complete if they bore children. A report of May 1603 indicated that James was considering "to visit the Archduke and the Infanta there (Flanders) himself, to treat of a marriage between the Prince and the Princess which the Infanta now goes withal."[72] At the time of the negotiations for the treaty of 1604 the king took the Archdukes' ambassador aside and, pointing to his three children, said he wished "with all his heart his cousins, your masters, to have just as many." Queen Anne more directly asked if they still had no children.[73]

Sterrell must have enjoyed the performance of *Measure for Measure*. He will have watched the reaction of the king to the Duke's lecture on bearing the sword of heaven. He will have been satisfied by the appearance of a religiously-affected Duke and his nun-like mate named Isabella, the two resembling so closely the sovereigns in Brussels whom he had served for near a decade and would yet serve many more years to come. It was a busy holiday season for him, overseeing the Palace of St. John's housing the Revels and its many activities. It was likewise a busy season for Shakespeare, the leading Court playwright. *Othello*, the Moor of Venice, had just been performed on November 1 and the Sunday following was a repeat performance of *The Merry Wives of Windsor*. The ensuing several weeks had scheduled performances of the *Comedy of Errors*, *Loves Labour's Lost*, *Henry V*, and the *Merchant of Venice*. Sterrell will have gone between his fashionable new dwelling in the White Horse tenement in Long Ditch, Westminster, or to rooms he maintained in his leasehold of the Revels Palace, or to an office at Whitehall where he assisted Worcester. The thoughts of rebellion he had entertained in the summer of 1603 were now put aside, replaced by efforts to ameliorate the conditions of Catholics in England and to secure tolerance through the eventual succession of James's heir. His employer and patron was, after Robert Cecil, the most influential member of the King's Council and Court, Worcester's wife and daughters were closely associated with the queen, and Worcester's sons were classmates and companions to the royal sons. Even as he was enjoying the entertainments of the Christ-

24. Measure for Measure

The Infanta Isabella Clara Eugenia (1566–1633), Archduchess of Austria (Artist: Frans Pourbus the Younger; Royal Collection Trust/© Her Majesty Queen Elizabeth II 2015).

mas and New Year's season, his special standing at Court and his proximity to the royal family, events again put Sterrell in jeopardy, the greatest of his long career. Letters came into the hands of government agents and were passed up to the king's principal minister, just as had occurred twenty years earlier, when Walsingham learned of the acts of "Kirby" in transporting seminary youth in the French ambassador's ship. Robert Cecil closed in on Thomas Phelippes and immediately caught him in lies, forcing the Decipherer to decode his own ciphers and to implicate his close associate, William Sterrell. Then Cecil turned to Sterrell.

25

Cecil's Interrogations
Phelippes's Lies and Sterrell's Equivocations

Winwood's Report

Robert Cecil was probably suspicious of Worcester's secretive secretary well before January 1605. Some in the government, besides Essex, knew of "Robinson's" work as early as 1592 when Sterrell was working in Flanders and sending back correspondence under that alias. In 1594, William Waad was an intermediary between Sterrell and some members of the Council who were aware of Sterrell's intelligence work. Cecil may have understood Sterrell was at work in the Boulant overtures between 1598 and 1602. He would have thought Sterrell was a double agent. But to which master is the double agent truly loyal? If either.

A contemporary of Sterrell from Magdalen College alerted Cecil to Sterrell's activities in Flanders that would have been troubling to one who thought Sterrell was spying *against* the Catholic refugees. Ralph Winwood had transferred to Magdalen in 1578 and was with the College for a number of years while Sterrell was a student, fellow and praelector. Later, as secretary to Sir Henry Neville, Winwood participated in the Anglo-Spanish negotiations at Boulogne in the summer of 1600. After a brief visit to London where he received instructions from Cecil, Winwood returned to Paris where, in the absence of Neville, he served as the queen's agent until August 1602. This was just at the time of the Archpriest controversy, and Winwood was in the middle of the intrigues surrounding it. One of the people who turned to Winwood was Charles Paget, who had fled Brussels and Liège to take shelter in Paris. Paget sought to curry favor with the English government by betraying his former associates in Brussels. One of those was Thomas James. Another: William Sterrell.

In April 1602, Winwood dispatched a group of letters, the Wicham/Derrick letters from 1594, of Sterrell to Fr. Sherwood, together with Sterrell's cipher sheets. These were surely supplied by Paget, filched by him from Fr. Sherwood. Winwood informed Cecil[1]:

> Right honorable I have often sollicited 143 to discover if during his ++++ in Flanders he knew any now in England which are pensioners to the enemy or any other that holdeth intelligence with him. Now this last week falling into the same discourse he named unto me one William Stirrell, who as he sayeth for many years hath had correspondence, first with Thomas Fitzherbert, since with Owen and Sherewood [Sherwood] a priest, and doth receive a pension by their means. I heretofore have known one of that name, sometimes of Magdalen College in Oxford, and since belonging to the Earl of Worcester, but whether he be the same man I may not affirm. Herewith I send your Honor many of his letters though signed with a contrary name, and the cifer and address of Sherewood, with an acquaintance of money received: all

which the party above named delivered to me yesterday in the afternoon. I have thought it convenient to advertise this, apart from my ordinary dispatch.

If Cecil had confronted Sterrell with these letters, Sterrell had a ready explanation: Sir William Waad was aware of the correspondence when it occurred. He was trying to gain cooperation of William Higham and the Catholics overseas to engage in the "traffick of Arbella" and to obtain intelligence about Spanish intentions towards peace. More difficult to explain would have been the report of long correspondence also with Fitzherbert and Owen. Cecil will have noted Winwood's report but probably took no action against Sterrell. After all, the intelligence from Paget was eight years old, and Cecil already had reason to doubt Paget after the tricks played on him by Phelippes (with Sterrell).

Phelippes Arrested

On January 25, 1605, Cecil gave a polite note to Thomas Windebank, clerk of the Privy Council, to bring "hither Mr. Phillips [Phelippes] because I would be glad to speak with him."[2] No one was to be allowed to deliver Phelippes any message or letter on the way. But London society learned of the arrest almost immediately. John Chamberlain wrote to his friend Ralph Winwood: "I heard yesterday that Phelippes the deciferer was apprehended and committed and all his papers seized: how far the matter may spread is not yet discovered, for it is very new. All that I could learn is that he held correspondence with one Owen an ancient fugitive about [close to] the Archduke."[3]

As Chamberlain's letter indicated, Phelippes correspondence with Hugh Owen had been discovered. Letters of "Vincent" to "Benson" were intercepted and were identified as from Phelippes to Owen. Hence the seizure of all of Phelippes' correspondence.

So extraordinary was the spying matter, and so sensitive, that the investigation was carried out by the king's Principal Minister and Secretary of State himself, Robert Cecil, now Lord Viscount Cranborne. No other proceeding of the time seems comparable. Not even the Attorney General, Edward Coke, seems to have been consulted. The day of the Windebank arrest of Phelippes, Cecil conducted an interrogation which took the form of his writing out a question, below which Phelippes would write his answer, followed immediately on the same sheet by another Cecil question, and so on over several sheets.

Cecil's first question: "What intelligence or correspondency by letters or messages do you hold with any persons in foreign parts? If any with whom?" Phelippes's first words echo his opening words in a letter to Essex in 1596[4]: "I have taken some care to entertain an ancient apposted Intelligence, which was set on foot in the late Queen's time for her service as your Lordship partly did know." The means, he goes on to explain, is letters sent "by the ordinary Dutch post of Antwerp." The writer is "not known to me otherwise than as I suppose by circumstances to be Owen," and the letters are sent "under a direction to Peter Hallyns."

Cecil demanded to know how many letters Phelippes had sent, where were copies, and whether they were in cipher as they were in the queen's time. Phelippes was under great pressure and immediately lied. A huge mistake. He said he only randomly kept copies, had ceased marking the dates and "of late time I did not use any cifer but open discourse." Holding back what he knew to the contrary, Cecil then asked what aliases were used. Owen used the name Simon de Witt, Phelippes said. As for the letters to Owen back from England, Owen "thinketh them to come from a friend of Mr. Sterrell's who was the first that set it afoot being employed by my lord of Essex." In fact—unknown to Owen and his master Archduke Albert, so Phelippes claims to Cecil—that friend is Phelippes himself.

Cecil knew Phelippes was lying and now repeated his question about the use of ciphers, asking: "Because you say you wrote not in cipher of late time, what do you call late time. And because you seem to have had no speech with Styrrill of late, set down when you spoke last with him, where and what he said to you." Phelippes compounded his guilt by repeating his lie:

> I write not in cifer since a little after the peace was concluded. I saw Mr. Stirrell upon Tuesday as I take it: He asked me then whether I used [continued] to write or no and I told him no. He said that Charles Paget haunted him again with his old accusation which Sir W. Wade had told him of long since and prayed me to speak to Sir W. Wade in it. And truly Mr. Stirrell doth not know the same intelligence was continued in any sort.

Phelippes was unaware of what prompted his arrest and his interrogation by the King's Minister. With the next question, Phelippes heart will have sunk, for it would now be clear what Cecil had in his possession. Cecil asked: "Whether did you ever write to one Benson or not, and whether do you know doctor Taylor or not, when spoke you with him and about what and where." Phelippes responded:

> I know the name of Benson which I have sometimes used. I know D. Taylor. I spake with him last as I take it on Sunday at dinner at a friends one Mr. Ball in Fetter Lane who had invited him and me and others. I had no serious talk with him I am sure for that I know him to be a man of no moment otherwise than desirous to do service for the peace.

These were interesting companions: Dr. Taylor was the Archdukes' agent and John Ball served the Spanish ambassador.

With that, Cecil now had Phelippes affix his signature, as did three witnesses who countersigned as "read in the presence of us": Thomas Windebank, Levynus Munck, and R. Percival. These were three officials well trusted by Cecil. Apparently, when this was done Cecil produced the evidence that established Phelippes was lying in his examination. Cecil held a group of intercepted letters written in the preceding weeks of January by "Vincent" to "Benson," to which name Phelippes had just admitted to using, who was Hugh Owen; this was not Simon de Witt. They employed cipher, the use of which Phelippes had moments before denied, "since a little after the peace was concluded"—i.e., August 1604. No, these in cipher were only a few weeks old. Cecil required Thomas Phelippes to write on the back of it, "I confess this to be my hand," in front of the same three witnesses who had just signed Phelippes's examination responses. Phelippes surely trembled as Cecil gave him one of the letters to decipher, a letter of January 9, 1605. But it would be several days before Phelippes would get it back to the Prime Minister. Cecil was thus probably ignorant of its contents when Sterrell was examined the day after Phelippes's interrogation.

Did Cecil believe Phelippes that Sterrell's service had terminated? Perhaps Sterrell was Cecil's bigger prize to catch and he had seized Phelippes first to build the case against Sterrell. Cecil arranged for examinations of two of Phelippes's servants, Edward Petre[5] and Abraham Ferkin,[6] and himself wrote out questions for Phelippes's brother, Stephen. The dates of the servants' examinations are uncertain. Petre gave information about Thomas Barnes. Ferkin implicated Barnes, Dr. Taylor, "Freeman," "Johnson," and "Mr. Matthew."

Freeman, as seen earlier, was Robert Spiller; however, the identity of "Freeman" was not established until after the Gunpowder Plot later in the year. "Johnson" was Richard Fulwood, probably the same "Johnson" whom Thomas Phelippes sought to have released from prison in 1601; Fulwood worked closely with Robert Spiller and Fr. Garnet.

Stephen Phelippes wrote out his answers the day after his brother was examined. Cecil specifically asked him about his knowledge of "Receipts by Styrrill or for Stirrill" and the names used to write to him. The answers of Stephen Phelippes show that he had been aware of his brother's and William Sterrell's correspondence abroad for some five or six years. As related earlier, Sterrell had given money to Stephen for the sake of Thomas while Thomas was in prison around 1595. On other occasions, Sterrell had Stephen "fetch" money for Thomas from different merchants, but he did not know the source of the money, though clearly it was from abroad. Thomas, he said, complained that he was not well dealt with in that he had nothing given him when the Constable of Castile was here, i.e., at the time of the Spanish peace treaty of August 1604.

Sterrell's Interrogation

The same day that Stephen Phelippes gave evidence, Sterrell responded to interrogatories written out in Robert Cecil's rapid scrawl. The first question:

1. How come you first to deal with Owen? What monies or rewards had you from that side either by way of gift, payment or account?

Sterrell's response is in a "secretary" hand, a fluid handwriting style that allowed rapid writing and limited the need to lift the pen from the paper when forming letters. It is in the first person but it may be the hand of a stenographer taking down Sterrell's oral testimony. Sterrell said that the first time ever he saw Owen or heard of his name was in the Castle of Antwerp. One Sherwin, a priest, brought Owen to Sterrell. It was by Owens's means that Sterrell was set at liberty. Sterrell did not explain that he had been seized in Antwerp from a mistaken identity; the alias he had chosen was the same as the name of another Englishman the Duke of Parma's men were trying to apprehend. Later, at the resort at Spa of the Ardennes near Liège, Sterrell again met Owen who sought to have Sterrell return to England and enter into correspondence with him. "At my return I acquainted the Earl [of Essex] with the matter and Mr. Phelippes whom the Earl then used. The Earl willed me to entertain the correspondence."

The second question concerned money.

2. How were you paid them, and who had any part of it with you?

Sterrell answered:

Owen promised then to send me 30 crowns monthly but never performed. Long after, he wrote to me to be more diligent and he would perform. I acquainted the Earl with it, he willed me to do so and wished me to get what I could. At length Owen sent it and continued but with such conditions as that by laying out my money for him for such things as he did want I got little by it and this is all he sent me for all my travail and forbearance of my money. This money with my own laid out was paid by the post of Antwerp. No man had any part with me of the 30 crowns which came always quarterly.

This testimony conflicted with what Stephen Phelippes told Cecil. According to Stephen, Sterrell had been a significant source of money for Thomas Phelippes.

Next, Cecil demanded justification for Sterrell's corresponding with an enemy of England.

3. Why did you hold correspondence with anybody there, not being warranted? What did Phillips answer you when you told that you heard your name was used to Owen?

Sterrell needed to make it clear immediately that his correspondence with traitors had been warranted. He had already said that he was in the service of Essex, and now he said he could prove it. Such proof was very important to him. In 1592 Sterrell had demanded that Thomas Phelippes provide him with proof that he was working for the government of her Majesty. Essex had provided it. So Sterrell was able to respond: "I never had correspondence there with any but in the late Queen's time. The Earl of Essex employed me. I have his passport to show and a letter." He went on to say that he had later told Phelippes not to correspond in his name. Since the coming of King James in 1603, Sterrell would have nothing to do with such correspondence and was privy to nothing more of it. Since the king's coming, he only met with Phelippes by chance and would immediately depart.

Did others know of the correspondence? Cecil knew well that a passport granted by a dead man could be forged. Phelippes had the reputation of being the English government's principal forger of documents at one time. Was there any one who could confirm William Sterrell's story?

4. Who were acquainted with your correspondence besides Mr. Bacon and Mr. Waad?

Sterrell's response is bold. He laid the foundation of the correspondence a decade earlier, when he prepared for just such a scene as he now played out. He invokes the protection of the deceased queen, Elizabeth. Phelippes had not mentioned the queen in his answers. Sterrell makes her a manager of his intelligence. Sterrell's response was certain to insure that Cecil could do little to him, at least publicly: "They were acquainted with this correspondence: the Queen Majesty, the Earl of Essex, Mr. Francis Bacon, Mr. William Wade, and Mr. Phillips." The first two were now dead. The Earl of Essex died in February 1601 and the queen in March 1603. Although Essex was executed for rebellion against the queen, his name was once again highly regarded, and King James had publicly praised Essex and had restored his estates to Essex's children. Two of the other three men Sterrell named were living and were highly placed. Francis Bacon was a counselor to the king, while William Waad was now lieutenant of the Tower of London. Sterrell could not mention them as being acquainted with his correspondence unless it were true, for if it were not true and Bacon or Waad testified to the contrary, Sterrell could be put to death for treason. He went on to say, "The three last were acquainted with it, every man in his turn as the Queen or the Earl would employ them." And Sterrell could not resist adding a statement to exculpate himself from deceit in his own dealings with Cecil. To dispel the conclusion that he had cozened Cecil or that he was not worthy of credit, he added: "And I was told by Mr. Phelippes that your lordship was privy to it also but I never spoke with your lordship about it." The last phrase is a tantalizing indication of familiarity between the two men, for it is implicit that they had spoken upon other matters. What other conversations had Cecil and Sterrell entertained together?

Sterrell's list of five was surely incomplete and Cecil would well have understood this. Whose name is missing? Sterrell's employer for the prior fifteen plus years: the Earl of

Worcester. Even Ralph Winwood who was out of England for much of the last decade knew of Sterrell as "belonging to the Earl of Worcester" ever since he had left Magdalen College and Winwood had so informed Cecil. It was convenient for both Cecil and Sterrell to pretend mutually that Worcester was entirely in the dark about his agent's extensive contacts with the fugitives abroad, a useful fiction.

Now Cecil turned to current payments. Was there a continuing pension from abroad flowing to Sterrell or to Phelippes?

5. What monies have you received since the King's coming and how much upon old reckonings and how much upon new and whether has Phillips or any other received in your name any money or merchandise since the King's coming?

Sterrell said that he had not received a penny or a gift since the king had come to London in 1603 except for £80 that had been due from the quarter before. He had given instructions not to send more money in his name.

Cecil had several more questions, but that page has been lost from the public records. They related to other matters involving Sterrell of which Cecil was already aware. One was the redemption of the jewels of the House of Burgundy that the Archduke sought. Cecil had known of that at the time of the Boulant correspondence touching upon peace. Sterrell responded:

> After the 30 Crowns had been continued some space of 2 years as I remember, they wrote that if I could find them some in good place that could negotiate the matter of peace and deal for the redeeming for the Archdukes jewells there should be procured £200 yearly for him. At that time Mr. Phelippes was appointed again to be my overseer by the Earl of Essex. He took hold of it, and handled the matter of peace and jewells in such sort as they paid it and continued it till the Christmas before the Queen died, but it came not till his Majesty that now is was come, and this was the last money that ever I did know of, 50£ was for him, 30£ for me, but I had laid out for them about that Christmas, for rebato ruffes, silk stockings, girdles and hangers, more the half of that I had.

Cecil finally took up the correspondence that the government had recently intercepted between "Vincent" and "Benson," the latest which Phelippes had undertaken. Sterrell said he knew of no money received by Phelippes since the king's accession, and he did not believe that the men on the other side knew Phelippes as Phelippes; they thought him some other person. He then defended his correspondence and said it had ended years earlier.

> I was sent over by the Earl of Essex to stay in the low countries and send him intelligence but by reason of the intercepting of my letters I was constrained to return. And her Majestie with the Earl of Essex did often acknowledge that by my means there was good intelligence came to them, but about 2 years before her Majestie died I did seldom write leaving the whole managing of the intelligence to Mr. Phelippes and the sole writing of it. The money came some time by post sometime by exchange.

Could Sterrell trust Phelippes not to betray Sterrell's much greater involvement than he admitted to? The answer is both yes and no. Yes, because Phelippes understood that his only hope not to remain in prison for life or to be executed lay with Sterrell and Sterrell's employer, the Earl of Worcester. So, Phelippes could do nothing to betray Sterrell. He had watched too many others be executed, despite full confessions, to think that he could win reprieve by inculpating Sterrell further than Cecil already knew. As Phelippes spun out confessions and justifications over the next couple of years, he took great care to exonerate Sterrell of all involvement since the coming of James in 1603. Just four days after his initial statements, Phelippes wrote a long letter to Cecil. Phelippes understands, as did Sterrell, that Cecil was only concerned with the intelligence activities since James became king.

Phelippes again told Cecil: "It is true that at the Q[ueen's] death all was broken off to our thinking. And in truth Sterrell knows no other at this day."⁷ Beyond this, Sterrell probably did not trust Phelippes and never had.

Phelippes knew, of course, of the letters coming in to England to "Hallins," but he probably never saw the contents of the letters in the "Anthony Rivers" series, which were the outgoing side of the correspondence. Sterrell and Spiller and Garnet surely kept Phelippes in ignorance of most of the activities of the Jesuits, even though Phelippes was advancing their cause. In fact, this is probably why Phelippes's "Vincent" letters were intercepted by the government; Phelippes had lost the more secure conveyance that the "Rivers" letters had enjoyed. Moreover, when the possibility arose, Phelippes sought to try to betray the Jesuits to Cecil. He first promised to try to keep the "Vincent-Benson" correspondence alive for the benefit of the king and then offered, should a decision to break it off be reached, he would "would undertake to point out your time to take the Jesuits' packet and to hunt themselves to[o] if your Lo. do not apprehend it to be better first to see what will be the course they begin to take with the Fr[ench] K[ing] for there goes the hare away."⁸

Cecil surely suspected that William Sterrell was telling him far less than the whole truth about his correspondence with the overseas fugitives. But what evidence had he? Nothing in Cecil's possession suggested a plot to overthrow the government and nothing suggested that Sterrell was himself practicing the Catholic religion or harboring priests or Jesuits. Even if Cecil had more, what could he do with it? Pressing Sterrell would have caused still greater problems, for it might implicate Sterrell's patron, Worcester. Could Cecil rupture his fruitful collaboration with Worcester? Might not the king side with Worcester, James's hunting and riding companion who was as useful to the monarchy as Cecil himself was? Better to keep after Phelippes who had few friends at Court (though occasionally useful and used). When time served an occasion, Cecil could take condign action on Sterrell. Still, it must have been galling to Cecil a few days after his questioning of Sterrell to get Phelippes's decipherment of the Phelippes/Vincent letter to Hugh Owen dated January 9. The ciphers had concealed a detailed account of deliberations of the king and Cecil with a few other close advisers about how to respond to Dutch forcible inspection of ships on the high seas. It was political intelligence of the highest order, an account and analysis of discussions of the English king's innermost circle on topics of great importance to England's relations with the Dutch, Flanders, and Spain. Cecil read an account of his own arguments in the closed meeting. The writer suggested that Cecil's motives in the discussions were less than honorable and forthright, observing that "there will be no other issue than I have heretofore told you if this be true, as I cannot see but it should unless the Lo. Vicount [Cecil] do that he seemeth to do *pour tant plus encherir la merchandize.*" [French phrase—*for the purpose of making the merchandise more costly*]. The enciphered report's basis in first-hand observation is clear: "The E[arl] of Worcester seconded the Lo. Wotton's opinion honorably and so did the E[arl] of Northampton substancially *who came in while they were reasoning the case.*"

Who could be Phelippes's source for such detail except the Earl of Worcester's secretary and agent, William Sterrell? Of course Cecil had to investigate the matter of Phelippes and Sterrell himself. The Earl of Worcester—Privy Councilor and Master of the Horse—was second only to Cecil in power and influence in the English government. Revelation of the fact that Worcester's closest confidante had for years been engaged in intelligence with the most notorious traitors abroad and with English Jesuits could have caused a crisis in government as great as the Essex Revolt just a few years earlier.[9] It was better not to sort through all of Phelippes's trunks of letters that had been seized to make a case against Sterrell or Phelippes. A public trial would have been a huge embarrassment, calling into question Cecil's own governance in the last years of Elizabeth's reign. Sterrell went quietly on his way and Phelippes was relegated, without legal proceedings, to prison in the Gatehouse and then to house arrest.[10] A few months later Cecil was able to put Worcester into an awkward position where his loyalty could be tested.

26

A Stir in Wales
The Whitsun Commotion, 1605

If discovery of Sterrell's involvement with Hugh Owen and other Catholic opponents of the government was a peril to Sterrell, a different threat was presented to Worcester only four months later by other assertive Catholics. These were stirring up trouble only a short distance from his castle at Raglan in Monmouthshire.

The outbreak of violence began on May 21, 1605, in tiny Allensmore, a few miles southwest of Hereford and twenty-odd miles northeast of Raglan. A Catholic woman, Alice Wellington, had been denied burial rites by the local vicar. Early on a Tuesday morning, an assembly of 40 or 50 Catholic men and women, bearing both arms and candles, laid the simple woman to rest. The vicar's vehement protests were unheeded, so he hurried to the Bishop of Hereford to name names among the burial party, mostly spinners and weavers by trade.

The defiant act of faith was an outgrowth of the mission activities of at least three Catholic priests active in the area. One was a Jesuit, Robert Jones, later to become Superior of his order in England and Wales and to reside with the family of the Earl of Worcester. Jones was already closely associated with Worcester's son-in-law, William Morgan and had "converted" Morgan's wife, Frances.[1] Sterrell must have known William Morgan for years. Along with two brothers, Edward and George, William had been an Oxford student residing with John Case while Sterrell was lecturing at Magdalen College. A second priest was Roger Cadwallader, who will be executed five years later. The third was James Morris, who used the *alias* of Jones.

The Bishop of Hereford, Robert Bennet, was ham-handed in dealing with controversies within his jurisdiction. He was unsuited for his position by experience and by temperament. He confessed his own inability to handle the situation: "I am a stranger in these parts." The malice of the locals was directed against him.

Rumors reached the Court that a thousand Catholics had banded together in arms. The constables sent by the justices had been forced to retire. The Venetian ambassador reported that the king and Council were meeting daily and knew not what course to pursue.[2] He noted that the countryside was full of Catholics and ripe for revolt "thanks to the despair to which the insupportable cruelty and extortions have driven them."

William Morgan was arrested and sent to London. Held initially at the Hermitage, Charing Cross, he was moved to the Tower of London at the suggestion of Sir William Waad. Morgan was examined by the Council on June 17 and by Chief Justice Popham and Attorney General Coke the day following but his statements produced little useful information.

The government decided to attempt to defuse the crisis. Simultaneously, Catholics in London and Wales saw the prudence of the same course. The hope was that the Earl of Worcester, known as a "Church Papist" and highly regarded as a Welsh leader, could pacify the region without bloodshed. He was lord-lieutenant of Glamorganshire and Monmouthshire as well as a member of the inner circle of the Privy Council. Probably it was at his own suggestion that he was sent into Wales and Herefordshire to effect a resolution.[3]

Both the Archpriest and the Jesuit Superior strove to bring about peace. George Blackwell, the Archpriest, issued a letter on June 22 to the Catholic clergy in England to "suppress all the late suspected attempts and proceedings for liberty."[4] He directed them "to give notice to all our brethren, especially to such as are in or about those parts, in which such unlawful matters are suspected to have been contrived or devised." Two days later, Garnet wrote to Rome for a papal brief condemning Catholics who took up arms. He reported that he had already hindered four tumults and had persuaded the rebels to send a messenger to Rome.[5]

By the end of June Worcester had left for Wales. Learning of his mission and of the displeasure of the king and Council, the Welsh Catholics sent three men to explain how the events had arisen and to persuade the government of their loyalty and aversion to rebellion. Ambassador Molin reported that the men were immediately arrested and condemned to death. The gallows was kept up in readiness but execution was stayed pending some report back from Worcester of his efforts.[6]

Arriving at Raglan, Worcester immediately set to work to resolve the situation. A week later he sent to the king, via Robert Cecil, an ingenious report of what he had found and done. Informing his Majesty of the general state of the area, he assured him "of the quiet state of the country" rather than providing an "exact account of particular men's disloyal actions."

As Worcester related, Bishop Bennet and all the Justices of the Peace of the shire were assembled by Worcester at Raglan. To the group Worcester manifested "the zealous care his Majesty continually took for establishing of God's true religion and suppressing of Popish superstition, as being the religion he was born in, bred up in, and when he came to years of Government constantly professed." Yet, he continued, the king had learned that "these kind of people did mightily increase," i.e., persons of the Popish persuasion. He placed all the blame on the local government—religious and secular. Such increase could only be attributed to two causes: "either want of preaching and good instruction, or through negligence of Justices of Peace or inferior ministers." He demanded that the Bishop give an account to the king and that likewise the Justices were to give satisfaction. Subtly undercutting the move in London to provide harsher laws against recusants, Worcester informed the king and Cecil that "I told them that his Majesty conceived there were laws sufficient and the same laws gave them power and authority."

The next night, Tuesday, there was a general search throughout the shire such that the whole shire might at one instant be searched. Each Justice had the duty in his particular division to search in all suspected houses for "priests, Jesuits and obstinate recusants." Not all of the results were in by the time Worcester wrote his Friday report. He planned to go into Herefordshire the next Monday to arrange for follow-up and cooperation in searches in the two shires. In the meantime, he had laid "persons underhand," i.e., spies, to discover these priests. About Fr. Robert Jones, SJ, who was ministering to his daughter and son-in-law, Worcester said nothing. But Worcester did allude to a priest and to his own Catholicism in a light-hearted manner, while simultaneously undercutting the policy of the Archbishop of Canterbury, Richard Bancroft.

Saying he was done with the serious matters, Worcester now was ready to inform on himself. Lightheartedly, he wrote: "it is good to be the first informer hoping that I shall the easier obtain his Majesty's pardon. I have of late conferred with a seminary priest, nay more I have been at confession with him, but though he confessed his knavery in being a priest, I sought for no remission of my sins at his hand." The priest came into his hands through Sir Roger Bodenham. Sir Roger had chanced upon the priest who immediately confessed that he was an agent of the Archbishop of Canterbury, Richard Bancroft. Bancroft (when Bishop of London) had fomented the Archpriest controversy by pitting secular priests against the Jesuits. Now Bancroft was following the same policy by subverting a secular priest to move among the Catholics of Herefordshire and inform on them. Worcester reported with apparent surprise that the priest was the government's man:

> When he came, I found him to be the priest that my Lord had acquainted me with before my departure. After I had rated him publicly I told him I had other matters to charge him with and took him aside, hoping to have received some intelligence at his hand; but he delivered no more than formerly I had received, saying that he verily thinks the priests are all fled. He is gone to Glamorganshire; if any be come thither, he has promised to give me intelligence.

That is, Worcester found that he was the same priest/agent that Bancroft (or Cecil; the reference to "my Lord" is deliberately ambiguous) had told Worcester of. Worcester denounced him publicly but took him aside for intelligence. However, the priest could tell him nothing new and thus Worcester let him go on his way. Worcester's actions will have rendered the priest ineffectual in his areas of activity as Catholics learned of his treatment. That is, if the priest was really a turncoat and working for the government.

But who was this apparently apostate priest? He was called "Rice Griffiths." But this was just his latest alias. He was in fact George Williams, one of the lads Sterrell had helped to board the French Ambassador's boat in 1585. He managed to arrive at Rheims in 1587, was ordained in 1588 and returned into England a year later. He was imprisoned with George Errington, one the two men whom Sterrell had spoken for in convocation in 1587.

Bishop Bennet complained bitterly of Williams/Griffiths. He called him an instrument of Rome. He blamed both Bancroft and Cecil for misleading him and for exposing him to physical danger and ridicule, writing angrily to Cecil:

> The Archbishop of Canterbury recommended unto me Rice Griffithes, whose name is George Williams, as a priest who had submitted, taken the oath, abjured his priesthood and promised special service, to give him access to my ear and his liberty. You also wrote me letters to the same effect 2 years since. He has made semblance of service, but of late I have found him a perfidious man, a sycophant to me and a mere agent and spy for the Papists; as appears by depositions I purpose to send, containing matter of his saying mass, seducing the people, reconciling, confessing, marrying, assuring the priests and recusants of a toleration, disclosing my purposes, hindering service, bringing more priests into these parts and such like. For these matters I apprehended and committed him. At the Assizes came letters from the Archbishop that the judges should forbear him, and transmit him to him, and he is dismissed upon bond to appear in the King's Bench next term; to the great applause of papists and great appalling of well affected men. He never did service worth the least thanks, nay all the increase of priests and recusants here has proceeded from his treachery; and as often as I have admitted him to my chamber, so often have I been exposed to danger of my life...."[7]

Although Worcester had allowed Griffiths/Williams to leave for Glamorganshire, Bishop Bennet was so incensed by Griffiths that he had him arrested, interrogated and bound over for prosecution at the King's Bench. These actions in turn offended the Archbishop of Canterbury.[8]

That the priest was turned over to Worcester by Sir Roger Bodenham was itself indicative of the contrived nature of Worcester's proceedings. A major actor in the stirs was Thomas Prichard whom Bishop Bennett identified as "a man of Sir Roger Bodenham."[9] And a list of recusant Catholics forwarded to Cecil by Bishop Bennet identified "the principal and most dangerous Recusants in the diocese of Hereford...."[10] The first name was "The ladie Bridgett Boddenham, wife to Sir Roger Boddenham, Knight of the Bath."

George Williams was surely an agent not unlike Sterrell himself, playing a very dangerous role—appearing to the English government that he was cooperating with it to betray Catholics while he was actually using that appearance to gain information and perform acts helpful to the Catholics. That was the conclusion reached by Bishop Bennett. Bancroft and Cecil probably agreed inwardly but preferred for George Williams to go away quietly rather than admit they had been made pawns.

Worcester concluded his report by telling Cecil that he was "as weary with examinations of silly [innocent or simple] creatures as ever I was in my life," and commenting that he had had no time to view his parks since arriving at Raglan. The import of the conclusion and the entire report was that the crisis had been no crisis at all.

Worcester's report of July 5 was received in London within a few days and was immediately sent to the king at Windsor Castle. The Earls of Suffolk [Thomas Howard], Northampton [Henry Howard], and Salisbury [Cecil] informed Worcester that James had read the report "to his great satisfaction" and willed them to return Worcester thanks for taking so good a course to publish to His Majesty's subjects his great care to prevent all practices to the prejudice of the established religion. Worcester's journey was a "visible sign" of that care. His stay in Wales (to enjoy his parks) or return was left to his discretion.[11]

By early August, Ambassador Molin reported back to his government that the Welsh affair was over far more easily than was expected. Worcester had returned, informing the government that the movement was far inferior in importance than had been represented. Worcester, Molin said, put a few men in prison more for show than for punishment.[12] Similar reports made their way back to Hereford where Bishop Bennett complained that he had heard that Worcester "had given me and all the justices a check for sending up such untrue allegations."[13] He had also heard that Archbishop Bancroft "had persuaded the King that all those tumults were nothing but a broken head or two."

Worcester emerges from the 1605 episode as having achieved a successful conclusion that pleased the king's government and the English Catholics.[14] He reiterated his strong support of his king and deftly undercut the authority of the Bishop of Hereford and the Archbishop of Canterbury on Worcester's own ground, where his family continued to practice their faith. Unfortunately for Worcester, Sterrell and English Catholics, the successful handling of the 1605 stirs was eclipsed within four months by a catastrophic event nearly fatal to the Catholic church in England.

27

The Gunpowder Treason

The Gunpowder Plot and Plotters

In the early hours of November 5, 1605, Sir Thomas Knevett and a small party of men entered a building under lease to Thomas Percy, a gentleman pensioner—a member of the king's personal bodyguard. There, in a ground-floor vault that extended beneath the chambers of the House of Lords, they encountered a tall man wearing a cloak, a dark hat and riding boots. He gave his name as John Johnson. His true name was Guy Fawkes. Close at hand, hidden by faggots and brushwood, were thirty-six barrels of gunpowder, a ton or so of explosives intended to blow up the members of Parliament and their king as they assembled. Within hours a massive manhunt was under way for Fawkes's co-conspirators.

The principal figures of the Gunpowder Plot were: Robert Catesby, Thomas Percy, the Wintour brothers (Thomas and Robert), the Wright brothers (John and Christopher) and Guy Fawkes. Also involved, but with lesser roles, were Sir Everard Digby, Ambrose Rookwood, Robert Keyes, Thomas Bates and John Grant. All were gentlemen. Many of these conspirators had been associated with the Essex uprising. Several were part of the Spanish

The Gunpowder Plot Conspiritors, 1605 (Thomas Bates; Robert Winter; Christopher Wright; John Wright; Thomas Percy; Guy Fawkes; Robert Catesby; Thomas Winter) (© **National Portrait Gallery, London**).

Treason of 1602–03 recounted above. Unlike earlier plots, there is no reason to believe these men were prompted by government provocateurs.

Some time in January 1604 Catesby, Thomas Wintour and Guy Fawkes initiated a plan to overthrow the government, and John Wright was soon brought in. Thomas Percy, a cousin and retainer of Henry Percy, ninth earl of Northumberland, hired a house at Westminster adjoining the Parliament house in May 1604. "John Johnson" (Fawkes) was installed in the property. A neighboring cellar was added to the Percy property in the following March, and in stages the gunpowder was brought in. The conspirators organized horses and escape houses in Warwickshire.

The grievances of the Plotters were understandable. Their religion was not tolerated, and they faced severe fines and imprisonment as practicing Catholics. The new king was not living up to the promises he had held out to Catholics before coronation. The treaty of peace in August 1604 ignored the interests of the Romanists. The government had stepped up the enforcement of the recusant statutes. Catholics were denied freedom of worship and of speech to argue for toleration. They could not seek democratic change in a hereditary monarchy. All observant Catholics were barred from Parliament, from government office and from attending university. But what did the Plotters expect to achieve? Blowing up the Parliament with all the members of the Commons and the Lords and the king would certainly disrupt government. Could they form a new government?

Robert Cecil probably learned of the plot well before October. However, its discovery was attributed to the delivery of a letter to William Parker, Baron Monteagle, on the evening of October 26 at his home of Hoxton. Monteagle, a Catholic, was among those arrested, fined and pardoned in the Essex rebellion. The letter was a vague warning that he should retire to the country and not attend the Parliament: "they shall receive a terrible Blow this Parliament, and yet they shall not see who hurts them." Concerned that he was being set up, he immediately took the letter to Robert Cecil. According to some accounts, the Lord Admiral Howard, the Earls of Northampton and Worcester, and the Lord Chamberlain were also present.[1] The king was away, so Cecil waited another five days to bring the Monteagle letter to his attention. The monarch was given the opportunity to puzzle over it until he himself arrived at the deduction (perhaps with hints and encouragement) that a great blow might mean that the Parliament building was to be blown up. Commands were given, and a search was conducted of the vault beneath the building, where the powder kegs and Guy Fawkes were discovered.

Word of the Plot quickly spread. The conspirators fled London. Catesby, Thomas Percy, and others took refuge in Holbeach House, on the borders of Staffordshire. Gunpowder there was accidentally ignited, and some of the conspirators were injured. Government forces attacked the next day. Catesby, Percy, and John and Christopher Wright were all killed; Thomas Wintour, Ambrose Rookwood, and a few others were captured.

Fawkes and Thomas Wintour were tortured and questioned over the next few days. The interrogators extracted written confessions; they implicated others. Seven conspirators were tried on Monday, January 27, 1606. The king and Cecil wanted the Attorney General Coke to make clear during the trial that the conspiracy preceded the king's accession and thus was not a response to James's policies towards the Catholics. The government was keen to place responsibility for the Plot on the Jesuits and their associates. The principal targets in England were the Jesuit Superior, Henry Garnet, and those closest to him, Oswald

Tesimond, John Gerard, Edward Oldcorne, and Thomas Strange. Cecil also wanted Coke to place much of the blame upon the exiles in the Low Countries. This he did in the trials of the first group of conspirators and in the trial of Henry Garnet.

John Gerard

Gerard initially sought refuge on familiar ground, the Blackfriars quarters held by the Fortescue family (and later acquired in the name of Shakespeare). A contemporary account states[2]:

> [A]fter the discovery of the plot, and when Father Gerard had been publicly denounced all over the kingdom, he suddenly appeared without notice at Mr. Fortescue's house disguised by a false beard and hair, and asked him to take him in, as he knew not where to hide his head. Looking upon him, Mr. Fortescue said, full of heaviness, "have you no one to ruin but me and my family?"

Fortescue was right to fear ruin, for the government had long watched the property closely. Lord Chief Justice Popham wrote to Cecil on the day of the discovery of the conspiracy, informing him that there were letters from abroad at "Fortescue's house by the Wardrobe."[3]

Gerard wrote an open letter denying involvement in the plot. He had many copies made and scattered about the London streets. He also wrote a letter to the lords of the Council asserting his innocence.[4] Next, Gerard turned to another close associate of Sterrell and Phelippes for protection: Dr. Robert Taylor, the agent of the Archdukes. Taylor took John Gerard into his residence.[5] Gerard also rented a house for a short time. On May 3, 1606, the day of Garnet's execution, Gerard left on a ship carrying diplomats and made his way to the Low Countries.[6]

Oswald Tesimond

Oswald Tesimond was of special interest to the government because Catesby apparently revealed the plot to Tesimond, who related it to Garnet under the seal of confession. Tesimond had been educated in York in "Le Horse Fayre" free school along with the leading conspirators, Guy Fawkes and John and Christopher Wright. A proclamation was issued for Tesimond's arrest, and he was caught in the streets of London. But Tesimond eluded his captor, escaping into Suffolk. Eventually, he crossed to the continent in a boat loaded with dead pigs.[7]

Nicholas Owen

Nicholas Owen was the lay Jesuit whom Sterrell had gotten out of prison in 1594. "Little John," as Owen was known, was with Oldcorne and Garnet at Hindlip, a home of the Abington family in Worcestershire, hiding in one of the small chambers he had constructed. After four days he emerged, pretending to be Garnet in an effort to save the Jesuit. He was taken to the Tower and there tortured after refusing to answer questions concerning Garnet and Oldcorne. He was hung up with weights attached to his feet, until "his bowels gushed out with his life."[8] Upon his dying on March 2, 1606, from torture, the government declared Owen to have committed suicide.

Henry Garnet

Despite Nicholas Owen's self-sacrifice, Henry Garnet and Edward Oldcorne were captured at the end of January at Hindlip. They were placed in the Tower. Garnet was interrogated dozens of times, eventually being connected with Phelippes through Richard Fulwood and Robert Spiller. Worcester was present on at least one occasion. There is no indication that Worcester said anything. It is likely that Worcester and Garnet were well-acquainted. The experience must have been excruciating for Worcester, but he had long lived a double life—loyal subject to two Protestant monarchs, secret supporter of Jesuit fugitives, and silent sponsor of an intelligence network. Cecil insulted Garnet and then apologized. Garnet reacquainted himself with Chief Justice Popham, reminding him that they had served together in the printing shop of Tottel years earlier.

The prosecutors put Garnet in a cell with Fr. Edward Oldcorne. A secret passageway allowed two agents to listen surreptitiously to the conversations of the two priests. They took notes of what they heard, little of which was of any worth.

Garnet managed some correspondence with Anne Vaux. Portions of the letters were written with orange juice. He continued as her spiritual advisor though telling her she would soon need another. He knew that the outcome of his confinement could have but one end.

Garnet's trial was held on March 28, 1606. Robert Cecil secured a special place for Dr. Taylor at Garnet's trial so that he could prepare a report for King Philip III. The evidence of guilt in the Gunpowder Plot consisted of Garnet's admission that on July 9, 1605, Catesby had inquired whether it was lawful to undertake an action good for the Catholic cause if it should not be possible to avoid the destruction of some innocent persons together with the guilty. Without knowledge of the action contemplated, Garnet answered that it was lawful. That evening, Garnet was found guilty, and sentenced to be hanged, disemboweled, and quartered. Later, the Countess of Suffolk told Dr. Taylor that Robert Cecil was not among those responsible for the execution of Garnet.[9]

On May 3, 1606, Garnet was taken from the Tower to St. Paul's Churchyard and there executed. The dismembered parts were thrown into a basket containing straw. A Catholic witnessing the execution took some of the bloody straw and gave it to a tailor's wife. A short time later, the visage of Garnet seemed to appear from the blood on the straw. For a few days the straw circulated among a small group of Catholics who marveled at the miracle of the straw. These included, among others, Dr. Taylor, Lord William Howard, Anne Vaux, and the Spanish and Venetian ambassadors.

Thomas Strange, Ben Jonson and Thomas Wright

On October 9, 1605, just weeks before the Gunpowder Treason, Ben Jonson was observed by a government agent among a party at Robert Catesby's lodgings (the Irish Boy

Inn) with several of the conspirators, including Catesby. Immediately after the discovery of the Gunpowder Plot, Jonson was called to the Privy Council to convey an unnamed priest to the Council with a promise of safe conduct. A warrant of the Privy Council of November 7 was issued to "Benjamen Johnson to let a certain priest know that offered to do good service to the State, that he should securely come and go to and from the LL's, which they promised in the said warrant upon their honors."[10] The next day Jonson replied to Cecil that he had attempted to locate the priest through the Venetian ambassador's chaplain but was unsuccessful.

Who was Jonson's priest? Fr. Thomas Wright, a former Jesuit, has been suggested.[11] Jonson had contributed a prefatory sonnet for Wright's treatise on the *Passions of the Mind*, probably soon after its completion. And Thomas Wright, on a safe-conduct signed by twelve councilors, spoke with Fawkes in the Tower. But Wright's account puts him on the scene only after the Plotter's principal statements—not before Sunday November 10.[12] Wright may have been a second-best, found by the Council after Jonson's mandate proved fruitless. If the purpose was to find a priest thought likely by the Council to impress Guy Fawkes, Wright was a poor candidate. The priest was dismissed from the Jesuits in the mid-1590s for favoring an accommodation with the English state. Coming openly to England in 1595, he surrendered to the authorities with promises of informing on Spanish machinations. Though a fervent Catholic whose effective proselytizing earned him spells of prison and exile, his notorious willingness to deal with the regime, and his alienation from the principal English Jesuits, would have made him repugnant to Fawkes and the other Plotters.

Another priest well-known to Ben Jonson by 1605 was Fr. Thomas Strange, SJ, a protégé of Frs. Garnet and Gerard. Strange was eagerly sought by the English government in 1605. A wealthy young man, educated at Oxford and trained in law at Gray's Inn, Strange was already Catholic before making the Ignatian spiritual exercises with the imprisoned priest John Gerard, who describes him as talented, wealthy, and cultivated. Strange lived for two years in London in close association with Fr. Garnet before becoming a lay Jesuit in Rome. He then worked in Dunkirk to turn captured English sailors to Catholic causes, and slipped back into England late in 1602 to help a young Eton and Oxford relative leave England for Catholic exile. Captured at Dover and examined by the Council, he was released with Cecil's influence (doubtless a tribute to Strange's family connections), but broke bail by going back across the Channel.

On returning to England in 1604 Strange wrote a book that he dedicated to his friend Robert Catesby. In 1605, probably on the occasion of Jonson's 33rd birthday in June, Strange gave Ben Jonson a Latin Bible, which Jonson then inscribed: "Ex dono D. Thomae Strange, 1605, Beniamin Ionsonius. Benedicam Dominum in omni tempore, semper laus eius in ore meo–Ps xxxiii" ["Gift of Master Thomas Strange, 1605, Benjamin Jonson. I will bless the Lord at all times, his praise always in my mouth—Psalm 33"].[13]

Strange was named on November 5, as linked with Gunpowder suspects, in the first of Chief Justice Popham's reports to Cecil on the Gunpowder Plot. Late on November 7, Strange was arrested north of Warwick, riding westwards to meet with Fr. Garnet. The sheriff of Warwickshire's letter informing Cecil of this is dated November 12. Among Strange's interrogators were Chief Justice Popham and Attorney General Coke. Coke alluded to an examination of Strange during the January 27, 1606, trial of the principal Gunpowder conspirators. After Fr. Garnet's arrest, the government undertook more detailed examinations of Strange. The government sought to use Strange for evidence against Garnet but even torture could not gain Strange's cooperation. Months of repeated rackings left Strange an invalid for life, but nothing ever implicated him in the Plot. London observers expected his trial in early 1606, but no charge was ever laid. He stayed in the Tower, long in solitary, interrogated from time to time, until in 1610 he was released (or by one report escaped). Worcester, it appears, subtly mitigated the harshness of his confinement.

Thomas Barnes (also Nuse and Southwick)

Because the English government was adamant that the Gunpowder Plot was coordinated with English exiles in the Low Countries, Thomas Phelippes and his associates were certain to come into suspicion. Phelippes had never explained satisfactorily his extended correspondence with Hugh Owen. In Brussels, Phelippes' long-time operative, Thomas Barnes, seized the initiative within days of learning of the Plot and approached Thomas Edmondes, the English ambassador, volunteering to return to England to cooperate with the government.[14] Barnes gave Edmondes a letter from Dr. William Gifford to the Pope's nuntio's secretary, and Edmondes passed this on to Cecil. Edmondes asked that Gifford's name not be revealed, for Edmondes had entered into a correspondence with Gifford with the hope of making good use of Gifford. In other words, Edmondes expected Dr. Gifford to serve as an English agent.

Barnes gave the appearance of turning on Catholic exiles, but Dr. Gifford was in fact long an opponent of Hugh Owen and the English Jesuits. Dr. Gifford had helped his brother George Gifford serve as a double agent/provocateur 1583–86 and was a close ally of Charles Paget and Thomas Morgan. The letter was certain to incite Cecil against Dr. Gifford, for it began that "the hope of the Catholics is in the death of Cecil." Owen and Phelippes had probably instigated the Barnes initiative. Within days, Barnes was on his way to England to see Cecil with a letter of Edmondes recommending him.[15]

Cecil suspected that there was some trickery involved with Barnes and Phelippes and so put Barnes to test, in an effort to entrap Phelippes. After meeting with Barnes, Cecil gave Barnes a passport to return to Brussels. Barnes was to use the alias of Thomas Wilson, which was the name of one of Cecil's chief aides. Cecil then immediately sent a letter to Sir Thomas Fane, lieutenant of Dover Castle, to stop anyone carrying a Cecil passport using the name Thomas Wilson.[16] A bepuzzled Fane was approached at Dover within a short time by a party of three, one of whom bore a passport signed by Cecil and one of whom was named Wilson, but he was *Edward* Wilson, not *Thomas*.[17] The passport carrier was William Nuse, another outward-bound agent employed by Cecil to spy in France and the Low Countries. Fane detained them by false pretenses until he received further word from Cecil, which evidently came shortly, and thereafter Nuse sent to Cecil a series of dispatches from the Continent.

Two weeks later, "Thomas Wilson" was brought to Sir Thomas Fane as he tried to cross the English channel at Dover. He tried to show his papers to Fane, but Fane put "Wilson's" portmanteau under lock and key and sent the package (with key) to Cecil and

Northampton to have the first view. Fane told "Wilson" that his name was not really Wilson but instead Acton, one of the Gunpowder conspirators. Immediately, "Wilson" informed Fane that his true name was Thomas Barnes and that Cecil's secretary Levinus Munck was privy to all that Barnes was doing. Fane then locked him in a chamber in Dover Castle awaiting further word from Cecil. Soon, Barnes was allowed to proceed on to the Low Countries. A short time after, Cecil described the incident to Sir Thomas Edmondes (the ambassador in Brussels), saying that he had been using Barnes to trap Phelippes.[18]

Within a short time of Barnes's return to the Low Countries, Dr. Gifford was ruined. The Archduke sent him into exile and ordered that he was never to return in the Archduke's lifetime.[19] Gifford attributed his downfall to Owen and Phelippes and their associates.[20] Barnes's ploy was successful. It prevented his name from being tied to the Gunpowder Plot. Probably it allowed him to convey intelligence between Hugh Owen and Thomas Phelippes. And it gave Barnes (and his associates) an opportunity to eliminate the influence of an Owen adversary at the Brussels Court. Bold strategy enabled the network to limit the effects of their worst crisis.

Both William Nuse and Thomas Barnes reported back to Cecil (through his assistant Levinus Munck) in letters addressed to "Monsieur Du Pre." Nuse used the initials NW and WN. Barnes used the symbol Π.[21] Nothing of significance back to Cecil appears to have proceeded from Nuse or Barnes nor from a third agent dispatched by Cecil.

The third man sent abroad by Cecil to draw out incriminating information from Catholic exiles was George Southaick or Southwick. To gain release from the Marshalsea, Southwick promised Cecil to betray Catholic priests even before the Gunpowder Plot.[22] He was described as a raw youth who "hath been at Rome and many a Mass in his days."[23] In January–February 1606, Cecil had Southwick doing intelligence work lurking about Cambridge before sending him abroad.[24] On June 16/26, 1606 Southwick met with Edmondes in Brussels and related to the ambassador how he had been faring with the Catholic exiles.[25] Edmondes reported that "Southwell" was well-received; there was "an extraordinary liking of him conceived by them all for the pregnancy of his spirit and for the discontentment which they suppose to have been given by hard dealing in England." Moreover, the man was well-recommended by the Archpriest. Southwick's favorable letter from Blackwell may be attributable to the Archpriest's poor judgment of character, demonstrated on multiple occasions.

After Southwick left Edmondes he was supposed to meet with Owen, but Owen declined, probably suspecting him to be a spy. Southwick went on to meet with Sterrell's friend Fr. Sherwood at Valenciennes and then traveled to Douay where he encountered other exiled English priests.

Barnes probably met with Edmondes at about the same time as Southwick and likewise went on to Douay at about the same time.[26] The reason he was leaving Brussels, Barnes informed Cecil (through Munck), was that "here I am utterly disgraced with Owen, and that for two special causes as he sayeth. First for that as he hears, I was the principal instrument or cause of Mr. Phelipps his commitment. Secondly because he is assuredly given to understand by letters out of England that all those directions which I received hence to write unto him, are in my L. of Salisburies custody, which poynt he urgeth so particularly, as he addeth, that they should be written by Mr. Baylies own hand, but how true these accusations are, you know." He was going shortly to Douay, "where I shall have better means to understand of the Jesuits violent proceedings than elsewhere, and also live at a more easy rate than in this place." Cecil no doubt read this letter of Barnes with interest, for it shows that Owen knew well that the man with whom he had corresponded was Phelippes, not some imaginary friend of Sterrell. Phelippes had initially tried to convince Cecil that Owen was ignorant of the identity of the person writing to him after Sterrell had been replaced by "Vincent."

Nuse in July 1606 became involved in another alleged plot against King James. Thomas Franceschi, the brother of Col. Jaques, entered England from the Low Countries with Nuse and with John Ball, an Irishman who was serving the Spanish ambassador. They met at the ambassador's lodgings in London. Nuse alleged to the Privy Council that they discussed a plan to betray one of the English outposts in the Netherlands.[27] Some talk suggested King James might be assassinated. The next day, Ball gave Nuse some sweetmeats, which soon made Nuse ill, and a physician declared that the food had been poisoned. Franceschi and Ball were arrested. Franceschi admitted to planning actions against one of the Netherlands towns but denied anything relating to King James. The Spanish ambassador distanced himself from Ball but took the matter up with King James.[28] Edmondes informed Cecil from Brussels that reports out of England suggested that Nuse had made his allegations only to procure himself benefits from the state.[29] A year later, Ball and Franceschi were both released, but Ball's reputation and his involvement with Phelippes came back to cause problems for Phelippes.

Phelippes and Robert Spiller

After the Gunpowder Plot, Robert Cecil sought further information from Phelippes, raising questions of his complicity. It will be recalled that Cecil had his suspicions about Phelippes and one "Freeman" when he first arrested Phelippes in January 1605. This association became very serious once "Freeman" was identified as Robert Spiller. Ambassador Edmondes reported to Cecil that Guy Fawkes had been accompanied into England by Robert Spiller, under another alias.[30] Both Phelippes's brother and a servant of Phelippes were interrogated about "Freeman." Phelippes had never acknowledged any involvement with "Freeman" (and had not volunteered such) and had denied using any aliases since the king's coming (April 1603). He had earlier admitted some feigned correspondence using the names Witt and Vincent. For a time in 1605, Phelippes may have had his liberty enlarged, but with the discovery of the Gunpowder Plot, he was again in prison.

On February 4, 1606, in a letter from the Gatehouse, Phelippes began to admit to Cecil his relationship with "Freeman," a relationship that was established by Phelippes so as to assist the state because of "Freeman's" credit with the Catholics abroad. He admitted that "Freeman" had come to him a day or two after the uncovering of the Gunpowder Plot and he now admitted Freeman's real name as Spiller, brother of Spiller of the Exchequer, and said that Spiller has told him that he–Spiller—worked for the Countess of Arundel. The Catholics, said Phelippes, knew that he [Phelippes] was contrary to them in religion and thus had never trusted him with serious matters. Spiller had used the name "Freeman" to disguise himself to Phelippes, and Spiller had "professed ever to be ready to further any service for the state and furnished me with sundry news in former times." Phelippes said he first became acquainted with Spiller in the late queen's time "when peace was first talked of," i.e., when the Burgundian jewels matter first arose.

Phelippes was playing a high stakes game, with his life at risk. Spiller, as Cecil knew, often was accompanied by Richard Fulwood and worked closely with Fr. Garnet, who had finally been captured and brought to London. Would Phelippes be linked to Garnet? Phelippes had already admitted to correspondence with Owen, and that correspondence had traveled in Fr. Garnet's packets.

Cecil knew that Thomas Phelippes was a notorious dissembler. To check out Phelippes newest tale, Cecil was again interrogating his brother, Stephen Phelippes. In a writing dated February 28, 1606, Stephen related that Thomas had communicated with him and had given him instructions.[31] Phelippes had instructed his brother that "Ball" (John Ball, on the staff of the Spanish envoy) was to be told that his relationship with Thomas Phelippes was a matter of state secret and that "Freeman" *alias* Spiller was to be advised to keep out of the way. Also, Thomas Barnes was to stay out of the way and to take away any letters coming to Phelippes. Stephen further admitted that he had gone to the Exchequer to meet with Spiller's brother. Henry Spiller told Stephen that his brother Robert was "far enough out of the way or out of their fingers."

Cecil obtained similar information about Thomas Phelippes from other sources. As related above, Cecil tested Phelippes's honesty by using Barnes in an effort to trap him. He had information on Phelippes also from other sources.[32] Showing the seriousness of Phelippes's case, Cecil moved Thomas Phelippes from the Gatehouse to the Tower. The suspicion of Phelippes had deepened from reports from someone that Phelippes' overseas correspondence had been with the connivance of the Jesuits in England. New allegations in March or early April against Phelippes had arisen since his February 4 declarations to Cecil. Interrogatories submitted for Fr. Henry Garnet to answer included questions about Phelippes's work with the Jesuits[33]:

"3. What he [Garnet] knoweth of Phelippes and the correspondency he hath with Owen and Baldwin, how long he hath been acquainted with the same?

"How many have come to Phelippes in his [Garnet's] Packetts, by what endorsement, and how often did he write back?

"What other advertisement did Phelippes send to him by Richard Fullwood?"

These questions to the doomed Garnet make clear that Cecil was very close to discovering the operation of the "Anthony Rivers" correspondence that Sterrell (with Phelippes's complicity) had conducted for years through Garnet's packets abroad. Had James's "little beagle" been more of a bloodhound, he may have tracked to earth Sterrell under his various epistolary aliases. Perhaps he did but decided to leave him be.

The responses Garnet may have given to these questions have not survived. Most likely, he took the secrets to his death knowing that they would lead to Worcester and Sterrell. But Phelippes was confronted with the allegations, perhaps by the Lieutenant of the Tower, Sir William Waad.[34] He responded in a prolix, confusing letter of April 1606 to Waad, which was intended for the king himself, as well as further submissions to Cecil.[35] Phelippes said he knew the king did not conceive well of Phelippes's proceeding, so he hoped to better the king's understanding. Without mentioning the name of William Sterrell, Phelippes told of an imaginary correspondent who had been "pressed to find somebody that should set afoote certain overtures touching peace and the jewels of the House of Burgundy and such like, Ph[elippes] was nominated and used for those purposes to the contentment of both sides as it fell out at sundry times: with not that it was known or so much as suspected that Ph[elippes] was the man that indeed managed all matters." Phelippes said he had then used his contacts to try to improve his own lot and he accepted substantial sums of money from the Spanish emissary. He suggested that Robert Cecil misunderstood his declarations, and that some of the suspicions of Phelippes grew from actions of Charles Paget. Rambling, Phelippes revealed that there had been certain letters to Verstegan. Involved in this were an imaginary correspondent, a friend, and "Freeman." It is clear that the friend and Freeman were two different people (the description of the role of the "friend" indicates that the friend was undoubtedly Sterrell, whose name Phelippes no longer invokes), and it is also clear that Phelippes was taking care that the news of "occurents" was still continuing to Verstegan after Phelippes was arrested in January 1605. To further explain his relationship with Freeman *alias* Spiller, Phelippes now told the background and tied his acquaintance with Spiller to the negotiation of the Burgundian Jewels. Speaking of himself the third person, and repeating much of what he had written to Cecil at the beginning of February, Phelippes, said:

> "Ph. acquaintance with Freeman grew in the late Q. time when as the first negotiation for the jewells of the house of Burgundy was set afoote and so increased as the Negotiations for peace multiplied. He always professed dutifull affection to the state offering his service from time to time to that purpose, and was able (as he did) to inform Ph. of the occurents abroad: and in that great quarrel between the Jesuits and the Seculars furnished Ph. with all the intelligence he had thereof whereof you Mr. Lieftenant [Waad] know the use was made."

So, now Phelippes wanted the king to know that Phelippes had been cooperating with Spiller and what he got from Spiller in return was intelligence about the struggles between the Jesuits and the Seculars, i.e., the Archpriest controversy. Thus the information that Phelippes had given directly to Robert Cecil for several years about the dissensions within the Catholics had **all** come from Spiller, a man close to Henry Garnet. Phelippes now went beyond his February 4 declaration to Cecil and took up the recent allegations that he had cooperated with Fr. Garnet and Richard Fulwood. He professed ignorance of matters as to which imputations had been made against him. He said he knew of Fulwood only as a messenger between Freeman (Spiller) and himself, who came like a blast of wind, not knowing when or from whence he came. He had never seen Garnet and never had anything to do with him. As to the accusation of having this correspondence in Garnet's mail packets, he made an equivocal denial: "If any letter delivered Fulwood for Freeman or which came by him from Freeman went or came in Garnet's packet it was more than Ph. knew: who sent most by the ordinary post. And as touching the having any money from Baldwin it was very impertinent for no such thing ever was." If Cecil had possessed the mass of letters that "Rivers" had sent to Owen, Verstegan and Persons that are examined in earlier chapters, he would have grasped the extent of the intelligence activities that had been performed out of the Court. But Phelippes was careful to make no mention of Sterrell's role in the movement of letters and funds overseas. In August 1606 Phelippes also petitioned unsuccessfully the Privy Council for relief from his imprisonment, cautiously letting Cecil know that he was circumventing Cecil's authority.[36] Although nothing further arose to link Phelippes to the Gunpowder Plot, the charges against John Ball and Tomaso Franceschi in mid–1606 led to further suspicious of Phelippes's duplicity.[37]

Phelippes, like Fr. Strange, was held in the Tower for years without a trial. The date of his release is unknown, but he seems to have been in prison for more than four years.[38]

"Freeman" *alias* Spiller returned to London and submitted himself in 1608. Cecil learned that Spiller was returned and sent for him. The Bishop of London reported to Cecil that Spiller was very willing to go to Cecil and that he "has taken the oath of allegiance and protested deeply his dislike of the Jesuits; as also his readiness to do the state any service."[39] With Garnet dead, Gerard overseas, Phelippes committed to his version of events that favored Spiller, and Sterrell silent, there was no case to be made against Spiller for treasonous correspondence. No letters bore the names of Spiller or Freeman, and his messenger Richard Fulwood was long gone.[40] Spiller continued for many years a manager of property for the Countess of Arundel.[41] The noblewoman and her son continued to be prominent at the Court of King James for years and Spiller's brother was a useful official of the government, so Spiller was unmolested. It is most doubtful that his profession of dislike for the Jesuits was sincere as he left a "good part of his wealth for the encrease and the advancement of the means of" Jesuits in exile.[42]

Hugh Owen and Fr. William Baldwin

Hugh Owen was implicated in the Gunpowder Plot almost immediately in a confession of Thomas Wintour and by Fawkes. Wintour said in a confession of November 23, 1605, that after the initial placing of gunpowder and firewood, Fawkes was sent to Brussels to inform Owen so that Owen could help the overthrow.[43]

The king himself directed Coke through Robert Cecil, to give emphasis to the existence of a Catholic conspiracy that was in place *before* James's accession. Its pre–1603 existence would mean that a Catholic plot was not a response to James's policies towards the Catholics, and it would justify those policies James took after assuming the crown. On the morning of the trial of Fawkes and other conspirators, Cecil sent the following instructions to Coke:

> First that you be sure to make it appear to the world that there was an employment of some persons to Spain for a practice of invasion as soon as the Q[ueen]'s breath was out of her body. The reason is this for which the King doth urge it. He saith some men there are that will give out and do, that only despair of the K[ing]'s courses on the Catholics and his severity drew all these to such works of discontentment; where by you it will appear that before his M[ajesty]'s face was ever seen, or that he had done anything in government, the k[ing] of Spain was moved, though he refused it, saying he rather expected to have peace.... *You must remember to lay Owen as foul in this as you can*.[44]

Cecil wrote to the English ambassador in Brussels to demand the extradition of Hugh Owen back to England. Owing to the seriousness of the changes, the Archduke did have Owen, Stanley and Baldwin arrested but he was unwilling to send a loyal aide and a Jesuit priest to certain death in England.

Owen received help from the Spanish in avoiding extradition. Of special importance were his many years of correspondence. In a memorandum that he intended to be circulated in the Spanish Council of State, he expressed his great anxiety for his papers[45]:

> There are the reports and plans for the reform of England, and the activities on behalf of the rights of the Most Serene Infanta. There are some letters, over the names of various English lords and many leading personages, which undertake by pledges of their persons and fortunes to assist his Majesty and his Highness whenever an opportunity came. Furthermore there are the original *avisos* for many years past and the

ciphers by which they can be read with the names of the correspondents as well as the manner used to forward their letters during the war and after. Among the above mentioned *avisos* are the ones which reveal a certain recent uprising which the late Queen tried to foster in these provinces when his Highness had left for his wedding in Spain. In them various great personages of these provinces are named as having intrigued in company with the Queen.

Here Owen was no doubt referring to the Coemans/Lanfranchi intrigues of 1599 in which Sterrell and Phelippes had played so important a role in revealing to Owen the "double treachery" undertaken while Archduke Albert was away from Brussels. Should anyone hostile see the file, Owen warned that "it will do great injury to his Majesty and be a betrayal of many English Catholics who are his devoted followers."[46] William Sterrell and his employer Worcester were surely the Englishmen most likely to be injured by the files that Owen wanted protected. Owen was included in a Parliamentary act of attainder in May 1606.[47]

Nearly three years after the Gunpowder Plot, Robert Cecil attempted to kidnap Hugh Owen and transport him back into England for treason. His instrument was Thomas Wilford, an Englishman who deserted the archduke's army and went to England, where he met with Cecil. Wilford's correspondence with Cecil and others in England was revealed to the Archduke's Court by Owen and Baldwin in July 1608. The plan was to draw Owen to a private home in Brussels, distract or murder Owen's own servants, and then bind Owen and throw him into a waiting coach to be taken to Antwerp for conveyance to England. Recruited by Wilford was a Captain Whitebread, who was supposed to carry certain letters to England at the end of July 1608. Whitebread betrayed Wilford. Responding to these serious accusations of violations of international standards, Cecil denied intentions of murder. But he admitted that he knew Wilford and had talked about his "liking that by some stratagem, he [Owen] might have been stolen into a ship and brought to England."[48]

Some suspicion was raised that Whitebread entrapped Wilford. Edmondes suggested that it was all a scheme of Owen.[49] Perhaps this was indeed the case, for Whitebread was evidently a participant in the Owen-Sterrell-Phelippes network. Owen (as "J.B.") had written Sterrell ("Robinson") in 1602 that "Monsr Boulant told me I might direct my letters to you as now I do to Guillame Whitbread."[50] And Stephen Phelippes in February 1606 provided information that his brother Thomas Phelippes had instructed that certain matters be referred to "one Whitebread" if Thomas Barnes were to come over.[51] The Cecil-Wilford kidnapping episode was embarrassing to Cecil, and it is not beyond likelihood that the 70 year old Owen had schemed his own kidnapping as a fitting retribution to Cecil for all the discomfort Cecil had caused Owen since the Gunpowder Plot.

So long as Owen remained in Brussels, he was a diplomatic problem between England and the Archdukes. Spain expressed its willingness to move Owen to the staff of its embassy in Rome, and Owen's pension was guaranteed to continue. The Archduke embraced the solution. Owen departed the place of his residence for some thirty-five years to travel by a safe route to Rome. There he could retire and be with his friends from the correspondence network of many years, Thomas Fitzherbert and Robert Persons. Loomie comments: "It was probably the most pleasant period of his life, living in honored retirement and security amid the baroque elegance of the Spanish embassy."[52] Owen died there in 1618 at the age of eighty. What stories he could have told!

William Baldwin was not so fortunate as Owen. Although he continued to live in Flanders and enjoyed the support of the Archduke, the English still hoped to gain his custody. On a journey to Rome in 1610, Baldwin was apprehended by soldiers of the Elector Palatine, Frederick IV. His disguise failed him when letters he carried for others revealed his identity. After an imprisonment in Heidelberg he was sent in chains by Frederick to King James. There was virtually no evidence to connect Baldwin with the Gunpowder Plot. Never tried, Baldwin spent the next eight years in the Tower. In June 1618, Baldwin was part of a group of Jesuits who were released and banished from England through the efforts of the Spanish ambassador, the Count of Gondomar. This release was after William Sterrell's intelligence work for the Archduke had resumed and perhaps Sterrell was able to help effect Baldwin's release. From 1622 to his death a decade later (age 69) Baldwin was rector of the English College in St. Omers.

Sterrell and Gunpowder

Of Sterrell at the time of the Plot we hear nothing. The silence of the record is striking. Less than a year earlier, Robert Cecil had discovered that Sterrell and Phelippes were together engaged in a long correspondence with Hugh Owen and other English fugitives whom Cecil now wished to tie closely to the Gunpowder Plot. Although Phelippes was again arrested and interrogated, William Sterrell seems not to have been bothered. We surmise that Sterrell avoided further activity with Garnet, Owen, Phelippes and the other fugitives after his January 1605 interrogation. Cecil could find no evidence of actions after that interrogation, and as far as could be determined from Phelippes's files, Sterrell's intelligence work had largely ceased about the time James came to the throne in 1603.

The Gunpowder Plot surely had a profound impact on William Sterrell's life. The Jesuit structure in England that Sterrell had worked with for more than a decade abruptly disintegrated. Most of the people with whom Sterrell was associated and who knew of his secret intelligence role were all suddenly dead or fled; if in England, they were in fear of their lives. Until more evidence is found, it appears that William Sterrell ceased to function as an intelligencer for the next dozen years after the Gunpowder Plot.

28

Conclusion: The State of the English Counter-Reformation after Gunpowder

For many generations to come, the Roman Catholic Church in England would bear the stigma of the plot to destroy the government. Many sensible people would distance themselves from that stigma. Even the Archpriest himself, Fr. Blackwell, decided that he and others should take the Oath of Allegiance, despite having earlier opposed it.[1] All was in disarray. As it became clear in succeeding years that no toleration was forthcoming and that Catholicism was likely to remain a clandestine religion, numerous Catholics followed the examples of Ben Jonson, Hugh Holland and others and conformed to the Church of England. Those who continued in the old faith, including Worcester's immediate family, often suffered repercussions for their religion.

From the mission of Campion and Persons to the capture of Fr. Garnet, the English Jesuits and their allies in France, the Low Countries, Spain and Rome had been the heart, the soul, and the intellect of the English Counter-Reformation. With Garnet's execution, with the death and escape of other Jesuits, and with the infamy and odium falling on Catholics generally after the Gunpowder Plot, the moving spirit of English Catholicism was gone. Worcester and his family, in distant Wales, continued to nourish the faith and supported the Jesuits, as did a number of other of other families we have covered where they were able. But Worcester, Sterrell and others began looking to a generation after James for relief of English Catholics. For now, the Counter-Reformation was effectively extinguished.

Worcester and Sterrell flourished at Court, especially in the seven years between the Gunpowder Plot and the death of Prince Henry in 1612. Sterrell was effectively impresario for at least one Ben Jonson queen's masque (*Love Freed from Ignorance and Folly*–1611). Perhaps it was for this supervisory role that King James's list of "Free Gifts from the Exchequer in the Eighth Year of the King's Reign, 1610–11" includes this item: "William Stirrel— - 50£," a reward of 10£ more than Sterrell allotted for Ben Jonson. Still later, Sterrell will return to intelligence work for the Archdukes, evidently at their invitation when his old friend Thomas Fitzherbert, now a Jesuit priest, was posted to their Court in Brussels around 1616. A hundred and fifty of Sterrell's beautifully written and clever letters from the period 1617–1626 survive in the Vienna Archives, with news of the English Court on many topics (including many discussions of the proposed match of Prince Charles with the Infanta of Spain). Probably he wrote many more. After the death of his long-time patron, Sterrell will marry and father a child, before dying in 1631, leaving an exquisite epitaph for himself in his last will and testament: *caelo tegitur qui non habet urnam.*[2] Heaven shelters those who have no grave. His final thoughts were on those martyrs whom the state had denied proper burial, Campion, Briant, Hartley, Southwell, Anne Line, Barkworth and many more.

Chapter Notes

Introduction to Selected Original and Reference Sources

The letters of "Anthony Rivers" have been studied by historians mainly in the extracts, not fully reliable, in Henry Foley, *Records of the English Province of the Society of Jesus*, i (London, 1877), pp. 1–62. The originals of twenty-five from the series are in the Westminster Diocesan Archive in Kensington, London; seventeenth century excerpts from several dozen others are in Collectanea which in the twentieth century were in Stonyhurst College, Lancashire, and the Archives of the Society of Jesus in Rome. The relevant "Stonyhurst" MSS are now held in the Jesuit archive in Mount St., London. The originals of a few "Rivers" letters are in the State Papers. Letters attributed to "Anthony Rivers" and collected by the 17th century copyist Christopher Grene, S. J., were transcribed by a priest (Fr. Kearns) around 1963. Archives of the Society of Jesus, London, Anglia 37. I have used a transcription of these made by Penelope Renold in 1963 and kindly supplied, along with typed transcripts of the surviving originals of the Rivers letters, by Fr. Thomas McCoog S. J., then Archivist of the Society of Jesus in London. An example of the citation used herein: Rivers to Ridolfo Perino, February 12, 1602 (AAW A7/25/185), where AAW stands for Archives of the Archbishop of Westminster and the volume is the seventh in the "A" series followed by item and page. Others are cited by the appropriate SP designation unless otherwise noted.

State Papers now housed in the United Kingdom's National Archives at Kew in London are identified as below. The convention followed, where possible, is to give the catalog number with volume and item number. For example, a letter of "J. B. to Peter Halyns" of April 30, 1600, from Liége is given as SP 15/34/30, and can be located as an item in the *Calendar of State Papers, Domestic Addenda, 1580–1625*, at pages 405–6. A letter of "John Petit to Pieter Halyns" of October 5/15, 1597, is from State Papers, Foreign, Flanders SP 77/5 fol. 233. In some cases, individual documents were examined at the National Archives at Kew. For the Calendar of State Papers Relating to English Affairs in the Archives of Venice, the citation will be to "CSPV," the volume of the calendar followed by the item number. Thus volume 10 of the *Calendar of State Papers Venice*, for 1603–7, item number 390, found on page 252, Molin to the Doge and Senate, June 19/29, 1605, is cited as CSPV 10:390. In many instances, the author has made use of microfilm of the original documents or photocopies obtained from the National Archives.

The *Calendar of State Papers relating to English Affairs (Spain)*, ed. Martin A. S. Hume (4 vols. London, HMSO, 1899) is cited as CSP Sp. followed by volume and page, for example, CSP Sp. 4:650, Thomas Fitzherbert (to Lerma?) November 30, 1599. The *Calendar of the state papers relating to Scotland and Mary, Queen of Scots* eds. William K. Boyd, et al. (13 vols., London, 1898–1969) is cited as CSP Scot. followed by volume and page, for example, CSP Scot. 8: 292–93, Charles Paget to Mary, 31 March 1586. Other State Papers are as follows:

SP 12 State Papers, Domestic, Elizabeth I
SP 14 State Papers, Domestic, James I
SP 15 State Papers, Domestic, Addenda
SP 52 State Papers, Scotland, Elizabeth I
SP 53 State Papers, Mary Queen of Scots
SP 77 State Papers, Foreign, Flanders
SP 78 State Papers, Foreign, France
SP 83 State Papers, Foreign, Holland and Flanders
SP 94 State Papers, Foreign, Spain
SP 99 State Papers, Foreign, Venice

Items from the *Calendar of the Manuscripts of the Most Hon. the Marquis of Salisbury, preserved at Hatfield House, Hertfordshire* (London, 1888–1973) are cited as "Hatfield Papers" by volume and page; for example: Hatfield Papers 17: 39, Thomas Phelippes to Cecil, January 29, 1605. In some instances, the author has made use of microfilm of the original documents available at the Folger Shakespeare Library in Washington, D.C.

Acts of the Privy Council are from John Roche Dasent et al., ed., *Acts of the Privy Council of England* (London: Her Majesty's Stationery Office, 1890-1964) and are cited APC followed by volume and page; for example a passport for Mush and Barnaby was issued at the request of Bancroft, signed by Cecil and Mr Secretary Herbert, dated September 10, 1601, is cited APC 31:205.

Middle Temple Records. Charles Henry Hopwood, ed., 3 vols. (London: Butterworth, 1904), are cited Middle Temple Records, vol.: page.

OED refers to noted entries in *Oxford English Dictionary* Second Edition on CD-ROM (v. 4.0)(2009).

ODNB refers to noted entries *Oxford Dictionary of National Biography*, ed. H. C. G. Matthew and Brian Harrison, 60 vols. Oxford: Oxford University Press, 2004.

Chapter 1

1. Waugh (1961), p. 83.
2. McCoog (1996a), p. 143 n. 50. Fr. Persons listed a number of gentlemen in the Gilbert Association, but the list is no doubt incomplete. He and Campion traveled separate paths during most of their mission, and he would be unaware of some of the people helping Campion. McCoog notes, for example, that Thomas James was probably a member of the Gilbert association; he greeted Campion and Emerson when they arrived in London, id. p. 143. William Sterrell should probably be counted as associated with the group.
3. Persons (1582), pp. 98-9.
4. A great victory over the Turks in 1571 in Greece by an alliance of the Venetians, Austrians, Spanish and the papacy. G. K. Chesterton's narrative poem, "Lepanto," celebrated Don John's victory.
5. Waugh (1961), p. 105.
6. Pollen (1914), p. 142.
7. Macray (1901) 3: 80-1.
8. This exchange occurred:
   William Fulke: Whatever you can bring, I have answered already in writing against others of your side. And yet if you can add anything, put it in writing and I will answer it.
   Campion: Provide me with ink and paper and I will write.
   Fulke: I am not to provide you ink and paper.
9. McCoog (1996b), p. 136; McCoog (1996a), pp. 154-55.
10. Among its verses:
    You thought perhaps when learned Campion dies
    His pen must cease, his sugared tongue be still
    But you forgot how loud his death it cries,
    How far beyond the sound of tongue and quill,
    You did not know how rare and great a good
    It was to write his precious gifts in blood.

Chapter 3

1. Sledd in CRS III pp. 203, 241.
2. SP 12/141/10, "—G[Ifford] to John Gifford, Esq.," August 5, 1580, from Paris: "...Sr in brief I thank almighty God I have not so evil spent my time but that I can live honorably in any country or university in Europe, when you shall forsake me, which I deem greatly you mean, in leaving me with beggarly maintenance. I protest unto you Sir I spent at my proceeding [travel and living] 100 and fifty crowns, whereof I had not a penny of you, but god has provided me (who can raise up for his servant unexpected succour) such friends as I trust will not fail me. truly it grieves me exceedingly that my own brother coming unto these parts, you sent me not one pound to bless me, not having relieved me but with twenty crowns in a whole year and half, and much more it cuts my heart that you send the poor youth so bare to beg his bread rather than to provide for him, he may be constrained to serve a stranger's pleasure all his life."
3. "I am not ignorant what you have given to all your daughters, I know well, there is none of them that ever did help or I think would help any of us with one penny."
4. SP 12/193/33 iii. Thomas Bayly to Giles Gifford, October 9, 1580.
5. The confession of Gilbert Gifford in Latin is in Hatfield Papers, 3: 346-349; a partial translation is in Hicks (1964), p. 113.
6. Barret to Agazarri, reprinted in Renold (1967), pp. 41-48.
7. Hicks (1964), pp. 18-19, quotes Persons as follows: "As among others did two young men of good family and rare talents named William and Gilbert Gifford, who coming to the seminary of Rheims helped much to form a faction amongst the scholars. Among other things they united closely with two lay gentlemen, Paget and Morgan, one English, the other Welsh, heads of the lay faction." See Persons, *Notes Concerning the English Mission*, C.R.S. IV, p. 69.
8. Wood (1691), 2: 381. Florio went with Barnes to Magdalen: "At which time, wearing a gown, he [Florio] was matriculated as a member of that house [Magdalen] in 1581, aged almost 36 years, and as a teacher and instructor of certain scholars in the University."
9. In self-justification, Bruno later portrayed Oxford and its professors as "a constellation of most obstinate pedantry, ignorance and presumption mingled with a rustic incivility which would provoke the patience of Job." He had, he claimed, debated with "a miserable doctor, who came forward on that grave occasion as a leader of the academy, [and] stumbled fifteen times over fifteen syllogisms, like a hen against the stubble." The Nolano was treated with "Incivility and Discourtesy."

10. Labanoff (1844), 5: 406, Marie Stewart to Mlle Marie de Castelnau, January 26, 1584.

11. CSP Scot. 7: 5, Mary Queen of Scots to Mauvissière January 5, 1584. She proposed a secret means of communication:

> the best and most secret writing is allum soaked in a little clear water twenty-four hours before one wishes to write, and to read it, it is only necessary to damp the paper in some basin of clear water. The secret writing appears white, sufficiently easy to read until the paper has dried again. You could write in this way on white taffeta or white cloth, especially fine linen, and to know between us when there is something written, cut from the piece of taffeta or linen a little piece from one of the corners. As to the papers which are ordinary memoirs write the letter "M" of this word" memoir" with the tail curled round.... I shall use the same if necessity requires.

Chapter 4

1. SP 12/160/29, April 1583; Pollen (1922), pp. xxxvii–xxxviii.

2. SP 12/160/29, April 1583. As elsewhere, the spelling has often been modernized.

3. Pollen (1922), p. 169, letter of Nuncio Castelli to Cardinal of Como, May 2, 1583. The letter is given in Italian in Knox, *Records*, p 412–13.

4. Pollen (1922), p. xxxix, citing Gentlemen Pensioners Rolls.

5. The mother of Sir Francis Englefield was an Elizabeth Throckmorton of Coughton, Warwickshire, and her brother, Sir George Throckmorton, was the father of Sir John Throckmorton of Feckenham.

6. Persons to Don Juan de Ideaques, June 30, 1597, transcription, Jesuit Archives, London, Persons 46/12/4 pp. 665–673. Another translation/transcription of this letter is found in Tierney-Dodd 3: lix-lxvii.

7. The proposition that Fagot was Giordano Bruno has been argued in scholarly detail by John Bossy in *Giordano Bruno and the Embassy Affair*. But it is very unlikely to be correct. It is clear from Bossy's own research that Bruno was in Paris on 28 March, o.s./ 7 April, n.s. 1583 with the English ambassador. Bossy (1991), p. 13.There is no indication that Bruno had any prior connections with the English or with any English agent. Probably he was trying to secure a passport to go to Oxford. Because the first letters under the name Fagot to Secretary Walsingham reported events of 14 April, o.s. 1583 in the French embassy in London, Bossy concludes that Bruno—to be Fagot—must have immediately come to London and settled in at the embassy "some time in April." Bossy himself recognizes that "we shall find no reason for thinking that Henri III sent Bruno to London on any kind of political or religious mission." Bossy (1991), p. 14. The only motivation Bossy can suggest for Bruno assuming the role of Fagot was money from Walsingham. Even assuming that Bruno left Paris as early as March 29, it is altogether improbable that within two weeks he could have reached London, settled in, and began to carry out arrangements to spy for Walsingham, a man there is no reason to believe he had ever known. Others who have examined the timing of Bruno's trip to England found that he had gone first to Oxford and that it "was apparently in the summer of 1583 that Bruno entered the Ambassador's house." Yates (1964), p. 90. In other words, the only reason for Bossy to believe that Bruno was in London in mid-April 1583 was that there were letters of Fagot from that time, and a reason for believing that Fagot was Bruno was that Bruno was in the embassy in mid-April 1583. That a man who had never been in England should suddenly know enough of English political matters to report on the identities and background of English and Scots visitors to the French embassy is wholly improbable. Though he dealt often with unsavory characters, one must also doubt that Walsingham would ever have looked for intelligence from a man such as Bruno, whom he presumably knew either not at all or only by reputation as an erratic, vagrant scholar.

8. "Memoir of Châteauneuf," Labanoff (1844), 6: 291. "Monsieur l'ambassadeur, vous avez grande intelligence et secrete avec la Reine d'Ecosse, mais croyez que je sais tout ce qui se fait en mon royaume; et puis j'ai été prisonnière du temps de la reine, ma soeur, je sais de quels artifices usent les prisonniers pour gagner des serviteurs et avoir de secretes intelligences."

9. Q. Z. (1584), "A Discoverie of the Treasons Practised and Attempted Against the Queenes Maiestie and the Realme, by Francis Throckmorton...." Throckmorton had confessed, said the paper, of a plan:

> Agreed on by the Scottish Queen and her confederates in france, and in other foreign parts, and also in England, for the invading of the realm.
> That the Duke of Guise should be the principal Leader and Executer of that Invasion....
> That the Duke of Guise had prepared the Forces, but there wanted two things, money, and the assistance of a convenient Party in England, to join with the foreign Forces.

10. Id. P 188. Paget "endeavoured in a sort to find the disposition of William Shelley, Esquier, how he might stand affected to give assistance to the treasons, although Paget discovered not directly his traiterous Intents to Shelley."

11. "Examination of Lord Henry Howard," December 11, 1585 CSP Scot. 6: 675–76. He was reexamined the next month, id. 7: 21–2.

12. Most historians have agreed on Gratley's role except for Fr. Pollen who, on slight evidence, asserted

that Gratley only later became a tool for Walsingham. Pollen (1919), pp. 67–73.

13. Walsingham was writing to Phelippes about Gratley as Foxley in May 1586; Morris (1874), p. 189. Letters of Gratley/Foxley to Walsingham are at SP 12/191/27 (July 24, 1586); SP 15/29/100 (April 20, 1586); SP 15/29/110 (May 28, 1586); SP 15/29/118–19 (June 18, 1586, June 21, 1586); SP 15/29/139 (August 9, 1586).

14. Morris (1874), pp. 189, 218–219, Phelippes to Walsingham, July 8, 1586.

15. SP 12/200/48, Gilbert Gifford to Phelippes, April 27/May 7, 1587. A number of other letters identified as Gilbert Gifford's show clearly that ♃ is Gilbert Gifford. SP 12/208/20, calendared as Gilbert Gifford to Walsingham ? January 23, 1588 (dated internally as February 2 under calendar used in Paris), has the Jupiter symbol noted on the back; this letter makes reference to another letter written by the writer to his uncle Offley. The next item in the state papers is SP 12/208/21, which is the letter to Monsieur Offley of the same date and signed "Gilb. Gifford." Another letter 10 days later, SP 12/208/48, February 2/12, 1588 is signed G Gifford, and the outside has the same Jupiter symbol. Other instances are cited below.

16. Bossy (1991), p. 193 (discusses the symbol's usage and where it appears). In *Under the Molehill*, Bossy (2001), p. 160 he backs away from his earlier statement that the symbol identified Fagot ; now he says the symbol can be found on other correspondence pertaining to Scotland, but the symbol Bossy describes does not appear to be the same usage. In fact, the endorsements reproduced in Bossy's plates IX (Fagot) and X (Fowler to Walsingham), Bossy (2001), pp. 158–59, are not at all alike. The use of ♃ in shown by Bossy on p. 157 (but not reproduced on Bossy's plate IX Fagot) is very much the same as when used with Gilbert Gifford. For use with Phelippes, see, e.g., "Phelippes to ♃ [Gilbert Gifford]," March ? 1587, SP 12/199/96; "♃ [Gilbert Gifford] to [Walsingham?]" Feb 2, 1588, SP 12/208/48. Thomas Barnes to Gilbert Curll, April 28, 1586, Pollen (1922) pp. 5–6 (♃ deciphered as Gilbert Gifford). Gilbert Curll to Barnaby, June 19/29, 1586, Pollen (1922), pp. 11–12. See also Florent Bacot to Phelippes, June 1590, SP 12/232/72: "desires some assistance for his friend, the spy, who signs ♃, who was in great necessity." Florent Bacot was a correspondent of Gilbert Gifford, "Gilbert Gifford to Florent Bacot," SP 12/208/90 (Feb.? 1588).

17. A *Mémoire* thought to be written by ambassador Châteauneuf comments of Gilbert Gifford that "the said gifford came from France where he was nourished seven or eight years among the Jesuits and had been in Italy and Spain and spoke very well all [these] languages." Labanoff (1844), 6: 279. This *Mémoire*, an incomplete fragment, is taken as though it were written by Châteauneuf but it is written in the third person and describes Châteauneuf as though it were by an aide: "pour lors était Ambassadeur en Angleterre pour le Roi de France, Messire Guillaume de L'aubespine, Baron de Châteauneuf-Sur-Cher, en Berry, Conseiller du Conseil-D'état du Roi, qui y était arrivé en Août 1585..." p. 276. The *Memoire* gives one pause for it could be taken as evidence against Gilbert Gifford being Fagot. This is because the *Memoire* treats Gifford as first appearing at the French embassy in December 1585. Yet there is a letter of Fagot to Walsingham that recounts a meeting of Fagot with Châteauneuf that probably dates from early September 1585. SP 12/206/80. It is calendared as December 1587. Bossy reprints and translates this letter of Fagot (1991), p. 234–37, and suggests its date as September, 1585. His reason for the dating is apparently based on the fact that Fagot's letter speaks of Girault, the butler of the embassy in the present tense. Yet in the latter part of September Girault is thought to have perished at sea when Mauvissière's boat was taken by pirates. Perhaps the *Memoire* was not actually written by Châteauneuf but by an aide who was not aware of a meeting in September. Perhaps Châteauneuf did not want to bring out he had been duped by Gilbert Gifford; Pollen has commented of the *Mémoire*: "There is an element of self-defence about the composition which may detract a trifle from its value here and there." Pollen (1922), p. liii. Or perhaps Fagot/Gifford invented the meeting with Châteauneuf for purposes of enhancing his credibility.

18. There has been much confusion over the years on Cherelles. Bossy (2001) pp. 14–28, traces this treatment by historians.

19. SP 15/30/69, Stafford to Walsingham, January 7, 1588: "I hear that [Gilbert Gifford] has ... brought Arnold [Arnault—Cherelles] in suspicion for dealing with you, and for being the great arm that is spoken of in Phelippes' letter...." Perhaps "great arm" refers to Cherelles as a copier of documents.

20. Bishop of Glasgow to Mary Stewart, March 21, 1586, CSP Scot. 8: 255–56: "A report of [Cherelles] has been made to their most Christian Majesties that Walsingham should have won him to the devotion of the Queen of England, and caused a chain of two hundred crowns to be given him; and on this account the said Sieur de Chasteauneuf has been told to send him back hither with all diligence."

Walsingham's spy Berden reported much the same to his master about June 1586, indicating the source of the story was the English ambassador. Berden said Stafford imparted "his said secrets to Charles Arundell and that he told him that M. Arnault [Cherelles], That Lately Attended Upon the French Ambassador here was a spy for the right Honourable your good master [Walsingham] and that he gave him at his first entertainment a chain of gold, upon his promise to perform that office; which matter was delivered to the Queen Mother [Catherine De Medici] who presently was much perplexed with the matter, and gave order to remove him from hence." [Thomas Rogers, alias Berden] to Francis [Mills? Walsingham's secretary], [June ?], CSP Foreign 1586-8, p. 34.

21. SP 12/168/34; in Foley Records 6: 723-25. At some point Phelippes was resident in Leadenhall but he no doubt maintained several places in London.

22. Wilson (2007), pp. 189-90.

Chapter 5

1. 23 Eliz. 1 c.1, "Act to retain the Queen's Majesty's subjects in their obedience."

2. The Spanish ambassador in England wrote to his monarch that the English "Queen has ordered letters to be written to the earls of Northumberland, Montague, Worcester, and Southampton, five barons, and three hundred gentlemen, who are held to be Catholics, and has ordered them to be imprisoned in the castles and strongholds, which, as I mentioned in a former letter, had been chosen for the purpose, in fear of a rising of Catholics here...." CSP Sp. 3:49, August 21, 1580.

3. Job Throckmorton himself got into religious troubles for his Puritanism a few years later. The printing press upon which the Mar-Prelate Tracts were published was set up at Haseley. In 1591 Job Throckmorton was acquitted of associating with religious malcontents.

4. The priest Slye identified was Fr. Roger Wakeman, a Douay trained priest who was already dead at the time of these testimonies. Arrested at the time of the Campion mission, he died in Newgate prison in November, 1582.

5. Once again, Slye probably had good information. The manor of Cookhill, on the borders of Worcestershire and Warwickshire, was home to William Fortescue and his young son Nicholas. Father and son were both zealous Catholics, and Nicholas later sheltered another religious man named Baker, the Benedictine monk David Baker.

6. He recalled that "[I]n the year 1558, when I was six years of age, a friend of mine told me for the first time that my father was dead, and he waited to see what would be my reply. I was silent for some time, as though meditating something; which he perceiving, and asking what it was, i replied that i grieved for the death of my parent, because when he would rise again on the Day of Judgment he would appear worm-eaten and full of holes."

7. CSP Scot. 8: 292-93, Charles Paget to Mary, 31 March 1586 ("Fitzherbert whom I recommended to your majesty has become the Queen Mother's man, and is allowed to receive what benefit he can from England.").

Chapter 6

1. Bossy (1991), p. 237. SP 12/206/80, wrongly calendared as 1587.

2. SP 78/14 (calendar p. 675); reproduced in Bossy (1991). pp. 238-240.

Chapter 7

1. "Instructions by Elizabeth to Sir Amias Powlet," CSP Scot. 7: pp. 585-86.

2. Thomas Morgan to Mary Stewart, July 10, 1585, CSP Scot. 8: 10, 12. In March 1586 Morgan wrote Mary that Poley had "employed" for him and Paget for 12 months, indicating Poley's involvement dates from on or before March 1585. March 21, 1586, CSP Scot. 8: 262, 273.

3. March 21, 1586, CSP Scot. 8: 262, 274: "By Blunt's influence and my advice he [Poley] is placed with Lady Sidney, the daughter of secretary Walsingham, and can therefor discover many things of value to your majesty. At my instigation he did acceptable service to the French ambassador on his first arrival in England. Your majesty may employ Poley safely for communication with the French Ambassador."

4. August 13, 1585, CRS 21, p. 78; same letters at SP 15/29/38, 39, 41. When the letters from France came in, Phelippes marked them with an X then later a B or 80. CRS 21, p. 78. The Calendar of State Papers has mistakenly identified a letter or two of B with Thomas Barnes when they were part of the reports of Berden.

5. "All this was told me by Thomas Fitzherbert, as a great secret, upon my showing him the three ciphers. I also understand by him that Thomas Throgmorton [brother of Francis Throckmorton] goes very shortly into Spain, to further the practices, and that Parsons is secretly in the camp of the Prince of Parma, to the like end, and shortly goes to Rome about it. Fitzherbert is likely to know of these matters, as he is secretary to all the persons before mentioned of our nation, and of the Jesuits' party. He has offered me a chamber in his house at Paris; but his commons are above my reach, and I must buy a bed, if I will be there; also he will want to borrow, and I have nothing to lend, being six crowns in debt. Yet it is a place most necessary, as he gives and receives intelligence, and his house is the place of common conference, and the lodging of Charles Arundell when at Paris...."

6. Pollen (1919), p. 85.

7. CSP Sp. 3: 577.

8. Pollen (1919), p. 85.

9. CSP Scot. 9: 530.

10. This and other related letters are reprinted in Pollen (1904), pp. 248-49, *passim*.

11. Thomas Barnes entered Trinity College, Oxford, in 1573 age 18. In 1576 he arrived at Douay and moved to the English College at Rome in 1580. He was a son of William Barnes of Barcheston and Tatlon (Talton, Tadlington), Worcestershire and Alice Middlemore, daughter of Thomas and Anne Middlemore of Edgbaston, Warwickshire. The connection to the Giffords of Chillington was through the

Throckmortons of Coughton who were common relations to both the Giffords and the Middlemores, leading Thomas Barnes and Gilbert Gifford to describe themselves as cousins. Thomas's brother William Barnes was a significant figure in the vicinity of Stratford-upon-Avon. William Barnes, a Catholic, was a member of the Middle Temple. Because their father had died in 1561, Thomas Barnes was probably partly raised by his brother William, who advanced money for his education on the Continent.

12. Pollen (1922), pp. cxxxii, 17. Barnes is not to be confused with Robert Barnewell, an Irish gentleman among those who were executed in the plot.

13. Phelippes wrote Walsingham of Gifford's proposal to this effect:

> If he [Walsingham] thinks Berden a fit man ... it needs but to get someone to disguise himself like a gentleman of ability to come and talk with the ambassador as Emilio Russo, and he to give that credit to Berden which would serve the turn hereafter.

Phelippes to Walsingham, July 17, 1586, CSP Scot. 8:530.

14. SP 12/202/38, Tho. Phelippes to ♃ (Gilbert Gifford).

15. Mary to Morgan, July 17, 1586, Labanoff (1844), 6: 423–24. She knew that Phelippes was said to be Walsingham's man and had earlier warned Châteauneuf that although he had promised to do her service, he was playing a double game. Mary to Châteauneuf, March 24, 1586, Labanoff (1844), 6: 262–63.

16. Anthony Babington to Robert Poley, [August] 1586, CSP Scot. 8: 658. The Latin phrase is a line from Apuleius, *Metamorphoses* (or *The Golden Ass*) 4.10.

17. In three stanzas, the first of which is:
> My prime of youth is but a frost of cares,
> My feast of joy is but a dish of pain,
> My crop of corn is but a field of tares,
> And all my good is but vain hope of gain.
> The day is past, and yet I saw no sun,
> And now I live, and now my life is done.

18. In a long document prepared for the trials of the conspirators by Sir John Puckering, George Gifford's name leads all the rest of the Babington conspirators. The summary of the charges and evidence against George Gifford:

> [Accusations.] That he had undertaken the killing of her majesty by the solicitation of one Persons a Jesuit, and the Duke of Guise, and had thereupon received of the Duke of Guise 800 pounds or crowns.
>
> [Evidence.] Savage, 10th and 11th August, by report of Gilbert Giffard. Ballard, 8th August, as he heard, and that George Giffard had sworn it to Persons. Ballard, 12th August, says he heard it of Gilbert Giffard. Ballard, 19th August, that he had told it to Babington and Dunn. Savage, 11th August, Gilbert Giffard told him that the Duke of Guise protested that if he caught George Giffard he should die for not performing it. Ticheborne, 29th August, Babington told him that George Giffard had received money of the Duke of Guise for undertaking to kill the Queen.
>
> George Giffard himself examined 23rd August, utterly denies that he ever knew Persons or Ballard, that he ever had any intelligence from the Duke of Guise or from any other from beyond the seas, or ever received any money from the Duke of Guise or from any beyond the seas.

CSP Scot. 8: 680–81, "Examinations of the Conspirators," September 6, 1586.

19. SP 12/192/42, 17 August 1586, "Examination of George Throckmorton."

20. Walsingham's report on prisoners in the Tower in November, 1586 noted: "G. Gyfforde—Her Majestie to be moved for his release with order to proceed in his voyage." CRS 2 p. 262, from SP 12/295/30. The queen was surely unaware of Gifford's actions on her behalf and Walsingham could not dismiss Gifford from prison on his own. He remained in the Tower in July 1588, as did three other of Walsingham's agents in the Babington Plot period: William Stafford, Michael Moody, and Robert Poley. CRS 2, p. 281, from 12/215/19.

21. Nicholl (1992), p. 164.

22. APC 19:210.

23. APC 24:251.

24. SP 14/62/28, Sir George Gifford to Salisbury (Cecil), March 15, 1611: "Has served 39 years without reward. Is in difficulties. Requests favour, as his Lordship's wife's kinsman, to obtain 2,000*l* worth of goods forfeited for not paying customs."

25. Gifford called upon Bernardino Mendoza in Paris and tried to get his endorsement for the Babington Plot, as Mendoza related to King Philip, August 13/3, 1586, CSP Sp. 3: 603–08. The meeting must have been held sometime late in July under the English calendar, as the letter to Philip said the dispatch had been waiting four days for want of a passport. An unnamed priest (perhaps Ballard?) had called on Mendoza some months earlier with a vague inquiry about help for a Catholic uprising, and in early May Mendoza learned of a plot of "four men of position who have the run of Queen's House" to kill the queen. CSP Sp. 3: 579. Gilbert Gifford implicated his own father as supporting the plot.

26. Stafford to Walsingham, January 25, 1585, quoted in Pollen (1922), p. xxxvi.

27. As we see it expressed in similar words by Pandarus in *Troilus and Cressida* [5.10]:

> **Pandarus.** world! world! thus
> is the poor agent despis'd! traitors and bawds, how earnestly are
> you set a work, and how ill requited! Why should our endeavour be
> so lov'd, and the performance so loathed?

28. SP 15/30/55, Dec. 1587, Sir Edward Stafford to Secretary Walsingham.

29. SP 12/200/48–50, April 26/May 7, 1587, Pollen (1922), p. 174. The reference to Heywood is to Fr. Jasper Heywood, a Jesuit, who wrote to Aquaviva, the head of the Jesuits, some time about 1586 that George Gifford had dealt with Fr. Persons about the slaughter of Elizabeth, and the whole matter was entrusted to Gifford to kill her. George Gifford promised to do so and then betrayed the whole affair, wrote Heywood. Reprinted in Pollen (1922), p. 172.

30. Stafford, the English ambassador, wrote Walsingham soon after Arundell's death: "No Man on this side served my turn as he did, and never the Spanish Ambassador nor his master [King Philip II] were better handled. I had the quickest and most correct advertisements out of Spain from him, and the Spanish Ambassador had that credit in him that he hid nothing that was reasonable from him." SP 15/30/226, Stafford to Walsingham, October 26, 1587. Walsingham's agent Berden reported in September 1585 that the other Catholics in Paris and Rome had come to suspect Charles Arundell of being a spy because of his time with Stafford, but after close examination were convinced that Arundell was with them. Berden noted: "The Pope is the more desirous to be persuaded of Charles Arundell in that he has been commended to him by the Duke of Guise for a meet man to have the conduct of an Army to invade his native country, and Arundell, suggested to the Pope certain plots how the country might be invaded."

31. SP 15/29/39.

32. Southwell (1953), pp. 18–19. English modernized for clarity.

33. Cooper (2012), p. 64.

34. Critical reflections can be found in one of the shrewdest observers of the Elizabethan legal system. In a play whose central theme is the nature of justice, Shakespeare's Portia in the role of a justice-dispensing judge observes:
> Ay, but I fear you speak upon the rack,
> Where men enforced do speak anything.
> [*Merchant of Venice*, 3.2].

35. Strickland (1858), pp. 426–27.

36. According to Phelippes himself, he had an "appearance before the lords and other Commissioners at Fotheringhay, he being commanded to attend upon the Secretary [Walsingham] hither with some papers that were in his custody and having obtained by special favor a special place among the Q[Ueen's] learned Counsell, and other officers attendant upon the Service within the very Parquet of the presence to see and hear what was done for that both Clerks of the Crown, Powle and Sandes being old and ignorant men, fombled out so untowardly the things they were to read by reason of their office, the said Phelips standing by was commanded to help them out and to read such letters and evidences as the Q[Ueen's] learned Counsell Produced." SP 14/1/119–20, May ?, 1603 (Apology of Phelippes for meddling in the cause of Mary Queen of Scots).

Chapter 8

1. When Don Juan of Austria was assigned the task of pacifying the Spanish Low Countries in 1577, he had advised King Philip of Spain that it was necessary that England be ruled by someone friendly to Spain but he had not persuaded Philip to any plan of action.

2. Mattingly (1959), p.121.

3. SP 12/198/18, February 7, 1587; SP 12/198/29, February 10, 1587.

4. SP 12/198/12, February 12, 1587. The searchers missed some evidence: In 1959 electricians working in the residence found a wooden box nailed to a joist in the roof. It had lain hidden there for nearly four centuries. It contained an ancient vellum, on which was written a list of indulgences, and it enclosed an *Agnus Dei* issued by the Pope. http://Jesuitinstitute.Org/Pages/Campion.Htm (last accessed November 19, 2014).

5. Summarizing the orders of the Privy Council at the beginning of 1588, one historian notes they reflect a general order of the Council to the effect that:
> [A]ll persons of standing who remained obdurate in their Catholic belief were restrained and compelled to surrender their arms, if they still possessed them; these were to be sold to well-affected subjects needing armor.... The more obstinate of the recusants were to be placed in close confinement; those less so were to be assigned to private homes where their conformity might be induced; a few, where the government thought leniency to be advisable, were permitted to remain in their homes under restrictions.

Trimble (1964), p. 134. E.g., SP 12/208/58 February 8, 1588 (Cambridge, Huntington); SP 12/208/66 February 12, 1588 (Leicestershire).

6. CSP Sp. 3: 573, King Philip to Mendoza, April 28, 1586.

7. CSP Sp. 3: 577, 603–07.

8. CSP Sp. 3: 536–37.

9. CSP Sp. 3: 639, October 20, 1586.

10. CSP Sp. 3: 201–02, Mendoza to Philip, October 29, 1581; CSP Sp. 3: 209–10, November 7, 1581.

11. CSP Sp. 4: 519, March 22, 1589.

12. CSP Sp. 4: 133, letter of September 2, 1587 ("Julius has informed me that Drake's voyage is abandoned, as he has been assured by letters of Cecil.").

13. Hume, the editor of the Spanish papers, believed it was Fitzherbert who was new intermediary. CSP Sp. 4: 541. He was surely correct.

14. Fitzherbert devotes four pages to his *Treatise Concerning Policy and Religion* (1606, 1610) to Henry III's error and want of judgment in having the Duke and Cardinal killed "whereof I am able to say much

of my own knowledge, for I was at the same time in his courte and pallace at Bloys in the service of his mother..." p. 35. To the defense that "reason of state required it" Fitzherbert responded that there must be a "necessary concurrence of the reason of state with conscience and religion" which concurrence had not been present. Id. p 36.

15. Loomie (1963a), p. 109.

16. Loomie comments that King Philip failed to consult adequately with the exiles: "For Englefield and other leading exiles a graver incident by far was the failure of King Philip's advisers to consult them before the Armada of 1588." "Englefield, Sir Francis," ODNB.

17. CSP Sp. 4: 9–10, Olivares to Philip (January 27, 1587). A little later, Olivares commented to the king that Persons "is worrying me to death to get the Pope to make him [Allen] archbishop of Canterbury" if the cardinalate was not forthcoming. CSP Sp. 4: 40, Olivares to Philip, March 16, 1587.

18. CSP Sp. 4: 37, "Memorial Presented to His Holiness Setting Forth the Advisability of Making Dr. Allen a Cardinal," March 14, 1587.

19. Allen (1587).

20. Allen (1588), pp. liv-lv. The date is given at the end of the pamphlet as April 28, 1588.

21. SP 12/211/15, June 12, 1588.

22. SP 12/211/56 June 24, 1588. .

23. These occurred at Denham, Bucks., in the home of Sir George Peckham, whose son Edmund was married to Fr. John Gerard's sister, Dorothy. These exorcisms were the basis of Modo, Mahu, Hobbididance, and Flibbertigibbet, in Shakespeare's *King Lear*, 3.4. See F. W. Brownlow, *Shakespeare, Harsnett, and the Devils of Denham* (Newark: U of Delaware Press 1993).

24. Janelle (1935), pp. 6–7: "In 1568, William Allen had founded a residential house for [English students], known as the English College or Seminary: there Catholic priests to be trained for the English mission field. To this College Southwell now became attached; but we hear that soon after his arrival he was 'received into Anchin College,' the Jesuit college at Douay, founded in 1569. This probably means that while, at the former, he resided and received tutorial instruction, at the latter he attended the regular course of classes." Devlin (1956), p. 23, notes that the "arrangement for Robert was that he should have board and lodging at the English College, and attend classes at the neighbouring Jesuit school."

25. Devlin (1956), pp. 228–29.

26. Brownlow (1996), p. 11.

27. Id.

28. Id.

29. Caraman (1951), p. 8.

30. Id., 10.

31. Id., 10–11.

32. Read (1925), 1:431. Alford (2012), p. 264, indicates that Lord Burghley came into possession of the Walsingham files ("The contents of Walsingham's secure cabinets moved to Burghley's own"); but this seems doubtful.

33. SP 12/202/41, quoted at length in Read (1925) 3: 286–87.

34. SP 12/202/38, Tho. Phelippes to ♃ (Gilbert Gifford), June ?, 1587 (sends him 150 crowns to be paid by Peter Hatchett).

35. Ungerer (1976) 1: 4–9; Hammer (1999), pp. 155, 194.

36. CSP Sp. 4: 123, Mendoza to King Philip, July 12, 1587.

37. Hutchinson (2007), pp. 214–15, 232–33.

38. Details on Standen's life and intelligence work is found in Paul E. J. Hammer's entry in the ODNB and in Hammer (1992), pp. 277–95. See also, Hicks (1960), *passim*, and Read (1925), 3: 289–92.

39. Read (1925), pp. 291–92.

40. McGrath (1967), p. 202. Fr. Pollen referred to the "Massacre of 1588" in collecting papers related to the executions of the period. CRS V, *Unpublished Documents* (1908), p. 150.

41. Baldwin (1931), *passim*, argues that *The Comedy of Errors* alludes to the execution of Fr. Hartley. Another secular priest executed at Shoreditch shortly before Hartley was William Gunter. He was from Raglan, Monmouthshire and enrolled at Douay in July 1583. He left Rheims for England in July, 1587 and was arrested a year later, on June 30, 1588. He was hung on August 28, 1588. Burton & Pollen (1914), pp. 366–71.

42. Howell (1809), p. 1255 ("Dr. Allen made a most villainous and slanderous Book, which was very hard to be got, in which was contained, that the Earl of Arundel was a procurer of the last Bull, and the procurer of the Invasion also. The Bull was some part read, and the Book itself was some part read also.") See also, p. 1262 ("Then were read ... the bull of Sixtus Quintus and several remarks made on Allen's Memorial to the English...)."

43. Howell (1809), p. 1255.

44. Devlin (1956), p. 198.

45. ODNB, "Persons, Robert."

Chapter 9

1. Morris (1874), p. 114, Morgan to Mary Queen of Scots, October 15, 1585.

2. Cecil (1915), p. 11.

3. Spedding (1861), 1: 251.

4. Phelippes's younger brother had been a secretary and confidante to Francis Bacon, a relationship that had led to some difficulties between Anthony Bacon and the younger Phelippes. Jardine & Stewart (1999), pp. 84, 103–04.

5. In Shakespeare's *Twelfth Night* Sir Toby uses *Thou* in speaking to his close friend Andrew Aguecheek but tells him to taunt the youth he is challenging by referring to him as "Thou":

Sir Toby. Go, write it in a martial hand; be curst and brief; it is no matter how witty, so it be eloquent and full of invention. Taunt him with the license of ink; if **thou** *Thou'st* him some thrice, it shall not be amiss; and as many lies as will lie in thy sheet of paper....

6. December 8, 1587—Hyp/A/17, fo 48r. [Bodleian Library]: the Latin entry translates: "By the consent of the parties the cause has been remitted to be treated and determined by the venerable man Lord Vice Chancellor and Doctor James, Dean of Christ Church."

7. Hatfield Papers 6: 511–12.

8. One translation of this passage is given as "The Earl of Worcester and his eldest son, who are dominant in Wales, hate Protestantism, and many of their tenants and followers are much devoted to the Catholic religion." *The Spectator*, July 19, 1862, p. 804. The letter is reprinted in its Latin original and its provenance explained in Mattingly (1957), pp. 325–339.

9. Statement of Taylor on entering the College at Rome, CRS 54 (1962), p. 83.

10. SP 12/242/33, Phelippes to Essex, with Essex's comments, May 30, 1592.

11. SP 12/246/60, Earl of Essex to Thomas Phelippes, n.d.

12. Clark (1931), p. 84, n. 1.

13. Harley (1997), p. 102.

14. Harley (1997), pp. 94–95.

15. Sir William Stanley wrote a letter to Walsingham on October 10, 1586 (before he turned) concerning Jaques, "his lieutenant whom he has loved very well in respect that Mr. Vice-Chamberlain put him in the place and also for 'sundry good parts' found in him" and who was now "thought to be one in the odious conspiracy against her Majesty." CSP Foreign, 21/2: 188–89. An agent of Robert Cecil in 1606 informed Cecil that Jaques told him that "by his wit he got out of the Fleet having been three years prisoner and yet my hand was in the treason with Babington and Titcheborne as Also in Sir William Stanley's revolt." Hatfield Papers 18:423, Captain William Newce to Cecil [1606].

16. The Earl "demanded what inwardness there was between you [Phelippes] and the Lord Treasurer." SP 12/238/137, William Sterrell to Phelippes, April? 1591.

17. Allen to Agazzari, March 6, 1584, in Renold (1967), pp. 71–9. A spy report from France on English Catholics from this period said that Lord Herbert and Sir Edward Herbert are friends at Court of the papists or "Friends to the Popish Conspirators." CSP Scot. 6: 7, "Extracts of Letters, August 21, 1583"; SP 15/29/148. Thomas Rogers to Sec. Walsingham, August 11, 1585. These two documents containing similar information are probably from August 1585 rather than the time indicated by the Scottish Calendar.

18. SP 12/238/138, Francis Bacon to Thomas Phelippes, April ?, 1591; Spedding (1861), 1: 252.

19. SP 12/250/63 (wrongly calendared as 1594?). When it was calendared in the State Papers the researchers thought it dated from 1594, apparently in the supposition that it touched on a proposal Bacon made early in 1594 for the Queen to negotiate with the King of Spain and the Archduke Ernest over the plots coming out of the Low Countries. Spedding (1861), 1: 306. The 1594 proposal of Bacon for the Queen to negotiate may very well have concerned William Sterrell, but this letter of Sterrell is most certainly from 1591. Clearly Sterrell had not been in the employ of Phelippes before this time, despite the letters in the Calendar of State Papers that mistakenly assigned a date before 1591.

20. A letter of William Sterrell to Thomas Phelippes, SP 12/238/137, tentatively dated April ? 1591 mentions £10 that Phelippes owes to Sterrell but nothing indicates what this is for.

21. SP 12/239/120 (calendared as August 2, 1591). Sterrell to Phelippes.

22. Cole is probably John Cole of St. Catherine Coleman, esq., Diocese of London, listed as a Recusant at liberty in a list dated 1592 in Hatfield Papers 4: 263–73, p. 267.

23. The details of this journey are gleaned from multiple documents: SP 12/239/120, Sterrell to Phelippes, August 2, 1591; SP 12/240/10, Henry Saintmain (Sterrell) to Phelippes, September 11, 1591; SP 12/241/45 (Sterrell) to Phelippes, February 13, 1592; SP 12/241/44, Instructions for Mr. Saintmain, February 1592; SP 12/243/118, endorsed, "Saint Main," undated.

24. Probably a man using the name Monsieur Cahart SP 12/240/12, M. Cahart to Monsieur Thomas Francquelin, September 12/22, 1591 (in French). Phelippes wrote on the outside that it was "From M. Cahart to Saintmain." Cahart seems to say that Francquelin (Saintmain/Sterrell) had not communicated the matter to M. Snowden who could easily have prevented the embarkation of the Italian.

25. SP 12/240/10, Henry Saintmain (Sterrell) to Phelippes, September 11, 1591: "I hope to have better fortune the next time, because I intend not hereafter to deal in such sorts that other men's negligence shall overthrow all my labors. Let any wise, indifferent man judge whether I took not the best course. If you had made that haste which I required the service had been fully performed. But if my hope be to go again, as I hope (because I would fain do something worthy of good reward) I will trust only to myself." SP 12/241/45 (Sterrell) to Phelippes, February 13, 1592: "I rest in the meantime very sorry that you seem to have doubted of the truth of my unfained relations, wherein if I dealt not sincerely with you, let him refuse my soul that hath redeemed it. Had Guerdon's [governor of Calais] ship been stayed as I directed, then had my faith appeared...."

26. SP 12/243/78, John Baxter (Fitzherbert) to Robinson ("the other watchword that you advised him to use from Lile at your being there"), December 1/11, 1592; SP 12/244/15, Sterrell to Phelippes, January 15, 1593, Fitzherbert "had written something in this letter in milk, but it will not appear, for he sends me word that he followed my directions from Lile."

27. SP 12/241/2, Sterrell to Phelippes, January 2, 1592.

28. For an example of Cutt's sharp dealings, see Hatfield Papers 7: 280.

29. Carleton (Sherwood) spent some time in London in 1586 not in prison. He was sighted by one of Walsingham's informants in the Castle Tavern with Walsingham's spy Berden and several Catholics whom Berden was spying on. CSP Scot. 8: 569, Francis Milles to Walsingham, July 30, 1586: "With Berd. supped Edward Shelley, who brought with him Carleton the Priest, one Higham lately condemned for hearing a mass, and enlarged out of the 'Compter,' and one Robert Gage" (Gage was among those executed seven weeks later in the Babington Plot). Edward Shelley was executed in the violent reprisals against Catholics after the failure of the Armada.

30. SP 12/241/2, Sterrell to Phelippes, January 2, 1593.

31. SP 12/240/10, Henry Saintmain (Sterrell) to Phelippes, September 11, 1591.

32. Strype (1824), 4: 259–60.

33. SP 12/240/34, Henry Saintmain to Thomas Phelippes, October 8, 1591.

34. "Now that I am come into your state, I must follow it, and will to the uttermost. If my Lord Treasurer do mean to send any man for intelligence, if you could work me to be the man, then I should both compass something for our selves, and yet yield him such contentment as every one shall not be able to do the like."

35. Phelippes must have taken exception to Sterrell's trying to bring Lord Burghley into the plans. Sterrell wrote to Phelippes that he was sorry that Phelippes has taken exception against Sterrell's last letter. SP 12/250/64 (wrongly calendared as 1594?). Sterrell says that he gave "no Cause, if it would please you to consider of it with indifference. You know that I may have evil happen and be discovered in some actions or be in danger some other way. If then I have good grounds, that is powerable [powerful] friends to stand upon I may be relieved easily by your and their good means. I beseech you therefor think not amiss of me if I love to tread sure. He that means to stand by it will look to sure footing as well backward as forward." He goes on to remark that the last time he went over only to see why they sent for him; this time he goes "To know what they do, and to be no secondary man among them." Sterrell would be content with Phelippes' simple promise, but Phelippes should not be offended that Sterrell seeks more anchor than one.

36. Kelsey (1998), p. 345.

37. Ungerer (1976), 1: 127.

38. The association with Don Pedro may well have related to Sterrell's probable acquaintance with Edward Winter. The latter had been a student at Oxford while Sterrell was a student. In 1589 Winter was taken prisoner while in Europe and by February 1590 was lodged in Antwerp castle. Winter sought to persuade the English government to arrange that he be given freedom in exchange for Don Pedro de Valdes; the Privy Council agreed in principle to the exchange. Winter and Don Pedro came to know each other well through a correspondence with one another. It is tantalizing to imagine that Sterrell met with Winter when Sterrell too found himself briefly detained in Antwerp Castle in 1592, a year before Winter's release. In August 1595 Winter married the Earl of Worcester's daughter, Anne Somerset. Hasler (1981), 3: 673–75. Perhaps the Somerset family was already allied with the Winter family, as their seats were not far distant, and Sterrell became involved with Don Pedro as Worcester tried to help Edward Winter. Or perhaps Sterrell knew Edward Winter from Oxford and became associated with Don Pedro in order to help Winter; if so, then Sterrell may have brought Anne Somerset together with Winter after the latter's release.

39. The "I" in "Ailiff" was transcribed by a printer of the Acts of the Privy Council as a "C."

40. Matriculation entry of December 8, 1578 age 15, Foster (1891), 1: 48. Sterrell, Ayliffe, and Skinner may have become friends at Oxford c. 1578–80; Sterrell may have encountered Skinner and Ayliffe when Skinner was a law student in London and Sterrell (as "Kirby") was appearing at the embassy of the French Ambassador, Monsieur Mauvissière.

41. Owen Lewis had much control over the development of the English College at Rome, and Sir Richard Shelley once complained that the hospice which became the College under Lewis had become "the exclusive preserve of Oxford men of plebeian origin." Quoted in Edwards (1995), p. 15. Richard Ayliffe fits perfectly into this description of the men favored by Owen Lewis.

42. Petti (1959), p. 57. The events were also noted in the records kept by the Spanish officials concerning Englishmen in the Low Countries who received pensions from Spain. The entry for 1596 of recommendations concerning those receiving pensions from the King of Spain described Skinner as "A gentleman of good birth, he was pensioned through the request of Cardinal Allen. 'Not being paid he fled to England to seek aid among his friends.' He was captured and condemned, but now it is understood that he lives at home; there is no reason to retain his name any further." Loomie (1963a), p. 258. Loomie elsewhere notes that Skinner was given a good pension of 40 escudos a month by the Spanish; Skinner said he did not need it as he claimed to have income of 3,000 escudos–roughly £750 a year. It is tempting to think that Skinner's confession under torture is the basis for Portia's observation when Bassanio says he lives upon the rack: "but I fear you speak upon the rack, Where men enforced do speak anything." *The Merchant of Venice*, 3.2.

43. Birch (1754), 1: 89, Standen to Anthony Bacon, October 22, 1592.

44. Loomie (1963b), p. 19; Verstegan (1959), p. 61, n. 6.

45. Jeaffreson (1887), 2: 215; Anstruther (1968), 2: 296.

Chapter 10

1. Wernham (1976), pp. 344–45; Nicholl (1992), pp. 234–35.

2. Robert Cecil was himself nearly imprisoned by Mondragon when in 1588, before the Armada, the Queen had sent him on a mission to the Low Countries. From Antwerp Cecil sent a letter stating that "Montdragon, who is governor of the citadel here, would have quickly laid his authority upon me, if I had not had a direct passport from his Altesse, for all my copy of the safe-conduct of the Commissioners and their train." The letter is reproduced in Cecil (1915), pp. 32–37 Mondragon's last major battle would be fought when he was more than 92. He conducted military operations from a chair overlooking the movement of troops towards battle, the plumes of his iron headpiece waving colorfully. He personally arranged a counter-ambush on this occasion and returned to Antwerp victorious against a far younger man, to which the historian Motley comments: "So far could the icy blood of ninety-two prevail against the vigour of twenty-eight." Motley (1871), 3: 341.

3. SP 12/248/53; SP 15/33/13, Hugh Owen to Sterrell, May 7, 1594. See below, p 308–09 n. 45 for discussion of this letter being separated into 2 parts of the Calendar. Ferdinando Robinson, an Englishman who was said to have served William Stanley as a mule keeper in the past, was returning to poison his old master in the water of Spa.

4. SP 12/242/38, Robinson, May? 1592 Liège. The full letter makes clear that the recipient is a friend waiting to hear from Sterrell in Middelburg and that Sterrell is sending him back to England—this was Staveley.

5. SP 12/242/68, Thomas Ferrers to Lord Burghley, June 30, 1592.

6. SP 12/242/3, Robinson to Mr. Morice at the Swan, Bishopsgate Street, May 1, 1592. Perhaps the prospect of Parma coming into France had been sufficient to lessen the siege. In France in December, Essex had written Lord Burghley: "The name of the Duke of Parma doth make a Frenchman startle...." Essex to Burghley, Devereux (1853), 1: 266.

7. SP 12/242/37, Robert Robinson to Mr Morice at the Sign of the Swan Without Bisbopsgate. A date on the back in Phelippes's hand says "May 1592."

8. The Infanta is alluded to as heir to France in Shakespeare's *The Comedy of Errors*: "Antipholus: Where France? Dromio: In her forehead, arm'd and reverted, making war against her heir" [a pun on hair]).

9. SP 12/242/38, Robinson, May? 1592 Liège; SP 12/242/3, Robinson to Mr. Morice, May 1, 1592.

10. SP 12/242/53, Robert Robinson to John Morice, June 13, 1592 (June 21is date given by Sterrell, n.s.). Another letter of Sterrell's in the State Papers was miscalendared and can cause confusion for historians. The letter is dated by Sterrell as January 2 but with no year. The Calendar puts it in 1592. It was actually written January 2, 1593. The letter discusses Cloudsley, whom Sterrell did not meet until later in 1592. The confusion is compounded by a note added by Phelippes himself to a letter of his to Essex that says "Touching Cloudesly." The letter was several weeks before Phelippes had heard of Cloudsley. When Phelippes was organizing his many letters he probably mis-remembered to whom the letter pertained.

11. SP 12/243/91.

12. Lennon (1981), p. 31.

13. Lennon (1981), pp. 40–41.

14. Lennon (1981), p.43.

15. Lennon (1981), p 47. Richard Stanihurst became a physician before returning to the Low Countries. His second wife died in 1602. Both his sons eventually took holy orders and entered the Jesuits. Stanihurst himself became a priest and for a time served as chaplain to Archduke Albert. A close friend of Richard Verstegan (another of Sterrell's associates), Stanihurst probably contributed to the writing of the *Conference About the Next Succession* that was completed in 1594. He also wrote an introductory verse for Verstegan's 1604 book, *Restitution of a Decayed Intelligence*.

16. Lennon (1981), p. 54; Loomie (1965 a), p. 147.

17. SP 77/5 fo. 355, J P to Halyns, May 25/June 4, 1598, Liège.

18. SP 12/242/3, Robinson to Mr. Morice, May 1, 1592; SP 12/242/38 Robinson May? 1592, Liège; SP 12/242/30, Robinson to Morice May 28, 1592; SP 12/242/37, Robert Robinson to Mr Morice, May 1592.

19. Verstegan reported these events in his newsletters to Fr. Persons, and it was surely part of the news shared among the English in the Low Countries. Petti (1959), pp. 57, 61. The index to this volume labels Skinner "Apostate." There's no basis for this. This man's fortitude in his faith was such that he was facing charges and confiscation of his property many years later solely because of his religion. Jeaffreson (1887), 2: 215 (Middlesex Records) lists Anthony Skinner and Edward Gage (Gadge) (Skinner's father-in-law) as recusants and William Iveson—St Andrews-in-Holborne January 16, 8 James 1 (1611); Skinner was again indicted in 12 James 1.

20. SP 12/242/30.

21. SP 12/242/37, Robert Robinson to Mr. Morice, May 1592.

22. SP 12/242/53, Robert Robinson to John Morice, June 13, 1592.

23. Sterrell said he had been "promised such a piece of Spanish velvet as you never did see better" but it would cost plenty. SP 12/242/30, Robinson to Morice, May 28, 1592.

24. SP 12/242/53, June 13, 1592. The Jesuits developed their own lines of correspondence with which William Sterrell became intimately involved under several other aliases.

25. SP 12/242/56, Robert Robinson to Mr. Morice, June 18, 1592.
26. SP 12/242/37, Robert Robinson to Mr Morice, May 1592.
27. SP 12/242/3, Robinson to Mr. Morice at the Swan, Bishopsgate Street, May 1, 1592.
28. SP 12/242/26, Robinson to ??, May 26, 1592; SP 12/242/30, Robinson to Morice, May 28, 1592; SP 12/242/53, Robert Robinson to John Morice, June 13, 1592; SP 12/242/56, June 18, 1592, Robert Robinson to Mr. Morice.
29. SP 12/242/26, Robinson to ??, May 26, 1592. Sterrell gave a new routing for letters: "To send to me you must take this course, the superscription of your letter thus to me must be thus a monsr. Robert Robinson demeurent au Liège, loge a l'ensigne de la lance Courone en la rue Seinte Huberte. It must be put in a cover and directed to a messenger in Dort who is called Jan de Bode van lac, ende graven Strat ende Silver Cloak. Your letter thus addressed will come to me."
30. He may have been the Thomas Ferrers who was a son of Sir Humphrey Ferrers of Tamworth, Warwickshire. He matriculated from Trinity College, Oxford, age 16 the same day as his older brother John, October 16, 1583. Foster (1891), 2:493; Hasler (1981), 2: 114–15. *Visitation of Warwickshire* 1619, pp. 5–7. He would have been about 25 when he encountered Sterrell in 1592. He was a cousin of Henry Ferrers of Baddesley Clinton, whose home was used on occasion by the Jesuits.
31. SP 12/242/68, Thomas Ferrers to Lord Burghley, 30 June 1592.
32. Foster (1891), 4: 1500. Hasler (1981) 3: 519, identifies Townshend as of Magdalen Hall but Clark (1887), p. 108 confirms that John Townshend, Norfolk, gent., 13, matriculated from Magdalen College November 24, 1581.
33. Hasler (1981), 3: 519. John Townshend was an MP in 1593, 1597, and 1601. He was fatally wounded in a duel in 1603, in which he killed another Magdalen College contemporary, Sir Matthew Browne.
34. SP 12/242/89, Ezekiel Staveley to Phelippes, Leadenhall, from Middleburgh, July 26, 1592. In recounting his exchange with Ferrers, Stavely told him that he worked for Essex, and Ferrers said that Essex was a kinsman of his. The person doing the Calendar of State Papers interpreted Stavely's writing as saying Stavely worked for "Lord of Casselis." The tailor's spelling was simply difficult; the name written is "Essiskes." The calendar editor interpreted as a "C" was the same letter signed below: "E" zechill Stavely. Essex had inherited the title of Lord Ferrers of Chartley because his family descended from the Sir Walter Devereux who had married the heiress of Lord Ferrers of Chartley. Lacey (1971), pp. 6–7. Thomas Ferrers was correct in claiming a kinship with Essex, and clearly the Calendar editor simply mis-read the handwriting.
35. SP 12/ 242/89, Staveley to Phelippes, July 26, 1592, from Middleburg. Obviously Sterrell had been right in trying to see that Burghley knew of his mission.
36. SP 12/242/103, Thomas Ferrers to Thomas Phelippes, August 6, 1592.
37. Id. The same greetings are included in the follow up letter of August 17, 1592, SP 12/242/107, Ferrers to Phelippes, from Middelburg.
38. SP 12/242/107, Ferrers to Phelippes, from Middelburg, August 17, 1592.
39. SP 12/241/44, "Instructions for Mr. Saintmain" February 1592.
40. Devereux (1853), 1: 295.
41. SP 12/242/37, Robert Robinson to Mr Morice at the Sign of the Swan Without Bishopsgate. See also SP 12/242/26 Robinson to ?? May 26, 1592. The Calendar of State Papers reads the name there as Hughes, but it is another letter of Sterrell's describing Reinold Bisley. In the original the name is in cipher with a decipher above it that is very indistinct; it is in the hand of Phelippes. The description is identical to that given in other letters for Bisley.
42. SP 12/242/26, Robinson, May 26, 1592.
43. SP 12/243/92 (the Calendar of State Papers has these as Dec.? 1592 but the document surely precedes the questioning in July 1592). Bisley was to be asked if he was not sent over by them secretly and whether he has or is promised a pension by the King of Spain or the Duke of Parma. Phelippes's questions concerned whether Bisley was bringing letters to one Webster who was a prisoner in the Marshalsea prison.
44. SP 12/242/33, Phelippes to the Earl of Essex, May 30, 1592. A note that appears to be Phelippes hand that may have been added years later says "Touching Cloudesly." But this was probably in error.
45. A dispatch of Ferrers from Middleburgh in late June said that he had heard that Stavely had left London some 14 days past; Ferrers's letter may have been dated new style, which would have meant it was from about June 20 and his information may have been a bit stale. SP 12/242/68, Thomas Ferrers to Lord Burghley, June 30, 1592,.
46. SP 12/242/88, notes of the examination of Renold Bisley, July 25, 1592.
47. The latter may have been Ingram Thwing, an Englishman in Brussels receiving a pension from the King of Spain, Loomie (1963a), p. 261; Petti (1959), p. 77. Or he may have been Edward Thwing, a priest who, like Bisley, was from York. Ordained in 1590, Edward Thwing went into England in about 1594; in 1600 he was executed by the government.
48. Another set of notes (undated) of Phelippes on Bisley state that Bisley was to be found at an Italian's house who was married to an Englishwoman and who kept a bowling alley in Bishopsgate Street. SP 12/243/94.
49. SP 12/241/118, "Reinold Boseley [To Cecil ?]," April 7, 1592.
50. Richard Verstegan reported to Baynes of Bisley's arrest. Petti (1959), p. 75.
51. See Pollen (1908), p. 214. Pollen made a con-

fused jumble of references to Sterrell and Bisley and Cloudsley in the Calendar of State Papers.

52. SP 12/241/118. This April 7 letter contains a number of the same points of information that Bisley tells to Phelippes later in July, such as that he was supposed to visit Sir William Courtney about an army to come into England, so there can be no doubt but "Boseley" (Beseley or Beeseley) and Bisley are the same man.

53. SP 12/245/92–93, Lord Buckhurst to Phelippes, September 8 & 10, 1593.

54. See the 1591 correspondence concerning Barnes. Moody was working through Robert Poley. Hatfield Papers 4: 138. September 27/October 7, 1591 (Moody to Heneage); Moody to ?, October 4 1591, Hatfield, Papers 4: 144; Burghley to Heneage, October 12 1591, Hatfield Papers 4: 147; "Poly" to Moody, October 1591, Hatfield Papers 4: 156.

55. SP 12/242/3, Robinson to Mr. Morice at the Swan, Bishopsgate Street, May 1, 1592.

56. SP 12/242/26, Robinson to ?? May 26, 1592. See also SP 12/242/37.

57. SP 12/249/110, notes for the Earl of Essex. These notes by William Waad, secretary to the Privy Council, for August 21, 1594, show that Essex was asked to write to the deputy governor of Flushing to "stay" Moody and "send him hither safe."

58. SP 12/249/103.

59. Dr. William Gifford reported in a letter in June 1595 that Moody had been arrested by Mondragon and placed in a secret prison. SP 12/252/66. Moody had been planning to return to England just at this time and had written Sir Thomas Heneage on arranging to bring things for him. Hatfield Papers 5: 213–14, May 20, 1595. Another letter of December 1596 reported that Moody had died three weeks earlier, though this date is uncertain. SP 12/256/29. A report of John Gyles to the Earl of Essex dated November 20, 1596 said that "Mr. Moody is banished out of the K. low countries." Hatfield Papers 6: 486.

60. SP 12/242/107, Ferrers to Phelippes, from Middelburg, August 17, 1592. Ferrers states in his letter to Phelippes: "The xvth ditto Mr Robert Robinson did come unto me, and Stavely with him. His desire was that I would disburse unto him x l [10 pounds] sterling, which he told me your worship would most willing repay in England, the which I was most willing to perform, and have paid unto him so much...." Sterrell may have used the money to go back to Antwerp or Brussels, for it was a few weeks more before he was again in England.

61. Gustav Ungerer has documented the laxness in security among Essex's brilliant counselors, and the leaks led several of the Earl's followers to resign or threaten to resign. Ungerer (1976), 1: 301–02.

62. SP 12/246/60, Earl of Essex to Thomas Phelippes.

63. Also referred to as Birkett, Burke, or Birkhead, he was a priest who was in England operating under the alias of George Lambton. In 1608 the Pope named Birkett to the presbitership of England to replace George Blackwell who had been the "Archpriest." Letter of Pope Paul V to Geo. Birkett, January 22, 1608, SP 14/31/11.

64. Walsingham's daughter, Frances, now receiving correspondence from Phelippes, as had her father.

65. This letter is found in the SP 12/243/13 and is reproduced in Spedding (1861), 1: 118–19. Spedding, who seemed ashamed that Bacon was involved at all in the distasteful business of spying, did not know quite what to make of it. He surmised, correctly, that the letter was among those seized by Robert Cecil in 1605 from Thomas Phelippes. The letters of Bacon among those seized "are to be regarded merely as specimens and fragments accidently cast up of the kind of services in which Essex employed him; not by any means as affording a complete account of his labours, even in this one kind." Id. p. 119.

66. SP 12/246/62.

67. Sterrell is describing a meeting with Essex or Bacon. Jardine and Stewart believe that the reference here is to Francis Bacon and that Sterrell was indignant at being sent to Bacon instead of going to Phelippes. Jardine & Stewart (1999), p. 130. There is reason to believe this is correct. However, it also is possible that Bacon was a peacemaker between Essex and Sterrell and that Sterrell had seen Essex himself. Sterrell is reluctant to put Essex's name in a letter but not Bacon's name; Essex is reluctant to put Sterrell's name in a letter but not Bacon's or Cloudsley's.

68. SP 12/243/118; SP 12/243/119.

69. SP 12/242/53.

Chapter 11

1. SP 12/246/ 63, Sterrell to Phelippes (reference to Old Paynter); SP 12/241/2, Sterrell to Phelippes ("if you send Paynter to the woman she shall deliver it"); SP 12/238/125 (I send [? torn] the letter which I would wish you to send away presently and so send the other by Painters father for we must needs have two posts); Robin Painter, SP 12/244/103; Robert Paynter, SP 12/250/61; Robert Paynter and old painter, SP 12/244/149. The elder Paynter was James Paynter (Painter) who was employed by the queen and secretary Walsingham as a courier. SP 15/27/55 (Thomas Copley to his cousin, Lady Walsingham, from Paris, January 3, 1582: "I have received by Painter, the post, your loving commendations."); SP 15/27/64 (Thomas Copley to Sec. Walsingham, from Paris, April 5, 1582: "Painter, the post, … has just arrived"); SP 15/27/69 (John de Critz to Sec. Walsingham, from Paris, April 21, 1582: "I hope you have received my last letter and the pictures by James Painter…"); SP 15/28/44 (Sir Edward Stafford to Sec. Walsingham, from Paris December 2, 1583: "After I had delivered my letters to Painter the post…"); SP 15/28/47 (William Parry to Sec. Walsingham, December 18, 1583: "Painter promised to take this letter

with him, but did not come for it…"); SP 12/184/59 (James Paynter to Walsingham, November 1585).

2. SP 12/243/15, Thomas Ferrers to Phelippes (with note of Sterrell), September 17, 1592.

3. Sterrell had expected "the vice admiral to set a man to dog him, and show him to the deputy and I would defray all charges. I fear that the vice admiral or some Dutch has played the jade. [a term of contempt]. The best is to send the description to justice Young and to Gravesend; that man brought letters and great directions concerning the chiefest points." Justice Young is Richard Young, a magistrate well-known as a strenuous torturer of Catholics. Some of Sterrell's letters were routed by Essex through Young. SP 12/244/36 (n.d.); SP 12/245/41, Essex to Phelippes.

4. SP 12/246/63 (n.d.) (about March 1593). Sterrell's experience with Quentin Pertry's handing off his letters in Middelburg had been a lesson.

5. The name used for Fitzherbert in the letters from Sterrell was John Baxter, and they were to be sent to Pierre Sage in Dieppe. SP 12/243/78, Thomas Fitzherbert (Rouen) to Pierre Sage, Dieppe, December 1/11, 1592. This Frenchman was to forward them to "Jehan Gaillo's, Postmaster, to Hold for John Baxter" or to send them to Fitzherbert in his own name at the Papal College, near St. Nicholas church.

6. SP 12/246/64, Sterrell to Phelippes, n.d. A courier bearing a letter called at Mistress Staveley's alehouse, but had forgotten the name of the man he was to leave it for. Sterrell wrote to Phelippes: "Among other things she told me that there was one that inquired of my Lord of Worcester's gentleman that should lay there but could not remember what name he used. Undoubtedly it was some sent from Owen to me for I left him direction to send to the White Goat without Bishopsgate."

7. OED, 7. a. A sign arranged or given to indicate a person; a word or material object employed to authenticate a person, message, or communication; a mark giving security to those who possess it; a password.

8. SP 12/246/61, Robinson to Phelippes, probably November 1592.

9. SP 12/243/78, John Baxter (Fitzherbert) to Robinson (Sterrell), December 1/11, 1592: "Your privy token of *cupio* I delivered to the party who willeth me to write unto you that he understandeth it well & will not refuse to pay such sums as by the same shall be demanded of him though it be without letter of exchange & so would he have you do in like sort when he shall send you the same though he thinketh it not amiss to use also as occasion shall serve the other watchword that you advised him to use from Lile at your being there, for *abundans cautella non nocet*."

10. SP 12/244/15, Sterrell to Phelippes, January 15, 1593.

11. Even Fitzherbert had difficulty with some of their tokens that he could not remember. He told Sterrell: "Some things concerning our old reckonings you write so obscurely as I can by no means understand them for that all my papers & notes of our former dealings are at Paris from whence i can by no means recover them by reason of the troubles [civil turmoil in Paris]." SP 12/243/78, John Baxter (Fitzherbert) to Robinson (Sterrell), 1/11 December 1592. Fitzherbert had left Paris for Rouen about 1588. Fitzherbert's statement here is strong evidence then that the correspondence between Fitzherbert and Sterrell dated from the mid-1580s or earlier.

12. According to Sterrell's statements to Phelippes, Fitzherbert and Owen were of different factions, and Owen would have resented Sterrell dealing with Fitzherbert but not vice-versa. SP 12/246/61, Robinson (Sterrell) to Phelippes (n.d.). This may have been true, but it is just as likely that this was a pose in Sterrell's dealing with Phelippes before he had entrenched Phelippes in work with Owen.

13. SP 12/243/78, John Baxter (Fitzherbert) to Robinson (Sterrell), 1/11 December 1592. Fitzherbert had received letters from Sterrell dated 12 October and 14 November and informed Sterrell that he had sent two letters on 23 August.

14. SP 12/244/98, ____ to Robinson from Dieppe, 30 March /9 April 1593.

15. SP 12/246/ 61, Robinson (Sterrell) to Phelippes (n.d.); SP 12/246/60, Earl of Essex to Thomas Phelippes.

16. SP 12/241/2. The Calendar of State Papers has this letter as January 2, 1592. However, a number of internal points make clear that the date was 1593.

17. "Yet surely Bisly doth but lie, for if I had such credit as he pretendth we should have heard something. If they suspect me then is Bisley set to discover me by them, so thinking to be even with [to have revenge on] me and Cloudsley lett pass for better proof.… You may do well to employ Cloudsley about the prisons, and let him find out Daniell who is either employed for the Queen or is a notable knave in no mean matter." The antecedents of Sterrell's pronouns are unclear. Are the "they" and "them" the Catholic exiles in the Low Countries or are they agents of the English government? Phelippes would have known.

18. Sterrell paid a Welshman to deliver the letter to Phelippes and to await a reply, telling Phelippes he "must make shift to understand his Welsh English, he comes out of the mountains of Wales."

19. SP 12/244/15, Sterrell to Phelippes, January 15, 1593.

20. "The death of Parma will either greatly help or hinder the King of France, for the proud Spaniard will fight, and so perhaps lose all, for he shall not easily carry the Wallons as Parma did. Owen's credit is in the wain unless the Cardinal [Allen] support him but Westmorland will tread him down. If Mansfield continue you must send some good intelligence to Fitzherbert—that is the way to do good, and write nothing else till I come." The reason Owen's influence would wain under Mansfield as governor

was that Mansfield was close to Charles Paget, now located in Brussels, and Owen and Paget were enemies. See statement of George Herbert to William Waad, August 27, 1595, Hatfield Papers 5: 353–54.

21. SP 12/244/ 26, Robinson (Sterrell) to Phelippes, January (?) 1593. "Cloudsley hath been with me this morning, but he cannot find Burkett.... Cloudsley thinks that if he goes to York, by means of his brother who is a priest and prisoner there he shall be able to find him or hear some certain news of him and some others. You may do well to talk with him concerning this point, if he go it were necessary that he had some note to some trusty justice who may advisedly apprehend such as he discovereth without scandalizing of Cloudsley." A report on priests in England sent to Lord Burghley in January 1593 listed a priest named Cloudsley in Lancashire. SP Addenda 15/32/ 64, reprinted in Foley Records 6: 743. Peter Cloudsley is probably the priest about whom in June 1585 Thomas Alfield, the martyr, was interrogated; he was asked as to his knowledge of (Christopher) Bagshaw and one Clowdsley. SP 12/179/ 61. A chronology of Catholic persecutions from this period indicated that about March 16, 1592, "Sir Peter Cloudsley, an old priest, [was] taken at Browne's house about Humslay [and] beaten with a wand. Both he and Browne were brought to York before the Council, who committed Sir Peter to John Stokes' house, the tipstaff..." Foley Records 3: 757.

22. SP 12/244/18, draft in Phelippes's handwriting dated 18 January 1593.

23. SP 15/30/ 58, William Sterrell to Phelippes (n.d.). The Calendar dates this as 1587?. However, the letter relates legislation that was anticipated, making clear that the 1593 Parliament was the time of the letter. Years later, after Robert Dudley had left his native England to reside in Florence with his new wife Elizabeth Southwell, the status of his marriage was of some embarrassment. Who was called to Rome to treat with the Pope to confirm the canonical validity of the marriage? Fr. Richard Sherwood, William Sterrell's friend and correspondent of many years standing. Anstruther (1968), 1: 314.

24. The "sickening record of treachery and crime" is told in vivid detail with original documents in Camm (1910), pp. 16–66.

25. Neale (1957), p. 316.

26. SP 12/245/65, Saint Main (Sterrell) to Phelippes (n.d.). The use of the alias at a time when Sterrell corresponded with Phelippes in his own name is explained most likely by the sensitive nature of the correspondence and perhaps that Sterrell was directing the letter to a different address than otherwise used. Sterrell wrote Phelippes:

> Good Sir may it please you to understand that I am importuned to know what shall become of those words which should be spoken in the Marshallsea [Prison] they are committed close prisoners so that none of them can come at me, I pray you, deal with him for the liberty of Mr. Brownell [Brenell] if it may be for by him I must learn something for Basset. He sent me word of Clark [Clearke] the priest his going to his house. I pray you let me hear from you concerning this point. The liberty I speak of is the enlargement in prison and such liberty as he had which was to be absent all day and lie at home at night.

The "Brenell" whose liberty Sterrell sought through Phelippes was Gratian Brownell, a bachelor of law from Oxford who was in the Marshalsea. When he was released from the Marshalsea is unclear. However, he was quite ill at the end of December 1592. SP 12/243/93, Young to Sir John Puckering, December 23, 1592 reprinted in CRS V pp. 213–15. The editor mistakenly discusses the relationship of Sterrell and Bisley in giving the background to this document, id. p. 214. Gratian Brownell was examined in the Marsalsea in April 1593 as part of a survey of all in prison for Popery. He had been in prison for six years and continued to answer the "Bloody Question." Strype (1824), 4: 257. Sterrell's effort to obtain the freedom of a Catholic prisoner while pursuing intelligence was part of his regular pattern.

27. SP 12/244/5. Examination of Thos. Clarke, January 7, 1593.

28. SP 12/245/138.

29. SP 12/245/98, Topcliffe to Burghley, September 19, 1593. For the allegations ultimately made against Bassett, see Camm (1910), App. B, pp. 385–89. The litany includes a fantastic charge that Bassett tried to poison Topcliffe by putting a spider in his drink.

30. SP 12/244/124, Thomas Phelippes to William Sterrell.

31. SP 12/245/65, Saint Main (Sterrell) to Thomas Phelippes. The daily death toll from the plague had risen to more than 30 on March 24, 1593 and continued to increase thereafter. Chambers (1923), 4: 348.

32. SP 12/246/64, Sterrell to Phelippes (n.d.). Sterrell also said he had been expecting some directions for a letter to Owen, indicating this letter was probably soon after SP 15/30/58, touching upon the party attended by Sir Henry Grey and others. Sterrell knew of a person going to Rome and could give intelligence on the seminaries there if the man could be advanced some money.

33. SP 12/244/103, Sterrell to Phelippes (n.d.).

34. Hopwood (1903), 1: 330.

35. SP 12/195/122, Sterrell to Phelippes (n.d.). The Calendar of State Papers assigned a date of 1586? to this letter. However, this is clearly wrong.

36. Compare Lord Saye in *2 Henry VI*, 4. 4.
Saye: So might your Grace's person be in danger.
The sight of me is odious in their eyes;
And therefore in this city will I stay
And live alone as secret as I may.

37. This is a quote from the chorus in Seneca's *Phaedra*, line 1123 and is sometimes given as "Quanti

Casus Humana Rotant!" or as "Quanti Casus, Heu, Magna Rotant!".

38. SP 12/199/46, Sterrell to Phelippes.
39. SP 12/195/123, Sterrell to Phelippes.
40. SP 12/250/61, Sterrell to Phelippes.
41. SP 12/250/62, Sterrell to Phelippes.
42. OED: † *to Make Leap Year Of*: (fig.) to pass over.
43. SP 12/244/123, Sterrell to Phelippes (6 April) 1593. Sterrell told Phelippes that he was polite but "God defend that ever I should need him so much as to intrude myself, yet if ever time serve I know he will need me or at least one of like faith."
44. SP 12/244/150. In the next few months her progresses took the queen to Croydon, Nonsuch, Oatlands and Windsor. Chambers (1923), 4:108.
45. Sterrell told Phelippes he would be satisfied if Phelippes would do two things: "The first is to let me have the remainder of such money as you promised me that i may furnish my chamber presently. The other is that as opportunity shall be offered, you would not be unmindful to prefer me to the service of some nobleman or other like to be employed. I doubt not but to discharge the duty of a secretary which is convenient sufficiency, as many others do. Loath I am to solicit the Earl in these two suits, hoping upon your courtesy and being desirous that all favours should be derived unto me by your means and mediations to the Earl." SP 12/244/150.
46. SP 12/244/149.
47. The events of late 1592 and early 1593 are recounted by Phelippes to Essex in December 1596. Hatfield Papers, 6: 511. After Sterrell returned in late 1592, Phelippes was partly superseded, and others around Essex worked with Sterrell. Among these were probably Francis Bacon, Anthony Bacon, and William Waad. William Sterrell's mission undertaken in 1591–92 was regarded as a failure that brought him into suspicion and disfavor all the way up to the queen of England. Part of the reason for the failure is that at some point in this mission the Catholics "accused our man as a dealer with the state (i.e., spying for the English side), which in some sort at his first going over he did not deny...."
48. Petti (1959), pp. 135–36. The spelling of Verstegan's letter is modernized. While Verstegan does not mention Sterrell's name, Petti recognized the description of Fitzherbert's friend as being Sterrell and it is probably correct. Id. p. 139, n. 16.
49. SP 12/250/60, Sterrell to Phelippes (n.d.).
50. SP 12/283/75 (i). Harvey's second wife was Camilla, daughter of a Florentine merchant named Vincent Guicciardini; she was sister of James Guicciardini, another agent of Essex. Jones (1933), p. 327. For examples of James Guicciardini's intelligences to Essex from Florence, see J. Guicciardini to Essex, Hatfield Papers, 6: 154–56, April 24, 1596; 7: 235, June 4, 1597.
51. It will be recalled that Thomas Ferrers had sent a report to Lord Burghley of Sterrell (Robinson) and Staveley from Middelburg less than a year earlier saying that Sterrell was "Now a Pensioner to the King of Spain and Hath 20 Crowns Per Month."
52. Breight (1996), pp. 113–14.
53. Id., 114–16.
54. Curtis Breight has argued that Robert Cecil "guided a covert operation to demonize and then destroy Marlowe." The continued efforts to prosecute Marlowe suggest strongly a desire of Cecil to undo Marlowe. Breight (1996), p. 129. Nicholl's view is that Marlowe's death was an Essex conspiracy.
55. SP 12/245/28, Sterrell to Phelippes—Gains Park.
56. The aunt of Sir William was Mary Fitzwilliam, whom we have encountered several times before, as wife first of John Shelley of Michelgrove and then of Sir John Guildford of Hemsted. The biographical information for Mary Fitzwilliam, wife first of John Shelley of Michelgrove and then of Sir John Guildford of Hemsted is gleaned from the *Visitations of Sussex*, p. 37, the ODNB (entries for her father Sir William Fitzwilliam (1460–1534) and Sir William Fitzwilliam (1526–99), and Bindoff (1982) (entries for Sir William Fitzwilliam, 2: 145 and her husband, Sir John Guildford, 2: 265). It is possible that Mary Fitzwilliam was not the aunt but the sister of the Sir William Fitzwilliam whose years were 1526–99. There were three generations in a row in which the head of the family was named Sir William Fitzwilliam of Milton, Northamptonshire and Gains Park Essex. Mary Fitzwilliam was probably a daughter of the second wife (Mildred Sackville) of the first Sir William Fitzwilliam.
57. du Maurier (1975), pp. 181–82; McClure (1979), 1: 76.
58. Devereux (1853), 1: 290. Essex was sworn in as a member of the Privy Council on February 25, 1593, and this undated letter must have been sent soon afterwards. Lacey (1971), p. 102:

> Mr. Bacon,-The Queen hath sent for me in such kindness this morning, as I must not refuse to go to her. I hear not of Mr. Philips [Phelippes]. I will acquaint you with my business, that you, upon conference with him, may do that which myself would have done. The Queen did require of me a draft of an instruction for matter of intelligence, seeming willing, now she hath sworn me one of her Council, to use my services that way. I persuade myself she doth it rather to try my judgment in it, than for any present necessity for instruction of any man that is to go. The places are Rheims and Rome. Mr. Philips hath known Mr. Secretary's [Essex's father-in-law, Walsingham] courses in such matters, so as I may have counsel from you, and precedents from him. I pray you, as your leisure will serve, send me your conceit [thoughts] as soon as you can, for I know not how soon I shall be called on. I will draw some

notes of mine own, which I will reform and enlarge by yours. In haste, this Friday morning,
Your most assured friend,
Essex.

59. Perez's biographer, Marañon (1953), p. 360, states that the second edition of the book was printed in England in 1593. Woodfield (1973) p. 107, gives the date as late 1593 or early 1594, remarking that "for the first and only time in his printing career he [Richard Field] made use of a completely fictitious imprint." In the printer's note in the book, the printer states (in Spanish) that he had little notice of the Spanish language.

60. Perez's chronicler Gustave Ungerer observes that the second edition was complete when Perez turned up in London in April 1593, and was ready to go to press as soon as the authorities were willing to license the printing. If Perez had to wait until 1594, the "delay must have been due to the resistance of Sir William Cecil and his partisans." Ungerer (1976), 2: 252.

61. Ungerer (1976), 1: 247.

62. The quote here is from the Calendar of State Papers, 1591–94, p. 358. The actual document, SP 12/245/42 does not say "The Informer" but simply "He." The letter is a hand other than Essex's and refers to Essex in the third person; yet, it no doubt is from Essex, probably written by one of his secretaries.

63. Devereux (1853), 1: 290-91 (undated letter of Essex to an unnamed agent). The Latin phrase signifies the agent should gain news of events rather than plans and deliberations of his correspondents.

64. SP 12/245/50, Phelippes to Sterrell, Gains Park, Epping, July 5, 1593.

65. Ungerer (1976), 1: 247.

66. Hatfield Papers 5: 26.

67. Id. p. 97, letter of January 28/February 7, 1595 of "W. Nicols" to "Sir Peter Hollins."

Chapter 12

1. Lisa Jardine and Alan Stewart begin their biography of Sir Francis Bacon with an exchange between Essex and Robert Cecil on the post of Attorney General in a coach as they left an interrogation of Dr. Lopez, suggesting how important the assassination charges were to the competition for the chief attorney position. Jardine & Stewart (1999), p. 11.

2. Jardine & Stewart (1999), p. 12.

3. Jardine & Stewart (1999), p. 155; Lacey (1971), p. 118.

4. Essex's evidence and sources are murky. Possibly his suspicions on Lopez had arisen from Roger Walton whose disappearance had caused Essex's ire earlier. Walton's contacts with Lopez were described by Robert Draper in an interrogation on February 5, 1594, SP 12/247/41.

5. Hammer (1999), p. 161: "This sudden change of fortunes was a very sweet moment for Essex. However grudgingly, Elizabeth was forced to recognize the value of his intelligence. For once, Burghley and Cecil were forced to dance according to his tune. Like the rest of the council, they had to demonstrate their concern for the queen's safety by throwing their full weight behind the investigation."

6. Confessions of John Annias, February 5, 1594, SP 12/247/44; February 8, 1594, SP 12/247/53; February 8, 1594, SP 12/247/54; confession of Hugh Cahill, February 21, 1594, SP 12/247/78; examination of Patrick Collen, February 6, 1594, SP 12/247/45; confession of Hugh Cahill, February 21, 1594, SP 12/247/78. There is a "Confession of William Polwhele," SP 12/246/49, tentatively dated December 1593, but this dating is probably off by a month.

7. *A True Report of Sundry Horrible Conspiracies* (1594), p. 17. This pamphlet, generally attributed to Lord Burghley, is available at Early English Books Online.

8. In a dispatch of August 7, 1592 to Lord Burghley, Thomas Jeffrey (an English merchant and intelligence agent in Calais) informed the Lord Treasurer that one Daniell, an Irish Catholic, had met with him and wished to pass intelligence of great importance to Lord Burghley. SP 12/242/104, Thos. Jeffrey to Lord Burghley, August 7, 1592.

9. SP 12/249/12 (confession of Henry Walpole, 13 June 1594); transcribed in CRS V pp. 252-3.

10. The Calendar dates the first confession of Polwhele as December 1593, SP 12/246/49, but the basis for this is unclear. The Calendar dates the first confession of Annias as January 1594, SP 12/247/33, but this is equally uncertain. The first firm dates for statements of Polwhele and Annias seem to be about February 5, 1594, i.e., after the prosecution of Dr. Lopez had begun in earnest.

11. SP 12/247/38 (February 4); SP 12/247/73 (February 21). William Tompson had been captured two years earlier, tortured and examined by Richard Young. He had confessed to a plot to set fire to English ships at Dieppe and then had escaped prison, SP 12/241/102 (examination of Wm. Thomson, *Alias* Carre); SP 12/247/33, confession of Jo. Annias.

12. In his examination of February 5, 1594 Annias said that he wrote to Manuel Louis (Tinoco) that he had resolved to become a true subject of the Queen and had sent John Daniel for his pardon. SP 12/247/44. When they were together in the Low Countries, Annias was "much ruled by him [Daniell]." SP 12/247/54–56.

13. SP 12/247/33.

14. SP 12/247/44.

15. SP 12/247/56.

16. SP 12/247/45; SP 12/247/52; SP 12/247/64; SP 12/247/76–77.

17. SP 12/247/38–39. One historian, Hume (1901), pp. 107–08, commented on these investigations: "it is not surprising to hear, as these plots were divulged through the Cecil organisation, that mysterious hints were indulged in that for his own ends the earl of

essex was more or less mixed up in the nefarious plans...."

18. SP 12/246/49, confession of December 1593: "there's no other way but two when she goes to walk or when she goes to a sermon. Take a dagger or a pistol and stab her or shoot her into the body for she takes no care of her goings. And if you can escape but two or three hours you are safe for ever."

19. SP 12/247/78, confession of Hugh Cahill, February 21, 1594.

20. SP 12/247/79, declaration by John Daniell, February 21, 1594.

21. SP 12/247/91, February 25, 1594.

22. Hatfield Papers 4: 474.

23. SP 12/247/44.

24. SP 12/247/54: He now recalled hearing that Hugh Owen had asked Thomas Butler, "who had then come from England, whether he was ever in the queen's stable or served there; whether the hay lies above the horses, or at Charing Cross; whether the great horses were there, and if there was a great store of hay and corn near, and that it would be good to set fire to it, whereby Her Majesty and the Council would be much discomforted."

25. Id.

26. Polwhele and his companion, Edward Codrington, were both identified at Rheims as "nobilis juvenis," that is, from respected families. Knox (1878), p. 245. In one of his statements, Polwhele said his companion to Rheims was "Arthur Canfand" but this clearly was not the case. He continued to be associated with Edward Codrington, as is clear from Codrington's confession in April 1594 when he was captured in Flushing. In Calais, Codrington had been awaiting news and support from Polwhele but had to leave there for want of money. Hatfield Papers 5: 178 (wrongly entered as [1595] as can be seen by noting the May 2, 1594 letter of Henry Thirkell to Lord Burghley, SP 12/248/90, who was captured at Flushing at about the same time as Codrington. Both Codrington and Thirkell got false passports from Fr. Scudamore (Skidmore) who "who could counterfeit Sir Thos. Baskerville's hand."). Burghley's can be seen by noting the Mayand support from Polwhele but had to leave there for want of money.

27. SP 12/247/45, February 6, 1594, examination of Patrick Collen before Sir Thos. Wilkes, Attorney General Thos. Egerton, Solicitor General Edw. Coke, and Rich. Young.

28. SP 12/247/38.

29. SP 12/247/44.

30. Id.

31. SP 12/247/73.

32. SP 12/248/41. Tompson, he said, was now a tapster at an inn in St. Omer.

33. SP 12/247/97. See also Dimock (1894), pp. 440–472.

34. SP 12/253/62.

35. SP 12/254/12. However, Daniel evidently met in person with Cecil on December 20, 1595, and followed with a letter again bewailing his fortune and seeking help from Cecil. He again reminded Cecil that at the "arraignment of all such as came hither about wicked practices, her Majesty's Attorney reported John Daniel to have been the first discoverer of those practices." Hatfield Papers, 5: 504.

36. SP 12/256/33.

37. Maclean (1864), p. 49.

38. ODNB, "Fitton, Mary."

39. For example, in the trial of Henry Garnett, Coke will recite the Jesuit missions to England going back to Campion and Persons. After the Spanish Armada, he continues in 1606, the Jesuits fell again to "secret and treasonable practices: for in the year 92 [sic], came Patrick Cullen, who was incited by Sir William Stanley, Hugh Owen, Jaques Fraunces, and Holt the Jesuit, and resolved by the said Holt to kill the queen; to which purpose he received absolution, and then the sacrament, at the hands of the said Jesuit, together with this ghostly counsel, that it was both lawful and meritorius to kill her. Nay, said, Jaques, that base laundress's son (who was a continued practiser both with this Cullen and others, to destroy her majesty) the state of England is and will be so settled, that unless mistress Elizabeth be suddenly taken away, all the devils in Hell will not be able to prevail against it, or shake it." Howell (1809), 2: 224–25.

40. SP 12/241/2 (incorrectly calendared as 1592). Phelippes would "do well to employ Cloudsley [a courier] about the prisons, and let him find out Daniell who is either employed for the queen or is a notable knave in no mean matter." Once again, Sterrell was using his position to ferret out the enemies of the Catholic cause.

41. SP 12/247/96, Windebank to Cecil, February 27, 1594.

42. Yorke and Williams were executed in February 1595. Hammer (1999), p. 158. I have been unable to determine the fate of Henry Young. Two recent writers have indicated that Young was a provocateur against Williams and Yorke. Breight (1996), pp. 124, 288 n. 53; Nicholl (1992), pp. 266–67, 283, 389. The fact that he is not mentioned by Daniell nor included in the recitations of traitors by Coke in later trials suggests that he likely was a government plant.

43. DNB (1897) "Sir William Stanley," p. 971: "He paid a visit to Rome in 1591 to consult with Allen and other enemies of the Queen. in the event of her death he urged that the Lady Arabella Stuart or Lord Strange (see Stanley, Ferdinando, Fifth Earl of Derby) should be recognised as her successor."

44. Dulles (1963), ch. 10; Montagu (1954).

45. SP 12/249/7, Sir Cuthbert Buckle, Mayor of London to Lord Burghley, June 7, 1594. The letter of Owen to Sterrell is found in the State Papers in two widely separated parts. The first four pages are in SP 12/248/53. The editor of the Calendar, published in 1867, thought the letter was from Owen to Phelippes. The last sheet is in SP 15/33/13 (CSP Domestic Ad-

denda, 1580–1625, p. 363, published in 1872). The editor of this later volume did not connect the fragment with the other fragment calendared five years earlier. The link between the two is facilitated by Owen's epistolary practice of writing at the foot of each page the first word of the next page. Placing the fragments side-by-side leaves no doubt about the fact that they are one letter.

46. Of the same name, John Fortescue. See Chambers (1930), 2: 166–67.

47. Id. "In after life [an unspecified date after 1598], John Fortescue and his wife retired to St Omer."

48. Deed of March 10, 1613, Chambers (1930), 2: 155.

49. Devlin (1956), p. 217. Devlin does not specify whether this son attended St. Omers. Chambers (1930), p. 169 says that one son was Edward, at the English College Rome. John's son, John, is thought to be the John Robinson who was to become the tenant of the Gatehouse after the Blackfriar's Gatehouse was acquired by William Shakespeare. A witness to Shakespeare's will was John Robinson, and this probably was the same John Robinson who was tenant of the Blackfriar's property by William Shakespeare.

50. Hatfield Papers 9: 186-7, May 31, 1599, Fra. Duckett to Richard Brother.

51. This steward Robinson was reported as hiding a priest named Richard Dudley and was said to be resident in May 1599 "over against Sir John Fortescue's door" in or opposite Blackfriars, not in Bishopsgate. Chambers (1930), 2: 169. And, a John Robinson was resident in Blackfriars in November 1596 (petition against Burbage's public theatre). Given the commonness of the name Robinson, the steward and the father of the Robinson who gave the letter to the Lord Mayor may be different people, or the steward may have had two properties or the son may have not truthfully identified the father.

52. Hatfield Papers 5: 40; letter of December 19, 1594.

Chapter 13

1. Foley Records 4: 45; endorsed "Father Garnet to Fr. Rob. Parsons, September 6, 1594." Address: "A Molto Mag. Sign., Il Sig. Marco Tusinga, Venezia."

2. Id. p 46. "it is a wonder to see how God hath protected our letters of late; for I could write of two or three several escapes almost miraculous, if I could declare it without revealing the means of my sending, which I should be very loath should appear in my letter, if it should chance to be taken."

3. Caraman (1951), p. 107.

4. SP 12/262/123.

5. Caraman (1951), p. 111 note 1.

6. SP 12/244/98. The letter is an abstract in the hand of Phelippes.

7. SP 12/240/10; Hatfield Papers 4: 625, Francis Derrick to Henry Wickham; Hatfield Papers 4: 626, Francis Derrick to Henry Wickham, October 9, 1594, n.s.

8. Three of the Wicham-Derrick letters touch on the Line-Heigham family: SP 12/283/75 iii, July 20, 1594; SP 12/283/75 ii, September 21, 1594; Hatfield Papers, 4: 626, October 9, 1594.

9. The stick-pin was a "Toothpick of gold weighing one ounce and little more containing in it one faire diamond one less diamond and five sparks of diamonds seven small rubies and one pearle pendant and 4 other small pearles." It was held in London by John Antonio Sark, an Italian merchant. SPD12/283/75 ix. Richard Sherwood assigned the jewel to William Sterrell's use in a note of July 27, 1594. That Sherwood is Derrick and Sterrell Wicham is confirmed by the fact that "Derrick" urges "Wicham" to redeem the jewel, and Sherwood has assigned the same to Sterrell.

10. SP 12/283/75 iv, August 20 [10?], 1594. Loomie identifies this Owen from the Spanish pension list as: "A relative of the Duchess of Feria, at whose request he was pensioned, he has served a long time, first in the Burgundian infantry and lately with the Spanish. He was recovering from a wound for a long time and for this reason his pension was transferred. He can now return to duty, he is an excellent soldier and highly honored." Loomie (1963a), p. 255. SP 12/206/78 n.d. "The Names of all such English captains as serve under the enemy in the Low Countries and are desirous to get passports to come over into England: ... Mr. Owen son to Mr Rc of Oxfordshire hath served under the Spaniards these x years & is a resolute fellow." See also Hodgetts (1999), pp. 415–30; Hogge (2002), pp. 291–300.

11. Hatfield Papers 4: 625, Francis Derrick to Henry Wickham, October 9, 1594. He was to obtain for "Throk" [Thomas or George Throckmorton] "a bandora or orphtrye of the new fashion, which hath the bridge and the stops slope, as well the treble as the other strings wired; the best you can find, wherein you must use the help of some who can skill in that instrument; and also to procure some principal lessons for the bandora of Holborne's making...." Sterrell was also requested to "send over some proper youth, cunning in music, specially in that instrument of the lute whose entertainment shall be such as I dare warrant you he shall well like and give you thanks." The bandora and the orphtrye [orphanion] were cittern-like instruments, essentially early guitars. Anthony Holborne was a well-known composer and luthier, second only to John Dowland in his time.

12. SP 12/283/75 I, Harry Wicham (Sterrell) to Francis Derick (Sherwood), June 1, 1594. The circumstances of this christening and Montague's commitment to his father-in-law's house (Lord Buckhurst) are discussed in Questier (2006) pp. 235–36.

13. Another brother, Edward, was a seminarian who died a Jesuit in the English College, Rome.

14. SP 12/249/64; SP 12/249/98; SP 12/249/103; SP 12/249/112. In an undated letter that is probably from 1595 or 1596 to Thomas Phelippes, Sterrell says he is sending a letter to warn George Throckmorton of danger and to advise him to come to Sterrell for his safety if he should be in London. SP 12/256/68 (Feb.? 1596).

15. Edwards (1995), pp. 258, 275; Loomie (1973b), 2: 8; Loomie (1972), p. 165; SP 12/281/20, Ralph Winwood to Cecil, July 16, 1601. Denounced for attending mass at the London residence of the Spanish Ambassador (Medoza), Thomas James was imprisoned for a time. He moved his commercial activities to Spain but maintained contact with a brother, Francis James, who remained in London. Like so many others associated with Sterrell, Thomas James was one of the young men who helped Edmund Campion and Robert Persons in their 1580–81 mission, as were three of the Throckmorton brothers.

16. SP 12/283/75 iv, August 10, 1594. The letter does not bear a year, and the Calendar of State Papers cataloged it as probably 1597; however, from the statements of the letter, it is clear that it was written in 1594. Among other news, it states that the Earl of Sussex was going to the christening of the King of Scotland's child. In August of 1594 Robert Radcliffe, 5th Earl of Sussex, was sent as ambassador-extraordinary to Scotland to assist at the baptism of James's eldest son, Henry. Compare letter of A. Bacon to F. Bacon of July 26, 1594 relating that Sussex was to go to the christening in Scotland because Cumberland was sick. See Birch (1754), 1: 181. During this period, Sterrell wrote every Saturday and August 10, 1594 was on Saturday. This same letter of Sterrell mentions his letters of July 20 and 27, and August 3, all of which were Saturdays in 1594.

17. "neque in hoc saeculo neque in futuro." See Matthew 2, 12:32—et quicumque dixerit verbum contra Filium hominis remittetur ei qui autem dixerit contra Spiritum Sanctum non remittetur ei *Neque in Hoc Saeculo Neque in Futuro*—And whosoever shall speak a word against the Son of man, it shall be forgiven him: but he that shall speak against the Holy Ghost, it shall not be forgiven him neither in this world, nor in the world to come.

18. CSP Sp. 3: 681, 688, Mendoza to Philip, December 24, 1586.

19. Dr. Gifford was close to Cardinal Allen. He continued a role at Rheims and sometimes acted for the college on official business with the papal nuncio in Brussels.

20. SP 15/31/26, May 31, 1589. This apparently is Phelippes write-up of Barnes's report.

21. SP 15/31/82, November 16/26, 1589. The editor of the Calendar thought this letter, addressed to John Whytsand, merchant, London, was from Charles Paget to Barnes, even transcribing the mention of Paget in the letter as "me." ("*I will send you* another *book in press, answering what was written in France of the death of the Queen of Scots,* touching *me and Morgan* sharply"; the document cipher has "Chas Paget" [in Phelippes's hand] above the cipher). Hicks (1964), p. 221, n. 665, correctly recognized that this and another letter or two were actually in Barnes's hand. During the period 1589–91, Barnes's identity in letters exchanged with Phelippes was given the symbol α with a dot above it. Another letter of "Clitheroe to" and of date of August 10/20, 1591 is in the English State Papers, see SP 12/239 (p. 85 of Calendar). The use of the name Gerard Burghet for mail to London related to Barnes began in 1589; a letter of Barnes from Brussels to Phelippes (addressed as John Whytsand, London) dated September 7/17, 1589, SP 15/31/44 told Phelippes he had sent something to him with the endorsement "A Monsieur Monsieur [sic] Gerarde Burghet francois, etc., by which subscription you were to demand it" for he was concerned about it miscarrying. Letters of Charles Paget to Barnes via the Burghet name are examined below.

22. SP 15/31/32, June 23, 1589. Answers to Owen's instructions, being suggestions for a letter from Thos. Barnes to Owen; CSP Foreign, 21/3: 491–93, Hugh Owens' Instructions to B.

23. Wernham (1987), p. 443, n. 24, citing CSP Scot. 10: 360, 369.

24. Wernham (1987), p. 443, n. 23.

25. Wernham (1987), p. 443, n. 25.

26. Barnes's dealing with Phelippes can be documented over a fifteen year period, while there is no evidence of Barnes dealing with Lord Burghley, and evidence from 1606 shows him not to be allied with Robert Cecil.

27. SP 53/19/108. This letter has been mistaken in the Calendar of Scottish Papers and in the writings of scholars. Phelippes notation that the letter was to Barnes was mistakenly read as "Baines" and the tentative dating was given as 1586. CSP Scot. 9: 29–30. The letter states that it is written on the first of October and refers to the fall of Hulst a short time earlier. Hulst fell on September 19, 1591, Motley (1871), 3: 115. It also refers to several people who were not in the Low Countries until after 1586. More importantly, as noted hereafter, Phelippes drafted a Barnes response to this letter a short time after receiving it in October 1591, SP 12/240/53, Phelippes' draft to Paget for Barnes, October 31, 1591.

28. SP 12/240/19, Ch. Paget to Mons. Giles Martin, Frenchman, London. Endorsed by Phelippes, "From Ch. Paget to Barnes." September 23/October 3, 1591.

29. Phelippes' draft to Paget for Barnes, October 31, 1591, SP 12/240/53. Whether such a letter was sent or received is not known.

30. SP 12/242/121, "James Young, Alias Dingley, a Priest, to Lord Burghley,." August 27, 1592. Handover (1957), p. 92–94, treats this as a plan for kidnapping Arbella. English fugitives more likely thought of Arbella as being held captive by the English as had been her aunt, Mary Queen of Scots; they would have been rescuing her, not kidnapping her.

31. "It was told me that there was on[e] Barnes who came from the councell here into Flaunders about 4 yeares agoe, did treate a mariage betwixt the prince of Parma and a lady called Arbella." confession of Henry Walpole, June 13, 1594, SP 12/249/13, transcribed, CRS V, *Unpublished Documents* p. 252 at 259.

32. BL, Lansdowne MS 71.2; E. St. John Brooks, TLS, February 27, 1937. The Countess of Shrewsbury ("Bess of Hardwick") to Burghley, September 21, 1592. Morley's admission in July 1592 to membership of the Chapel Royal most likely is not attributable to Lord Burghley but to his close relationship with William Byrd, the Catholic composer and musician who was first sworn in as a gentleman of the Chapel Royal in February 1572.

33. Some scholars have doubted that Thomas Morley could have been tutor to Arbella because of his employment at St. Paul's. But employment, whether as tutor or organist or university praelector, was not a continuous relationship during the early modern period, and Morley could easily have had several roles (as indicated by his presence in the Low Countries in 1591). E.g., Nicholl (1992), pp. 340-42. Nicholl and others have held out the possibility that "Morley" the tutor was Christopher Morley, i.e., Marlowe.

34. Hatfield Papers, 4: 144, Moody to ?, October 4, 1591. Moody's symbol for himself was an M superimposed on an upside-down M, with a horizontal bar through them. The Hatfield Calendar mistakenly identifies Moody's addressee as Essex in several of the letters. Hatfield Papers, 4: 144, October 4/14, 1591. The letters are addressed to "The Most Honourable Knighte" followed by a symbol. His correspondent almost certainly is Sir Thomas Heneage, not Essex. When Burghley then writes on October 12, 1591 that he has seen Moody's writings to Heneage we can be assured that Moody has been writing to Heneage, not to Essex, Hatfield Papers 4: 147, Burghley to Heneage, October 12 1591.

35. Hatfield Papers 4: 156, draft as from "Poly" to Moody, October 1591,.

36. There is discussion of Moody's potential intelligence service for them in two letters of Moody to Burghley in May 1591, indicating that he was employed to convey secret messages to Charles Paget. SP 12/238/155, May 18, 1591; SP 12/238/185, May 27, 1591. Moody had written Sir Thomas Heneage seeking employment in December 1590. Hatfield Papers, 4: 77.

37. SP 12/239/148, "Account of the Chief Points in Ricroft's Declaration of Moody's Bad Proceedings."

38. SP 12/239/164. The Calendar has this as "Mr. U." Charles Nicholl reads it as "Mr V" and this would be Sir Thomas Heneage, the Vice-Chamberlain. Nicholl (1992), p. 341.

39. SP 12/241/118, "Reinold Boseley [Bisley] [To Cecil ?]," April 7, 1592.

40. SP 12/239/148. Account of the chief points in Ricroft's declaration of Moody's bad proceedings.

41. Renold (1967), pp. 209-216.

42. SP 12/242/30, Robinson to Morice, May 28, 1592; SP 12/242/37, Robert Robinson to Mr. Morice; SP 12/242/26, May 26, 1592; SP 12/242/3, Robinson to Mr. Morice, May 1, 1592.

43. SP 12/242/81, Chas. Paget to Bartolomeo Rivero, *Alias* Thos. Barnes, London.

44. The significance of the imputation of bastardy was not lost on the chief legal adviser to Burghley and Cecil, Sir Edward Coke: he wrote in the margin of Williamson's deposition "note the disabling of Arbella." Handover (1957), p. 109:

45. The highlighted Spanish term in the report is a translation of "para afloxarlo mas," derived from the older spelling of the verb "aflojar," meaning to loosen, slacken, relax, let loose; to relent, debilitate; to grow weak, to abate; to grow cool in fervor or zeal; to lose courage; to come loose.

46. Hatfield Papers 5: 251-252. The authorship of the *Conference*, under the pseudonym Doleman, has been contentious since the appearance of the work. On the controversy, see Hicks (1957-8), pp. 104-37; Pollen (1903b), pp. 517-32; Loomie (1965a), pp. 145-155 (1965a); Holmes (1980), pp. 415-429. Loomie is surely correct that Stanihurst, a historian who contributed to Holinshed's *Chronicles*, likely had a hand in the drafting of the *Conference* while in Spain.

47. *Conference About the Next Succession*, p. 191 (1681 edition; pages missing from the EEBO edition). The belief in the high standing of Arbella as claimant was shared by many. One of Robert Cecil's secretaries also placed her just after James, adding that she was "by some thought more capable than he (James), for that she is English borne (the want whereof, if our Lawyers opinions be corant, is the cause of his exclusion)." Wilson (1936), p. 2.

48. *Conference About the Next Succession*, pp. 200-02 (1681 ed.).

49. *Conference About the Next Succession*, p. 196.

50. *Conference About the Next Succession*, p. 185 of 1681 edition; p. 241 of EEBO edition.

51. Hatfield Papers 4: 625, Francis Derrick to Henry Wickham, October 9, 1594. A second letter of the same date of "Derrick" to "Wickham" covered much the same ground. Hatfield 4: 626. Perhaps they were sent via separate routes to assure delivery.

52. Lodge (1838), 3: 14, Worcester to Shrewsbury, June 19, 1603.

53. SP 12/241/25, report by Robert Bainbridge January 25, 1592. Nicholas Williamson was said in the report to be in the service of Shrewsbury. When he was arrested and interrogated in 1594/95, he showed that he was very knowledgeable about the Low Countries intelligencers who were at that time working with William Sterrell.

54. Lodge (1838), 3: 39, Worcester to Shrewsbury, September 24, 1603.

55. Lodge (1838), 3: 88, Worcester to Shrewsbury, February 2, 1604.

Chapter 14

1. Hatfield Papers, 3: 112.
2. Hogge (2005), p. 227.
3. SP 12/239/87. Fr. Cecil may have been related to the family of Lord Burghley.
4. McGrath (1967), p. 179. The Bloody Question or variants on it were published by Lord Burghley in a pamphlet under the cumbersome but descriptive title: "A Particular Declaration or Testimony of the Undutifull and Traiterous Affections Borne Against Her Majestie by Edmond Campion, Jesuite and Other Condemned Priests, Witnessed by Their Own Confessions: In Reproofe of Those Slanderous Bookes and Libels Delivered Out to the Contrary by Suche as Are Malitiously Affected Towards Her Majestie and the State." For other "Bloody Questions" of a similar framing, see Holmes (1982), pp. 31–32, 44–46.
5. Caraman (1951) p. 99.
6. Caraman (1951) p. 102.
7. In January 1594 Essex said in a letter to the Earl of Derby that Sir Thomas was "so much my friend as without question I should take (i.e., receive or hire) any man upon his word...." Lodge (1838), 2: 450. The printed heading of this letter identifies this as January 17, 1595 but this is clearly a typographical error as there are several references showing this letter to be in answer to a letter of December 19, 1593 from Derby to Essex. The man whom Essex retained against the disfavor of Derby was identified as Bolds or Bolts, possibly John Bolt.
8. Caraman (1951), p. 238, quoting from Stonyhurst MSS.
9. Persons to Fr. Creswell, October ??, 1595, transcript in Jesuit Archives, London, 46.12.3, c. p 512.
10. A surprising number of examples survive that show Sterrell's prison visitations. SP 12/240/34; SP 12/245/65; SP 12/256/69.
11. Hatfield Papers, 6: 490–93.
12. Hatfield Papers, 7: 520, letter of December 22, 1597.
13. Caraman (1951), p. 35.
14. Freedman (1983), p. 109.
15. Mateer (1997), p. 29. Mateer observes that Bolt was closely employed by Sir John Petre for several years (about 1587–93), spending "long periods in London, probably as Petre's city agent.... When Sir John was in town Bolt accompanied him everywhere, functioning as his personal servant and perhaps even as a bodyguard on his master's nocturnal round of social and business engagements." Id. pp. 32–3.
16. SP 12/248/37.
17. SP 12/248/38.
18. Hatfield Papers 12: 704.
19. SP 12/249/85. The letter is not in the hand of Sherwood and is identified in the Calendar as a copy. The Calendar summary or paraphrase presents a misimpression of the letter. Roger Line was already in the Low Countries, and had been since 1591. The letter actually states: "Commend me most hertily to your good sister & tell her from me that I would gladly she were here with her owne husband where I trust she should better recover her health than where she is, and she should find me ready to do her all the comfort & pleasure I possibly can."
20. ODNB, "Waad, Sir William."
21. Caraman (1951), pp. 140–41, and notes 240–41.
22. Caraman (1951), p. 83.
23. SP 15/32/64, reproduced in Foley Records 6: 742–44.
24. Caraman (1995), p. 74.
25. The Latin description is by Fr. Henry Garnet, Brownlow (1996), p. 13.
26. Quoted McDonald & Brown (1967), p. xxxi. The text of the letter is reprinted in Hood (1926), pp. 47–9.
27. Devlin (1956), p. 324.

Chapter 15

1. A Sterrell letter of September 21, 1594, told Fr. Sherwood: "I perceive I have put you to silence, yet you might think I would take it unkindly. I will do more for you than you think for I shall have opportunity to see you shortly. There shall come an Ambassador to Ernestus. I am in suit to come with him, ... Adieu 21 of September. Yours even as his own. Ha: Wicham." SP 12/283/75 ii.
2. Spedding (1861), 1: 305–07. Wernham (1987), p. 443, covers the proposed Wilkes mission and its cancellation. He concluded that it was "natural enough that some of Elizabeth's ministers, Burghley in particular, should consider making yet another attempt to drive a wedge between the governments in Brussels and Madrid upon the coincidence of the discovery of the Lopez Plot with the arrival in the Spanish Netherlands of a new Governor-General who perhaps might not quite see eye to eye with his Spanish master."
3. Hatfield Papers 5: 12–14, letters of Privy Council to Mons. Richardot and of Queen Elizabeth to Archduke Ernestus.
4. SP 12/250/35, letter of November 19, 1594. The diplomatic career of Wilkes is given in SP 12/246/52. Wilkes was a friend of the Earl of Essex. SP 12/244/92, Essex to Wilkes March 27, 1593.
5. Hatfield Papers vol. 5 p. 26. 1594, Dec. 2.
6. The editors of the Calendar of State Papers assumed that "Hallins" was Thomas Phelippes, for notes in his handwriting are often found on the letters. But Phelippes was simply cataloging and storing the correspondence that was directed to Sterrell. Most of the letters addressed to "Hallins" are in SP 77/5 and 77/6.
7. As related earlier, while Sterrell was in the Low Countries in 1592, he directed some of his letters for Phelippes to "Mr. Morice" at the Swan, Bishopsgate, in London. The address was actually

that of Ezekiel Staveley, a tailor and sometime courier; Staveley's wife would see to it that the correspondence reached its proper destination.

8. The postscript to the December 2 letter states "Your old friend Fitsher [Fitzherbert] is here long since, who told me of late he had written to you and wondered he had no answer, and sent the same by means of the friend who brought you and me first acquainted. You shall do well to answer him." The friend who first made Owen and Sterrell acquainted was probably Fr. Richard Sherwood. When Sterrell first went into the service of Essex through Thomas Phelippes in 1591, he had already been a correspondent with Fitzherbert for some time.

9. SP 12/283/75 ii, Harry Wicham to Derrick. "I am afeard you are to open with '38 (Paget): he deals with one [symbol] (Poley) the vilest [symbol] (spy) that ever was and so you may undo '44 (Sterrell)."

10. Pistol referred to Sir Thomas Heneage, and Pistol's man was Robert Poley.

11. As we saw earlier, Paget communicated with Burghley and Cecil through Michael Moody, and just six weeks before Owen's December 2 letter to Sterrell, Moody had written to Poley "I hope you will come with this ambassador [Wilkes] as a thing very necessary...." Hatfield Papers 5: 8, John Bristowe [M. Moody] to [Poley], October 17, 1594.

12. Hatfield Papers 5: 26, December 2, 1594.

13. "Cloves" was deciphered to (Car:) by another hand in the original, as were other names in the letter.

14. Hatfield Papers 5: 34–35, Archduke Ernest to King of Spain, December 10/20, 1594.

15. Gatacre was included on a nationwide list of recusants in 1592 as Francis Gatacre of Swinnerton. Hatfield Papers 4: 272.

16. Knox (1878), p. 282 (Joannes Catacreus).

17. SP 12/249/72, August 13, 1594. On the Thatcher family, see Foley Records 6: 561–62.

18. *List and Analysis of State Papers, Foreign Series, Elizabeth I*, vol. 6 (ed. R.B. Wernham, London, 1993), pp. 76-7 (Sir Edmund U[ve]dall to Burghley, February 12, 1595).

19. Hatfield Papers 5: 63.

20. Loomie (1963a), p. 102.

21. Foley Record 3: 577, n. 8.

22. *List and Analysis of State Papers, Foreign Series, Elizabeth I*, vol. 6 (ed. R.B. Wernham, London, 1993), p. 76 item 32 (1993).

23. He had gone on to Douay for a year and then to Rheims for some two years, then to Liège and then back to Rheims and Douay for several more years. From there he was in Italy and then again back to Douay for seven or eight more years, with visits to Paris, Rouen and other towns in France. Eight or nine months before apprehension, he was in Brussels and met with Francis [Hugh] Owen "A Pensioner of the King of Spain." Three months before, he was in Brussels meeting with Father Holt and had exchanged greetings with Jaques and Sir William Stanley, who had known George Somerset's father. He had also met with Charles Paget, who had given him word of his father's death and that his father had left him some means. George was now "Extreme Poor" and was returning to England to present himself to the Privy Council and submit to their favor.

24. A letter of Dr. William Gifford to Thomas Throckmorton of May, 1595 reported "Catequay was taken meeting George Somerset at Flushing, to go to England, sent to the Council, and let go." SP 12/252/8. Catequay is a variation of "Catacreus," which is how Gatacre's name was entered in the Douay Records where Dr. Gifford was a lecturer who would have known Gatacre from there or from being in Brussels in late 1594. An examination of the original document and Phelippes transcription of it, SP 12/252/9, confirm the identity of "Catequay" as Gatacre, for they state: "Catequaye Mr. Fitzherberts brother and George Somersett...."

25. Hatfield Papers, 5: 105: "About eight days ago there passed into England one William Sterrell, an Englishman, who told me he was employed in these parts by your Honour; and understanding so much by him also by English merchants i let him pass."

26. On May 20, 1595, Verstegan wrote to Baynes in Rome, "Sir William Stanley and Mr. Owen are as yet bothe here with me, ..." Petti (1959), p. 234.

27. Hatfield Papers 5: 97, "W. Nicols" to Sr Peter Hallins, London coopman, February 7, 1595, n.s.

28. Sterrell already knew Persons: a January 1592 letter of Sterrell's had informed Phelippes that he might go to Spain, where he would expect "to find no small credit with Persons the Jesuit." SP 12/241/10. Sterrell probably had met with Persons during the Campion-Persons mission in 1580-81.

29. Persons to Fr. Creswell, October ??, 1595, transcript in Jesuit Archives, London, 46.12.3. These letters brought by Sterrell were perhaps the same that Persons showed soon after to a friend: "Father Persons ... shewed me letters out of England certifying the death of Father Sowthwell [Southwell], Father Walpoole, the imprisonment of Father Gerret [Gerard], Fr. Bertlet [Birket?] and Father Creswell." Hatfield Papers 5: 448–49, November 10/20, 1595.

30. The status of Sir Francis Englefield's lands has been traced by Geoffrey de C. Parmiter (1975) (1977).

31. The facts are recited in Coke's Reports, "Englefield's Case" (1591) 7 Co. Rep. 11b; in Popham, "Sir Francis Englefield's Case," (1591) Poph 18, 79 Eng.Rep. 1139; and in "Sir Francis Englefield's Case," (1591), 4 Leonard, 137.

32. Birch (1754), 1: 202–03.

33. Rolston reported to Bacon: "Robert Parsons the jesuit, for his great learning and singular judgment in the affairs of the world, and his skill in the French, Italian, and Spanish ... had more credit in effect than Sir Francis Englefield, tho' in outward show it appeared otherwise. He had free access to the King, when he thought proper, and was highly esteemed by the Spanish clergy, by which means he

had lately founded the English college in Valladolid." Birch (1754), 1: 202.

34. Sir Francis Englefield to the King of Spain, September 8, 1596, reprinted and translated from the Spanish in Tierney-Dodd 3: xlviii-liii. "Having served your majesty for more than forty years, ... I cannot, at a moment when it appears that the Almighty is about to remove me from the world, refrain from addressing to your majesty these few lines. They are the last that you will receive from me in this life (for I have ordered that they shall not be delivered until after my death)...."

35. CSP Sp., 4: 670. "Report of the Council of State on a Letter of Thomas Fitzherbert, Begging a Cardinal's Hat for Father Persons," dated September 26, 1600. The pope was considering appointing Arthur Pole as an English cardinal, but Fitzherbert asserted that Persons should be elevated first.

36. CSP Sp. 4: 628–29: Persons to Idiaquez.

37. The Duke of Feria urged King Philip in January 1597 (and had made the same arguments to Archduke Albert) to take strong measures against the faction in Flanders supporting James of Scotland as successor to the English crown. He urged the king to send Charles Paget, William Tresham, and Ralph Ligon to Sicily where they could work no further mischief and to reprimand others of the faction. The Duke praised highly Hugh Owen, Fr. Holt and Thomas Fitzherbert; the Scottish faction had been working against Owen and Holt. Duke of Feria to the King of Spain, January 3, 1597, Tierney Dodd 3:liii.

38. CSP Sp. 4: 633. Hume, the editor of the Calendar initially wrote the name as "Stevello" but later recognized that he had gotten Sterrell's name wrong. Hume (1901), p. 221.

39. Strype (1824), 4: 385, 390.

40. Arber, *Stationers Register*, 2: 713.

41. Oxford, Bodley Library, English Hist. B. 172f. 1-2, copy of the I.P.M., dated May 27, 1597. A. J. Loomie first noticed this document (1963a), pp. 50–51, but did not connect Thorpe to the publisher of Shakespeare, Jonson, Marston and others.

42. *Calendar of Patent Rolls, Philip & Mary 1554–1555* (H M Stationery Office 1936) p. 52, March 4, 1555.

43. Parmiter (1977), p. 20. Trappes-Lomax (1951), p. 133 gives a date of 1586 but this is clearly in error. Some sources on the history of the manor have incorrectly identified the date of death of Sir Francis as 1586 or 1587. See E. Crittall (ed.), *A History of Wiltshire*, ix, 191 (Oxford, 1970), citing V. C. H. Berks. iii 407: "...Englefield was attainted in 1585 and all his lands were formally forfeited to the Crown. Two years later he died. Wootton Bassett then passed to his nephew Francis...."

44. However, they were still held in "tail male"; after the accession of James, Francis Englefield was granted the reversionary rights of Wotton Basset and others in Wiltshire. Entry of August 1, 1605, CSP Dom. 1603–10, p. 230.

45. Burke (1844), p. 184.

46. In 1572 there was a double wedding of the Dormer and Browne (Montagu) families—Lord Montagu's son Anthony married Sir William Dormer's daughter Mary Dormer, and Sir William Dormer's son Robert married Lord Montagu's daughter Elizabeth Browne. Chambers (1923), 1: 163.

47. A second Spanish armada did sail in the next month after Persons's memorandum and after Englefield's advice. A fleet of eighty-one large ships left Lisbon and Coruña in October 1596. Under the command of Don Martin de Padilla—the Adelantado (governor) of Castile—they were to sail to Brittany and seize Brest. This would have provided an excellent location from which to launch further attacks against England, in the manner suggested by Persons, though Persons had suggested using Ireland or Scotland for a base. A successful taking of Brest would have helped overcome the humiliation inflicted by the raid on Cadiz that the Earl of Essex and Lord Howard of Effingham had successfully mounted in the previous June and July. However, as in 1588, the weather was against the Spaniards in 1596. Padilla's fleet was scattered by a storm, and thirty-two of the ships were lost. Kamen (1997), p. 308.

48. Martin & Finnis (2003a), pp. 1–43.

49. Hatfield Papers, 6: 511–13, Phelippes to Essex, December 9, 1596. This correspondence to Essex probably fell into the hands of Robert Cecil after the execution of Essex in 1601.

50. The excerpts were on separate pages from the letter proper and were calendared in the Hatfield Papers according to the dating of the excerpts and thus are found earlier in the same volume. Hatfield Papers 6: 490–93. A nearly identical copy of these notes is in the State Papers, SP 12/260/118. It is clear from internal references in the letter to Essex that this letter and the Nicols/Hallins excerpts were together. The copy of the excerpts (and notes on the Hallins/Nicols correspondence) sent with the letter to Essex is in the Hatfield Papers and the copy in the State Papers was the copy Phelippes kept in his file, which files were seized by Cecil in 1605. Evidently, Phelippes was concerned that Essex might think that the extracts were misleading, so the next day, December 10, 1596, he sent on to Essex the originals of two of the letters of Nicols. Hatfield Papers 6: 516, Thomas Phelippes to the Earl of Essex, December 10, 1596. This explains why in Hatfield Papers 6: 481 there appears a more complete copy of the letter of "Thomas Nicols to Peter Halyns" dated November 19, 1596 that is excerpted on page 491–92; likewise, in Hatfield Papers 6: 493 there appears a more complete copy of the letter of "Thomas Nicols to Peter Halyns" dated November 26, 1596 that is excerpted on page 492–93.

51. Hatfield Papers, 6: 512, Phelippes to Essex, December 9, 1596.

52. Hatfield Papers 6: 513, Phelippes to Essex, De-

cember 11, 1596 (mis-calendared as December 9); Hatfield Papers 6: 516–17, Phelippes to Essex, December 10, 1596.

53. This appears to be a misrepresentation by Phelippes, but one necessary to justify Phelippes's proposal. Phelippes's statement here corresponds with the seeming distrust between Owen and Sterrell in the Wicham/Derrick letters.

54. The letter of Dr. William Gifford to Thomas Throgmorton (Throckmorton) with the cover letter of Phelippes to Burghley is in the State Papers, SP 12/252/66.

55. As detailed below, Phelippes and Sterrell were brought separately before Cecil in January 1605 to account for the correspondence they had been conducting with Owen. SP 14/12/32, Phelippes's examination, January 25, 1605; SP 14/12/37, Answers of William Sterrell, January 26, 1605. Each admitted that it continued up to the accession of James in March 1603 and perhaps beyond. Sterrell was sent on his way, no doubt because of the great power and influence of his patron, the Earl of Worcester. But Phelippes spent much of the next five years in prison because of this correspondence with Hugh Owen.

56. Hatfield Papers 17: 39, Thomas Phelippes to Cecil, January 29, 1605.

57. See Hicks (1964), p. 124 n. 352 for an example of the confusion the Sterrell/Phelippes ruse has brought about. Hicks thought that with an enlarged photo of the name that was crossed out on one of the letters, he was able to determine the "Monk's" real name was "Jehan Batson." The name that was crossed out most likely was Jhean Baxter, one of the letter-drop names used by Sterrell, Phelippes and Thomas Fitzherbert. See above, p. 300 for example of another letter using this name. There was an Englishman named Petit, see Loomie (1963a), pp. 35, 256–57, in the Low Countries, but the intelligencers merely used the name to mislead the English government.

58. Hatfield papers, 6: 512.

59. If Sterrell received letters from "Nicols," who was Owen, why then the name Petit? The letters of "Petit" were sometimes showed to Essex, Robert Cecil or the Queen, and for this purpose Sterrell, Phelippes and Owen pretended they came from a "Monk at Liège." That is to say, the Nicols name (and a few others) was used for correspondence directed to Sterrell, while the "J.B." or "Petit" letters were intended to be shared at Court.

Chapter 16

1. At least forty-one letters to "Hallins/Halyns" still exist and are held in the Public Record Office's Flanders Papers. They are all in the same hand, and form the greater part of a series extending from November 1594 to 1604, which includes (i) letters in that hand from "John Petit," "J.P.B," and "J.B." to "Halyns" (ii) letters in that hand from "J.B." to "Mr Robinson," (iii) letters in a different hand or hands to "Halyns" from "Thomas Nichols," and "W. Nichols," and (iv) letters in another different hand to "Halyns" from "J. Sauf." The author of the letters from "J.B.," "John Petit," "J.P.B.," and "Thomas Nicols" or "W. Nicols" is Hugh Owen, who was based throughout this period in Brussels, though often purporting to write from Liège. The different handwriting is explained when "Nicols" tells "Hallins": "you must excuse me for I am forced to use another man's hand for security." Hatfield Papers 5: 97, W. Nicols to Sr Peeter Hallins, February 7, 1595, n.s. Another Hallins letter example is SP 15/34/30, J. B. to Peter Halyns April 30, 1600, from Liège.

2. SP 77/6 fol. 34, J. B. to Halyns, 18/28 August 1599 Brussels ("What I have written was for the good of Her Majesty").

3. SP 78/42 fol. 88 (c. April, 1600).

4. Hatfield Papers 17: 39, Thomas Phelippes to Cecil, January 29, 1605.

5. SP 77/5 fol. 233, John Petit to Pieter Halyns. October 5/15, 1597, Liége.

6. *King Lear*, 1.2: "for when thou gav'st them the rod and putt'st down thine own breeches...."

7. SP 77/6 fol. 178, J.B. to Halyns, June 14/24, 1600, Liège.

8. SP 77/5 fol. 326, J. P. to Peeter Halyns, March 7, 1598. Phelippes's notation on the outside was "The Sc[ot] speakes of war with England."

9. CSP Sp. 4:650, Thomas Fitzherbert (to Lerma?) Nov 30, 1599.

10. SP 12/283/20.

11. SP 77/6 fol. 293, Advices—signature erased, September 7/17, 1601.

12. SP 12/282/2, Phelippes to Cecil, October 3, 1601.

13. SP 12/281/19, Cecil to Lord Burghley, July 15, 1601,.

14. Hatfield Papers 17:39, Thomas Phelippes to Cecil, January 29, 1605. Phelippes's claims that his identity was not known to Owen, and that Sterrell was perplexed about how to keep the secret, need not and cannot be taken as accurate accounts of what Owen and Sterrell knew.

15. Church historians, such as Fr. Christopher Grene, S. J., thought that Anthony Rivers was a Jesuit and preserved letters in that name or in his handwriting as part of the history of the Society. Letters under names such as Fenner, Cordale and Renzo that reached Fr. Persons and others may not have been preserved, one suspects, because the letters did not seem to be part of the religious history.

"Rivers" is the name of the Englishman most visibly and admirably involved in fostering good relations with Burgundy in the late fifteenth century, Anthony Woodville, second Earl Rivers, whom someone familiar with late sixteenth century usage could imagine signing himself Anthony Rivers, just as Sterrell's master the fourth Earl of Worcester always signed himself E. [or Edward] Worcester. There was a Somerset family connection to Anthony Woodville.

16. The intercepted packets are reconstructed in Martin & Finnis (2002a), 39–74.

17. Verstegan was the main conduit for money going into England to Thomas Phelippes and William Sterrell (and perhaps the Jesuits too); and "Jacob Samander" is another name for "J.S." and "J. Sauf," who are unquestionably aliases of Verstegan in his capacity as a participant in the incoming J.B. (etc.) correspondence of Owens with "Halyns" (etc.), and in an outgoing series of letters to Owen (as "Benson") from "Vincent" (= Phelippes). Thus Vincent writes to Benson, in cipher, on January 10, 1605: "Since the writing hereof, we understand from the factor of the arrival of our letters of the 5 and 12 of December, as also of the cheese [= money] by Samander, for the which I thank you…" SP 14/12/16.

18. It is the hand used at the end of a letter from "W. Nicols" of February 7, 1595, n.s., and in a letter of "Thomas Nicols" of November 19, 1596, n.s.

19. The identity of "A. L." is perhaps Adrien de Langhe, who was made prisoner of the English garrison at Flushing in May 1594. SP 12/248/101, May 11, 1594.

20. SP 77/6/27.

21. His handwriting, both in secretary and italic, has an extraordinary eccentricity: a small semi-circle (such as continental writers often use for an umlaut or dieresis) placed, in tic-like fashion, above the letters "u" and "v" in many but by no means all their appearances. For an instance, signed by Verstegan, see SP 12/252/15 (letter of May 10/20, 1595; amusingly, this letter was given to Verstegan's clandestine colleague Thomas Phelippes, doubtless by Burghley, for deciphering of the occasional numerical cipher codes; and Burghley, one conjectures, will have admired Phelippes's wonderful ability to decipher number codes—where one number, e.g., 107, stands for a proper name—from only one example; to maintain verisimilitude, the code's probable co-author, Phelippes, left one of the numbers undeciphered). For another example of the eccentricity, see Petti (1959), p. xlx (facing page 1), lines 3 (two instances) and 10 (one instance).

22. Hatfield Papers 6: 491.

23. Thus "Thomas Nicols" (Owen) to "Peter Halyns," November 19, 1596, Hatfield Papers 6:484, says: "My host has sent the Holland cheese by such shipping and travellers as you gave direction." And "Tho. Nicols" to "Pieter Halins," November 26, 1596, Hatfield Papers 6:493 says: "The other cheeses promised are sent already, as you appointed. W is for wool [intelligence]. In the latter end of January we will knit up all accounts, and what you have laid out shall be answered. If You take great travel [= travel or travail/work], I hope to get for a pot of wine for your recompense."

24. SP 14/12/35.

25. SP 77/6 fol. 21, J. B. to Halyns, May 31/June 10, 1599, Liège. "I sent my host in antwerp (unto whom I gave charge to send my letters to the post) two gloves of sundry sort to be sent unto you praying you to cause to be made of each fashion a dozen pair & the like leather (or better if it may be had) for men & women but let be left unbuttoned at the wrist, it may be done here according to their fancies that shall wear them. in any case let them be finely sewed & good leather."

26. SP 12/271/33, "George Fenner" to "Giulio Piccioli, or Bernardo Edlyno, Venice," June 30, 1599.

27. SP 12/271/107, Francis Cordale to "His Partner Balthazar Gybels, Antwerp," July 21, 1599.

28. SP 77/6 fol. 48, J.B. to Halyns, September 29, 1599, n.s.

Chapter 17

1. *Twelfth Night,* 2.5.

2. See Hatfield Papers 5: 34–35, Archduke Ernest to King of Spain, December 10/20, 1594; "Memorial for the Archduke Ernest Governor of the Low Countries, Regarding English Persons and Affairs in Their Relation to the Government of Flanders, 1594" reprinted in Knox (1878), pp. 401–408.

3. CSP Sp. 4: 628–29, Persons to Idiaquez.

4. SP 12/265/63, December 26, 1597. Paget expressed a desire to do service to both the queen of England, whose subject he was, and to the king of Spain, who had supported him in his banishment. The editor of the Calendar of State Papers thought this letter was directed to Secretary Cecil, evidently because the letter mentions favor shown to Paget's nephew as does another later letter to Cecil. However, the recipient is not otherwise identified; it may have been sent through Barnes and never delivered to the intended recipient, whomever it was. The letter mentions an earlier visit of Barnes to Paget, and Barnes apparently did no work for Robert Cecil before 1605. Barnes worked for Phelippes who at this time in 1597 and 1598 was operating on behalf of Essex, albeit while Phelippes also pretended to do some favors for Robert Cecil. Paget was uncertain who favored his restoration; still later, Paget thought Barnes was working for Essex.

5. Cf. Wernham (1994), p. 213.

6. Wernham (1994), p. 231.

7. SP 77/5 fol. 326, J. P. to Peeter Halyns, February 25/March 7, 1598.

8. SP 78/42 fol. 88 (c. April-May, 1600).

9. SP 77/5 fol. 327, Jacques de Boulant to (Robinson), March 23/April 2, 1598.

10. Wernham thought that Cecil rather than Phelippes sent the letters to the Queen, and he misread Phelippes' memo to say that the Queen sent instructions by "Mr Carew"; R. B. Wernham (1994), p. 246. Reading the same documents, Lafleur de Kermaingant thought Cecil had been designated by the Queen to guide the response to the Boulant overture. *Mission De Jean De Thumery,* 1: 209–11 (Paris, 1886).

Phelippes in fact had written "Mr Carm." abbreviating "Carmarthen." As Phelippes later confessed, "His Lo: [Essex] communicating the whole with the Q: by her commandment Sterrell had order to proceed as was required. And so by many things which passed to and fro much light was gotten. I was then a prisoner in the Fleet yet managed it wholye to her Highness contentment sometime by the entremise of my Lord of Essex sometime by Mr. Carmarthen." Hatfield Papers 17:39, Thomas Phelippes to Cecil, January 29, 1605.

11. Hatfield Papers 17:39, Thomas Phelippes to Cecil, January 29, 1605, microfilm of original at Folger Library. Phelippes may have forgotten that he had more recently pretended to write to Mons. Boulant in dealing with Cecil. In a letter of May 4, 1602, Phelippes had conveyed to Cecil some supposed intelligences from Rome about the Appellant controversy and told Cecil that he heard "nothing of the letters that went out to Monsr. Boulant..." SP 12/284/4, Thomas Phelippes to Cecil, May 4, 1602.

12. SP 78/42 fol. 88 (c. April-May, 1600).

13. SP 12/266/116, Charles Paget to Barnes (M. Gerard Burghert), April 17/27, 1598. "I pray you signify to me with whom you deal about [my] affairs, that I may know to whom I am beholding and so worthily acknowledge the same."

14. Persons to Don Juan de Idiaques, June 30, 1597, transcription, Jesuit Archives, London, Persons 46/12/4 pp. 665-673.

15. Edwards (1995), pp. 216-20.

16. SP 12/244/35.

17. SP 15/33/95, Charles Paget to Thomas Barnes, March 1598. "The Earl of Essex's father was very good to my brother and myself ... I would be glad to be brought into his good grace; employ yourself to the uttermost to do him pleasure; if you think good, impart our talk in the Capello to him, and though Secretary Cecil does no show himself willing to pleasure me, yet I will not cease to honour and serve him for his virtues." This is a copy of the letter in Phelippes hand. An abstract of it, deciphered, is found at SP 15/34/1 among with a collection of such abstracts that Phelippes maintained of the Paget-Barnes correspondence.

18. Paget later wrote: "The substance of my speeches in the Capello was, that if the Queen will grant me a pardon and restore me my livings, I will spend the remainder of my life in her service, my religion excepted." On this, Phelippes wrote a comment in the margin: "His speech in the Capello was otherwise, and not so general, whatsoever he says." SP 15/34/10, Charles Paget to Thomas Phelippes, June 3, 1599.

19. SP 12/266/116, Charles Paget to Barnes (M. Gerard Burghert); SP 12/267/8, Charles Paget to Barnes (M. Gerard Burghert).

20. Paget recounts letters to him from Barnes dated April 22 and May 13 that gave Paget "great consolation." SP 15/33/97, Charles Paget to Barnes, June 10, 1598. This letter, too, is among the abstracts at SP 15/34/1.

21. Id. "touching the services it is expected I may do, by reason of my acquaintance with the Jesuits, I was never a favourite of theirs, because I have ever misliked the courses of Fathers Parsons and Holt, and have not only told them plainly thereof, but advertised the Cardinals and the Pope of the same, which has made them proceed with great fury against me and some others. Let the Queen be assured that the Jesuits cannot abide to hear of peace, and especially between her and the King of Spain, as it will be the break up of all the plots and practices for England, of which I hope to discover some before long, and to diminish their credit in all parts."

22. SP 12/267/67, June 1598, "A Proposition of Charles Paget for Calling the Jesuits Out of England, by Means of the French King, During the Treaty."

23. Persons to Cajetan, Naples August 22, 1598, transcription, Jesuit Archives London Box 46/12/5 fol. 912.

24. Edwards (1995), pp. 226-27. Edwards believed that the secret person giving help was Simon Willis, an aide to Robert Cecil who was dismissed in 1602. However, there is no reason to think that the letters of Paget to Barnes ever got to Robert Cecil for Willis to have access to them. The reason why the originals of the April 27 and May 8 letters ended up in the State Papers is that they were among the many papers seized from Phelippes's files in 1605 when he was arrested.

25. Persons to Peña, Naples August 22, 1598, transcription, Jesuit Archives London Box 46/12/5 fo. 955-57.

26. Loomie (1963a), p. 255. A report made in 1600 on Spanish pensioners in the Low Countries now said of Paget: "He corresponds with the Queen of England and some of her Council. His own letters show he is willing to gain a pardon; he is completely dedicated to the Scottish faction, and left for France six months ago...."

27. SP 12/268/112, Paget to Barnes November 20, 1598 (copy in Phelippes hand); SP 15/33/101, Paget to Barnes, November 24, 1598. Abstracts of these same letters, also in Phelippes's hand, are found at SP 15/34/1.

28. Turner was certainly an opportunist and a slippery fellow, but it was to him that Paget entrusted letters he sent to England. Thomas Edmondes from Paris a few weeks later told this story of the Turner saga: "One Turner an Englishman that is lately come out of the low Countries hath addressed himself to me and acquainted me that having embarked himself a month since at Dover to have come into France, he was taken on the seas by a Shallop of Graveline, and therefore forced as he sayeth to pretend that he was going to serve Sir William Stanley by the which means he was well received and favored by the English priests and fugitives there, and was brought by Sir William Stanley to the Archduke who

dealt with him to employ himself to burn part of her Majesty's navy at rochester, wherein he promised to do his endeavor. He delivered me these inclosed letters which he received from Mr. Paget to convey to his sister the Lady Walgrave, and the other from Mr Tresham to his brother Sir Thomas Tresham but neither of them importeth matter of knowledge, your honor shall also herewith receive a note that he hath made of the names of the English that he saw in those parts." Butler (1913), pp. 371–72, Edmondes to Cecil, September 12, 1598.

29. SP 12/268/112, Paget to Barnes, November 26, 1598.

30. SP 12/268/112, Paget to Barnes, November 30, 1598.

31. SP 15/34/1, Charles Paget to Thomas Barnes (in hand of Phelippes). Paget was reported as "extremely affected to the Queen's proceedings, and a great hinderer of the King of Spain's courses." His enemies had good credit "and every word they speak brings me in question of disgrace." Phelippes and Sterrell engaged in the same trick on William Tresham, another English fugitive who was associated with Paget. He too looked to Essex and Barnes for a return to England and soon came to realize he had been tricked and identified to the Jesuits, the Pope and the Archduke as seeking the Queen's mercy. See SP 15/34/2, William Tresham to Essex, March 10 1599; SP 15/34/6, William Tresham to Thomas Barnes April 14, 1599; SP 15/34/14, William Tresham (from Paris) to Barnes June 18, 1599. In this last, Tresham sought to have a letter to Essex conveyed through Sir Anthony Standen.

32. SP 12/270/93, Paget to Barnes, April 24, 1599; SP 12/270/94, Paget to Cecil, April 24, 1599.

33. SP 15/34/7, Phelippes to Charles Paget, addressed to J. Auguste, Scotchman Porte St. Michel, Paris (draft of what was sent to Paget).

34. SP 15/34/10, Charles Paget to Thomas Phelippes, June 3, 1599.

35. At about the same time Paget again wrote to Barnes. SP 15/34/12, Paget to Barnes, June, 1599 Paris. Phelippes's abstract suggests Paget was irritated: his speeches in the Capello were not well-understood or reported. He expressed chagrin about his contacting Edmondes, saying it might have been regarded as indiscreet if he had not gone through Edmondes in treating for a pardon from the Queen.

36. SP 12/271/10, Paget to Barnes, June 15, 1599. In a draft letter, Barnes (with Phelippes suggesting the language) replied indignantly and asserted "there must be no blame about divulging the Jesuits' matter; it was sent to the Queen, and it is not known into whose hands it came afterwards." SP 12/271/24, Barnes to Paget, June [24?], 1599.

37. S.P. 77/5, fol. 25. This letter is quoted in Hicks (1964), p. 124, n. 352.

38. SP 12/271/74, July 4/14, 1599.

39. Quoted in Edwards (1995), p. 228 (apparently quoting from *Winwood's Memorials*, 112). The ambassador had advised giving support to Paget in exchange for discovery. SP 12/271/29, June 27, 1599, Sir Henry Neville to Sec. Cecil "They reserve more particular discoveries [of the Jesuit faction] till they see what hope there is of obtaining their suit. Paget says he has almost been bereft of his living by some advertisements he sent over out of the Low Countries."

Chapter 18

1. Loomie (1963a), pp. 77–8. Lanfranchi, an Italian banker in Antwerp, had been used by Lord Burghley to try to drive a wedge between the Duke of Parma and Spain in August 1590 as recounted earlier. Lanfranchi was Burghley's man to show a deciphered message that indicated malice the Spanish held toward Parma. Wernham (1987), p. 443.

2. Loomie (1963a), p. 78.

3. Hatfield papers 9:138 "Carlo Lanfranchi to Horatio Scali." As are other letters catalogued by Cecil's secretary, this bears the endorsement "Carlo Lanfranchi to my Master." On May 2, 1599, n.s., April 22, o.s. Lanfranchi wrote Cecil from Antwerp, saying of Coemans, who had just left London: "You must not think it strange if you hear nothing from the friend who has just left you; those to whom he must refer the matter are some way off this place, where it will not be easy for him to go. But he has left Brussels, and I hope will soon be back." The implication is that Coemans had to coordinate with the Brabant nobility, and it would be difficult to travel to the Dutch lands. On May 8, 1599, n.s. Lanfranchi again wrote to Cecil from Antwerp, mentioning his letter of May 2, and saying that "Counsellor Cumans" would soon be passing from this place (Antwerp) and would bring the main facts and some details about a friend and would "Finish off the matter energetically." Hatfield papers 9:148 "Carlo Lanfranchi to Horatio Scali."

4. SP 12/271/19 "Jo. Nicols" in "Middleburgh" June 21/July 1, 1599.

5. SP 77/6 fol. 21, J. B. to Halyns, May 31/June 10, 1599, Liège.

6. SP 12/281/79, Levinus Munck to Cecil, September 9, 1601. Munck told Cecil of Coemans: "for all his secrecy, his coming was known 10 days ago, as i was informed by the post from Antwerp, and you [Cecil] had been advertized from Brussels."

7. Butler (1913), pp. 48, 49, 104, 109.

8. SP 77/6 fol. 32, J. B. to Halyns, July 28 /August 7, 1599, Liège.

9. SP 77/6 fol. 34, J. B. to Halyns, 18/28 August 1599, Brussels.

10. SP 77/6 fol. 48, J. B. to Halyns, September 19/29, 1599, Brussels. Phelippes echoes this same Spanish proverb a few months later in a note: "The Archduke's Secretary was dealt with on the behalf of Charles Paget seeking to be reconciled again with the Archduke offering some service with condition to be paid his arrearages of his pension. It was an-

swered in a Spanish proverb—*Hagase El Milagro Y Haglo El Diablo*. His service must precede his reward it seemeth." SP 12/275/34, July 22/August 1, 1600 "In Secret."

11. SP 77/6 fol. 40B, J. B. to Halyns, August 29/September 8, 1599.

12. Goodman (1925), p. 40, quoting Rowland Whyte to Sir Robert Sidney, Sydney Papers, 2: 175: "upon Thursday the Lord Chamberlain feasted him [Verreyken], and there in the after noone his plaiers acted before Vereiken, Sir John Old Castell, to his great contentment."

13. John Chamberlain, the London letter-writer, wrote to his friend Dudley Carleton on 5 March about the close companionship between Ralegh and Verreyken:

> Our peace goes but slowly on, and when all is done it is thought it will prove but a cessation, or truce, for seven or ten years at most. Neither do I think any great persons shall be employed in the treaty, when Sir Walter Raleigh is like to be second in the commission as himself says in secret. He attends the ambassador [Verreyken] much by the Queen's appointment, and carries him up and down to see sights and rarities hereabout. He has had him at [St.] Pauls, at Westminster, at Whitehall and wherenot.

McClure (1979), 1:91, letter of 5 March 1600.

14. Goodman (1925), p. 46.

15. SP 12/274/106, "Written Under Confidence 17 Aprilis 1600." Thomas Phelippes apparently had a personal stake in the Palavicino debt. From 1595 on Phelippes was in debt to the queen for more than £11,000 and the queen was indebted to Palavicino for still more. Some efforts were made for the debt of Phelippes to the queen be used to satisfy the queen's debt to Palavicino. See Phelippes's letter of March 28, 1596 to Robert Cecil expressing his hope that he may be "rid of the Queen's tempestuous displeasure" by assuming part of the queen's debt to Palavicino, which Phelippes had discussed with Palavicino. Hatfield Papers 6:118.

16. One dated April 14 is a draft to Cecil and the other is dated April 17. The latter, addressed to Cecil, has on the outside a notation by Cecil's secretary of April 18 "Mr Thomas Phillips to My Mr [Master]." SP 12/274/103, "Minute to Mr. Secretary Touching Device of Intelligence"; SP 12/274/107, Thomas Phelippes to Sec. Cecil, April 17, 1600.

17. SP 14/12/37–38, January 26, 1605. It is highly unlikely that Essex would have taken this matter in hand in April 1600. He was confined and in the Queen's severe displeasure and had been for the prior 7 months or so. Possibly the reference to the peace and the jewels relates back to the initial Boulant peace overtures of early 1598. But we find no reference to the jewels before the April 1600 note of Phelippes. And there is every indication that Essex was opposed to peace with Spain and the Low Countries. Essex's enemies—Lord Cobham and Ralegh—seem to have benefited initially from the "Jewels" and peace proceedings, though it probably contributed to their convictions for treason.

18. Sydney Papers 2: 462, Rowland Whyte to Sir Robert Sidney, May 16, 1600: "The marriage of the other Lord Harbert and Mrs Anne Russell is at a stay till her Majesty appoint a day...."

19. The commission was led by the English ambassador to France, Henry Neville, and also included Robert Beale, John Herbert, and Thomas Edmondes.

20. SP 12/275/8, Phelippes to Cecil, June 16, 1600.

21. SP 77/6 fol. 174, Jean le Clerque to Vincent Orwell, May 27/June 6, 1600. That this letter is the one to which Phelippes has reference in his letter to Cecil is seen in the fact that the Leclerque letter refers to Boulogne (Bullen) as "St. Hubert" and Phelippes's letter parenthetically informs Cecil: "the party hath failed being at St Hubert Bullen (which is meant by St. Hubert)...."

22. "Il vous fault garder vre [vostre] credit, aultrement on protestera contre vous qui vous redonderoit a grand dommage perte & deshonneur qui est pire.'"

23. This is the same Harrison who confessed to a substantial role for the government in the Babington Plot and execution of Mary Queen of Scots. Thomas Harrison had formerly been employed by Walsingham to spy on the seminarians at Douay.

24. SP 77/6 fol. 204, Letter from Brussels, signature erased, August 31/September 10, 1600. "I heard there was in company of the English commissioners one Harrison a craftie-headed fellow but yet not his crafts master in that he intended, for he sought to play the spy but went about it so openly and apparently that his own errours berayed him, he haunted much the Spanish ambassador's chaplain (who was a spaniard's son born in antwerp but brought up in England and so speaketh English)." In March 1599 Harrison wrote to Lord Cobham that Cecil, through his secretary Willis, had accepted Harrison's offers of service in the Low Countries. SP 12/270/56, Thomas Harrison to Cobham, March 14, 1599. Two years later "Rivers"(Sterrell) wrote to Fr. Persons what happened to this man, whom he described as a kinsman of Sir John Fortescue and follower of the late Earl of Essex in his prosperity. Harrison had been "employed for some service at Boulogne when the Commissioners there met about the treaty of the peace, hath ever since continued thereabout, and busied himself as it is thought more in French affairs than he had commission, by occasion whereof he was lately under colour of further employment, called home by the Admiral, and upon his arrival was sent prisoner to the Tower." Rivers to Ridolfo Perino, February 12, 1602 (AAW A7/25/183–86).

25. Handover (1959), p. 219.

26. Id. 219.

27. SP 12/275/121. The connections between Cob-

ham's family and Phelippes were long-standing. Phelippes served his uncle, Sir Henry Brooke (Cobham), in France c. 1579–81. Phelippes served in the Parliaments of 1584 and 1586 for Hastings and probably owed his seat to William Brooke, 10th Lord Cobham (d. 1597), brother of Sir Henry and father of Henry, 11th Lord Cobham. Hasler (1981), 3: 219–20.

28. SP 12/279/33, Phelippes to Lord Cobham, March 23, 1601.

29. Stone (1956), p. 86.

30. SP 12/279/122, Phelippes to Lord Cobham, June 28, 1601.

31. SP 12/279/33, Phelippes to Lord Cobham, 23 March 1601.

32. It was Sterrell, rather than Phelippes, who had the regular use of the Jesuits' secure system of transmitting mail from London to Antwerp and Brussels. On lay associates of Phelippes and Sterrell who were involved in this system, see Martin & Finnis (2006), pp. 209–12.

33. SP Flanders 77/6 fol. 260,—to Mr. Boulant with 2 translations.

34. Hurault (1931), pp. 44–5.

35. Hatfield Papers 6:409, September 30, 1596, Sir Anthony Ashley to Cecil.

36. Hatfield Papers 6:118, March 28, 1596, Phelippes to Cecil.

37. SP 12/271/80, Thos. Phelippes to his cousin Wm. Phelippes, attending the Lord Treasurer, July 6, 1599.

38. SP 77/6 fol. 279, H. Boulant to Mr. Robinson, June 12/22, 1601.

39. SP 12/279/122, Phelippes to Cobham, June 28, 1601.

40. SP 12/281/79, Levinus Munck to Cecil, September 9, 1601.

41. SP 12/283/26, "The Heads of Letters Written 9 and 23 Jan and 6 Feb for to Sound in What Terms They Be on the Other Side."

42. SP 12/283/26.

43. SP 77/6 fol. 313, fol. 317–8 (hand of Thos. Phelippes); fol. 319–21 (hand of Levinus Munck, secretary to Robert Cecil), H. Boulant to Robinson, 2 copies and translation, February 5/15, 1602.

44. SP 77/6 fol. 328, Richardot's memorial to Fortado (Hand of Thos Phelippes), February 20/March 2, 1602.

45. The quotation here is from SP 77/6 fol. 436, "The Proceedings with M. Boulant About Peace" which itself paraphrases "Richardot's Memorial to Fortado," SP 77/6 fol. 328. This latter is a Phelippes translation from the Spanish of the declaration sent by Richardot to Fortado, a copy of which is BL Stowe 167, ff. 312–13.

46. Rivers to Ridolfo Perino, February 12, 1602 (AAW A7/25/183–86). Sterrell's patron, the Earl of Worcester, was now (since June 30, 1601) a privy councilor, and Sterrell was thus inward with the Council's deliberations. (The highly regular pattern of Sterrell's "Rivers" correspondence makes it reliably certain that a virtually identical letter went in the same packet via Antwerp, addressed to Owen in Brussels under some such name as Bernardo Edlyno): see Martin & Finnis (2002a), pp. 40–46.

47. Cecil may have preceded the overture to "Boulant" by secret—perhaps duplicitous—communications through a priest he was using as a spy. On December 22, 1601 Rivers/Sterrell wrote to his overseas correspondents that for consideration of peace "it is thought Barwis hath twice been in Flaunders, and is now going a third tyme, and with him An ... Skynners brother, imployed as it [is] thoughte underhand *by the* Secretarye to deal with the Nuncio as from the Catholicke partye, to bee mediator for the entertainment of an other treaty of peace, yet so as the other part should seem to desyre it...." One cannot say for certain whether the Rivers letter of February 12 alludes to the overture to Boulant or to the earlier Barwise effort but the former is more likely. Cecil is unlikely to have made use of Barwise with the knowledge of the privy councillors.

48. Rivers to Ridolfo Perino, February 12, 1602 (Westminster VII n. 25). This Rivers/Sterrell letter provided extensive intelligence and political analysis.

49. SP 12/283/26, Phelippes's notes of letter of February 6, 1602.

50. Rivers to Ridolfo Perino, March 10, 1602 (AAW A7/30/201). The "matter of peace [which] was in some sort on foot, broached by us and well entertained on the other part, now ... hangeth in suspense, but with little probability of any good success."

51. Rivers to Ridolfo Perino, March 17, 1602 (AAW A7/32/205–06). "The conceipt of some likelihood of peace is clean quailed [faded, withered]; it stands with our policy, but to keep the wars of the low countries on foot, and for ourselves, it must be all as we will, or no dealing, but had the Irish action stood firm, we would willingly have embraced any though not altogether honorable conditions, *tempora mutantur* etc. [times change and we change with them]."

52. SP 77/6 fol. 332, "Answer to M. Boulant Touching Overture of Peace," March 27, 1602 (State Papers Calendar wrongly shows this as March 17/27; it should have been calendared as March 27/6 April). Although it was intended to precede the Edmondes/Fortado letter, its journey to Brussels was delayed several months by a miscarriage of the post, and the Archduke unfortunately received the Fortado letter first.

53. Edmondes to Fortado, March 28, 1602, BL Stowe 167, ff 318–319 (in French), ff. 320–25 (English draft of same).

54. SP 77/6 fol. 436, "The proceedings with M. Boulant about peace—1602." That Cecil is the "friend" alluded to by "Robinson" is confirmed by the reference to the "quiver" simile in a subsequent description of this Boulant episode by Phelippes in

which he referred to the "Boulant" and Fortado overtures: "so as Mr. Secretary [Cecil] said they seemed to be shafts both taken out of one quiver." Another indication that Cecil was responsible for the response to Boulant is a letter in which Phelippes had conveyed to Cecil some supposed intelligences from Rome about the Appellant controversy; he told Cecil that he heard "nothing of the letters that went out to Monsr. Boulant…" SP 12/284/4, Thomas Phelippes to Cecil, May 4, 1602.

55. Edmondes to Fortado, March 28, 1602, Stowe MSS., 167, ff. 318r-319v. An English draft of this letter is also in the Stowe MSS., 167, ff. 320r-325v.

56. Rivers to Ridolfo Perino, March 30, 1602 (AAW A7/33/207-08).

57. Rivers to Ridolfo Perino, April 7, 1602 (AAW A7/35/211-12).

58. Rivers to Ridolfo Perino, April 28, 1602 (AAW A7/39/223-26).

59. SP 77/6 fol. 436, "The Proceedings with M. Boulant About Peace—1602."

60. SP 77/6 fol. 341, J. B. to Robinson, May 19/29,1602.

61. SP 77/6 fol. 348, _____ to Robinson, June 29/July 9, 1602; SP 77/6 fol. 436.

62. SP 77/6 fol. 332, "Answer to M. Boulant Touching Overture of Peace," March 27, 1602.

63. Letters to Robert Cecil on the whereabouts of Lord Cobham from both Phelippes and Ralegh confirm this. Ralegh's letter of August 13, 1601 is reprinted in Latham & Youings (1999), pp. 205-06 ("My Lord Cobhame stayd here butt on night but went on for Cornwale."). Phelippes' letter is dated August 21, 1601 and states that Cobham "Is in the West Country," SP 12/281/60.

64. SP 12/281/19, Cecil to Lord Burghley (Cecil's brother), July 15, 1601.

65. Maclean (1864), p. 116. Cecil to Sir George Carew, June 30, 1602. Cobham and Ralegh are not named but scholars there is no doubt that they were the friends referred to.

66. Handover (1959), p. 279.

67. Hatfield Papers 12: 227, Davison to Cecil, July 16, 1602.

68. Id.: "[M]ost of the things being old and out of fashion, and the stones and pearl for the most part greatly decayed in their goodness and lustre; so as if her Majesty can quit her hands of them for so much as the principal debt amounts to (not more than about £28,700), she shall make a very good bargain."

69. Hatfield Papers 12:256.

70. Hatfield Papers 12: 469, Charles Comte d'Arenberg to Lord Cobham, November 12/22, 1602: "Je vous supplie, Monsieur, me voulloir tant obliger de me faire entendre librement sur cela vostre opinion, ne faisant doubte d'une bonne responce bien agreable, vous asseurant que je m'employeray tant affectueusement par de ca en ce faict comme je voy que la calamite en quoy le pais et generallement tout la Chrestiente est le requiert."

71. SP 14/1/57, Cobham to James, April 29, 1603. "as i was writing unto your Majesty I received this enclosed from the Count Arenberg betwixte whom and me, during the life of my late mistress, there was by her appointment, intelligence and good correspondence holden."

72. Birch (1848), 1:12, Cecil to Parry, August 4, 1603.

Chapter 19

1. Lambeth Palace Library MS 657 f. 108v letter of E Reynolds to Essex May 6, 1596. "The Earle of Worcester is returned from the funerals but hath not yet executed his place of Deputy Mr of the horse." Worcester was formally made Deputy Master by January 1598.

2. Harley (1997), pp. 93-98. At Christmas time in 1589, Byrd was a guest of the Petres at Ingatestone Hall; fellow guests included Edward Somerset (his first Christmas as Earl of Worcester) and his wife Elizabeth, Countess of Worcester, and there was, of course, music-making.

3. Devereux (1853), 1:395; Spedding (1862), 40.

4. Lacey (1971), p. 204.

5. The position was not without hazards. In 1599, Rowland Whyte wrote to Sir Robert Sydney of an equine accident to Worcester: "My Lord of Worcester helping the Queen from her horse, her horse trod on his foot, and this morning she went to see him." Rowland Whyte to Sir Robert Sidney, Sydney Papers, II, 381.

6. Hatfield Papers 14:106; unsigned. endorsed: "My L. in Favor of My L. of Worcester to Her Matie." Essex set forth in the spring of 1599. In *Henry V*, Essex's departure was explicitly alluded to. The playwright expressed hope that Elizabeth's general would return from Ireland with the success that Henry enjoyed at the Battle of Agincourt:

Were now the general [Essex] of our gracious empress
(As in good time he may) from Ireland coming,
Bringing rebellion broachèd on his sword,
How many would the peaceful city quit,
To welcome him! [*Henry V*, 5. 1. 22-34].

7. SP 12/271/34, George Fenner" to "His Partner Baltazar Gybels, Antwerp," June 30, 1599.

8. SP 12/271/33, "George Fenner" to "Giulio Piccioli, or Bernardo Edlyno, Venice," June 30, 1599.

9. He echoed a letter of the Council written to Essex June 10, 1599: "Her Maj. pleasure is that you do not longer continue him [Southampton] in that place and charge of General of the Horse…" Devereux (1853), 2:43. That Sterrell's information was not derived from Court gossip is indicated by comparing his letters of June 30 with John Chamberlain's letter of June 28 "The Earl of Rutland is returned out of Ireland upon commandment, and the Earl of Southampton said to be either come or coming…" SP 12/271/30, John Chamberlain to Dudley Carleton, June 28, 1599.

10. SP 12/271/33, "George Fenner" to "Giulio Piccioli, or Bernardo Edlyno, Venice," June 30, 1599.

11. Devereux (1853), 2:40–41.

12. SP 12/271/106, Francis Cordale to "Hum. Galdelli or Gioseffo Tusinga, Vinegia," July 22, 1599; SP 12/271/107, Francis Cordale to "His Partner Balthazar Gybels, Antwerp," July 21, 1599; SP 12/271/108, Francis Cordale to Marco Tusinga, Vinegia, July 22, 1599.

13. Id. "The favour and affection of the common people still is addicted to the Earl of Essex rather as is thought hoping by his means some way to be freed from their intolerable exactions than for any special love to his person for did they once see him in adversity they would no more respect him than they did the late Duke of Norfolk: And it is probable they would be as ready to follow any that gave show of greatness or likelihood to procure them some immunities, for never were they more oppressed and subject to all servile conditions."

14. Rowland Whyte to Sir Robert Sidney, October 4, 1599, Sydney Papers, 2:398–99.

15. This intrusion was made a matter of charge against Essex by the Privy Council on September 29, 1599 (Whyte to Sydney, September 30, in *Sydney Papers* 2:129), but the charge was not repeated in the proceedings of June 1600.

16. Thomas Birch (1754) 2:454 (which has *A* for *In*); Worcester's quotation is from *Tristia* bk. 2, ll. 107–8. The contemporary understanding of these lines is evidenced by Bartholomew Merula's commentary (*P. Ovidius Nasonis Libri De Tristibus*, Venice 1511, 19ᵛ) and by George Sandys' translation of 1632, quoted in Bate (1993), p. 163. That understanding could be expressed thus:

> "Even what one does by mis*fortune* must be expiated, so the Gods hold,
>
> And mis*chance* gets no mercy from an offended divinity."

17. SP 77/6 fol. 178, J. B. to Halyns, June 14/24, 1600, Liège. "From Holland is it written also that my lord of Essex's matter was heard afore the Council & some others of mark & learning. He much commended for his discreet & modest behavior in his answers so as that there is great hope conceived that her majesty will of her benignity restore him to her grace as in times past. Sir Robert Cecil is highly commended for his wise & temperate manner of proceedings in that matter showing to have no gall, although perhaps he had been galled if not by the Earl yet by some of his dependants by employing his endurance & credit with her majesty in favor of the said Earl. He hath won great credit at home among wise men & no less abroad where he is not known but by name." Despite the fact Essex was an anti-Spanish warrior, he was far more likely to be well-disposed towards the English Catholics than his rival, Robert Cecil.

18. Rawson (1911), p. 225.

19. Rowland Whyte to Sir Robert Sidney, May 16, 1600, Sydney Papers, 2: 462: "The marriage of the other Lord Harbert and Mrs Anne Russell is at a stay till Her Majesty appoint a day...."

20. Hicks (1955), p. 123, quoting a letter of June 21, 1600 from London to Persons.

21. Devereux (1853), 2:111–12.

22. As the term was expiring, Essex pressed hard for the renewal. He wrote the queen of the "great number of hungry and annoying creditors" who left him without rest. Devereux (1853), 2:125–26. The Farm of Sweet Wines "is both my chiefest maintenance and mine only means of compounding with the merchants to whom i am indebted." Silence was her answer.

23. AAW A7/1/1-4, Sterrell/Rivers to Ridolfo Perino (Persons), January 13, 1601.

24. Excited by the prospect of high political action, a small party of Essex's coterie persuaded the Lord Chamberlain's acting company to perform Shakespeare's *Richard II*—in which a monarch is deposed—just before they were to call upon the queen.

25. Drafts of two long letters—dated February 11 and 18—bearing a signature of "Vincent Hussey" survive, together with the notes of various speeches on Essex's revolt given in Star Chamber proceedings held on February 13, 1601. The drafts and the notes are in different hands but on the same pages, indicating that the two writers worked together. One hand is that of Phelippes (the two draft letters)—and the other (the notes of the Star Chamber) appears to be the hand of William Sterrell. In the place where Phelippes annotated papers for his files, is the legend—in Phelippes' hand—"11 Febr 1600 [1601] the accident of the Erle of Essex enterprise." Sterrell would have been present at the Star Chamber proceeding as secretary to Worcester; Phelippes had no such access. Vincent Hussey was the identity the two used in lower level correspondence to the Flanders fugitives, and it is clear that this is to whom the final letters were sent when the February 18, draft states "My last to you was per Samander at the 11ᵗʰ of this month...." Jacob Samander was one addressee of the Flanders correspondence, even mentioned by name in the "Jean Leclerque" letter which Phelippes had given to Cecil in June 1600. The draft of the letter of February 18 summarizes the notes from the Star Chamber speeches. We surmise from these, and from similar drafts of other letters, that Sterrell would dictate letters to Phelippes, which the two men would edit as they worked together. The February 18 letter adds details of the Star Chamber proceeding not in the notes, indicating again the likelihood that the writer was present at the proceedings and dictated the contents of the draft letter. For example, Lord Keeper Egerton's speech is presented in the notes with no personal observations, but the February 18 letter reports the speech and then comments: "This was the substance of his Lordship's speech; but though usually ready of speech, he was

in great perturbation, and obliged to break off, drowned in tears."

26. Cobbett's State Trials, 1:1337.
27. Id., 1:1344.
28. Id. 1:1351.

Chapter 20

1. AAW A7/54/269, Rivers (Sterrell) to Ridolfo Perino (Persons), July 28, 1602. This chapter is derived from Martin & Finnis (2006).
2. Anstruther (1968), p. 42.
3. Anstruther (1968), pp. 13–17; ODNB.
4. Law (1896), 2:xvii.
5. Indeed, the letters appointing Blackwell were dispatched in a Jesuit packet to Garnet for delivery. Pollen (1916), p. 29. Anstruther (1968) pp. 39–41; ODNB.
6. See Tierney-Dodd 3: 49–50, cxxx-cxxxi. Renold (1958), pp. 227–8, makes a case that this first appeal was really a pretext for an attempt, gestating before the Archpriest's appointment, to gain control of the English Catholic mission. The principal actors in this concerted undertaking were Charles Paget and the Rev. Dr. William Gifford in Flanders, and Frs. Christopher Bagshaw, Thomas Bluet, John Mush and John Colleton in England.
7. Pollen (1916), p. 46. Blackwell formally approved a work written by Fr. Thomas Lister, S. J., an eleven page *Treatise of Schism (Adversus Factiosos)* calling for excommunication of schismatics such as the Appellants. Pollen (1916), pp. 39–40; Law (1896), 1:99; Law (1889), pp. lxxxii- lxxxiii.
8. Law (1896). 1:210–26.
9. In August, 1601, the Pope issued his eirenic judgment on the second appeal, admonishing the Archpriest at least as much as the dissident priests, and commanding the dropping and silencing of all charges of schism pertaining to the first appeal. Some have thought that this second papal ruling might well have headed off the third appeal had not the Archpriest withheld publishing it to the secular clergy until January 1602. But considering the specifically anti-Jesuit character of the third appeal, and its backdoor propulsion by the government, it seems unlikely that Blackwell's latest misjudgment made any such decisive difference. The dissidents later argued that the Archpriest kept the papal brief of August 17, 1601 secret lest its prohibition of publications on the controversies prevent Persons' first book against the Appellants, the *Briefe Apologie*, from going into circulation (which it did in the first half of January 1602).
10. Usher (1910), 1:39–67 gives an account of Bancroft's manifold operations against Puritan sectaries (such as the Marprelate pamphleteers) from 1584 to 1593.
11. Soon after Bancroft came to the see of London, one of the turbulent longtime detainees at Wisbech, Fr. Ralph Ithell, defected from Catholicism and went to live at Bancroft's residence, becoming a minister in the state church around the beginning of 1598: Renold (1958), pp. 32, 318–9, 323–4.
12. See Law (1896), 1:226–241 (forty-five articles of enquiry, with replies to them by Bagshaw, after Nov. 1600 and before February 1601). *True Relation* emerged anonymously in London about September 1601. It was reprinted by Law as the bulk of his *Jesuits and Seculars*.
13. *Briefe Apologie*, fo. 70^r.
14. When he was captured on first landing as a missionary priest in May 1585, Bagshaw was carrying ciphers for corresponding with Charles Paget, Pollen (1916), p. 32.
15. On the character and fate of this remarkable dossier, see Renold (1958), pp. xviii–xxii, noting that a rough draft of the articles survives in Bancroft's hand.
16. A passport for Mush and Barnaby was issued at the request of Bancroft, signed by Cecil and Mr. Secretary Herbert, dated September 10, 1601, APC 31:205. Bagshaw and Bluet were banished into France and Germany only, along with another seminary priest and a friar, by order of the whole Council dated October 21, 1601: APC 31: 299–300; also 316. For details of which priests were involved and where they went after leaving England, see letters of the papal nuncio in Flanders, dated October 1601-January 1602, n.s., in Louant (1942), 3: 270, 275, 288–9, 291, 293–4.
17. Anstruther (1968). ODNB. Bossy (1965), p. 84, explains how this turncoat priest made himself the "dominant figure in the group."
18. Scott (1902), 52–3 (diary entry in or before February 1603).
19. Parmelee (1994), pp. 853–72, 865; Jenkins (1947), pp. 180 ff. William Jones, a Puritan printer, attacked Bishop Bancroft for promoting Papist books: SP 14/8/22, [May] 1604. His allegations were essentially correct. Fr. Persons in Rome knew long before: in his *Briefe Apologie*, fo.163^v, he wrote: *"these books were printed in England by consent of the heretics,* but yet in some secrecy for avoiding the knowledge of Catholics more than of the enemy. Nay, now it is further known how the matter of this printing hath passed under the protection of my Lord of London...." A listing of the pamphlets of both sides, with bibliographical information, is in Milward (1977), pp. 116–126.
20. R. Bancroft, *A Sermon Preached at Paules Crosse the 9 of Februarie ... by Richard Bancroft D. of Divinitie* (March, 1589); R. Bancroft, *A Survay of the Pretended Holy Discipline* (1593); R. Bancroft, *Daungerous Positions and Proceedings, Published and Practised Within the Iland of Brytaine Under Pretence of Reformation* (1593).
21. Carlson (1981), p. 59. See also Black (1997), p. 712 ("Bancroft ... is usually credited with the [pamphlet] strategy").
22. Paul (1950), p. 96; Brownlow (1993), pp. 68–

70, 187–88. Bancroft's chaplain Samuel Harsnett is the attributed author of *Declaration of Egregious Popish Impostures* (mid-1603) (famous as a source for *King Lear*), but Bancroft has been thought to have had an authorial hand: Paul (1950), 92. On September 16, 1602, Rivers/Sterrell wrote, probably alluding to the *Declaration*: "The Bishop of London is very busy with three Chaplains, and as many scribes, in composing some new book against Jesuits…": AAW A7/60/284. In later years, Bancroft as archbishop of Canterbury would be chief organizer of the translation of the King James Bible. Nicolson (2003), 65–83.

23. On October 19 he told Garnet that he felt he needed a year's repose: Persons to Garnet, October 19, 1602, n.s., in Edwards (1995), p. 279.

24. When Persons arrived in Rome in March 1597, where he was to remain based until his death in 1610, he promised to supply Cardinal Pietro Aldobrandino with regular news from London. "I am sending your eminence by Mr Roger [Baines], Cardinal Allen's secretary, certain reports on English affairs which he has extracted from certain letters written to me, and i shall go on doing the same henceforward, when letters come from there … as long as i remain here in Rome." Persons to Aldobrandino, Rome May 2, 1597, n.s. (Italian), Vatican Archives, Borghese, iii, 124.g.2, fo. 5 (olim 3); transcript and translation by Leo Hicks SJ, Jesuit Archive, Mount Street, 46/12/4, 604–5.

25. "Discorso sopra la proposta, che s'ha a fare, per quanto si dice, a Vostra Santitá da alcuni sacerdoti Inglesi a nome della Regina d'Inghilterra circa il dar liberta di conscienza ai Catholici di quel regno," Jesuit Archive, Rome, MSS Anglia, i, fo. 101, transcription and translation by Leo Hicks SJ in Jesuit Archive, Mount Street, London, 1203 (Italian), 1215–6 (English). This part of the memorandum is not reproduced in the version from the Inner Temple Petyt MSS printed in Law (1896), 2: 76–81.

26. Five of their six stated points of petition dated March 6, 1602, n.s., Law (1896), 2: 103, are aimed in the general direction of the Jesuits.

27. Thus, the Venetian ambassador to Rome reported on March 9, 1602, n.s. that the four priests in Rome are "to beg for recall of the Jesuits from England in return for which the Queen would not forbid the exercise of the Roman rite provided there was no sedition and secrecy." SP 99/1061 pp. 497–98; on May 11, n.s. he reports the French ambassador affirming that the Queen would not oppose the quiet use of the Catholic rite, SP 99/1078, p. 503.

28. Frangipani, who in the autumn and early winter of 1601 had extensive interviews with three Appellants and another pro-Appellant priest from England, seems to have been in no doubt that, though the three denied it, a primary aim of the Appellant party was the withdrawal of the Jesuits from England, Louant (1942), 3:271 (letter of October 5, 1601, n.s.), 3:276 (October 10, n.s.), 3:289 (November 23, n.s.), 3:290 (December 7, n.s.), 3:294 (December 28, quoting the nuncio in Paris), 3:331 (August 22, 1602, n.s.). Persons early in 1602 wrote in his *Manifestation*: "we have seen letters both from Germany, Flanders, Venice, Rome, Paris and Other Places … the common agreeing in this, that they [Appellants] are messengers sent by the Queen and Counsel of England to the Pope to offer liberty of conscience upon condition, that the Jesuits with the Archpriest & his friends may be recalled out of England." Persons (1602), fo. 71r.

29. This authorization was strictly a breach of the ancient statute of Praemunire and the Henrician legislation forbidding appeals to Rome. In due course, Puritans would take this kind of point in public criticism of Bancroft and Cecil (as well as Buckhurst, Fortescue, and Whitgift) for their countenancing of papists in face of the law: see, e.g., (Blount) to (Persons), February 17, 1603, Stonyhurst MSS Anglia, iii, no. 9; Foley (1877), 1:19 (there misdated 1602).

30. Arch. Vat., Borghese, iii, g. 1, fo. 70^v (paper fos. 69–70^v): "Cavato D'una Lettera D'un Gentilhuomo Laico Di Londra il 29 Di Gennaro 1603").

31. Person's prefatory epistle to the *Briefe Apologie* bears a date of July 20, 1601 but, according to Pollen, "*Revision in England* and Printing in Flanders Was Delayed…" Pollen (1916), p. 102 (emphasis added). The manuscript was sent to Antwerp where it was edited by Sterrell's correspondent Richard Verstegan and printed under the imprint of Arnot Coninx. The 500 page book then appeared in England about January 1602. Petti (1963), p. 102. Persons' *Appendix* and *Manifestation*, appearing later in 1602, were handled in the same way by Verstegan/Coninx.

32. SP 12/279/85, May 16, 1601. Her Majesty's ship the *Lion* halted a boat at Tilbury Hope that was carrying a group of about 15 youths of good families. Their destination was Calais, from which they intended to set forth to seminaries. They were in the company of a man called Thomas Johnson of Bankside, said to be a waterman. The report of the apprehension said that John Hake, a tailor of Southwark, had secured the boat for the youth and that "it is signified that Johnson is a special man to carry away these young gent."

33. SP 12/282/2, Phelippes to Cecil, October 3, 1601. Phelippes' confessions to Cecil in 1605 and 1606 repeatedly identify Fulwood as going by the alias of Johnson, and Phelippes acknowledged frequent contacts with him.

34. SP 12/279/109, Phelippes to Cobham, June 13, 1601.

35. Hatfield Papers 12: 230–32. The letters of Sterrell (Fenner/Cordale/Rivers) discuss Barwise on several occasions, noting that he is to be released from prison and banished; SP 12/271/33, Fenner to Giulio Piccioli or Bernardo Edlyno, June 30, 1599. Rivers later reports of Barwise as "hop[ing] for liberty," letter of March 17, 1602, AAW A7/32/206 (In Foley (1877) 1: 24), and as having "little reputation," letter to Ridolfo Perino,

March 30, 1602, AAW A7/33/208 (in Foley (1877) 1: 26). See also Rivers to Ridolfo Perino, December 22, 1601, AAW A7/9/33; Rivers to Ridolfo Perino, February 12, 1602, AAW A7/25/185; Rivers to Ridolfo Perino, May 26, 1602, AAW A7/44/240.

36. Barwise's reliable information probably came from the Archpriest Blackwell himself, who had foolishly trusted Barwise by having him help examine and discipline one of the dissident priests who was in the Clink with Barwise. Law (1889), p. lxxxvii.

37. Loomie (1973b), 1:1-2. Loomie notes that Spiller was still publicly identified as a recusant in 1626.

38. Loomie (1973b), 1:1. For over twenty years from 1602, Henry Spiller, a secret Catholic, was in charge of collecting the fines and sequestrations from recusant Catholics nationwide. Loomie identified Robert Spiller as the son of Sir Henry in Loomie (1963b), p. 15 but corrected this to brother of Sir Henry in Loomie (1973b), p. 1.

39. Only when he was imprisoned after the Gunpowder Plot did Phelippes explain his relationship with Spiller to Cecil, saying it arose during the negotiation for the Burgundian jewels and in that "great quarrel between the Jesuits and the Seculars." The information that Phelippes had given directly to Robert Cecil for several years about the dissensions within the Catholics had *All* come from Spiller, a man close to Henry Garnet. SP 14/20/51, April? 1606, the Tower, Thomas Phelippes to Lieutenant of the Tower (Waad) for the King. See also SP 14/18/63, Phelippes to Cecil, February 4, 1606 where Phelippes said he knew Spiller attended the Countess of Arundel and that his brother was with the Exchequer.

40. SP 12/286/17, Richard, Bishop of London, to Sec. Cecil (December 1602).

41. On July 6, 1601 (Stonyhurst MSS, Coll. P, 537-8), Garnet tells Persons that "new appeals and the journey of the four [to Rome] is threatened daily."

42. Short excerpt by Christopher Grene of Rivers to Persons in Stonyhurst MSS Coll. P ii, fo. 584 (modern fo. 279). It appears in November Bluet went, with Frs. Bagshaw and Barnaby, to Flanders to see the papal nuncio Frangipani, while Frs Mush and Champney went to Paris to see Henri IV's minister Villeroy. Bossy (1965), pp. 81-4, describes Bagshaw's decision to go no further than Paris, and his replacement as intellectual leader of the party by Fr. John Cecil, who made himself the "dominant figure in the group." The four who journeyed on to Rome were Frs. Bluet, Cecil, Mush and Champney. As Bossy's account details, they now went with the support they had sought from Henri IV.

43. Tierney-Dodd 3: cxlvi-ii.

44. SP Flanders, 77/6 fol. 326-27, February 16/26, 1602. Baldwin, from the camp at Ostend, reported that "Doctor Bagshaw and some others of that crew are gone up towards Rome.... They were courted and countenanced in Paris by Paget, Morgan and the rest of the Scottish faction, whereby we may gather that they are all birds of one feather. They hold (as i hear) divers consultations in Mignon College. God grant they bring not forth a like tragedy to that of Babington."

45. AAW A7/9/34, Rivers to Ridolfo Perino, December 22, 1601. The Copley book was "full of apparent falsehoods and slanders. All contain such unpleasing matter devised of mere malice, as they cannot but be ungrateful unto you." It was surely *An Answer to a Letter of a Jesuited Gentleman by His Cousin*. Copley, a poet and mercurial personality, was from a strongly Catholic family. One of his sisters was the second wife of Richard Stanihurst, and he was a cousin of Robert Southwell. Another sister was Margaret Gage, who was condemned but reprieved in 1591 for harboring a priest and again arrested in 1601 for the same cause, along with Ann Line (who suffered execution). Responding to it, Persons recalled Copley's days as a student in the English college at Rome, an "idle-headed boy," "light witted" enough to ascend the pulpit with a rose in his mouth. Persons, *Manifestation*, 96v.

46. Hatfield Papers 12: 47, Bancroft to Cecil, February 8, 1602.

47. SP 12/183/40, Privy Council to Bancroft, February 1602 (no signatories).

48. AAW A7/29, 200, Rivers to Perino, March 3, 1602: "the Lord Keeper and the Chief Justice do much mislike that by favour of the Bishop of London the discontented have such liberty."

49. "The unquiet priests here nothing relent, but are rather in jollity; they boast that their agents Mush, Champney and Bluet are already at Rome. One of good account told me, and i dare warrant it for truth, that Mr Secretary of late said that he found himself abused by those priests, disavowing all good conceit of them, adding that he well perceived that they did notably cogg and lie touching the encouragement given them by the two nuncios of France and Flanders to proceed of their voyage. And as to the *Apologie* and *Appendix* he said that the style of these was much more grave and sensible than the others; especially he showed a dislike of the *Quodlibets* [By William Watson], as written with great and apparent levity, etc." AAW A7/30/201, Rivers to Perino, March 10, 1602.

50. AAW A7/32/205, Rivers to Perino, March 17, 1602. The date of all but five of the twenty-five relevant Rivers letters proves to be a Wednesday.

51. Id.

52. Law (1896), 2:2 (February 20, 1602).

53. Law (1896), 2: 2.

54. Law (1889), p. cvi.

55. Law (1896), 2: 6. In a letter of March 31, 1602 the appellants again emphasized the books that were recently sent to Persons. Mush to Edward Farrington (Bennett), reprinted in Tierney-Dodd 3: clvi-clix. Persons was charging them with "heretical propositions contained in certain English books set out

since we came, they say, by Mr. Watson. These we must answer, when Father Persons has set them down in writing...." These books certainly included some that were sent by Sterrell, such as the English version of Watson's *Quodlibettes* and Copley's *Answer*; perhaps all on Persons' list came from Sterrell. Tierney prints Persons' list in Tierney-Dodd 3: clviii n. 1.

56. Mush diary, Law (1896), 2: 6-7. In a letter into England a few weeks later, Mush was more positive about the French role: "We are safe under the protection of the King of France; otherwise we had been fast at the first ... the French ambassador is a father to us." Mush to Edward Farrington (Bennett), March 31, 1602, reprinted in Tierney-Dodd 3: clvi-clix.

57. Most are from Cecil's files; some are endorsed by one of his secretaries, and bear in Phelippes's hand the letter's address to Her Majesty's Principal Secretary. They are dated May 4, June 4, July 30, August 21, and November 3. A final letter dated December 6 may or may not have been accompanied by an enclosure from Rome.

58. SP 12/284/4, May 4, 1602, Phelippes to Cecil with April 27/17, 1602 letter of Rome. Persons' authorship of this April 27/17 relation is clear from its postscript reference to "a new book lately imprinted and to come for England," of which there "is as yet only one of them in England." The postscript's exact description of the title, the chapter headings, and size and length of the book precisely fit the published edition of Persons's *Manifestation*.

59. Law (1896), 2: 193-4; also 2:11 (Mush's diary for April 15, 1602, n.s.), and 2:146-7 (letter from the Appellants dated April 15.).

60. Mush's diary for April 15, n.s.: "They [the two cardinals] were offended also with us, for that our adversary Parsons and his had told them we cried all over the City, *victoria, victoria,* which was a mere calumny, and so we told the Cardinals, but they seemed not to believe us, but Arigone said we on both sides were *terribiles*." Law (1896), 2: 11.

61. In 1965 John Bossy would treat the ruling as the substantial disposition of the whole appeal, a "nasty setback for Fr. Persons ... and for the Spaniards who were supporting him." Bossy (1965), p. 85: he summarizes it as "a statement exonerating them for their conduct in england and by implication censuring the Archpriest," and seems to attribute it to "a period of intensive lobbying on [ambassador] Béthune's part."

62. Rivers picks up this theme in his letter of June 2, AAW A7/45/241: "I have seen their propositions for Bishops, Archpriests, Assistants, Sindixes *et quid non? Spectatum admissi risum teneatis amici?*" The quotation ("If you were given a viewing [of such a hybrid], my friend, could you help laughing?") aptly recalls Horace's polemic against disordered art, at the beginning of *Ars Poetica*.

63. AAW A7/42/235-6, Rivers to Ridolfo Perino, May 5, 1602.

64. On July 7, 1602 Sterrell gave his most authoritative summary of the provenance of the Appellants' books. AAW A7/50/254, Rivers to Perino.

65. AAW A7/44/239, Rivers to Ridolfo Perino, May 26, 1602.

66. SP 12/284/25, June 4, 1602, Phelippes to Cecil with May 15/25, 1602 letter from Rome.

67. AAW A7/50/253, Rivers to (Persons), July 7, 1602. "I have now received two of yours the 25th of May and 15[Th] of the last [June], the continuance of the relation from the 27 of April till the 25th of May."

68. Stonyhurst MSS, Anglia A.iii. fo. 13 (modern fos. 20-23). This is clearly a draft, with deletions and interlineated changes.

69. Stonyhurst MSS, Coll. P ii. fos. 450-52 (modern fos. 133-5). This is the fair copy, with the same content and in evidently the same hand as SP 12/284/25i.

70. SP 12/284/25ii.

71. It is not possible to say with certainty whether Cecil received the Roman version (3) now SP 12/284/25i, or rather the Sterrell copy (4), now *Ibid.* no. 25ii. Doubtless one of the two was found in Phelippes' papers and linked by the Public Record Office or the *Calendar* with the other.

72. "their course *here* [is] *far different* (as it seems) from [w]hat they hold there with you. And, further, it is noted that, whereas, in their said books, the greatest subject of all their invectives is father Persons, here they have not hitherto so much as named him in all their writings given up...."

73. Hatfield Papers 12: 555.

74. As recently as April 19, 1602, two men—Duckett and Collins—had been executed for this Appellant publishing venture, as Sterrell recounted to Persons. AAW A7/39/224, Rivers to Perino, April 28, 1602: "...at the same time was also arraigned one James Duckett a layman as a felon for divulging a book written by Mr Southwell in answer to the Proclamation [of 1591], being of this accused by one Bullock a stationer that had concurred to the printing of the same." Sterrell described the overbearing of the jury by the Chief Justice and gave what must be an eye-witness account of the execution and of Duckett's edifying death. The Appellants' sponsor, Bancroft, had not bestirred himself to save these pawns in the game.

75. *A Manifestation,*. 78^r.

76. Id., fo.78^r.

77. Persons, *Manifestation*, 70^r.

78. Id., fo 80r.

79. SP 12/284/88, July 30, 1602, Phelippes to Cecil, with abstract of SP 12/284/25I; SP 12/284/89, July 30, 1602, Phelippes to Cecil with June 23, 1602 notes of the proceedings of the priests of April 27 and May 25 and references to letters of June 22 and July 6.

80. "[T]he Chief Justice the day before their execution going to the court to know the queen's pleasure, she willed him to proceed, adding that she beshrewed his heart if he spared them or any other of their coat [religion]."

81. SP 12/284/89i.
82. AAW A7/54/269, Sterrell/Rivers to Perino, July 28, 1602: "My very dear Sir, I have received yours of the *22th* [sic] of the *last* [June], and *6th of this present month* [July] together, wherein you acknowledge other two of mine; many more are either by this arrived with you, or well on their way towards you. ... I have seen the continuance of the *relation till the 23 of June*, as I did the *two former* [i. e. April 27 and May 25]" (emphases added).
83. AAW A7/59/282, Rivers to Perino September 1, 1602.
84. SP 12/284/106 with 106i.
85. He sent one on August 17, n.s. to Sterrell/Rivers, too late to be included in this transmission to Cecil. AAW A7/61/285, Rivers to (Persons), September 22, 1602.
86. The Appellants "have obtained none of their demands." The summary is in five terse points: "1. the Archpriest is to continue his office as before, without any other associated unto him; 2. the Fathers of the Society are not for any their [the Appellants'] pretences to be called out of England; 3. all the seminaries are to be governed as before; 4. all their [the Appellants'] books are condemned; 5. they must not deal any more with the Council or others in authority in prejudice of their companions." The Appellants have, however, obtained restitution of their faculties, with "certain admonitions to the Archpriest to deal with them more respectively for the time to come, and i know not what else about his not conferring so much with the fathers [Jesuits]—and this at the fathers' special instance and request...."
87. AAW A7/57/275, Rivers to Perino, August 25, 1602.
88. AAW A7/61/286, Rivers to (Persons), September 22, 1602.
89. Once again, the Roman draft of this relation has survived. Stonyhurst MSS, Anglia, iii, no. 22, in the same hand as the draft relation of May 25, n.s., and headed: "Concerning the Business of the Appellant Priests in Rome from the 1 of August Until the 14 of September." Cecil had other reports of the proceedings in Rome up to late August, from two of the principal backers of the Appellants in Paris, Charles Paget and James Hill. Paget reported to Cecil that Persons and Fitzherbert had written to Hugh Owen about the Rome proceedings, and he summarized what Persons and Fitzherbert had said in their presumably intercepted letters to Owen; the points are similar to what Phelippes had just passed on to Cecil. SP 12/285/6, September 15, 1602, Charles Paget to Secretary Cecil; SP 12/285/7, September 15, 1602, James Hill to Secretary Cecil. Hill's letter is of the same date as Paget's and speaks of an enclosure which is not identifiable in the State Papers.
90. Reprinted in Tierney-Dodd 3:clxxxiv; McGrath (1967), p. 297. A draft of the proclamation survives "With Considerable Differences" and "Much Corrected by Cecil." SP 12/285/55.

91. On October 12, n.s., the Brief made on October 5 had been released to the parties in Rome. Late that night Persons finished his final relation of the whole sequence. SP 12/285/46ii, headed by Sterrell "the last relation about the business of the Appellant Priests in Rome, from the 14th of 7th [September] unto the 12th of Oct. 1602. Wherein also the final determination of his Holiness is recounted." The final sheet also begins Sterrell's transcription of "The answer of T. C. to a letter of his friend in Perugia concerning the last Brief of his Holiness dated the 5th of October about the determination of the English affairs," dated October 14, n.s.—a letter explaining the respects in which the papal brief is better than it looks from the point of view of Jesuits and supporters of the Archpriest. Sterrell says on November 17 (Rivers to Perino, AAW A7/67/303): "I know it [the brief] will be grievous to many; for my own part the letter to Perugia hath well satisfied me, and i conclude with others *sic ut quimus quando ut volumus non licet* [when we can't get what we want, we make do with what we can]." Persons' relation of October 12 carries the account on from September 14, n.s., in some detail, and gives a rapid but not unfair summary of the Brief. In the State Papers, Sterrell's transcription of it is now bundled with the transmission to Cecil of November 3, and perhaps it was indeed enclosed with that. But more probably, we think, it was sent on to Cecil later, conceivably even as late as December 6, when Phelippes wrote to Cecil with an enclosure concerning the Appellants, touching also on their continuing attempt, as Phelippes reports, to launch yet another appeal, "one last attempt against the Archpriest's authority" and "to remove all Jesuits out of England." SP 12/286/3.
92. AAW A7/60/284, "Thomas Neevell" to Perino, September 16, 1602.
93. Tierney-Dodd 3: clxxxiv-clxxxviii.
94. AAW A7/68/306, Rivers to Perino, December 15, 1602.
95. SP 12/287/51, Rivers to Perino, March 9, 1603 (intercepted, together with similar letters of the same date to "Giacomo Creleto" (Hugh Owen and Fr. William Baldwin SJ, Brussels) (*Ibid.*, no. 50) and "Giovanni Battista Galfredi" (Richard Verstegan, Antwerp) (no. 52).
96. Sterrell/ "Rivers" noted to Persons in a letter of July 7, 1602 AAW A7/50/253–54, "When the Bishop [Bancroft] saw the new book of the *Manifestation, etc.*, he exulted beyond measure, saying this would stir up the contrary party to more invective writings, which was the main point that he most levelled [aimed] at; he termed both sides knaves, but the Appellants good instruments to serve the State."
97. AAW A7/87, a document endorsed in Bancroft's hand "Reasons of the Proceedings Held with the Secular Priests," and also, perhaps in the same hand, "May 1603"; headed "The True Reasons of Her Majesty's Late Proceedings with Recusants, Which Made Men Dream of Some Intended Toleration";

and for the rest believed to be in the hand of one of Bancroft's clerks.

98. CRS 2, 213–18 (Stonyhurst MSS, Coll. P f. 444) (Persons to Sterrell/Rivers, July 6, 1603). He said: "their odious clamors here [in Rome] against the pretense of the said lady infanta made our present king [James] so many friends in this court, as, partly by that and by the ordinary emulations against Spain, and by assurances given by Scottish men and some English also, that this man would be Cath[Olic] or at least give full liberty of Conscience, all this [papal] court ran after him in such manner, as that all others that did not take the same course were thought either partial or passionate."

99. He says he is "humbly to desire you that you will not think that I surcease upon any disgust or other dislike, but will ever be ready to serve you and yours to the uttermost of my poor abilities, and if it shall appear that you are willing I continue as before, I shall think no labour too much, nor omit any opportunity for the performance."

100. SP 12/287/52, "Anthony Rivers" to Gio. Battista Galfredi, Venice," March 9, 1603.

101. He wrote Baldwin: "I shall willingly continue the trade, but if sometimes scanted of time, and pressed with other occasions, I give not so full satisfaction as you expect, I must pray to be excused and that of other friends may supply till fitter opportunity." SP 12/287/50, "Anthony Rivers" to "Giacomo Creleto, Venice," March 9, 1603.

102. "My cousin and Ortelio have, and do acquaint you, with a secret which i have imparted with them, for the intercepting of letters. Be alert, for we are eager set and very barren of good intelligence from those parts, for all other matters I refer you to their discourses. This matter of letters is written as i suppose *by Mr Henry, and so with my commendations to my Brother William adieu. Ortelio.* By this hand you will know I conceal nothing from Ortelio." The packet of letters with which this was sent was intercepted by the English government.

Chapter 21

1. "A Career Despite Dad's Advice," *New York Times*, September 2, 2002.
2. Corsini was agent of the Grand Duke of Florence. His brother Bartolomeo was used to pass intelligence letters from Anthony Standen to Walsingham c. 1587. See Hicks (1960), pp. 96, 119.
3. Hotson (1954), pp. 201–02.
4. Hotson (1954), pp. 181–182.
5. AAW A7/1/1–4, Sterrell/Rivers to Ridolfo Perino (Persons), January 13, 1601.
6. Quoted in Hotson (1954), pp. 199–200.
7. AAW A7/1/1–4, Rivers to Ridolfo Perino, January 13, 1601.
8. Id.
9. Quoted Hotson (1954), p. 193.
10. AAW A7/1/1–4, Sterrell/Rivers to Ridolfo Perino (Persons), January 13, 1601.
11. AAW A7/39/225–26, Sterrell/Rivers to Ridolfo Perino (Persons), April 28, 1602.
12. AAW A7/9/33–4, Sterrell/Rivers to Ridolfo Perino (Persons), December 22, 1601.
13. AAW A7/25/183–86, Sterrell/Rivers to Ridolfo Perino (Persons), February 12, 1602.
14. AAW A7/29/197–200, Sterrell/Rivers to Ridolfo Perino (Persons), March 3, 1602.
15. AAW A7/30/201, Sterrell/Rivers to Ridolfo Perino (Persons), March 10, 1602.
16. AAW A7/32/205, Sterrell/Rivers to Ridolfo Perino (Persons), March 17, 1602.
17. AAW A7/35/211–12, Sterrell/Rivers to Ridolfo Perino (Persons), April 7, 1602.
18. Westminster vii, n. 47, 247, Sterrell/Rivers to Ridolfo Perino (Persons), June 9, 1602.
19. AAW A7/49/251–52, Sterrell/Rivers to Ridolfo Perino (Persons), June 30, 1602.
20. Baptist Hicks (1551?–1629), knighted 1603, later first Viscount Campden (ODNB).
21. AAW A7/49/251–52, Sterrell/Rivers to Ridolfo Perino (Persons), June 30, 1602.
22. Id.
23. Id.
24. AAW A7/53/257–58, Sterrell/Rivers to Ridolfo Perino (Persons), July 21, 1602.
25. AAW A7/54/269–70, Sterrell/Rivers' to Persons, July 28, 1602, written in the left-hand margin near the end.
26. AAW A7/57/275–76, Sterrell/Rivers to Ridolfo Perino (Persons), August 25, 1602.
27. AAW A7/59/281–82, Sterrell/Rivers to Ridolfo Perino in Vinegia, September 1, 1602 Wednesday. Sterrell/Rivers used this phrase three times: "sic ut quimus quando ut volumus non licet." When what we want is not possible, we do what we can. It is most likely from Terence's *Andria* (sic ut quimus, aiunt, quando ut volumu' non licet).
28. AAW A7/67/303, Sterrell/Rivers to Ridolfo Perino, November 17, 1602.
29. AAW A7/68/305–06, Sterrell/Rivers to Ridolfo Perino, December 15, 1602.
30. Much Ado: "I had my good wit out of the 'Hundred Merry Tales.'"—a famously bad joke book first published 1526.
31. SP 12/287/51, Sterrell/ Rivers to "Ridolfo Perino, Venetia," March 9, 1603.
32. SP 12/287/52, "Anthony Rivers" to "Gio. Battista Galfredi," Venice, March 9, 1603.
33. Loomis (1996), pp. 482–509.
34. CSP Scot (1858) 2: 577.

Chapter 22

1. Nicholls (1995b), p. 822.
2. Nicholls (1995a), p. 922, La Renzi's testimony of July 19, 1603:

3. Hatfield Papers 15: 218.
4. Nicholls (1995a)., p. 922; Howell (1809), 2: 8. The evidence adduced at Ralegh's trial from an examination of La Renzi was that Cobham came to Arenberg's lodgings within five days after Arenberg's arrival in London. Cobham's written confession is to the same effect. SP 14/2/94, Cobham to the Lords, July 1603.
5. Nicholls (1995c), p. 38.
6. Howell (1809), 2: 18.
7. Loomie (1972), p. 168, citing Simancas E K 1631/5, Sessa to Philip III, March 20, 1601.
8. Loomie (1972), p. 170, indicates he was awarded this post on October 4/14, 1602, but probably did not take it up until March 1603; Loomie (1971a), p. 12.
9. Hopwood (1903), 1: 316. Moore is a member of Parliament in 1601 and later is attorney for a group of Catholics—including William Shakespeare—in a title suit concerning a Catholic refuge center in Blackfriars, London.
10. The instructions that Cecil gave for the trial of the Gunpowder Plotters directed Coke to commend Monteagle for his role in exposing the Plot "because it is so lewdly given out that he was once of this Plot of Powder and afterward betrayed all to me." SP 14/19/94.
11. Hatfield Papers 17: 512, statement of November 26, 1605, quoted in Loomie (1971a), pp. 10–11.
12. For another treatment of the visits and planning, see Pollen (1903a), pp. 572–85; he includes a discussion/summary of Creswell's memoir of the events. It is likely that Thomas James was working with Wintour, for the young man from Worcestershire was otherwise unknown to the court of Philip, and James was in Madrid when Wintour arrived. Loomie discusses the evidence that James was involved, Loomie (1971a), p. 12.
13. Wintour's confession, Hatfield Papers 17: 513, indicates that Tesimond was with him. Loomie (1971a), pp. 42–46, recognized that Tesimond was in Spain around this time but insisted that Tesimond had preceded Wintour and was there only for the purpose of encouraging the Spanish to oppose the French support of the Appellants. Yet Loomie did not doubt the accuracy of the report given to Albert on July 3, 1603 that "[s]ome months before the Queen died, the English Catholics sent to Spain two people to present to his Majesty the miseries they suffered." Loomie surmises the second person was Thomas James. It appears that Thomas James had last been in England about July or August 1601 and had then gone back to Brussels and Paris before returning to Spain in early January 1602. The sense of the reports of the time seems to be that Wintour and a companion were sent together by the English Catholics. Perhaps Loomie was as eager to distance the Jesuits from complicity in the Spanish Treason as Cecil and Coke were to taint them with it. Guy Fawkes in 1605 confessed that Thomas Wintour told him that the year before Elizabeth died he was sent by Catesby and others into Spain with Tesimond, in order to propose to the Spanish king to send an army to Milford Haven, at which time the Catholics were endeavouring to collect 2,000 or 1500 horse to join with the Spanish army; the king promised to place 100,000 crowns at their disposal. Jardine (1846), 2: 273.
14. Loomie (1971a), pp. 12–13, citing E 2512/61; E 2512/64.
15. Loomie (1963a), pp. 194–95 (spelling modernized).
16. Lonchay & Cuvelier 1: 40; Loomie (1963a), p. 195, citing E 617/226, identifies the Spaniard seeking the intelligence connection as Juan de Velasco, the Constable of Castile.
17. Hatfield Papers 17: 39, Thomas Phelippes to Cecil January 29, 1605.
18. Loomie (1963a), p. 174; also Loomie (1971a), p. 21 n. 4.
19. Loomie (1971a), p. 13, citing E 2512/71–5, Spanish copy of letter to Creswell, October 13/23, 1602.
20. Loomie (1971a), p. 15, citing CSP Sp 1587–1603 pp. 719–29 (at 720) *Consulta* of February 1, 1603, n.s.
21. Loomie (1971a), p. 15, citing CSP Sp 1587–1603 pp. 719–29 (at 720) *Consulta* of 1 February 1603, n.s.; March 8/18 1603 Creswell informs Lerma that he is "Pressed Urgently from England to Send Them a Reply: Either Yes, or No" and asks for two confidential papers from England to be considered by Philip; Loomie (1971a), p. 16.
22. CSP Sp 1587–1603, pp. 719–29. "Report of the Council of State to Philip III on the English Succession, February 1, 1603.
23. Id. P 726.
24. Id. P 728.
25. Id. Pp. 729–37. "Report of the Council of State to Philip III on the English Succession, March 2, 1603.
26. Id. P. 734.
27. On November 25, 1605 Guy Fawkes confessed that christopher wright had been in Spain about two months before Fawkes arrived there, and on November 30 confessed that he was told by Cresswell that Wright was in Spain on the same business: Jardine (1846), 2: 273–4. Other than their Yorkshire background, little is known of the biographies of Christopher and John Wright.
28. Loomie (1971a), P. 18, Citing E 840/129, "Relacion De Antonio Dutton," May 18, 1603.
29. Loomie (1971a), P. 19, Citing May 13/23, E 840/130.
30. Loomie (1971a), P. 21 Citing E 840/131.
31. E 622/96–97.
32. The arrival of Albert in Brussels is described in Duerloo (2012), Pp. 42–43. Sterrell's two visits to Flanders on behalf of unnamed earls are related above in Persons's 1596 memorandum.
33. It was Grene's description of Rivers as

Garnet's companion, CRS 2, 213, Collectanea P. F. 444.

34. E 622/97.

35. SP 12/287/50, "Anthony Rivers" to "Giacomo Creleto, Venice," March 9, 1603.

36. He told Albert: "Some months before the Queen died, the English Catholics sent to Spain two people to present to his Majesty the miseries they suffered. They wished to show how ready they were to assist any design to reduce that kingdom to the Catholic faith."

37. They had come to Tassis' lodgings "at a late hour of the night to protect ourselves from certain spies." Quoted in Loomie (1963b), p. 16, citing E 840/109.

38. The full text of Fawkes's memory version is in Loomie (1971a), pp. 61–63 (E 840/126). Loomie comments that the mystery man's "denunciations of James as a Scottish heretic [in the report given Albert July 3, 1603] are virtually identical with the special oral report which Fawkes had already carried into Spain." Id., p 24.

39. Howell (1809), 2:170: "Presently after whose Death [the Queen] was *Christopher Wright*, another Messenger sent over into *Spain* by *Garnet* (who likewise did write by him to *Creswell*, for the furtherance of the Negotiation) *Catesby* and *Tresham*, in the name and behalf of all the Romish Catholicks in *England*; as well to carry news of her Majesty's Death, as also to continue the aforesaid Negotiation for an Invasion and Pensions, which by *Tho. Winter* had before been dealt in. And in the *Spanish* Court, about two Months after his arrival there, doth *Christopher Wright* meet with *Guy Fawkes*; who upon the 22d of *June* was employed out of *Flanders* from *Brussels* by Sir *William Stanley, Hugh Owen* (whose Finger hath been in every Treason which hath been of late Years detected) and *Baldwyn* the Legier Jesuit in *Flanders*; from whom likewise the said *Fawkes* carried Letters to *Creswell* in *Spain*, for the countenancing and furtherance of his affairs."

40. Loomie (1971b), pp. 303–06.

41. Loomie (1971a), p. 30.

42. SP 14/14/40 (1605), reprinted in Foley 4:370–71.

43. Details of his life are conflicting, but it is clear that he was active in Wales. McCoog (1994), p. 160; Matthias (1963), p. 40; Foley 7: 553. The "Lister" mentioned in the same report was Fr. Thomas Lister, S.J., a supporter of Garnet and the Archpriest in 1599–1601 who wrote a *Treatise of Schism (Adversus Factiosos)*, calling for excommunication of schismatics such as the Appellants. Pollen (1916), pp. 39–40; Law (1896), 1:99; Law (1889), pp. lxxxii- lxxxiii.

44. SP 14/14/40 (1605), reprinted in Foley Records 4:371: "whereas the whereas the said Mr. Morgan, the younger, was busy about armour presently after the queen's death, though the matter be made up, yet it is thought, and so muttered, that his meaning was to have indeed taken up arms. And Jones, the Jesuit, the firebrand of all, was then in his company." The same report identified "Mr. Morgan, the younger, of Lanternham" as the man "who hath married the Lady Frances" meaning Frances Somerset, Worcester's daughter.

45. Hatfield papers, 17, p. 513, statement of November 26, 1605. He said that if the Spanish forces "were small, and trusted upon succor here, then I thought Milford Haven more convenient, being in parts where they could not be offended with the Queen's powers until their friends might have time to assemble."

46. Patent by the Queen at Westminster, countersigned by Sir Thomas Egerton (Lord Keeper of the Great Seal,), December 2, 1599 (42 Elizabeth), Lansdowne MSS 207a, fo. 359. In *Notices and Remains of the Family of Tyrwhitt*, this patent of appointment as sheriff in December 1999 is miscited and mistaken for an appointment as Lieutenant of the county; in fact it is in the standard form set out, e.g., in Michael Dalton, *Officium Vicecomitum: The Office and Authority of Sherifs* (London, 1623), f. 3^v

47. Martin & Finnis (2003c), pp. 556–69.

48. SP 14/3/7, Waad to Cecil, August 4, 1603.

49. Catesby's sister Anne and Tyrwhitt's aunt Mary were each married to brothers in the Browne family, sons of Viscount Montague. Pollen (1919), p. 45: "Viscount Montague's daughters-in-law were: Mary, daughter of Sir William Dormer; Mary, daughter of Sir Robert Tyrwhitt [married to Sir George Browne]; Anne, daughter of Sir William Catesby [married to Sir Henry Browne]." Burke (1844), p. 89 (under Browne of Kiddington).

50. Stone (1948), p. 37, n. 1, citing PRO Lord Chamberlain's Office, Recognizances for Debt, pp. 192–5.

51. SP 14/16/16, November 6, 1605. Sir Edward Hoby wrote to Sir Thomas Edmondes, the English ambassador in Brussels concerning Tyrwhitt: "I understand that Tyrwhitt, which married my Lady Bridget, and also Sir Everard Digby, are gone to the rebels, who have left Warwickshire, and are gone into Worcestershire: but of the flying hand, and little strength, not daring to come into any good town." Printed in Birch (1848), 1: 39.

52. SP 77/6 fol. 436, The proceedings with M. Boulant about peace—1602.

53. Hatfield Papers 17: 39, Thomas Phelippes to Cecil, 29 January 1605.

54. SP 14/20/51, Phelippes to Lieutenant of the Tower (Waad) for the King April? 1606. Because this Phelippes statement was shortly after the Gunpowder Plot in which the English government claimed Owen was complicit, Phelippes was reluctant to raise Owens' name; he asserted the contact had been made "In Mancicidor's Name."

55. Id. The "Former Correspondence" was surely the "Boulant" letters, again suggesting that the 1603 Boulant memorandum was to Lord Kinloss. The reference to Dr. Taylor's negotiations is explored below. After Phelippes spent about two months in the Gate-

house prison in 1605, Lord Kinloss seems to have given some backing to Phelippes' story, and with Cecil's approval Phelippes was allowed to remove to his own house for confinement. Hatfield Papers 17: 88, Phelippes to Cecil, March 7, 1605; 17: 111–12, Phelippes to Cecil, March 28, 1605; *Id.*, p. 128, Phelippes to Cecil, April 3, 1605.

56. Lefèvre (1925), pp. 697–714.

57. Id., pp. 704–05; Lonchay (1918), I: 26, nos. 50–51. After the discovery of the Gunpowder Plot and the obloquy heaped upon Hugh Owen by Cecil and Coke for his alleged role in it, Phelippes placed even greater emphasis on his "negotiation" as having been "in truth and substance with Mancicidor a person of honor and professing friendship with the State...." Phelippes said his more recent correspondence had actually been "in Baylyes [Richard Bayley] hand an assistant to him [Owen] in his service under the Secretary [Mancicidor]." SP 14/20/51, Phelippes to Lieutenant of the Tower (Waad) for the King, April? 1606.

58. Loomie (1963b), pp. 18–20.

59. Loomie 1973b), p. 9, n. 9.

60. It was surely Robert Taylor, law scholar of Douay, to whom a government informer named Simon Knowles referred in a 1594 statement about Taylor's transport of youths. SP 12/248/48: "Arrived at Calais last Tuesday, hastening there to find Taylor, a student at law dwelling at Douay, whom he saw in busy talk before at St. Omer, with Bray and Smith, the Jesuits, which Taylor often comes to England, and carries over the youths."

61. SP 14/12/35, January 26, 1605. Cecil must have thought "Freeman" was the priest named Oswald Needham who was one of the "appellants" willing to take the oath to the Queen and may have been of the sort to cooperate with Phelippes. See Foley Records 1: 55. This would appear to confirm that Cecil thought Phelippes was supplying him information from an anti-Jesuit source in 1601–02. Stephen Phelippes also acknowledged that Thomas Phelippes talked of the recipient of letters at Antwerp "which I have heard named by the name of Verstegin [Verstegan] but what he is that serves to attend about the Archd[Uke's] Court I know not."

62. SP 14/18/63, Phelippes to Cecil, February 4, 1606.

63. Hatfield Papers 15: 216–17.

64. SP Flanders 77/8 fo 16ᵛ, January 6, 1606, Edmondes to Cecil: "I have been also informed, that the person that passed the last time from hence into England, in the company of Guy Fawkes, is one Spiller that then went under the name of Bellamy. It is said that he is brother to Spiller the Attorney of the Exchequer."

65. Fr. Henry Garnet must have had a close relationship the family of Sterrell's friend Anthony Skinner. A copy of Robert Southwell's *A Short Rule of Good Life*, written between 1589 and 1591 or early 1592, was bound with other pieces, and the volume was among books donated in 1659. The Southwell work is preceded by the date 1597 and a Latin epigram, *Eterna Prepones Cadueris* (Prepare for eternal things lest you fall), followed by the initials "H. G.," i.e., Henry Garnet. At the end of the Southwell text are blank pages on which are written the names of the children of William Skinner: Anthony, Bennet, Martha and John, with their birthdays and ages shown as they were in 1597. Thus, what this appears to be is Garnet's copy of Southwell's book, and he has written in the names and ages of the Skinner family: a pastoral activity of priests for many centuries. Brown (1989), pp. 134–35.

66. Archivo General de Simancas, Estado 622/84, "Relacion del dor Roberto Tayllero de lo que se ha tratado" ("la tercera persona ... es conocido de Hugo Hoen."), dispatched to Spain from Brussels in July 1603.

67. Loomie (1973b), I: 9; see also, Loomie (1963b), pp. 18–19.

68. Loomie (1963b), pp. 18–19; Estado 622/84, "Relacion del dor Roberto Tayllero de lo que se ha tratado"; Estado 622/83 "La relacion que en Inglaterra ha dado el Doctor Roberto Tayllero."

69. Hatfield Papers 18: 238–39, Sir Thomas Lake to Cecil, August 17, 1606.

70. Hatfield papers 17: 39, Thomas Phelippes to Cecil, January 29, 1605.

71. Loomie (1963b), p. 19; Lonchay & Cuvelier, 1: 156.

72. Loomie (1969), p. 55. The Spanish money to Cecil has long distressed historians admiring of Cecil. The classic defence of Cecil is given by Gardiner (1887), 1: 216: "It is possible that, as soon as the peace was concluded,—thinking as he did that it was likely to be permanent,—he offered to do those services for the Spanish Government which, as long as it was a friendly power, he could render without in any way betraying the interests of his own country; whilst, with his very moderate standard of morality, he did not shrink from accepting a pecuniary reward for what he did."

73. See Somerset (1997), p. 24. Somerset notes the rumors that Countess Suffolk was Robert Cecil's mistress; King James himself may have poked fun at the relationship.

74. The report on the Councilors is reprinted and translated in Loomie (1973b), 1: 2–9.

75. Loomie (1963b), p. 15.

76. Loomie (1963b), p. 18.

77. Estado 622/84, pp. 5–6. Fr. Loomie thought this statement was simply taken from the report of the mystery visitor to Albert of July 3, 1603 and was not an authentic report by Taylor. Loomie was persuaded that Garnet's "actual correspondence" to Rome was more reflective of the Jesuit's outlook. In the correspondence Loomie referred to, Garnet expressed concern that discontent might lead to persecution. Of course, what Garnet may have worried over was a hare-brained scheme like that of William Watson in the Bye Plot, not a coordinated interven-

tion by the Archduke and the Spanish. The thesis that the Spanish somehow garbled Taylor's report with the mystery figure's statements to the Archduke several weeks earlier is far-fetched and not supported by the internal structure of the three Spanish documents.

78. See below for Cardinal Bentivoglio's characterization of Albert as "a prince of impenetrable secrecy."

79. Tierney-Dodd 4: 37 ("The Catholics' Supplication Unto the King's Majesty, for Toleration of Catholic Religion in England," reprinted id. lxxii-lxxiv); Anstruther (1953), p. 260.

80. SP 14/3/2, August 2, 1603, Sir Richard Lewkenor Chief Justice of Chester to the Council; SP 14/3/13, August 6, 1603, Sir Richard Lewkenor to the Council. Lewknor interrogated Francis Plowden (who had entered Oxford with Skinner in 1577 and followed him to the Middle Temple in 1582) about an intercepted letter to Skinner. Plowden was the second son of Edmund Plowden, one of the most prominent jurists of the age. He told Sir Richard Lewkenor that Anthony Skinner and his wife had been staying with Plowden's family at their estate of Shiplake for some months; before that Skinner was living in London. Plowden discussed the July 17 meeting with the Council and king of the Catholic group had included Plowden and Skinner. His uncle Ralph Sheldon was a means to meet with John Talbot of Grafton, Thomas Throckmorton and Sir Thomas Tresham and other Catholics so that they could further their suit for favor from the king. Plowden said the Catholics had discussed whether it was lawful to seek to further their cause through the ambassador of the king of Spain but they had concluded that although lawful it might be ill taken by the king that his subjects should seek or procure means for his favor by any foreign prince or ambassador.

81. Estado 622/224: "Relacion Hecha Por El Doctor Taylor Y Su Companero Al Padre Superior." A mrginal note in the document identifies the companion to Taylor as the man who introduced him to the Countess of Suffolk; that person was, of course, Skinner. Summary in French in Lonchay & Cuvelier, 1: 164.

82. Loomie (1973a), p. 70.

83. Loomie (1963b), p. 31. Taylor and Spiller are seen in a Frenchman's report of his experiences in England. This account is from Harley (1997), p. 143. See Hatfield Papers 17: 611–12. As Charles de Ligny was on his way from Cambrai, he encountered two men thought to be disguised Jesuits at Gravelines: "Dr. Noiriche," (surely Dr. Taylor), and "Speelleer," a servant of Henry Garnet. "Speelleer's" brother is identified as an attorney with a Catholic wife; Robert Spiller's brother was an attorney with the Exchequer. De Ligny said the two men needed someone who knew Italian, Latin and French, and he went to work for them. They went to a house of Garnet's, some five miles from London; this was probably White Webbs. He also was taken to Spiller's house in London. On another occasion, the Frenchman was taken to another large house outside of London where Garnet, William Byrd and others played music. De Ligny's hosts asked him to deliver some letters for them. But instead of going directly back to France, he returned to London and was arrested; his books included a composition of music by William Byrd dedicated to Henry Howard, Earl of Northampton.

84. Dodd (1938b), p. 643.

85. Loomie (1973b), 1: 87, Philip III to Pedro de Zuñiga, October 27, 1606.

86. Loomie (1971a), p. 45.

87. Caraman (1951), pp. 205, 257; Wadsworth (1629), p. 26: Wadsworth, a Catholic apostate, speaks of Henry Taylor, secretary to the Spanish Ambassador Gondamor, his mother living at St. Omers and her late husband Dr. Taylor who "had done for their Society [Jesuits], in protecting in his Chamber that Jesuit Father *Gerat* [Gerard], a complotter of the Gunpowder Treason, and then interpreter to the Spanish Embassador in England...."

88. Loomie (1973a), p. 74. The younger Taylor was brought up in the trade of intelligencer. A spy's report of 1604 described in detail "Doctor Taylors Sonne" who was meeting with Hugh Owen in Brussels. Owen had given him diverse letters and dispatched him to London. The spy, Thomas Allison, then encountered young Taylor again at Calais as both traveled to England: "he was then disguised and in a suit of very poor clothes almost like a rogue, which made me take the more regard to him when i remembered Owen's speeches and thought him to be a physician's son, and a lusty bold fellow. I was jealous [suspicious] that he might have some action in hand some way or other, and it fell out we came over in a French Bottom together, & I perceived his Packett of Letters and that he had a good store of gold...." Allison was going to have young Taylor searched at Dover but they encountered a storm and landed at a place where no search was taken. Allison warned that Taylor might attempt to poison all the Councilors. Dodd (1938a), pp. 163–64 (Report of Thomas Allyson [Allison]).

89. Hatfield Papers 17: 39, Thomas Phelippes to Cecil, January 29, 1605.

90. SP 14/20/51, Phelippes to Lieutenant of the Tower (Waad) for the King, April? 1606. After the Constable of Castile came in 1604 for the signing of a peace treaty, Phelippes was at first slighted but then rewarded with 500 Crowns [£125] and later he was assigned 5000 Crowns [£1250]. This may be compared to the amount that Ralegh at trial was said to have expected: £1,500. Phelippes indicates that some money was paid to him through "Freeman"/Spiller as "Ayuda De Costa" and may have been paid out of funds offset by funds paid in Brussels to the Jesuit Baldwin as coming from England. Phelippes portrays himself as in and out of favor with the representatives from the Archduke and from Spain.

91. Persons to Rivers, July 6, 1603; CRS 2, pp. 213–18 (Stonyhurst MSS, Coll. P, fol. 444). The letter is not actually addressed to Rivers, but Fr. Grene who collected and copied a great many letters of Persons and others surmised that the recipient of this letter was to be Persons' correspondent who had written to Persons as Rivers. The surviving copy must have been a copy retained by Persons, a usual practice for Persons.

92. Born in 1572, Lilly spent seven years as a London apothecary and then was eight or nine years in the Clink for his Catholicism. He was a servant of John Gerard and Henry Garnet and became well acquainted with Anne Line. When John Gerard escaped from the Tower of London in 1597, John Lilly helped him over a wall and was one of the men who oared the Thames to carry Gerard away. In 1599 John Lilly was arrested in a government raid on a house maintained by Anne Line and another woman; Mistress Line was present, and John Gerard escaped. Sterrell reported Lilly's capture and imprisonment in the Tower to Persons in a letter that the government intercepted. SP 12/271/108, Francis Cordale to Marco Tusinga, Vinegia, July 22, 1599. Sterrell was no doubt an old acquaintance of Lilly. After torture and imprisonment, Lilly escaped and made his way to Rome. He entered the Society of Jesus under the hands of Persons in February 1602.

93. Loomie (1973b), 1: 20, Constable of Castile to Philip III, August 16, 1604. This was earlier the conclusion of Spanish ambassador, Juan de Tassis, Count of Villa Mediana, who conveyed his opinion to King Philip III that the religious question should be left until after a treaty was concluded. Hicks (1960), p. 199.

Chapter 23

1. Chambers (1923), 2: 225; 4: 334–35.
2. Henslowe's Diary (Greg, ed.) p. 180. Twelve pages of the printed Diary list all the advances and outlays of Henslowe to Worcester's company August 17, 1602 through May 9, 1603, pp. 179–190. See also Chambers (1923), 2: 220–240.
3. Chambers (1923), 1: 100. In recounting some of the authorizations given by the Earls of Suffolk (Lord Chamberlain) and Worcester, Chambers observed: "These Lords, one as Lord Chamberlain, the other as Master of the Horse, seem regularly to have had the supervision of emptions and provisions for masks given at the royal expense." Id. I, 209.
4. Philip Henslowe recorded in his *Diary*: "Begininge to playe agayne by the kynges licence & layd owt sense for my lord of worsters men." This was again at the Rose Theater. Greg (1904), p. 190.
5. A draft of the King's patent is reproduced in Chambers (1923), 2: 229–30.
6. The King's licence of Lawrence Fletcher, William Shakespeare, seven other named associates, and others, to be in effect the King's Men or playing company is dated May 19, 1603: *Patent Rolls 1 James I, Pars 2, Membr. 4*; there are drafts of 17 and 18 May; the lease to William Sterrell of the Hospital (House, Palace) of St. John of Jerusalem is undated but issued in May 1603; SP 15/35/22 (May 1603). In the Signet docquet book, the entry for Sterrell's grant is just after the entries for grants to William Broderick and John Norton that were dated May 17, 1603 and just before a grant to Robert Wrothe that was dated May 22. PRO Docquet pages for May 1603 (SO 2.2). In the Index for the Bills of Privy Signet, which are indexed alphabetically in chronological order, the entries for Southampton, Sterrell and Shakespeare are in that order and show their grants are for May 1603. Phillimore (1890), p. 62. Southampton's pardon was granted May 16, 1603, and the Shakespeare license grant was May 17–19. Most likely, the grant to Sterrell was May 17, 1603. An examination of the grant in the Public Record Office shows it to have been accompanied by a note to the new king: "This wherewith +++ a grant to be made by yr. Majtie unto William Sterrell out of the keeping of your Majesty's house of St. John's of +++ [Jerusalem] for term of his life, going under your hand…." This is followed by a document of August 6, 1603: "Lease to William Stirrill of the Late Priory of St. John's, of Jerusalem. [Docquet]."

Gurr (1996), pp. 112–3, rightly remarks that "what happened in May 1603 was unique both in its timing among the great flurry of activities that attended James's accession, and in the history of company patronage. Who prompted the patent to be issued so early in James's frenetic round of decision-making and new appointments it is impossible to say … the matter must have been surprisingly high on the agenda either of James himself or of one of his senior advisers at the English court." The contiguity in the official records of the licence and the lease suggests that behind both was one and the same figure, vastly more senior and influential in James's court: Edward, Earl of Worcester.

7. See also Heywood (1612), p. 40 (dedicated to the Earl of Worcester): "the palace of S. Johnes … hath belonged to … the Office of the Revels, where our court playes have been in late daies yearley rehearsed, perfected, and corrected before they come to the publicke view of the prince and the nobility." St. John's ceased to be used for these purposes, and Sterrell's lease was terminated, in or about February 1608. In tracing the history of the Priory of Clerkenwell, Walter Thornbury comments that at this location the Master of Revels resided "with all his tailors, embroiderers, painters and carpenters, and all artificers required to arrange court plays and masques." From St. John's, the Master "licensed all plays all plays, regulated the stage for thirty-one years, and passed no less than thirty of Shakespeare's dramas, commencing with Henry IV and ending with Anthony and Cleopatra…. The court revels were all rehearsed in the great hall at St. John's." Thornbury (1873), 2: 315.

8. For example, in 1610, Sterrell was made impresario or supervisor for the year's Court masque, *Love Freed from Ignorance and Folly*. The performance was designed and timed to influence Anglo-French diplomacy at a crucial shift in European diplomatic relations following the assassination of King Henry IV of France. In recognition of his role, King James gave Sterrell a special grant, greater than the payment allocated the masque's author, Ben Jonson, or his collaborator, Inigo Jones. Herford & Simpson, 10: 528. Nichols (1827), 2: 411.

9. Loomie (1963b), p. 54. Tassis wrote the King of Spain in June 1604 "Since my arrival here from the Court of his Majesty [Archduke Albert], Taylor has served me reliably on every occasion. Through his hands I exchange letters with the Countess [of Suffolk] and her husband [Lord Chamberlain Suffolk], and Northampton [uncle of Suffolk], for they trust him." He probably knew many of the priests in hiding from their days at Douay.

10. Loomie (1963b), p. 38.

11. Chambers (1923), 4: 169–170.

12. Loomie (1971b), p. 307, citing E 2586, fol. 153, Zuniga to Philip, November 8, 1608.

13. Lodge (1838), 3: 88–89, Worcester to Shrewsbury, February 2, 1604.

14. John Florio, in the dedicatory epistle to his translation of Montaigne's essays addressed to Lady Bedford acknowledges his debt to her; she had encouraged him to complete the work in her house and had read his manuscript. Sterrell, too, had read the manuscript: he or his brother were retelling stories from it among the lawyers of the Middle Temple prior to its publication. Sorlien (1976), p. 153.

15. SP 14/12/44, Thomas Phelippes to Visct. Cranborne (Cecil), January 31, 1605.

16. Persons to Sir Anthony Standen, Sept., Oct., & Nov. 1603-4, "The Tenor of Three Letters…" Transcription in Jesuit Archives London, letters of Persons, Box 46.12.6 (transcriptions) f. 1437.

17. SP 15/35/61, Standen to Person, December 17/27, 1603. Sterrell, as "Ortelio Renzo," wrote "Giovanni Antonio Frederico" January 31, 1604 that among other things recounted Standen's imprisonment. SP 14/6/37, Ortelio Renzo to Giovanni Antonio Frederico, January 31, 1604. Though this letter appears to have been intercepted, one with the same information probably reached Persons in Rome. Persons related much of the same information in a letter to the Pope of May 11, 1604. Transcription in Jesuit Archives London, letters of Persons, Box 46.12.6 (transcriptions) f. 1475-80. Persons told the Pope "That I had been informed from England that it was not my letter but one of Standen's written to me that was captured, or rather intercepted by the English ambassador to Paris: and this by the treachery and disloyalty of some one of the disaffected Englishmen residing in Paris…."

18. Akrigg (1962), p 22. Worcester humorously alluded to the king's preferences for sport to Shrewsbury. Lodge (1838), 3: 40–41, Worcester to Shrewsbury, September 24, 1603: "Now, where your Lordship thinks that stag and buck hunting being out we shall ply matters of state, know, my good Lord, that we are, and like to be, more violent for the hare than ever we were for the buck or stag ; and we will chase royally, if all go not as we could wish."

19. Willson (1956), p. 186.

20. Lodge (1838), 3: 110–11, Worcester to Shrewsbury, December 4, 1604.

21. Sterrell took a lease of the White Horse tenement in Long Ditch, for 40 years on December 4, 1604; information kindly provided by Dr. Richard Mortimer, Keeper of the Muniments, Westminster Abbey, email to author, October 17, 2000.

22. Lodge (1838), 3: 88–89, Worcester to Shrewsbury, February 2, 1604.

23. AAW A7/29/197–200, Rivers to Augustino Cornelio in Venegia, April 4, 1604.

24. The Coronation entertainments, the Panegyre and the Althorpe entertainments were bound together in a 1604 volume, Hereford & Simpson (1925), 7: 83–131. Edward Blount was publisher and "V. S.," Valentine Simmes, the printer. Chambers (1923), 3: 391; Ferguson (1968), p. 22; STC 14756. From the beginning of his career Simmes had strong ties to Catholics. Worcester and Sterrell were in a position to choose or influence who would participate in Court functions and who would publish the books arising from the Court functions and entertainments.

25. Id. "The 19th of the same the King rode in his robes from Whitehall to Westminster Church, where the Bishop of Durham preached; that done he went on foot to the Parliament House, with all the nobility before him, the earl of Arundell carrying his train, being seated under his estate [canopy], he made a speech of an hour long, which because it is in print, and I mean now to send it you, I forbear farther to speak of."

26. Lindley (1998), p. ix.

27. Chambers (1923), 3: 277–281.

28. Lee (1972), p. 56, Carleton to Chamberlain, January 15, 1604.

29. SP 14/6/37, "Ortelio Renzo to Giovanni Antonio Frederico" January 31, 1604. Carleton made the same observation about the precedence shown the Spaniard on the occasion of the *Vision of 12 Goddesses*: "The Spaniard thinks he hath carried away by being first feasted … and invited to the greatest mask; and the French seems to be greatly discontented that he was refused to be admitted to the last, about which he used unmannerly expostulations with the king and for a few days troubled all the court; but the queen was fain to take the matter upon her, who as a masker had invited the Spaniard as the Duke [of Lennox, who was responsible for the earlier masque] before had done the French, and to have them both there could not well be without bloodshed." Lee (1972), p. 55, Carleton to Chamberlain, January 15, 1604.

30. Two months earlier, *Othello*, featuring a blackamoor, had been performed at Court.

31. Thomas Phelippes estimated the total cost to be between £4,000 and £8,000 "To execute the Queen's fancy." SP 14/12/16 (Vincent—Phelippes) to Benson (Owen), January 10, 1605.

32. Hereford & Simpson (1925), 10:442, identify the "La. Hebert" of the *Masque of Blackness* as the daughter of Henry Herbert, second earl of Pembroke, and Mary Sidney. All that is known of this Anne Herbert is that she died young and unmarried. Their identification is mistaken, for Anne Russell Somerset was "Lady Herbert" in 1605.

33. The letter of "Vincent" to "Benson" (Phelippes to Owen), January 10, 1605, SP 14/12/16, reports in detail the diplomatic contretemps between the French and the Spanish ambassadors.

34. Prominent musicians who have been identified as Catholic whose travels provided opportunity for clandestine communications include Peter Phillips, Thomas Morley and John Dowland. Morley studied with the Catholic composer William Byrd, and perhaps Phillips did too. After leaving London at a young age, Phillips lived in Douay, Rome, Genoa, Spain, France, Antwerp and finally Brussels where he spent many years as organist for Archduke Albert. For Phillips's career, see Petti (1958), on Morley see SP 12/240/19, September 23, 1591 and SP 12/240/53, October 31, 1591. On Dowland, see Poulton (1982). Both Morley and Dowland were students at Oxford while William Sterrell was lecturing there. Both Morley and Dowland, as well as William Byrd, dedicated works to Robert Cecil. See also Chiasson-Taylor (2006).

35. Philip Sidney wrote his father-in-law, Secretary Walsingham:

> I wrote a letter to you by Will, my Lord of Leicester's jesting player, enclosed in a letter to my wife [Walsingham's daughter], and I never had answer thereof. It contained something to my lord of Leicester and council, that some way might be taken to stay my lady there. I since diverse times have writ to know whether you had received them, but you never answered me that point. I since find that the knave delivered the letters to my lady of Leicester.

Sir Philip Sidney's letter to Sir Francis Walsingham, dated at Utrecht on March 24, 1586. Bruce (1844), Pp. 89–90. There has been controversy over whether the jesting Will was actually Will Kemp or someone else. A William Kemp received a pension from the King of Spain "to secure service," for activities in the Low Countries at about this time. Loomie (1963a), p. 252.

36. Sir Thomas Kemp was a "A "notorious papist" in Kent. SP 12/203/61. One of his daughters married Sir Thomas Shirley and she was mother of Thomas, Anthony and Robert Shirley. See ODNB, "Kemp, Will" for discussion of Will Kemp's connection with the Catholic family in Kent.

37. Hasler (1981), 3:375–377.

38. There was also a small community associated with the estate. In his little book called *Kemps Nine Daies Wonder*, Kemp does not mention the Petres. Twice in the book he makes clear he plans to go to Rome.

39. ODNB, Anthony Shirley.

40. SP 77/6/258.

41. Davies (1967), pp. 135–36.

42. SP 77/6 fo. 271, J.B. to Halyns., May 13/23, 1601 Liège.

43. Chambers (1923), 2: 326.

44. Day (1607).

45. An anonymous play, *The Return from Parnassus*, has Kemp meeting with the Emperor of Germany. Chambers (1923), 2: 326. This was Emperor Rudolph II, whose court was at Prague and who was the eldest brother of Archduke Albert.

46. A Revels warrant dated February 28, 1602, is for the payment of £10 to "William Kempe and Thomas Heywood servants to the Earl of Worcester." It was for a performance by Worcester's Company of January 3, 1602. Chambers (1923), 4: 167.

47. Davies (1967), p. 128.

48. Davies (1967), p. 138.

49. Notes from the examination of Henry Walpole, June 17, 1594, Pollen (1908), pp. 260–61.

50. "Allen, Parsons, Holt receive all their intelligences that i know of by Verstegan, unless Covert give the Cardinal some now and then; also Hopkins and I think Middleton do give owen his, besides Verstegan; and Tippin I take it gives F. Holt intelligences, and he and Mr. Owen I heard since my departure from Brussels to St. Omers, were with Ibara, as with Cosmo before, to whom they gave all. At my being there i could not hear or perceive he used any Englishman much, but rather Fr. Creyton and Vincent Zelander, but my stay was very short. Now whence all these fetch their intelligences in England, I know not: Verstegan takes from Garnet for Parsons and Holt and as I remember he told me from Spillor [Spiller]. Something they have by comers and goers, as Hassenet and such like, which is all that i remember." Id. p. 262.

51. Id. p. 265.

52. Id. p. 257 (June 13/14 1594).

53. Dodd (1938a), p. 167, report of Thomas Allyson [Allison].

54. Chambers (1923), 2: 304, 320, 328. Gurr (1996), *passim*, traces Browne and Greene.

55. Schrickx (1986), p. 122.

56. Chambers (1923), 2: 529.

57. Chambers (1923), 2: 167; Schrickx (1986), p. 214.

58. Schrickx (1986), p. 214.

59. In 1608 a warrant was issued for payments for John and Caleb Hassenet for "Feats of activity by them performed upon a vaughting horse," Chambers (1923), 4: 174, and the Hassenet brothers took their show to the Low Countries, performing in Ghent

March 27, 1609, Schrickx (1986), p. 214. No doubt they carried letters and messages with them.

60. Birch (1760), pp. 48–49.

61. John Chamberlain to Ralph Winwood, October 12, 1605, McClure (1979), 1: 208.

62. In January 1605 Thomas Somerset was made a Knight of the Bath along with Prince Charles, the future king. At Henry's creation as Prince of Wales in June 1610, these two Somerset boys were made Knights of the Bath.

Chapter 24

1. Barnaby & Wry (1998), pp. 1225, 1226. John Klause properly cautions that it is "not sufficiently appreciated that the fundamental conflict of principles in *Measure for Measure* is not between justice and mercy but between justice and the law." Klause (2008), p. 241.

2. George Whetstone's two-part play *Promos and Cassandra* (1578), and *Epitia* (1583), an Italian play by Giraldi Cinthio.

3. Shakespeare had dedicated two of his earliest works, *Venus and Adonis* (1593) and *Rape of Lucrece* (1594), to the Earl of Southampton and he, like the courtiers in the 1604 audience, knew well that a Juliet (Elizabeth Vernon) and a Claudio (Southampton) were imprisoned in 1598 when Mistress Vernon's pregnancy appeared and Southampton returned from France to marry her in secret. Elizabeth released them but banished them from her Court.

4. One of James's favorite young courtiers, William Herbert (3rd Earl of Pembroke). In 1600, Mary Fitton had become pregnant with Herbert's child without the benefit of marriage, with the upshot that Queen Elizabeth imprisoned him for a time. Mary Fitton was placed in the care Lady Margaret Hawkins for the duration of her pregnancy. Pembroke refused to marry her. Their infant died at birth. Indeed, it would have been difficult not to make the association as William Herbert's brother, Philip (created Earl of Montgomery five months later) was married the day after the performance of *Measure for Measure* in an elaborate ceremony in which James I played a prominent part.

5. Judge not, that ye be not judged.
For with what judgment ye judge, ye shall be judged:
and with what measure ye mete, it shall be measured to you again.
And why beholdest thou the mote that is in thy
brother's eye, but considerest not the beam that is in thine own eye?
Or how wilt thou say to thy brother, Let me pull out
the mote out of thine eye; and, behold, a beam is in thine own eye?
Thou hypocrite, first cast out the beam out of thine
own eye; and then shalt thou see clearly to cast out the mote out of
thy brother's eye.

Matthew vii, 1–5; see also Mark iv, 24 and Luke vi, 38. Critics have detected thirty or more biblical passages embedded in the play. Fulton (2010), p. 121. The 1604 audience would likely know that this passage is preceded by the admonition that also expresses like treatment of likes, a measure for a measure: "if you will forgive men their offences, your heavenly Father will forgive you also your offences, but if you will not forgive men, neither will your Father forgive you your offences."

6. Shakespeare was aware of the Greek and Roman tradition of Sophocles and Seneca, playwrights at the seat of government, using their art to speak truth to power and to community, albeit with indirection. Sophocles employed tales of Thebes and Troy to teach Athenians of the need for humility and wisdom in government and the dangers of strict interpretation of religious law. Shakespeare used his position as court playwright to comment on and critique contemporary controversies, albeit indirectly, setting them in different environs and different environs.

7. See above, p. 141–42, 312 n. 7.

8. In contrast, the poet's *Rape of Lucrece,* where Tarquin "pens [Lucrece's] piteous clamors in her head" with "the nightly linen that she wears" as he rapes her, absolves Lucrece (despite her sense of sin) of guilt:

Let sin, alone committed, light alone
Upon his head that hath transgressed so;
Let guiltless souls be freed from guilty woe.
[*Rape*, lines 1480–82].

When Lavinia is raped by Demetrius and Chiron in *Titus Andronicus*, it is clear that she is wholly innocent and victimized in losing her chastity. Though Lucrece and Lavinia die to prevent family shame, there is nothing but innocence about them, and this contributes to the tragedy. They may lose their lives, but Shakespeare's readers have no reason to suppose their souls. Isabella's refusal is the greatest departure of Shakespeare from his sources. In neither Whetstone's *Promos and Cassandra* nor Cinthio's *Epitia* does the sister of the condemned man refuse to render up her chastity.

9. Might there not be a charity in sin
To save this brother's life? [*Measure*, 2.4].

10. Sweet sister, let me live.
What sin you do to save a brother's life,
Nature dispenses with the deed so far
That it becomes a virtue. [*Measure*, 3.1].

11. See the discussions of Fr. Sugar and Grissold (a layman) below. Many other instances could be cited. Although the English government often asserted the executions were not for religious belief, the fact that pardon was generally available for those renouncing the Catholic religion makes it clear that recusancy was the ultimate factor.

12. Simpson (1867), pp. 131–32. Holmes (1982),

p. 85, notes that the call for recusancy preceded Campion/Persons: "Nicholas Sander wrote in 1567 forbidding Catholics to have 'fellowship' with protestants 'in marriage, in prayer and in all the service of God.'"

13. Bossy (1975), p. 124; Bossy (1973), pp. 91–105.

14. The English state church recognized only the sacraments of baptism and the Lord's supper (communion) and rejected the Catholic belief of the real presence of Christ in the latter.

Measure seems to allude to the issue of the real presence in the Eucharist when a troubled Angelo, struggling with his temptation, says:

> Heaven in my mouth,
> As if I did but only chew His name. [*Measure*, 2.4].

15. Article XXII Purgatory of the 39 Articles of the Church of England that were adhered to after 1571.

16. Lucio exclaims to her:

> I hold you as a thing enskied [in heaven] and sainted
> By your renouncement, an immortal spirit
> And to be talked with in sincerity
> As with a saint. [*Measure*, 1.4].

17. Oh, cunning enemy that, to catch a saint,
> With saints dost bait thy hook! Most dangerous
> Is that temptation that doth goad us on
> To sin in loving virtue. [*Measure*, 2.2].

With this passage, Angelo identifies himself as saint, which is in keeping with Puritan doctrine of God electing certain living humans for salvation (without respect of good works), who are thus the "Visible Saints" among the faithful.

18. In a letter to Oxford University in January 1582, the Earl of Leicester, the University's Chancellor, expressed his and the Privy Council's complaint about the toleration of "secret and lurking Papists among you, which seduce your youth and carry them over by flockes to the Seminaries beyond Seas."

19. Tierney-Dodd 4: lxxxvii.

20. Morris (1875), pp. 143–44: "William Byrd and Helen his wife *praesentantur* for popish recusants. He is a gentleman of [the] King's Majesty's chapel and as the minister and churchwardens do hear Byrd, with the assistance of one Gabriel Colford who is now at Antwerp, hath been the Chief and principal *seducer* of John Wright son and heir of John Wright of Kelvedon in Essex gent and of Anne Wright the daughter of the said John Wright the elder. And the said Ellen Byrd as it is reported and as her servants have confessed have appointed business on the Sabbath day for her servants of purpose to keep them from Church and hath also done her best endeavour to *seduce* Thoda Pigbone her now maid servant to draw her to poperie as the maid hath confessed."

21. Hereford & Simpson 1: 220–22.

22. *Measure*, 3.2. Simpson (1899), p. 37: "Similarly, the lawfulness of the use of equivocation, when the truth is unjustly demanded, is laid down by the Duke in 'Measure for Measure' in precise terms: 'Pay with falsehood false exacting.'".

23. Milward (2005), P. 181. Milward dismisses it as a "minor item in the characterization of the duke-turned-friar ... that the Catholic spectators or readers would have had no difficulty in accepting his disguise with a willing 'suspension of disbelief.'"

Similarly problematic is the Duke's statement about Angelo at confession [3.1].

24. Id. p. 186.

25. Jardine (1851), pp. 80–81: "In like manner, one beyng convented in the Bishopps courte because he refuses to take such a one to his wyfe as he had contracted wth *per verba de praesenti*, having contracted with an other privyly before, so that he cannot be husband to her that claymeth hym, may answere that he never contracted with her *per verba de praesenti*, understanding that he did not so contract that it was a marriage; for that is the fynal intention of the judge to knowe whether there were a sufficient marriage between them or no, that so he may give true sentence. and otherwise the judge would geve sentence that he should be wth that woman which is not his wife, and so there shoulde be an error in the judgement. Even so may one in this case answere to the remote intention of the lawe and of the judge...."

26. Garnet explains how "we may use some equivocall word wch hath many significations, and we understand it in one sense, wch is trewe, although the hearer conceave the other, wch is false." Id. p. 48. He gives, as his example, the ambiguity that may be found in the word "lie." "[If] one should be asked whether such a straunger lodgeth in my house, and I should aunswere, 'He lyeth not in my house,' meaning that he doth not tell a lie there, althoughe he lodge there." The Clown uses Garnett's very words to equivocate to Desdemona as to the location of Lieutenant Cassio:

> Desdemona. Do you know, sirrah, where Lieutenant Cassio lies?
> Clown. I dare not say he lies anywhere.
> Desdemona. Why, man?
> Clown. He's a soldier; and for one to say a soldier lies, is stabbing.
> Desdemona. Go to! Where lodges he?
> Clown. To tell you where he lodges, is to tell you where I lie.
> Desdemona. Can anything be made of this?
> Clown. I know not where he lodges, and for me to devise a lodging,
> and say he lies here or he lies there, were to lie in mine own throat. [*Othello*, 3.4].

Many scholars have noted the apparent allusion to Fr. Garnet in *Macbeth* [2.3], and Shakespeare's *Phoenix and Turtle* memorializes the martyrdom of Garnet's assistant, St. Anne Line, and Shakespeare devotes a stanza to Fr. Garnet. Finnis & Martin (2003a), pp. 12–14.

27. Tierney-Dodd 4: lxxxv.

28. In the first, "We beseech your majesty to yield us as much favour, as others of contrary religion to that, which shall be publicly professed in England, shall obtain at your hands. For, if our faults be like, or less, or none at all, in equity our punishment ought to be like, or less, or none at all." Id. lxxiii. The supplication of 1604 called attention to the toleration of puritanism, which "is neither suppressed with penalties, nor oppressed with indignities." Id. lxxxv. In the second, they offered themselves as sureties, they would "stand bound, life for life," for the performance of their allegiance. Id. lxxxvi.

29. McIlwain (1918), p. 20. "I confesse, where I thought (by being gracious at the beginning) to win all mens hearts to a loving and willing obedience, I by the contrary found, the disorder of the countrie, and the losse of my thankes to be all my reward." James advised his son not to be like Angelo—"a Tyran would enter like a Saint while he found himselfe fast vnder-foot, and then would suffer his vnrulie affections to burst foorth." p. 20.

30. Tierney-Dodd, 4: app. 1.

31. LaRocca (1984), p. 27.

32. Tierney-Dodd 4:40–41.

33. Hatfield Papers, 16: 174–195. When the Privy Council inquired of the assize judges as to the reason for the executions, one explained: "we offered, if they would come to the church, pray for the King, and conform, to labour to the King for them. But they, as they had done divers times before, refused so to do." This report confirms the account given by a witness to the proceedings collected in Challoner (1839), p. 11:

"a justice of peace said to him, Grissold, Grissold, go to church, or ellse, God judge me, thou shalt be hanged. Then God's will be done, quoth he. After that, the judge asked him again, if he would go to church? I have answered you, my lord, enough for that matter, I will not. Then thou shalt be hanged, said the judge."

34. Id., p. 10: "Be it known unto you, good people, that i come hither to die for my conscience. The undersheriff answered, thou diest, not for thy conscience, but for treason. To which he replied, you do me wrong. There is none can touch me for treason; it is for conscience I Die."

35. "Bear witness, good people. That I die here not for theft, nor for felony; but for my conscience." Challoner (1839), p. 12.

36. Childs (2014), p. 220.

37. The father of John and Robert Grissold left three pounds in his will to Anthony Skinner's father. Camm (1910), p. 320. It was a Skinner of Rowington who drew John Grissold into the service of Anne Vaux. Childs (2014), p. 166. Multiple Grissolds were indicted for recusancy in September 1592 in Warwickshire. SP 12/243/76. Richard and John Grissold were identified as "notorious papists and fugitives" who were "either beyond the seas or lurking in England." John Grissold in another report of the same time was indicted in both Tamworth and Rowington "for a most willfull Recusant... Is certainly inhabiting in neither place but is accompted a wandering rogue, and one that laboreth to seduce others to Papistrie."

38. Finnis & Martin (2003a), pp. 12–14.

39. Foley Records 7: 1362, (March 11, 1601). On the scaffold, Barkworth called out: "I come here to die, being a Catholic, a Priest, and a religious man, belonging to the Order of St Benedict, by which Order this Kingdom of England was first converted." Id. p. 1365.

40. 13 Eliz. c. 2.

41. ODNB, "Mayne, Cuthbert."

42. Fr. Gerard related that priest/prisoners' cells were frequently searched for *Agnus Deis*—"From time to time our cells were entered and a search made for altar plate, *Agnus Deis*, and relics." Caraman (1951), p. 5.

43. Anstruther (1968), p. 341.

44. In 5.1 Lucio refers to the Friar/Duke as "A saucy friar, A very scurvy fellow" with the meaning of "insolent."

45. Bald (1953), p. 34. Fr. Persons, writing to Rome, relates Bishop Aylmer's mistreatment of a 16-year-old Catholic maiden who, for defending the papacy under his interrogation, was sent for whipping in a house of correction for prostitutes. Hicks (1942), p. 81 (Latin), p. 89 (English translation); for the *Virgo* sent to the brothel see also letter of Persons dated November 17, 1580, id. pp. 53, 60; Kenny (1982), pp. 40–41.

46. Halper (2001), pp. 223–24. Stephen Greenblatt has written of James's actions as producing "salutary anxiety" in onlookers; they are made aware of their own status as subjects of the king and of the king's repressive power. Greenblatt (1988), pp. 136–137.

47. As Melvin Seiden puts it, "Angelo is the duke's man; his job is the duke's neglected job; his sexual, legal, and political principles are the duke's—at least at the outset … there can be no evading the fact that the duke and his deputy are bonded by a set of shared moral assumptions." Seiden (1990), pp. 20–21.

48. McIlwain (1918), p. 43. "A king is as one set on stage, whose smallest actions and gestures, all the people gazingly do behold."

49. Rudolf II remained King of Hungary throughout 1604; the other relevant archdukes were Rudolf's brothers Matthias, Maximilian and Albert, who were seeking in 1604 to overcome the mad rule of Rudolf. Duerloo (2012). pp. 252–58.

50. Jonathan Israel has said "it seemed as if theirs was a model instance of a princely court restoring unity and harmony to a torn and divided society." Israel (2003), p. 2. On Albert's death, one of the Spanish king's council commented that his loss "has been a great one, for his rule was such that having found the three estates (the nobles, church and towns) of those provinces utterly corrupted he reduced them to proper order and obedience." Id.

51. As described by Hugo de Schepper and Geoffrey Parker, "in the Habsburg Netherlands the executive and the judiciary were one and the same." de Schepper & Parker (1976), p. 244. They note that the Privy Council, which was only required to clothe the archdukes' commands in legal language, "could issue letters of *abolitie* (pardon), *gratie ende remissie* (which saved sentenced murderers from execution), or *rehabilitatie* (which reversed a previous sentence). All were freely and frequently used." Id., p. 246.

52. This made him *Priest* of a named church, Santa Croce in Gerusalemme, one of the seven principal churches in Rome. Duerloo (2012), p. 23.

53. Duerloo (2012), p. 23.

54. Duerloo (2012), p. 23.

55. Bradbrook (1987), p. 9 ("The Duke, who is as ruthlessly efficient in his means as he is benevolent in his ends, proceeds to apply the third degree with the skill of a grand inquisitor...").

56. Gless comments "Isabella's name ... itself appears to suggest Catholicism, specifically Spanish Catholicism." Gless (1979), p. 102. Halper (2001), p. 239 notes Isabella is the Spanish version of Elizabeth.

57. After her husband died in 1621 she exchanged her courtly robes for the dress of a Poor Clare, although she continued as governor of the Netherlands. In October 1621, she became a member of the Franciscan Third Order, and after a year's novitiate she made her profession in 1622. She was also a generous patron of the Poor Clares at Ghent.

58. Duerloo (2012), p. 29. Indeed, the phrase "to use it for my time" was especially apt for Albert, for the title he and Isabella received as sovereigns was conditional; if they had no children, the sovereignty reverted to Spain.

59. Duerloo (2012), p. 32.

60. The Duke's resort to and relation with Friar Thomas has a close parallel to Archduke Albert and his confessor, the Dominican Fray Iñigo de Brizuela, an advisor of "*mucha discreción y prudencia.*" Israel (2003) p. 5. Brizuela later became Bishop of Segovia and president of the Council of Flanders because of his knowledge of the personalities and affairs of the Spanish Netherlands. Albert looked to him for spiritual and political guidance and sent him on diplomatic missions. The counterpart to Isabella's nun, Francisca, was the Infanta Isabella's confessor Padre Fray Andrés de Soto, of the order of Saint Francis. van Wyhe (2004), pp. 411–45. All of these details would be well-known to Sterrell, who had made multiple visits to Brussels while providing intelligence to them and while representing the interests of Worcester and English Catholics.

61. de Schepper & Parker (1976), p. 241: "He decided that the Netherlands should be handed over, not to his son the future Philip III, but to his daughter Isabella, who was to marry her cousin Albert, archduke of Austria and (since 1596) the king's governor-general in Brussels."

62. Loomie (1965b), p. 507.

63. Loomie (1971b), 303–16.

64. Isabella's brother was Philip III (crowned King of Spain 1598), while Anne's was Christian IV of Denmark (crowned 1596).

65. Wilson (1936), p. 5.

66. Despite allegations of Arenberg involvement in the Main Plot of Cobham and Ralegh, the English government did not believe that Arenberg posed any threat.

67. Duerloo (2012), p. 166.

68. Duerloo (2012), p. 143–145.

69. Duerloo (2012), p. 168.

70. Duerloo (2012), p 174.

71. As a recent historian has noted, "one can not perhaps call the age of Albert and Isabella a 'Golden Age.' But there can be no doubt that it was an era of glittering cultural achievement centred round a princely court which itself stood at the centre of the European stage." Israel (2003), p. 2.

72. Hatfield Papers 16: 237; Duerloo (2012), p. 74. Isabella seems to have been pregnant at the time. The couple, however, never were able to have a child.

73. Duerloo (2012), p 76.

Chapter 25

1. SP 12/283/75, Ralph Winwood to Cecil, April 10, 1602. The person passing the documents to Winwood is identified as "143," whom the Calendar suggests is Colville. But Colville would have had no access to the Wicham/Derrick letters back in 1594. Paget, however, was in Brussels at that time and in the very letters passed on, Sterrell had pointedly warned "Derrick" (Sherwood) that he was too open with Paget. Paget denounced other agents. Paget told Ralph Winwood of Thomas James, and Winwood had informed Robert Cecil about James in the summer of 1601. Winwood was repeating Paget when he named Thomas James as "a hard and desperate Ruffian, who hath lived in great inwardness with Persons the Jesuit." Quoted from Sawyer (1725), 1: 341, Winwood to Cecil, Paris, July 15, 1601; Loomie (1972), pp. 165, 169.

2. SP 14/12/31, January 25, 1605, Cecil to Windebank.

3. McClure (1939) 1: 202. Winwood had become England's diplomatic Agent to the States-General of the United Provinces (States).

4. See above, p. 83. Hatfield Papers 6: 511–13, Phelippes to Essex, December 9, 1596: "It is now above five years ago that, finding an old decayed intelligence between Sterrell and the fugitive traitors on the other side, I did for the Queen's service, accept an offer made me of restoring the same, knowing much good might be wrought thereon."

5. SP 14/12/34, January ?, 1605, examination of Edward Pettar or Petre.

6. SP 14/12/33, January ? 1605, examination of Abraham Ferkin.

7. Hatfield Papers 17: 39, Thomas Phelippes to Cecil January 29, 1605.

8. SP 14/12/44, Thomas Phelippes to Cecil, January 31, 1605.

9. Nearly four centuries later the English government acted in the same manner when it discovered a high level government employee was a Communist agent of the Soviet Union. This was Anthony Blunt. He was a member of the infamous Cambridge spy ring which included Kim Philby, Guy Burgess and Donald Maclean. They did work for the Soviet Union before and after World War II. Blunt was a relative of the queen, and he was the keeper of the royal family's art. Like Sterrell, he had a brilliant scholastic career, at Cambridge rather than Oxford, and he was a Fellow of Trinity College. Like Sterrell, he worked in British intelligence but was a double agent. And like Sterrell, Blunt after discovery of his role continued to work in the government; he was learned, highly intelligent and useful, and so his spying past was essentially overlooked and kept secret for years by the government itself.

10. In a letter intended for King James, SP 14/20/51, April? 1606, Phelippes indicated that he had been allowed to move to his own house about the end of March 1605 to remain prisoner for 12 months. He was still in the Gatehouse prison on March 28, 1605, Hatfield Papers 17: 111–12, Phelippes to Cecil, and on April 3, 1605, Hatfield Papers 17: 128, he thanks Cecil for showing him favor by "This Change of Prison, Which I Reckon as Good as a Full Liberty...."

Chapter 26

1. Worcester's family had been Catholic for years. Jones's claim to have converted Frances Somerset and others of her family likely refers to her willingness to become openly recusant rather than continue as a "Church Papist," a Roman Catholic who conformed outwardly to the Church of England. Sometime about 1605 she and her husband pledged to support Jesuit missionaries in both North and South Wales. Mathias (1963), p. 84.

2. CSPV 10:390, Molin to the Doge and Senate, June 19/29, 1605. Mathias (1963), treats the dates of Molin's dispatches as though they were old style; it appears from internal references that they are given new style to correspond with the calendar used on the Continent. All of Molin's dispatches are dated herein with this assumption of old style/new style as dates.

3. The likelihood that he voluntarily undertook the potentially difficult project is suggested by a document from 1607. Its authorship is unknown. After attributing the outbreak to the presence of an agent provocateur, the document states that so alarmed were the local inhabitants that "they requested that the leading Catholics of London, such as the Archpriest with some of his reverend assessors, or the Jesuit Fathers and others, who possessed more authority over the Catholics, should immediately send some gentlemen into those parts with full authority to assist in allaying the excitement." Quoted in Mathias (1963), p. 107. This, the account reported, was done, referring obviously to Worcester.

4. Reprinted in Tierney-Dodd 4: cx.

5. CSP 1603–1610, p. 228; reprinted in Tierney-Dodd 4: cix.

6. CSPV 10: 397, Molin to the Doge and Senate, July 3/13, 1605.

7. Hatfield Papers 17: 361, Bennett to Cecil, August 9, 1605.

8. Hatfield Papers 17: 389, Bennett to Cecil, August 24, 1605. A report of the examinations of "Rice Griffiths alias Williams, a seminary priest" by Paul de la Hay to Cecil was to the same effect as Bennett's complaints: evidence from many witnesses established that Griffiths said mass, administered the sacrament, heard confessions, gave absolution and solemnized marriages. Hatfield Papers 17: 456, de la Hay to Cecil, October 16, 1605. He betrayed both the Archbishop of Canterbury and the Bishop of Hereford by passing on information to recusants and priests to allow them to escape. Evidently Griffiths *Alias* Williams went so far as encouraging young Catholic lads to go abroad and study for the priesthood, as he had. Mathias notes that "James Griffiths, who entered the English College, Rome, on November 7, 1611, stated that it was through the care and industry of his mother that he was reconciled to the Church of Rome 'by a certain priest of Hereford, now dead, named Mr. Williams.'" Mathias (1963), p. 19.

9. SP 14/14/52, Bp. of Hereford to the Earl of Salisbury, June 22, 1605.

10. SP 14/14/53.

11. Hatfield Papers 17: 314.

12. CSPV 10: 408, Molin to the Doge and Senate. July 31/August 10,1605.

13. Hatfield Papers 17: 360–61, Bennett to Cecil, August 9, 1605.

14. Worcester's role has been seriously misunderstood by some Catholic historians. Fr. Philip Caraman, for example, describes him thus: "Worcester's role among the Councillors was perhaps the most sinister ... [He] had been very active against Catholics at the disturbance in Herefordshire.... He was one of [Cecil's] most useful tools." Caraman (1964), p. 349. To the contrary, Worcester was acting at the instigation of the Archpriest, Fr. Garnet and the Jesuits, and other concerned Catholics. Far from being a tool, he outwitted Cecil and the Protestant bishops at every turn in dealing with the king and the Council.

Chapter 27

1. Haynes (1994), p. 81; Edwards (1973), pp. 116–17.

2. Hotson (1937), p. 181; Chambers (1930), 2: 168.

It appears that Gerard attempted to lodge some of the conspirators at the Gatehouse before the plot was revealed. This does not mean Gerard knew of the plot itself.

3. SP 14/216/10. The property adjoining the Gatehouse, belonging to Henry Percy, 9th Earl of Northumberland, was probably searched thoroughly. Though Northumberland did not use it for his residence, his servant Thomas Percy was one of the plotters who had rented the building which was used for the gunpowder. Northumberland himself was imprisoned in the Plot and remained in the Tower until 1621.

4. Caraman (1951), pp. 203–04, 256.

5. Caraman (1951), p. 257; Wadsworth (1629), p. 25.

6. Caraman (1951), pp. 209, 258–59. Sterrell (and Worcester) probably saved another Jesuit by timely warning John Gerard of an impending search. John Gerard had brought Thomas Everett (Everard) to Catholicism and the priesthood. For biography on Thomas Everard, Foley Records 2: 399–409. Upon learning of the Gunpowder Plot, Everett had gone to a house in London, and someone reported to the government the presence of a priest. Gerard recounts that "the fact reached the ears of the Council. And as he [Everett] is something of my height, and has black hair, Cecil thought it was I of whom notice was given him, and said to a private friend of his, 'Now we shall have him,' naming me." Morris (1871), p. clxxx. Gerard sent warning to Everett before the search was made. How was Gerard in a position to know what Cecil had told a "private friend" about Gerard? There can be very few "private friends" of Cecil who also would have been in a position to know Gerard and to convey to Gerard the very words of Robert Cecil. The "private friend" was surely Worcester or Sterrell, and Sterrell would have reported the words to warn Gerard.

7. Caraman (1951), p. 205 n. 2. ODNB.

8. Morris (1871), p. 186.

9. Loomie (1969), p. 41.

10. Hereford & Simpson (1925), 1: 202–03.

11. Teague (1998), pp. 249–252; Riggs (1989), pp. 67–68.

12. Richard Broughton, *English Protestants Plea, and Petition...* (Saint-Omer: C. Boscard) (1621) (STC (2nd ed.) / 3895.5), 59.

13. Hereford & Simpson (1925), 1: 263; Martin & Finnis (2005), pp. 12–13.

14. Edmondes wrote to Cecil that he was addressed by an Englishman "calling himself by the name of Barnes, who as it seemeth is employed to make relation to the Pope's Nuntio of the proceedings of the Catholics in England, and he professing a desire to deserve the good opinion of the State promiseth to make discovery of the business, wherein he shall be employed...."

15. Hatfield Papers 17: 504, Edmondes to Cecil, November 22, 1605.

16. Hatfield Papers 17: 559, Cecil to Sir Thomas Fane, December 24, 1605. Cecil insisted that his instructions be carried out "privately as may be, for therein consists the life of the service."

17. Hatfield Papers 18:10–11, Fane to Cecil, January 8, 1606.

18. Hatfield Papers 18: 49–51: "Concerning Thomas Philips [Phelippes] it is true that both before from the Lord Arundel before his coming over, and since from you, and now lately from Barnes I have been informed of his continuing correspondency with owen, ever since Owen was committed prisoner and thereupon hath been brought in question and his house suddenly searched. In his examination he hath not denied his correspondency, but protesteth it was not with any evil purpose but only to draw on thereby some reward for his former troubles. He is committed close prisoner, and what course shall he further taken you shall be advertised. For Barnes he is now returning again into Flanders with many vows and promises to continue to do good service. As he was at Dover with my pass, carrying a letter from Phelippes to Owen (of Barnes's own handwriting, wherewith I was before acquainted) he was suddenly stayed by order from the Lord Warden upon suspicion that he was one Acton, a traitor of the late conspiracy, who is yet untaken; the description of Acton agreeing almost in all parts with Barnes's person. Whereupon his papers and letters being sent to my Lord of Northampton, I thought fit not to defer any longer the calling of Phelippes into question, which till then i had forborne, hoping by Barnes's means to have discovered some further matter than before i could do. You may have an eye of Barnes's proceeding there, and as you see cause advertise me of it."

19. Hicks (1963), p. 214.

20. Gifford wrote to Sir Thomas Edmondes: it "proceedeth from Owen and Baldwin's wicked and false information, charging me with a letter written in cipher into England and sent back by Phelippes that I was and had been always most faithful to my King [James]." Id., p. 215. Edmondes followed up on Gifford's assertions by saying that Gifford suspected that "Barnes hath betrayed to Owen a letter of his which he committed to him to carry into England, whereof there is great likelihood and that therein the overflowing of his pen might transport him to make some unpleasing mention of these prince's proceedings." Id. p 217, quoting Edmondes to Cecil, July 16, 1606, S.P. 77/8, f. 143. Precisely what this letter was is uncertain. It appears that Dr. Gifford must have written a document concerning the Gunpowder Plot that was carried by Barnes into England in December 1605 and that it was an embarrassment to the Archduke. See Hicks (1963), p 234 n. 29 and Willaert (1905), 7 : 605 n. 3. The ambassador of the Archdukes in London, Hoboken, wrote in April 1606 that Gifford had maintained a close correspondence with Cecil and Northampton to the detriment of the Catholics and the Archduke. Id. p 606.

21. The identification of Barnes as author of two letters to "Du Pre" as Π is clear, for the outside of the first says "Th. B. from St. Omers," (SP 77/8 fo. 95, April 26/May 6, 1606) and the second says "Barnes to Me from Brussells" (SP 77/8 fo. 121, 1606 June 16/26).

22. Hatfield Papers 17: 456, Southaick to Cecil, October 17, 1605; id., 17: 469–70, Southaick to Cecil, October 27, 1605.

23. Dodd (1938b), p. 644; Edwards (2002), pp. 22–33.

24. Hatfield 18: 46, Dr. Dupont (Deputy Vice-Chancellor of Cambridge) to Cecil, February 9, 1606: "Affirming that he has been employed by the Ambassador of France in certain intelligences unto your Lordship, and that you have accepted well of his service and gave him 15*l*. I shall most willingly attend your good pleasure whether you will have any further stay or inquiry made of him." Cecil immediately had Dupont send Southaick back to Cecil. Hatfield 18: 49, Dr. Dupont to Cecil, February 11, 1606.

25. Edmondes referred to Southaick as Southwell, and Southwick signed a letter to Edmondes as "George Southwell, Alias Sowthwick." SP 77/8 ff. 126–27.

26. Edmondes dated his letter re: Southwick as June 16, 1606 and he was probably using the English calendar though in Brussels. Barnes wrote from Brussels giving the date as "This xxvith of June stilo novo 1606," which was June 16 on the English calendar.

27. Hatfield Papers 18: 197–200, Cecil to Edmondes, July 12, 1606.; Gardiner (1887) 1: 344–47.

28. Hatfield Papers 18: 204, Don Pedro de Cuniga (Zuniga), Spanish ambassador, to Cecil, July 17, 1606. See also Hatfield 18: 259–63, Cecil to Edmondes with enclosures, August 27, 1606.

29. Hatfield Papers 18: p 227, Edmondes to Cecil, August 6, 1606.

30. Edmondes to Cecil: "I have been also informed, that the person that passed the last time from hence into England, in the company of Guy Fawkes, is one Spiller that then went under the name of Bellamy." SP Flanders 77/8 fo. 16ᵛ, January 6, 1606.

31. SP 14/18/124, February 28, 1606, Stephen Phelippes—information.

32. Hatfield Papers 18: 49–51.

33. Hatfield Papers 18: 25–27, April 1606.

34. SP 14/20/50, April 29, 1606, Thomas Phelippes to Cecil: "I perceive by that Mr Levinus dealt with me about[?] not long before that some confessions of Garnett should do me harm which till I know particularly I know not how to answer directly."

35. SP 14/20/51, Phelippes to Lieutenant of the Tower (Waad) for the King April? 1606. SP 14/20/50, April 29, 1606. The dates of the interrogatories to Garnet and the letter of Phelippes were probably about mid-April 1606 for on April 17, 1606 Waad wrote to Cecil that Phelippes's servant could apprehend Fullwood. Hatfield Papers 18: 113–14, Waad to Cecil.

36. Hatfield Papers 18: 268, Phelippes to Cecil, August 1606.

37. It is beyond the scope of the present work to trace the subsequent career of Phelippes. He continued to scheme from prison and used his wife as a conduit. Hatfield Papers 19: 397, December 1607?, Mary Phelippes to Cecil.

38. ODNB, "Phelippes, Thomas."

39. Hatfield Papers 20: 109, March 20, 1608.

40. Loomie (1963a), p. 258.

41. Loomie (1973b) 1: 1–2; Hervey (1921), pp. 23, 25, 258; L. Stone (1965), p. 413. Loomie notes that Spiller was still publicly identified as a recusant in 1626.

42. Loomie (1973b) I: 1–2.

43. SP 14/216/114, Declaration of Thomas Wintour. "Mr. Catesby wished us to consider whether it were not now necessary to send Mr. Fawkes over, both to absent himself for a time as also to acquaint Sir William Stanley and Mr. Owen with this matter. We agreed that he should; provided that he gave it them with the same oath that we had taken before, viz., to keep it secret from all the world. The reason why we desired Sir William Stanley should be acquainted herewith was to have him with us so soon as he could, and, for Mr. Owen, he might hold good correspondency after with foreign princes. So Mr. Fawkes departed about Easter for Flanders and returned the later end of August [1605]. He told me that when he arrived at Brussels, Sir William Stanley was not returned from Spain, so as he uttered the matter only to Owen, who seemed well pleased with the business, but told him that surely Sir William would not be acquainted with any plot as having business now afoot in the Court of England, but he himself would be always ready to tell it him and send him away so soon as it were done."

44. SP 14/19/94, letter of January 27, 1606; Loomie dates and partly quotes this letter in Loomie (1971a), p. 42.

45. Loomie (1963a), p. 85.

46. Loomie (1963a), p. 85.

47. Dodd (1938b), p. 648; Loomie (1963a), p. 84.

48. Edwards (1985), p. 151 (quoting Cecil to Edmondes September 24, 1608).

49. Edwards (1985), p. 149. "The best excuse that I can make for wilford is that it is a thing of Owen's and Baldwin's own hatching by the setting of Whitebread on work to engage him therein, and afterwards to betray him."

50. SP 77/6 fo. 341, May 19/29, 1602, J. B. to Robinson.

51. SP 14/18/124, February 28 1606, Stephen Phelippes—information.

52. Loomie (1963a), p 92.

Chapter 28

1. On the complexity of the Oath and Catholic responses, *See* Questier (1997), pp. 311–329.

2. The haunting Latin phrase has inspired writers who have included Sir Thomas More (*Utopia*) and St. Augustine (*City of God*). Sterrell will have looked to the same source on which they drew: Lucan, *Pharsalia* (also known *as de bello civili*), Book IX. After the decisive battle of Pharsalia which makes him ruler of the Roman world, Julius Caesar (in Lucan's account) maliciously denies burial to the countless thousands of dead soldiers of Pompey's defeated army. As Caesar breakfasts gloating over the dreadful scene, the poet speaks to him. His rage at the dead flouts humanity. And it is a futile anger; all will be swallowed up in the final conflagration of this world; and whether Caesar's spirit after death ascends or descends, just so high or low he will find spirits of these dead fellow citizens. And meanwhile, *caelo tegitur qui non habet urnam*. Sterrell was surely reflecting on numerous martyrs, dead fellow citizens, he had known who were denied the rituals of burial in a religious civil conflict that spanned his life.

Bibliography

Adams, Joseph Quincy. 1917. *Shakespearean Playhouses*. New York: Houghton Mifflin.
Adams, Reginald H., ed. 1986. *Memorial Inscriptions of St John's College Oxford*. Oxford: St. John Baptist College and Oxford Historical Society.
Akrigg, G. P. V. 1962. *Jacobean Pageant: Or, the Court of King James I*. Cambridge: Harvard University Press.
Alford, Stephen. 2012. *The Watchers: A Secret History of the Reign of Elizabeth I*. New York: Bloomsbury.
Allen, P. S. 1923. "The Birth of Thomas North," *English Historical Review* 37: 565–6.
Allen, William. 1587. *The Copie of a Letter*. Antwerp 1587, access EEBO.
_____. 1588. *Admonition to the Nobility and People of England*. Antwerp [?] 1588, access EEBO.
Allison, A. F. and D. M. Rogers. 1994. *The Contemporary Printed Literature of the English Counter-Reformation Between 1558 and 1640*, vol. ii. Aldershot, Hant, England: Scolar Press.
Anstruther, Godfrey. 1953. *Vaux of Harrowden: A Recusant Family*. Newport, Monmouthshire: Johns.
_____. 1968. *The Seminary Priests: A Dictionary of the Secular Clergy of England and Wales 1558–1850, I Elizabethan 1558–1603*. Ware: St. Edmund's College.
Bald, R. C., ed. 1953. *An Humble Supplication to Her Maiestie by Robert Southwell*. Cambridge: Cambridge University Press.
Baldwin, T. W. 1924. "Shakespeare's Jester: The Dates of *Much Ado* and *As You Like It*," *Modern Language Notes* 39: 447–55.
_____. 1931. *William Shakespeare Adapts a Hanging*. Princeton: Princeton University Press.
_____. 1944. *Small Latine and Lesse Greeke*. Urbana: University of Illinois Press.
_____.1950. *On the Literary Genetics of Shakspere's Poems and Sonnets*. Urbana: University of Illinois Press.
Barnaby, Andrew & Joan Wry. "Authorized Versions: *Measure for Measure* and the Politics of Biblical Translation," *Renaissance Quarterly* 51: 1225–1254. 1998.
Bate, Jonathan. 1993. *Shakespeare and Ovid*. Oxford: Oxford University Press.
Bednarz, James P. 1983. "Imitations of Spenser in *A Midsummer Night's Dream*," *Renaissance Drama* 14: 79–102.
Beer, Barrett L. 1998. *Tudor England Observed: The World of John Stow*. Thrupp, Stroud, Gloucestershire: Sutton Pub.
Bevington, David and Peter Holbrook, eds. 1991. *The Politics of the Stuart Court Masque*. Cambridge [England]: Cambridge University Press.
Bindoff, S. T., ed. 1982. *The House of Commons, 1509-1558*, 3 vols. London: Secker & Warburg.
Birch, Thomas. 1754. *Memoirs Of the Reign of Queen Elizabeth*. London: Printed for A. Millar.
_____. 1760. *The Life of Henry Prince of Wales*. London: Printed for A. Millar.
_____. 1848. *The Court and Times of James the First*, 2 vols. London: Printed for A. Millar.
Black, Joseph. 1997. "The Rhetoric of Reaction: The Martin Marprelate Tracts. 1588–89. Antimartinism, and the Uses of Print in Early Modern England," *Sixteenth Century Journal*, 28: 707–725.
Blits, Jan H. 2003. *The Soul of Athens: Shakespeare's A Midsummer Night's Dream*. New York & Oxford: Lexington Books.
Blomefield, Francis. 1805. *An Essay Towards a Topographical History of the County of Norfolk*, vol. I. [1726] 2nd ed. London: Printed for W. Miller.
Bloxam, John Rouse. 1857. *A Register of the President, Fellows, Demies ... Of ... Magdalen College*, vol. III. Oxford.
Boas, F. S. and Greg, W. W. 1922. *The Christmas Prince*. London: Printed for the Malone Society, by F. Hall at the Oxford University Press.
Bossy, John. 1973. "The English Catholic Community, 1603–1625," in *The Reign of James VI and I*, ed. A. G. R. Smith. London, 1973.
_____. 1975. *The English Catholic Community, 1570–1850*. London, 1975.
_____. 1965. "Henri IV, the Appellants and the Jesuits," *Recusant History*, 8: 80–122.
_____. 1991. *Giordano Bruno and the Embassy Affair*. New Haven: Yale University Press.
_____. 2001. *Under the Molehill: An Elizabethan Spy Story*. New Haven: Yale University Press.
Bradbrook, M. C. 1965. *English Dramatic Form: A History of Its Development*. London: Chatto & Windus; New York, Barnes & Noble.

_____. 1987. "Authority, Truth, and Justice in *Measure for Measure*" in *William Shakespeare's Measure for Measure*. New York: Chelsea House.

Bradney, Joseph Alfred. 1914. *A History of Monmouthshire from the Coming of the Normans into Wales Down to the Present Time*. Vol. 2, [Part 3], Vol. 2, [Part 3]. London: Mitchell, Hughes and Clarke.

Breight, Curtis C. 1996. *Surveillance, Militarism and Drama in the Elizabethan Era*. New York: St. Martin's Press.

Brennan, Michael G., ed. *The Travel Diary (1611–1612) of an English Catholic, Sir Charles Somerset*. Leeds: Leeds Philosophical & Literary Society.

Brooks, Harold F., ed. 1979. *A Midsummer Night's Dream*. Arden Edition of the Works of William Shakespeare. Bristol: Methuen.

Brown, Nancy Pollard. 1989. "Paperchase: The Dissemination of Catholic Texts in Elizabethan England," *English Manuscript Studies* 1: 120–43.

Brownlow, F. W. 1993. *Shakespeare, Harsnett, and the Devils of Denham*. Newark: University of Delaware Press.

_____. 1996. *Robert Southwell*. New York: Twayne.

Bruce, John. 1844. "Who Was 'Will, My Lord of Leycester's Jesting Player,'" *Shakespeare Society Papers*, 1:89–90.

Budiansky, Stephen. 2005. *Her Majesty's Spymaster: Elizabeth I, Sir Francis Walsingham, and the Birth of Modern Espionage*. New York: Viking.

Bullough, Geoffrey. 1957–1966. *Narrative and Dramatic Sources of Shakespeare*. London : Routledge and Kegan Paul; New York: Columbia University Press.

Burke, John. 1844. *A Genealogical and Heraldic History of the Extinct and Dormant Baronetcies of England, Ireland, and Scotland*. London: J.R. Smith.

Burton, Edwin Hubert, and John Hungerford Pollen. 1914. *Lives of the English Martyrs*. Second series. *The Martyrs declared Venerable. Volume I. 1583–1588*. Edited by E.H. Burton ... and J.H. Pollen. London: Longmans & Co.

Butler, D. C. 1904. "Dr. William Gifford in 1586," *The Month*. March, 1904, pp. 243–58.

Butler, Geoffrey G. 1913. *The Edmondes Papers*. Roxburghe Club, London: J.B. Nichols and Sons.

Butler, Guy. 1983. "Shakespeare and Two Jesters," *Hebrew University Studies in Literature and the Arts*, 11: 161.

Camm, Bede. 1910. *Forgotten Shrines: An Account of Some Old Catholic Halls and Families in England, and of Relics and Memorials of the English Martyrs*. London: Macdonald & Evans.

Caraman, Philip.1964. *Henry Garnet, 1555–1606, and the Gunpowder Plot*. London: Longmans.

_____. 1995. *A Study in Friendship: Saint Robert Southwell and Henry Garnet*. St. Louis: Institute of Jesuit Sources.

_____, ed. 1951. *John Gerard: The Autobiography of an Elizabethan*. London: Longmans.

Carlson, Leland H. 1981. *Martin Marprelate, Gentleman*. San Marino: Huntington Library.

Carter, Charles H. 1964. *The Secret Diplomacy of the Hapsburgs, 1598–1625*. New York: Columbia University Press.

Catholic Church, Armand Louant, Léon van der Essen, and Ottavio Mirto Frangipani. 1924. *Correspondence d'Ottavio Mirto Frangipani*. Rome: Institut historique belge.

Cecil, Algernon. 1915. *A Life of Robert Cecil*. London: Murray.

Challoner, Richard. 1839. *Memoirs of Missionary Priests*. Philadelphia: John T. Green.

Chambers, E. K. 1923. *The Elizabethan Stage*, 4 vols. Oxford: Clarendon Press.

_____. 1930. *William Shakespeare*, 2 vols. Oxford: Oxford University Press.

_____. 1944. *Shakespearean Gleanings*. Oxford: Oxford University Press.

Chambrun, Clara Longworth. 1935. *My Shakespeare, Rise! Recollections of John Lacy, One of His Majesty's Players*. Stratford-on-Avon: Shakespeare Press.

Cheney, Edward P. 1926. *A History of England from the Defeat of the Armada to the Death of Elizabeth*. New York: Longmans, Green and Co.

Chiasson-Taylor, Rachelle A. M. 2006. *Musicians and Intelligence Operations, 1570–1612: Politics, Surveillance, and Patronage in the Late Tudor and Early Stuart Years*. Ph. D. dissertation, McGill University.

Childs, Jessie. 2014. *God's Traitors: Terror and Faith in Elizabethan England*. Oxford: Oxford University Press.

Clark, Andrew, ed. 1887. *Register of the University of Oxford* II/i. Oxford: Oxford Historical Society.

Clark, Arthur. 1931. *Thomas Heywood*. Basil Blackwell: Oxford, 1931.

_____.1951. *Chepstow, Its Castle and Lordship*. [Newport? Mon.] Newport & Monmouthshire Branch of the Historical Association.

Collins, Arthur., ed. 1746. *Letters and Memorials of State [Sydney Papers]*. 2 vols. London, cited as Sydney Papers.

Cooper, John. 2012. *The Queen's Agent: Sir Francis Walsingham and the Rise of Espionage in Elizabethan England*. New York: Pegasus Books.

Crehan, J. H. 1964. "Shakespeare and the Sarum Ritual," *The Month* 32: 47–50.

Crittall, Elizabeth, ed. 1970. *A History of Wiltshire*. Vol. 9. Oxford: Oxford University Press.

Davies, David William. 1967. *Elizabethans Errant*. Ithaca, N.Y.: Cornell University Press.

Day, John, William Rowley, and George Wilkins. 1607. *The Travailes of the Three English Brothers*. [London]: Printed at London for John Wright and are to bee sold at his shoppe. Access EEBO.

de Groot, John Henry. 1946. *The Shakespeares and "The Old Faith."* New York: King's Crown Press.

de Kermaingant, Laffleur. 1886. *Mission De Jean De Thumery*. Paris: Firmin-Didot.

de Schepper, Hugo and Geoffrey Parker. 1976. "The Formation of Government Policy in the Catholic Netherlands Under 'The Archdukes,'1596-1621," *English Historical Review*, 91: 241-254.

Devereux, W., ed. 1853. *Lives and Letters of the Devereux, Earls of Essex,1540-1646*. 2 Volumes. London: J. Murray.

Devlin, Christopher. 1956. *The Life of Robert Southwell, Poet and Martyr*. London: Longmans, Green and Co.

Dimock, Arthur. 1894. "The Conspiracy of Dr. Lopez," *English Historical Review*, 9:440-72.

Dodd, A. H. 1937. "Two Welsh Catholic Emigres," *Bulletin of Celtic Studies* 8: 346-48.

_____. 1938a. "A Spy's Report, 1604," *Bulletin of Celtic Studies*. 1938. 9:154-67.

_____. 1938b. "The Spanish Treason, the Gunpowder Plot, and the Catholic Refugees," *English Historical Review* 53: 627-50.

Donaldson, Ian. 2011. *Ben Jonson: A Life*. New York: Oxford University Press.

Donno, Elizabeth S. 1962. *Sir John Harington's a New Discourse of a Stale Subject, Called the Metamorphosis of Ajax: A Critical Annotated Edition*. London: Routledge.

Draper, John W. 1936. "*As You Like It* and 'Belted Will' Howard," *Review of English Studies* 12: 440-44.

Duerloo, Luc. 2012. *Dynasty and Piety: Archduke Albert. 1598-1621 and Habsburg Political Culture in an Age of Religious Wars*. Burlington, Vt.: Ashgate.

Duffy, Eamon. 1992. *The Stripping of the Altars*. New Haven, CT: Yale University Press.

Dulles, Allen. 1963. *The Craft of Intelligence*. New York: Harper & Row.

Du Maurier, Daphne. 1975. *Golden Lads: Sir Francis Bacon, Anthony Bacon, and Their Friends*. Garden City, N.Y.: Doubleday.

Eccles, Mark. 1934. *Christopher Marlowe in London*. Cambridge, Mass: Harvard University Press.

_____. 1982. "Brief Lives: Tudor and Stuart Authors," in *Studies in Philology*, vol. 79. Fall 1982.

Edwards, Francis. 1964. *The Dangerous Queen*. London: Geoffrey Chapman.

_____. 1973. *The Gunpowder Plot: The Narrative of Oswald Tesimond Alias Greenway*. Folio Society.

_____. 1985. "The Attempt in 1608 on Hugh Owen, Intelligencer for the Archdukes in Flanders," *Recusant History* 17: 140-57.

_____. 1995. *Robert Persons: The Biography of an Elizabethan Jesuit 1546-1610*. St. Louis, Missouri: Institute of Jesuit Sources.

_____. 2002. "The First Earl of Salisbury's Pursuit of Hugh Owen," *Recusant History* 26: 2-38.

_____. 2006. *The Succession, Bye and Main Plots of 1601-1603*. Dublin: Four Courts Press.

Ferguson, W. Craig. 1968. *Valentine Simmes: Printer to Shakespeare, Jonson, Marlowe ... and Other Elizabethans*. Charlottesville, VA: Bibliographical Society of the University of Virginia.

Finnis, John. 2005. "'The Thing I Am': Personal Identity in Aquinas and Shakespeare," *Social Philosophy & Policy* 22: 250-282; also in Ellen Frankel Paul, Fred. D. Miller & Jeffrey Paul, eds. *Personal Identity*. Cambridge & New York: Cambridge University Press, 250-282.

_____, and Martin, Patrick. 2003a. "Shakespeare's Intercession for *Love's Martyr*," *Times Literary Supplement*, no. 5220, April 18th, 12-14.

_____, and Martin, Patrick. 2003b. "An Oxford Play Festival of February 1582. *Notes & Queries* 248:391-4.

Norfolk, Henry Granville Fitzalan-Howard. 1857. *The Lives of Philip Howard, Earl of Arundel, and of Anne Dacres, His Wife*. London: Hurst and Blackett.

Foakes, R. A. Ed. 1984. *A Midsummer Night's Dream*. The New Cambridge Shakespeare. Cambridge & New York: Cambridge University Press.

Foley, Henry. Ed. 1877-1883, *Records of the English Province of the Society of Jesus*, 7 Vols. London, Cited as Foley Records Volume.

Foster, Joseph. 1891. *Alumni Oxonienses: The Members of the University of Oxford, 1500-1714*, 4 Vols. Oxford: Parker, 1891.

Fraser, Antonia. 1969. *Mary Queen of Scots*. London: Weidenfeld & Nicolson.1996.

_____. *Faith and Treason: The Story of the Gunpowder Plot*. New York: Doubleday.

Freedman, Sylvia. 1983. *Poor Penelope: Lady Penelope Rich, an Elizabethan Woman*. Abbostbrook, Bourne End, Bucks: Kensal Press.

Froude, J. A. 1925. *English Seamen in the Sixteeenth Century*. London: G.G. Harrap.

Fulton, Thomas. 2010. "Shakespeare's Everyman: *Measure for Measure* and English Fundamentalism," *Premodern Shakespeare*: A special issue of *Journal of Medieval and Early Modern Studies* 40. 1. 2010: 119-47.

Gardiner, Samuel R. 1887. *History of England from the Accession of James I to the Outbreak of the Civil War 1603-1642*, 10 vols. London: Longmans, Green, and Co.

Gless, Darryl J. 1979. *Measure for Measure, the Law, and the Convent*. Princeton, N.J.: Princeton University Press.

Goodman, Nathan Gerson. 1925. *Diplomatic Relations Between England and Spain, 1597-1603*. Philadelphia, Pa: [University of Pennsylvania?].

Greenblatt, Stephen. 1988. *Shakespearean Negotiations: The Circulation of Social Energy in Renaissance England*. Berkeley: University of California Press.

Greg, Walter W., ed. 1904. *Henslowe's Diary*. London: Bullen.

Guiney, Imogen. 1939. *Recusant Poets*. New York: Sheed & Ward.

Gurr, Andrew. 1996. *The Shakespearian Playing Companies*. Oxford: Oxford University Press.

Halliwell, J. O., ed. 1845. *Poetical Miscellanies from*

a MS. Coll. of the Time of James I. London: T. Richards.

Halper, Louise. 2001. "Measure for Measure: Law, Prerogative, Subversion," 13 *Cardozo Stud. L. & Literature* 221.

Hammer, Paul E. J. 1992. "An Elizabethan Spy Who Came in from the Cold: The Return of Anthony Standen to England in 1593," *Historical Research* 65: 277–95.

―――. 1999. *The Polarisation of Elizabethan Politics: The Political Career of Robert Devereux, 2nd Earl of Essex, 1585–1597*. Cambridge: Cambridge University Press.

Handover, P. M. 1957. *Arbella Stuart, Royal Lady of Hardwick and Cousin to King James*. London: Eyre & Spottiswoode.

―――. 1959. *The Second Cecil 1563–1604*. London: Eyre & Spottiswoode.

Harley, John. 1997. *William Byrd: Gentleman of the Chapel Royal*. Aldershot, England: Scolar Press.

Hasler, P. W. 1981. *The House of Commons, 1558–1603*, 3 vols. London: Her Majesty's Stationery Office.

Haynes, Alan. 1994. *The Gunpowder Plot*. Stroud, England: A Sutton.

Heath, Charles. 1806. *Historical and Descriptive Accounts of the Ancient and Present State of Ragland Castle*. Monmouth: Printed and sold by him, in the market place.

Herford, C. H., P. Simpson, and E. M. Simpson. *Ben Jonson*, eds. 1925. 11 vols. Oxford, 1925–52, cited as Herford and Simpson.

Hervey, M. 1921. *Life and Correspondence and Collections of Thomas Howard, Earl of Arundel*. University Press: Cambridge.

Heywood, Thomas. 1612. *An Apology for Actors*. London: Okes.

Hicks, Leo, SJ. 1942. *Letters and Memorials of Father Robert Persons SJ*. London, Catholic Record Society no. 39.

―――. 1955. "Sir Robert Cecil, Father Parsons and the Sucession," *Archivum Historicum Sociatatus Iesu* 24:95–139.

―――. 1957-8. "Father Robert Persons, S. J. and the Book of Succession," *Recusant History*, 4: 104–37.

―――. 1960. "The Embassy of Sir Anthony Standen," *Recusant History*, 5: 91–127; 184–222.

―――. 1963. "The Exile of Dr William Gifford from Lille in 1606," *Recusant History*, 7 214–38.

―――. 1964. *An Elizabethan Problem: Some Aspects of the Careers of Two Exiled Adventurers*. New York: Fordham University Press.

Hodgetts, Michael. 1999. "The Owens of Oxford." *Recusant History*, 24:415–30.

Hogge, Alice. 2002. "Closing the Circle: Nicholas Owen and Walter Owen of Oxford," *Recusant History*, 26:291–300.

―――. 2005. *God's Secret Agents*. New York: Harper.

Holleran, James V. 1999. *A Jesuit Challenge: Edmund Campion's Debates at the Tower of London in 1581*. New York: Fordham University Press.

Holmes, Peter J., ed. 1980. "The Authorship and Early Reception of a Conference About the Next Succession to the Crown of England," *The Historical Journal*, 23:415–429.

―――. 1981. *Elizabethan Casuistry*. London, Catholic Record Society no. 67.

―――. 1982. *Resistance and Compromise: The Political Thought of the Elizabethan Catholics*. Cambridge [Cambridgeshire]: Cambridge University Press.

Honan, Park. 2005. *Christopher Marlowe: Poet and Spy*. Oxford: Oxford University Press.

Hood, Christobel M. 1926. *The Book of Robert Southwell: Priest, Poet, Prisoner*. Oxford: Oxford University Press.

Hotson, Leslie. 1937. *I, William Shakespeare*. London: J. Cape.

―――. 1954. *The First Night of Twelfth Night*. London: R. Hart-Davis.

―――. 1952. *Shakespeare's Motley*. Oxford: Oxford University Press.

Howard, Charles. 1817. *Historical Anecdotes of some of the Howard Family*. New edition. L.P. W. Clarke: London.

Howard, Henry. 1834. *Indications of Memorials, Monuments, Paintings, and Engravings of Persons of the Howard Family, and of Their Wives and Children ... [etc.]*. Corby Castle: [publisher not identified].

―――. 1857. *The Lives of Philip Howard, Earl of Arundel and of Anne Dacre, His Wife*. London: Hurst and Blackett.

Howell, Thomas Bayley, ed. 1809. *Cobbett's Complete Collection of State Trials and Proceedings for High Treason and Other Crimes and Misdemeanors*, 2 vols. London: T C. Hansard.

Hubault, Gustave. 1856. *Michel De Castelnau: Ambassadeur En Angleterre*. Paris: Impr. Belin.

Hume, Martin A. S., ed. 1899. *Calendar of State Papers Relating to English Affairs. Spain*. London, HMSO.

―――. 1901. *Treason and Plot; Struggles for Catholic Supremacy in the Last Years of Queen Elizabeth*. London: J. Nisbet.

Hurault, André, Sieur de Maisse. 1931. *A Journal of All That Was Accomplished by Monsieur De Maisse Ambassador in England from King Henri IV to Queen Elizabeth Anno Domini 1597*, G. B. Harrison and R. A. Jones, eds. Bloomsbury [London]: Nonesuch Press.

Hutchinson, Robert. 2007. *Elizabeth's Spy Master: Francis Walsingham and the Secret War That Saved England*. London: Phoenix.

Inns of Court (London), and Charles Henry Hopwood. 1903. *A Calendar of the Middle Temple Records*. Edited by C.H. Hopwood.

Israel, Jonathan. 1997. *Conflicts of Empires: Spain, the Low Countries and the Struggle for World Supremacy*. London: Hambledon.

Janelle, Pierre. 1935. *Robert Southwell the Writer: A Study in Religious Inspiration*. New York: Sheed & Ward, Inc.

Jardine, David. 1846. *Criminal Trials*, 2 vols. London: M. A. Nattali.

_____, ed. 1851. [Garnet's] *Treatise on Equivocation*. London: Longman, Brown, Green, and Longmans.

Jardine, Lisa and Alan Stewart. 1999. *Hostage to Fortune: The Troubled Life of Francis Bacon, 1561–1626*. New York: Hill and Wang.

Jeaffreson, J. C., ed. 1887. *Middlesex County Records*, 4 vols. London: Middlesex County Records Society.

Jenkins, Gladys. 1947. "The Archpriest Controversy and the Printers, 1601–1603," *The Library*, V [5th series], 2:180–86.

Jones, Deborah. 1933. "Lodowick Bryskett and His Family," pp. 243–362, in Charles J. Sisson, ed. *Thomas Lodge and Other Elizabethans*. Cambridge, Mass.

Jones, Emrys. 1977. *The Origins of Shakespeare*. Oxford: Oxford University Press.

Kamen, Henry. 1997. *Philip of Spain*. New Haven: Yale University Press.

Kaula, David. 1975. *Shakespeare and the Archpriest Controversy*. The Hague: Mouton.

Kelly, Christine. 1987. *Blessed Thomas Belson: His Life and Times 1563–1589*. Gerrards Cross: Colin Smythe.

Kelsey, Harry. 1998. *Sir Francis Drake*. New Haven: Yale University Press.

Kenny, Anthony. 1982. "Reform and Reaction in Elizabethan Balliol, 1559–1588," in John Prest, ed. *Balliol Studies*, 17–52. London: Leopard's Head Pr.

Kilroy, Gerard. 2005. *Edmund Campion: Memory and Transcription*. Aldershot: Ashgate.

Kingsford, Lethbridge. 1923. "Essex House, Formerly Leicester House and Exeter Inn," *Archaeologia* 73: 1–54.

Klause, John. 2000. "Politics, Heresy, and Martyrdom in Shakespeare's Sonnet 124 and *Titus Andronicus*," in Schiffer, James, ed. 2000. *Shakespeare's Sonnets: Critical Essays*. New York: Garland. 219–40.

_____. 2002. "*The Phoenix and Turtle* in Its Time," in Moisan, Thomas and Bruster, Douglas, eds. 2002. *In the Company of Shakespeare: Essays in Honor of G. Blakemore Evans*. Madison [NJ]: Farleigh Dickinson University Press. 206–229.

_____. 2008. *Shakespeare, the Earl and the Jesuit*. Madison [NJ]: Fairleigh Dickinson University Press.

Knight, Ellen E. 1980. "*The Praise of Music*: John Case, Thomas Watson, and William Byrd," *Current Musicology*, 30: 37–51.

Knox, Thomas Francis, ed. 1878. *The First and Second Diaries of the English College, Douay*. London: D. Nutt.

Labanoff, Alexandre, ed. 1844. *Lettres. Instructions et Mémoires De Marie Stuart. Reine d'Écosse*, 7 vols. London.

Lacey, Robert. 1971. *Robert, Earl of Essex*. New York: Atheneum.

LaRocca, John. 1984. "'Who Can't Pray with Me Can't Love Me': Toleration and Early Jacobean Recusant Policy, "*Journal of British Studies* 23: 22–36.

Law, Thomas Graves. 1896. the *Archpriest Controversy: Documents Relating to the Dissensions of the Roman Catholic Clergy, 1597–1602*, 2 Vols. London: Camden Society.

_____. 1889. a *Historical Sketch of the Conflicts Between Jesuits and Seculars in the Reign of Queen Elizabeth*. London: D. Nutt.

Lawrence, W. J. 1928. *Shakespeare's Workshop*. Oxford: B. Blackwell.

Lee, A. G. 1964. *The Son of Leicester*. London: Gollancz.

Lee, Maurice, ed. 1972. *Dudley Carleton to John Chamberlain, 1603–24*. New Brunswick, N.J.: Rutgers University Press.

Lefèvre, Joseph. 1925. "Juan De Mancicidor, Sécretaire D'état Et De Guerre De L'archiduc Albert, 1596–1618," *Revue Belge De Philologie Et D'histoire*, 4: 697–714.

Lennon, Colm. 1981. *Richard Stanihurst*. Blackrock, County Dublin: Irish Academic Press.

Lewis, C. S. 1954. *English Literature in the Sixteenth Century Excluding Drama*. Oxford: Clarendon Press.

Lindley, David. 1998. *Court Masques: Jacobean and Caroline Entertainments, 1605–1640*. Oxford: Oxford University Press.

Lloyd, David, and Charles Whitworth. 1766. *State Worthies* [originally *The Statesmen and Favourites of England*. 1665]. London: Printed for J. Robson.

Loades, David. 2007. *The Cecils: Privilege and Power Behind the Throne*. Kew: National Archives.

Lodge, Edmund. 1838. *Illustrations of British History*, 3 vols. 2d ed. London: J. Chidley.

Lonchay, Henri, and Joseph Cuvelier. *Correspondance De La Cour d'Espagne Sur Les Affaires Des Pays-Bas Au XVII Siècle*, 6 vols. Brussels, 1923–30. Cited as Lonchay & Cuvelier.

Loomie, Albert J. 1963a. *The Spanish Elizabethans*. London: Burns & Oates.

_____. 1963b. "Toleration and Diplomacy," *Transactions of the American Philosophical Society*, n. s., 53/6. 1963.

_____. 1965a. "Richard Stanyhurst in Spain: Two Unknown Letters of August 1593," *Huntington Lib. Q.* 28: 145–55. 1965.

_____. 1965b. "Philip III and the Stuart Succession in England, 1600–1603," *Revue Belge De Philologie Et d'Histoire*, 43: 492–514.

_____. 1969. "Sir Robert Cecil and the Spanish Embassy," *Bulletin of the Institute of Historical Research* 42: 30–57.

_____. 1971a. "Guy Fawkes in Spain," *Bulletin of the Institute of Historical Research* Special Supplement No. 9.

_____. 1971b. "King James I's Catholic consort," *Huntington Lib. Q.*, 34:303–16.

_____. 1972. "Thomas James: The English Consul of Andalucia," *Recusant History* 11:165–178.

_____. 1973a. "Francis Fowler II, English Secretary of the Spanish Embassy, 1609" *Recusant History*, 12/2 pp. 70–78.

_____. 1973b. *Spain and the Jacobean Catholics*, vol. I: *1603–1612*. Catholic Record Society no. 64

Loomis, Catherine. 1996. "Elizabeth Southwell's Manuscript Account of the Death of Queen Elizabeth I. With Text." *English Literary Renaissance* 26. 3: 482–509.

Macray, William Dunn. 1897. *The Register of the Members of St. Mary Magdalen College, Oxford*, vol. II. *Fellows 1522–1575*. London: Frowde.

_____. 1901. III. *Fellows 1576–1648. A Register of the Members of St Mary Magdalen College, Oxford*. London: Frowde.

Madan, Falconer. 1895. *The Early Oxford Press*. Oxford: The Clarendon Press.

Marañon, Gregorio. 1953. *Antonio Perez*, Charles D. Ley, trans. New York.

Martin, Patrick H. and Finnis, John M. 2002a. "The Identity of 'Anthony Rivers,'" *Recusant History* 26: 39–74.

_____. 2002b "Tyrwhitt of Kettleby, Part I: Goddard Tyrwhitt, Martyr, 1580," *Recusant History* 26: 301–313.

_____. 2003a. "Thomas Thorpe, 'W. S,' and the Catholic Intelligencers," *English Literary Renaissance* 33: 1–43.

_____. 2003b. "*Caesar*, Succession, and the Chastisement of Rulers," *Notre Dame Law Review* 78: 1045–1074

_____. 2003c. "Tyrwhitt of Kettleby, Part II: Robert Tyrwhitt, a Main Benefactor of John Gerard SJ, 1599–1605," *Recusant History* 27: 556–569

_____. 2005. "Benedicam Dominum: Ben Jonson's Strange 1605 Inscription," *Times Literary Supplement*, November 4th, 12–13,

_____. 2006. "The Secret Sharers: 'Anthony Rivers' and the Appellant Controversy, 1601–2," *Huntingdon Library Quarterly* 69/2: 195–237.

Mateer, David. 1997. "William Byrd, John Petre and Oxford Bodleian Ms Mus. Scholar. E. 42,. " *Research Chronicle of the Royal Musical Association* 29: 21–46.

Mathias, Roland. 1963. *Whitsun Riot*. London: Bowes & Bowes.

Mattingly, Garrett. 1957. "William Allen and Catholic Propaganda," in *Aspects De La Propagande Religieuse*. Geneva: Droz. 325–339.

_____. 1959. *The Armada*. Boston: Houghton Mifflin.

McClure, Norman Egbert, ed. 1979. *The Letters of John Chamberlain*. 2 vols. Westport, Conn.: Greenwood Press.

McCoog, Thomas M. 1988. "'The Slightest Suspicion of Avarice': The Finances of the English Jesuit Mission," *Recusant History* 19: 103–23.

_____. 1994. *English and Welsh Jesuits, 1555–1650*, 2 vols. Catholic Record Society nos. 74–75.

_____. 1996a. *The Society of Jesus in Ireland, Scotland, and England, 1541–1588*. Leiden: E.J. Brill.

_____. 1996b. "'Playing the Champion': The Role of Disputation in the Jesuit Mission," *The Reckoned Expense*, McCoog, ed. Woodbridge, Suffolk: Boydell Press.

McDonald, James H. and Nancy Pollard Brown, eds. 1967. *The Poems of Robert Southwell*. Oxford: Clarendon Press.

McGrath, Patrick. 1967. *Papists and Puritans Under Elizabeth I*. London: Blandford Press.

McIlwain, Charles Howard, ed. 1918. *The Political Works of James I*. Cambridge, Mass.: Harvard University Press.

Milward, Peter. 1973. *Shakespeare's Religious Background*. Bloomington: Indiana University Press.

_____. 1977. *Religious Controversies of the Elizabethan Age: A Survey of Printed Sources*. Lincoln: University of Nebraska Press.

_____. 2005. *Shakespeare the Papist*. Naples, Fla.: Sapientia Press of the Ave Maria University.

Montagu, Ewen. 1954. *The Man Who Never Was*. Philadelphia: Lippincott.

Morris, John, ed. 1871. *The Conditions of Catholics Under James I. Father Gerard's Narrative of the Gunpowder Plot*. London: Longmans, Green, & Co.

_____, ed. 1874. *The Letter-Books of Sir Amias Poulet*. London: Pickering and Co.

_____. 1875. *The Troubles of Our Catholic Forefathers, Second Series. "The Life of Father William Weston, S. J."* London: Burns and Oates.

_____. 1881.*The Life of Father John Gerard*. London: Burns and Oates.

Motley, John Lothrop. 1871. *History of the United Netherlands. 1590–1600*, vol. 3. New York: Harper & Brothers.

Munday, Anthony. 1587. "*A Discoverie of Edmund Campion*" in *Holinshed's Chronicles of England*, Vol. 4. London: Johnson [u.a.].

Neale, Sir John Ernest. 1953. *Elizabeth I and her Parliaments*. London: Cape.

Newdigate, C. A. 1931. "A New Chapter in the Life of B. Robert Southwell, S. J.," *The Month* 157: 246–54.

Nicholl, Charles. 1992. *The Reckoning: The Murder of Christopher Marlowe*. London: Jonathan Cape.

Nicholls, Mark. 1991. *Investigating Gunpowder Plot*. Manchester [u.a.]: Manchester University Press.

_____. 1995a. "Sir Walter Ralegh's Treason: A Prosecution Document. " *English Historical Review* 110:902–924.

_____. 1995b. "Treason's Reward: The Punishment of Conspirators in the Bye Plot of 1603," *The Historical Journal* 38/4:821–42.

_____. 1995c. "Two Winchester Trials: The Prosecution of Henry Brooke, Lord Cobham, and Thomas Lord Grey of Wilton, 1603," *Institute of Historical Research*, 68: 26–48.

Nichols, John. 1827. *The Progresses and Public Pro-*

cessions of Queen Elizabeth. London: Printed by and for John Nichols and Son .

Parker, Geoffrey. 1972. *The Army of Flanders and the Spanish Road 1567-1659*. Cambridge: Cambridge University Press.

———. 1979. *Spain and the Netherlands, 1559-1659*. Short Hills, N.J.: Enslow Publishers.

———. 1998. *The Grand Strategy of Philip II*. New Haven: Yale University Press.

Parmelee, Lisa Ferraro. 1994. "Printers, Patrons, Readers, and Spies: Importation of French Propaganda in Late Elizabethan England," *Sixteenth Century Journal*, 25: 853-72.

Parmiter, Geoffrey de C. 1975. "Plowden, Englefield and Sandford: I," *Recusant History* 13:159-177.

———. 1977. "Plowden, Englefield and Sandford: II," *Recusant History* 14:9-25.

Parsons, Robert. 1973. An Epistle of the Persecution of Catholickes in Englande (1582) [by] Robert Persons. [Menston]: [Scolar P.].

———, and Humphrey Leech. 1973. A Manifestation of the Great Folly, 1602. Menston [England]: Scolar Press.

Paul, Henry N. 1950. *The Royal Play of Macbeth*. New York: Octagon Books.

Petti, Anthony G., 1957. *A Study of the Life and Writings of Richard Verstegan*. c. 1550-1640. thesis London University.

———. 1958. "Peter Philips, Composer and Organist, 1561-1628," *Recusant History* 4: 48-60.

———. 1963. "A Bibliography of the Writings of Richard Verstegan. C. 1550-1641." *Recusant History* 7: 82-103.

———, ed. 1959. *The Letters and Despatches of Richard Verstegan*. London: Catholic Record Society no. 52.

Phillimore, W. P. W., ed. 1888. *Visitations of Worcestershire, 1569*. London: Harleian Society, 1888.

———. 1890. *An Index to the Bills of Privy Signet*. London: Printed for the British Record Society, 1890.

Plummer, Charles, ed. 1887. *Elizabethan Oxford: Reprints of Rare Tracts*. Oxford: Clarendon Press.

Pollen, John Hungerford. 1903a. "The Accession of King James I," *The Month* 101: 572-85;

———. 1903b. "The Question of Elizabeth's Successor," *The Month* 101: 517-32.

———. 1904. "Dr. William Gifford in 1586," *The Month* 103:243-56, 348-66.

———. 1908. *Unpublished Documents Relating to the English Martyrs*. London, Catholic Record Society no. 5.

———. 1914. "Introduction," *Campion's Ten Reasons*. London. 1-29.

———.1916. *The Institution of the Archpriest Blackwell*. London: Longmans, Green.

———. 1922. *Mary Queen of Scots and the Babington Plot*. Edinburgh: Printed by T. and A. Constable for the Scottish History Society.

———, Philip Howard Arundel, and William MacMahon. 1919. *The Ven. Philip Howard, Earl of Arundel, 1557-1595: English martyrs, vol. II*. London: Privately printed for the Society by Harrison & Sons.

Poulton, Diana. 1982. *John Dowland*. Berkeley, Calif: University of California Press.

Prior, Roger. 2000. "Gascoigne's *Posies* as a Shakespearian Source," *Notes and Queries* 245: 444-49.

Pritchard, Arnold. 1979. *Catholic Loyalism in Elizabethan England*. Chapel Hill: University of North Carolina Press.

Questier, Michael. 1997. "Loyalty, Religion and State Power in Early Modern England: English Romanism and the Jacobean Oath of Allegiance," *The Historical Journal*, 40/2. Jun., 1997. 311-329.

———. 2006. *Catholicism and Community in Early Modern England*. Cambridge, UK: Cambridge University Press.

Q. Z. 1584. "A Discoverie of the Treasons Practised and Attempted Against the Queenes Maiestie and the Realme, by Francis Throckmorton." June 15, 1584. reprinted *Harleian Miscellany* 3:182-93. London, 1745.

Ralegh, Walter, Agnes M. C. Latham, and Joyce A. Youings. 1999. *The Letters of Sir Walter Ralegh*. Exeter: University of Exeter Press.

Rawson, Maud Stepney. 1911. *Penelope Rich and Her Circle*. London: Hutchinson & Co.

Read, Conyers. 1925. *Mr. Secretary Walsingham and the Policy of Queen Elizabeth*. 3 vols. Oxford: Clarendon Press.

Renold, Penelope. 1958. *The Wisbech Stirs*. London, Catholic Record Society no. 51.

———. 1967. *Letters of William Allen and Richard Barret, 1572-1598*. London, Catholic Record Society no. 58.

Riggs, David. 1989. *Ben Jonson*. Cambridge, Mass.: Harvard University Press.

Robinson, John Martin. 1995. *The Dukes of Norfolk*. Chichester, West Sussex: Phillimore.

Rowse, A. L. 1965. *Times, Persons, Places*. London: Macmillan.

Ryland, John William. 1922. *Records of Rowington*. Vol. II, Vol. II.

Salisbury, Robert Cecil, George Carew Totnes, and John Maclean. 1864. *Letters from Sir Robert Cecil to Sir George Carew*. [Westminster]: Printed for the Camden Society.

Sawyer, Edmund, ed. 1725. [Ralph Winwood]. *Memorials of Affairs of State in the Reigns of Queen Elizabeth and King James* I, 3 vols. London: Ward.

Schmitt, Charles B. 1983. *John Case and Aristotelianism in Renaissance England*. Kingston [Ont.]: McGill-Queen's University Press.

Schoenbaum, Samuel. 1975. *William Shakespeare: A Documentary Life*. Oxford: Clarendon Press.

Scott, Harold Spencer, ed. 1902 *The Journal of Sir Roger Wilbraham*. London: Officers of the Royal Historical Society.

Schrickx, Willem. 1986. *Foreign Envoys and Traveling Players in the Age of Shakespeare and Jonson*. Wetteren: Universa.

Seiden, Melvin. 1990. *Measure for Measure: Casuistry and Artistry*. Washington, D. C.: Catholic University of America Press.

Simpson, Richard. 1867. *Edmund Campion: A Biography*. Edinburgh:Williams and Norgate.

———. 1896. *Edmund Campion: A Biography*. London: John Hodges.

———, and Henry Sebastian Bowden. 1889. *The Religion of Shakespeare*. London: Burns & Oates.

Smith, Alan Gordon. 1936. *The Babington Plot*. London: Macmillan.

Smith, J. C. and E. De Selincourt. 1912. *The Poetical Works of Edmund Spenser*. Oxford: Oxford University Press.

Sorlien, Robert Parker. 1976. *The Diary of John Manningham of the Middle Temple 1602–1603*. Hanover, N. H.: Published for the University of Rhode Island by the University Press of New England.

Southern, A. C. 1950. *Elizabethan Recusant Prose, 1559–1582*. London: Sands.

Southwell, Robert. 1953. *An Humble Supplication to Her Majestie*, R. C. Bald, ed. Cambridge.

Spedding, James, Robert L. Ellis, and Douglas D. Heath. 1857-74. *The Works of Francis Bacon*. London: Longman.

Spedding, James, ed. 1861. *Letters and Life of Francis Bacon*, 2 vols. London: Longman.

Stevenson, W. H. & Sadler, H. E. 1939. *The Early History of St. John's College Oxford*. Oxford: Oxford Historical Society.

Stone, Lawrence. 1948. "The Anatomy of the Elizabethan Aristocracy," *Economic History Review* 18: 1-53.

———.1956. *An Elizabethan: Horatio Palavicino*. Oxford: Clarendon Press.

———. 1965. *Crisis of the Aristocracy*. Oxford: Clarendon Press.

Strong, Roy. 1977. *The Cult of Elizabeth: Elizabethan Portraiture and Pageantry*. London: Thames & Hudson.

Strickland, Agnes. 1858. *Lives of the Queens of Scotland*, VII. Edinburgh and London: Blackwood.

Strype, John. 1821. *The Life and Acts of John Aylmer*. Oxford: Clarendon Press.

———. 1824. *Annals of the Reformation*, 4 vols. Oxford: Clarendon Press.

Teague, Frances. 1998. "Jonson and the Gunpowder Plot." *Ben Jonson Journal* 5: 249–252.

Thornbury, Walter. 1873. *Old and New London: A Narrative of Its History, Its People, and Its Places*, 3 vols. London: Cassell, Petter, & Galpin.

Tierney, M. A. *Dodd's Church History of England*, 5 vols. London: C. Dolman, 1839-43. cited as Tierney-Dodd vol. :page.

Trappes-Lomax, T. B. 1951. "The Englefields and Their Contribution to the Survival of the Faith in Berkshire, Wiltshire, Hampshire and Leicestershire" *Biographical Studies. Recusant History*. 2: 131–148.

Trimble, W. R. 1964. *The Catholic Laity in Elizabethan England*. Cambridge.

Ungerer, Gustav. 1976. *A Spaniard in Elizabethan England: The Correspondence of Antonio Perz's Exile*, 2 vols. London:Tamesis Books.

Usher, Roland G. 1910. *Reconstruction of the English Church*. New York: D. Appleton.

Vickers, Brian. 1996. *Francis Bacon: A Critical Edition of the Major Works*. Oxford: Oxford University Press.

van Wyhe, Cordula. 2004. "Court and Convent: The Infanta Isabella and Her Franciscan Confessor, Andrés De Soto," *The Sixteenth Century Journal* 35: 411–45.

Wadsworth, James. 1629. *The English Spanish Pilgrim*. London.

Walsham, Alexandra. 1993. *Church Papists: Catholicism, Conformity and Confessional Polemic in Early Modern England*. Woodbridge, Suffolk, UK: Boydell Press.

———. 1999. *Providence in Early Modern England*. Oxford: Oxford University Press.

Ward, G. R. M., ed. 1840. *The Statutes of Magdalen College Oxford Now First Translated and Published*. Oxford and London.

Waugh, Evelyn. 1961. *Edmund Campion, Jesuit and Martyr*. London: longmans, Green & Co.

Wernham, R. B. 1976. "Christopher Marlowe at Flushing in 1592," *English Historical Review* 91: 344–5.

———. 1987. "Queen Elizabeth I, Emperor Rudolph II and Archduke Ernest," in E. I. Kouri & Tom Scott, eds. *Politics and Society in Reformation Europe*. London: Macmillan, 1987. 437–52.

———. 1994. *The Return of the Armadas: The Last Years of the Elizabethan War Against Spain 1595–1603*. Oxford: Clarendon Press.

Wilcox, John. 1941. "Putting Jaques into 'As You Like It,'" *Modern Language Review* 36: 388–394.

Willaert, Leopold. 1905. "Negotiations Politico-Religieuses Entre l'Angleterre Et Les Pays-Has Catholiques. 1598-1625. D'apres Les Papiers D'etat Et De L'audience Conserves Aux Archives Générales Du Royaume De Belgique a Bruxelles," *Revue D. Histoire Ecclésiastique*, vi. 1905 47–54, 566–581, 811–826; vii. 1906 585–607; viii. 1907 81–101, 305–311, 514–532; iv. 1908 52–61, 736–745.

Williams, Neville. 1964. *Thomas Howard Fourth Duke of Norfolk*. London: Barrie & Rockliffe.

Williamson, Hugh Ross. 1951. *The Gunpowder Plot*. London: Faber and Faber.

Williamson, J. Bruce. 1924. *The History of the Temple, London*. London: J. Murray.

Willson, David Harris. 1956. *King James VI and I*. London: Jonathan Cape.

Wilson, Derek. 2007. *Sir Francis Walsingham: A Courtier in an Age of Terror*. London: Constable.

Wilson, Thomas. 1936. "The state of England anno dom. 1600," ed. F. J. Fisher. *Camden Miscellany, XVI*, CS, 3rd ser., 52. London: Camden Society.

Wood, Anthony à, and Philip Bliss. 1820. *Athenae Oxonienses: an Exact History of all the Writers and Bishops Who have had Their Education in the University of Oxford* 4. 4. London: Rivington.

Woodfield, Denis B. 1973 *Surreptitious Printing in England, 1550–1640*. New York: Bibliographical Society of America, 1973.

Yates, Frances A. 1934. *John Florio: The Life of an Italian in Shakespeare's England*. Cambridge: Cambridge University Press.

_____. 1964. *Giordano Bruno and the Hermetic Tradition*. London, Routledge & Kegan Paul.

Index

Page numbers in ***bold italics*** indicate pages with illustrations.

Agnus dei 66, 256
Alabaster, William 145
Alba, Duke of 22
Albert (Hapsburg), Archduke 131, 152–54, 162–64, 166–68, 171–72, 175–78, 218, 223–25, 228–33, 257–60, 265, 286
Aldobrini, Cardinal 246
Aldred, Solomon 42, 54–55, 57
Alfield, Thomas 13, 14
Allen, William 2, 7, 19, 25, 29, 30, 36, 53, 55, 60, 71, 72, 73, 76, 77, 78, 84, 93, 103, 126, 129, 130, 131, 15, 137, 138, 148, 194, 223, 234, 247
Alleyn, Edward 84
Allison, Thomas 247
Andrew, Cardinal 175–77
Angelo (*Measure*) 249–57
Anjou, Duke of 42
Anne, Queen (Stewart) 139, 226, 239–40, 257, 259–60
Annias, John 120–27
Antonio, Dom, Prior of Crato (Portuguese pretender) 70, 75
Appellants 165, 194–207, 235
Archer, Fr. James 121–22
Archpriest 165, 194–207, 224, 272–73, 284, 288
Arenberg, Count *see* Ligne, Charles de
Arnault, Jean seigneur de Cherelles 35
Arundell, Charles 31, 34, 53, 61, 70, 75, 294, 295, 297
Audley, Thomas 39
Ayliffe, Richard 88, 92–93, 97–98, 109, 125
Aylmer, John 58, 195

Babington, Anthony 47, 50, 54, 56–59, 61, 63, 65–66, 73, 115, 202
Babington Plot 21, 31–32, 34–36, 50–52, 55, 57–60, 62, 67, 69–70, 72, 86, 91, 104, 137, 168, 170, 173, 202, 219, 239
Bacon, Ann 117
Bacon, Anthony 81, 100, 117–18, 153
Bacon, Sir Francis 53, 81, 85, 87, 100, 104–05, 113, 116–18, 120, 123, 125, 129, 147, 186–87, 267
Bacon, Nathaniel 100

Bagshaw, Christopher 193–95, 201, 205
Baines, Richard 57
Baldwin, Fr. William 129, 172, 207, 212, 222, 225, 231–32, 235, 283–87
Bales, Christopher 74
Ball, John 265, 282–84
Ballard, Fr. John 34, 50–51, 54–55, 61–6, 137, 168, 173
Bancroft, Richard Bishop 191, 193–203, 205–06, 273–74
Barker, Edward 61
Barkworth, Fr. Mark 255, 289
Barnes, Thomas 34, 51, 55–56, 82, 132–33, 167, 169, 171, 193, 265, 280–81, 283, 286
Barnwell, Robert 54
Barrett, Richard 25
Barrowes/Barwise, Robert 123, 197–98, 207
Basilikon Doron 254, 256
Bassett, William 44, 111–12, 157
Bates, Thomas **275**
Bayley, Richard 129, 178
Bedford, Earl of 12, 190
Bedford, Lady 241
Beesley, George 74
Bellamy, Robert 89, 91, 142
Bennet, Bishop Robert 271–74, 341
Bennet, Fr. William 77
Bentivoglio, Guido 259
Berden, Nicholas 42, 44, 51–53, 56, 62, 67, 69, 72, 76
Berkeley, Sir Richard 129
Berlaymount, Count 96–97
Birkbeck, Fr. William 98
Birket/Burkett, Fr. George 105, 108–10
Bisley, Reinhold 101, 102–04, 106, 108–10, 135
Blackwell, Fr. George 44, 85, 194–95, 206, 221, 224, 230, 272, 281, 287–88
Bloody Question 141–42, 144, 251, 253
Blount, Sir Charles, Lord Mounjoy 146, ***236***
Blount, Sir Christopher 52, 146, 191–92
Bluet, Fr. Thomas 194–95, 198, 201
Bodenham, Sir Roger 273–74
Boleyn, Anne 40

Bolt, John 143–44
Bond of Association 36, 37, 51, 63, 65
Borghese, Cardinal 202
Borromeo, Cardinal Carlo 7
Boulant, Jaques (alias) 161–62, 164, 167–68, 175, 177, 180–185, 13, 218, 227–28, 233, 263, 268, 286
Bowes, Robert 133, 138
Briant, Fr. Alexander 13, 14, 141, 255, 289
Brooke, George 219–20
Brooke, Henry, 11th Baron Cobham 23, 47–48, 53, 144, 149, 162, 180–81, 184–85, 197, 219–21, 233, 256
Browne, Edward 84
Browne, Mary (Wriothesley), Countess of Southampton 93, 151, 157
Browne, Robert 247
Brydges Eleanor 19
Brydges, Edmund 19
Buc, George 239–40
Buc, Robert 239
Buckhurst, Lord *see* Sackville, Thomas
Bunny, Edmund 7
Burghert, Gerard (alias) 169, 171
Burghley, Lord *see* Cecil, William
Burgundian Jewels 177, 0179, 180–85, 197, 220, 268, 283–84
Bussy/Bushy, Sir John 82
Bye Plot 185, 218–21, 225–26
Byfield, William 46
Byrd, William 14, 15, 86, 139, 144, 186, 253

Cadwallader, Roger 271
Cahill, Hugh 120–27
Cajetan, Cardinal 170–71, 194–95, 317
Campion, Fr. Edmund 6–*14*, 15, 20, 38–42, 54, 69, 97, 104, 141, 143, 145, 150, 246, 255, 289
Campion's Brag 10, 12–3
Carey, George, Lord Hunsdon, Lord Chamberlain ***190***, 212
Carey, Henry, Lord Hunsdon, Lord Chamberlain 35, 47–8, 60
Carmarthen, Richard 128, 159, 168
Case, Dr. John 26, 28, 211, 271
Castelnau, Michel de, Sieur de la

353

Mauvissière 25, 26–28, 32–35, 45–49, 82, 91
Catesby, Robert 221, 226, *275*–79
Catholic League 55, 81
Cecil, Fr. John 73, 140, 195
Cecil, Sir Robert, Viscount Cranborne, Earl of Salisbury 3, 59, *79*, 80–81, 87, 102, 104, 107, 116–17, 120–25, 128, 134–35, 138–40, 143, 148, 150, 159, 161–64, 166–85, 187–89, 192–208, 210–15, 218–20, 227–30, 232–33, *236*, 241, 247, 262–70, 272–74, 76–87
Cecil, William, Lord Burghley 36, 43, 63–65, 69–70, 72, 75, 79–81, 87, 92, 92, 99, 101, 103–04, 106, 109, 114, 117, 121–22, 124, 126–28, 131, 133–36, 138–40, 144–45, 150–51, 169, 175–76, 186, 188
Chadderton, Henry 43
Chaloner, Sir Thomas 241, 247
Chambers, E. K. 238–39
Champney, Anthony 195–96, 247
Charke, William 10
Charles IX, King (France) 28
Chassaigne, Girault de la (Jero) 45–48
Châteauneuf, Guillaume de l'Aubespine, Baron de 33, 35, 46, 49, 52, 56, 64, 69
Cherelles *see* Arnault
Christoval, Don Count Mondragon 96, 100, 103–04, 121
Cicero 11, 84
Clark, Fr. Thomas 112
Clark, Fr. William 219
Claudio (*Measure*) 249–53, 255
Clement VIII, Pope 235
Clifford, George, Earl of Cumberland *190*, 209, 228–29, 231, 233
Clifford's Inn 39
Clitheroe/Clitherow, Margaret 13, *141*, 252
Clitheroe/Clitherow, Fr. William 134, 172, 310
Cloudsley, Fr. Peter 97, 109
Cloudsley, Thomas 97, 104–05, 107–10, 115
Coemans, Jerome 175, 77, 181–82, 186
Coke, Sir Edward 111, 117, 20, 123–25, 129, 143, 19, 195, 206, 214, 216, 219, 247, 264, 271, 276–77, 280, 285
Collen, Patrick 120-2
Comedy of Errors 260
Compton, Lord William 108
Conference about the Next Succession 132, 136–38, 169–70, 259
Copley, Anthony 155, 198, 203, 219, 226
Copley, Helen (Stanihurst) 98
Copley, Sir Thomas 98
Cordale, Francis (alias) 147, 164, 166
Corsini, Filippo 208
Courcelles, Mons. 26, 31, 42
Cowper, John 41
Coxe, Richard 83

Creswell, Fr. Joseph 221–23, 225, 246
Crichton, William 29
Critz, John de 79
Curll, Gilbert 34, 56, 65
Cutt, Robert 90–91

Dacre, Anne (Howard), Countess of Arundel 17, 20, 60, 66, 78, 192, 197–98, 228–30, 239, 242, 282, 285
Dacre, Elizabeth (Howard) 20
Dacre, Margaret (Sackville) 20, 77
Dacre, Thomas 20
Daniel, Samuel 241, 243
Daniell, John 104, 109–10, 115, 120–27, 170
Davison, William 185
Deane, Fr. William 76
Decem Rationes (Ten Reasons) 11–12, 76, 82
Denne, Edmund 46
Denny, Christopher 58
Devereaux, Robert, Earl of Essex 27, 71, 80–83, 85, 87–89, 91–93, 95, 97–98, 100–06, 108, 113–18, 120, 122–27, 130, 132, 140, 142–46, 148–52, 155–60, 162, 165, 169–70, 172, 179–80, 186–93, 213–14, 221, 241, 247, 263–68, 270
Digby, Sir Everard 275, 331
Dodwell, Thomas/Edward 35, 46–48, 60, 84
Dormer, Jane, Duchess of Feria 131, 150, 157
Dormer, Mary 131, 150, 157
Dormer, Sir Robert 157
Drake, Elizabeth 92
Drake, Sir Francis 68, 75, 92, 297
Drake, Richard 92
Dudley, Ambrose, Earl of Warwick 39
Dudley, Robert (son of Leicester) 110
Dudley, Robert, Earl of Leicester 6, 8, 12, 26–28, 39, 43, 52, 69, 74, 82, 245
Duke Vicentio (*Measure*) 249–59
Dunn, Henry 54
Dutton, Anthony (alias) 221, 223, 225

East, Dorothy (Fitzherbert) 14, 42, 70
Eaton, Fr. Reginald 226
Edlyno, Bernardo (alias) 166
Edmondes, Sir Thomas 170, 172, 176–78, 183–84, 280–82, 286
Edward IV, King 18, 82
Egerton, Sir Thomas 61, 123, 124, 140, 188, 191, 199, 212
Elizabeth I, Queen *see* Tudor, Elizabeth
Emerson, Ralph 7
Empresa, Enterprise 21, 29, 30–33, 35, 37, 51, 52, 61, 154, 170, 221–22
Englefield, Francis (nephew) 153, 155–59

Englefield, Sir Francis 31, 71, 108, 129, 131, 151–56, 221, 234
Englefield, John 153
English College, Rome 2, 10, 14, 23, 25, 34, 154, 222
Equivocation, doctrine 6, 74, 141–42, 253–54
Ernest, Archduke 137–39, 147–48, 152, 167
Errington, George 83, 273
Escobar, Antonio de 70

Fagot, Henry (alias) 25, 32–36, 45–46, 48–49, 56, 61, 90
Faille, Charles della 259
Fairfax, John 41
Fane, Sir Thomas 280–81
Farnese, Alessandro, Duke of Parma 54, 67–69, 72, 81, 86, 96–97, 102, 106, 109, 127, 133, 135–36, 148
Farnese, Prince Rainutio 132–37
Fawkes, Guy 50, 218, 221, 225, 229, 275–77, 279, 282, 285, 329, 330–31, 342–43, 348
Fenner, George (alias) 147, 164, 166
Feria, Duke of 131, 140, 144–45, 150–51, 154, 156, 182
Ferkin, Abraham 228, 265, 340
Ferrers, Thomas 96, 99–101, 104, 107, 115, 149
Field, Richard 117, 119
Fitton, Mary 124
Fitzalan, Henry, Earl of Arundel 43
Fitzherbert, Dorothy *see* East, Dorothy
Fitzherbert, Sir Anthony 41
Fitzherbert, Thomas 7, 11–12, 14, 41–43, 47, 52–53, 70–71, 75, 78, 86, 89–90, 93, 96, 105–12, 115, 118, 129–32, 134, 137, 140, 144, 148–57, 163, 168, 207, 221, 263–64, 286, 288
Fitzwilliam, Mary (Shelley) (Guildford) 43, 98
Fleming, Thomas 129
Florio, John 26–27, 49, 241
Florio, Michael Angelo 26–27
Fortado, Mr. 182–84, 227, 320–21
Fortescue, Sir John 122, 127
Franceschi, Giacomo de (Capt. Jaques) 86, 121–24, 149–51, 172
Franceschi, Thomas 282, 284
Francis II, King (France) 26, 28
Francis/Frauncis, Clare 89
Francisca (*Measure*) 253, 258, 339
Frangipani, Ottavio 179, 324–25
Freeman (alias) *see* Spiller, Robert
Frizer, Ingram 115
Fulwood, John 197
Fulwood, Richard 197, 207, 266, 278, 283–85

Gage, Edward 44, 93
Gage, John 43–44, 186
Gage, Thomas 44

Gama, Estevan Ferrera de 123, 125
Garnet/Garnett, Fr. Henry 57, 73, 129–30, 142–4, 154, 160–61, 165, 192, 194, 197–99, 204, 206–7, 219, 221, 224, 229–33, 235, 239, 247, 254–55, 266, 269, 272, 276, 278, 280, 283–85, 288
Garret, Edward 121
Gatacre, Francis 41, 313
Gatacre, John 149–51, 157, 313
Gentleman Pensioner(s) 19, 23, 29, 59, 275
Gerard, Fr. John 47–48, 50, 73–74, 77, 129–30, 140–46, 192, 226, 232, 277, 279
Gerard, Sir Thomas 47, 142
Gifford, Edward 24
Gifford, George 2–3, 19, 23–24, 29–33, 35–37, 51, 54–55, 58–62
Gifford, Gilbert 19, 23–25, 31, 33–35, 42, 49–57, 60–61, 67, 69–70, 75–76, 193
Gifford, John 23
Gifford, Richard 19
Gifford, Dr. William 19, 23–5, 29–31, 33–34, 51, 54–55, 60–62, 67, 121, 133, 169, 172, 193–94, 280–81
Grant, John 275
Gratley, Edward 34, 51, 54–55, 60, 193
Gray, Sir Harry 110
Gray, Fr. Robert 112
Grays Inn 18, 30, 53, 279
Greene, Thomas 240, 247
Gregory XIII, Pope 7, 31
Greville, Fulke 16, 27–29
Grey, Jane 22, 27
Griffiths, Rice (alias) 273, 341
Grissold, John 255
Grissold, Robert 255
Guildford, Sir John 43
Guildford, Thomas 43
Guilford/Guildford, Sir Henry 43–44, 145, 186, 216
Guilford/Guildford, Richard 46, 98
Guise, Henry, Duke of 3, 26, 29–33, 35–37, 42, 51–52, 58–59, 61–62, 67, 70, 168, 170
Gunpowder Plot 1–3, 160, 221, 226, 229, 232, 266, 275–88
Gwinne, Matthew 27

Hallins/Halyns, Peter (alias) 98, 119, 147–48, 151–52, 158–67, 173, 176, 189, 193, 228, 269
Hamlet 80, 187, 251
Hanmer, Meredith 10
Harrison, Thomas 53, 57, 179
Hartley, Fr. William 11, 76, 289
Harvey, Francis 115, 132, 149
Hassenet, John 246–47, 336
Hatton, Sir Christopher 34, 65, 86, 150
Haynes, William 58
Heneage, Sir Thomas 93, 134, 135, 136, 164, 303, 311, 313
Henry III, King (France) 26–28, 42, 63, 67, 70

Henry IV, King (Navarre) 81, 90, 97, 116–17, 12, 167, 175, 208, 235
Henry V 260
Henry VII, King 22, 82, 126, 132
Henry VIII, King 17–18, 22, 40
Henslowe, Philip 233, 247
Herbert, William, Earl of Pembroke 124, 250
Hesketh, Richard 121, 125–27
Heywood, Fr. Jasper 61, 297
Heywood, Thomas 86, 334, 336
Higham/Heigham, William 91, 130–31, 140, 144, 147, 192, 264
Hilliard, Nicholas 135
Hoby, Sir Edward 111
Hodges, William 19
Hodgson (jailer) 29
Hodgson, Christopher 54
Holroyd, Michael 208
Holt, Fr. William 86, 94, 102, 105–08, 121–22, 124, 133–34, 136, 147–48, 155, 170, 247
Howard, Charles, Earl of Nottingham 187, **190**, 213, **236**, 276
Howard, Henry, Earl of Northampton 32–33, 35, 78, 230, 232, **236**, 274, 276
Howard, Katherine, Countess of Suffolk 229–31, 233, 239–40, 244, 278
Howard, Philip, Earl of Arundel 16, 20, 23, 29, 33–34, 43, 72, 76–77, 100, 230, 239
Howard, Thomas, Duke of Norfolk 16, 100, 239
Howard, Thomas, Earl of Suffolk 78, 230, 232, 239–40, 274, 276
Howard, Lord William 20, 77, 230, 239, 278
Huddlesford, Henry 41
Huguenots 1, 67
Humphrey, Lawrence 13
Hussey, Vincent (alias) 165–66, 176

Ibarra, Stephano 120–23
Idiaquez, Juan de 70
Idiaquez, Martin de 154
Isabella (*Measure*) 249–56, 258, 260
Isabella Clara Eugenia, Infanta 97, 152, 162–64, 177, 206, 218, 220–21, 227, 229, 233–34, 244, 249, 251, 257–60, **261**

James, Thomas 7, 131, 221–24, 234, 263
James, Dr. William 83
James VI and I, King 2–3, 22, 27, 78, 86, 90, 132–33, 137–38, 151, 159, 161–63, 165, 173, 185, 206, 210–16, 218–21, 223–27, 229–30, 232–36, 238–43, 247–51, 253–57, 259–60, 267–69, 274, 276, 282–83, 285, 287–88
Jeffrey, Thomas 121–22
Jewel, John 3
Johnson, Elizabeth 59
Jones, Inigo 244, 334

Jones, Richard 84
Jones, Fr. Robert 226, 271–72, 330
Jonson, Ben 57, 158, 242, 244, 253, 278–79, 288
Joyeuse, Duke de 45

Kemp, Will 245–46
Keyes, Robert 275
King Lear 1
King's Men 239–40, 333
Kirklande, Christopher 40
Knevett, Sir Thomas 275
Knollys, Henry 19
Knollys, Robert 19
Knollys, Sir William 19, 190–91, 211

Lake, Sir Thomas 215, 227–31, 233
Lanfranchi, Carlos 133, 175–77, 286
Leicester, Earl of *see* Dudley, Robert
Leroy, John/Jean 176–77
Lessius, Leonard 73
Leveson, Sir Richard 124
Lewis, Owen Bishop of Cassano 93
Lewknor, Lewis 244, 332
Ligne, Charles de, Count Arenberg 97, 180, 185, 219–20, 229, 233, **236**, 240, 247, 259–60
Lindley, David 243
Line, Anne (Higham) 91, 130, 144–45, 191–92, 252, 255, 289
Line, Richard 145
Line, Roger 130, 144, 192
Loomie, Fr. Albert 176, 286
Lopez, Roderigo 70, 120, 123–25, 147
Lord Chamberlain's Men 239, 245
Love Freed from Ignorance and Folly 288
Love's Labours Lost 260
Loyola, Ignatius 6

Mabbe, James 248
Main Plot 185, 218–19, 221, 225
Manifestation of the Great Folly 201–03
Manners, Bridget (Tyrwhitt) 226
Manners, Roger, Earl of Rutland 190–91, 226
Mansfield, Count 137, 148
Mariana (*Measure*) 250, 254
Markham, Sir Griffin 219, 226
Marlowe, Christopher 57, 95, 113, 115–16
Marprelate, Martin (pseudonym) 196
Marshalsea, Prison 9–11, 42–44, 47–48, 92, 112, 127, 281
Maude, Bernard 51, 54, 57
Mauvissière, seigneur de *see* Castelnau, Michel de
Measure for Measure 240, 245, 249–62
Medici, Catherine de 18, 26, 28, 42, 70
Medina Sidonia, Duke 68

Mendoza, Bernardino de 32–33, 53–54, 67, 69–70, 75, 132, 219
Merchant Adventurers 95–96, 99, 115
Merchant of Venice 120, 260
Meres, Anthony 82
Merry Wives of Windsor 260
Middle Temple 39, 41, 86, 108, 112–13, 186, 221
Mikulin, Grigori Ivanovich 209
Milward, Fr. Peter 253
Molin, Nicolo 272, 274
Moody, Michael 57, 64, 95, 101–04, 106, 121, 134–38, 164, 169
Morgan, Edward 271
Morgan, George 271
Morgan, Thomas 24–25, 29, 30–31, 33–36, 51–54, 56–57, 62, 67, 75, 80, 137, 168, 198, 280
Morgan, William 226, 271
Morley, Thomas 134–36, 139
Munck, Levinus 181, 265
Munday, Anthony 13, 57, 104
Mush, John 195–96, 198–201

Nau, Claude 60, 61, 65
Neevell/Nevell, Thomas (alias) 164, 205
Neville, Edmund 37
Neville, Sir Henry 180, 263
New Inn 113–14
Newgate, prison 64
Nicols, William (alias) 119, 148, 152, 158–60, 165, 176
Nix, William 29–30, 36, 58
Norfolk, Duke of *see* under Howard
Norris, Sir John 81
Northumberland, Countess of *see* Percy, Anne
Northumberland, Earl of *see* Percy, Henry
Norton, William 46, 98, 186
Nuse, William 280–82

Oath of Supremacy 46, 82, 85
Office of Revels 238–39, 260, 334, 336
Offield, Clement 58, 59
Oldcorne, FR. Edward 73–74, 277–78
Oldnall, Alice (Skinner) 39
Oldnall, John 39
Olivares, Count 71, 222–23
O'Neill, Hugh, Earl of Tyrone 187–88, 214
Order of the Garter 86, 139, 189, 215, 226
Orsino, Don Virginio 208–10
Orwell, Vincent (alias) 147, 161, 165–66, 176, 179
Osbaldeston, Fr. Edward 112
Othello 254, 260
Ousley, Nicholas 75
Ovid 26, 188–89
Owen, Francis 131
Owen, Henry 157
Owen, Hugh 43, 86, 96, 100, 102, 104–10, 119, 121–38, 143, 147–55,
158–68, 170, 172, 175–80, 182–84, 187, 189, 207, 212, 215, 222, 225, 228–29, 231–34, 241, 244, 246–47, 263–67, 269, 271, 280–87
Owen, Nicholas 10, 140, 142, 144, 157, 277–78
Oxford, colleges: Balliol 6, 194; Christ Church 13, 43–44, 83; Exeter 10, 39, 47; Gloucester Hall, 194; Lincoln, 23; Magdalen 12–13, 27, 48, 82, 84–85, 88, 92, 100, 139, 215, 241, 248, 263, 268, 271; St. John's 6, 11, 139
Oxford, Earl of *see* Vere, Edward de

Page, Fr. Francis 192, 203
Paget, Charles 24–25, 29–31, 33–36, 51–54, 56, 61–62, 67, 75, 121, 133–34, 136–38, 148, 154, 164, 167–75, 193–95, 198, 263–65, 280, 284
Palavicino, Sir Horatio 180–81
Palmer, Captain 45–46
Parham, Sir Edward 219
Parker, Matthew 43
Parker, William Lord Monteagle 221, 276
Parma, Duke of *see* Farnese, Alessandro
Parry, William 21, 36–37, 51, 53–54, 60, 67, 168, 170
Parry Plot *see* Parry, William
Paul VI, Pope 144
Paulet, Sir Amias 51, 53, 56, 81
Paynter, James 107
Paynter, Robert 107, 110, 115
Pembroke, Earl of *see* Herbert, William
Percy, Anne, Countess of Northumberland 18–19
Percy, Sir Charles 215
Percy, Henry, Earl of Northumberland 18, 30–34, 36, 62
Percy, Mary 102–03
Percy, Thomas, Earl of Northumberland 17–19
Perez, Antonio 75, 92, 116–19, 121, 123–24
Persons, Robert 2, 5–13, **14**, 23, 25, 29, 31, 36, 42–44, 47, 71, 74, 76, 7, 1, 08, 115, 129–32, 137, 141–43, 146, 148, 151–58, 164–65, 167–74, 182–83, 187, 189–90, 193–207, 209–211, 213, 215, 221–25, 227, 234–36, 240–41, 245–46, 286, 288
Pertry, Quintin 99, 100
Pertry, Simon 99
Petre/Pettar, Edward 265, 340
Petre, Sir John 143, 186
Petre, Lady 43
Petre, Sir William 10, 86, 143, 186, 245
Phelippes, Stephen 166, 228, 265–66, 283, 286
Phelippes, Thomas 24, 25, 33–35, 51–57, 60, 62, 65, 79–85, 87–92, 34–35, 97–112, 114–20, 125–26,
128–29, 132–35, 144, 147–48, 151, 158–66, 168–86, 189, 193, 197–205, 207, 213–14, 222, 227–30, 233, 238, 241, 244, 262, 264–70, 278, 280–87
Philip II, King 29, 31, 53, 67–71, 75, 96, 8, 108, 117, 152–5, 175, 222, 229, 258–59
Philip III, King 221, 225, 244, 278
Phoenix and Turtle 192, 255
Pius V, Pope 6, 17, 89
Plowden, Francis 232, 332
Poley, Robert 50–53, 57, 62, 104, 115–16, 131, 135–38, 148, 164, 169, 197, 207
Pollen, Fr. John Hungerford 52–53
Polwhele, William 121–27
Pounde, Fr. John 43
Pounde, Thomas 9–10, 43
praemunire 38, 45, 201, 324
Puckering, John 61, 91, 296, 305

Queen Anne's Company 239
Questor, Matthew 219–20

Ralegh/Raleigh, Sir Walter 28, 59, 81, 90, 94, 178, 180, 184–85, 216, 219–21, 233
Ramus, Peter 26
Read, Conyers 76
Recusant, recusancy 41, 59, 69, 89, 112, 232, 236, 240, 249, 250–57, 272–74, 276
Renzo, Ortelio (alias) 14, 164, 206–07, 243, 316, 334–35
Rich, Penelope (Devereaux) 143–44
Richardot, Jean 148, 178, 182–83, **236**
Richardson, Roger 40
Ricroft, John 135
Ridolfi, Robert di, Plot of 18, 22, 50
Rivers, Anthony (alias) 161, 164–66, 182–83, 197–98, 200–01, 203–04, 206–09, 222, 224, 234, 240, 269, 283–84
Robinson, John 126–27
Robinson, Robert (alias) 89, 91, 95–96, 99–101, 105, 107, 125–27, 130, 142, 161, 164–66, 168, 181–84, 193, 227, 233, 286
Rogers, Thomas *see* Berden, Nicholas
Rolston, Anthony 54, 93, 153
Rookwood, Ambrose 226, 275–76
Roscarock, Nicholas 10
Rowington Manor 39–41, 255
Rowlands, Richard *see* Verstegan, Richard
Rowsham, Fr. Stephen 55
Russell, Anne (Somerset) 189, 209

Sackville, Jane 131
Sackville, Robert 20, 77
Sackville, Thomas (son of Buckhurst) 222
Sackville, Thomas, Lord Buckhurst, Earl of Dorset 20, 77, 102,

103, 131, 162, 178, 181, 196, 216, **236**
Salisbury Court 25–27
Salusbury, Thomas 54
Samander, Jacob (alias) 165, 179
Samier/Samerie, Henry 32
Santa Cruz, Marquis of 68
Sauf, J. (alias) 165
Saunders, William 41
Savage, John 51, 54
Scudamore/Skidmore, John 121
Sessa, Duke of 171, 221–22, 245
Shakespeare, William 2, 80, 82, 245, 248, 251, 253, 255–56, 258, 260, 277
Sheffield, Lord Edmund 8, **190**
Sheldon, Ralph 232
Shelley, Edward 76
Shelley, Elizabeth (Guildford, Gage) 43–44, 186
Shelley, John 43–44, 98
Shelley, Margaret 43
Shelley, Mary (Fitzwilliam, Guildford) 98
Shelley, Richard 44
Shelley, William 31–33, 43–44, 46, 62, 77, 84
Shelley, Sir William 43
Sherwin, Ralph 7, 10, 11, 13, 14, 141
Sherwood, Fr. Richard (alias Carleton) 86, 89–91, 94, 96, 107–08, 121, 129–32, 138, 140, 144, 154, 192, 207, 263, 281
Shirley, Sir Anthony 245–46
Shirley, Sir Thomas 245
Shrewsbury, Earl of *see* Talbot
Sidney, Sir Philip 16, 27–29, 52, 81, 95, 246
Sidney, Sir Robert 95, 102, 133, 191
Simmes, Valentine 157
Sixtus V, Pope 67, 71, 77, 258
Skeres, Nicholas 115–16
Skinner, Anthony 39–41, 47, 70, 5, 87–89, 92–93, 97–98, 125, 156, 229–33, 235, 255
Skinner, William 39–41
Sledd, Charles 23–25
Slye, Thomas 40–41
Smith, Andrew 91
Smith, Richard 8
Somerset, Anne (Percy), Countess of Northumberland 30, 103
Somerset, Anne (Winter) 300
Somerset, Catherine (Petre) 143, 186
Somerset, Charles 248
Somerset, Edward (son) 248
Somerset, Edward, 4th Earl of Worcester 15, 18, 30, 44, 84–88, 93, 98, 107–10, 113, 114, 116, 139, 143, 145, 149, 157, 160, 162, 179, 182, 186–191, **190**, 193, 204, 208, 209, 211, 215, 216, 217, 222, 223, 226, 227–31, 238–48, 260, 268–74, 276, 278, 280, 283, 286, 288
Somerset, Elizabeth (Guilford/Guildford) 186, 215
Somerset, Elizabeth (Windsor) 30, 98

Somerset, Frances (Morgan) 271
Somerset, George 102, 103, 149, 150, 151
Somerset, Henry 85, 179, 189, 209, 217, 244
Somerset, Thomas (1529–86) 18, 19, 30, 84, 103, 149
Somerset, Thomas (1579–1649) 215, 240, 244
Somerset, William (d. 1597) 85, 86
Somerset, William, 3rd Earl of Worcester 18, 19, 29, 30, 87, 103
Somerset House, Treaty of 236, 240, 249, 276
Sotehill, Henry 82
Sotehill, Sir Gerard 2
Southampton, Countess of *see* Browne, Mary (Wriothesley)
Southampton, Earl of *see* Wriothesley, Henry
Southwark, Synod of 9, 252
Southwell, Elizabeth 305
Southwell, George (Sowthwick) 342
Southwell, Katherine (Sterrell) 82
Southwell, Fr. Robert 11, 57, 58, 62, 73, 74, 77, 124, 125, 131, 142–146, 202, 256, 281, 289
Southwick, George 280–81
Spanish Treason 219, 221, 226, 229–31, 234
Spiller, Henry 282–83, 285
Spiller, Robert (alias Freeman) 78, 197–98, 207, 225, 228–31, 233, 239, 255, 266, 269, 278, 282–85
Spirit Orthon 160, 164, 224
Stafford, Sir Edward (alias Julius) 36, 42, 55, 60, 64, 67, 70, 75, 107
Stafford, William 64
Stafford Plot 64
Standen, Anthony 75–76, 118, 128, 241
Stanihurst, James 97
Stanihurst, Richard 97–98, 123, 129
Stanihurst, Walter 97–98
Stanley, Ferdinando, Lord Strange, Earl of Derby 86, 126–27, 212
Stanley, Sir William 69, 71, 86, 93, 96, 102, 104, 106, 109, 121–24, 126–27, 134, 147, 150–51, 172, 222, 225–26, 231–32, 285
Staveley, Ezekiel 92, 94–97, 100–01
Stephens, Edward 47
Sterrell, Henry (brother) 82, 113
Sterrell, Henry (father) 8, 82
Sterrell, William, Agent for Catholics 2, 84–85, 89, 103, 111–12, 149, 224–25; aliases—Cordale 164, 166, Fenner 147, 164, 166, Hallins, Peter 98, 119, 147–48, 151–52, 158–67, 173, 176, 189, 193, 228, 269, Kirby 47–48, 84, Nevell 164, 205, Orwell 147, 161, 165–66, 176, 179, Renzo, Ortelio 14, 164, 206–07, 243, 316, 334–35, Rivers, Anthony 161, 164–66, 182–83, 197–98, 200–01, 203–04, 206–09, 222, 224, 234, 240, 269,

283–84, Robinson, Robert 89, 91, 95–96, 99–101, 105, 107, 125–27, 130, 142, 161, 164–66, 168, 181–84, 193, 227, 233, 286, Saintmain 89, 94, 106, Wicham 130–31, 263; appellants controversy—193–207; Cecil, interrogation by—263–70; correspondents—Baldwin 179, 207, Fitzherbert 43, 71, 107–08, 118, Holt 107–08, Owen 107, 126–27 (*see* Hallins, Peter), Persons 12 (*see* Rivers, Anthony), Sherwood 107–08, 131, Skinner 70, 85, 88, Verstegan 119, 148, 151, 165, 207, 214, 284
Stevens, Fr. Richard 43
Stewart, Prince Charles 243, 288
Stewart, Prince Henry 243, 248
Stewart/Stuart, James *see* James, King
Stewart/Stuart, Mary Queen of Scots 14, 17–26, 28–37, 40, 42–43, 47, 50–67, 69–72, 76, 80–81, 84, 91, 101, 103, 118, 126, 130, 132, 137–38, 144, 168, 173, 186, 218, 234
Stradlinge, Arthur 46
Strange, Fr. Thomas 277–80, 285
Stransham, Fr. Edward 52
Stuart, Arabella/Arbella 102, 116, 126, 130–39, 144, 147, 212, 214, 219, 240, 242, 264
Sugar, Fr. John 255–56
Swinnerton, Elizabeth (Gatacre) 41
Synod of Southwark 9, 252

Talbot, Edward 139
Talbot, George, Earl of Shrewsbury 24, 50, 139
Talbot, Gilbert, Earl of Shrewsbury 136, 139, **190**, 214, 240–41
Talbot, Henry 139
Tassis, Juan de, Count of Villa Mediana 225, 230–32, **236**, 239, 330, 333–34
Taylor, Dr. Robert 179, 219–20, 224, 228–33, 235, 239, 265, 277–78
Taylor, Fr. William 85
Tesimond, Oswald (alias Greenwell or Greenway) 221–22, 224, 229, 234, 277
Theatrum crudelitatum haereticorum 13, **141**
Throckmorton, Francis 31–33, 36, 54, 58, 61, 131
Throckmorton, George 31, 58–59, 131
Throckmorton, Job 39–40, 44
Throckmorton, Sir John 31
Throckmorton, Margery 31
Throckmorton, Thomas 31, 33, 121, 131
Throckmorton Plot 21, 30–37, 39, 43, 51, 53, 55, 67, 87, 131, 153, 219
Tichborn, Fr. Thomas 203
Tichbourne, Chidiock 7, 54, 58
Tilney, Charles 54, 239

Tilney, Edmund 239–40
Tinoco, Emanuel Luis 123, 125
Tiro, M. Tullius 84
Tissue, Robert (alias) 169
Tompson, William 121, 123
Topcliffe, Richard 44, 58, 111–12, 141–43, 146
Townshend, John 100, 302
Townshend, Roger 100
Trappes, des Mons. 64
Tresham, Francis 192, 221
Tresham, Sir Thomas 232
Tudor, Elizabeth, Queen 2–3, 6–7, 11–13, 16–19, 21–23, 26, 32, 35–37, 42–44, 48, 56, 63–64, 67–68, 75, 79–83, 85–88, 93–94, 101–06, 109–11, 117, 120–28, 135–36, 146–47, 158–60, 162–63, 168–69, 171, 177–78, 180, 183, 186–**190**, 194–95, 199, 203, 208–17
Tudor, Mary, Queen 18, 50, 155
Tunstall, James 84
Tyburn 10–11, 13, 15, 52, 76, 255
Tyrell, Fr. Anthony 54
Tyrwhitt, Goddard 9
Tyrwhitt, Nicholas 8–9
Tyrwhitt, Robert 226
Tyrwhitt, Sir Robert 8, 82, 226

Ungerer, Gustav 92
Unton, Edward 69
Uvedall, Sir Edmund 131, 149–51

Valdés, Don Pedro de 92, 300
Vallenger, Stephen 13
Vaux, Anne 247, 255, 278
Vaux, Lord 73
Vega, Antonio de 70
Velasco, Juan de, Constable of Castile 222, 228, **236**, 244, 266
Vere, Edward de, Earl of Oxford 16, 20

Verreyken, Louis 178
Verstegan/Rowlands, Richard 13–4, 43, 92–93, 115, 119, 129–30, 132, 137, 141, 148–54, 158, 165, 168, 172, 179, 182, 187, 198, 207, 212, 214–15, 222, 247, 284
Vision of the Twelve Goddesses 243

Wade/Waad, Sir William 48, 58, 129–31, 138, 140, 142–44, 147, 159–60, 182, 192, 263–65, 267, 271, 283–84
Walpole, Fr. Henry 121, 134, 247, 307, 311, 336
Walsingham, Sir Francis 2–3, 18–25, 27, 29–37, 40, 42, 44, 46, 48–59, 61–65, 67–70, 72, 74–7, 79–80, 87, 91, 101, 118, 128, 133–34, 136, 144, 147, 169, 193–94, 197, 202, 245, 262
Walton, Roger 107
Ward, Margaret 76, 201, 252
Warren, Thomas 83
Watkinson, Fr. Robert 203
Watson, Fr. William 76, 195, 198, 201, 203, 219
Waugh, Evelyn 10
Wellington, Alice 271
Westmorland, Earl of 17, 86, 107–08, 136
Weston, Fr. William 34, 72, 73, 145, 194
Whip/Whipp, William 101, 102, 104
Whirret, William 41
Whitebread, Guillame 286
Wilbraham, Sir Roger 195
Wilford, Thomas 286
Wilkes, Sir Thomas 137, 139, 147–48, 150, 179
Williams, George 46, 273
Williams, Richard 103, 121, 149

Williams, Sir Roger 81
Williamson, Nicholas 136–37, 147
Wilson, Derek 1
Wilson, Thomas 80, 259, 280
Wilson, Fr. Thomas 44
Windebank, Thomas 123, 125, 264–65
Windsor, Edward 54, 61
Windsor, William 29, 98
Winter, Sir Edward 216
Wintour/Winter, Robert 221, **275**
Wintour/Winter, Thomas 221–26, 229, 234, **275**, 276, 285
Winwood, Sir Ralph 180, 207, 263–64, 268
Worcester, Earl of *see* Somerset, William, Worcester, relations with
Worcester's Men 238, 239, 245, 247, 333, 336
Worthington, Dr. Thomas 121, 147
Wright, Christopher 221, 223–25, **275**, 276–77
Wright, John 221, **275**, 276–77
Wright, Fr. Thomas 145, 152, 157–58, 278–79
Wriothesley, Henry, Earl of Southampton 151, 187–88, 190–91, 241, 250
Wyatt's Rebellion 22

Yardley, Roger 57
Yates, Francis 69
Yelverton, Sir Christopher 192
Yorke, Edmund 103, 121–22, 125, 147
Young, Henry 121
Young, Richard 61, 62, 121, 122
Younger, Fr. James 134

Zúñiga, Don Pedro de 230

www.ingramcontent.com/pod-product-compliance
Ingram Content Group UK Ltd.
Pitfield, Milton Keynes, MK11 3LW, UK
UKHW050544150426
5217IPUK00026B/2061